PORTRAIT OF AMERICA

NINTH EDITION

VOLUME 2

From Reconstruction to the Present

STEPHEN B. OATES

UNIVERSITY OF MASSACHUSETTS, AMHERST

CHARLES J. ERRICO

NORTHERN VIRGINIA COMMUNITY COLLEGE

HOUGHTON MIFFLIN COMPANY

BOSTON   NEW YORK

This book is dedicated in loving memory to our mothers:

Florence Baer Oates

Mary Sybil Errico

These caring, gifted women introduced us to the world of literature, inspired us by their example, and gave us unstinting support throughout our college and professional careers.

Publisher: Patricia Coryell
Sponsoring Editor: Sally Constable
Senior Development Editor: Jeff Greene
Senior Project Editor: Jane Lee
Editorial Assistant: Carrie Parker
Senior Art and Design Coordinator: Jill Haber
Senior Photo Editor: Jennifer Meyer Dare
Composition Buyer: Chuck Dutton
Associate Strategic Buyer: Brian Pieragostini
Senior Marketing Manager: Katherine Bates
Marketing Assistant: Lauren Bussard
Cover Design Manager: Anne S. Katzeff

Cover Image: Smithsonian American Art Museum, Washington, DC/Art Resource, NY.

Printed in the U.S.A.

Library of Congress Control Number: 2006928362

Instructor's exam copy:
ISBN 13: 978-0-618-73225-8
ISBN 10: 0-618-73225-X

For orders, use student text ISBNs:
ISBN 13: 978-0-618-64297-7
ISBN 10: 0-618-64297-8

1 2 3 4 5 6 7 8 9-MP-10 09 08 07 06

CONTENTS

children making their way home after school. Laskin's vivid
description of the blizzard is haunting. As he says, the storm was a
tragic example of a dream gone wrong for pioneers who had moved
west in search of a prosperous new life. For countless pioneer families,
the promise of the Homestead Act proved to be a cruel joke. The storm
that killed their children demonstrated "that the land they had desired so
fervently and had traveled so far to claim wasn't free after all."

Theodore Roosevelt believed that she was one of those infamous muckrakers, more interested in filth than the truth. Tarbell ignored those insults. In 1906, her tenacity and willingness to make personal sacrifices resulted in a federal antitrust suit against the ignoble Rockefeller and his mighty Standard Oil Company.

depression in its history. Textbooks explain in detail the economic reasons for the crash of 1929 and the ensuing Depression, but none captures the human suffering and the failure of early relief efforts better than Watkins's prize-winning *The Great Depression,* a companion to the popular PBS television series, from which this selection is excerpted.

In 1932, when Franklin D. Roosevelt was first elected president, the Great Depression was in its cruelest year, with unemployment escalating and banks foreclosing on farmers' homesteads at an alarming rate. In 1933, President Roosevelt responded to the crisis with the Agricultural Adjustment Administration for farmers and the National Recovery Administration for the unemployed. Roosevelt scholar James MacGregor Burns assesses these and other measures of the early New Deal, 1933-1934, and argues that Roosevelt's approach to the Depression was not a coherent, far-sighted program of reform, but a series of experiments that reflected Roosevelt's empirical temper.

IX.   A WORLD AT WAR (1937–1945)   202

An eminent and prolific historian takes us inside the White House on the eve of America's entry into World War II. With insight and sensitivity, Goodwin describes the complex personalities and backgrounds of Franklin and Eleanor Roosevelt and intoduces us to a diverse cast of characters who visited and befriended them. We learn how two extraordinary people gained strength of character through adversity. By sheer willpower, Franklin triumphed over an attack of polio that crippled both legs. His ordeal gave him "a greater sympathy and understanding of the problems of mankind." For her part, Eleanor had to overcome the terrible hurt of her husband's infidelity. By doing so, she found "new avenues of fulfillment" and became the most influential first lady in American history. When Pearl Harbor plunged the nation into war in December 1941, the president's remarkable partnership with Eleanor would serve him well in the perilous years ahead.

This provocative selection makes it clear that the American government knew about Hitler's death camps for European Jews and other prisoners and the dreadful "Final Solution" to "the Jewish question" as early as August 1942. Many critics argue that

Roosevelt should have bombed the hideous gas chambers at Auschwitz and the railroad tracks leading to that murderous prison. The author contends that "mainstream Jewish opinion was against the whole idea." It is "abhorrent" to contemplate the number of helpless concentration camp prisoners that Allied bombs would have killed. Inmates already loaded into cattle cars would have perished from thirst and heat while waiting the "few days" the Germans needed to rebuild damaged track. Roosevelt believed that the best way to save Jewish lives was to win the war as swiftly as possible.

the flesh-and-blood King from the dust of history. The selection traces King's intellectual and spiritual development that culminated in his philosophy of nonviolence; seeks to explore his personality, including his human flaws, with empathy and understanding; and assesses his accomplishments as an internationally acclaimed spokesman for the civil rights movement and the protest against the Vietnam War.

helped shape his performance in office. He was upbeat, witty, and supremely optimistic. But Reagan's other "salient traits" were his coldness, his inaccessibility, and his penchant for thinking only about the big picture and thus missing crucial details. Even so, Brookhiser credits Reagan with being the lead player in bringing about momentous historic events like the crumbling of the Berlin Wall, the collapse of the Soviet Union, the relegation of Communism to "the ash-heap of history," and the end of the Cold War that had plagued the planet for almost half a century.

One of America's most eminent historians discusses six critical errors of the United States and the Soviet Union that helped cause and sustain the Cold War. Stressing the importance of the perception of events in understanding the past, Schlesinger shows how exaggeration and misunderstanding on the part of both countries escalated Cold War tensions, once to the very brink of nuclear holocaust.

XV.   FROM THE TECHNOLOGICAL REVOLUTION TO MODERN TERRORISM   370

We are living in the midst of a technological revolution whose historical significance has already surpassed that of the Industrial Revolution. The advent of the computer is perhaps the most important technological achievement of all. Among other things, the computer has revolutionized how we communicate, gain access to information, wage war, and conduct business and countless other operations. This selection is an intimate portrait of "one of the most important minds and personalities" of the computer era: the Harvard dropout and fiercely competitive computer wizard who built Microsoft into a "near monopoly" in the field of desktop computer systems and software. By the late 1990s, Microsoft had a market value of $160 billion, and Bill Gates had become the richest person and most famous businessman in the world.

Gaddis discusses the lessons of September 11, 2001, from a historical perspective. Focusing on the post–Cold War decade, he explains how the failures and shortcoming of American foreign policy created anti-American feelings in much of the world. The events of September 11, he warns, thrust us into a new era that is "bound to be more painful than the one we've just left."

PREFACE

Good history begins with a good story.

—JAMES WEST DAVIDSON
AND MARK HAMILTON LYTLE

The ninth edition of *Portrait of America* is the work of two historians who care deeply about the teaching of American history. We realize that many students enter undergraduate history courses and advanced placement high school programs with the impression that the study of history entails little more than names and dates. We are convinced that the superb readings in *Portrait of America* demonstrate that this is a misconception and that studying history can in fact be a profoundly enriching experience. This is because *Portrait of America* stresses the human side of the American past, suggesting how the interaction of people and events shaped the course of American history. We chose selections for this anthology that make history live by telling a good story, and that were written for students, not for professional historians. The essays, narratives, and biographical portraits gathered here humanize American history, portraying it as a story of real people who actually lived, people with whom we can identify. We hope that the anthology is an example of humanistic history at its best, the kind that combines scrupulous and engaging scholarship with a compelling narrative style. Because college survey audiences are not professional ones, they might enjoy reading history if it is presented in an exciting and accessible form.

There is another reason why students will find *Portrait of America* edifying: it showcases the writings of some of America's most eminent historians. Volume Two contains excerpts from critically acclaimed, best-selling books by Margaret MacMillan and Doris Kearns Goodwin, both famous authors.

The prizes our contributors have won testify to their important places in the galaxy of American letters. Pulitzer Prize winners include Edmund Morris, David McCullough, James MacGregor Burns, Arthur M. Schlesinger, Jr., and Doris Kearns Goodwin. In addition, Eric Foner, John Lewis Gaddis, and Arthur M. Schlesinger, Jr., have all won the prestigious Bancroft Prize. Stephen B. Oates, an elected member of the Society of American Historians, received the Robert F. Kennedy Memorial Book Award, two Christopher Awards, and fellowships from the Guggenheim Foundation and the National Endowment for the Humanities. Many of the other contributors also earned significant literary and scholarly recognition. Thus *Portrait of America* offers readers a unique opportunity to learn from a lineup of historians and writers with national and even international reputations.

The ninth edition of Volume Two has been extensively revised. It contains seven new selections of superior literary and historical merit. They make this the strongest edition of *Portrait of America* yet published. The new readings are:

- James Oliver Horton and Lois E. Horton's graphic story of the black experience during Reconstruction, when the former slaves' dreams of true equality and a better life were obstructed by southern white violence and racial oppression;
- David Laskin's haunting description of the ferocious blizzard of 1888 that shocked migrants to the Dakota and Nebraska frontier and that killed hundreds of their children;
- William and Mary Lavender's vivid account of the suffragists who suffered cruel imprisonment for crusading for women's right to vote;

- Margaret MacMillan's inspired and insightful story of a sickly Woodrow Wilson and his losing struggle for American participation in the League of Nations;
- James West Davidson and Mark Hamilton Lytle's fascinating analysis of how the bigotry of native-born white Anglo-Saxon Protestants contributed to the execution of two obscure Italian immigrants named Sacco and Vanzetti;
- James MacGregor Burns's riveting account of the Great Depression of the 1930s and President Franklin D. Roosevelt's efforts to end it by bold and pragmatic experimentation;
- Richard Brookhiser's brilliant examination of Ronald Reagan's personality and of his role in such momentous events as the collapse of the Soviet Union and the end of the Cold War.

The ninth edition retains the best and most popular selections of the previous edition. We hope that *Portrait of America* remains as balanced as ever, for it offers samplings of virtually every kind of history—men's and women's, black and white, social and cultural, political and military, urban and economic, national and local—so that students can appreciate the rich diversity of the American experience.

Portrait of America contains several important features that help students learn from its contents. Each selection is preceded by a glossary that identifies important individuals, events, and concepts that appear in the reading. Introductions set the selections in proper context and suggest ways to approach studying them. They also tie all the selections together so that they can be read more or less as connected episodes. Study questions following the selections raise significant issues and encourage students to make comparisons and contrasts between selections. The questions also help students review the readings and suggest points for class discussion.

The anthology is intended for use largely in college survey courses. It could be used as a supplement to a textbook or to a list of paperback readings. Or it could serve as the basic text. *Portrait of America* could also be used effectively in advanced placement high school classes. The book is organized into fifteen parts according to periods or themes; each part contains two or three related selections. This organization allows readers to make comparisons and contrasts between different events or viewpoints.

With this edition, we are introducing a new website. On this website, instructors and students will find a number of selections that appeared in the seventh and eighth editions, but are not included in the ninth edition primarily for reasons of length. With this website, we can keep the print version of *Portrait of America* to a reasonable length and still make available many popular selections from those editions.

We could not have assembled the ninth edition without the generous help of others. Robert Kinson, Elza M. England, and Denise Pattee Pargas assisted us at crucial points in the preparation of the manuscript, and we are most grateful to them. At Northern Virginia Community College, Alice Reagan helped identify new selections, and Betty Pasqualini assisted with formatting the manuscript. Jay Boggis did a superb job of copyediting the manuscript, and we are most grateful to him. We also want to thank the following professors for taking time out from their busy schedules to review the volume: Richard Aquila, Pennsylvania State University, the Behrend College; Terri Halperin, University of Richmond; Gordon Patterson, Florida Institute of Technology; and Vivian Talbot, Weber State University.

S. B. O.
C. J. E.

PART ONE

A Troubled Peace

1 *"Call Me Mister"*: The Black Experience During Reconstruction

JAMES OLIVER HORTON AND LOIS E. HORTON

For African Americans in North and South alike, the Civil War had profound religious meaning from the beginning. Hundreds of thousands, writes historian Vincent Harding, "believed unwaveringly that their God moved in history to deliver his people, and they had been looking eagerly, praying hourly, waiting desperately for the glory of the coming of the Lord. For them, all the raucous, roaring guns of Charleston Harbor and Bull Run, of Antietam and Fort Pillow, of Shiloh and Murfreesboro and Richmond were the certain voice of God, announcing his judgment across the bloody stretches of the South, returning blood for blood to the black river." During the course of that war, African Americans believed, God did deliver them. He drove out the rebels and slaveholders, just as he had once driven out the Hittites and Canaanites. With the Confederacy's collapse, as one song went, "slavery chain done broke at last."

> *Slavery chain done broke at last!*
> *Broke at last! Broke at last!*
> *Slavery chain done broke at last!*
> *Gonna praise God till I die!*

Some reacted to their liberation with cautious elation. When a young Virginia woman heard her former masters weeping over the capture of Jefferson Davis, she went down to a spring alone and cried out, "Glory, glory, hallelujah to Jesus! I's free! I's free!" Suddenly afraid, she looked about. What if the white folks heard her? But seeing no one, she fell to the ground and kissed it, thanking "Master Jesus" over and over. For her, freedom meant hope—hope that she could find her husband and four children who had been sold to a slave trader.

Others celebrated their liberation in public. In Athens, Georgia, they danced around a liberty pole; in Charleston, they paraded through the streets. Many African Americans, however, were wary and uncertain. "You're joking me," one man said when the master told him he was free. He asked some neighbors if they were free also. "I couldn't believe we was all free alike," he said. Some African Americans, out of feelings of obligation or compassion, remained on the home place to help their former masters. But others were hostile. When a woman named Cady heard that the war was over, she decided to protest the cruel treatment she had suffered as a slave. She threw down her hoe, marched up to the big house, found the mistress, and flipped her dress up. She told the white woman, "Kiss my ass!"

For Cady, for the young black woman of Virginia, for hosts of other African Americans, freedom meant an end to the manifold evils of slavery; it meant the right to say what they felt and go where they wanted. But what else did freedom mean to them? As black leaders of Charleston said, it meant that blacks should enjoy full citizenship, have the right to vote, and run for political office. It meant federal protection from their former masters lest they attempt to revive slavery. And it meant economic security in the form of land, so that the blacks could exercise self-help and be economically independent of their former masters.

If the end of the war was a time of profound hope for black Americans, it was a monumental calamity for most southern whites. By turns, they were angry, helpless, vindictive, resigned, and heartsick. Their once-beloved Confederacy was devastated. Its towns and major cities, Richmond and Atlanta, were in rubble. Former rebel soldiers returning home found their farm and plantation houses ransacked and even burned down, their barns destroyed, their fields burned, and their livestock gone. As one historian says, "Many [white southerners] were already grieving over sons, plantations, and fortunes taken by war; losing their blacks was the final blow." Some masters shot or hanged African Americans who proclaimed their freedom. That was a harbinger of the years of Reconstruction, for most white southerners were certain that their cause had been just and were entirely unrepentant about fighting against the Union. A popular ballad captured the mood in postwar Dixie:

> Oh, I'm a good ole Rebel, now that's just what I am
> For this fair land of freedom I do not care a damn.
> I'm glad I fit against it, I only wish't we'd won
> And I don't want no pardon for nothin' what I done. . . .
>
> I hates the Yankee nation and everything they do
> I hates the Declaration of Independence too
> I hates the glorious Union, 'tis dripping with our blood
> And I hate the striped banner, I fit it all I could. . . .
>
> I can't take up my musket and fight 'em now no mo'
> But I ain't gonna love 'em and that is certain sho'
> And I don't want no pardon for what I was and am
> And I won't be reconstructed and I don't care a damn.

In Washington, Republican leaders were jubilant in victory and determined to deal firmly with southern whites in order to preserve the fruits of the war. But what about the new president, Andrew

Johnson? A profane, hard-drinking Tennessee Democrat who bragged about his plebeian origins, Johnson had been the only southern senator to oppose secession openly. He had sided with the Union, served as war governor of Tennessee, and became Lincoln's running mate in 1864, on a Union ticket comprising both Republicans and War Democrats. As a result of the assassination of Lincoln, Johnson was now president, and he faced one of the most difficult tasks ever to confront an American chief executive: how to bind the nation's wounds, preserve African American freedom, and restore the southern states to their proper places in the Union.

Lincoln had contemplated an army of occupation for the defeated South, thinking that military force might be necessary to protect the former slaves and prevent the old southern leadership from returning to power. Now there was such an army in the conquered rebel states, and a great number of these Union troops were black.

In the following selection, historians James Oliver Horton and Lois E. Horton help you feel the soaring hope and terrible pain of emancipated blacks as they endured the transition from slavery to freedom in the postwar years. Instead of being passive and undeserving recipients of freedom (as an earlier generation of historians portrayed them), African Americans reached out and seized control of their destinies. They set about defining and exercising freedom for themselves, searched across the war-torn South for lost family members, established independent black churches, and struggled against an unrepentant white South determined to maintain white supremacy. With the acquiescence of President Johnson, white leaders in conquered Dixie adopted infamous black codes that severely restricted the freedom of the former slaves. In the story the Hortons tell, you will read about how southern African Americans had to endure Jim Crow segregation, poll taxes aimed at preventing blacks from voting, and the night-riding violence of the Ku Klux Klan. You will also read accounts of how African Americans had the courage to stand up to white prejudice and fight back.

For the blacks, the first troubled year of Reconstruction ended joyously with the ratification of the Thirteenth Amendment, which abolished slavery in America formally and forever. Nevertheless, as the Hortons remind us, "slavery still has an impact on Americans more than a century after its abolition. . . . As Americans, we must understand slavery's history if we are ever to be emancipated from its consequences."

GLOSSARY

BLACK CODES   These were local laws adopted by white-dominated state governments early in Reconstruction in the conquered South. Such notorious statutes virtually kept the freedmen in a state of servitude. These laws placed severe restrictions on the ownership of land and the ability of the former slaves to move freely in order to seek better jobs. The black codes were a product of white southern governments that came into power under President Johnson's lenient Reconstruction plan. One historian described them as the "slave codes revisited."

BROWN, JOHN   Brown had earned his reputation in "Bleeding Kansas" as an implacable antislavery warrior. Kansas, therefore, had a special appeal to African American migrants. Before the Civil War, freestate and pro-slavery settlers fought a vicious guerrilla war over the status of slavery there. The free-state majority finally won control of the territorial government. In 1861, Kansas entered the Union as a free state.

CARPETBAGGERS   Northerners, including former soldiers, who migrated to the South in search of economic opportunities. Many were teachers and nurses who came to assist the freedmen. Named for the bags that carried their belongings, the carpetbaggers were resented by white southerners who resisted any changes in race relations.

DUNN, OSCAR J.   Black lieutenant governor of Louisiana, Dunn was born into slavery. He was self-educated and during Reconstruction became an outspoken advocate of black suffrage.

EXODUSTERS Name given to some six thousand former slaves who fled the South for the freedom of the western frontier, where they hoped to obtain nominally free land under the Homestead Act. The Exodusters homesteaded twenty thousand acres of land, much of it only marginally productive. "I asked my wife did she know the ground she stands on," one Louisiana Exoduster remembered. "She said, 'No!' I said it is free ground, and she cried like a child for joy."

FIFTEENTH AMENDMENT (1870) The right of United States citizens to vote could not be denied, this amendment said, "on account of race, color, or previous conditions of servitude." After Reconstruction, the white-dominated southern states used poll taxes, literacy tests, and grandfather clauses to prevent blacks from voting or holding political office. This rendered the great amendment meaningless for almost a century.

FOURTEENTH AMENDMENT (1868) Despite President Johnson's opposition, the Republican majority in Congress approved this significant amendment, which prohibited individual states from depriving American citizens "of life, liberty, or property, without due process of law." The next selection recounts the "checkered history" of the Fourteenth Amendment.

FREEDMEN'S BUREAU Established by congressional statute in March 1865, the Bureau of Freedmen, Refugees, and Abandoned Lands, popularly known as the Freedmen's Bureau, attempted to provide food and schools for the former slaves, to help them secure jobs, and to make certain they received fair wages.

GRANDFATHER CLAUSES Sometimes called "understanding clauses" or the "good character clauses," they were provisions built into southern state constitutions to ensure that poor and illiterate whites could vote, while blacks could not. Historian C. Vann Woodward referred to these "artfully devised" clauses as "loopholes" in the voting barriers "through which only white men could squeeze."

GRANT, ULYSSES S. This former Union general served as president from 1869 to 1877. As chief executive, Grant did try to stop terrorist activities in the South, but otherwise did little to help the freedmen achieve true social, political, or economic freedom. As the Civil War ended, he advised President Johnson to remove the African American troops from the South.

HAMPTON, WADE Governor of South Carolina and United States senator, Hampton represented white southerners who wanted to "redeem" the South by expelling carpetbaggers, scalawags, and freedmen from state governments and reestablishing white supremacy in Dixie.

HAYES, RUTHERFORD B. Former governor of Ohio and a Republican, Hayes served as president from 1877 to 1881. Hayes defeated Democrat Samuel J. Tilden in the controversial presidential election of 1876. Tilden won the popular vote, but the outcome in the electoral college depended on disputed ballot counts in three southern states. The Republican and Democratic leaders agreed to a compromise in 1877 that awarded Hayes the presidency in exchange for removing federal troops from the South.

JIM CROW LAWS Southern state and local laws that enforced segregation and discriminated against African Americans. The term "Jim Crow" derived from the name of a song sung by Thomas Rice in a black minstrel show before the Civil War.

JOHNSON, ANDREW President from 1865 to 1869 and a product of the poor white South, Johnson had no sympathy for those who wanted to achieve true racial equality. He defied congressional Reconstruction measures and was impeached for political reasons. By one vote, the Senate failed to convict him, but Johnson was virtually powerless after the impeachment proceedings.

KU KLUX KLAN Following the Civil War, this secretive paramilitary organization emerged in the South and used violence and intimidation to subdue the freedmen.

LIBERIA In 1821, the American Colonization Society helped establish this settlement in West Africa as a haven for American black colonists. Over the next decade, several thousand free blacks voluntarily migrated to Liberia.

LITERACY TEST In the years after Reconstruction, white southern leaders adopted literacy tests, which, like poll taxes, were designed to prevent freedmen from voting. Poor and illiterate whites were exempted from taking literacy tests because of carefully written "grandfather clauses." The Hortons sum up such discrimination against African Americans: "Starting in 1890 in Mississippi, and then spreading across the South, a constellation of laws restricted the [elective] franchise to whites only."

REVELS, HIRAM RHODES In 1870, Revels, a minister and an educator, became the first African American to serve in the Unites States Senate. A Mississippi Republican, Revels left the Senate a year later to become president of Alcorn Agricultural College (now Alcorn University).

SCALAWAGS Native southern whites who became Republicans during Reconstruction, scalawags resented being ruled by the planters and supported the legal and political rights of the freedmen.

SHARECROPPING Lacking the money to acquire their own land in the South, many former slaves became sharecroppers. They rented plots of land from their former masters who paid them with shares of their crops. For African Americans, the sharecropping system was an odious form of exploitation. As the Hortons explain: "Unequal resources and power . . . led to white landowners' binding black sharecroppers to the land through real or contrived indebtedness."

SHERMAN, WILLIAM TECUMSEH "Bill" Sherman, of course, was the Union general whose army cut a huge swath of destruction across the Confederacy in the last year of the war. But in Hortons' story, he did something else that only made white southerners hate him all the more. On January 16, 1865, from his headquarters in Savannah, he issued Special Field Order 15, which confiscated certain portions of Confederate plantations and farms in the area for the exclusive use of the freedmen. Six months later, forty thousand black farmers were cultivating their own forty-acre plots along the coastal areas of Georgia and South Carolina. President Johnson later returned this property to its prewar white owners and expelled the former slaves from the land.

STANTON, EDWIN M. Lincoln's Secretary of War, Stanton approved of Sherman's Special Field Order 15, which gave the freedmen an opportunity to farm confiscated Confederate land.

SOUTHERN HOMESTEAD ACT (1866) Congress designated forty-four million acres of public land in five southern states for settlement by the freedmen and by whites who had remained loyal to the Union. Few benefited from this legislation. Much of the land was unsuitable for farming, and few former slaves had the resources to wait for the revenue that would follow their first successful crop.

TENURE OF OFFICE ACT (1867) By the terms of this federal statute, no federal official confirmed by the Senate could be removed until the Senate had approved a successor. When President Johnson removed Secretary of War Stanton in 1868, he violated this law and was impeached as a consequence. The senate, however, failed to convict him.

THIRTEENTH AMENDMENT (1865) This momentous amendment ended slavery in the United States. Southern resistance to change and northern complacency would delay any significant improvement in race relations for another one hundred years.

A t the end of the war it was not clear how the reuniting America would define black freedom, although it was clear that slavery was dead. In January 1865, by a vote of 121 to 24, Congress passed the Thirteenth Amendment to the U.S. Constitution, providing for the total abolition of American slavery. Ratified before the year was out, it seemed to many whites and blacks to be the fulfillment of the American Revolution. At last all Americans would have the promise of liberty and justice found in the Declaration of Independence. First, however, the country faced the task of ensuring the survival of people made destitute by slavery and the war. The immediate needs of the freed people were great, greater than could be met by the efforts of the private philanthropies that had been active during the war. In March 1865, before the fall of Richmond, the government had established the Bureau of Refugees, Freedmen, and Abandoned Lands, placing it in the War Department. The Freedmen's Bureau established operations in every department of the occupied South and provided aid to impoverished whites as well as freed slaves. Bureau agents established schools for the freed people and registered legal marriages for former slaves. Attempting to restore order to the war-ravaged southern plantation economy, and to bring in tax money to support federal assistance, agents negotiated millions of labor contracts, many between freed people and their former owners. As state governments were reestablished, the Bureau also oversaw voter registration.

Freed people had definite ideas about the meaning of freedom. Some took new names to denote their new status, as some black people had done after they escaped from slavery before the war, calling themselves Freeman or Freedman, for example. Some

Excerpts from James Oliver Horton and Lois E. Horton, *Slavery and the Making of America* (New York: Oxford University Press, 2005), pp. 207, 209–227, 230–231. Copyright © 2005 by Oxford University Press, Inc. Reprinted by permission of Oxford University Press, Inc.

Ratified in December, 1865, the Thirteenth Amendment guaranteed freedom to four million former slaves like those shown here. Most desired "forty acres and a mule"—that is, land and the tools to make it productive so that they could become economically self-sufficient. But most freedmen failed to achieve their dream when the sharecropping system, which replaced slavery, bound them to work land owned by white southerners. (Lightfoot Collection)

dropped slave names given to them by their masters in favor of the names they had been known by in the slave quarters. Others who had been known by a succession of names as they were sold from owner to owner, settled on the name of the fairest or kindest master. Some took the names of masters they had when they were parted from family members. In this way, they hoped, it would be easier for husbands, wives, mothers, fathers, or children to find them.

Freedom meant keeping families together and finding lost family members. In slavery many people had tried to keep track of family members who were sold away. Slaves and free blacks whose occupations let them travel through the South had provided

important links, carrying information and messages between people separated by slavery. Many men, like Maryland's Charles Ball who had run away twice from farther south, had endured the hardships of escaping in order to return to wives and children whom they had been forced to leave behind. Even in the same area, husbands and wives owned by different planters had sometimes gone without sleep and risked harsh punishment in order to see their mates. Tamar Grandy and her husband were both slaves in eastern North Carolina in the early 1800s. She was sold to a Georgia trader but escaped and traveled a hundred miles to return to her husband and her mother. Her husband lived twenty-five miles away from where she was in hiding. For years he came to visit her, leaving home as soon as he finished his work, spending part of the night with his wife, and walking the long distance back in order to arrive home before sunrise, when he would be called to the fields.

With freedom came relief from the slaves' greatest fear—having family members sold away. Touching reunions occurred during and after the war. Ben and Betty Dodson found each other in a refugee camp. They had been sold to separate masters twenty years before, and he had spent all that time searching for her. One Virginia mother found her eighteen-year-old daughter in a refugee camp. The girl had been sold away when she was just an infant. Finding children who had been sold away when they were young or finding the parents who had been sold away when the children were young was exceedingly difficult. With each succeeding sale, a child may have been given a different name, and intervening years made it difficult to recognize the adult who was once someone's child. For such children to be able to find their families required a slave community that kept the children's family histories alive during long periods of separation. Even with the community's help, however, reuniting families was often impossible. Slave mortality was high, especially in the lower South, and it was likely that people sold down the river many years before had not survived until freedom came.

The seemingly insurmountable odds notwithstanding, freed people traveled great distances, tracking down every lead, in efforts to find their families. They questioned every person they met from the area where their relative was last heard of. Freedmen's Bureau teachers and missionaries wrote thousands of letters for the illiterate freed people, following every rumor that someone had seen or heard of their relatives. People placed advertisements in newspapers, giving information about the missing person's former life, personal characteristics, injuries, and scars: Nearly a generation after the Civil War, newspapers still carried such ads:

Information Wanted, of Caroline Dodson, who was sold from Nashville, Nov. 1st, 1862, by James Lumsden to Warwick, (a trader then in human beings), who carried her to Atlanta, Georgia, and she was last heard of in the slave pen of Robert Clarke, (human trader in that place), from which she was sold. Any information of her whereabouts will be thankfully received and rewarded by her mother. Lucinda Lowery, Nashville.

Land ownership was also important to the freed people. For many ex-slaves, the promise of self-sufficiency, independence, and opportunity that freedom represented rested on the ownership of land. Various military commanders had allowed former slaves to work land abandoned by fleeing Confederates, and rumors persisted that the federal government would eventually grant land to the freed people. On January 16, 1865, just months before the South's surrender, U.S. General William T. Sherman took time from his devastating Georgia campaign to meet with twenty black community leaders in Savannah and discuss the issue of confiscated Confederate land in Georgia, South Carolina, and northern Florida. Secretary of War Edwin M. Stanton joined the discussions and approved Sherman's Special Field Order 15, declaring that "the islands from Charleston south, the abandoned rice-fields along the rivers for thirty miles back from the sea, and the country bordering the St. Johns River, Florida, are reserved and set apart for the settlement

of the [N]egroes now made free by the acts of war and the [Emancipation] proclamation of the President of the United States." Each family was to be issued forty acres and an army mule to use in its cultivation. A few months later, the plan seemed confirmed by the government's placement of responsibility for refugees, freedmen, and abandoned lands in the same department.

In the spring of 1865, as the war came to an end, Vice President Andrew Johnson from Tennessee replaced the slain president in the oval office. Johnson had been Lincoln's wartime political choice, another strategy to hold the slave-holding border states, and was a political conservative. The new president spent the early days of his administration granting amnesty to former Confederate military leaders and handing out pardons wholesale to Confederates. White southerners needed simply to swear loyalty to the United States and agree to support the abolitionist provisions of the Thirteenth Amendment to have their property and general citizenship rights restored. Members of the southern aristocracy who had led the Confederacy in its war on the United States quickly applied for and received pardons. Thus, most of the land was returned to its prewar owners, and the former slaves who had been living on and cultivating the land during the last year of the war were expelled. Former abolitionists in Congress were never successful in their attempts to pass legislation granting former slaves land from the thousands of acres of confiscated Confederate land still under federal control. Ultimately, left without this foundation for independence, the freed people were forced to depend on former slaveholders to employ them or rent them land to farm.

Once pardoned and returned to political power, men from the planter class passed new laws reinstating much of their control over black people. In an attempt to re-create the southern racial etiquette of slave days, they punished black farm laborers for questioning white landlords, attacked black businessmen and their establishments for being too successful or competitive, attacked black students for displaying too much intelligence, confronted blacks who dressed too well or too neatly, and assaulted white people for encouraging black aspirations. Angered and distressed by the growing independence of their former slaves, planters complained that freed people were unwilling to work for what the planters considered reasonable wages. According to one Texas planter, the exorbitant wages offered by white employers with no sense of the "proper racial hierarchy" had spoiled the former slaves and led them to have outrageous expectations. Planters believed this had encouraged an inappropriate feeling of equality among the newly freed blacks.

After emancipation many African Americans did try to withdraw from the workforce. As a mark of their freedom, some men wanted their wives to be able to leave the fields and keep house for their families. Virtually all blacks wanted their children to be able to attend school, and some black people did demand respect from southern whites. As one former Georgia slave explained, many blacks vowed to take "no more foolishness off white folks." Long-standing customs and laws governing interracial contact in the South were designed to reinforce white supremacy. Whites addressed a black man as "boy" and a black woman as "girl" no matter how old they were, and either might be addressed as "nigger." The title of Uncle or Aunty that whites used for elderly blacks was the closest thing to respect an African American could expect. In Helena, Arkansas, after the war, when an elderly former slave addressed a white man on the street as "Mr." the white man followed the prewar convention and replied "Howdy uncle." The black man was insulted, made it clear they were not related, and demanded, "Call me Mister."

From the standpoint of former slaves, such confrontations were part of an effort to make freedom a reality of daily life in the South, a reality that white southerners were anxious to avoid. What ensued was a determined struggle between African Americans seeking dignity and respect and southern whites attempting to maintain the principle of white supremacy. White leaders argued that only strong restrictive measures would restore the black workforce to its prewar level of usefulness. Many southern

states enacted black codes, limiting the freedom of former slaves and returning them to near slavery. Vagrancy provisions imposed fines and jail time on unemployed African Americans, forcing former slaves into low-paying agricultural jobs and ensuring white planters a steady supply of cheap plantation labor. Without land, the ability to bargain for jobs, or the right to vote or hold office, southern blacks stood only marginally above their former slave position.

Almost all southern blacks were agricultural workers, and without land of their own, they had to depend on white land-owners for work. After the war cash was in short supply in the South, so landowners offered shares of the crop instead of wages in return for black labor. Sharecropping, as this system was called, seemed an equitable solution to the problem. Sharecroppers lived on the land, worked it as if it were their own, brought in the crop, and were entitled to a portion of the harvest at the end of the season. For landowners this ensured an agricultural labor force without the need for cash, and for sharecroppers it offered an approximation of the independent family farm. Unequal resources and power, however, led to white landholders' binding black sharecroppers to the land through real or contrived indebtedness.

Essentially, the bonds of debt peonage replaced the chains of slavery, and planters could control their labor force almost as completely as slaveholders had controlled theirs. To purchase seed, tools, teams of mules or horses, and other supplies, impoverished sharecroppers were forced to rely on credit advanced against the following year's crop. They also purchased food, clothing, and other necessities on credit, either at stores operated by the landowner or at independently owned stores in the vicinity. Interest rates were generally high and sharecroppers found themselves falling further and further into debt each season. "[Landowners] didn't pay everything they promised," recalled one Arkansas sharecropper. When he attempted to appeal to local authorities, he found that a white man's accounting superseded any argument an African American could offer. "They said figures didn't lie," he reported. He understood

Before the Civil War, most southern states barred slaves from learning to read and write. During Reconstruction, the establishment of black schools made it possible for the former slaves, children and adults alike, to obtain an education. As the Hortons conclude, "education was an important mark of their freedom and represented their hope for a better future." (Cook Collection, Valentine Richmond History Center)

that this could be a very dangerous situation, for any black man who questioned a white man's word was putting his life at risk. "You know how that was," he explained, "You dassent dispute a [white] man's word then."

Henry Blacke sharecropped for much of his adult life. He later explained, "[N]o matter how good accounts you kept, you had to go by [the white landowners'] account, and—now brother, I'm telling you the truth about this—it has been that way a long time." White southerners seemed to operate with a different set of ethics when dealing with blacks. As one Freedmen's Bureau official put it, white "men who are honorable in their dealings with their white neighbors will cheat a Negro without feeling a single twinge of their honor." Whites argued that the survival of southern civilization demanded completely controlling blacks, and, as in slavery, any black person who showed signs of contesting their control must be brought into line immediately. A Freedmen's Bureau official described white attitudes toward blacks in the Reconstruction South saying, "Wherever I go . . . I hear the people talk in such a way as to indicate that they are yet unable to conceive of the Negro as possessing any right at all." Even among "honorable" white men, he noted, "to kill a Negro [white southerners] do not deem murder; to debauch a Negro woman they do not think fornication; to take the property away from a Negro they do not consider robbery."

The Republican-controlled Congress attempted to protect African American rights, but President Johnson fought efforts to strengthen and broaden the powers of the Freedmen's Bureau and to pass a Civil Rights Act nullifying the black codes and providing citizenship rights to black people. Johnson campaigned widely for Democratic candidates in the Congressional election of 1866. He spoke against Republican candidates, attacked programs to aid the former slaves, and referred to some of the strongest supporters of the U.S. war effort against the Confederacy as traitors to the nation. Even the most moderate Republicans were outraged, and, after Republicans made substantial gains in the election, they joined with their more radical colleagues in solid opposition to the president. The Republican Congress passed the Civil Rights Act of 1866 and the Fourteenth Amendment, which wrote its provisions guaranteeing black citizenship into the Constitution. They took control of reconstructing southern state governments, passing measures limiting the power of the old southern elites and calling for new state constitutions.

Congress also passed several measures to limit Johnson's power, including the Tenure of Office Act. According to that law, the president could not dismiss any cabinet member appointed with the advice and consent of the Senate until the Senate had approved a successor. In early 1868, Johnson violated this law, and the Republican-dominated House of Representatives voted to impeach him. Although Johnson was saved from being removed from office by one vote in the Senate, his presidency was so weakened that he ceased to be a significant obstruction to

Congressional plans for reconstructing the South. Under Congressional Reconstruction, African Americans were allowed to participate in the state conventions that drew up the new constitutions, constitutions that gave blacks the right to vote. In South Carolina, Mississippi, Louisiana, and other southern states where blacks formed either a majority or a substantial proportion of the population, African Americans attained political power.

In 1866, pressured by abolitionists in Congress, the federal government passed the Southern Homestead Act, giving former slaves and whites who had remained loyal to the United States preferential access to 44 million acres of public land in five southern states for one year. The land, however, was poor—rocky, infertile, marshy, or otherwise unsuitable for farming. Penniless former slaves found it impossible to support themselves while waiting for the first crop, and few could take advantage of the program. A few blacks pooled their meager resources and bought some decent farmland. In Charleston two hundred freed people formed a land investment group called The Freemen's Land and Home Society and collectively purchased a 600-acre plantation on Remley's Point near the city, paying about ten dollars an acre. Many soldiers pooled their military pay and bought small plots, but the vast majority remained landless.

The ratification of the Fifteenth Amendment to the U.S. Constitution in 1870, outlawing the use of race to disenfranchise voters, brought more black men to the polls. Black women, too, were active in southern politics, even though, like white women, they could not vote. They attended political meetings and rallies and were a strong arm of the Republican Party, especially in the South where African American political power was most significant during Reconstruction. According to one historian, in South Carolina, "Freewomen as well as children left the rice fields when it was time to register, attended political meetings and rallies where their influence over the lowcountry vote was recognized and manipulated, and were found at the polls on election days." The presence of so many black women at political events apparently made some white Republicans uneasy. In Charleston, white Republicans attempted to convince black men to "leave their wives at their firesides, or, better still, to 'cut grass.'" The effort was apparently unsuccessful, for black women continued to be active advisers to their male representatives and participated in almost every phase of the voting process, except actually casting a ballot. Black leaders generally encouraged black women's participation in politics and recognized important, sometimes nontraditional, roles for them. During the mid 1870s black women armed with clubs patrolled polling places in South Carolina to keep order and protect Republicans who came to vote.

With large numbers of freed African Americans in the South and 10 percent to 20 percent of southern white males still disqualified from voting because of their rebellion against the United States, blacks were a majority of the electorate in five southern states. Their votes provided the foundation for the Republican Party in the South, a party that had not existed there before the war. Blacks found allies among white Republicans from the North who came to the South during and after the war. Southern Democrats called these whites carpet-baggers after the bags in which many carried their possessions, denoting their newcomer status. Although generally characterized as political opportunists, most were teachers and nurses who came to aid and educate former slaves.

The southern Democrats' most venomous charges were leveled at those people called scalawags, white southerners who became Republicans or supported the Republican Party. Such southern whites who allied themselves with blacks were the targets of public ridicule and violence. This was especially true with the rise of such vigilante political terrorist groups as the Knights of the White Camilla, The Pale Face Brotherhood, and others organized in the mid- to late-1860s in an effort to frustrate Republican rule and force black people back to a place of servitude in southern society. The longest lasting and most notorious of these groups was a social club formed in Tennessee in 1866 that became the Ku Klux Klan. It was led by the former slave trader, Confederate general, and notorious commander of the Fort Pillow massacre, Nathan Bedford Forrest.

These groups used intimidation and violence to discourage blacks and white Republicans from voting. In the spring of 1866, whites invaded the black community in Memphis, Tennessee. When newly discharged black soldiers and local freedmen defended themselves against the marauding whites and city police, forty-six blacks and two whites died. The political motivation was clear when a local newspaper called the riot proof that "the southern men will not be ruled by the [N]egro.". . .

In 1868 Republican and former general Grant replaced Andrew Johnson as president. Congress reacted to the continuing southern violence in the early 1870s by enacting a number of anti-Klan measures, which the president signed into law. In 1871 Grant suspended the writ of habeas corpus in nine South Carolina counties where the Klan was particularly active, making it easier to arrest people suspected of terrorist activity, and sent in federal troops to augment the government's efforts to quell the violence. Congress launched an extensive investigation of the Klan and political terrorism in the South, and the federal officials arrested and indicted hundreds of whites in Mississippi, South Carolina, and North Carolina for their participation in terrorist activity. Some observers were surprised that, in addition to poor whites, many of those arrested for such crimes were professional men, doctors, lawyers, ministers, and college professors.

Seeing African Americans hold political office especially incensed white southern Democrats. They accused blacks of being ignorant, incompetent people attempting to rise above their naturally subservient place in society. The vast majority of southern blacks were illiterate at the end of the war, but most black political leaders were educated. Oscar J. Dunn, who became lieutenant governor of Louisiana, for example, was born a slave but had been able to educate himself. Many, like Dunn, were self-educated, but many others had been formally educated. Hiram Rhodes Revels, a freeborn North Carolina barber and an ordained African Methodist Episcopal minister, became America's first black U.S. senator in 1870. He was a Republican who represented Mississippi for one year, completing the term of Jefferson Davis, who had given up his Senate seat in 1861 to become president of the Confederacy. Revels was well educated, having attended a Quaker seminary in Indiana and Knox College in Illinois. After his term in the Senate, Revels served as president of Mississippi's Alcorn Agricultural College (now Alcorn University), the first land-grant college for black students. . . .

Hundreds of African Americans, former soldiers, abolitionists, businessmen, ministers, lawyers, and teachers, helped guide southern governments for a brief time in the turbulent years of Reconstruction. Many had been born in the South, had left to work and live in the North, in Canada, or in Europe, and returned to take advantage of the unprecedented opportunities for community service and black political leadership. Facing incredible economic and political problems, they worked with white Republicans and even some white Democrats to rebuild the South. In the years between the end of the Civil War and the first decade of the twentieth century, more than six hundred African Americans served in state legislatures, twenty were elected to the U.S. House of Representatives, and two were elected to the U.S. Senate.

During Reconstruction, federal and state government efforts held the promise of improving many people's lives in the South. The majority of the delegates to the South Carolina constitutional convention were black, and 57 out of the 124 blacks had been slaves. This convention passed a number of progressive measures in 1868: abolishing racial discrimination in voting, schools, and the militia; protecting married women's property rights; establishing the state's first divorce law and the first free public school system; providing for elected rather than appointed judges; and abolishing dueling, imprisonment for debt, and property requirements for voting and holding office. The Freedmen's Bureau established and ran more than four thousand schools in the South, open to whites as well as blacks. Many of these schools served areas where there had previously

been no public education. The bureau ended most of its aid programs in 1868 but continued to operate schools that educated students from kindergarten to college until 1872. For the freed people, education was an important mark of their freedom and represented their hope for a better future. Since many slaves had been legally prohibited from learning to read and write, education was doubly important to them. About 95 percent of slaves were illiterate in 1863, but by 1877 more than six hundred thousand black children were in elementary schools. . . .

Southern Democrats were determined to reinstate the racial control of the prewar South and to further this aim tried to ensure black economic dependence and discourage black education. They used many methods in their postwar campaign, but violence became their signature. Outbreaks of racial violence, generally called riots but often seeming more like open rebellion, continued during the 1870s. Throughout the South, violence was the common political tool of those bent on returning to absolute and unquestioned white domination. Leading southern Democrats routinely rationalized the most heinous crimes if they helped "save southern civilization." Wade Hampton of South Carolina, who served as governor and U.S. senator, rallied his political colleagues by arguing that almost any illegal action, even murder, was completely acceptable if done in the name of white supremacy. He urged Democrats to do all in their power to "control the vote of at least one Negro, by intimidation, purchase, keeping him away or as each individual may determine, how may best accomplish it." Then he moved to the deadly specifics. "Never threaten a man individually. If he deserves to be threatened, the necessities of the times require that he should be killed."

African Americans did not meekly submit, however. They used whatever power they had to enforce the law and protect themselves and their communities. Black judges issued arrest warrants, and black sheriffs jailed white terrorists. Armed African Americans, especially war veterans, confronted white vigilante groups. Many black veterans had retained their military weapons, and some formed militia units to protect their communities. In Wilmington, North Carolina, black troops arrested the white chief of police when he refused to surrender his weapon as ordered, and in Victoria, Texas, blacks lynched the white killer of an African American townsman. In South Carolina, when a Confederate veteran stabbed a black Army sergeant for refusing to leave a railroad car in which white women were seated, black soldiers decided the veteran was guilty and shot him.

Southern whites quickly realized that racial intimidation could not be effective so long as these black militia units existed, and they tried to legally disarm and disband them. White Republican officials in the South were sometimes willing to accede to white petitions in order to gain the cooperation of prominent local citizens. As black militia units were disbanded, African American communities were left open to attack from the growing number of terrorist groups. Blacks were forced to depend on the law for protection, an increasingly unlikely possibility as conservative whites returned to power, or to defend themselves. In 1868, for example, black Mississippi politician Charles Caldwell was wounded by a white man. He shot and killed his assailant but was then charged with murder. Such confrontations were common, but Caldwell's acquittal by an all-white jury on the grounds of self-defense was unusual. . . .

Black voters in South Carolina constituted a majority, but white Democrats were determined to keep African Americans away from the polls. Blacks in some communities demanded their rights, and some whites chafed at what they considered African American arrogance. Such insults, the white southerners contended, "no white people upon earth had ever to put up with before." Whites in the small town of Hamburg on the Savannah River in South Carolina complained that they were forced to give way to black parades and were treated with disrespect and even arrested "on the slightest provocation" by the local black police. Tensions exploded during the country's centennial celebration on July 4, 1876, when a parading black militia company forced a local white farmer's son and son-in-law to halt

their carriage. Although Dock Adams, the militia commander, opened the ranks to let them through after some contention, the next day the farmer brought charges against Adams for impeding his travel. The black militia confronted armed white men in the town, and a well-known Democratic politician demanded that Adams disarm his militia company. He refused, the men began fighting, and the black militiamen retreated to the armory. Hundreds of whites from Augusta, Georgia, just across the river, invaded Hamburg to answer the challenge, bringing a cannon to aid in avenging the insult to their racial honor. The whites killed the town's black marshal and killed at least five other blacks after they had been captured. Blacks killed one young white man. The white mob also looted and vandalized African American homes and businesses. A grand jury indicted seven whites for murder and dozens more as accessories, but all were acquitted.

As the violence increased and it became clear that African Americans were not safe anywhere in the South, growing numbers of blacks began to reconsider colonization. African Americans from several southern states met in New Orleans in December 1875 to discuss migrating to the independent West African nation of Liberia. The racial troubles in America created substantial interest in Liberia, and not only among southern blacks. Northern blacks faced less continual violence but confronted discouraging racial discrimination in public places, in the job market, and in housing. In 1878, one colonization group in Pennsylvania received almost fifty thousand inquiries from African Americans considering migration possibilities.

Although many were interested in West Africa, many more African Americans looked to lands in the American West as a place of opportunity and a safe haven. A few people made their way to New Mexico, Arizona, Colorado, and Oklahoma. Groups of North Carolina and Mississippi blacks migrated to Nebraska, and others looked to the frontier state of Kansas. Exodusters, as migrants to the American frontier were called, led by such men as former slave Benjamin "Pap" Singleton from Tennessee, moved their families from the Deep South westward into Kansas during the 1870s. Kansas had a special appeal: it had plenty of unoccupied land and was associated in the minds of African Americans with the Underground Railroad and John Brown. For them, it was an abolitionist territory that had battled proslavery forces and finally entered the Union as a free state. By the mid-1870s many southern blacks were taken with "Kansas Fever" fueled by rumors of free land, free transportation, and free supplies. The reports were largely exaggerated, but they did draw thousands from the violent South to the promise of a new life. By 1878 the town of Nicodemus, Kansas, boasted a population of seven hundred African Americans, all recent migrants from the Deep South. In April of the next year, hundreds more Exodusters traveled up the Missouri River by steamboat to the eastern Kansas settlement of Wyandotte.

Most African Americans did not leave the South. They did not have the resources, debts bound them to the land on which they sharecropped, or family ties held them in place. The proportion of blacks living in the South had dropped from 94 percent at the start of the Civil War to 84 percent by 1880, but the vast majority were still southerners. For this vast majority of black people in America, their brief political influence was rapidly fading. In the presidential election of 1876, pitting Democrat Samuel J. Tilden against Republican Rutherford B. Hayes, both parties claimed victory in Louisiana, South Carolina, and Florida, and thus the presidency. When an electoral commission sustained Hayes's claim, Democrats in Congress refused to certify the election. After the chaos of civil war and the disruption of the Reconstruction, the nation was in no mood for such political uncertainty. From every quarter—business interests, state and local governments, churches, and universities—came the demand that the election be settled quickly. A series of meetings led to a compromise where-by the Republican, Hayes, would take the presidency. Democrats would not contest economic policies benefiting Republican business interests, and in return the Hayes administration would remove the last U.S. troops from the South, leaving southerners to handle civil stability and civil rights in their states. The compromise that saved the nation from uncertainty and placed the Republican in the White House had been struck at African Americans' expense.

In the following years Southern Democrats, assisted by rulings of the U.S. Supreme Court, removed federal protections for black rights in the South. The court weakened or struck down much of the preceding decades' civil rights legislation and placed the responsibility for enforcing the Fourteenth and Fifteenth amendments on the states. Southern blacks denied the right to vote or lacking legal protection found their only recourse was to state authority. As conservative Democrats moved into positions of power at all levels of southern state governments, there was little recourse at all. Starting in 1890 in Mississippi, and then spreading across the South, a constellation of laws restricted the franchise to whites only. Poll taxes generally put the vote financially out of reach for sharecroppers and other poor blacks. Literacy testing was often devised and administered so that no black person, no matter how educated, could qualify to vote. Meanwhile, a clause in state regulations safeguarded the voting rights of illiterate whites by waiving the literacy requirement for voters deemed people of good conduct or whose grandfathers had voted before 1860, a time when almost all southern blacks were slaves.

Other laws provided for racial segregation in public accommodations, transportation, and almost every phase of life. The Mississippi Plan, and the host of laws that followed in every southern state and many border states, were the foundation for the extensive southern system of racial segregation often called the Jim Crow system. The Jim Crow segregation system was named after a character played by white actor, Thomas Dartmouth "Daddy" Rice. In the 1840s and 1850s, Rice blackened his face and danced, playing Jim Crow, a racial stereotype born of the white imagination. By the mid-1890s it was clear that Reconstruction's promise of real freedom was coming to an end, and there seemed little blacks could do about it. . . .

. . .Yet Reconstruction was not a total failure. Slavery was ended, and black people no longer faced the awful prospect of having their children and other family members sold away from them. African Americans made great gains in literacy and education, and a few even managed to acquire land. The Constitution was changed: the Thirteenth Amendment abolished slavery, the Fourteenth Amendment guaranteed African Americans citizenship rights, and the Fifteenth Amendment forbade the denial of voting rights on account of race. Constitutional guarantees may not have been honored, but they established legal principles to which plaintiffs could appeal. African Americans had struggled before the Civil War to end slavery and during Reconstruction to attain citizenship rights, and they continued their struggle for full freedom through the twentieth century. . . .

Despite the progress made against racial injustice, slavery still has an impact on Americans more than a century after its abolition. Its legacy remains in the history and heritage of the South that it shaped, in the culture of the North where its memory was long denied, in the national economy for which it provided much of the foundation, and in the political and social system it profoundly influenced. Slavery and its effects are embedded in the national culture and in the assumptions and contradictory ideals of American society. The central issues under debate today—issues involving race, class, region, religion, and national identity—are all imperfectly understood without the historical context of American slavery and without an understanding of the means by which a freedom-loving people rationalized their tolerance of slavery's development. Although it is troubling to consider, it is nonetheless true that slavery was, and continues to be, a critical factor in shaping the United States and all of its people. As Americans, we must understand slavery's history if we are ever to be emancipated from its consequences.

QUESTIONS TO CONSIDER

1 Describe the accomplishments of the Freedmen's Bureau in helping blacks make the transition from slavery to freedom. Before the Civil War, the cruel domestic slave trade broke up black families. What actions did the freedmen take to find lost family members and what obstacles often impeded their efforts?

2 Why did the former slaves need to own land to achieve true independence? Contrast the actions of William Tecumseh Sherman and Andrew Johnson on the distribution of confiscated Confederate lands to the freedmen. Why did sharecropping prevent the freedmen from becoming independent landowners?

3 What immediate impact did the Fourteenth and Fifteenth amendments have on the rights of former slaves? How was this important legislation compromised by southern whites who feared and resisted any change in race relations?

4 In what ways did the carpetbaggers and scalawags try to help the freedmen? In what ways was the Southern Homestead Act supposed to benefit the former slaves? Did it benefit them? Describe the accomplishments of the Republican governments in the former Confederate states, governments in which African Americans participated. How did such governments keep "the promise of improving many people's lives in the South"?

5 What motivated some African Americans to migrate to Liberia and to the American frontier? Why did most of the former slaves remain in the South?

6 What was the compromise that settled the disputed presidential election of 1876? Why do the authors contend that it "had been struck at African American expense"? In what ways did poll taxes, literacy tests, and other Jim Crow measures severely restrict the freedom of the former slaves?

2 The Checkered History of the Great Fourteenth Amendment

ERIC FONER

In the following selection, Eric Foner, today's foremost historian of the Reconstruction era, recounts the dramatic and controversial history of the great Fourteenth Amendment. Because it promised equality of all Americans before the law, Foner states that it was "one of the most important lasting consequences of the immense changes produced by the war."

To place Foner's story in historical context, it would be well to pick up the Reconstruction story with what was transpiring in the nation's capital in 1865 and 1866. Andrew Johnson's soft, conciliatory reconstruction policy enraged Republican leaders on Capitol Hill. As we saw in the previous selection, the president not only opposed granting black men the right to vote but also allowed former Confederates to return to power in the southern states. Johnson also stood by when ex-rebel legislators enacted black codes that reduced blacks to a virtual condition of peonage, and he hotly opposed congressional interference in the reconstruction process. He even urged southern states to reject the Fourteenth Amendment, pushed through Congress by the Republicans, which would protect southern blacks. The amendment would prevent the states from adopting laws that abridged "the privileges or immunities of citizens of the United States." It would also bar the states from depriving "any person of life, liberty, or property, without due process of law," or from denying any person the "equal protection of the law." Johnson did more than just oppose the amendment; he damned Republican leaders like Charles Sumner of Massachusetts and Thaddeus Stevens of Pennsylvania, calling them tyrants and traitors. He even campaigned against the Republican party in the 1866 off-year elections. As a consequence, he alienated moderate as well as radical Republicans, who soon united against him. When the 1866 elections gave the Republicans huge majorities in both houses of Congress, they took control of Reconstruction and set about reforming the South themselves, granting blacks the right to vote and hold office.

Thus the stage is set for Foner's brilliant essay on one of the most important constitutional amendments in American history. In the short run, the equal protection clause had little effect on the lives of the former slaves. Southern white resistance and northern complacency resulted in what Foner calls "a new system of racial subordination" that sought to eliminate black voting, institute racial segregation, and place severe restrictions on "blacks' economic power."

Moreover, the great Fourteenth Amendment itself underwent a drastic reinterpretation. When Reconstruction ended in 1877, the United States entered what Mark Twain called the Gilded Age, a conservative era dominated by big businessmen and their corporate monopolies. In this period, reflecting the spirit of the times, the Supreme Court changed the original purpose of the Fourteenth Amendment: the Court's new interpretation turned it into an instrument for the protection of corporations. At the same time, the Court acquiesced in the ruthless oppression of black people in the white supremacist South.

But decades later, in the activist 1960s and 1970s, a progressive Supreme Court not only returned the Fourteenth Amendment to its original purpose, but also expanded it to protect the rights of "aggrieved groups of all sorts—blacks, women, gays, welfare recipients, the elderly, the disabled." More than a century after its ratification, this powerful amendment, first conceived in "imperfect compromise" during Reconstruction, has become today (in Foner's words) "the most important bulwark of the rights of American citizens." What follows is the fascinating story of how that came to be.

GLOSSARY

BLACK CODES   See glossary in previous selection.

BROWN v. BOARD OF EDUCATION OF TOPEKA (1954) The Supreme Court's landmark decision that ruled that state-initiated racial segregation violated the equal protection guarantee of the Fourteenth Amendment. This was because separation inherently meant inequality.

DRED SCOTT v. SANDFORD (1857) With a majority of southerners as justices, the Supreme Court ruled that neither Congress nor the territories could outlaw slavery. Five justices maintained that to do so would violate the property rights clause of the United States Constitution. Since slaves were property, the Court said that they could not be United States citizens.

FIFTEENTH AMENDMENT   See glossary in previous selection.

JOHNSON, ANDREW   See glossary in previous selection.

PLESSY v. FERGUSON (1896) This Supreme Court decision upheld "separate but equal" accommodations for whites and African Americans. The majority of justices argued that the ruling was consistent with the equal protection clause guaranteed by the Fourteenth Amendment.

RECONSTRUCTION ACT OF 1867 Provided the freedmen with the right to vote and "launched the short-lived period of Radical Reconstruction during which, for the first time in American history, a genuine interracial democracy flourished."

SANTA CLARA COUNTY v. SOUTHERN PACIFIC RAILROAD In a strange twist the Supreme Court ruled in this case that a corporation was a person under the law. By this decision, the Fourteenth Amendment forbade states to interfere with a corporation's activities, like the regulation of working conditions.

STEVENS, THADDEUS A Radical Republican leader in the House of Representatives, he devoted his career to the struggle against slavery and for the equal rights of the freedmen. He promoted the Fourteenth Amendment and the confiscation and distribution of former rebel lands to the newly freed slaves, and he was a major force in the impeachment trial of Andrew Johnson.

SUMNER, CHARLES One of the leading Radical Republicans in the Senate, he too was a committed idealist who advocated complete civil and political equality for African Americans. "More than any of his political contemporaries," writes his biographer, David Herbert Donald, "Sumner realized that the future of American democracy depended on the ability of the white and black races to live together in peace and equality."

TRUMBULL, LYMAN This Illinois senator and his colleague, Senator John Sherman of Ohio, thought that suffrage for the freedmen was "a political liability." Both men represented the moderate wing of the Republican party that desired a free labor economy in the South. They joined the Radicals who desired more drastic changes only after President Johnson opposed the Fourteenth Amendment and stuck adamantly to his prosouthern policy.

On June 13, 1866, Thaddeus Stevens, the majority floor leader in the House of Representatives and the nation's most prominent Radical Republican, rose to address his congressional colleagues. His subject was the Fourteenth Amendment to the Constitution—which, after months of deliberation and innumerable drafts and redrafts, was about to receive final approval by Congress. Its purpose was to secure the fruits of Union victory in the Civil War by guaranteeing equal civil rights for the freed slaves and loyal governments in the South.

Born during George Washington's administration, Stevens had enjoyed a public career that embodied, as much as anyone's, the struggle against the "Slave Power" and for equal rights for black Americans. In 1837, as a delegate to Pennsylvania's constitutional convention, he had refused to sign the state's new frame of government because it abrogated the right of African Americans to vote. As a member of Congress during the 1850s, he had fought against the expansion of slavery and, during the secession crisis, opposed compromise with the South. Once the Civil War began, he was among the first to advocate the emancipation of slaves and the enrollment of black soldiers.

During the era of Reconstruction that followed the war, Stevens insisted that the South was a "conquered province," which Congress could govern as it saw fit. He was the most prominent advocate, for example, of distributing land to former slaves so that they might have an economic foundation for their freedom. Like other Radicals, he believed that Reconstruction was a golden opportunity to purge the nation of the legacy of slavery and create a society whose citizens enjoyed equal civil and political rights, secured by a powerful and beneficent national government. "The whole fabric of southern society must be changed," he declared, "and never can it be done, if this opportunity be lost." Stevens's speech

Thaddeus Stevens was the driving force behind the Fourteenth Amendment, but controversy followed this champion of the freedmen. In the superstitious nineteenth century, his clubfoot was deemed a sign of evil. Although he never married, there were many rumors about his relationship with an African American housekeeper with whom he lived for many years. (Library of Congress)

on June 13 was an eloquent statement of this political creed:

In my youth, in my manhood, in my old age, I had fondly dreamed that when any fortunate chance should have broken up for awhile the foundation of our institutions, and released us from obligations the most tyrannical that ever man imposed in the name of freedom, that the intelligent, pure and just men of this Republic . . . would have so remodeled all our institutions as to have freed them from every vestige of human oppression, of inequality of rights, of the recognized degradation of the poor, and the superior caste of the rich. . . . This bright dream has vanished [quoting Shakespeare's *The Tempest*] "like the baseless fabric of a dream." I find that we shall be obliged to be content with patching up the worst portions of the ancient edifice, and leaving it, in many of its parts, to be swept through by the . . . storm of despotism. Do you inquire why, holding these views and possessing some will of my own, I accept so imperfect a proposition? I answer, because I live among men and not among angels.

A few moments later, the Fourteenth Amendment was approved by the House. The result was never in doubt because, with the southern states still unrepresented, the Republican party commanded an overwhelming majority. The final vote was 120–32, well above the required two-thirds majority. Three days later, having been approved by the Senate shortly before the House vote, the amendment was sent to the states for ratification. It became part of the Constitution on July 28, 1868.

The Fourteenth Amendment prohibited the states from abridging the equality before the law of American citizens, provided for a reduction in representation in Congress should any state deprive male citizens of the right to vote, excluded Confederates who had previously taken a constitutional oath from holding state or federal office, and prohibited payment of the Confederate debt. It was one of the most important lasting consequences of the immense changes produced by the Civil War and the subsequent political crisis of Reconstruction, especially the struggle between the president and Congress over control of Reconstruction policy.

In late May 1865, six weeks after he succeeded the martyred Abraham Lincoln, Pres. Andrew Johnson announced his plan for reuniting the nation, launching the era of presidential Reconstruction. Although a staunch Unionist from Tennessee, Johnson was an inveterate racist and a firm defender of states' rights. The essentials of his Reconstruction plan allowed white southerners to establish new state governments—which were required by Johnson to abolish slavery, repudiate secession, and abrogate the Confederate debt but otherwise accorded a free hand in controlling local affairs. When these new governments quickly enacted the repressive Black Codes, most northern Republicans turned against the president. As one observer put it, the Black Codes seemed designed to "restore all of slavery but its name." Meanwhile, the election of "rebels" to leading offices in the South

Andrew Johnson from Tennessee remained loyal to the Union and became Lincoln's vice president at the end of the Civil War. The former senator was motivated by his devotion to the Constitution and his disdain for the planter class. With his poor southern white background, Johnson opposed granting political rights to the freedmen. His lenient Reconstruction program allowed former Confederates to take office in southern state governments, and he permitted these governments to enact the infamous black codes, which virtually reenslaved African Americans in the South. (Library of Congress)

and reports of violence directed against both freed people and northern visitors reinforced the conviction that Johnson's plan played into the hands of the southern Democrats.

When the Thirty-ninth Congress (elected in November 1864) finally assembled in December 1865, Radical Republicans, led by Stevens, called for abrogation of the Johnson-authorized state governments and the establishment of new ones based on equality before the law and universal manhood suffrage. The Radicals, however, didn't control the Republican party. Occupying the political middle ground was the moderate Republican majority, led in Congress by Sen. Lyman Trumbull of Illinois and Sen. John Sherman of Ohio. Unenthusiastic about black suffrage—which they viewed as a political liability in the North and an experiment whose outcome couldn't be predicted in the South—Trumbull, Sherman, and their allies were nonetheless fully committed to ensuring "loyal" governments in the former states of the Confederacy and protecting the elementary rights of freed slaves in a society organized on the basis of free labor rather than slavery. Eventually, however, Johnson's policies, and the actions of the state governments created under his supervision, drove them into the Radicals' arms, uniting the entire Republican party against the president.

Much of the ensuing debate over Reconstruction revolved around the problem, as Trumbull put it, of defining "what slavery is and what liberty is." The Civil War had greatly enhanced the power of the national state. Especially because of the service of two hundred thousand black men in the Union army and navy, the war had also put the question of black citizenship on the national agenda. By early 1866, moderates had concluded that equality before the law—enforced, if necessary, by national authority—had become an inevitable consequence of emancipation and a condition for restoring the South to full participation in the Union. These principles were embodied in the Civil Rights Act of 1866, a precursor to the Fourteenth Amendment that outlined the rights all Americans were to enjoy regardless of race. These included the rights to make contracts, bring lawsuits, and enjoy equal protection of the security of person and property. Johnson's veto of this measure and its repassage by Congress in April 1866 marked the final breach between the president and the Republican party. It was the first time in American history that a significant piece of legislation became law over a president's veto.

Beyond impelling congressional Republicans to devise their own Reconstruction plan, Johnson's intransigence persuaded them to write their understanding of the consequences of the Civil War into the Constitution, there to be secure from shifting electoral majorities. The result was the Fourteenth Amendment, adopted by Congress after months of committee deliberations and a series of alterations on the House and Senate floors. Some Republicans wished to disqualify leading Confederates from voting; others wanted to include both "universal amnesty" for "rebels" and "universal suffrage" for black men. But these proposals failed to win the support of most Republicans. In its final form, the amendment was a compromise on which all Republicans could unite.

This process of compromise, however, as Stevens's June 13 speech suggests, resulted in a text that didn't fully satisfy the Radicals. The Fourteenth Amendment, as enacted, didn't abolish existing state governments in the South, nor did it guarantee blacks the right to vote; indeed, in one section, it offered each southern state, once readmitted to the Union, the alternative of allowing black men to vote and retaining the state's full representation in Congress or continuing to disenfranchise blacks and suffering a loss of representation proportionate to the black percentage of the state population. (No penalty applied, however, when women were denied the right to vote, an omission that led many advocates of women's rights to oppose ratification of the amendment.)

The Fourteenth Amendment had five sections in all, three of which have little importance today—those barring Confederates from office, dealing with the Confederate debt, and reducing a state's representation in Congress if men are denied the right to vote. (This last provision was never enforced, even during the decades when southern states disenfranchised most black voters.) Nonetheless, the Fourteenth Amendment has since become, after the Bill of Rights, the most important constitutional change in the nation's history. Its heart was Section 1, which declared that all persons born or naturalized in the United States were both national and state citizens. Section 1 also prohibited states from abridging the "privileges and immunities of citizens"; depriving them "of life, liberty, or property without due process of law"; and denying them "equal protection of the laws." It thus established, as Thaddeus Stevens told the House, the principle that state laws "shall operate equally upon all." Later he added, "I can hardly believe that any person can be found who will not admit that . . . [it] is just."

In keeping with constitutional authority the principle that equality before the law, regardless of race, could and should be enforced by the national government, the Fourteenth Amendment permanently transformed the definition of American citizenship and refashioned relations between the federal government and the states as well as those between individual Americans and the nation. We live today in a legal and constitutional system shaped profoundly by the Fourteenth Amendment.

During the 1866 Congressional elections, ratification of the Fourteenth Amendment became the central issue of the campaign. That fall, the president embarked on an unprecedented speaking trip across the North, known as the "swing around the circle." Its primary purpose was to drum up support for candidates associated with Johnson's National Union party—mostly northern Democrats who supported the president's Reconstruction policies. Yet Johnson also took the opportunity to rally whatever opposition to ratification he could. Again and again, he called for reconciliation between North and South, insisting that suffrage requirements and citizens' rights should be left to the states. Johnson also engaged in impromptu debates with hecklers, intimating that Stevens and the other Radicals were traitors. For their part, Republicans defended the amendment as necessary to secure the emancipation of the slaves and prevent Confederates from controlling the South.

The outcome of the midterm elections was continued Republican dominance in Congress and a clear mandate for Stevens and the Radicals. Johnson, however, continued his intransigent opposition to the amendment, urging southern legislatures to refuse to ratify it. And during the winter of 1866–1867, every southern state, except Tennessee, indeed rejected the amendment. With southern state governments thus having thoroughly discredited themselves in the eyes of nearly all Republicans, moderate and radical alike, party leaders concluded that only by establishing entirely new governments in the south could Reconstruction be accomplished. In March 1867, on the penultimate day of its postelection session, the Thirty-ninth Congress passed, over Johnson's veto, the Reconstruction Act of 1867. This gave the right to vote to black men in the South and launched the short-lived period of Radical Reconstruction during which, for the first time in American history, a genuine interracial democracy flourished. In March 1870, the Fifteenth Amendment, prohibiting any state from depriving citizens of the right to vote because of race, became part of the Constitution. What Republican leader Carl Schurz called "the great Constitutional revolution" of Reconstruction was complete. "Nothing in all history," exulted abolitionist William Lloyd Garrison, equaled "this wonderful . . . transformation of four million human beings from . . . the auction-block to the ballot-box."

In general, the Acts and Amendments of Reconstruction reflected the intersection of two products of the Civil War era: the newly empowered national state and the idea of a national citizenry enjoying equality before the law. In fact, rather than embodying a threat to liberty (as Jefferson had perceived it), the federal government had now become "the custodian of freedom," declared Charles Sumner, the abolitionist senator from Massachusetts. The rewriting of the Constitution during Reconstruction promoted a sense of the document's malleability and further suggested that the rights of individual citizens were intimately connected to federal power. This was a substantial departure from the pre–Civil War period, when disenfranchised groups were far more likely to draw inspiration from the Declaration of Independence than from the Constitution. (After all, the only mention of equality in the original Constitution came in the clause granting each state an equal number of senators.)

For example, the Bill of Rights, ratified in 1791, defined civil liberties in terms of state autonomy. Its language—"Congress shall pass no law. . ."— reflected the Jeffersonian belief that concentrated power was a threat to freedom. The Reconstruction amendments, however, which included the Thirteenth Amendment abolishing slavery, assumed that rights required political power to enforce them. These amendments, therefore, not only authorized the federal government to override state actions that deprived citizens of equality but also concluded with sections empowering Congress to "enforce" the amendments with "appropriate legislation." The Reconstruction amendments, especially the Fourteenth, transformed the Constitution from a document primarily concerned with federal-state relations and the rights of property into a vehicle through which members of vulnerable minorities could stake a claim to substantive freedom and seek protection against misconduct by all levels of government.

Limiting the privileges of citizenship to white men had long been intrinsic to the practice of American democracy. In 1857, in deciding *Dred Scott v. Sandford,* the Supreme Court had declared that no black person could be a citizen of the United States. Racism, federalism, a belief in limited government and local autonomy—Reconstruction challenged all these principles of nineteenth-century political culture. So deeply rooted were they, in fact, that only during an unparalleled crisis could they have been superseded, even temporarily, by the vision of an egalitarian republic embracing black Americans as well as white under the protection of the federal government. Indeed, it was precisely for this reason that the era's laws and constitutional amendments aroused such bitter opposition. The underlying principles—that the federal government possessed the power to define and protect citizens' rights, and that blacks were equal members of the body politic—were striking departures in American law. It isn't difficult to understand why President Johnson, in one of his veto messages, claimed that federal protection of African-American civil rights, together

Frederick Douglass was a runaway slave, the author of a popular autobiography, the editor of the North Star, *perhaps the most dynamic of the abolitionist spokesmen, and the greatest black man of his generation. He was also a champion of the women's rights movement. (The National Archives)*

with the broad conception of national power that lay behind it, violated "all our experience as a people."

Reconstruction proved fragile and short lived. Its end is usually dated at 1877, when federal troops were withdrawn from the South (as a consequence of the contested 1876 presidential election) and white-supremacist Democrats regained control of southern state governments. But retreat from the idea of equality was already underway prior to 1877, as traditional ideas of racism and localism reasserted themselves during the early 1870s and violence disrupted the southern Republican party. This transition accelerated after 1877, when Supreme Court interpretation of the Fourteenth Amendment increasingly eviscerated its promise of equal citizenship. Deciding the 1873 Slaughterhouse Cases, for example, the Court severely restricted the rights protected under the amendment, ruling that these comprised only those rights that owed their existence to the federal government—such as traveling on navigable waterways, running for federal office, and being protected on the high seas. Clearly, *these* rights were of limited concern to most former slaves. All other rights, the Court ruled, were derived from state, not national, authority, and with these the amendment had "nothing to do."

Next came the 1883 Civil Rights Cases, which invalidated a federal law prohibiting unequal treatment of blacks in public accommodations on the grounds that the Fourteenth Amendment barred only *legal* discrimination, not the actions of private individuals. Finally, the Court's famous 1896 decision in *Plessy* v. *Ferguson* decreed that state-mandated racial segregation didn't violate the Fourteenth Amendment's equal protection clause because "separate" could be equal. By the turn of the twentieth century, therefore, the states had been given carte blanche to nullify the Reconstruction amendments and civil rights laws. A new system of racial subordination was put in place in the South, centered on the elimination of black voting, racial segregation, and the severe restriction of blacks' economic opportunities. And these blatant violations of the Fourteenth and Fifteenth Amendments occurred with the acquiescence of the North, as reflected in the Supreme Court rulings.

Meanwhile, the Court made use of the Fourteenth Amendment in a manner that Thaddeus Stevens could never have imagined—as a barrier against governmental regulation of corporate behavior. In 1886, in *Santa Clara County* v. *Southern Pacific Railroad,* the Court declared that a corporation was a "person" under the law and thus couldn't be deprived of the "privileges and immunities" specified in the amendment's first section. This principle underpinned a long legal era during which the Court held that "liberty of contract"—the right of corporations to operate without state interference such as regulation of working conditions, limitation of working hours, and so on—was the real intention of

the Fourteenth Amendment. Not until the late 1930s did the Court abandon this liberty-of-contract jurisprudence.

The Fourteenth Amendment's checkered history, however, is also the history of evolving American ideas about civil rights and civil liberties. During the first half of the twentieth century, the Court slowly took up the work of applying Fourteenth Amendment protections to the citizens' rights enumerated in the Bill of Rights. That is, the Court began to rule that states must respect the same civil liberties that the first ten amendments to the Constitution protect against federal intrusion. This process, called "incorporation" by legal historians, began shortly after World War I, when the Court responded to extensive censorship by wartime authorities with an opinion that obligated states under the Fourteenth Amendment to refrain from unreasonable restrictions on the freedoms of speech and of the press. Soon afterward, it invalidated state laws that required all students to attend public schools and prohibited teachers from instructing in languages other than English (measures directed against schools established by churches and immigrant groups). The amendment's guarantee of equal liberty, it declared, included the right to bring up children and practice religion free from governmental interference.

During the 1950s and 1960s, led by Chief Justice Earl Warren, the Court again turned to the Fourteenth Amendment as a source not only for the racial justice envisioned by its framers but also for a vast expansion of civil liberties for all Americans. In 1954, in the *Brown* v. *Board of Education* decision that overturned *Plessy,* the Warren Court ruled that state-sanctioned racial segregation violated the Fourteenth Amendment's equal protection clause because separation was inherently unequal. In subsequent decisions, it struck down state laws that sought to destroy civil rights organizations by requiring them to disclose lists of their members; and in *New York Times* v. *Sullivan* (1964), it greatly expanded the legal protections given newspapers and other media by requiring that plaintiffs in libel suits prove that the defamatory remarks in question were made out of either malice or a "reckless disregard" for the truth. Reversing its long history of compliance with racial injustice, the Supreme Court had become by the end of the 1960s the Congress's leading ally in the struggle for racial justice.

The Warren Court continued the process of incorporation until the states were required to abide by virtually every clause in the Bill of Rights—from such literal guarantees as protection against unreasonable searches and seizures and the right to a speedy trial to inferred rights, including the right of indigent defendants to publicly appointed legal counsel. During this period, the Court struck down numerous state and local measures, including some mandating prayer in public schools, that violated the First Amendment's ban on government support for religion.

Meanwhile, generating even greater controversy, it discovered under the aegis of the Fourteenth Amendment some entirely new rights that the states couldn't abridge. Most dramatic of these was the right to "privacy," embodied in the 1965 *Griswold* decision overturning a Connecticut law that prohibited the use of contraceptive devices and in *Roe* v. *Wade* (1973), which created the constitutional right to terminate a pregnancy. This "rights revolution" undertaken by the Warren Court elevated the status of the Fourteenth Amendment until it became the major constitutional provision to which aggrieved groups of all sorts—blacks, women, gays, welfare recipients, the elderly, the disabled— appealed in seeking to expand their legal rights and social status.

Today, amid the continuing controversies over abortion rights, affirmative action, the rights of homosexuals, and many other issues, the Court's interpretation of the Fourteenth Amendment remains a focus of judicial as well as political debate. An imperfect compromise when added to the Constitution during Reconstruction, the amendment has since become the most powerful bulwark of the rights of American citizens. We haven't yet created the "bright dream" of which Thaddeus Stevens spoke in his June 1866 speech, but thanks to the reinvigoration of the Fourteenth Amendment by the twentieth-century Supreme Court, more Americans enjoy more rights and more freedoms today than ever before in our history.

QUESTIONS TO CONSIDER

1 Consider the long career of Thaddeus Stevens. What issues did he champion and what frustrations did he face? Why would Foner state that Stevens viewed Reconstruction as a "golden opportunity"?

2 Why would Foner describe the Fourteenth Amendment as "one of the most important lasting consequences of the immense changes produced by the Civil War and the subsequent political crisis of Reconstruction?" After its passage, do you think that race should have been a factor when determining legal equality? In what ways was its original purpose later compromised in Supreme Court rulings such as *Plessy* v. *Ferguson* and *Santa Clara County* v. *Southern Pacific Railroad?*

3 Why would Foner state that the Reconstruction amendments made the Constitution a document "through which members of vulnerable minorities could stake a claim to substantive freedom and seek protection against misconduct by all levels of government"? Before Reconstruction, why did the Declaration of Independence, more so than the Constitution, provide hope for the downtrodden and oppressed?

4 Why did the mood of the country in the conservative period following the fall of the Radical Republicans erode the original purpose of the Fourteenth Amendment? How would Thaddeus Stevens have viewed the Slaughterhouse Cases, the 1883 Civil Rights Cases, and the separate but unequal society that emerged?

5 The Fourteenth Amendment's checkered history reflected the changing values of the country. Explain how, during probusiness eras, it has protected

corporations more than people. Why did it fail to prevent racial discrimination at the end of the nineteenth century? How did it help spark a "second reconstruction" nearly sixty years later, after a ground-breaking decision from the Warren Court?

6 The Fourteenth Amendment, initially passed to help guarantee equality under the law for the freedmen, became a vehicle in the twentieth century to help many other groups—women, gays, the elderly, and the disabled. Is this a violation or a natural extension of its original intent? Examine the rationale for decisions that applied the Fourteenth Amendment to issues like abortion, school prayer, and the rights of the accused. Are we now approaching that "bright dream" envisioned by Thaddeus Stevens?

PART TWO

Conquest of the West

3 Sitting Bull and the Sioux Resistance

ROBERT M. UTLEY

In the forty years after the Civil War, American pioneers conquered and exploited an immense inner frontier that lay between California and the Mississippi River. It was an area as diverse as it was expansive, a region of windy prairies, towering mountains, painted deserts, and awesome canyons. Heading east out of California or west from the Mississippi, Americans by the thousands poured into this great heartland, laying out cattle ranches and farms, building towns and mining camps, and creating a variety of local and state governments. People moved to the frontier for various reasons: to start a new life, seek glory and adventure, strike it rich in a single, fabulous windfall, and prevail over the West's challenging environment.

Still, the winning of the West was not all romance. Driven by the aggressive, exploitive imperatives of their culture, American pioneers—especially whites—infiltrated Indian lands and hunting grounds, and conflicts between settlers and Indians broke out all across the frontier line, thus opening a gruesome chapter in the westward movement after the Civil War. The fact was that white-dominated America tended to regard the Indians as savages who deserved violent treatment. If these "ignorant nomads" blocked the advance of Christian civilization across the West, they should be "removed." And so, terrible fights erupted whenever whites and Indians came into contact. Trying to reduce the violence, the government sent out additional federal troops, including several African American regiments; instead of enforcing existing treaties, the soldiers usually defended whites who violated the pacts, which only provoked the Indians all the more.

In 1867, the federal government decided to confine the Indians to small, remote reservations in areas of the West spurned by United States settlers. Herein lies a paradox, for the whites' handling of the Indians in the late 1860s contrasted sharply with the way they treated southern blacks. The Congress that approved the small reservation policy, with its philosophy of strict segregation and inequality for western Indians, was the same Congress that attempted to give African American men in the South political rights equal to those of white men.

But many Indian bands refused to surrender their ancient hunting grounds, refused to be herded onto reservations and made to "walk the white man's road," and they fought back tenaciously. None did so with more resolve than the warrior elements of the proud, buffalo-hunting Lakota (or Sioux) of the northern Plains, who united behind Sitting Bull and vowed to throw the white invaders out of Lakota country. Sitting Bull, the great holy man and war chief of the Hunkpapa Lakota, is the subject of the selection by Robert M. Utley, a distinguished historian and biographer of the American West. Based on his biography, The Lance and the Shield: The Life and Times of Sitting Bull *(1993), Utley's essay affords rare insight into Lakota culture and what happened to it when it collided with a rapacious, acquisitive invader whose superior military power, forked tongue, and deadly diseases brought doom to Native Americans everywhere.*

As Utley points out, the government's small-reservation policy, which was implemented by treaties in 1868, split the Lakota into two camps. The agency Indians, under the leadership of Red Cloud of the Oglala Sioux, accepted reservation life and tried to adapt to it. The nonreservation Indians, headed by Sitting Bull, elected to fight the United States Army in a desperate attempt to save "the free life of old." Indeed, rising to the unprecedented position of head chief of all the Lakota, Sitting Bull assembled the most formidable Indian force in the West, one that on a hot June day in 1876 massacred George Armstrong Custer and 262 men of the United States Seventh Cavalry in the Battle of the Little Bighorn in Montana. But it was a Pyrrhic victory for the Lakota and their Cheyenne allies: in the fall, the army trapped them and compelled them to surrender. Sitting Bull escaped to Canada, and his followers ended up in out-of-the-way reservations in the Dakota Territory.

The other western tribes met the same fate. Overwhelmed by superior firepower and faced with starvation, because whites were exterminating the buffalo, the Indians' "commissary," the Native Americans had no choice but to abandon their way of life and submit to segregation on small reservations in the Dakotas, Oklahoma, New Mexico, Oregon, Idaho, and Montana. The federal government systematically obliterated Indian culture and tribal organization, placed the Indians on individual plots of land, and ordered them to become farmers and accept the culture of their conquerors. By 1890, thanks to generations of bloodletting and sickness, scarcely 200,000 Indians remained in the United States, compared with the 2 million Indians in North America at the time of the European discovery.

Meanwhile, Sitting Bull himself returned from Canada and surrendered to the military, which placed him on the Standing Rock Reservation as a prisoner of war. Here, as Utley says, the Indian agent—a petty tyrant—attempted to destroy Sitting Bull's reputation among his incarcerated people. Yet the great Lakota war chief and holy man remained indomitable: he accepted schooling for his offspring but rejected all other government efforts to make Indians into "imitation whites."

Defeated and broken in spirit, many reservation Indians turned to religion for comfort in a hostile world. First the Indians of Nevada, then the Lakota and other Plains Indians took up the Ghost Dance, a sacred ritual that reaffirmed tribal unity and prophesied the return of the old days, when the buffalo would be plentiful again and the Indians would be free of the white invaders. Intimidated by such a "frightful conglomeration of rituals and customs," as one white put it, the United States government outlawed the Ghost Dance. But Sitting Bull and his people kept on dancing. Indeed,

Sitting Bull became "the high priest of the religion at Standing Rock," which put him on a collision course with the Indian agent and his Lakota police. Utley recounts the violent, ironic climax to Sitting Bull's life and goes on to observe that he lost his struggle with white Americans, not because of any personal failing but because of "impersonal forces beyond his control or even his understanding." As you study Sitting Bull's life, the evolution of his three distinct personalities, and his tragic end, you might want to consider this question: Which do you think was the better way for the Indians to deal with the white invaders—the appeasement of Red Cloud, or the uncompromising resistance of Sitting Bull?

GLOSSARY

ARROW CREEK, BATTLE OF (AUGUST 13, 1872)   Here Sitting Bull performed a feat of bravery that awed his followers: he seated himself and calmly smoked his pipe within range of the soldiers' guns.

BLACK HILLS (SOUTH DAKOTA)   Sacred Lakota domain called Paha Sapa; gold miners invading the Black Hills helped ignite the Great Sioux War of 1876.

BROTHERTON, MAJOR DAVID H.   Accepted Sitting Bull's surrender in 1881.

CRAZY HORSE   An Oglala Lakota and the greatest of all the Sioux war chiefs, he also fought to drive the white invaders away and save the old ways.

CROW FOOT   Sitting Bull's favorite son, who died with him in the confrontation with Indian police in 1890.

CROWS   Plains Indian tribe and traditional enemy of the Lakota.

FORT LARAMIE TREATY (1868)   Set aside all of present-day South Dakota west of the Missouri River as the Great Sioux Reservation.

FOUR HORNS   Sitting Bull's uncle who was wounded in the Battle of Killdeer Mountain.

GHOST DANCE RELIGION   Begun by a Paiute messiah named Wovoca, the Ghost Dance movement swept the Plains Indians incarcerated on reservations; it prophesied the end of the white invaders and the return of the buffalo and all previous generations of Indians.

HUNKPAPA   Sitting Bull's division of the Lakota; the other six divisions were Miniconjou, Sans Arc, Two Kettle, Bruele, Oglala, and Blackfeet Sioux (not to be confused with the Blackfeet tribe that lived and hunted northwest of the Lakota).

KILLDEER MOUNTAIN, BATTLE OF (JULY 28, 1864)   A "calamitous" defeat for the Lakota that pointed up the futility of the Indians' fighting an open battle with well-armed soldiers.

LITTLE BIGHORN, BATTLE OF (JUNE 25, 1876)   More than two thousand Sioux warriors "massacred" Lieutenant Colonel George Armstrong Custer and his 265 men in this remote location in southeastern Montana.

LONG KNIVES   Indian name for white soldiers armed with rifles and bayonets.

McLAUGHLIN, JAMES   Agent of the Standing Rock Lakota Reservation who tried to shape the Indians into "imitation whites" and to destroy Sitting Bull's reputation.

RED CLOUD   Chief of the Oglala Sioux, Red Cloud led Indian resistance to the Bozeman Trail and the three forts that guarded it. The trail ran through Indian country in Montana and Colorado. Red Cloud's raids and the so-called "Fetterman Massacre" forced the United States in 1868 to abandon the trail and the forts and to "regard the Powder River country as 'unceded Indian country.'" As Utley says, Red Cloud had "won his war."

SULLY, GENERAL ALFRED   Commanded United States Army forces in the Battle of Killdeer Mountain.

SUN DANCE   The central ceremony in the sacred life of the Lakota; in it the dancers engaged in self-sacrifice and self-torture in order to gain the favor of the Great Mysterious and ensure a successful buffalo hunt.

WAKANTANKA   Lakota word for the Great Mysterious.

WICHASHA WAKAN   Lakota term for a holy man such as Sitting Bull.

itting Bull's fighting days ended on July 20, 1881, when he led his little band of faithful headmen into the cramped office of the commanding officer at Fort Buford, Dakota Territory. All were shabbily dressed and gaunt from the hunger of their Canadian exile. Sitting Bull, once the mightiest chief of the Lakota Sioux, wore a threadbare calico shirt and black leggings; a tattered, dirty blanket was loosely draped around his waist. Suffering a severe eye infection, he had tied a kerchief turbanlike around his head and drawn it partly across his eyes. Beneath, his dark seamed face with jutting nose and chin and perpetually downturned mouth registered both resignation and despair.

His men grouped behind him, the Sioux chief sat next to the blue-clad soldier chief. Placing his Winchester rifle beneath the chair, Sitting Bull drew to him his five-year-old son Crow Foot. Major David H. Brotherton opened the council by setting forth the terms on which the surrender would be received. In fact, they were no terms at all, since the U.S. government's adamant insistence on unconditional surrender had put off this day until starvation left no other recourse.

After the officer ceased speaking, Sitting Bull slumped in his chair, silent and glum. Brotherton invited him to speak. He sat motionless for five minutes—as if in a trance, thought one witness. He said a few words to his men, then gestured to Crow Foot, who picked up his father's rifle and handed it to the army officer. Then Sitting Bull spoke in words that the interpreter translated:

I surrender this rifle to you through my young son, whom I now desire to teach in this manner that he has become a friend of the Americans. I wish him to learn the habits of the whites and to be educated as their sons are educated. I wish it to be remembered that I was the last man of my tribe to surrender my rifle. This boy has given it to you, and he now wants to know how he is going to make a living.

"Sitting Bull" by Robert M. Utley, *MHQ: The Quarterly Journal of Military History,* Vol. V, No. 4 (Summer 1993). Reprinted by permission.

The ceremony at Fort Buford marked the end, at age fifty, of Sitting Bull's career as a warrior, war leader, and tribal war chief, a career that had begun at the age of fourteen, when he counted his first coup on a Crow Indian. He had achieved power and distinction in other fields, too—as a *wichasha wakan,* a holy man; as a band chief; and finally, a post unique in Sioux history, as supreme chief of all the Lakota tribes. His war honors and trophies, however, provided his greatest satisfaction. That he understood the tragic symbolism of giving up his rifle he betrayed in a song composed to connect what had been to what would be: A warrior / I have been / Now / It is all over / A hard time / I have.

What "had been" began in 1831 with Sitting Bull's birth into a distinguished family of the Hunkpapa tribe, one of the seven tribes of Teton or Lakota Sioux. A nomadic people, the Lakotas occupied the high plains between the Missouri River and the Bighorn Mountains while ranging north to the British possessions and south as far as the Platte and Republican rivers. Together, they numbered between 15,000 and 20,000 people. Other Sioux lived to the east—Yanktons and Yanktonais east of the Missouri River, and Dakotas, or Santees, in Minnesota.

At the age of fourteen, his name was not yet Sitting Bull but Jumping Badger, although his deliberate and willful ways had earned him the nickname Hunkesni, or "Slow." Much against his parents' counsel, Slow insisted on accompanying a war party of ten men striking westward from the Powder River in search of horses and scalps of the enemy Crow tribe. Unproven lads often tagged along on such expeditions as errand boys. They learned the ways of war without actually fighting.

On the third day out, crossing a divide, the party spotted a dozen mounted Crows gathered in conference beside a creek. Whooping and shouting, the Lakotas raced down the slope in a headlong charge. Startled, the Crows spread out to receive the attack. But one Crow spurred his horse to escape. Slow, mounted on a sturdy gray horse his father had given him, his naked body painted yellow from head to foot and hung with colorful strands of beads, shrieked a war cry and galloped in pursuit. The powerful gray swiftly overtook the quarry. Pulling abreast, Slow smashed his adversary with a tomahawk and knocked him from his mount. Another warrior hurried in to finish the act and count second coup. In fierce fighting, the Sioux killed all but four of the Crows, who fled the field.

In a jubilant ceremony at the home village, Slow donned his first white eagle feather, emblem of a first coup, and entered one of the world's most highly developed warrior societies. His mother presented him with the beaded, feathered lance that became his favorite offensive weapon. His father presented a shield bearing a sacred design that appeared to him in a dream. From his father also came his own name, to replace Slow and resonate in the history of not only the Sioux but their enemies as well: Tatanka-Iyotanka, Sitting Bull.

As Sitting Bull's adolescent years fell behind in the 1840s, he took on his adult build. With a heavy, muscular frame, a big chest, and a large head, he impressed people as short and stocky, although he stood five feet ten inches tall. His dark hair reached to his shoulders, often braided with otter fur on one side, hanging loose on the other. A severe part at the center of the scalp glistened with a heavy streak of crimson paint. A low forehead surmounted piercing eyes, a broad nose, and thin lips. Although dexterous afoot and superbly agile mounted, he was thought by some to be awkward and even clumsy.

In adulthood Sitting Bull developed into the Hunkpapa incarnate, the admired epitome of the four cardinal virtues of the Lakotas: bravery, fortitude, generosity, and wisdom. "There was something in Sitting Bull that everybody liked," one of his tribesmen recalled. "Children liked him because he was kind, the women because he was kind to the family and liked to settle family troubles. Men liked him because he was brave. Medicine men liked him because they knew he was a man they could consider a leader."

Sitting Bull evolved three distinct personalities. One was the superlative warrior and huntsman, adept at all the techniques of war and the hunt, boastful of his deeds, laden with honors and ambitious for more, celebrated and rewarded with high rank by his people. Another personality was the holy man, suffused with reverence and mysticism, communing constantly with Wakantanka, the Great Mysterious, dreaming sacred dreams and carrying out the rites and ceremonies they mandated, entreating for the welfare of his people, offering sacrifices ranging from a buffalo carcass to his own flesh. A third was the good tribesman, a man of kindness, generosity, and humility, unostentatious in dress and bearing, composer and singer of songs, a friend of children and old people, peacemaker, sportsman, gentle humorist, wise counselor, and leader. That he excelled in all three realms testified to uncommon merit.

The Lakota culture was hardly a generation old at the time of Sitting Bull's birth. Only around the beginning of the nineteenth century did the Lakotas become fully mounted on horses and begin to acquire guns. Horses and guns enabled them to seize and defend their rich hunting grounds, to follow the great migrating herds of buffalo that shaped their distinctive way of life, and by the middle of the nineteenth century to evolve into the proud and powerful monarchs of the northern Great Plains. Ironically, by furnishing the horses and guns, white people made possible the Lakota way of life; then, in less than a century, they destroyed it.

In the years of Sitting Bull's youth, the Hunkpapas had little conception of the white world. The only whites they knew were traders based at posts along the Missouri River. From them, or other tribes acting as intermediaries, came the horses and guns, along with other useful manufactures. Whites in substantial numbers lived 500 miles to the southeast; the Hunkpapas sensed no threat from them. Their hostility was reserved for enemy tribes such as the Crows, Flatheads, Assiniboines, and Arikaras.

By Sitting Bull's thirtieth birthday, however, the white world had begun to intrude alarmingly on the Hunkpapas. Treaty makers, government agents, and soldiers had begun to appear along the upper Missouri in the 1850s, and by the 1860s the menace had grown

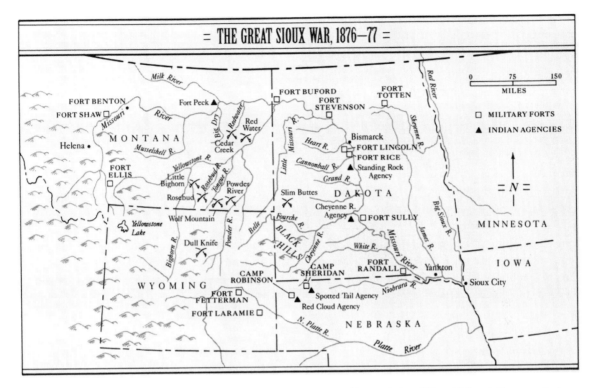

= THE GREAT SIOUX WAR, 1876–77 =

(From The Lance and the Shield *by Robert M. Utley. Maps* *by Jeffrey L. Ward. Copyright © 1993 by Jeffrey L. Ward.*

Reprinted by permission of Henry Holt and Company, Inc.)

distressingly clear. Settlers fingered up the river valleys to the south. Emigrants bound for the gold mines of western Montana killed the buffalo and grazed their livestock on the choice grasses. The voracious boilers of the steamboats consumed the timber stands in the river valleys. The Hunkpapas began to add the whites to their list of enemies.

By this time Sitting Bull had participated in many war expeditions. These were usually limited both in objectives and in scale, though large-scale expeditions and pitched battles sometimes occurred. He had performed many feats of bravery that won the applause of his people and membership in the men's societies that played a major part in Lakota life. He became a war chief of the Hunkpapa tribe. His very name struck terror in the hearts of enemy warriors. Observing this effect, his comrades sometimes disconcerted an opponent by shouting, "Tatanka-Iyotanka tahoksila!"—"We are Sitting Bull's boys!"

Sitting Bull and his "boys" fought for a variety of motives. Where their range overlapped with that of others, they fought for control of hunting grounds. They fought in defense against the aggressions of others; for plunder, chiefly the horses that constituted the prime measure of wealth; for revenge of injuries real and fancied; for glory and the strictly prescribed war honors that determined prestige and leadership.

In any battle, whatever the scale, the Hunkpapas, like all Plains Indians, fought in time-honored fashion. Singly and in knots they galloped back and forth, firing arrows or musket balls at the enemy. Sometimes they gathered in bunches for a thrust aimed at overrunning their foes. Each man indulged in a variety of flashy escapades to display bravery; he followed a leader only when it suited his convenience or inclination. In any such encounter, Sitting Bull's role was chiefly, through exhortation and example, to inspire men to exhibit ever greater personal daring and to join with him in whatever tactical move circumstances seemed to dictate. Neither he nor any other chief "commanded," as whites used the term.

Typifying this mode of combat and Sitting Bull's part in it was the Lakotas' most memorable fight with an enemy tribe. This occurred in the winter of 1869–70, and they remembered it as the Thirty-Crows-Killed battle.

Sitting Bull's band wintered that year in Montana, along the Missouri River and Big Dry Creek. In the middle of the winter, amid bitter cold and deep snow, two Hunkpapa boys were returning from a day of hunting when a party of thirty Crows cut their trail in the snow. Except for two men mounted on one pony, the Crows were afoot. The two hurried to overtake the boys and succeeded in killing one. Wounded, the other escaped to carry word to the Hunkpapa village.

At once Sitting Bull organized a revenge expedition of about 100 warriors. Guided by the surviving boy, the men found their enemies posted behind rock breastworks at the head of Big Dry Creek. As dawn broke, the Hunkpapas attacked. A few on each side had firearms, but most had only bow and arrows. The Hunkpapas fought in the usual fashion, each man for himself, each striving for deeds of bravery and the coups that added to war honors. Although outnumbered more than three to one, the Crows enjoyed the advantages of defense from a fortified position. Steady in their own bravery, they sold their lives dearly. But as the morning hours slipped by, the Hunkpapas gradually took their toll on the Crows.

Like his warriors, Sitting Bull charged as chance presented and retreated when the fire grew too hot. Once he darted to the breastworks and reached across with his bow to count three coups. Finally, as noon approached, he and his comrades surged forward, leaped the walls, and in desperate hand-to-hand fighting killed the last of the Crows. Hunkpapa casualties were much lighter: Thirteen died and seventeen limped off with serious wounds.

This style of combat worked well enough against an enemy practicing the same style, as Crows, Assiniboines, and other Plains tribes did. Pursued in battles with white people, especially white soldiers, it had severe drawbacks.

Sitting Bull's Hunkpapas and other Lakotas of the upper Missouri had their first combat with United States troops in 1863–64. In two summer campaigns, Generals Henry H. Sibley and Alfred Sully led formidable expeditions to the Dakota plains, at first to round up Santee Sioux fugitives from the Minnesota uprising of 1862, then to punish Lakotas who had interfered with the migration to the newly discovered Montana mines.

Almost certainly, Sitting Bull fought in the battles of Dead Buffalo Lake and Stony Lake, July 26 and 28, 1863. He may have been at Whitestone Hill on September 3, 1863. He unquestionably played a leading part in the battles of Killdeer Mountain and the Badlands, July 28 and August 7–9, 1864. In all these fights, the Indians relied on their traditional techniques, and in all they suffered severe to calamitous defeats.

Killdeer Mountain should have shown the Sioux the perils of trying to take on the soldiers in open battle. As many as 1,400 lodges representing four Lakota tribes traced the southern edge of a low range of rugged, wooded mountains falling away on the north to the Little Missouri badlands. A series of buttes and ridges, separated by deep gorges, rose stairlike to the dominating mountain mass. In this natural fortress, emboldened by a force exceeding 2,000 warriors, the Sioux felt confident of routing the approaching army of General Sully.

With 2,200 cavalry and artillery, Sully advanced across the parched plains from the south. Judging the terrain too broken for mounted action, he dismounted and pushed forward on a broad front of skirmishers. Horseholders, then wagons and artillery, brought up the rear.

The Indians came out to meet him. Resplendent in paint and war costume, they sat their ponies in little clusters on every hill and ridge facing the blue lines and curling around their flanks. When within range, the two forces opened fire.

For five miles the fighting roiled northward toward the village at the foot of Killdeer Mountain, the Lakotas attacking in typical fashion. Despite their numbers, however, they could not slow the steady advance of the soldiers.

Mounted on a fast sorrel and armed with musket and bow and arrows, Sitting Bull fought with his usual bravery. As the soldiers launched a final assault aimed at the village itself, he saw a bullet slam into the back of his revered uncle, Chief Four Horns. "I am shot," yelled Four Horns, clinging grimly to his mount.

Sitting Bull dashed to the rescue, seized the horse's bridle, and, as his young nephew White Bull steadied the injured man, led the way into a sheltering thicket. There Sitting Bull gave Four Horns water to drink, applied medicine to the wound, and bandaged it. The bullet remained inside, Four Horns said; he could feel it and it hurt. (Later he recovered and explained that the bullet had dropped into his stomach and never bothered him again.)

While Sitting Bull doctored his uncle, the soldiers won final victory, scattering men, women, and children into the mountains and seizing the village. The next day they methodically destroyed everything that could benefit the Indians. Lodges, meat, robes, utensils—all went up in flames. The troops counted more than a hundred Sioux bodies left on the battlefield; how many dead and wounded were carried away is not known. By contrast, Sully reported casualties of two killed and ten wounded.

The Sibley-Sully campaigns, especially Killdeer Mountain, gave Sitting Bull his first taste of battle with the Long Knives. They did not, he discovered, fight like Indians. Instead they fought in organized formations, obedient to commands of their officers, and brought overwhelming firepower to bear. Their rifled muskets claimed greater range, accuracy, and hitting force than the feeble smoothbore trade muskets of the Indians. The soldiers' cannon in particular were frightening and deadly.

The lessons were clear: Acquire better firearms, and avoid open battle with the Long Knives, relying instead on the hit-and-run tactics at which the Sioux excelled. Sitting Bull's record suggests that he fully grasped the first lesson, only partly the second. Not surprisingly in view of the dictates of culture, neither he nor any other chief ever thought to fight in disciplined formations maneuvered by a hierarchy of command.

The Battle of Killdeer Mountain heralded two decades of conflict with the Long Knives. As whites edged onto the northern Great Plains, soldiers came to protect them. Their "war houses" on the Missouri River, along with the steamboats that carried people and merchandise to the Montana mines, infuriated the Sioux. No chief took a more uncomplicated or inflexible view of this invasion than Sitting Bull. Except for traders, he held, the whites must all get out of Lakota domain and quit traveling through it. If they would not go peaceably, they would be driven out.

It now fell to Sitting Bull to embody the spirit of Lakota resistance to the white threat. Throughout the late 1860s he led the Hunkpapa offensive against the whites. In this aggressive war, he wielded his favorite attack weapon, the lance, which symbolized his role as the offensive arm of the Hunkpapa tribe.

Principal objectives of the offensive were the military posts of the upper Missouri: Forts Rice, Stevenson, Totten, and Buford. Permanent abodes of the detested Long Knives, the forts stood for the resolve of the whites to possess Lakota territory. The campaign took the form mainly of raids near the forts. Logging details, stock herders, mail riders, and travelers bound for the mines periodically ran afoul of nearby war parties.

Sioux usually regarded direct assaults as risks not worth the prospective gain, but twice they launched such attacks, in each instance with Sitting Bull in the lead. The first occurred at Fort Rice on July 28, 1865. In four hours of desperate fighting, the garrison of "Galvanized Yankees"—Confederate prisoners enlisted for Indian duty—held the defenses and drove off the assailants with well-directed rifle and artillery fire. The second clash occurred on December 24, 1866, when Sitting Bull and his warriors seized the outbuildings of Fort Buford and battled their foes until routed by artillery and charging infantry.

Sitting Bull's offensive on the upper Missouri paralleled an even more determined one to the west, in the Powder River country, over the same issues. Spearheaded by Red Cloud's Oglala tribe, Lakotas fought to close the Bozeman Trail to the Montana mines and get rid of the three forts the army had built to guard travelers. Unlike Sitting Bull, Red Cloud won his war. In the Fort Laramie Treaty of 1868, the United States yielded the three forts and agreed to regard the Powder River country as "unceded Indian country." There the Sioux could live so long as the buffalo sustained their way of life.

The Treaty of 1868 profoundly shaped the destiny of both Red Cloud and Sitting Bull. Besides the unceded territory, it defined a Great Sioux Reservation—all the present state of South Dakota west of the Missouri—and bound all Sioux to settle there eventually. Within a few years Red Cloud and many of his followers had settled there, launching him on a career as mediator between his people and government authorities.

For his part, Sitting Bull scorned the treaty, the reservation, and everything else associated with the whites (except trade goods, especially arms and ammunition). He had not signed this or any other treaty, and never would. He intended to live as always, following the buffalo, raiding Crows and Assiniboines, and defending his homeland. "You are fools," he had lectured some agency Indians, "to make yourselves slaves to a piece of fat bacon, some hard-tack, and a little sugar and coffee."

In Red Cloud and Sitting Bull, the Treaty of 1868 personalized two powerful magnetic poles of leadership. Red Cloud emerged as the principal chief of the agency Lakotas, those who chose to live within the Great Sioux Reservation and accept government dole. Sitting Bull emerged as the principal chief of the nonreservation Lakotas, who ranged the plains country in the free life of old. Indeed, he had his followers proclaim him supreme chief of all the Lakotas. Such a post had never existed, but his force of personality gave it substance.

The Sitting Bull bands, the "northern Indians," the "hunting bands," or simply the "hostiles," in the white lexicon, numbered about 450 lodges, about 4,000 people including about 800 fighting men.

Sitting Bull in 1885, four years after his surrender. The great Lakota was both a holy man and a war chief who embodied the four cardinal virtues of his people: bravery, fortitude, generosity, and wisdom. The crucifix he wears in this photograph was supposedly presented to him by a Jesuit missionary in 1868. (Library of Congress)

Ranging the valleys of the Yellowstone River and its southern tributaries, many bands came together in the summer for the annual sun dance and perhaps a communal buffalo hunt and a big war expedition against an enemy tribe. In the winter they scattered to remote valleys to sit out the cold, hungry months. In the warm season their numbers swelled with reservation kin out for a summer's lark. In the frigid season their numbers dwindled as rations at the agencies beckoned.

In the aftermath of the Treaty of 1868, with the Lakotas increasingly divided into reservation and nonreservation factions, Sitting Bull called off his offensive against the Missouri River forts. From now on he would fight the white people only in defense of his homeland—the Powder and Yellowstone country that roughly coincided with the unceded territory of the treaty. Sitting Bull's last raid on Fort Buford occurred in September 1870. Now the shield instead of the lance symbolized his role among Lakotas.

Staunchly backing Sitting Bull in his new defense posture was the greatest of all Lakota war leaders—Crazy Horse of the Oglalas. He shared Sitting Bull's aversion to the reservation and the ways of the white people. To the hunting bands, he was a chief second in stature only to Sitting Bull.

Of more ambiguous conviction was another war chief, Gall of the Hunkpapas. Close to Sitting Bull since childhood, Gall tended to take counsel in expediency. Sometimes he even slipped into the Hunkpapa agency at Grand River to sample government rations.

The defensive policy expressed itself most forcibly in the opposition of the hunting bands to the Northern Pacific Railroad. In the summers of 1872 and 1873, they fought army units escorting company surveyors marking out a rail route in the Yellowstone Valley. This was the heart of Lakota hunting grounds and the more valuable to them because only recently wrested from the Crows at great cost in blood.

At the Battle of Arrow Creek on August 13, 1872, Sitting Bull performed one of his most memorable feats of bravery. Urged on by Sitting Bull and Crazy Horse, Lakota and Cheyenne warriors struck engineers and their cavalry guardians in the bend of a dry streambed in the upper Yellowstone Valley.

As the sun rose on the battlefield, all eyes turned in wonder to Sitting Bull, who staged a spectacle of bravery so imaginative that it surpassed all others that day. Getting his pipe and tobacco pouch from his horse, he walked from the bluffs out into the open valley to within enemy range. Seating himself on the ground, he shouted, "Who other Indians wish to smoke with me come." As Sitting Bull calmly and with studied deliberation filled the bowl with tobacco, his nephew White Bull, Gets-the-Best-Of, and two

Cheyennes ventured into the open and seated themselves beside the chief.

The "smoking party," as White Bull termed it, was a terrifying experience. After kindling the tobacco, Sitting Bull puffed placidly, then passed the pipe to his companions. With pounding hearts, each puffed vigorously and passed it quickly down the line. Throughout he said nothing, just looked around and smoked quietly as bullets kicked up dirt and sang through the air. When all the tobacco had burned, Sitting Bull picked up a stick, thoroughly cleaned the bowl, and stowed the pipe in its pouch. He rose and slowly walked back to the admiring knots of fellow tribesmen. The other smokers ran back.

This ingenious exhibition, so captivating to people who placed great emphasis on daring, added to Sitting Bull's long list of valorous deeds. It reinforced his reputation for bravery and answered those who, in the worsening factionalism of the early 1870s, mocked his pretensions. It was, White Bull remembered, "the bravest deed possible."

After 1873 the Northern Pacific faded from the Lakotas' list of grievances. In four inconclusive battles and a few skirmishes, they had expressed their violent opposition, but they had not stopped the railroad. The Panic of 1873 did that, and the railhead rested at Bismarck, on the Missouri, until after other events had neutralized the Sioux.

Although furious, the Sitting Bull bands offered no violent opposition to a far more blatant assault on their territory. Blazing the "Thieves' Road" into the Black Hills, the Custer Expedition of 1874 saw only a few Lakotas and fought none. But the discovery of gold set off a rush that doomed the Indians' possession of the hills.

It also confronted the administration of President Ulysses S. Grant with a hard dilemma. The Black Hills lay within the Great Sioux Reservation, inarguably guaranteed the Indians by the Treaty of 1868. Yet miners flocked to the hills, and the electorate demanded that the government legalize the invasion. In part because of intimidation by the Sitting Bull bands, however, the reservation chiefs refused to sell.

Not until the independent bands yielded to government control, federal officials concluded, could they buy the Black Hills.

A rationale was necessary to force the hunting bands onto the Great Sioux Reservation. They had not interfered with the gold rush, and although they had not signed the Treaty of 1868, it sanctioned their residence in the unceded territory. The defensive policy of Sitting Bull and Crazy Horse, furthermore, left only the thinnest pretext for military force. But their young men had raided Crows, Assiniboines, and Arikaras, as they had always done. They had also terrorized whites on the upper Yellowstone, more in fear of what might happen than of what had happened. In these treaty violations by people who had never subscribed to a treaty, the government found its excuse to order the Sitting Bull bands to the reservation or face military action. Such were the origins of the Great Sioux War of 1876.

Even when confronted with the government's ultimatum in their winter villages, Sitting Bull and his fellow chiefs did not understand that a war was brewing. They were minding their own business and had no plans to fight the white soldiers. Then, on March 17, 1876, cavalry stormed through a village on Powder River, killing two and wounding several others; now the hunting bands knew the Long Knives had declared war.

Sitting Bull drew the winter camps together for self-defense. As spring gave way to summer, reservation Indians began to make their way westward, to join in the defense. By late June his village had swollen from 3,000 to 7,000 people, from 800 to 1,800 warriors.

Now forty-five, Sitting Bull no longer took the lead on the battlefield. He was the "old man chief" and holy man whose judgment and counsel guided the policies and decisions of the allied tribes. Crazy Horse, Gall, and other fighters set the example in combat.

At a sun dance early in June, in supplication to Wakantanka, Sitting Bull gave 100 pieces of flesh from his arms. He also fasted and danced while gazing at the sun. Just below the sun he saw soldiers and horses bearing down on an Indian village. They rode upside down, their feet to the sky, their heads to the earth with hats falling off. A voice proclaimed: "These soldiers do not possess ears. They are to die." The vision and prophecy thrilled his people.

Soldiers were coming—three armies from three directions. They were led by General Alfred H. Terry, Colonel John Gibbon, and "Three Stars," George Crook. With Terry rode "Long Hair," George Armstrong Custer. On June 17, 1876, Sitting Bull's warriors confronted General Crook on the upper reaches of Rosebud Creek. Shoshone and Crow auxiliaries broke the Sioux charge and saved Crook's force from being overrun. Sitting Bull, his arms cut and useless from the sun-dance sacrifice, ranged the lines, exhorting the warriors. Crook limped back to his supply base.

The Battle of the Rosebud did not fulfill Sitting Bull's prophecy. Crook's soldiers had not fallen into the Sioux camp and died. But a week later, Long Hair Custer and his cavalrymen fell into the Sioux camp. It sprawled sleepily in the Little Bighorn Valley on that hot Sunday of June 25, 1876. As depicted in the sun-dance vision, many soldiers died.

A stunned white world gave Sitting Bull all the credit. The "Napoleon of the Sioux," the *New York Herald* labeled him two weeks later, and in subsequent issues self-appointed experts explained how such a catastrophe had happened. One of them declared that the famed Jesuit missionary Father Pierre-Jean De Smet had taught Sitting Bull to speak and read French; the chief had then studied French histories of the Napoleonic Wars and "modeled his generalship after the little Corsican corporal." An army officer, who should have known better, wrote, "The tactics of Sitting Bull seem to have been those pursued by the great Napoleon in his famous campaign of 1814, and were the same practiced by General Lee at Richmond in 1864–65." Soon the nation would be told that Sitting Bull, in a youthful guise, had attended West Point.

In such fantasies a dazed public and a mortified army sought explanations for the disaster that had befallen a supposedly elite regiment and its valiant commander. They wanted to believe that Custer's 7th Cavalry had been overwhelmed by superior numbers commanded by a military genius, the Napoleon of the Sioux.

The truth, of course, was that, as at Killdeer Mountain and all other encounters with Plains tribes, there had been no Indian general at the Little Bighorn. As one of his followers pointed out, "The chief might give orders to fight but he does not direct how to proceed."

The Indians did not win the battle because of generalship or even leadership. They won because they outnumbered the enemy three to one, because they were united, confident, and angry, and above all because the threat to their women and children fired every man with determination to save his family. The Indians won, too, because their foes let themselves be beaten in fragments. Both in the valley and on the battle ridge where the "last stand" occurred, command and control collapsed, discipline evaporated, and men panicked, which left the initiative to the Indians.

If whites ascribed Napoleonic genius to Sitting Bull in 1876, in less than a decade they had produced another interpretation. On the reservation, abetted by Indians currying favor with the Great Father, white officials now said Sitting Bull had not participated in the battle at all; he had remained in his teepee making medicine, or fled to the hills in terror, even abandoning his family, or skulked somewhere else safely out of danger.

In truth, at the Battle of the Little Bighorn, Sitting Bull was a chief several times over whose bravery no one questioned. He was far more valuable as a counselor than as a fighting man. Leave that to the young warriors striving for glory. Chiefs were expected to fight only to protect noncombatants, and that is what he did when soldiers led by Major Marcus Reno threatened the women and children at the upper end of the village.

After that threat receded, he could have withdrawn with honor. Instead he continued to fire at the soldiers and shout encouragement to the warriors, hovering on the edge of the fighting until everyone left to confront Custer downstream. Then he posted himself at the village's northern end, where many women and children had collected. More than enough men swarmed on the battle ridge to wipe out Long Hair, which they did in less than an hour.

Sitting Bull's significance at the Little Bighorn lay not in flaunting bravery, or directing the movements of warriors, or even inspiring them to fight. It lay instead in leadership so wise and powerful that it drew together and held together a muscular coalition of tribes, one so infused with his defiant cast of mind that it could rout Three Stars Crook at the Rosebud and rub out Long Hair Custer at the Little Bighorn. Never had the Sioux triumphed so spectacularly—and they never would again. For that triumph, more than any other chief they could thank Sitting Bull.

But the triumph contained the seeds of defeat. A stunned nation lashed back, and the Sioux country swarmed with regiments of "Custer avengers." By the spring of 1877, most of the hunting bands had surrendered and gone to the reservation, setting the stage for the government to seize the Black Hills and legalize the invasion.

Sitting Bull could not stomach such humiliation. With a die-hard following he crossed the "medicine road" into the land of the Grandmother. There he got along famously with the queen's redcoats, the North-West Mounted Police, and formed his first close ties to white men. But the buffalo were disappearing in Canada as they were in the United States, and "Bear Coat"—General Nelson A. Miles—watched the boundary like a hawk. After four years of hardship, starvation overcame humiliation, and young Crow Foot handed his father's rifle to Major Brotherton.

The final decade was one of despair. After nearly two years as a prisoner of war, Sitting Bull went to the reservation. At Standing Rock Agency, Agent

James McLaughlin's goal was to transform his charges into imitation whites. He sought to make them into tillers of the soil embracing Christianity, Americanism, and the customs and values of the white people. Sitting Bull refused to be made over. He accepted what he thought would be beneficial, such as schooling for his children and grandchildren, and rejected the rest. Finding him unpliable, McLaughlin launched the campaign of ridicule and derision that included the imputation of cowardice at the Little Bighorn.

Hunger, disease, a decade of cultural breakdown, and another land grab made the Sioux reservations fertile ground for the Ghost Dance religion that took root in 1890. It promised a new world, without whites, peopled by all the generations of Indians that had gone before, and stocked with an abundance of buffalo and other game. Whether Sitting Bull truly believed, he functioned as the high priest of the religion at Standing Rock. The government decided to remove him to a distant military post.

Irony and tragedy stalked Sitting Bull's final days. Not the Long Knives of old, but *ceska maza,* "metal breasts" (for their police badges) of his own tribe, closed in on their former leader. At dawn on December 15, 1890, a platoon of Indian policemen forced their way into his cabin on Grand River and placed him under arrest. Excited Ghost Dancers crowded around the cabin, and his own son Crow Foot, now fourteen, taunted him for giving up. The volatile confrontation blew up in a paroxysm of gunfire and hand-to-hand fighting. Sitting Bull went down, shot at close range in the chest and the back of the head by *ceska maza.* Crow Foot died too, beaten and shot by enraged policemen.

The Hunkpapas, even those who had forsaken the old ways, knew McLaughlin's portrait of Sitting Bull to be grotesquely flawed. They well remembered he had been a magnificent warrior, an inspiring war chief, a statesman and political leader of vast wisdom, a holy man of marvelous power, and to his last day a leader of compelling force.

The world remembers Sitting Bull not for what he achieved in his own culture but for his battle against the westward movement of the American people. It is this battle that gives him nearly universal name recognition beyond his own culture. In this struggle, as both lance and shield, his inflexibility served him well. He acted on faultless reasoning: The land of the Lakotas belonged to the Lakotas, and no whites had any right to be there. He fought to keep them out, and when that failed, he fought to defend his people and his territory from invasion. He lost not because of failings of leadership or, given his cultural outlook, failings of judgment, but because of impersonal forces beyond his control or even his understanding.

QUESTIONS TO CONSIDER

1 How did Lakota culture change during the nineteenth century? What effect did white settlers have on that culture throughout the century?

2 What was the traditional Lakota manner of fighting, and what values did it highlight? Why did this style of warfare not work against white troops, and what lessons does Robert Utley think Sitting Bull should have learned from this?

3 Describe Sitting Bull and his three "personalities." Discuss the stance he took toward whites, and compare it with that taken by Red Cloud. Which one of them do you think was right and why?

4 What were the principal interests of Americans in Sioux territory, and how did Americans generally react to Sitting Bull's effort at resistance? How did the United States government deal with the Lakota Sioux? How and on what pretext did they finally break the resistance of Sitting Bull's people?

5 What is the significance of the Ghost Dance religion and of Sitting Bull's tragic death? How do you feel about Utley's conclusion that Sitting Bull lost, not because of any personal or cultural failings but because of forces beyond his control?

4 Death on the Prairies: The Murderous Blizzard of 1888

DAVID LASKIN

With the Indians out of the way, Americans were free at last to conquer the vast Great Plains that reached from Texas to the Canadian border in the center of the country. Westering farmers had stopped at the edge of this enormous grassland because its arid climate and shallow topsoil seemed unsuited to agricultural techniques devised in the East. But after the Civil War came the development of new farming techniques and new machinery such as the windmill, the chilled-iron plow, and the combine—all of which made agriculture feasible on the windy prairies. As a consequence, farmers from east of the Mississippi swarmed there during the postwar years, some claiming 160 acres free under the 1862 Homestead Act, most buying their land from speculators or the railroads. In the 1880s alone, more than one million people poured onto the Great Plains from the Great Lakes states. Meanwhile, after the failure of Reconstruction, African Americans headed west as well; they were sodbusters, cowboys, speculators, miners, lawmen, desperadoes, and cavalrymen. Asian and Mexican Americans were present, too, all contributing to the drama of frontier conquest. The pioneers lived in all manner of homes—from dugouts to sod houses—battling tornadoes, hail, dust storms, blizzards, prairie fires, and grasshopper plagues in an endless struggle to make new lives for themselves on the nation's last frontier.

The westering experience tended to break down traditional male and female "spheres," which stripped women of all political and legal rights and restricted them to the home while their husbands had jobs and careers in the outside world and ran political affairs. As modern scholarship has demonstrated, frontier women were not chained to the home but were close to equal partners with their menfolk: in addition to their household chores, the women helped their husbands hunt, gather water and fuel, and plant and harvest.

As David Laskin points out in the following selection, male and female migrants to the Dakota and Nebraska frontier were shocked by its violent shifts in weather. Who back East or down South could have conceived of a land where the temperature could fall eighteen degrees in just three minutes? Who would have guessed that farmers and school children could start their days in shirtsleeves, without heavy overcoats, only to experience wind chills that night that were forty degrees below zero?

On January 12, 1888, the most murderous blizzard of that region suddenly struck the Dakota and Nebraska prairie. As Laskin says, "One moment it was mild, the sun was shining, a damp wind blew fitfully out of the south—the next moment frozen hell had broken loose." The ferocity of the storm killed hundreds of children making their way home after school. Thus it was called "the children's blizzard." Neither the children who survived the storm nor their parents would ever forget that terrible day.

Laskin's vivid description of the blizzard of 1888 will haunt you long after you have read his account. In Laskin's view, the storm was a tragic example of a dream gone wrong for pioneers who had migrated west in search of a prosperous new life. They learned that "the sudden storms, the violent swings from one meteorological extreme to another, the droughts and torrents and killer blizzards were not freak occurrences but facts of life on the prairie." For countless pioneer families, the promise of the Homestead Act proved to be a cruel joke. The storm that killed their children demonstrated "that the land they had desired so fervently and had traveled so far to claim wasn't free after all."

GLOSSARY

CARNEGIE, ANDREW   A Scottish immigrant and a self-made man, Carnegie founded the Carnegie Steel Company. In 1900, it became the largest industrial corporation in the world (see selection 5). In 1878, Carnegie won the steel contract to build the Brooklyn Bridge (see selection 6).

DEPRESSION OF 1893   The greatest economic depression the United States had yet experienced, the depression (or "panic") of 1893 was a product of agricultural and industrial expansion that had produced a surplus of goods. Railroad companies had built too many miles of track, and farmers had borrowed too heavily, forcing many to lose their land as crop prices fell.

EDISON, THOMAS ALVA   From his modern research laboratory in Menlo Park, New Jersey, Edison promised "a minor invention every ten days and a big thing every six months or so." Known as the "Wizard of Menlo Park," a man with little formal education, Edison produced two "big things": the phonograph in 1877 and the electric light, a product of experiments with carbon filaments, in 1879.

GALVESTON HURRICANE   This storm of September 8, 1900, was the deadliest hurricane in American history thus far. It devastated this southeastern Texas city, killing over ten thousand people. Galveston was left in ruins with $30 million damage ($700 million in today's dollars).

GARLAND, HAMLIN   A product of rural Iowa, Garland wrote novels such as *Son of the Middle Border* (1890) that described the bleak lives of settlers on the Great Plains.

HOMESTEAD ACT (1862)   Legislation that provided 160 acres of government land on the rugged prairie frontier to anyone who promised to live and work on it for five years.

The only requirement was a ten dollar registration fee. Between 1862 and 1900, almost six hundred thousand families received free homesteads on forty-eight million acres of land.

HYPOTHERMIA   A medical condition that occurs when a person's body temperature drops significantly below normal. Hypothermia starts when the core body temperature falls below 35 degrees Celsius (95 degrees Fahrenheit).

JOHNSTOWN FLOOD   On May 31, 1889, heavy rains forced the old South Fork Dam in Johnstown, Pennsylvania, to break, resulting in a deadly flood that killed over 2,209 people in that workingclass city.

MORGAN, J. PIERPONT   In the Gilded Age, Morgan was the most powerful and influential figure in the world of American finance. He established the first billion-dollar company, the United States Steel Corporation.

POWELL, JOHN WESLEY   An explorer and geologist, Powell was a professor at Illinois Wesleyan University and director of the United States Geological Survey.

ROCKEFELLER, JOHN D.   A Cleveland merchant, Rockefeller used ruthless and often illegal methods to build the Standard Oil Company that, by 1879, produced 90 percent of America's oil refining needs (see selection 8).

SCRIBNER, CHARLES   A New York publisher, Scribner started *Scribner's Monthly* in 1870. Eleven years later, he changed its name to the *Century Magazine*.

VANDERBILT, CORNELIUS   Nicknamed the "Commodore," Vanderbilt earned millions in the shipping business. Later in life, he built the New York Central Railroad that controlled over 4,500 miles of track from New York City to Chicago.

On January 12, 1888, a blizzard broke over the center of the North American continent. Out of nowhere, a soot gray cloud appeared over the northwest horizon. The air grew still for a long, eerie measure, then the sky began to roar and a wall of ice dust blasted the prairie. Every crevice, every gap and orifice instantly filled with shattered crystals, blinding, smothering, suffocating, burying anything exposed to the wind. The cold front raced down the undefended grasslands like a crack unstoppable army. Montana fell before dawn; North

Dakota went while farmers were out doing their early morning chores; South Dakota, during morning recess; Nebraska as school clocks rounded toward dismissal. In three minutes the front subtracted 18 degrees[*] from the air's temperature. Then evening gathered in and temperatures kept dropping steadily,

---

[*]All temperatures are Fahrenheit unless otherwise indicated.

Excerpt from pp. 1–8, 198–202, 267–271 from *The Children's Blizzard* by David Laskin. Copyright © 2004 by David Laskin. Reprinted by permission of HarperCollins Publishers.

hour after hour, in the northwest gale. Before midnight, windchills were down to 40 below zero. That's when the killing happened. By morning on Friday the thirteenth, hundreds of people lay dead on the Dakota and Nebraska prairie, many of them children who had fled—or been dismissed from—country schools at the moment when the wind shifted and the sky exploded.

Chance is always a silent partner in disaster. Bad luck, bad timing, the wrong choice at a crucial moment, and the door is inexorably shut and barred. The tragedy of the January 12 blizzard was that the bad timing extended across a region and cut through the shared experiences of an entire population. The storm hit the most thickly settled sections of Nebraska and Dakota Territory at the worst possible moment—late in the morning or early in the afternoon on the first mild day in several weeks, a day when children had raced to school with no coats or gloves and farmers were far from home doing chores they had put off during the long siege of cold. But the deadly quirks of chance went deeper and farther than circumstance or time of day. It was the deep current of history that left the prairie peculiarly vulnerable to the storm.

For nearly all of the nation's short life span, the grasslands at the heart of the country had been ignored, overlooked, skirted, or raced over. On maps the words *Great American Desert* hovered vaguely between the Mississippi River and the Rocky Mountains, and the rest was left blank or faintly labeled Indian Territory. But then, after the Civil War, when the swelling cities of the East Coast settled down to the serious business of industrial capitalism, the Great American Desert was reborn and rechristened. Suddenly this immense expanse of open land was not waste, but paradise—and like paradise, it was free, or all but free. Railroad companies flush with millions of acres of government land grants promised new settlers the sky and sold them the earth at irresistible prices. Under the Homestead Act, the U.S. government gave every comer 160 acres free and clear in exchange for the investment of a small filing fee and five years of farming. The dream of free land let loose a stampede. In the three decades after 1870, some 225 million acres of the continent's heartland

were broken, stripped of sod, and planted with crops—more land than had been "improved" in the preceding 263 years of white settlement in the United States. On the last frontier was enacted the greatest human migration the earth had yet endured.

It was late in the day to be an American pioneer. While Thomas Edison was making the first moving pictures in New Jersey, while electric lights shone from Chicago skyscrapers raised on steel skeletons, while Vanderbilts, Carnegies, Morgans, and Rockefellers were adorning their neo-Gothic and Renaissance palaces with the treasures of Europe, homesteaders in Dakota warmed themselves in sod huts at fires of buffalo bones. It wasn't that the sodbusters didn't know that elegant Pullman sleeping cars skimmed over the train tracks at the edges of their wheat fields or that the future price of that wheat depended on tycoons in New York and the number of mouths to feed in Russia. Whether they had come from Europe in the reeking steerage of immigrant ships or boarded converted cattle cars in Chicago, Saint Paul, or New York, they had witnessed with their own eyes the newborn marvels of the industrial world. Someday, they believed, these marvels would be theirs. If they worked hard enough, if their children worked hard enough, the land in time would provide.

And so the settlers of the prairie banked on the future and put their trust in land they loved but didn't really understand. They got down to work so quickly they didn't have time to figure out the vagaries of soil and climate, the cycles of the seasons, the fickle violent moods of the sky. Deprived of both the folk wisdom born of deep familiarity with a single place and the brash abstractions of the new science, the pioneers were vulnerable and exposed. There hadn't been time to put up fences. Children waded into tall grass and vanished. Infants were accidentally dropped in snowdrifts. Infections flourished in the primitive, unsanitary claim shanties.

Coded messages hummed through the telegraph wires strung alongside the train tracks, but settlers' farms were too far from the offices where the messages were received and decoded to do them any good. When the cloud descended from the northwest and filled the air with snow, they had no warning. Unaware of the risk, they wandered out in pursuit of a single precious cow and lost their way between sod hut and barn. Their fuel gave out, their roofs blew off, their animals suffocated. Their children froze to death in the furrows of their fields.

"All around no-one knew of any-one else's predicament," wrote a Dakota pioneer after the storm, "so each acted as he or she thought fit and people survived or died according to their temperament. You can't preach about it. If a young fellow had every penny of his cash tied up in an uninsured herd of cattle . . . what would most of us have done? No-one knew THEN that this was the day which was to be remembered when all the days of 70 years would be forgotten."

One of the many tragedies of that day was the failure of the weather forecasters, a failure compounded of faulty science, primitive technology, human error, narrow-mindedness, and sheer ignorance. America in 1888 had the benefit of an established, well-funded, nationwide weather service attached to the Army and headed by a charismatic general—yet the top priority on any given day was not weather, but political infighting. Forecasters—"indications officers," as they were styled then—insisted their forecasts were correct 83.7 percent of the time for the next twenty-four hours, but they were forbidden to use the word *tornado* in any prediction; they believed that America's major coastal cities were immune to hurricanes; they relied more on geometry and cartography than on physics in tracking storms; they lacked the means and, for the most part, the desire to pursue meteorological research. "[T]he promise of a science of profound interest to the scholar and of vast usefulness to the people is being rapidly realized," wrote explorer and geologist Major John Wesley Powell of meteorology in 1891. "While the science has not yet reached that stage when directions can be successfully given at what hour it is wise to carry an umbrella on a showery day, it has reached that stage when the great storms and waves of intense heat or intense cold can be predicted for all the

land in advance of their coming so as to be of great value to all industries of the land. All the discomforts of the weather cannot be avoided, but the great disasters can be anticipated and obviated." Mighty rhetoric—and many believed it. But in truth, when it came to weather prediction, government forecasters in the last decades of the nineteenth century were still relying more on empirical observations and even proverbs of the "red sky at night, sailor's delight" school than on a sound scientific understanding of the atmosphere. Many of the "great storms and waves of intense heat or intense cold" escaped them altogether—or were mentioned in their daily "indications" too late, too vaguely, too timidly to do anyone any good. When it came to "great disasters," they knew far less than they thought they knew.

It was the age of confidence. Arrogance was epidemic.

The officer in charge of the experimental indications office that had been established in Saint Paul for the express purpose of predicting blizzards and outbreaks of extreme cold on the prairie did not entirely miss the January 12 storm. He knew before midnight on January 11 that it would snow in Dakota Territory and Nebraska the following afternoon and get colder that night. His indications "verified." But they helped few, if any, people in the region escape or protect themselves. Warnings were not posted in time. No one reading the indications for that day would have guessed that an historic storm was bearing down on them. Those in positions of authority neither recognized nor cared about the forecasting failure. To the extent that knuckles got rapped as a result of the storm, it had to do with sleet-covered sugar plantations in the Deep South, not frozen children on the prairie.

It was the Gilded Age. Disaster meant financial ruin.

Even in a region known for abrupt and radical meteorological change, the blizzard of 1888 was unprecedented in its violence and suddenness. There was no atmospheric herald. No eerie green tinge to the sky or fleecy cirrus forerunner. One moment it was

January 12, 1888
The Advance of the Cold Wave

The settlers on the prairie were not prepared for the dramatic changes in weather conditions they faced in this new land. On January 12, 1888, a low-pressure system swept a frigid arctic air mass down from Canada. "The cold front raced down the undefended grasslands like a crack unstoppable army. Montana fell before dawn; North Dakota went while farmers were out doing their early morning chores; South Dakota, during morning recess; Nebraska as school clocks rounded toward dismissal. In three minutes the front subtracted 18 degrees from the air's temperature."

mild, the sun was shining, a damp wind blew fitfully out of the south—the next moment frozen hell had broken loose. The air was so thick with fine-ground wind-lashed ice crystals that people could not breathe. The ice dust webbed their eyelashes and sealed their eyes shut. It sifted into the loose weave of their coats, shirts, dresses, and underwear until their skin was packed in snow. Farmers who had spent a decade walking the same worn paths became disoriented in seconds.

The pioneers of the prairie, even those who had lived there only a few seasons, were accustomed to seeing hail rip open the bases of enormous black clouds and winds of summer fire stream out of the west. They had crouched by their stoves for dark days and nights while winter gales blew without ceasing. They had watched houses get sucked in whirling fragments up the bases of funnel clouds. But nobody had any idea that the atmosphere was capable of a storm like this.

The blizzard of January 12, 1888, known as "the Schoolchildren's Blizzard" because so many of the victims were children caught out on their way home from school, became a marker in the lives of the settlers, the watershed event that separated before and after. The number of deaths—estimated at between 250 and 500—was small compared to that of the Johnstown Flood that wiped out an entire industrial town in western Pennsylvania the following year or the Galveston hurricane of 1900 that left more than eight thousand dead. But it was traumatic enough that it left an indelible bruise on the consciousness of the region. The pioneers were by and large a taciturn lot, reserved and sober Germans and Scandinavians who rarely put their thoughts or feelings down on paper, and when they did avoided hyperbole at all costs. Yet their accounts of the blizzard of 1888 are shot through with amazement, awe, disbelief. There are thousands of these eyewitness accounts of the storm. Even those who never wrote another word about themselves put down on paper everything they could remember about the great blizzard of 1888. Indeed, it was the storm that has preserved these lives from oblivion. The blizzard literally froze

a single day in time. It sent a clean, fine blade through the history of the prairie. It forced people to stop and look at their existences—the earth and sky they had staked their future on, the climate and environment they had brought their children to, the peculiar forces of nature and of nature's God that determined whether they would live or die. . . .

"Everything changes; nothing does," the poet James Merrill wrote in a poem called "After the Fire." The effects of disaster, no matter how extreme, do not last forever. We bury our dead, nurse the wounded, rebuild, and get on with our lives. Today, aside from a few fine marble headstones in country graveyards and the occasional roadside historical marker, not a trace of the blizzard of 1888 remains on the prairie. Yet in the imagination and identity of the region, the storm is as sharply etched as ever: *This is a place where blizzards kill children on their way home from school.* To understand why and how the deadliest Midwestern blizzard happened the way it did is to understand something essential about the history of the American prairie—indeed about the history of America itself.

We'll never know how many spent that night out on the prairie. It had to be at least several thousand, most of them in the southern and eastern parts of Dakota Territory, in the eastern half of Nebraska, and in southwestern Minnesota. Northern Dakota was largely spared because the storm blew through so early that people remained home and kept their children in. Iowa, though it received the heaviest snow, also suffered relatively few casualties. The storm didn't hit there until late in the day, when evening was gathering and farmers and their children were back home. But in southern Dakota and Nebraska the timing could not have been worse. . . .

The catalog of their suffering is terrible. They froze alone or with their parents or perished in frantic, hopeless pursuit of loved ones. They died with the frozen bloody skin torn from their faces, where they had clawed off the mask of ice again and again. Some died within hours of getting lost; some lived through the night and died before first light. They were found standing waist deep in drifts with their hands frozen to barbed-wire fences, clutching at straw piles, buried under overturned wagons, on their backs, facedown on the snow with their arms outstretched as if trying to crawl. Mothers died sitting up with their children around them in fireless houses when the hay or coal or bits of furniture were exhausted and they were too weak or too frightened to go for more.

A young Dutch couple in Minnesota died kneeling side by side with their hands held high above their heads.

A nine-year-old Nebraska boy named Roman Hytrek was walking the prairie with his dog when the storm overtook them. That evening the dog turned up scratching at the door of a neighbor's house. Roman's empty coat was found in March. Eventually a search party recovered the boy's body. Roman had died alone leaning against the side of a hill. They speculated that he had unbuttoned his coat so that he could cradle his dog next to him in it and that the wind ripped it from his shoulders. . . .

William Klemp, a newly married Dakotan in the full vigor of young manhood, left his pregnant wife at home and went out in the storm to care for their livestock. He never returned. A few weeks later, Klemp's wife gave birth to a son. It was spring when they found his body in a sod shanty a mile from the house. Klemp's face had been eaten away by mice and gophers.

In the region that would soon become the state of South Dakota there were deaths in thirty-two of the forty-four counties east of the Missouri River. Every pioneer who wrote a memoir, every family that recorded its history included a story of someone who died in the blizzard. Every story is heartbreaking.

Lois Royce, a young teacher of a Nebraska country school, huddled on the open prairie all night with three of her pupils—two nine-year-old boys and a six-year-old girl. The children cried themselves to sleep. Lois stretched out on the ground, lying on her side with her back to the wind and the children

cradled in the hollow of her body. She covered their sleeping bodies with her cloak. The boys died first. Lois felt one of the bodies cease to breathe and go cold. Then, a few hours later, the other. The boys went in silence. The little girl, Hattie Rosberg, had begged her teacher through the night for more covers to keep her warm. She died at daybreak deliriously crying, "I'm so cold, mama, please cover me up." When the air had cleared enough to see, Lois left the three dead children lying together and crawled on her hands and knees a quarter of a mile to the nearest farmhouse.

In Dakota's Beadle County . . . Robert Chambers, a farmer in his early thirties, was outside watering cattle with his two sons and their Newfoundland dog when the weather turned. The older boy, who was eleven, suffered from rheumatism, so Chambers sent him home before the storm got bad. He thought that he and nine-year-old Johnny could drive the cattle to the barn themselves. The dog would know the way. But . . . father and son were overtaken and bewildered. When Chambers realized there was no hope of finding their farmhouse, he burrowed into a drift, wrapped Johnny in his jacket and vest (neither of them had come out with overcoats), and told the boy to get into the hollow out of the wind. Robert Chambers stood in the storm shouting for help as long as his voice held. The dog barked frantically. But no one heard them over the wind.

By evening Chambers was too cold to do anything but lie down in the snow next to his son. He put the dog beside them for extra warmth. Johnny could feel how frigid his father's body was. He urged his father to get up and to look for the line of the trees they had planted by the house. But Chambers would not leave his son.

As the night wore on, father and son talked about death. Chambers assured Johnny that they would survive and repeated over and over that the boy must lie still. Johnny knew that his father was freezing to death. At some point the boy dozed off. When he woke, his father was still alive, but barely. Chambers told his son to pray and that he would pray with him.

At daylight a rescue party heard the Newfoundland barking and found them. The snow had drifted so deeply that Johnny was entirely buried but for a small opening by his mouth. The dog was standing guard. Robert Chambers was dead.

The Westphalen girls, Eda and Matilda, also died in the night. Though born five years apart, the daughters of German immigrants, the girls had grown close to each other in the tragedies that had befallen their family during the past few years. Diphtheria struck the Westphalens in the winter of 1883. Two days before Christmas, six-year-old Frederick died. Six weeks later, their father, Peter, deranged by grief, hanged himself. Since then their mother had managed alone with six children. The winter of the blizzard, Eda was thirteen, Matilda, eight. The storm hit when the girls were at their country school in a hilly section of eastern Nebraska near the railroad town of Scribner (named by an Eastern railroad official for his son-in-law, New York publisher Charles Scribner). The teacher, Nellie Forsythe, told the children to go home. Eda and Matilda left together. The schoolhouse was halfway up the side of a smooth rounded hill; their house was a mile due north at the bottom of a valley cut by a creek. Usually it was an easy walk downhill across the fields. But in the storm the girls had the wind in their faces. No matter how they struggled against it, the northwest wind pushed them east into a series of ravines. For a while they wandered in circles. Then they drifted east and south with the wind. Only when they came to a wire fence did Eda realize they had gone in the wrong direction. They needed to turn around—but turning meant walking into the wind. Matilda failed, and Eda took off her wraps and covered her younger sister.

Most victims of hypothermia curl up on their sides and die in a fetal position. Eda and Matilda died facedown. Very likely they dropped while fighting to walk into the wind. Once they fell, they must have lost consciousness very quickly. They lay on the snow a few feet apart on the side of a hill. The windward side. All night the wind blew snow over their bodies, covering them and laying them bare again.

In the course of the night, the haystack in which Etta Shattuck had taken refuge became her prison. The hay had become so compacted and heavy with drifting snow that it pinned Etta in the small hollow she had dug for herself. As the temperature plunged, the fibers tightened. Etta's torso stayed fairly warm, but the cave was so shallow that she was unable to shelter her legs or feet. Exposed to the cold, her legs turned to blocks of wood. She was powerless to escape.

Etta drifted in and out of consciousness, but she never fell into a deep sleep. She felt mice rustling through the stack and nibbling at her wrists and somehow that comforted her. It seemed miraculous that something else was alive in the storm. When she was most alert, Etta prayed. She moved her lips and tried to summon the voice to sing hymns. She ran the words through her mind, but the sound that came from her mouth was hardly more than labored breathing. She was glad as never before that she had found God. God had brought her to the haystack; she was sure of it. God would guide the steps of a rescuer. Etta had faith. She knew she would be saved.

At some point in the night the wind died down enough for her to hear coyotes howling. That keening yelp. Or maybe it was still the wind. Etta's eyes fluttered open and the air looked a little brighter. It must be morning. Whoever had forked the prairie grass into this stack would come. Etta tried her voice to see if she could cry out for help. She could move her mouth and neck and shoulders. But her body was caught in the vise of the frozen haystack and her legs were paralyzed. The hymns and prayers would keep her going until someone came and pulled her out.

If nothing else, as long as she could sing and pray, Etta could ward off deep sleep—the sleep from which she would never rouse herself. . . .

"I have seen the Dread of Dakota. A genuine blizzard and am now ready to leave anytime, that we can sell," pioneer wife Sadie Shaw wrote to relatives back east from her Dakota homestead in Douglas County. *"Oh, it was terrible.* I have often read about Blizzards but they have to be *seen* to be fully *realized."*

The Shaws did not sell. . . . There were many such threats and much misgiving after the blizzard of 1888, but few families left—at least not right away. The weather finally moderated. Summer came and the prairie turned hot and dry. Day after day the sun sucked the moisture out of the black soil of the prairie. Grieving families got on with their lives, prayed for rain, had more children.

The blizzard of January 12, 1888, did not put an end to the great white endeavor of settling and taming the prairie, but it did mark a turning point, a change of mood and direction. The Dakota boom had ended. Immigration to the prairie frontier slowed to a trickle in the last years of the 1880s. A time of reckoning and taking stock had set in. A new mood of caution, suspicion, and bitterness took hold. "Good bye, Lord, I am going west," Arthur Towne remembered the church deacon shouting as Dakota-bound families streamed out of their Vermont village in 1881. By the close of the decade the joy was gone and the Townes were exhausted. "It did seem as if the whole James River valley was just a dumping ground for blasted hopes," Towne's mother told him wearily. "The holiday spirit of eight years before had entirely vanished," wrote Hamlin Garland of the sullen mood of the decade's end. "The stress of misfortune had not only destroyed hope, it had brought out the evil side of many men. Dissension had grown common. Two of my father's neighbors had gone insane over the failure of their crops. . . . [S]omething gray had settled down over the plain. Graveyards, jails, asylums, all the accompaniments of civilization, were now quite firmly established. . . . No green thing was in sight, and no shade offered save that made by the little cabin. On every side stretched scanty yellowing fields of grain, and from every worn road, dust rose like smoke from crevices."

The truth was beginning to sink in: The sudden storms, the violent swings from one meteorological extreme to another, the droughts and torrents and killer blizzards were not freak occurrences but facts of life on the prairie. This was not a garden. Rain did not follow the plow. Laying a perfect grid of mile-sided squares on the grassland did not suppress the chaos of the elements. The settlers had to face the facts. Living here and making a living off this land was never going to be easy.

Weather that takes lives and destroys hopes presents a moral quandary. Call it an act of God or a natural disaster, somebody or something made this storm happen. But what? . . . Were the immigrant parents themselves to blame for uprooting their families from the relatively safe enclaves of the Ukraine, Vermont, Prussia, and Norway and exposing them to the brutal cold fronts and lows that sweep down off the Canadian Rockies?

Or should one condemn an economic system that gave some families mansions on Summit Avenue and left others so poor that they would risk their children and their own lives for the sake of a single cow? They called it "The School Children's Blizzard" because so many of the victims were so young—but in a way the entire pioneer period was a kind of children's disaster. Children were the unpaid workforce of the prairie, the hands that did the work no one else had time for or stomach for. The outpouring of grief after scores of children were found frozen to death among the cattle on Friday, January 13, was at least in part an expression of remorse for what children were subjected to every day—remorse for the fact that most children had no childhood. This was a society that could not afford to sentimentalize its living and working children. Only in death or on the verge of death were their young granted the . . . long columns of sobbing verse, the stately granite monuments. A safe and carefree childhood was a luxury the pioneer prairie could not afford.

"The dark, blinding, roaring storm once experienced, ever remains an actual living presence, that has marked its pathway with ruin, desolation and death," wrote South Dakota historian Caleb Holt Ellis in 1909. "The 12th of January, 1888, is, and long will be, remembered, not only by Dakotans, but by many in the northwest, not for the things we enjoy, love, and would see repeated; but for its darkness, desolation, ruin and death, spread broadcast; for

Homesteaders, many of whom were recent immigrants, took advantage of the free land offered by the federal government and moved west in hopes of finding a better life. The family shown here poses in their Sunday best against the background of their modest sod house. Alas, many of these families saw their dreams shattered by violent storms, voracious insects, and topsoil too shallow for growing crops. As David Laskin concludes, "the land that they had desired so fervently and had traveled so far to claim wasn't free after all." (© Bettmann-CORBIS)

the sorrow, sadness and heartache that followed in its train." To this day, nearly a century after Ellis wrote these words, the storm remains "an actual living presence" in the region. Mention the date to anyone whose family experienced the storm and you'll get a story of death or narrow escape. "There are those who say that that storm was no worse than others we have had," wrote Austen Rollag fifty years later, "but those who speak thus could not have been out of the house but sitting around the stove. I have seen many snowstorms in the more than sixty years I have been living here, but not one can compare with the storm of January 12, 1888."

The memories still burn. They burn all the fiercer because sorrow, sadness, and heartache did indeed follow in the blizzard's train. Drought ravaged the prairie in the early 1890s. Thousands who had borrowed against their homesteads went bankrupt in the financial panic that inaugurated the depression of 1893. Farm income slipped steadily in the last decades of the nineteenth century. The price of corn fell by half between the mid-1870s and the 1890s. A great exodus commenced on the prairie. By the time the rains returned late in the 1890s, over 60 percent of the pioneer families had abandoned their homesteads. Settlers came back, tried to make a go of it in the Dakotas or even farther west—and once again got burned out, frozen out, and blown away. Outmigration is on the rise once more. Nearly 70 percent of the counties in the Great Plains states have fewer people now than they did in 1950. These days nearly one million acres of the plains are so sparsely populated that they meet the condition of frontier as defined by the Census Bureau in the nineteenth century. Seven of our nation's twelve poorest counties are in Nebraska. As whites flee to cities and coasts, Native Americans and the bison that sustained them for thousands of years are returning. Indian and buffalo populations have now reached levels that the region has not seen since the 1870s. The white farmers and townspeople who remain would shun you for daring to say it, but in large stretches of prairie it's beginning to look like European agricultural settlement is a completed chapter of history. "It's time for us to acknowledge one of America's greatest mistakes," wrote Nicholas D. Kristof on the op-ed page of the *New York Times,* "a 140-year-old scheme that has failed at a cost of trillions of dollars, countless lives and immeasurable heartbreak: the settlement of the Great Plains."

The blizzard of January 12, 1888, was an early sign of that mistake. In the storm that came without warning, the pioneers learned that the land they had desired so fervently and had traveled so far to claim wasn't free after all. Who could have predicted that the bill would arrive with a sudden shift of wind in the middle of a mild January morning? A thousand storms of dust and ice and poverty and despair have come and gone since then, but this is the one they remember. After that day, the sky never looked the same.

QUESTIONS TO CONSIDER

1 Why does Laskin state that the horrible blizzard of 1888 "hit the most thickly settled sections of Nebraska and Dakota Territory at the worse possible moment"? Describe the dramatic change in temperatures that accompanied this storm. Why were the humble people of this raw region of the prairie prone to take risks, even in the face of a devastating blizzard?

2 In the post–Civil War years, what factors encouraged the stampede of settlers into America's heartland, which earlier had been thought to be a worthless desert? Compare the lifestyle of these "sodbusters" to the luxuries enjoyed by the wealthy industrial tycoons back East.

3 Compare twenty-first-century weather forecasting (satellite imagery, the technology of the Weather Channel) with that of the late nineteenth century. What advance warning did the prairie settlers have of the blizzard of 1888?

4 This selection describes many personal stories of humble people who faced tragedy with an inner courage that is both compelling and memorable. Which of these stories touched you the most and why? Try to imagine yourself as a settler caught in the killer blizzard of 1888. Imagine what you and your children would have experienced, and explain whether you would have stayed or left that violent land.

5 Describe the change in "mood and direction" caused by the blizzard of 1888 on settlers living on the prairie and people who thought about moving there. Why does Laskin conclude "that most children had no childhood" on the bleak prairies?

6 Why do some historians conclude that "the settlement of the Great Plains" was "one of America's greatest mistakes"? How has the population of that rugged region changed over the past sixty years?

PART THREE

The New Industrial Order

5 The Master of Steel: Andrew Carnegie

ROBERT L. HEILBRONER

From the 1820s on, the United States industrialized at an impressive rate. But the real boost came during the Civil War, when the United States Congress created a national currency and banking system, enacted homestead legislation, and appropriated federal aid for a transcontinental railroad. Such measures, argues historian James M. McPherson, provided "the blueprint for modern America." From the crucible of civil war emerged a new America of big business, heavy industry, and commercial farming that became by 1880 "the foremost industrial nation" in the world. The federal government played a crucial role in the postwar boom. One Republican administration after another not only maintained a protective tariff to minimize foreign competition but gave away millions of dollars' worth of public land to railroad companies, adopted a hard-money policy that pleased big business, and—except for the Interstate Commerce and Sherman Antitrust Acts, both adopted because of popular unrest—cheerfully refused to regulate or restrict the consolidation of America's new industrial order.

It was during the Gilded Age (as Mark Twain called it), an era between Robert E. Lee's surrender at Appomattox and the turn of the century, that American capitalism, growing for decades now, produced mighty combinations that controlled most of the nation's wealth. The leaders of the new industrial order comprised a complex gallery of individuals popularly known as the robber barons. There had, of course, been many rich Americans before the Gilded Age, people who made fortunes from traffic in lands and goods. But the post–Civil War robber barons were a different breed, for they controlled the essential tools of the booming industrial economy itself: railroads (the nation's basic transportation system), banking, and manufacturing. They eliminated competition, set prices, exploited workers, and commanded the awe or fear of an entire generation. Enough of them were rags-to-riches individuals, the kind celebrated in the novels of Horatio Alger, to encourage the notion of the American dream at work, a dream that in the United States all who were capable could rise to the top. Some of the tycoons were gaudy vulgarians such as one H. A. W. Tabor. Finding a portrait of Shakespeare hanging in a Denver opera house that he had built, Tabor demanded that the portrait be replaced with his own, storming, "What the hell has Shakespeare done for Denver?" Others were industrial pirates such as Jay Gould, a consumptive rascal who made his money by various nefarious means.

But other entrepreneurs fit a different pattern: like the rapacious capitalist played by Michael Douglas in the movie Wall Street, *they were obsessed with the power that wealth brought them. An example was Cornelius "Commodore" Vanderbilt, who began his career as a ferryboatman, rose to ownership of riverboats (hence his nickname), and went on to become a railroad magnate who owned a transportation empire worth $80 million and lived in splendor in a Manhattan mansion. This rowdy, profane man loved to win in any way he could, once proclaiming, "Law? What do I care about the law. H'ain't I got the power?"*

Then there was John D. Rockefeller, a quiet, penny-pinching millionaire whose Standard Oil Company became one of the nation's most powerful monopolies. Indeed, Rockefeller's business methods, stressing the virtues of order, organization, and planning, set the example of modern business organization. Unlike other Gilded Age entrepreneurs, however, Rockefeller had little interest in money for money's sake. At the end of his life, through foundations named after him, he donated millions of dollars to religious activities, medical research, and higher education.

And then there was steel magnate Andrew Carnegie, the subject of the insightful portrait that follows. Another self-made man, Carnegie was at one time the richest person in the world. Perhaps more than any other tycoon, he embodied the spirit of the age, a man who not only created but advocated and celebrated industrial power. He defended democracy, capitalism, and the Anglo-Saxon race, and he even argued that evolution produced millionaires such as he, ignoring the fact that such folk enjoyed generous government benefits, not to mention the help of federal troops serving as strikebreakers. Yet Carnegie also acted on his own self-proclaimed sense of duty: having amassed a prodigious fortune, he proceeded to give almost all of it away during his lifetime. In him, Robert L. Heilbroner sees both the failures and the integrity of Gilded Age America.

GLOSSARY

ALGER, HORATIO   Gilded Age author whose heroes rose from poverty to greatness and thus fulfilled the "American dream."

AMERICAN FEDERATION OF LABOR   Organized in 1886 with Samuel Gompers as president, the AFL was an association of trade unions whose membership consisted exclusively of skilled workers.

CARNEGIE CORPORATION OF NEW YORK   After making his fortune, Andrew Carnegie established this "first great modern" philanthropic foundation.

CARNEGIE, McCANDLESS & COMPANY   Andrew Carnegie's British-American steel company and the nucleus of his steel empire.

FRICK, HENRY   Self-made millionaire who amalgamated his coke empire and Andrew Carnegie's steelworks and assumed "the active management of the whole." Frick, Captain William Jones, and Charles Schwab constituted "the vital energy" of the Carnegie empire.

GOSPEL OF WEALTH   Andrew Carnegie's philosophy (in a book of that title) that the millionaire has a duty to distribute wealth while still alive.

JONES, CAPTAIN WILLIAM One of a "brilliant assemblage" of men around Andrew Carnegie, "a kind of Paul Bunyan of steel," who was inventive in handling machinery and talented at dealing with people.

KNIGHTS OF LABOR America's first major labor union, founded in 1869. By 1886, its membership numbered more than 700,000.

MORGAN, J. P. Wealthy banker who purchased the Carnegie steel empire in 1901 for $492 million; it became the core of the United States Steel Company.

PULLMAN, GEORGE Developed the Pullman railroad sleeping car and joined forces with Andrew Carnegie to form the Pullman Palace Car Company.

SCHWAB, CHARLES Assistant manager of Andrew Carnegie's Braddock plant and another of the brilliant men surrounding Carnegie.

SCOTT, THOMAS A. Superintendent of the Pennsylvania Railroad and Andrew Carnegie's boss who first encouraged him to invest in stock.

UNITED STATES STEEL COMPANY J. P. Morgan merged the Carnegie empire with other interests to create this huge corporation, which controlled more than 60 percent of America's steel production.

WOODRUFF, T. T. When Andrew Carnegie bought a one-eighth interest in Woodruff's company, Woodruff began production of the first sleeping car for trains.

Toward the end of his days, at the close of World War I, Andrew Carnegie was already a kind of national legend. His meteoric rise, the scandals and successes of his industrial generalship—all this was blurred into nostalgic memory. What was left was a small, rather feeble man with a white beard and pale, penetrating eyes, who could occasionally be seen puttering around his mansion on upper Fifth Avenue, a benevolent old gentleman who still rated an annual birthday interview but was even then a venerable relic of a fast-disappearing era. Carnegie himself looked back on his career with a certain savored incredulity. "How much did you say I had given away, Poynton?" he would inquire of his private secretary; "$324,657,399" was the answer. "Good Heaven!" Carnegie would exclaim. "Where did I ever get all that money?"

Where he *had* got all that money was indeed a legendary story, for even in an age known for its acquisitive triumphs, Carnegie's touch had been an extraordinary one. He had begun, in true Horatio Alger fashion, at the bottom; he had ended, in a manner that put the wildest of Alger's novels to shame, at the very pinnacle of success. At the close

of his great deal with J. P. Morgan in 1901, when the Carnegie steel empire was sold to form the core of the new United States Steel Company, the banker had extended his hand and delivered the ultimate encomium of the times: "Mr. Carnegie," he said, "I want to congratulate you on being the richest man in the world."

It was certainly as "the richest man in the world" that Carnegie attracted the attention of his contemporaries. Yet this is hardly why we look back on him with interest today. As an enormous money-maker Carnegie was a flashy, but hardly a profound, hero of the times; and the attitudes of Earnestness and Self-Assurance, so engaging in the young immigrant, become irritating when they are congealed in the millionaire. But what lifts Carnegie's life above the rut of a one-dimensional success story is an aspect of which his contemporaries were relatively unaware.

Going through his papers after his death, Carnegie's executors came across a memorandum that he had written to himself fifty years before, carefully preserved in a little yellow box of keepsakes and mementos. It brings us back to December, 1868, when Carnegie, a young man flushed with the first taste of great success, retired to his suite in the opulent Hotel St. Nicholas in New York, to total up his profits for the year. It had been a tremendous year and the calculation must have been

---

"The Master of Steel: Andrew Carnegie" by Robert L. Heilbroner. Reprinted from *American Heritage*, August 1960, pp. 4–9, 107–111, by permission of the author.

extremely pleasurable. Yet this is what he wrote as he reflected on the figures:

Thirty-three and an income of $50,000 per annum! By this time two in years I can so arrange all my business as to secure at least $50,000 per annum. Beyond this never earn—make no effort to increase fortune, but spend the surplus each year for benevolent purposes. Cast aside business forever, except for others.

Settle in Oxford and get a thorough education, making the acquaintance of literary men—this will take three years of active work—pay especial attention to speaking in public. Settle then in London and purchase a controlling interest in some newspaper or live review and give the general management of it attention, taking part in public matters, especially those connected with education and improvement of the poorer classes.

Man must have an idol—the amassing of wealth is one of the worst species of idolatry—no idol more debasing than the worship of money. Whatever I engage in I must push inordinately; therefore should I be careful to choose that life which will be the most elevating in its character. To continue much longer overwhelmed by business cares and with most of my thoughts wholly upon the way to make more money in the shortest time, must degrade me beyond hope of permanent recovery. I will resign business at thirty-five, but during the ensuing two years I wish to spend the afternoons in receiving instruction and in reading systematically.

It is a document which in more ways than one is Carnegie to the very life: brash, incredibly self-confident, chockablock with self-conscious virtue—and more than a little hypocritical. For the program so nobly outlined went largely unrealized. Instead of retiring in two years, Carnegie went on for thirty-three more; even then it was with considerable difficulty that he was persuaded to quit. Far from shunning further money-making, he proceeded to roll up his fortune with an uninhibited drive that led one unfriendly biographer to characterize him as "the greediest little gentleman ever created." Certainly he was one of the most aggressive profit seekers of his time. Typically, when an associate jubilantly cabled: "No. 8 furnace broke all records today," Carnegie coldly replied, "What were the other furnaces doing?"

It is this contrast between his hopes and his performance that makes Carnegie interesting. For when we review his life, what we see is more than the career of another nineteenth-century acquisitor. We see the unequal struggle between a man who loved money—loved making it, having it, spending it—and a man who, at bottom, was ashamed of himself for his acquisitive desires. All during his lifetime, the moneymaker seemed to win. But what lifts Carnegie's story out of the ordinary is that the other Carnegie ultimately triumphed. At his death public speculation placed the size of his estate at about five hundred million dollars. In fact it came to $22,881,575. Carnegie *had* become the richest man in the world—but something had also driven him to give away ninety per cent of his wealth.

Actually, his contemporaries knew of Carnegie's inquietude about money. In 1889, before he was world-famous, he had written an article for the *North American Review* entitled "The Gospel of Wealth"—an article that contained the startling phrase: "The man who dies thus rich dies disgraced." It was hardly surprising, however, if the world took these sentiments at a liberal discount: homiletic millionaires who preached the virtues of austerity were no novelty; Carnegie himself, returning in 1879 from a trip to the miseries of India, had been able to write with perfect sincerity, "How very little the millionaire has beyond the peasant, and how very often his additions tend not to happiness but to misery."

What the world may well have underestimated, however, was a concern more deeply rooted than these pieties revealed. For, unlike so many of his self-made peers, who also rose from poverty, Carnegie was the product of a *radical* environment. The village of Dunfermline, Scotland, when he was born there in 1835, was renowned as a center of revolutionary ferment, and Carnegie's family was itself caught up in the radical movement of the times. His father was a regular speaker at the Chartist rallies, which were an almost daily occurrence in Dunfermline in the 1840's, and his uncle was an impassioned orator for the rights of

Andrew Carnegie, in his mid-twenties when photographed here in 1861, was the son of Scottish working-class radicals and the product of a stern religious upbringing. In his younger days, he thought that the amassing of wealth was "one of the worst species of idolatry." However, he abandoned his plans to retire at thirty-five in order to devote his energies to self-improvement and benevolent enterprises. Instead, he became one of the richest men the world had ever known. (Courtesy, Carnegie Corporation of New York)

the working class to vote and strike. All this made an indelible impression on Carnegie's childhood.

"I remember as if it were yesterday," he wrote seventy years later, "being awakened during the night by a tap at the back window by men who had come to inform my parents that my uncle, Bailie Morrison, had been thrown in jail because he dared to hold a meeting which had been forbidden . . . It is not to be wondered at that, nursed amid such surroundings, I developed into a violent young Republican whose motto was 'death to privilege.'"

From another uncle, George Lauder, Carnegie absorbed a second passion that was also to reveal itself in his later career. This was his love of poetry, first that of the poet Burns, with its overtones of romantic egalitarianism, and then later, of Shakespeare. Immense quantities of both were not only committed to memory, but made into an integral—indeed, sometimes an embarrassingly evident—part of his life: on first visiting the Doge's palace in Venice he thrust a companion in the ducal throne and held him pinioned there while he orated the appropriate speeches from *Othello.* Once, seeing Vanderbilt walking on Fifth Avenue, Carnegie smugly remarked, "I would not exchange his millions for my knowledge of Shakespeare."

But it was more than just a love of poetry that remained with Carnegie. Virtually alone among his fellow acquisitors, he was driven by a genuine respect for the power of thought to seek answers for questions that never even occurred to them. Later, when he "discovered" Herbert Spencer, the English sociologist, Carnegie wrote to him, addressing him as "Master," and it was as "Master" that Spencer remained, even after Carnegie's lavishness had left Spencer very much in his debt.

But Carnegie's early life was shaped by currents more material than intellectual. The grinding process of industrial change had begun slowly but ineluctably to undermine the cottage weaving that was the traditional means of employment in Dunfermline. The Industrial Revolution, in the shape of new steam mills, was forcing out the hand weavers, and one by one the looms which constituted the entire capital of the Carnegie family had to be sold. Carnegie never forgot the shock of his father returning home to tell him, in despair, "Andra, I can get nae mair work."

A family council of war was held, and it was decided that there was only one possible course—they must try their luck in America, to which two sisters of Carnegie's mother, Margaret, had already emigrated. With the aid of a few friends the money for the crossing was scraped together, and at thirteen Andrew found himself transported to the only country in which his career would have been possible.

It hardly got off to an auspicious start, however. The family made their way to Allegheny, Pennsylvania, a raw and bustling town where Carnegie's father again sought work as an independent weaver. But it was as hopeless to compete against the great mills in America as in Scotland, and soon father and son were forced to seek work in the local cotton mills. There Andrew worked from six in the morning until six at night, making $1.20 as a bobbin boy.

After a while his father quit—factory work was impossible for the traditional small enterpriser—and Andrew got a "better" job with a new firm, tending an engine deep in a dungeon cellar and dipping newly made cotton spools in a vat of oil. Even the raise to $3 a week . . . could not overcome the horrors of that lonely and foul-smelling basement. It was perhaps the only time in Carnegie's life when his self-assurance deserted him: to the end of his days the merest whiff of oil could make him deathly sick.

Yet he was certain, as he wrote home at sixteen, that "anyone could get along in this Country," and the rags-to-riches saga shortly began. The telegraph had just come to Pittsburgh, and one evening over a game of checkers, the manager of the local office informed Andrew's uncle that he was looking for a messenger. Andy got the job and, in true Alger fashion, set out to excel in it. Within a few weeks he had carefully memorized the names and the locations, not only of the main streets in Pittsburgh, but of the main firms, so that he was the quickest of all the messenger boys.

He came early and stayed late, watched the telegraphers at work, and at home at night learned the Morse code. As a result he was soon the head of the growing messenger service, and a skilled telegrapher himself. One day he dazzled the office by taking a message "by ear" instead of by the commonly used tape printer, and since he was then only the third operator in the country able to turn the trick, citizens used to drop into the office to watch Andy take down the words "hot from the wire."

One such citizen who was especially impressed with young Carnegie's determination was Thomas A. Scott, in time to become one of the colorful railway magnates of the West, but then the local superintendent of the Pennsylvania Railroad. Soon thereafter Carnegie became "Scott's Andy"—telegrapher, secretary, and general factotum—at thirty-five dollars a month. In his *Autobiography* Carnegie recalls an instance which enabled him to begin the next stage of his career.

One morning I reached the office and found that a serious accident on the Eastern Division had delayed the express passenger train westward, and that the passenger train eastward was proceeding with a flagman in advance at every curve. The freight trains in both directions were standing on the sidings. Mr. Scott was not to be found. Finally I could not resist the temptation to plunge in, take the responsibility, give "train orders" and set matters going. "Death or Westminster Abbey" flashed across my mind. I knew it was dismissal, disgrace, perhaps criminal punishment for me if I erred. On the other hand, I could bring in the wearied freight train men who had lain out all night. I knew I could. I knew just what to do, and so I began.

Signing Scott's name to the orders, Carnegie flashed out the necessary instructions to bring order out of the tangle. The trains moved; there were no mishaps. When Scott reached the office Carnegie told him what he had done. Scott said not a word but looked carefully over all that had taken place. After a little he moved away from Carnegie's desk to his own, and that was the end of it. "But I noticed," Carnegie concluded good-humoredly, "that he came in very regularly and in good time for some mornings after that."

It is hardly to be wondered at that Carnegie became Scott's favorite, his "white-haired Scotch devil." Impetuous but not rash, full of enthusiasm and good-natured charm, the small lad with his blunt, open features and his slight Scottish burr was every executive's dream of an assistant. Soon Scott repaid Andy for his services by introducing him to a new and very different kind of opportunity. He gave Carnegie the chance to subscribe to five hundred dollars' worth of Adams Express stock, a company which Scott assured Andy would prosper mightily.

Carnegie had not fifty dollars saved, much less five hundred, but it was a chance he could ill afford to miss. He reported the offer to his mother, and that pillar of the family unhesitatingly mortgaged their home to raise the necessary money. When the first dividend check came in, with its ornate Spencerian flourishes, Carnegie had something like a revelation. "I shall remember that check as long as I live," he subsequently wrote. "It gave me the first penny of revenue from capital—something that I had not worked for with the sweat of my brow. 'Eureka!' I cried, 'Here's the goose that lays the golden eggs.'" He was right; within a few years his investment in the Adams Express Company was paying annual dividends of $1,400.

It was not long thereafter that an even more propitious chance presented itself. Carnegie was riding on the Pennsylvania line one day when he was approached by a "farmer-looking" man carrying a small green bag in his hand. The other introduced himself as T. T. Woodruff and quite frankly said that he wanted a chance to talk with someone connected with the railroad. Whereupon he opened his bag and took out a small model of the first sleeping car.

Carnegie was immediately impressed with its possibilities, and he quickly arranged for Woodruff to meet Scott. When the latter agreed to give the cars a trial, Woodruff in appreciation offered Carnegie a chance to subscribe to a one-eighth interest in the new company. A local banker agreed to lend Andy the few hundred dollars needed for the initial payment—the rest being financed from dividends. Once again Andy had made a shrewd investment: within two years the Woodruff Palace Car Company was paying him a return of more than $5,000 a year.

Investments now began to play an increasingly important role in Carnegie's career. Through his railroad contacts he came to recognize the possibilities in manufacturing the heavy equipment needed by the rapidly expanding lines, and soon he was instrumental in organizing companies to meet these needs. One of them, the Keystone Bridge Company, was the first successful manufacturer of iron railway bridges. Another, the Pittsburgh Locomotive Works,

made engines. And most important of all, an interest in a local iron works run by an irascible German named Andrew Kloman brought Carnegie into actual contact with the manufacture of iron itself.

None of these new ventures required any substantial outlay of cash. His interest in the Keystone Bridge Company, for instance, which was to earn him $15,000 in 1868, came to him "in return for services rendered in its promotion"—services which Carnegie, as a young railroad executive, was then in a highly strategic position to deliver. Similarly the interest in the Kloman works reflected no contribution on Carnegie's part except that of being the human catalyst and buffer between some highly excitable participants.

By 1865 his "side" activities had become so important that he decided to leave the Pennsylvania Railroad. He was by then superintendent, Scott having moved up to a vice presidency, but his salary of $2,400 was already vastly overshadowed by his income from various ventures. One purchase alone—the Storey farm in Pennsylvania oil country, which Carnegie and a few associates picked up for $40,000—was eventually to pay the group a million dollars in dividends in *one* year. About this time a friend dropped in on Carnegie and asked him how he was doing. "Oh, I'm rich, I'm rich!" he exclaimed.

He was indeed embarked on the road to riches, and determined, as he later wrote in his *Autobiography,* that "nothing could be allowed to interfere for a moment with my business career." Hence it comes as a surprise to note that it was at this very point that Carnegie retired to his suite to write his curiously introspective and troubled thoughts about the pursuit of wealth. But the momentum of events was to prove far too strong for these moralistic doubts. Moving his headquarters to New York to promote his various interests, he soon found himself swept along by a succession of irresistible opportunities for money-making.

One of these took place quite by chance. Carnegie was trying to sell the Woodruff sleeping car at the same time that a formidable rival named George

Pullman was also seeking to land contracts for his sleeping car, and the railroads were naturally taking advantage of the competitive situation. One summer evening in 1869 Carnegie found himself mounting the resplendent marble stairway of the St. Nicholas Hotel side by side with his competitor.

"Good evening, Mr. Pullman," said Carnegie in his ebullient manner. Pullman was barely cordial.

"How strange we should meet here," Carnegie went on, to which the other replied nothing at all.

"Mr. Pullman," said Carnegie, after an embarrassing pause, "don't you think we are making nice fools of ourselves?" At this Pullman evinced a glimmer of interest: "What do you mean?" he inquired. Carnegie quickly pointed out that competition between the two companies was helping no one but the railroads. "Well," said Pullman, "what do you suggest we do?"

"Unite!" said Carnegie. "Let's make a joint proposition to the Union Pacific, your company and mine. Why not organize a new company to do it?" "What would you call it?" asked Pullman suspiciously. "The Pullman Palace Car Company," said Carnegie and with this shrewd psychological stroke won his point. A new company was formed, and in time Carnegie became its largest stockholder.

Meanwhile, events pushed Carnegie into yet another lucrative field. To finance the proliferating railway systems of America, British capital was badly needed, and with his Scottish ancestry, his verve, and his excellent railroad connections Carnegie was the natural choice for a go-between. His brief case stuffed with bonds and prospectuses, Carnegie became a transatlantic commuter, soon developing intimate relations both with great bankers like Junius Morgan (the father of J. P. Morgan), and with the heads of most of the great American roads. These trips earned him not only large commissions—exceeding on occasion $100,000 for a single turn—but even more important, established connections that were later to be of immense value. He himself later testified candidly on their benefits before a group of respectfully awed senators:

For instance, I want a great contract for rails. Sidney Dillon of the Union Pacific was a personal friend of mine.

Huntington was a friend. Dear Butler Duncan, that called on me the other day, was a friend. Those and other men were presidents of railroads . . . Take Huntington; you know C. P. Huntington. He was hard up very often. He was a great man, but he had a great deal of paper out. I knew his things were good. When he wanted credit I gave it to him. If you help a man that way, what chance has any paid agent going to these men? It was absurd.

But his trips to England brought Carnegie something still more valuable. They gave him steel. It is fair to say that as late as 1872 Carnegie did not see the future that awaited him as the Steel King of the world. The still modest conglomeration of foundries and mills he was gradually assembling in the Allegheny and Monongahela valleys was but one of many business interests, and not one for which he envisioned any extraordinary future. Indeed, to repeated pleas that he lead the way in developing a steel industry for America by substituting steel for iron rails, his reply was succinct: "Pioneering don't pay."

What made him change his mind? The story goes that he was awe-struck by the volcanic, spectacular eruption of a Bessemer converter, which he saw for the first time during a visit to a British mill. It was precisely the sort of display that would have appealed to Carnegie's mind—a wild, demonic, physical process miraculously contained and controlled by the dwarfed figures of the steel men themselves. At any rate, overnight Carnegie became the perfervid prophet of steel. Jumping on the first available steamer, he rushed home with the cry, "The day of iron has passed!" To the consternation of his colleagues, the hitherto reluctant pioneer became an advocate of the most daring technological and business expansion; he joined them enthusiastically in forming Carnegie, McCandless & Company, which was the nucleus of the empire that the next thirty years would bring forth.

The actual process of growth involved every aspect of successful business enterprise of the times: acquisition and merger, pools and commercial piracy, and even, on one occasion, an outright fraud in selling the United States government overpriced and underdone steel armor plate. But it would be as foolish to maintain that the Carnegie empire grew by trickery as to deny that sharp practice had its place. Essentially what lay behind the spectacular expansion were three facts.

The first of these was the sheer economic expansion of the industry in the first days of burgeoning steel use. Everywhere steel replaced iron or found new uses—and not only in railroads but in ships, buildings, bridges, machinery of all sorts. As Henry Frick himself once remarked, if the Carnegie group had not filled the need for steel another would have. But it must be admitted that Carnegie's company did its job superlatively well. In 1885 Great Britain led the world in the production of steel. Fourteen years later her total output was 695,000 tons less than the output of the Carnegie Steel Company alone.

Second was the brilliant assemblage of personal talent with which Carnegie surrounded himself. Among them, three in particular stood out. One was Captain William Jones, a Homeric figure who lumbered through the glowing fires and clanging machinery of the works like a kind of Paul Bunyan of steel, skilled at handling men, inventive in handling equipment, and enough of a natural artist to produce papers for the British Iron and Steel Institute that earned him a literary as well as a technical reputation. Then there was Henry Frick, himself a self-made millionaire, whose coke empire naturally complemented Carnegie's steelworks. When the two were amalgamated, Frick took over the active management of the whole, and under his forceful hand the annual output of the Carnegie works rose tenfold. Yet another was Charles Schwab, who came out of the tiny monastic town of Loretto, Pennsylvania, to take a job as a stake driver. Six months later he had been promoted by Jones into the assistant managership of the Braddock plant.

These men, and a score like them, constituted the vital energy of the Carnegie works. As Carnegie himself said, "Take away all our money, our great works, ore mines and coke ovens, but leave our organization, and in four years I shall have re-established myself."

But the third factor in the growth of the empire was Carnegie himself. A master salesman and a skilled diplomat of business at its highest levels, Carnegie was also a ruthless driver of his men. He pitted his associates and subordinates in competition with one another until a feverish atmosphere pervaded the whole organization. "You cannot imagine the abounding sense of freedom and relief I experience as soon as I get on board a steamer and sail past Sandy Hook," he once said to Captain Jones. "My God!" replied Jones. "Think of the relief to us!"

But Carnegie could win loyalties as well. All his promising young men were given gratis ownership participations—minuscule fractions of one per cent, which were enough, however, to make them millionaires in their own right. Deeply grateful to Jones, Carnegie once offered him a similar participation. Jones hemmed and hawed and finally refused; he would be unable to work effectively with the men, he said, once he was a partner. Carnegie insisted that his contribution be recognized and asked Jones what he wanted. "Well," said the latter, "you might pay me a hell of a big salary." "We'll do it!" said Carnegie. "From this time forth you shall receive the same salary as the President of the United States." "Ah, Andy, that's the kind of talk," said Captain Bill.

Within three decades, on the flood tide of economic expansion, propelled by brilliant executive work and relentless pressure from Carnegie, the company made immense strides. "Such a magnificent aggregation of industrial power has never before been under the domination of a single man," reported a biographer in 1902, describing the Gargantuan structure of steel and coke and ore and transport. Had the writer known of the profits earned by this aggregation he might have been even more impressed: three and a half million dollars in 1889, seven million in 1897, twenty-one million in 1899, and an immense forty million in 1900. "Where is there such a business!" Carnegie had exulted, and no wonder—the majority share of all these earnings, without hindrance of income tax, went directly into his pockets.

Nevertheless, with enormous success came problems. One of these was the restiveness of certain partners, under the "Iron-Clad" agreement, which prevented any of them from selling their shares to anyone but the company itself—an arrangement which meant, of course, that the far higher valuation of an outside purchaser could not be realized. Particularly chagrined was Frick, when, as the culmination of other disagreements between them, Carnegie sought to buy him out "at the value appearing on the books." Another problem was a looming competitive struggle in the steel industry itself that presaged a period of bitter industrial warfare ahead. And last was Carnegie's own growing desire to "get out."

Already he was spending half of each year abroad, first traveling, and then, after his late marriage, in residence in the great Skibo Castle he built for his wife on Dornoch Firth, Scotland. There he ran his business enterprises with one hand while he courted the literary and creative world with the other, entertaining Kipling and Matthew Arnold, Paderewski and Lloyd George, Woodrow Wilson and Theodore Roosevelt, Gladstone, and of course, Herbert Spencer, the Master. But even his career as "Laird" of Skibo could not remove him from the worries—and triumphs—of his business: a steady flow of cables and correspondence intruded on the "serious" side of life.

It was Schwab who cut the knot. Having risen to the very summit of the Carnegie concern he was invited in December, 1900, to give a speech on the future of the steel industry at the University Club in New York. There, before eighty of the nation's top business leaders he painted a glowing picture of what could be done if a super-company of steel were formed, integrated from top to bottom, self-sufficient with regard to its raw materials, balanced in its array of final products. One of the guests was the imperious J. P. Morgan, and as the speech progressed it was noticed that his concentration grew more and more intense. After dinner Morgan rose and took the young steel man by the elbow and engaged him in private conversation for half an hour while he plied him with rapid and penetrating questions; then a few

In his late years, Carnegie turned again toward the idealism of his youth. Declaring that his riches had come to him as a "sacred trust" to administer for the good of humanity, he endowed numerous philanthropies and managed to give away 90 percent of his wealth before he died. (Carnegie Corporation of New York)

weeks later he invited him to a private meeting in the great library of his home. They talked from nine o'clock in the evening until dawn. As the sun began to stream in through the library windows, the banker finally rose. "Well," he said to Schwab, "if Andy wants to sell, I'll buy. Go and find his price."

Carnegie at first did not wish to sell. Faced with the actual prospect of a withdrawal from the business he had built into the mightiest single industrial empire in the world, he was frightened and dismayed. He sat silent before Schwab's report, brooding, loath to inquire into details. But soon his enthusiasm returned. No such opportunity was likely to present itself again. In short order a figure of $492,000,000 was agreed on for the entire enterprise, of which Carnegie himself was to receive $300,000,000 in five per cent gold bonds and preferred stock. Carnegie jotted down the terms of the transaction on a slip of paper and told Schwab to bring it to Morgan. The banker glanced only briefly at the paper. "I accept," he said.

After the formalities were in due course completed, Carnegie was in a euphoric mood. "Now, Pierpont, I am the happiest man in the world," he said. Morgan was by no means unhappy himself: his own banking company had made a direct profit of $12,500,000 in the underwriting transaction, and this was but a prelude to a stream of lucrative financings under Morgan's aegis, by which the total capitalization was rapidly raised to $1,400,000,000. A few years later, Morgan and Carnegie found themselves aboard the same steamer en route to Europe. They fell into talk and Carnegie confessed, "I made one mistake, Pierpont, when I sold out to you."

"What was that?" asked the banker.

"I should have asked you for $100,000,000 more than I did."

Morgan grinned. "Well," he said, "you would have got it if you had."

Thus was written *finis* to one stage of Carnegie's career. Now it would be seen to what extent his "radical pronouncements" were serious. For in the *Gospel of Wealth*—the famous article combined with others in book form—Carnegie had proclaimed the duty of the millionaire to administer and distribute his wealth *during his lifetime*. Though he might have "proved" his worth by his fortune, his heirs had shown no such evidence of their fitness. Carnegie bluntly concluded: "By taxing estates heavily at his death, the State marks its condemnation of the selfish millionaire's unworthy life."

Coming from the leading millionaire of the day, these had been startling sentiments. So also were his views on the "labor question" which, if patronizing, were nonetheless humane and advanced for their day. The trouble was, of course, that the sentiments were somewhat difficult to credit. As one commentator of the day remarked, "His vision of what might

be done with wealth had beauty and breadth and thus serenely overlooked the means by which wealth had been acquired."

For example, the novelist Hamlin Garland visited the steel towns from which the Carnegie millions came and bore away a description of work that was ugly, brutal, and exhausting: he contrasted the lavish care expended on the plants with the callous disregard of the pigsty homes: "the streets were horrible; the buildings poor; the sidewalks sunken and full of holes. . . . Everywhere the yellow mud of the streets lay kneaded into sticky masses through which groups of pale, lean men slouched in faded garments. . . ." When the famous Homestead strike erupted in 1892, with its private army of Pinkerton detectives virtually at war with the workers, the Carnegie benevolence seemed revealed as shabby fakery. At Skibo Carnegie stood firmly behind the company's iron determination to break the strike. As a result, public sentiment swung sharply and suddenly against him; the St. Louis *Post-Dispatch* wrote: "Three months ago Andrew Carnegie was a man to be envied. Today he is an object of mingled pity and contempt. In the estimation of nine-tenths of the thinking people on both sides of the ocean he has . . . confessed himself a moral coward."

In an important sense the newspaper was right. For though Carnegie continued to fight against "privilege," he saw privilege only in its fading aristocratic vestments and not in the new hierarchies of wealth and power to which he himself belonged. In Skibo Castle he now played the role of the benign autocrat, awakening to the skirling of his private bagpiper and proceeding to breakfast to the sonorous accompaniment of the castle organ.

Meanwhile there had also come fame and honors in which Carnegie wallowed unashamedly. He counted the "freedoms" bestowed on him by grateful or hopeful cities and crowed, "I have fifty-two and Gladstone has only seventeen." He entertained the King of England and told him that democracy was better than monarchy, and met the German Kaiser: "Oh, yes, yes," said the latter worthy on being introduced. "I have read your books. You do not like kings." But Mark Twain, on hearing of this, was not fooled. "He says he is a scorner of kings and emperors and dukes," he wrote, "whereas he is like the rest of the human race: a slight attention from one of these can make him drunk for a week. . . ."

And yet it is not enough to conclude that Carnegie was in fact a smaller man than he conceived himself. For this judgment overlooks one immense and irrefutable fact. He did, in the end, abide by his self-imposed duty. He did give nearly all of his gigantic fortune away.

As one would suspect, the quality of the philanthropy reflected the man himself. There was, for example, a huge and sentimentally administered private pension fund to which access was to be had on the most trivial as well as the most worthy grounds: if it included a number of writers, statesmen, scientists, it also made room for two maiden ladies with whom Carnegie had once danced as a young man, a boyhood acquaintance who had once held Carnegie's books while he ran a race, a merchant to whom he had once delivered a telegram and who had subsequently fallen on hard times. And then, as one would expect, there was a benevolent autocracy in the administration of the larger philanthropies as well. "Now everybody vote Aye," was the way Carnegie typically determined the policies of the philanthropic "foundations" he established.

Yet if these flaws bore the stamp of one side of Carnegie's personality, there was also the other side—the side that, however crudely, asked important questions and however piously, concerned itself with great ideals. Of this the range and purpose of the main philanthropies gave unimpeachable testimony. There were the famous libraries—three thousand of them costing nearly sixty million dollars; there were the Carnegie institutes in Pittsburgh and Washington, Carnegie Hall in New York, the Hague Peace Palace, the Carnegie Endowment for International Peace, and the precedent-making Carnegie Corporation of New York, with its original enormous endowment of $125,000,000. In his instructions to the trustees of this first great modern foundation, couched

in the simplified spelling of which he was an ardent advocate, we see Carnegie at his very best:

Conditions on erth [*sic*] inevitably change; hence, no wise man will bind Trustees forever to certain paths, causes, or institutions. I disclaim any intention of doing so . . . My chief happiness, as I write these lines lies in the thot [*sic*] that, even after I pass away, the welth [*sic*] that came to me to administer as a sacred trust for the good of my fellow men is to continue to benefit humanity . . .

If these sentiments move us—if Carnegie himself in retrospect moves us at last to grudging respect—it is not because his was the triumph of a saint or a philosopher. It is because it was the much more difficult triumph of a very human and fallible man struggling to retain his convictions in an age, and in the face of a career, which subjected them to impossible temptations. Carnegie is something of America writ large; his is the story of the Horatio Alger hero *after* he has made his million dollars. In the failures of Andrew Carnegie we see many of the failures of America itself. In his curious triumph, we see what we hope is our own steadfast core of integrity.

QUESTIONS TO CONSIDER

1 Robert L. Heilbroner suggests that Andrew Carnegie was interesting because of the contrasts in his character: the conflict between his Calvinist simplicity and his overpowering urge to accumulate wealth. What are the sources of Carnegie's contradictory character?

2 Describe Carnegie's personal "gospel of wealth." Did he live up to his own ideals? Why do you think he was attracted to the teachings of his "master," evolutionist Herbert Spencer?

3 All his life, Carnegie insisted upon his hatred of aristocratic privilege, yet he lived a life of magnificence in his Scottish castle, and he courted the acquaintance of famous politicians, scholars, and royal personages. How did he justify his actions? Did he

see himself as a different sort of aristocrat? Why did he go back to Britain to live?

4 Carnegie left a rich legacy of philanthropies, most notably the vast network of libraries that has developed into our present public library system. How was the money to fund these philanthropies obtained in the first place? Why do you think Carnegie—and many others—failed to see the contrast between the good money could do and the way it was made? How might wealthy people in the Gilded Age have viewed the lives of the working poor?

5 How does what Heilbroner calls the "failure" of Andrew Carnegie reflect the failure of America in the Gilded Age? What were the social and economic consequences of the *Gospel of Wealth* and of huge concentrations of capital in late nineteenth-century America?

6   The Brooklyn Bridge: A Monument to American Ingenuity and Daring

DAVID McCULLOUGH

Imagine the wide-eyed wonder of European immigrants, approaching New York City by ship, when they first glimpsed the towering Brooklyn Bridge across the East River. As David McCullough says in the following selection: "Its enormous granite towers loomed higher than anything anyone had ever seen, higher than the topgallant sails of the square-riggers coursing the river, higher than any building in New York, or any structure then on the North American continent."

This marvelous technological achievement was not only "the proudest symbol of America's greatest city," but also "much that is best about America." The late nineteenth century had produced many wonders, such as Thomas Edison's phonograph, George Eastman's Kodak camera, and Alexander Graham Bell's telephone. But nothing symbolized America's technological genius more than the enormous suspension bridge that stretched a mile across New York's East River. The bridge was all the more remarkable because it was free of the corruption, exploitation, and unfair business practices most often associated with the Gilded Age.

The story of the Brooklyn Bridge is also a tale of familial love and dedication. John A. Roebling, who had perfected the suspension bridge, designed the structure but died of "a freak accident" while surveying the Brooklyn shore. His son, Washington Roebling, a Civil War veteran on the Union side, took over his father's work, and it was this indomitable man and his persevering wife, Emily Warren Roebling, who saw the bridge through to its completion in 1883. The building of this magnificent structure involved more than steel and granite; it is a testament to a family's love and dedication to a common goal.

On another level, McCullough's portrait of the bridge and its builders represents urban history at its best. The labor force was remarkably diverse, including "men of every color and kind, from every corner of the globe." There were blacks up from the South, farm boys in from the countryside, and immigrants from across the sea. Such folk helped make New York the largest, most diverse, and most vibrant city in America.

In sum, the Brooklyn Bridge was a tremendous technological achievement, a family story, and a symbol of America's changing urban landscape. As you read the trilogy of essays in this section of Portrait of America, *think about how they are interrelated. It was the powerful steel industry of Andrew Carnegie, the subject of the previous selection, that furnished the steel for the bridge's cables. And it was the immigrants, treated in selection 7, who provided part of the manpower that built this American phenomenon.*

GLOSSARY

BATTLE OF THE LITTLE BIGHORN (JUNE 25, 1876)   See *Little Bighorn* in glossary in selection 3.

BENDS   A disease that results in extreme pain to the extremities, abdomen, and chest. Washington Roebling had made repeated dives into the strong currents of the East River to inspect the foundation of the bridge. He suffered the bends, caused by leaving the compressed air of deep water too quickly.

ROEBLING, EMILY WARREN   Washington's young wife, who helped supervise the construction of the Brooklyn Bridge after her husband was stricken with the bends. "In little time, she was conversant with every detail and became Washington's most valuable and trusted aide."

ROEBLING, JOHN A.   Builder who left Germany in the 1830s to make his fortune in America. His suspension bridges in Niagara, Pittsburgh, and Cincinnati were already completed when he started his project for a mammoth structure across New York's East River. He died of tetanus before finishing "his crowning work, his masterpiece."

ROEBLING, WASHINGTON   John's son and a Civil War hero. His dedication to completing the Brooklyn Bridge was partly motivated by his desire to build a monument to his father.

SCHUYLER, MONTGOMERY   The architectural critic who praised the Brooklyn Bridge as the most "durable monument" of its age—more important than a shrine, a fortress, or a palace.

TWEED RING   Corrupt political bosses were in control of many of the large cities in the late nineteenth century, but few were more powerful than William Marcy Tweed, who ran New York City at the time that the Brooklyn Bridge was being constructed. The three-hundred-pound Tweed and his Tammany Hall henchmen used graft to rob city treasuries of untold millions.

There is something particularly appealing about a bridge, almost any bridge, but the Brooklyn Bridge surpasses all.

In its day, it was the biggest, most famous bridge in the world, the most beautiful of suspension bridges, and the most dramatic testament yet to American technical ingenuity and daring. More than a mile long, it spanned New York's East River with "one great leap," as was said. Its enormous granite towers loomed higher than anything anyone had ever seen, higher than the topgallant sails of the square-riggers coursing the river, higher than any building in New York, or any structure then on the North American continent.

"You see great ships passing beneath it," wrote a visitor from abroad "and you will feel that the engineer is the great artist of our epoch and you will own that these people have a right to plume themselves on their audacity."

It was the thing everyone from the hinterlands was told not to miss seeing ("If ever you get to New York"), and the first New World spectacle beheld by tens of millions of immigrants as their inbound ships came up the harbor. As nothing else ever had, the bridge indicated that there was no place like New York, no place like America in the wondrous nineteenth century.

The heroic story of its construction is well known. Its position in American life is unrivaled, and as remarkable as anything about this infinitely unprecedented structure is that it has never lost that position. It remains not only the proudest symbol of America's greatest city and a thrilling work of architecture, but an enduring symbol of much that is best about America. And this, it happens, was just as its designer, the brilliant John A. Roebling, had promised from the start with characteristic immodesty.

If built according to his plans, he said, the bridge would stand down the ages as a stunning example of engineering and a great work of art.

That the bridge rose out of the Gilded Age, with its rampaging corruption, its infamous Tweed Ring and the Grant administration, the very heyday of

---

David McCullough, "The Brooklyn Bridge," from *American Greats* by Robert Wilson. Copyright © 1999 by Robert Wilson. Reprinted by permission of Public Affairs, a member of Perseus Books, L. L. C.

The Brooklyn Bridge was one of the most majestic and daring technological achievements of its age. In this 1912 photograph, New Yorkers enjoy the boardwalk, where they could escape "up and out and over the river, higher than they had ever been, to take in the spectacular panorama and breathe air fresh from the sea." (© The New York Times)

shoddy in nearly everything, makes the promise and its fulfillment all the more outstanding.

Himself an immigrant, Roebling had left Germany in the 1830s to find his destiny "in all that space" of America, and on arriving, he had taken the multitude of projects he saw under construction—highways, railways, canals—as the natural expression of an enlightened, self-governing people. It was John A. Roebling who perfected the suspension form, with bridges at Niagara, Pittsburgh, and Cincinnati. The bridge over the East River was to have been his crowning work, his masterpiece, but he died of tetanus in 1869, after a freak accident while making the initial surveys on the Brooklyn shore.

Only his son, Col. Washington Roebling, a Civil War hero, was qualified to take up the work in his place, and if dedication, high intelligence, decisiveness, and extraordinary courage are qualities to be especially admired, he was the most admirable of men. He carried on in the face of trials and setbacks never foreseen by his father, and with the ever-present knowledge that if the bridge succeeded, it would be his father's triumph, while should it fail, it would be his failure.

Washington Roebling had a gift for being always where he was needed, no matter the danger. In the crucial first stages, he was in and out of the great caisson foundation beneath Brooklyn tower, down below the river more often than anyone, to the point where he was stricken by the "bends," the dreaded caisson disease. The pain was excruciating and caused, as no one yet understood, by coming out of compressed air too rapidly.

As a result, he spent the better part of fourteen years in confinement, watching over the work with a telescope from a window in his house in Brooklyn Heights. To see that his orders were carried out, and to appraise progress on the bridge for him first hand, his wife, Emily Warren Roebling, went back and forth to the site several times daily. It was she who dealt with the press and the trustees of the project. In little time, she was conversant with every detail and became Washington's most valuable and trusted aide.

Nearly all of the work was exceedingly dangerous. How many others were eventually felled by the bends, how many were killed or maimed in building the towers or stringing the steel cables is not known—it is a measure of the time that nobody bothered to keep such records. But the cost in suffering and loss of life was considerable. Probably twenty-five or more were killed before the work ended.

The labor force was the epitome of "diversity," as we would say. Men of every color and kind, from every corner of the globe would later boast that they helped build the Brooklyn Bridge—New England farm boys new to the city, African Americans up from Maryland and Virginia, Irish and Italian immigrants in droves, English, Welsh, Swedes, Germans. Sailors proved particularly adept at the high-wire work.

Further, it was an enterprise led by youth, as suited a project that in concept and detail was virtually all pioneering and where physical stamina and creative energy counted for more than experience. Roebling, the only one who knew from experience how his father's bridges were built, was all of thirty-two when he took charge as chief engineer. The average age of the assistant engineers was thirty-one. Emily Roebling was twenty-six.

Because Roebling was never seen, rumors spread that he had lost his mind, and that if truth be known, this greatest, most daring of projects was in the hands of a woman.

The towers were completed the summer of 1876, the summer of the Centennial and the Battle of the Little Big Horn. The "spinning" of the cables commenced at once.

When the long span over the river was far enough finished for the first horse and carriage to cross, it was Emily Roebling who rode in it, carrying a rooster, as a symbol of victory, while from the rigging overhead the men waved their hats and cheered. If ever I could go back in time to witness an event, it would be this.

Construction ended, the bridge was opened on May 24, 1883. It had taken fourteen years. The fireworks in celebration that night were the most spectacular ever seen.

On reflection, some saw this clearly as an achievement of far-reaching importance. "It so happens," wrote the architectural critic Montgomery Schuyler, "that the work which is likely to be our most durable monument, and to convey some knowledge of us to the most remote posterity, is a work of bare utility; not a shrine, not a fortress, not a palace, but a bridge."

Like other ambitious projects then under way in New York, such as the Metropolitan Museum and Central Park, the bridge was an emphatic commitment to the ideal of the city, intended as a grand-scale enhancement to city life.

On Sundays and holidays, people could escape from the narrow, congested streets of the city to walk the bridge, to go up and out over the river, higher than they had ever been, to take in the spectacular panorama and breathe air fresh from the sea. Thousands came, year in, year out, to stroll the famous pedestrian promenade, a boardwalk unlike any to be found on any bridge ever built. By design, it was placed above the vehicular traffic so as not to impede the view, the Roeblings being what might be called civilized civil engineers.

Initially, the bridge had been launched by Brooklyn people who saw that Manhattan was running out of space in which to expand. If a connection could be made, they thought, then surely the overflow would come Brooklyn's way. No one had yet imagined that a city might grow upward instead of out.

As it happened, it was the bridge itself, with its immense scale and use of steel, that marked the start of high-rise New York. Steel for girders and steel rope or cable for elevators would make possible the skyscraper and the vertical city of the twentieth century.

Though dwarfed by modern New York, and by the colossal Verrazano Bridge down the harbor, the Roebling masterpiece is still an American treasure beyond compare, beloved in a way nothing else built in America has ever been. Its towers are still the loftiest towers of stone to be seen. (The towers of the larger suspension bridges built since are of steel.) It is still acclaimed by architectural critics and figures time and again in movies, advertisements, and television commercials. Photographers find it irresistible. It is photographed, without cease, from every angle in all seasons, in every kind of light.

It remains a reminder of other days, yet serves still as an indispensable main artery. Trucks and automobiles, as unimaginable to the builders as were skyscrapers, stream across in both directions twenty-four hours a day.

And on good days, the crowds still come to walk the promenade and experience the thrill of the view, the same lift of spirits felt by so many for more than a century. It remains what it was, the greatest of bridges, the Brooklyn Bridge, made in America, its appeal defying time, a symbol now no less than ever of brave work nobly done.

QUESTIONS TO CONSIDER

1 Of all of the great technological achievements of the late nineteenth century, what made the Brooklyn Bridge the symbol of American accomplishment? As McCullough observes, the awe-inspiring structure convinced those who first viewed it to believe that "there was no place like New York."

2 In what sense was building the Brooklyn Bridge largely a product of a family's devotion to each other? What were the separate roles played by John, Washington, and Emily Warren Roebling?

3 Describe the ethnic and racial backgrounds of the young labor force that built the Brooklyn Bridge. Why does McCullough conclude that the giant steel and granite structure represented America's diversity?

4 Why was the Brooklyn Bridge "a grand-scale enhancement to city life"? How did average New Yorkers use it on Sundays and holidays to experience something they had never seen or felt before?

5 Reflecting on selection 5 on Andrew Carnegie, explain why the modern American city of the late nineteenth century could never have developed without the steel industry. Besides the Brooklyn Bridge, in what other ways did steel change the New York landscape?

6 Why does McCullough conclude that the Brooklyn Bridge is "a symbol now no less than ever of brave work nobly done"?

7 A Little Milk, a Little Honey

DAVID BOROFF

The Gilded Age witnessed an enormous surge of immigration from Europe, as the romantic lure of America seemed to draw more people than ever. For Europeans, as one historian has noted, "America was rich, America was good, America was hope, America was the future." They came over by the millions, crowding into American cities and swelling the bottom ranks of American labor. Between 1850 and 1910, some 22,800,000 immigrants arrived in the United States, more than three-fourths of them after 1881. There was also a significant shift in the source of immigration. The "old" immigrants were from western and northern Europe—Britain, Ireland, Germany, and the Scandinavian countries. But in the 1890s, most immigrants were from eastern and southern Europe—Russia, Serbia, Austria-Hungary, and Italy—and most were Jewish or Catholic. When these people arrived in America's northeastern cities, they invariably antagonized native-born Protestants, who unfairly blamed them for America's growing urban problems.

The major gateway of the new immigration was New York City, where the population swelled from 1.5 million in 1870 to a spectacular 5 million by 1915. The constant stream of new arrivals made New York the largest and most ethnically diverse city in America. In fact, by 1900, more than three-fourths of New York's citizenry was foreign born. Among them were several hundred thousand eastern European Jews, most of whom settled in the crowded and tumultuous Lower East Side, where they lived in conditions that contrasted sharply with the dream of America that had brought them here.

David Boroff provides a vivid picture of the Jewish immigrants, who first began arriving in New Amsterdam (later New York) in 1654. His focus, however, is on the period after 1880, when Jewish immigration was, as he puts it, "in flood tide." Boroff's lively narrative not only captures the immigrant experience but points out the influence of the Jewish immigrants on the United States and America's influence on them.

In significant ways, the Jewish immigrant experience mirrored that of other ethnic groups newly arrived in America. Italians, Poles, Slovaks, Greeks, and Irish also congregated in "immigrant ghettos" in which they tended to recreate the features of the Old World societies they had left behind. While the ghetto had its bleak side, it nevertheless afforded ethnic groups "a sense of belonging," of "cultural cohesiveness" that assuaged the pain of leaving their homelands and starting over in a strange, often overwhelming new land.

GLOSSARY

AUSWANDERERHALLEN   Emigrant buildings in Hamburg.

CANTOR   In a synagogue's religious service, this officer performs the liturgy and sings or chants the prayers.

CASTLE GARDEN   The huge building, situated at the foot of Manhattan, where immigrants were cleaned and interrogated after their arrival.

CHEDERS   Hebrew schools.

COFFEE HOUSE   The most popular cultural institution in the Jewish ghetto.

GEHENNA   Hell.

GENTILE   People who are not Jewish.

GREENHORN, OR GREENER   Pejorative term for newly arrived immigrants.

JEWISH DAILY FORWARD   Socialistic Yiddish newspaper, edited by Abraham Cahan.

LANDSLEIT   Jewish term for fellow townsmen.

MAX HOCHSTIM ASSOCIATION   Energetically recruited girls to work as prostitutes.

NEW YORK INDEPENDENT BENEVOLENT ASSOCIATION   An organization of pimps.

ORTHODOX JEW   One who adheres faithfully to traditional Judaism, who is devoted to the study of the Torah, attends synagogue daily, and takes care to observe the Sabbath, Jewish holy days, dietary laws, and religious festivals.

"PIG MARKET"   Functioned as the labor exchange on the Lower East Side.

POGROM   Organized massacre of Jews.

SHTETL   Typical small Jewish town in Europe.

WHITE PLAGUE   Immigrants' term for tuberculosis.

YIDDISH   The Hebrew-German dialect and the main vehicle for a Jewish cultural renaissance between 1890 and World War I.

ZHID   Yiddish word for "leave."

It started with a trickle and ended in a flood. The first to come were twenty-three Jews from Brazil who landed in New Amsterdam in 1654, in flight from a country no longer hospitable to them. They were, in origin, Spanish and Portuguese Jews (many with grandiloquent Iberian names) whose families had been wandering for a century and a half. New Amsterdam provided a chilly reception. Governor Peter Stuyvesant at first asked them to leave, but kinder hearts in the Dutch West India Company granted them the right to stay, "provided the poor among them . . . be supported by their own nation." By the end of the century, there were perhaps one hundred Jews; by the middle of the eighteenth century, there were about three hundred in New York, and smaller communities in Newport, Philadelphia, and Charleston.

Because of their literacy, zeal, and overseas connections, colonial Jews prospered as merchants, though there were artisans and laborers among them. The Jewish community was tightly knit, but there was a serious shortage of trained religious functionaries. There wasn't a single American rabbi, for example, until the nineteenth century. Jews were well regarded, particularly in New England. Puritan culture leaned heavily on the Old Testament, and Harvard students learned Hebrew; indeed, during the American Revolution, the suggestion was advanced that Hebrew replace English as the official language of the new country. The absence of an established national religion made it possible for Judaism to be regarded as merely another religion in a pluralistic society. The early days of the new republic were thus a happy time for Jews. Prosperous and productive, they were admitted to American communal life with few restrictions. It is little wonder that a Jewish spokesman asked rhetorically in 1820: "On what spot in this habitable Globe does an Israelite enjoy more blessings, more privileges?"

From David Boroff, "A Little Milk, a Little Honey," *American Heritage,* October/November 1966, Vol. 17, No. 6. Reprinted by permission of American Heritage, Inc. Copyright © Forbes, Inc., 1966.

The second wave of immigration during the nineteenth century is often described as German, but that is misleading. Actually, there were many East European Jews among the immigrants who came in the half century before 1870. However, the German influence was strong, and there was a powerful undercurrent of Western enlightenment at work. These Jews came because economic depression and the Industrial Revolution had made their lot as artisans and small merchants intolerable. For some there was also the threatening backwash of the failure of the Revolution of 1848. Moreover, in Germany at this time Jews were largely disfranchised and discriminated against. During this period, between 200,000 and 400,000 Jews emigrated to this country, and the Jewish population had risen to about half a million by 1870.

This was the colorful era of the peddler and his pack. Peddling was an easy way to get started—it required little capital—and it often rewarded enterprise and daring. Jewish peddlers fanned out through the young country into farmland and mining camp, frontier and Indian territory. The more successful peddlers ultimately settled in one place as storekeepers. (Some proud businesses . . . made their start this way.) Feeling somewhat alienated from the older, settled Jews, who had a reputation for declining piety, the new immigrants organized their own synagogues and community facilities, such as cemeteries and hospitals. In general, these immigrants were amiably received by native Americans, who, unsophisticated about differences that were crucial to the immigrants themselves, regarded all Central Europeans as "Germans."

Essentially, the emigration route was the same between 1820 and 1870 as it would be in the post-1880 exodus. The travellers stayed in emigration inns while awaiting their ship, and since they had all their resources with them, they were in danger of being robbed. The journey itself was hazardous and, in the days of the sailing vessels when a good wind was indispensable, almost interminable. Nor were the appointments very comfortable even for the relatively well to do. A German Jew who made the journey in

1856 reported that his cabin, little more than six feet by six feet, housed six passengers in triple-decker bunks. When a storm raged, the passengers had to retire to their cabins lest they be washed off the deck by waves. "Deprived of air," he wrote, "it soon became unbearable in the cabins in which six sea-sick persons breathed." On this particular journey, sea water began to trickle into the cabins, and the planks had to be retarred.

Still, the emigration experience was a good deal easier than it would be later. For one thing, the immigrants were better educated and better acquainted with modern political and social attitudes than the oppressed and bewildered East European multitudes who came after 1880. Fewer in number, they were treated courteously by ships' captains. (On a journey in 1839, described by David Mayer, the ship's captain turned over his own cabin to the Jewish passengers for their prayers and regularly visited those Jews who were ill.) Moreover, there was still the bloom of adventure about the overseas voyage. Ships left Europe amid the booming of cannon, while on shore ladies enthusiastically waved their handkerchiefs. On the way over, there was a holiday atmosphere despite the hazards, and there was great jubilation when land was sighted.

There were, however, rude shocks when the voyagers arrived in this country. The anguish of Castle Garden and Ellis Island was well in the future when immigration first began to swell. But New York seemed inhospitable, its pace frantic, the outlook not entirely hopeful. Isaac M. Wise, a distinguished rabbi who made the journey in 1846, was appalled. "The whole city appeared to me like a large shop," he wrote, "where everyone buys or sells, cheats or is cheated. I had never before seen a city so bare of all art and of every trace of good taste; likewise I had never witnessed anywhere such rushing, hurrying, chasing, running. . . . Everything seemed so pitifully small and paltry; and I had had so exalted an idea of the land of freedom." Moreover, he no sooner landed in New York than he was abused by a German drayman whose services he had declined. "Aha! thought I," he later wrote, "you have left home and kindred in order to get away from the disgusting Judaeo-phobia and here the first German greeting that sounds in your ears is hep! hep!" (The expletive was a Central European equivalent of "Kike.") Another German Jew who worked as a clothing salesman was affronted by the way customers were to be "lured" into buying ("I did not think this occupation corresponded in any way to my views of a merchant's dignity").

After 1880, Jewish immigration into the United States was in flood tide. And the source was principally East Europe, where by 1880 three-quarters of the world's 7.7 million Jews were living. In all, over two million Jews came to these shores in little more than three decades—about one-third of Europe's Jewry. Some of them came, as their predecessors had come, because of shrinking economic opportunities. In Russia and in the Austro-Hungarian empire, the growth of large-scale agriculture squeezed out Jewish middlemen as it destroyed the independent peasantry, while in the cities the development of manufacturing reduced the need for Jewish artisans. Vast numbers of Jews became petty tradesmen or even *luftmenschen* (men without visible means of support who drifted from one thing to another). In Galicia, around 1900, there was a Jewish trader for every ten peasants, and the average value of his stock came to only twenty dollars.

Savage discrimination and pogroms also incited Jews to emigrate. The Barefoot Brigades—bands of marauding Russian peasants—brought devastation and bloodshed to Jewish towns and cities. On a higher social level, there was the "cold pogrom," a government policy calculated to destroy Jewish life. The official hope was that one third of Russia's Jews would die out, one third would emigrate, and one third would be converted to the Orthodox Church. Crushing restrictions were imposed. Jews were required to live within the Pale of Settlement in western Russia, they could not Russify their names, and they were subjected to rigorous quotas for schooling and professional training. Nor could general studies be included in the curriculum of Jewish religious schools. It was a life of poverty and fear.

Nevertheless, the *shtetl,* the typical small Jewish town, was a triumph of endurance and spiritual integrity. It was a place where degradation and squalor could not wipe out dignity, where learning flourished in the face of hopelessness, and where a tough, sardonic humor provided catharsis for the tribulations of an existence that was barely endurable. The abrasions and humiliations of everyday life were healed by a rich heritage of custom and ceremony. And there was always Sabbath—"The Bride of the Sabbath," as the Jews called the day of rest—to bring repose and exaltation to a life always sorely tried.

To be sure, even this world showed signs of disintegration. Secular learning, long resisted by East European Jews and officially denied to them, began to make inroads. Piety gave way to revolutionary fervor, and Jews began to play a heroic role in Czarist Russia's bloody history of insurrection and suppression.

This was the bleak, airless milieu from which the emigrants came. A typical expression of the Jewish attitude towards emigration from Russia—both its hopefulness and the absence of remorse—was provided by Dr. George Price, who had come to this country in one of the waves of East European emigration:

Should this Jewish emigrant regret his leave-taking of his native land which fails to appreciate him? No! A thousand times no! He must not regret fleeing the clutches of the blood-thirsty crocodile. Sympathy for this country? How ironical it sounds! Am I not despised? Am I not urged to leave? Do I not hear the word *Zhid* constantly? . . . Be thou cursed forever my wicked homeland, because you remind me of the Inquisition. . . . May you rue the day when you exiled the people who worked for your welfare.

After 1880, going to America—no other country really lured—became the great drama of redemption for the masses of East European Jews. (For some, of course, Palestine had that role even in the late nineteenth century, but these were an undaunted Zionist cadre prepared to endure the severest hardships.) The assassination of Czar Alexander II in 1881, and the subsequent pogrom, marked the beginning of the new influx. By the end of the century, 700,000

Jews had arrived, about one quarter of them totally illiterate, almost all of them impoverished. Throughout East Europe, Jews talked longingly about America as the "goldene medinah" (the golden province), and biblical imagery—"the land of milk and honey"—came easily to their lips. Those who could write were kept busy composing letters to distant kin—or even to husbands—in America. (Much of the time, the husband went first, and by abstemious living saved enough to fetch wife and children from the old country.) Children played at "emigrating games," and for the entire *shtetl* it was an exciting moment when the mail-carrier announced how many letters had arrived from America.

German steamship companies assiduously advertised the glories of the new land and provided a one-price rate from *shtetl* to New York. Emigration inns were established in Brody (in the Ukraine) and in the port cities of Bremen and Hamburg, where emigrants would gather for the trip. There were rumors that groups of prosperous German Jews would underwrite their migration to America; and in fact such people often did help their co-religionists when they were stranded without funds in the port cities of Germany. Within Russia itself, the government after 1880 more or less acquiesced in the emigration of Jews, and connived in the vast business of "stealing the border" (smuggling emigrants across). After 1892, emigration was legal—except for those of draft age—but large numbers left with forged papers, because that proved to be far easier than getting tangled in the red tape of the Tzarist bureaucracy. Forged documents, to be sure, were expensive—they cost twenty-five rubles, for many Jews the equivalent of five weeks' wages. Nor was the departure from home entirely a happy event. There were the uncertainties of the new life, the fear that in America "one became a gentile." Given the Jewish aptitude for lugubriousness, a family's departure was often like a funeral, lachrymose and anguished, with the neighbors carting off the furniture that would no longer be needed.

For people who had rarely ventured beyond the boundaries of their own village, going to America was an epic adventure. They travelled with pitifully little money; the average immigrant arrived in New York with only about twenty dollars. With their domestic impedimenta—bedding, brass candlesticks, samovars—they would proceed to the port cities by rail, cart, and even on foot. At the emigration inns, they had to wait their turn. Thousands milled around, entreating officials for departure cards. There were scenes of near chaos—mothers shrieking, children crying; battered wicker trunks, bedding, utensils in wild disarray. At Hamburg, arriving emigrants were put in the "unclean" section of the *Auswandererhallen* until examined by physicians who decided whether their clothing and baggage had to be disinfected. After examination, Jews could not leave the center; other emigrants could.

The ocean voyage provided little respite. (Some elected to sail by way of Liverpool at a reduction of nine dollars from the usual rate of thirty-four dollars.) Immigrants long remembered the "smell of ship," a distillation of many putrescences. Those who went in steerage slept on mattresses filled with straw and kept their clothes on to keep warm. The berth itself was generally six feet long, two feet wide, and two and a half feet high, and it had to accommodate the passenger's luggage. Food was another problem. Many Orthodox Jews subsisted on herring, black bread, and tea which they brought because they did not trust the dietary purity of the ship's food. Some ships actually maintained a separate galley for kosher food, which was coveted by non-Jewish passengers because it was allegedly better.

Unsophisticated about travel and faced by genuine dangers, Jewish emigrants found the overseas trip a long and terrifying experience. But when land was finally sighted, the passengers often began to cheer and shout. "I looked up at the sky," an immigrant wrote years later. "It seemed much bluer and the sun much brighter than in the old country. It reminded me on [sic] the Garden of Eden."

Unhappily, the friendly reception that most immigrants envisioned in the new land rarely materialized. Castle Garden in the Battery, at the foot of Manhattan—and later Ellis Island in New York Harbor—proved to be almost as traumatic as the journey itself. "Castle Garden," an immigrant wrote, "is a large building, a Gehenna, through which all Jewish arrivals must pass to be cleansed before they are considered worthy of breathing freely the air of the land of the almighty dollar. . . . If in Brody, thousands crowded about, here tens of thousands thronged about; if there they were starving, here they were dying; if there they were crushed, here they were simply beaten."

One must make allowances for the impassioned hyperbole of the suffering immigrant, but there is little doubt that the immigration officials were harassed, overworked, and often unsympathetic. Authorized to pass on the admissibility of the newcomers, immigration officers struck terror into their hearts by asking questions designed to reveal their literacy and social attitudes. "How much is six times six?" an inspector asked a woman in the grip of nervousness, then casually asked the next man, "Have you ever been in jail?"

There were, of course, representatives of Jewish defense groups present, especially from the Hebrew Immigrant Aid Society. But by this time, the immigrants, out of patience and exhausted, tended to view them somewhat balefully. The Jewish officials tended to be highhanded, and the temporary barracks which they administered on Ward's Island for those not yet settled soon became notorious. Discontent culminated in a riot over food; one day the director—called The Father—had to swim ashore for his life, and the police were hastily summoned.

Most immigrants went directly from Castle Garden or Ellis Island to the teeming streets of Manhattan, where they sought relatives or *landsleit* (fellow townsmen) who had gone before them. Easy marks for hucksters and swindlers, they were overcharged by draymen for carrying their paltry possessions, engaged as strikebreakers, or hired at shamelessly low wages.

"Greenhorn" or "greener" was their common name. A term of vilification, the source of a thousand cruel jokes, it was their shame and their destiny. On top of everything else, the immigrants had to abide

Dated 1900, this photograph shows Hester Street in New York's Lower East Side at the peak of Jewish immigration from Eastern Europe. The Jewish neighborhoods were characterized by an integration of domestic life and commercial activity. One avenue of economic activity for these immigrants was the pushcart, which could be rented at low rates. Crowded and impoverished as it was, *the Lower East Side teemed with cultural vitality. It was, as author David Boroff puts it, "a vibrant community, full of color and gusto, in which the Jewish immigrant felt marvelously at home." (Seaver Center for Western History Research, Los Angeles County Museum of Natural History)*

the contempt of their co-religionists who had preceded them to America by forty or fifty years. By the time the heavy East European immigration set in, German Jews had achieved high mercantile status and an uneasy integration into American society. They did not want to be reminded of their kinship with these uncouth and impoverished Jews who were regarded vaguely as a kind of Oriental influx. There was a good deal of sentiment against "aiding such paupers to emigrate to these shores." One charitable organization declared: "Organized immigration from Russia, Roumania, and other semi-barbarous countries is a mistake and has proved to be a failure. It is no relief to the Jews of Russia, Poland, etc., and it jeopardizes the well-being of the American Jews."

A genuine uptown-downtown split soon developed, with condescension on one side and resentment on the other. The German Jews objected as bitterly to the rigid, old-world Orthodoxy of the immigrants as they did to their new involvement in trade unions. They were fearful, too, of the competition they would offer in the needle trades. (Indeed, the East

Europeans ultimately forced the uptown Jews out of the industry.) On the other side of the barricades, Russian Jews complained that at the hands of their uptown brethren, "every man is questioned like a criminal, is looked down upon . . . just as if he were standing before a Russian official." Nevertheless, many German Jews responded to the call of conscience by providing funds for needy immigrants and setting up preparatory schools for immigrant children for whom no room was yet available in the hopelessly overcrowded public schools.

Many comfortably settled German Jews saw dispersion as the answer to the problem. Efforts were made to divert immigrants to small towns in other parts of the country, but these were largely ineffective. There were also some gallant adventures with farming in such remote places as South Dakota, Oregon, and Louisiana. Though the Jewish pioneers were brave and idealistic, drought, disease, and ineptitude conspired against them. (In Oregon, for example, they tried to raise corn in cattle country, while in Louisiana they found themselves in malarial terrain.) Only chicken farming in New Jersey proved to be successful to any great degree. Farm jobs for Jews were available, but as one immigrant said: "I have no desire to be a farm hand to an ignorant Yankee at the end of the world. I would rather work here at half the price in a factory; for then I would at least be able to spend my free evenings with my friends."

It was in New York, then, that the bulk of the immigrants settled—in the swarming, tumultuous Lower East Side—with smaller concentrations in Boston, Philadelphia, and Chicago. Far less adaptable than the German Jews who were now lording it over them, disoriented and frightened, the East European immigrants constituted a vast and exploited proletariat. According to a survey in 1890, sixty per cent of all immigrant Jews worked in the needle trades. This industry had gone through a process of decentralization in which contractors carried out the bulk of production, receiving merely the cut goods from the manufacturer. Contracting establishments were everywhere in the Lower East Side, including

the contractors' homes, where pressers warmed their irons on the very stove on which the boss's wife was preparing supper. The contractors also gave out "section" work to families and *landsleit* who would struggle to meet the quotas at home. The bondage of the sewing machine was therefore extended into the tenements, with entire families enslaved by the machine's voracious demands. The Hester Street "pig market," where one could buy anything, became the labor exchange; there tailors, operators, finishers, basters, and pressers would congregate on Saturday in the hope of being hired by contractors.

Life in the sweatshops of the Lower East Side was hard, but it made immigrants employable from the start, and a weekly wage of five dollars—the equivalent of ten rubles—looked good in immigrant eyes. Moreover they were among their own kin and kind, and the sweatshops, noisome as they were, were still the scene of lively political and even literary discussions. (In some cigar-making shops, in fact, the bosses hired "readers" to keep the minds of the workers occupied with classic and Yiddish literature as they performed their repetitive chores.) East European Jews, near the end of the century, made up a large part of the skilled labor force in New York, ranking first in twenty-six out of forty-seven trades, and serving, for example, as bakers, building-trade workers, painters, furriers, jewellers, and tinsmiths.

Almost one quarter of all the immigrants tried their hands as tradesmen—largely as peddlers or as pushcart vendors in the madhouse bazaar of the Lower East Side. For some it was an apprenticeship in low-toned commerce that would lead to more elegant careers. For others it was merely a martyrdom that enabled them to subsist. It was a modest enough investment—five dollars for a license, one dollar for a basket, and four dollars for wares. They stocked up on pins and needles, shoe laces, polish, and handkerchiefs, learned some basic expressions ("You wanna buy somethin'?"), and were on their hapless way.

It was the professions, of course, that exerted the keenest attraction to Jews, with their reverence for learning. For most of them it was too late; they had to reconcile themselves to more humble callings. But it was not too late for their children, and between 1897 and 1907, the number of Jewish physicians in Manhattan rose from 450 to 1,000. Of all the professions it was medicine that excited the greatest veneration. (Some of this veneration spilled over into pharmacy, and "druggists" were highly respected figures who were called upon to prescribe for minor—and even major—ills, and to serve as scribes for the letters that the immigrants were unable to read and write themselves.) There were Jewish lawyers on the Lower East Side and by 1901 over 140 Jewish policemen, recruited in part by Theodore Roosevelt, who, as police commissioner, had issued a call for "the Maccabee or fighting Jewish type."

The Lower East Side was the American counterpart of the ghetto for Jewish immigrants, as well as their glittering capital. At its peak, around 1910, it packed over 350,000 people into a comparatively small area—roughly from Canal Street to Fourteenth Street—with as many as 523 people per acre, so that Arnold Bennett was moved to remark that "the architecture seemed to sweat humanity at every window and door." The most densely populated part of the city, it held one sixth of Manhattan's population and most of New York's office buildings and factories. "Uptowners" used to delight in visiting it (as a later generation would visit Harlem) to taste its exotic flavor. But the great mass of Jews lived there because the living was cheap, and there was a vital Jewish community that gave solace to the lonely and comfort to the pious.

A single man could find lodgings of a sort, including coffee morning and night, for three dollars a month. For a family, rent was about ten dollars a month, milk was four cents a quart, kosher meat twelve cents a pound, herring a penny or two. A kitchen table could be bought for a dollar, chairs at thirty-five cents each. One managed, but the life was oppressive. Most families lived in the notorious "dumbbell" flats of old-law tenements (built prior to 1901). Congested, often dirty and unsanitary, these tenements were six or seven stories high and had four apartments on each floor. Only one room in each three or four room apartment received direct air and sunlight, and the families on each floor shared a toilet in the hall.

Many families not only used their flats as workshops but also took in boarders to make ends meet. [Journalist and reformer] Jacob Riis tells of a two-room apartment on Allen Street which housed parents, six children, and six boarders. "Two daughters sewed clothes at home. The elevated railway passed by the window. The cantor rehearses, a train passes, the shoemaker bangs, ten brats run around like goats, the wife putters. . . . At night we all try to get some sleep in the stifling, roach-infested two rooms." In the summer, the tenants spilled out into fire escapes and rooftops, which were converted into bedrooms.

Nevertheless, life on the Lower East Side had surprising vitality. Despite the highest population density in the city, the Tenth Ward had one of the lowest death rates. In part, this was because of the strenuous personal cleanliness of Jews, dictated by their religion. Though only eight per cent of the East European Jews had baths, bathhouses and steam rooms on the Lower East Side did a booming business. There was, of course, a heavy incidence of tuberculosis—"the white plague." Those who were afflicted could be heard crying out, *"Luft! Gib mir luft!"* ("Air! Give me air!"). It was, in fact, this terror of "consumption" that impelled some East Side Jews to become farmers in the Catskills at the turn of the century, thus forerunning the gaudy career of the Catskill Borscht Belt resort hotels. The same fear impelled Jews on the Lower East Side to move to Washington Heights and the Bronx, where the altitude was higher, the air presumably purer.

Alcoholism, a prime affliction of most immigrant groups, was almost unknown among Jews. They drank ritualistically on holidays but almost never to excess. They were, instead, addicted to seltzer or soda water . . . which they viewed as "the worker's champagne." The suicide rate was relatively low, though higher than in the *shtetl,* and there was always a shudder of sympathy when the Yiddish press announced that someone had *genumen di ges* (taken gas).

The Lower East Side was from the start the scene of considerable crime. But its inhabitants became concerned when the crime rate among the young people seemed to rise steeply around 1910. There was a good deal of prostitution. The dancing academies, which achieved popularity early in this century, became recruiting centers for prostitutes. In 1908–9, of 581 foreign women arrested for prostitution, 225 were Jewish. There was the notorious Max Hochstim Association, which actively recruited girls, while the New York Independent Benevolent Association—an organization of pimps—provided sick benefits, burial privileges, bail, and protection money for prostitutes. The membership was even summoned to funerals with a two-dollar fine imposed on those who did not attend. Prostitution was so taken for granted that Canal Street had stores on one side featuring sacerdotal articles, while brothels were housed on the other.

Family life on the Lower East Side was cohesive and warm, though there was an edge of shrillness and hysteria to it. Marriages were not always happy, but if wives were viewed as an affliction, children were regarded as a blessing. The kitchen was the center of the household, and food was almost always being served to either family or visitors. No matter how poor they were, Jewish families ate well—even to excess—and mothers considered their children woefully underweight unless they were well cushioned with fat.

It was a life with few conventional graces. Handkerchiefs were barely known, and the Yiddish newspapers had to propagandize for their use. Old men smelled of snuff, and in spite of bathing, children often had lice in their hair and were sent home from school by the visiting nurse for a kerosene bath. Bedbugs were considered an inevitability, and pajamas were viewed as an upper-class affectation. Parents quarrelled bitterly—with passionate and resourceful invective—in the presence of their children. Telephones were virtually unknown, and a telegram surely meant disaster from afar.

The zeal of the immigrants on behalf of their children was no less than awe-inspiring. Parents yearned for lofty careers for their offspring, with medicine at the pinnacle. In better-off homes, there was always a piano ("solid mahogany"), and parents often spent their precious reserves to arrange a "concert" for their precocious youngsters, often followed by a ball in one of the Lower East Side's many halls.

To be sure, the children inspired a full measure of anxiety in their parents. "Amerikane kinder" was the rueful plaint of the elders, who could not fathom the baffling new ways of the young. Parents were nervous about their daughters' chastity, and younger brothers—often six or seven years old—would be dispatched as chaperones when the girls met their boy friends. There was uneasiness about Jewish street gangs and the growing problem of delinquency. The old folks were vexed by the new tides of secularism and political radicalism that were weaning their children from traditional pieties. But most of all, they feared that their sons would not achieve the success that would redeem their own efforts, humiliations, and failures in the harsh new land. Pressure on their children was relentless. But on the whole the children did well, astonishingly well. "The ease and rapidity with which they learn," Jacob Riis wrote, "is equalled only by their good behavior and close attention while in school. There is no whispering and no rioting at these desks." Samuel Chotzinoff, the music critic, tells a story which reveals the attitude of the Jewish schoolboy. When an altercation threatened between Chotzinoff and a classmate, his antagonist's reaction was to challenge him to spell "combustible."

The Lower East Side was a striking demonstration that financial want does not necessarily mean cultural poverty. The immigrant Jews were nearly always poor and often illiterate, but they were not culturally deprived. In fact, between 1890 and World War I, the Jewish community provides a remarkable chapter in American cultural history. Liberated from the constrictions of European captivity, immigrant Jews experienced a great surge of intellectual vitality. Yiddish, the Hebrew-German dialect which some people had casually dismissed as a barbarous "jargon," became the vehicle of this cultural renascence. Between 1885 and 1914, over 150 publications of all kinds made their appearance. But the new Yiddish journalism reached its apogee with the *Jewish Daily*

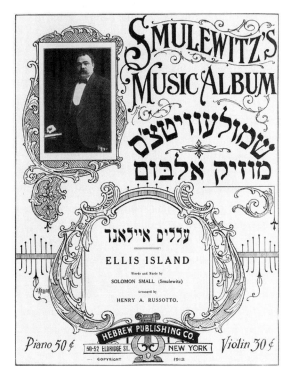

Yiddish sheet music from 1912. The song celebrates Ellis Island, which had replaced Castle Garden in 1892 as the point of entry for immigrants. A culture within a culture, Jewish New York had its own schools, newspapers, publishing houses, literary and musical circles, and a thriving Yiddish theater. (Sheet Music Collection, The John Hay Library, Brown University)

Forward under the long editorial reign of Abraham Cahan. The *Forward* was humanitarian, pro-labor, and socialistic. But it was also an instrument for acclimatizing immigrants in the new environment. It provided practical hints on how to deal with the new world, letters from the troubled (*Bintel Brief*), and even, at one time, a primer on baseball ("explained to non-sports"). The *Forward* also published and fostered an enormous amount of literature in Yiddish—both original works by writers of considerable talent, and translations of classic writers.

In this cultural ferment, immigrants studied English in dozens of night schools and ransacked the resources of the Aguilar Free Library on East Broadway. "When I had [a] book in my hand," an immigrant

wrote, "I pressed it to my heart and wanted to kiss it." The Educational Alliance, also on East Broadway, had a rich program designed to make immigrant Jews more American and their sons more Jewish. And there were scores of settlement houses, debating clubs, ethical societies, and literary circles which attracted the young. In fact, courtships were carried on in a rarefied atmosphere full of lofty talk about art, politics, and philosophy. And though there was much venturesome palaver about sexual freedom, actual behavior tended to be quite strait-laced.

But the most popular cultural institution was the café or coffee house, which served as the Jewish saloon. There were about 250 of them, each with its own following. Here the litterateurs sat for hours over steaming glasses of tea; revolutionaries and Bohemians gathered to make their pronouncements or raise money for causes; actors and playwrights came to hold court. For immigrant Jews, talk was the breath of life itself. The passion for music and theater knew no bounds. When Beethoven's Ninth Symphony was performed one summer night in 1915, mounted police had to be summoned to keep order outside Lewisohn Stadium, so heavy was the press of crowds eager for the twenty-five-cent stone seats. Theater (in Yiddish) was to the Jewish immigrants what Shakespeare and Marlowe had been to the groundlings in Elizabethan England. Tickets were cheap—twenty-five cents to one dollar—and theatergoing was universal. It was a raucous, robust, and communal experience. Mothers brought their babies (except in some of the "swellest" theaters, which forbade it), and peddlers hawked their wares between the acts. There were theater parties for trade unions and *landsmanschaften* (societies of fellow townsmen), and the audience milled around and renewed old friendships or argued the merits of the play. The stage curtain had bold advertisements of stores or blown-up portraits of stars.

There was an intense cult of personality in the Yiddish theater and a system of claques not unlike that which exists in grand opera today. The undisputed monarch was Boris Thomashefsky, and a theater program of his day offered this panegyric:

Tomashefsky! Artist great!

No praise is good enough for you!

Of all the stars you remain the king

You seek no tricks, no false quibbles;

One sees truth itself playing.

Your appearance is godly to us

Every movement is full of grace

Pleasing is your every gesture

Sugar sweet your every turn

You remain the king of the stage

Everything falls to your feet.

Many of the plays were sentimental trash—heroic "operas" on historical themes, "greenhorn" melodramas full of cruel abandonments and tearful reunions, romantic musicals, and even topical dramas dealing with such immediate events as the Homestead Strike, the Johnstown Flood, and the Kishinev Pogrom of 1903. Adaptability and a talent for facile plagiarism were the essence of the playwright's art in those days, and "Professor" Moses Horwitz wrote 167 plays, most of them adaptations of old operas and melodramas. The plays were so predictable that an actor once admitted he didn't even have to learn his lines; he merely had to have a sense of the general situation and then adapt lines from other plays.

There was, of course, a serious Yiddish drama, introduced principally by Jacob Gordin, who adapted classical and modernist drama to the Yiddish stage. Jewish intellectuals were jubilant at this development. But the process of acculturation had its amusing and grotesque aspects. Shakespeare was a great favorite but *"verbessert und vergrossert"* (improved and enlarged). There was the Jewish *King Lear* in which Cordelia becomes Goldele. (The theme of filial ingratitude was a "natural" on the Lower East Side, where parents constantly made heroic sacrifices.) *Hamlet* was also given a Jewish coloration, the prince becoming a rabbinical student who returns from the seminary to discover treachery at home. And *A Doll's House* by Ibsen was transformed into *Minna,* in which a sensitive and intelligent young woman, married to an ignorant laborer, falls in love with her boarder and ultimately commits suicide.

Related to the Jewish love of theater was the immigrant's adoration of the cantor, a profession which evoked as much flamboyance and egotistical preening as acting did. (In fact, actors would sometimes grow beards before the high holydays and find jobs as cantors.) Synagogues vied with each other for celebrated cantors, sometimes as a way of getting out of debt, since tickets were sold for the high-holyday services.

The Lower East Side was a vibrant community, full of color and gusto, in which the Jewish immigrant felt marvelously at home, safe from the terrors of the alien city. But it was a setting too for fierce conflict and enervating strain. There were three major influences at work, each pulling in a separate direction: Jewish Orthodoxy, assimilationism, and the new socialist gospel. The immigrants were Orthodox, but their children tended to break away. *Cheders* (Hebrew schools) were everywhere, in basements and stores and tenements, and the old custom of giving a child a taste of honey when he was beginning to learn to read—as symbolic of the sweetness of study—persisted. But the young, eager to be accepted into American society, despised the old ways and their "greenhorn" teachers. Fathers began to view their sons as "free-thinkers," a term that was anathema to them. Observance of the Law declined, and the Saturday Sabbath was ignored by many Jews. A virulent antireligious tendency developed among many "enlightened" Jews, who would hold profane balls on the most sacred evening of the year—Yom Kippur—at which they would dance and eat nonkosher food. (Yom Kippur is a fast day.) And the trade-union movement also generated uneasiness among the pious elders of the Lower East Side. "Do you want us to bow down to your archaic God?" a radical newspaper asked. "Each era has its new Torah. Ours is one of freedom and justice."

But for many immigrants the basic discontent was with their American experience itself. The golden province turned out to be a place of tenements and sweatshops. A familiar cry was *"a klug of Columbus!"* ("a curse on Columbus") or, "Who ever asked him, Columbus, to discover America?" Ellis Island was called *Tremindzl* (Island of Tears), and Abraham Cahan, in his initial reaction to the horrors of immigration, thundered: "Be cursed, immigration! Cursed by those conditions which have brought you into being. How many souls have you broken, how many courageous and mighty souls have you shattered." The fact remains that most Jewish immigrants, in the long run, made a happy adjustment to their new land.

After 1910, the Lower East Side went into a decline. Its strange glory was over. New areas of Jewish settlement opened up in Brooklyn, the Bronx, and in upper Manhattan. By the mid-twenties, less than ten per cent of New York's Jews lived on the Lower East Side, although it still remained the heartland to which one returned to shop, to see Yiddish theater, and to renew old ties. By 1924 Jewish immigration into the United States was severely reduced by new immigration laws, and the saga of mass immigration was done. But the intensities of the Jewish immigrant experience had already made an indelible mark on American culture and history that would endure for many years.

QUESTIONS TO CONSIDER

1 Compare the migration experience of Jewish immigrants to America in the periods before and after 1880. In what ways did the experience become easier or more difficult? How did the immigrants themselves change?

2 For some Jewish immigrants, America was "the land of milk and honey," whereas others cursed Columbus and called Ellis Island the "Island of Tears." Discuss the reality of the Jewish immigrant experience hidden behind both images of America.

3 Analyze the reasons for the ambivalent feelings and divisions that developed between newer eastern European Jewish immigrants and those Jews, usually of German origin, who had been settled in the United States for several generations.

4 The lure of land in the New World brought generations of Europeans to America. Why did the bulk of eastern European Jewish immigrants choose to remain in urban industrial centers such as New York City? Was there anything about their *shtetl* experience that made Jews more adaptable to city life?

5 Boroff says, "The immigrant Jews were nearly always poor and often illiterate, but they were not culturally deprived." What evidence is there to support this statement?

PART FOUR

Reform and Expansion

8 The Lady Versus Goliath: Ida Tarbell Takes on Standard Oil Co.

PAULA A. TRECKEL

In the Gilded Age, politics became a big business, too, as the mighty industrialists poured money into government circles at an unprecedented rate. Men now entered politics for the same reason they went into business: to make their fortunes. The new politics even derived much of its vocabulary from the world of industry. "A political party," contended American statesman William H. Seward, "is in one sense a joint stock company in which those who contribute the most direct the action and management of the concern." The United States Senate became known as the Millionaires' Club, because only the rich and powerful seemed able to get in. A sizable portion of both major parties not only vigorously defended the industrial barons but eagerly accepted their campaign contributions. A number of politicians shamelessly took bribes as well.

In the 1880s, the two national parties—the Republicans and Democrats—had a monopoly on American politics, and neither was responsive to the grassroots of America. The industrial consolidation had left many victims in its wake—workers, farmers, consumers, and small or aspiring business and professional people who wanted their share of opportunity and wealth. They had little chance for success as long as the wealthy captains of industry—men like Andrew Carnegie, J. Pierpont Morgan, and John D. Rockefeller—ruled the country, including its politicians. Such business moguls were determined to eliminate competition to their business empires by ruthless and sometimes illegal means.

Unable to persuade the federal government and the two major parties to redress their grievances, the victims of industrial consolidation launched their own reform movements. American farmers organized alliances to protect themselves against the big industrialists who ran the country. The alliance movement was an effort at cooperative agriculture to free farmers from "the furnishing merchants," banks, trusts, and railroads. The alliances, in turn, led to political organization, first in the People's party of Kansas (which drew men and women alike to its banners) and ultimately in the national People's party, or the Populist party, in 1892. According to Populist historian Lawrence Goodwyn, the agrarian revolt that culminated in the Populist crusade constituted "the largest democratic mass movement in American history." And the objective of that mass movement was to restore government to the people.

Another reform-minded group of the era was a cadre of investigative journalists associated with McClure's Magazine. Founded by Samuel Sidney McClure, the journal was dedicated to exposing and finding solutions to the social and economic ills that plagued industrial America. Soon McClure gathered around him "a team of journalists" known popularly as "muckrakers." Theodore Roosevelt gave them that name because he thought them too obsessed with social evils, with raking up the muck, or filth, of American society.

In the sprightly selection that follows, Paula A. Treckel tells the story of Ida Tarbell, "the foremost 'lady muckraker' of her time" Rejecting marriage because it would have restricted her freedom, Tarbell chose journalism as her profession (she also wrote a popular biography of Abraham Lincoln) and in 1894 joined McClure's Magazine staff in New York City. There she became a member of McClure's "muckraking" team of investigative reporters—Ray Stannard Baker, Lincoln Steffens, and William Allen White. By now, the pressure for reform had led to the passage of the Sherman Anti-Trust Act of 1890, which outlawed monopolies and other restraints of trade. But, as Treckel says, the measure was difficult to enforce "against America's powerful industrialists."

In 1903, Tarbell went after one of the country's mightiest trusts, Standard Oil Company, owned by millionaire John D. Rockefeller. When apprised that she was preparing an exposé of his company, Rockefeller derided her as "Miss Tarbarrel" and compared her to a worm that if ignored would disappear. But "Miss Tarbarrel" was undaunted. Through tenacity and painstaking research, she produced "The History of Standard Oil," which serialized in McClure's Magazine. Her exposé helped the government break up Rockefeller's huge monopoly, and it made Tarbell one of the most celebrated women in the land. What follows is the tale of how this amazing woman slew the American Goliath.

GLOSSARY

BAKER, RAY STANNARD A writer for *McClure's Magazine* who examined corruption and violence in the labor union movement. He stated, "I learned that common human suffering and common human joy, if truly reported, never grow stale." In his introduction to *The Shame of the Cities,* he added that America's problems could be resolved through "good conduct in the individual, simple honesty, courage, and efficiency."

FEDERAL TRADE COMMISSION (1914) One of the accomplishments of Woodrow Wilson's New Freedom, it represented a noble effort to oversee the practices of large corporations. It investigated complaints and could order companies to resolve the problems that surfaced. Many of its early members were conservatives who responded to only the most grievous of misdeeds.

McCLURE, SAMUEL SIDNEY Irish immigrant who established an influential newspaper chain and a magazine, *McClure's Magazine,* that focused on the major problems of his day. Ida Tarbell was one of many talented young writers that McClure hired. Although his inexpensive mass circulation journal contained fiction, essays on science, and profiles of leading figures like Thomas Edison, investigative journalism became its most prominent feature.

MONOPOLY   A company or group of companies that controls a market so completely, as Carnegie did with steel or Rockefeller with oil, that a particular corporate entity can dictate supply and prices and thus destroy competition.

MUCKRAKER   Theodore Roosevelt inadvertently coined this word. He compared the young reform-minded writers who published articles for *McClure's Magazine* to the man in *Pilgrim's Progress* who was so busy raking the "muke" (filth) that he never noticed the celestial crown over his head. Nonetheless, the American people were enthralled with writing like Upton Sinclair's portrayal of the meat-packing industry, Ray Stannard Baker's lurid description of the labor movement, and Lincoln Steffen's tale of a corrupt alliance between business and politics.

OIL REFINERY   Rockefeller invested in this business, which converted crude oil to useful commodities such as kerosene that provided both light and heat for America's homes and businesses. His base of operation was Cleveland, Ohio, which was close to the oil fields of western Pennsylvania and abutted the shipping lanes of Lake Erie.

PROGRESSIVE MOVEMENT   A reform movement that started at the state level with governors like Robert LaFollette in Wisconsin and moved to the national level from 1901 to 1914 during the presidential administrations of Theodore Roosevelt, William Howard Taft, and Woodrow Wilson. In seeking railroad regulation and antitrust legislation, the progressives championed the interests of farmers, laborers, and consumers.

REBATES   Kickbacks to large corporations from the railroads. As public carriers, the railroads could not practice discrimination in the rates they charged, yet they depended on their better customers to stay in business. Rockefeller used this illegal strategy to gain favorable transportation rates that smaller companies could not demand.

SHERMAN ANTI-TRUST ACT (1890)   Under pressure from reformers and consumer advocates, Congress enacted this measure, which made it illegal for corporations to destroy competition or to be "in restraint of trade or commerce." Although it regulated some business combinations, its language was vague, and corporations continued to eliminate competition and form monopolies.

SIDDALL, JOHN   Tarbell's youthful assistant who helped her gather evidence on the illegal activities of the Standard Oil Company. He and other employees at *McClure's Magazine* made certain that the accusations against the giant oil corporation were accurate and that Rockefeller could not charge the magazine with libel.

SOUTH IMPROVEMENT COMPANY   A Rockefeller enterprise that combined the largest and most powerful railroads and oil refineries. Its resources were so great that it destroyed competition.

STANDARD OIL COMPANY   It dominated the business of refining oil. By 1881, through illegal and sometimes cutthroat tactics, Rockefeller had 90 percent of this lucrative industry under his control and had established a monopoly that strangled competition. Tarbell's writings forced a reluctant federal government to dismantle this mammoth trust in 1911.

STEFFENS, LINCOLN   One of S. S. McClure's staff of investigative authors. He wrote a series of articles exposing corruption in Minneapolis that involved business and political leaders.

TARBELL, FRANKLIN   Ida's father, who hoped that he might profit through the manufacture of oil tanks that would transport the "black gold" to the refineries. Rockefeller used illegal rebates to destroy small operators like him. Ida learned from her father's misfortunes that "it was your privilege and duty to fight injustice."

TRUST   A method of combining resources that avoided the antimonopoly laws established by many states to prohibit one corporation from holding stock in another. Rockefeller, for example, had stockholders of various oil companies delegate their interests to Standard Oil "trustees" who made decisions that benefited the entire entity. Thus, one body managed and directed the interests of many companies.

TUTTLE, HENRY B.   A co-owner in a produce shipping firm, he gave Rockefeller a job as a bookkeeper and, in Treckel's words, "launched one of the most successful careers in American business."

WHITE, WILLIAM ALLEN   A well-known journalist and later a leading internationalist who argued for aid to the beleaguered democracies of England and France. The popularity of the Progressive movement surprised him. "The thing that constantly amazed me," noted White, "was how many people were with us."

The *Lion and the Mouse* made its Broadway debut on Saturday, November 25, 1905. The play told the tale of "the richest and the ablest and the hardest and the most unscrupulous" millionaire in America, John Burkett Ryder, and his confrontation with Miss Shirley Rossmore, a young woman of "clear moral intensity." The story opened with Miss Rossmore's father, a judge, accused of accepting securities from Ryder in exchange for making judicial decisions in the millionaire's favor. To prove her father's innocence, Miss Rossmore—the "mouse" to Ryder's "lion"—set out to expose the millionaire's criminal activities.

Unlikely as it may appear, the plot of this Broadway melodrama was snatched from the headlines of the day. It was loosely based on the story of Ida M. Tarbell and her investigation of millionaire John D. Rockefeller and his Standard Oil Company monopoly. Although it lacked the Broadway play's love story and happy ending, Tarbell's investigation of how Rockefeller achieved domination of the oil industry had more than its share of intrigue, crime, and corruption. Tarbell used her sense of moral outrage, passion for justice, and historian's eye for detail to reveal the inner workings of Rockefeller's business empire to the world. Her work helped lead to the prosecution of Standard Oil by the United States government and the company's subsequent dismantling in 1911.

Ida Minerva Tarbell was born on November 5, 1857, in the frontier town of Hatch Hollow, Pennsylvania, one of the rough and rowdy oil boomtowns of the region. Her father, Franklin Tarbell, hoped to make his fortune in the young industry by manufacturing tanks to hold the black gold taken from beneath the Pennsylvania hills. As a child, Ida saw how boom and bust cycles swept through the dirty, oil-slick communities that dotted the countryside and witnessed the horrors of accidents—fires and explosions—that plagued the industry.

"Lady Muckraker" by Paula A. Treckel. This article is reproduced from the June 2001 issue of *American History Illustrated* with permission of PRIMEDIA Special Interest Publications (History Group), copyright *American History Illustrated,* and the author.

This 1905 photograph shows Ida Tarbell at work in her study. The "lady muckraker" made the public aware of the corrupt and monopolistic practices of the Standard Oil Company. (Tarbell Archives, Pelletier Library, Allegheny College)

In 1872, suddenly and without warning, the region's railroads—the link necessary to bring the oil to market—doubled their shipping rates, deeply cutting the independent producers' profits. Then word leaked out that the railroads had favored a mysterious Cleveland-based outfit called the South Improvement Company by giving it rebates, in direct violation of federal law. Young Ida watched as her father and his friends crusaded against this menace to their livelihood. Violence swept the oil fields of western Pennsylvania as vigilantes destroyed the South Improvement Company's oil cars and burned out the men who joined or sold out to that organization. "It was my first experience in revolution," Tarbell recalled. She learned "it was your privilege and duty to fight injustice."

The force behind the threatened takeover of the region's oil production was John D. Rockefeller, a man who had risen from humble beginnings to become one of the nation's wealthiest and most powerful industrialists. Born in upstate New York in 1839, Rockefeller was the son of con artist William Avery Rockefeller and his long-suffering wife, Eliza. The family's poverty soon taught John the importance of saving and investing money and fired his dreams of becoming wealthy. "Some day, sometime, when I am a man, I want to be worth a-hundred-thousand-dollars," he confided to a friend. "And I'm going to be, too—some day." The somber boy found spiritual comfort in the Baptist church, which instilled in him the values of self-reliance and self-improvement and the belief that hard work would be rewarded both on earth and in heaven. Throughout his life John turned to his church for practical lessons in living.

When the Rockefeller family moved to Cleveland, Ohio, 16-year-old John sought work to help support his family. "I did not go to any small establishments," he recalled. "I did not guess what I would be, but I was after something big." During a meeting with Henry B. Tuttle, partner in a produce-shipping firm, Rockefeller boldly stated, "I understand bookkeeping, and I'd like to get work."

"We'll give you a chance," Tuttle said, and he hired the boy to handle the company's books, thereby launching one of the most successful careers in American business.

John worked hard and invested his clerk's salary in local grain and livestock businesses. By age 18 he had made enough money to start his own produce business with Englishman Maurice Clark. When the Civil War dramatically increased the price of commodities, the young Rockefeller invested his profits in a local oil refinery. Refineries bought crude oil from the oil producers and processed it into products such as kerosene. Cleveland was then the center of the refining industry because it was close to the oil-rich fields of western Pennsylvania, and its location on Lake Erie provided an easy means of shipping the valuable commodities it produced. Over time John D. Rockefeller purchased several more refineries in the area; in 1870 he incorporated his holdings as Standard Oil.

As America's industry boomed in the years following the Civil War and railroads became an ever-more important force, Rockefeller used every advantage—legal and illegal—that the market allowed. One tactic was to secure reduced rates from railroads by guaranteeing them volume shipments on a regular basis. When other companies refused to join forces with Rockefeller or agree to control the production and price of oil, he drove them out of business. Ida Tarbell saw for herself the effect of Rockefeller's machinations when he formed an alliance between three of the most powerful railroads and a handful of oil refiners, called it the South Improvement Company, and used it as a tool to gain further dominance. Using such tactics, Standard Oil's 40 companies gained control of 90 percent of the nation's oil refining industry by 1881.

In addition to buying refineries, Rockefeller sought control of the oil fields themselves. He built his own transportation network of pipelines and tankers, and marketed his products both at home and abroad. Rockefeller's efforts produced added benefits as well. He introduced cutting-edge technology and efficiency to the oil industry. And as the cost of processing petroleum dropped, so too did prices for fuel oil and lighting products.

While John D. Rockefeller was ruthlessly cornering the nation's oil market, Ida Tarbell was attending college in western Pennsylvania. From an early age she had planned to become an independent, professional woman,. "I would never marry," she pledged. "It would interfere with my plan; it would fetter my freedom." In 1876 she enrolled as a freshman at Allegheny College in Meadville, Pennsylvania. She was the only woman in her class. Following her graduation in 1880, Tarbell taught for a year before joining the staff of the Meadville, Pennsylvania, *Chautauqua Assembly Herald,* a publication of the Chautauqua Assembly's Literary and Scientific Circle.

During her six years at the *Chautauquan,* Tarbell learned the art and craft of journalism. She started out as a researcher and eventually assumed the duties, if not the title, of managing editor. Nevertheless, Tarbell longed for more. In church one Sunday, a visiting minister thundered, "You're dying of respectability!" at his complaisant congregation and spurred Tarbell to action. In 1889 she decided to try supporting herself with her own pen. The young journalist left the *Chautauquan* and headed for France.

Tarbell was ready for a new beginning. In Paris she made friendships that lasted a lifetime and reinvented herself as a historian, researching the life of French Revolutionary heroine Madame Manon Phlipon de Roland. To support herself, Tarbell wrote articles on French life for American news syndicates. One story, "The Paving of the Streets of Paris by Monsieur Alphand," piqued the interest of editor Samuel Sidney McClure, founder of *McClure's Magazine*. McClure had emigrated from Ireland in 1866, and in 1884 he had established one of the earliest U.S. newspaper syndicates. A dynamic, energetic man—Rudyard Kipling described him as a "cyclone in a frock coat"—McClure launched his magazine in 1893 to campaign for solutions to the pressing problems of the day. He was always looking for fresh, talented writers to join his staff. On a trip to Paris in the summer of 1892, he bounded up the stairs of Ida Tarbell's apartment building and into her life, changing it forever.

McClure asked Tarbell if she would come to New York to work at his magazine. Reluctant to give up her hard-earned independence, she agreed only to submit occasional articles to *McClure's* while she completed her biography of Madame Roland. But by 1894, Tarbell was unable to financially support herself, and she returned to the United States with her unfinished Madame Roland manuscript and joined the staff of *McClure's* in New York.

Ida Tarbell returned to a nation still reeling from the panic caused by the stock market crash of 1893. More than 15,000 businesses had failed, and at least one third of all manufacturing workers had lost their jobs. Midwestern farmers also suffered as they faced rising interest rates and falling crop prices. Tarbell's own family's financial distress clouded her homecoming. Her father had become an independent oil producer just as Standard Oil forced an increase in the price of the region's crude oil. Refiners were reluctant to buy crude from small, independent producers like Franklin Tarbell, and he had to mortgage the family's

Titusville home to pay his debts. One of his friends committed suicide when his own business failed.

The nation as a whole was changing, evolving from a largely agrarian economy into a more industrial one. With the change came abuses—not just the great concentration of wealth in the hands of a few industrialists such as Andrew Carnegie and Rockefeller, but also urban corruption, boss politics, and child labor. The Progressive Movement emerged in response to these issues and prompted Congress to pass the Sherman Anti-Trust Act in 1890, making it illegal to monopolize or restrain trade through unfair collaborations or conspiracies. The law was vague, however, and authorities had difficulty enforcing it against America's powerful industrialists.

At *McClure's* a team of journalists—Tarbell, Lincoln Steffens, William Allen White, and Ray Stannard Baker—reflected Progressive concerns in their articles about some of the era's excesses. Yet not everyone approved of this new breed of journalism. Although he knew and befriended many of the magazine's writers, including Tarbell, President Theodore Roosevelt publicly complained that these journalists focused only upon society's evils. "In Bunyan's *Pilgrim's Progress*," he said, "you may recall the description of the Man with the Muck-rake, the man who could look no way but downward with the muck-rake in his hands; who was offered a celestial crown for his muck-rake, but who would neither look up nor regard the crown he was offered, but continued to rake to himself the filth of the floor." The president's comments gave a name to the new generation of investigative journalists, with Ida Tarbell the foremost "Lady Muckraker" of her time.

McClure's January 1903 issue epitomized the work of the muckrakers. Lincoln Steffens contributed an article about political corruption in Minneapolis, part of his "Shame of the Cities" series. Ray Stannard Baker wrote about corruption and violence in the labor union movement in a piece called "The Right to Work." The issue also included an installment in a series by Ida Tarbell on "The History of Standard Oil," one of the most important exposés of the twentieth century.

The proliferation of industrial trusts interested *McClure's* staff members. They decided the best way to approach the subject would be to tell "the story of a typical trust to illustrate how and why the clan grew," recalled Tarbell. "How about the greatest of them all—the Standard Oil Company?" Tarbell decided she wanted to tackle the project, and she traveled to Europe where Sam McClure and his family were vacationing while he recovered from exhaustion. Tarbell expected to stay only a week while she pitched her idea to the publisher, but he asked her to join them in their travels. Finally, after visiting Switzerland and Italy, McClure approved Tarbell's story idea. She later admitted, "It had been a strong thread weaving itself into the pattern of my life from childhood on." Tarbell later explained to critics who charged that her work was motivated by personal concerns, "We were undertaking what we regarded as a legitimate piece of historical work. We were neither apologists nor critics, only journalists intent on discovering what had gone into the making of this most perfect of all monopolies."

Tarbell had no shortage of material to draw upon. Congress had been investigating Standard Oil almost continually since the company's creation in 1870 when it was suspected of receiving rebates from railroads and violating free trade. In the years since, government investigators had generated volumes of testimony, a massive collection of documentary evidence, as well as countless newspaper and magazine articles. These resources provided Tarbell with the foundation for her work, although at first she found the sheer mass of material at her disposal overwhelming. "The task confronting me is such a monstrous one that I am staggering a bit under it," she lamented. Aided by a young, eager assistant, John Siddall, she spent a year researching her subject before *McClure's* announced the series to readers.

Initially Tarbell was going to write the story in three parts—in the end she wrote 19. Dissecting the inner workings of Standard Oil with the precision of a surgeon wielding a scalpel, she exposed espionage and industrial terrorism. In one example, Tarbell detailed the testimony of Mrs. Butts, whose

On his ninety-first birthday, John D. Rockefeller hardly looked like the ruthless oil magnate who called Tarbell "Miss Tarbarrel." He maintained a religious faith based on "dividends of righteousness." Like Andrew Carnegie, he gave much of his huge fortune away. (Courtesy of the Rockefeller Archive Center)

oil company had a regular customer in New Orleans. A Standard Oil representative approached the customer and "made a contract with him to pay him $10,000 a year for five years to stop handling the independent oil and take Standard Oil." Tarbell also told of a young office boy in a Standard Oil plant who was told to destroy some company papers when the name of his Sunday school teacher, an independent oil refiner, caught his eye. The records contained information, collected by railroad freight clerks in Standard Oil's pay, about his teacher's oil shipments. Armed with such inside knowledge, the great trust could act against its competition by sidetracking rail cars, interfering with or destroying rivals' shipments, or pressuring buyers to cancel orders. By showing how the corporation worked in collusion with the railroads and carefully explaining its elaborate system of rebates and "drawbacks," Tarbell meticulously built her case against the great monopoly.

Rockefeller himself refused to meet with the woman he privately called "Miss Tarbarrel," and he met her series with stony silence. One day, while strolling in the grounds of his Cleveland home, a friend asked Rockefeller why he did not respond to Tarbell's charges. "Not a word!" he interrupted. "Not a word about that misguided woman." Then he pointed to a worm on the ground nearby. "If I step on that worm I will call attention to it," Rockefeller said. "If I ignore it, it will disappear."

Tarbell understood Rockefeller's need for silence. "His self-control has been masterful," she said; "he knows, nobody better, that to answer is to invite discussion, to answer is to call attention to the facts in the case." This, she was confident, he would not do. She also never feared that Rockefeller would take steps to silence her. "What had we to be afraid of?" she declared.

The journalist's curiosity got the best of her, however, when John Siddall learned that Rockefeller planned to give a talk in October 1903 to the Sunday school at the Euclid Avenue Baptist Church in Cleveland. She could not resist the opportunity to get a peek at the man. On that crisp October morning, Tarbell and Siddall arrived early at the church and awaited Rockefeller's entrance. Tarbell vividly recalled the moment when she first saw him: "We were sitting meekly at one side when I was suddenly aware of a striking figure standing in the doorway. There was an awful age in his face—the oldest man I had ever seen, I thought, but what power!" She recalled that his voice was "Clear and utterly sincere. He meant what he was saying. He was on his own ground talking about dividends, dividends of righteousness." When the talk ended, Tarbell and Siddall slipped out to get a good seat in the gallery, from where they could see the Rockefeller pew. Tarbell noted, "It was plain that he, and not the minister, was the pivot on which the audience swung."

Tarbell's findings strengthened the United States government's case against Standard Oil. Following publication of her series, President Roosevelt decided to make an example of the great oil trust.

On November 15, 1906, the government charged the Standard Oil Company of New Jersey and its 70 affiliates with violating the Sherman Anti-Trust Act. The company and its trustees were eventually found guilty of creating a monopoly, conspiring to restrain and control interstate commerce through the use of railroad rebates and drawbacks, controlling pipelines, conducting industrial espionage, and illegally eliminating competition from the marketplace. Following a series of appeals, the Supreme Court upheld the original decision against Standard Oil in May of 1911, and the mighty monopoly was broken up. Rockefeller retained stock in Standard Oil of New Jersey and the 33 independent subsidiaries created by the Supreme Court's decision. Ironically, the break-up of the trust made Rockefeller the world's richest man with a net worth of $900 million in 1913. And by the time of his death at age 98 on May 23, 1937, John D. Rockefeller was more widely known as "the world's greatest philanthropist" than the great "Lion" of the industrial age.

In addition to prompting the government's suit against Standard Oil, Ida Tarbell's series, published in two volumes as *The History of the Standard Oil Company* in 1904, contributed to the passage of new laws to protect competition in the marketplace. In 1914 the government established the Federal Trade Commission to oversee business activities.

Despite an illustrious career—in 1922 the *New York Times* included her as one of the "Twelve Greatest Living American Women"—Ida Tarbell never equaled *The History of Standard Oil*. Historian and Rockefeller biographer Allan Nevins declared, "It was the best piece of business history that America had yet produced." Before Tarbell's death on January 6, 1944, a young history professor asked her, "If you could rewrite your book today, what would you change?"

"Not one word, young man," she proudly replied, "Not one word."

QUESTIONS TO CONSIDER

1 Compare Rockefeller's climb to financial fortune with that of Andrew Carnegie, the subject of selection 5. How had both men in their youth showed initiative and the ability to invest wisely? Do you admire them for their energy or condemn them for their ruthlessness in taking advantage of labor and destroying competition?

2 Rockefeller's control of an industry reduced prices for fuel oil and lighting products such as kerosene. Why then did the federal government conclude that his actions were destructive? Compare Rockefeller's business and the government's reaction to it with the present-day court actions against Bill Gates and the claim that Microsoft unfairly destroyed competition. (See selection 31 for a portrait of Gates.)

3 Describe the economic problems that plagued Ida Tarbell's America when she returned home from Paris. How did the young writers at *McClure's Magazine* hope to solve these problems? What was Theodore Roosevelt's opinion of their efforts?

4 How had the Standard Oil Company affected Tarbell's life? Do you think that her personal feelings motivated her attack on Rockefeller? What did she discover about the giant oil corporation?

5 What did Rockefeller mean when he discussed "dividends of righteousness" at the Euclid Avenue Baptist Church? Why do you think that Tarbell was so anxious to see him?

6 Once Tarbell's charges against Rockefeller's giant oil monopoly became widely known, what did the federal government do in response? Did Rockefeller's wealth increase or diminish as a result of Tarbell's claims and the resultant government action? Again, reflect back to selection 5 and compare Rockefeller's reputation with that of Carnegie when both men were in the twilight of their careers.

9 America's First Southeast Asian War: The Philippine Insurrection

DAVID R. KOHLER AND JAMES W. WENSYEL

The last quarter of the nineteenth century marked the second age of imperialism, a time when the industrial nations of Europe—Britain, Germany, France, Belgium, and Russia—claimed colonies in Africa and spheres of influence in distant China. The United States, flexing its imperial muscles in the 1890s, was also alive with "aggressive, expansionistic, and jingoistic" sentiments. In 1893, with the help of 150 marines from a United States cruiser, American residents in Hawaii deposed the queen of the islands, set up a provisional government, and clamored for annexation. In 1898, the United States formally annexed Hawaii, thus expanding American territory and interests in the Pacific. In 1898–1899, the United States gained additional Pacific possessions in a controversial war with Spain, by then a second-rate power whose old empire in the Americas had all but disintegrated.

American expansionists, cheered on by a truculent yellow press, did not cause the war with Spain. But American policymakers and business leaders did use it as a means to extend American economic and political power. The war itself grew out of deplorable conditions in Cuba, caused by decades of Spanish misrule. A series of Cuban revolts and Spanish atrocities, which the American press exaggerated, aroused Americans' sympathy for the Cubans, whose cause seemed identical to that of the American patriots in 1776. In February 1898, American sentiment turned to outrage when the United States battleship Maine *blew up in Havana harbor, killing 260 American sailors.*

The cause of the explosion was never established, but American expansionists—among them, Assistant Secretary of the Navy Theodore Roosevelt—blamed Spain and demanded war. Overnight a slogan caught the imagination of the country: "Remember the Maine! To hell with Spain!"

In March, President William McKinley demanded that Spain agree to negotiations that would grant independence to Cuba. Faced with the possibility of a disastrous war in a distant hemisphere, Spain tried to maneuver, declaring an armistice with Cuban insurgents but hedging on Cuban independence. By then, both President McKinley and Congress were prepared for war. When Congress adopted a resolution recognizing Cuban independence, Spain retaliated by declaring war on the United States; the next day, Congress responded in kind.

Less than a week later, the American Asiatic Squadron under Commodore George Dewey won a dazzling victory in Manila Bay in the Spanish-held Philippines. As it turned out, Roosevelt had secured the command for Dewey and had directed him to prepare for action two months before official hostilities commenced. The United States also invaded Cuba, where Theodore Roosevelt gained national fame as colonel of the Rough Riders. After ten weeks of fighting, Spain capitulated, giving up control of Cuba and surrendering Puerto Rico, Guam, and the Philippines to the United States. For Secretary of State John Hay, it had been "a splendid little war."

Much has been written about the Spanish-American War and the United States empire that emerged from it. Much less is known about an important offshoot of that war—an American military campaign against Philippine insurgents that lasted three years, involved 126,000 United States troops, and resulted in 7,000 American and some 216,000 Filipino casualties. The United States learned a number of hard lessons about fighting against nationalist insurgents in distant Asian jungles, but sixty years later another generation of Americans forgot those lessons when plunging into a similar conflict in Vietnam. In the selection that follows, David R. Kohler, a naval special warfare officer, and James W. Wensyel, a retired army officer and the author of several books, narrate American involvement in the Filipino insurrection of 1898–1902, showing how it grew out of the Spanish-American War and the American bid for empire. The authors point out the influence of the Indian wars on American tactics in the Philippines, and they draw several significant parallels between the Philippine conflict and America's involvement in Vietnam. It was the Philippine conflict that generated strategic hamlets, free-fire zones, and search-and-destroy missions—terms that were later seared into the history of American involvement in Vietnam. As experienced military men, Kohler and Wensyel contend that future American leaders should ponder the lessons of the Philippine and Vietnamese conflicts before embarking on similar adventures.

GLOSSARY

AGUINALDO Y FAMY, GENERALISSIMO DON EMILIO   Commander of the Filipino nationalists who fought the Spaniards and then the Americans in an effort to achieve Philippine independence.

BOLO KNIFE   This sharp-edged instrument was the Filipino revolutionary's main weapon.

DEWEY, COMMODORE GEORGE   Commander of the American Asiatic Squadron, which sank the Spanish fleet in the Battle of Manila Bay, May 1, 1898.

GRAYSON, WILLIAM "WILLIE" WALTER   The Philippine insurrection began when he and his fellow soldiers seized Filipino nationalists within their picket line and firing broke out between the American and Filipino camps.

GUERRILLA WARFARE   Like the Vietcong and North Vietnamese sixty years later, the Filipinos eschewed conventional, Western-style warfare of pitched battles and dispersed throughout the countryside conducting "hit-and-run operations by small bands."

MACABEBES   Filipino mercenaries from the central Luzon province of Pampanga who fought for Spain and the United States against their own countrymen.

MacARTHUR, GENERAL ARTHUR   Assuming command of United States forces in 1900, he initiated new tactics designed to isolate the Filipino guerrillas from the villages that supported them; his tactics gave rise to strategic hamlets, free-fire zones, and search-and-destroy operations.

MAHAN, ADMIRAL ALFRED THAYER   United States naval strategist who contended that sea power and overseas colonies were the keys to national power; his writings greatly influenced American imperialists such as Theodore Roosevelt and Henry Cabot Lodge.

MERRITT, MAJOR GENERAL WESLEY   Commanded the United States Philippine Expeditionary Force, sent to oust the Spaniards from the islands.

SANTAYANA, GEORGE   Spanish-born philosopher, poet, and educator who observed that those who do not learn from the mistakes of the past are doomed to repeat them.

SMITH, BRIGADIER GENERAL JACOB W. "HELL-ROARING JAKE"   Veteran of the Wounded Knee Sioux massacre of 1890; when the insurgents on Samar Island massacred fifty-nine American soldiers, "Hell-Roaring Jake" Smith ordered his men to burn and kill their way across the island in retaliation.

TAFT, WILLIAM HOWARD   Headed a United States civilian commission that took over the Philippine colonial government in 1901.

USS *MAINE*   The mysterious sinking of this American battleship was the catalyst of the Spanish-American War.

"WATER CURE"   American method of torture devised in retaliation for Filipino acts of terrorism (booby traps and assassination); a bamboo reed was placed in an insurgent's mouth, and water, often salted or dirty, was poured down his throat until he was so painfully bloated that he talked.

"WHITE MAN'S BURDEN"   Racist concept, popular among American imperialists, that whites had a "moral responsibility" to uplift and civilize supposedly inferior dark-skinned people such as the Filipinos.

Guerrilla warfare . . . jungle terrain . . . search and destroy missions . . . benevolent pacification . . . strategic hamlets . . . terrorism . . . ambushes . . . free-fire zones . . . booby traps . . . waning support from civilians at home. These words call forth from the national consciousness uncomfortable images of a war Americans fought and died in not long ago in Southeast Asia. But while the phrases may first bring to mind America's painful experience in Vietnam during the 1960s and '70s, they also aptly describe a much earlier conflict—the Philippine Insurrection—that foreshadowed this and other insurgent wars in Asia.

The Philippine-American War of 1898–1902 is one of our nation's most obscure and least-understood campaigns. Sometimes called the "Bolo War" because of the Filipino insurgents' lethally effective use of razor-sharp bolo knives or machetes against the American

expeditionary force occupying the islands, it is often viewed as a mere appendage of the one-hundred-day Spanish-American War. But suppressing the guerrilla warfare waged by Philippine nationalists seeking self-rule proved far more difficult, protracted, and costly for American forces than the conventional war with Spain that had preceded it.

America's campaign to smash the Philippine Insurrection was, ironically, a direct consequence of U.S. efforts to secure independence for other *insurrectos* halfway around the world in Cuba. On May 1, 1898, less than a week after Congress declared war against Spain, a naval squadron commanded by Commodore George Dewey steamed into Manila Bay to engage the Spanish warships defending that nation's Pacific possession. In a brief action Dewey achieved a stunning victory, sinking all of the enemy vessels with no significant American losses. Destroying the Spanish fleet, however, did not ensure U.S. possession of the Philippines. An estimated 15,000 Spanish soldiers still occupied Manila and the surrounding region. Those forces would have to be rooted out by infantry.

David R. Kohler and James W. Wensyel, from *American History Illustrated* (January/February 1990), 19–30. Original title: "Our First Southeast Asian War," Reprinted through the courtesy of Cowles Magazines, publisher of *American History Illustrated*.

President William McKinley had already ordered a Philippine Expeditionary Force of volunteer and regular army infantry, artillery, and cavalry units (nearly seven thousand men), under the command of Major General Wesley Merritt, to "reduce Spanish power in that quarter [Philippine Islands] and give order and security to the islands while in the possession of the United States."

Sent to the Philippines in the summer of 1898, this limited force was committed without fully considering the operation's potential length and cost. American military and government leaders also failed to anticipate the consequences of ignoring the Filipino rebels who, under Generalissimo Don Emilio Aguinaldo y Famy, had been waging a war for independence against Spain for the past two years. And when American insensitivity toward Aguinaldo eventually led to open warfare with the rebels, the American leaders grossly underestimated the determination of the seemingly ill-trained and poorly armed insurgents. They additionally failed to perceive the difficulties involved in conducting military operations in a tropical environment and among a hostile native population, and they did not recognize the burden of fighting at the end of a seven-thousand-mile-long logistics trail.

Asian engagements, the Americans learned for the first time, are costly. The enterprise, so modestly begun, eventually saw more than 126,000 American officers and men deployed to the Philippines. Four times as many soldiers served in this undeclared war in the Pacific as had been sent to the Caribbean during the Spanish-American War. During the three-year conflict, American troops and Filipino insurgents fought in more than 2,800 engagements. American casualties ultimately totaled 4,234 killed and 2,818 wounded, and the insurgents lost about 16,000 men. The civilian population suffered even more; as many as 200,000 Filipinos died from famine, pestilence, or the unfortunate happenstance of being too close to the fighting. The Philippine war cost the United States $600 million before the insurgents were subdued.

The costly experience offered valuable and timeless lessons about guerrilla warfare in Asia; unfortunately, those lessons had to be relearned sixty years later in another war that, despite the modern technology involved, bore surprising parallels to America's first Southeast Asian campaign.

ORIGINS

America's war with Spain, formally declared by the United States on April 25, 1898, had been several years in the making. During that time the American "yellow press," led by Joseph Pulitzer's *New York World* and William Randolph Hearst's *New York Journal,* trumpeted reports of heroic Cuban *insurrectos* revolting against their cruel Spanish rulers. Journalists vividly described harsh measures taken by Spanish officials to quell the Cuban revolution. The sensational accounts, often exaggerated, reminded Americans of their own uphill fight for independence and nourished the feeling that America was destined to intervene so that the Cuban people might also taste freedom.

Furthermore, expansionists suggested that the revolt against a European power, taking place less than one hundred miles from American shores, offered a splendid opportunity to turn the Caribbean into an American sea. Businessmen pointed out that $50 million in American capital was invested in the Cuban sugar and mining industries. Revolutions resulting in burned cane fields jeopardized that investment. As 1898 opened, American relations with Spain quickly declined.

In January 1898 the U.S. battleship *Maine* was sent to Cuba, ostensibly on a courtesy visit. On February 15 the warship was destroyed by a mysterious explosion while at anchor in Havana harbor, killing 262 of her 350-man crew. The navy's formal inquiry, completed on March 28, suggested that the explosion was due to an external force—a mine.

On March 29, the Spanish government received an ultimatum from Washington, D.C.: Spain's army in Cuba was to lay down its arms while the United States negotiated between the rebels and the Spaniards. The Spanish forces were also told to abolish all *reconcentrado* camps (tightly controlled areas, similar to the strategic hamlets later tried in Vietnam, where peasants were regrouped to deny food and intelligence to insurgents and to promote tighter security). Spain initially rejected the humiliation of surrendering its arms in the field but then capitulated on all points. The Americans were not satisfied.

On April 11, declaring that Spanish responses were inadequate, President McKinley told a joint session of Congress that "I have exhausted every effort to relieve the intolerable condition . . . at our doors. I now ask the Congress to empower the president to take measures to secure a full and final termination of hostilities in Cuba, to secure . . . the establishment of a stable government, and to use the military and naval forces of the United States . . . for these purposes. . . ."

Congress adopted the proposed resolution on April 19. Learning this, Spain declared war on the 24th. The following day, the United States responded with its own declaration of war.

The bulk of the American navy quickly gathered on the Atlantic coast. McKinley called for 125,000 volunteers to bolster the less than eighty-thousand-man regular army. His call was quickly oversubscribed; volunteers fought to be the first to land on Cuba's beaches.

The first major battle of the war, however, was fought not in Cuba but seven thousand miles to the west—in Manila Bay. Dewey's victory over Spanish Admiral Patricio Montojo y Pasarón (a rather hollow victory as Montojo's fleet consisted of seven unarmored ships, three of which had wooden hulls and one that had to be towed to the battle area) was wildly acclaimed in America.

American leaders, believing that the Philippines would now fall into America's grasp like a ripe plum, had to decide what to do with their prize. They could not return the islands to Spain, nor could they allow them to pass to France or Germany, America's commercial rivals in the Orient. The American press rejected the idea of a British protectorate. And, after four hundred years of despotic Spanish rule in which

Filipinos had little or no chance to practice self-government, native leaders seemed unlikely candidates for managing their own affairs. McKinley faced a grand opportunity for imperialistic expansion that could not be ignored.

The debate sharply divided his cabinet—and the country. American public opinion over acquisition of the Philippines divided into two basic factions: imperialists versus anti-imperialists.

The imperialists, mostly Republicans, included such figures as Theodore Roosevelt (then assistant secretary of the navy), Henry Cabot Lodge (Massachusetts senator), and Albert Beveridge (Indiana senator). These individuals were, for the most part, disciples of Alfred Thayer Mahan, a naval strategist who touted theories of national power and prestige through sea power and acquisition of overseas colonies for trade purposes and naval coaling stations.

The anti-imperialists, staunchly against American annexation of the Philippines, were mainly Democrats. Such men as former presidents Grover Cleveland and Rutherford B. Hayes, steel magnate Andrew Carnegie, William Jennings Bryan, union leader Samuel Gompers, and Mark Twain warned that by taking the Philippines the United States would march the road to ruin earlier traveled by the Roman Empire. Furthermore, they argued, America would be denying Filipinos the right of self-determination guaranteed by our own Constitution. The more practical-minded also pointed out that imperialistic policy would require maintaining an expensive army and navy there.

Racism, though demonstrated in different ways, pervaded the arguments of both sides. Imperialists spoke of the "white man's burden" and moral responsibility to "uplift the child races everywhere" and to provide "orderly development for the unfortunate and less able races." They spoke of America's "civilizing mission" of pacifying Filipinos by "benevolent assimilation" and saw the opening of the overseas frontier much as their forefathers had viewed the western frontier. The "subjugation of the Injun" (wherever he might be found) was a concept

grasped by American youth—the war's most enthusiastic supporters (in contrast to young America's
opposition to the war in Vietnam many years later).

The anti-imperialists extolled the sacredness of independence and self-determination for the Filipinos.
Racism, however, also crept into their argument, for
they believed that "protection against race mingling"
was a historic American policy that would be reversed by imperialism. To them, annexation of the
Philippines would admit "alien, inferior, and mon-
grel races to our nationality."

As the debate raged, Dewey continued to hold
Manila Bay, and the Philippines seemed to await
America's pleasure. President McKinley would ultimately cast the deciding vote in determining America's role in that country. McKinley, a genial, rather
laid-back, former congressman from Ohio and one-
time major in the Union army, remains a rather ambiguous figure during this period. In his Inaugural
Address he had affirmed that "We want no wars of
conquest; we must avoid the temptation of territorial
aggression." Thereafter, however, he made few
comments on pacifism, and, fourteen weeks after becoming president, signed the bill annexing Hawaii.

Speaking of Cuba in December 1897, McKinley
said, "I speak not of forcible annexation, for that
cannot be thought of. That, by our code of morality, would be criminal aggression." Nevertheless, he
constantly pressured Madrid to end Spanish rule in
Cuba, leading four months later to America's war
with Spain.

McKinley described experiencing extreme turmoil,
soul-searching, and prayer over the Philippine annexation issue until, he declared, one night in a dream the
Lord revealed to him that "there was nothing left for
us to do but to take them all [the Philippine Islands]
and to educate the Filipinos, and uplift, and civilize,
and Christianize them." He apparently didn't realize
that the Philippines had been staunchly Roman
Catholic for more than 350 years under Spanish colo-
nialism. Nor could he anticipate the difficulties that,
having cast its fortune with the expansionists, America
would now face in the Philippines.

PROSECUTING THE WAR

Meanwhile, in the Philippine Islands, Major General
Wesley Merritt's Philippine Expeditionary Force
went about its job. In late June, General Thomas
Anderson led an advance party ashore at Cavite. He
then established Camp Merritt, visited General
Aguinaldo's rebel forces entrenched around Manila,
and made plans for seizing that city once Merritt arrived with the main body of armed forces.

Anderson quickly learned that military operations
in the Philippines could be difficult. His soldiers,
hastily assembled and dispatched with limited prior
training, were poorly disciplined and inadequately
equipped. Many still wore woolen uniforms despite
the tropical climate. A staff officer described the
army's baptism at Manila: ". . . the heat was oppressive and the rain kept falling. At times the trenches
were filled with two feet of water, and soon the
men's shoes were ruined. Their heavy khaki uniforms were a nuisance; they perspired constantly, the
loss of body salts inducing chronic fatigue. Prickly
heat broke out, inflamed by scratching and rubbing.
Within a week the first cases of dysentery, malaria,
cholera, and dengue fever showed up at sick call."

During his first meeting with Dewey, Anderson
remarked that some American leaders were considering annexation of the Philippines. "If the United
States intends to hold the Philippine Islands," Dewey
responded, "it will make things awkward, because
just a week ago Aguinaldo proclaimed the independence of the Philippine Islands from Spain and seems
intent on establishing his own government."

A Filipino independence movement led by
Aguinaldo had been active in the islands since 1896
and, within weeks of Dewey's victory, Aguinaldo's
revolutionaries controlled most of the archipelago.

Aguinaldo, twenty-nine years old in 1898, had
taken over his father's position as mayor of his
hometown of Kawit before becoming a revolutionary. In a minor skirmish with Spanish soldiers, he
had rallied the Filipinos to victory. Thereafter, his

popularity grew as did his ragtag but determined army. Aguinaldo was slight of build, shy, and soft-spoken, but a strict disciplinarian.

As his rebel force besieged Manila, Aguinaldo declared a formal government for the Philippines with himself as president and generalissimo. He proclaimed his "nation's" independence and called for Filipinos to rally to his army and to the Americans, declaring that "the Americans . . . extend their protecting mantle to our beloved country . . . When you see the American flag flying, assemble in numbers: they are our redeemers!" But his enthusiasm for the United States later waned.

Merritt put off Aguinaldo's increasingly strident demands that America recognize his government and guarantee the Filipinos' independence. Aguinaldo perceived the American general's attitude as condescending and demeaning.

On August 13, Merritt's forces occupied Manila almost without firing a shot; in a face-saving maneuver the Spanish defenders had agreed to surrender to the Americans to avoid being captured—and perhaps massacred—by the Filipino insurgents. Merritt's troops physically blocked Aguinaldo's rebels, who had spent weeks in the trenches around the city, from participating in the assault. The Filipino general and his followers felt betrayed at being denied a share in the victory.

Further disenchanted, Aguinaldo would later find his revolutionary government unrepresented at the Paris peace talks determining his country's fate. He would learn that Spain had ceded the Philippines to the United States for $20 million.

Officers at Merritt's headquarters had little faith in the Filipinos' ability to govern themselves. "Should our power . . . be withdrawn," an early report declared, "the Philippines would speedily lapse into anarchy, which would excuse . . . the intervention of other powers and the division of the islands among them."

Meanwhile, friction between American soldiers and the Filipinos increased. Much of the Americans' conduct betrayed their racial bias. Soldiers referred to the natives as "niggers" and "gugus," epithets whose meanings were clear to the Filipinos. In retaliation,

the island inhabitants refused to give way on sidewalks and muscled American officers into the streets. Men of the expeditionary force in turn escalated tensions by stopping Filipinos at gun point, searching them without cause, "confiscating" shopkeepers' goods, and beating those who resisted.

On the night of February 4, 1899, the simmering pot finally boiled over. Private William "Willie" Walter Grayson and several other soldiers of Company D, 1st Nebraska Volunteer Infantry, apprehended a group of armed insurgents within their regimental picket line. Shots were exchanged, and three Filipino *insurrectos* fell dead. Heavy firing erupted between the two camps.

In the bloody battle that followed, the Filipinos suffered tremendous casualties (an estimated two thousand to five thousand dead, contrasted with fifty-nine Americans killed) and were forced to withdraw. The Philippine Insurrection had begun.

GUERRILLA WARFARE

The Americans, hampered by a shortage of troops and the oncoming rainy season, could initially do little more than extend their defensive perimeter beyond Manila and establish a toehold on several islands to the south. By the end of March, however, American forces seized Malolos, the seat of Aguinaldo's revolutionary government. But Aguinaldo escaped, simply melting into the jungle. In the fall, using conventional methods of warfare, the Americans first struck south, then north of Manila across the central Luzon plain. After hard marching and tough fighting, the expeditionary force occupied northern Luzon, dispersed the rebel army, and barely missed capturing Aguinaldo.

Believing that occupying the remainder of the Philippines would be easy, the Americans wrongly concluded that the war was virtually ended. But when the troops attempted to control the territory they had seized, they found that the Filipino revolutionaries were not defeated but had merely changed strategies.

United States troops sent to the Philippines found the tropical climate and terrain "almost as deadly as combat." The first contingent of soldiers arrived wearing woolen uniforms. Thousands of *Americans fell victim to dysentery and malaria. (Keystone-Mast Collection, California Museum of Photography, University of California, Riverside)*

Abandoning western-style conventional warfare, Aguinaldo had decided to adopt guerrilla tactics.

Aguinaldo moved to a secret mountain headquarters at Palanan in northern Luzon, ordering his troops to disperse and avoid pitched battles in favor of hit-and-run operations by small bands. Ambushing parties of Americans and applying terror to coerce support from other Filipinos, the insurrectionists now blended into the countryside, where they enjoyed superior intelligence information, ample supplies, and tight security. The guerrillas moved freely between the scattered American units, cutting telegraph lines, attacking supply trains, and assaulting straggling infantrymen. When the Americans pursued their tormentors, they fell into well planned ambushes. The insurgents' barbarity and ruthlessness during these attacks were notorious.

The guerrilla tactics helped to offset the inequities that existed between the two armies. The American troops were far better armed, for example, carrying .45-caliber Springfield single-shot rifles, Mausers, and then-modern .30-caliber repeating Krag-Jorgensen rifles. They also had field artillery and machine guns. The revolutionaries, on the other hand, were limited to a miscellaneous assortment of handguns, a few Mauser repeating rifles taken from the Spanish, and antique muzzle-loaders. The sharp-edged bolo knife was the revolutionary's primary weapon, and he used it well. Probably more American soldiers were hacked to death by bolos than were killed by Mauser bullets.

As would later be the case in Vietnam, the guerrillas had some clear advantages. They knew the terrain, were inured to the climate, and could generally count on a friendly population. As in Vietnam, villages controlled by the insurgents provided havens from which the guerrillas could attack, then fade back into hiding.

Americans soon began to feel that they were under siege in a land of enemies, and their fears were heightened because they never could be sure who among the population was hostile. A seemingly friendly peasant might actually be a murderer. Lieutenant Colonel J. T. Wickham, commanding the 26th Infantry Regiment, recorded that "a large flag of truce enticed officers into ambushes . . . Privates Dugan, Hayes, and Tracy were murdered by town authorities . . . Private Nolan [was] tied up by ladies while in a stupor; the insurgents cut his throat . . . The body of Corporal Doneley was dug up, burned, and mutilated . . . Private O'Hearn, captured by apparently friendly people was tied to a tree, burned over a slow fire, and slashed up . . . Lieutenant Max Wagner was assassinated by insurgents disguised in American uniforms."

As in later guerrilla movements, such terrorism became a standard tactic for the insurgents. Both Filipinos and Americans were their victims. In preying on their countrymen, the guerrillas had a dual purpose: to discourage any Filipinos disposed to cooperate with the Americans, and to demonstrate to people in a particular region that they ruled that area and could destroy inhabitants and villages not supporting the revolution. The most favored terroristic weapon was assassination of local leaders, who were usually executed in a manner (such as beheading or burying alive) calculated to horrify everyone.

By the spring of 1900 the war was going badly for the Americans. Their task forces, sent out to search and destroy, found little and destroyed less.

The monsoon rains, jungle terrain, hostile native population, and a determined guerrilla force made the American soldiers' marches long and miserable. One described a five-week-long infantry operation: ". . . our troops had been on half rations for two weeks. Wallowing through hip-deep muck, lugging

a ten-pound rifle and a belt . . . with 200 rounds of ammunition, drenched to the skin and with their feet becoming heavier with mud at every step, the infantry became discouraged. Some men simply cried, others slipped down in the mud and refused to rise. Threats and appeals by the officers were of no avail. Only a promise of food in the next town and the threat that if they remained behind they would be butchered by marauding bands of insurgents forced some to their feet to struggle on."

News reports of the army's difficulties began to erode the American public's support for the war. "To chase barefooted insurgents with water buffalo carts as a wagon train may be simply ridiculous," charged one correspondent, "but to load volunteers down with 200 rounds of ammunition and one day's rations, and to put on their heads felt hats used by no other army in the tropics . . . to trot these same soldiers in the boiling sun over a country without roads, is positively criminal. . . . There are over five thousand men in the general hospital."

Another reported that the American outlook "is blacker now than it has been since the beginning of the war . . . the whole population . . . sympathizes with the insurgents. The insurgents came to Pasig [a local area whose government cooperated with the Americans] and their first act was to hang the 'Presidente' for treason in surrendering to Americans. 'Presidentes' do not surrender to us anymore."

NEW STRATEGIES

Early in the war U.S. military commanders had realized that, unlike the American Indians who had been herded onto reservations, eight million Filipinos (many of them hostile) would have to be governed in place. The Americans chose to emphasize pacification through good works rather than by harsh measures, hoping to convince Filipinos that the American colonial government had a sincere interest in their welfare and could be trusted.

As the army expanded its control across the islands, it reorganized local municipal governments and trained Filipinos to take over civil functions in the democratic political structure the Americans planned to establish. American soldiers performed police duties, distributed food, established and taught at schools, and built roads and telegraph lines.

As the war progressed, however, the U.S. commanders saw that the terrorism practiced by Aguinaldo's guerrillas was far more effective in controlling the populace than was their own benevolent approach. Although the Americans did not abandon pacification through good works, it was thereafter subordinated to the "civilize 'em with a Krag" (Krag-Jorgensen rifle) philosophy. From December 1900 onward, captured revolutionaries faced deportation, imprisonment, or execution.

The American army also changed its combat strategy to counter that of its enemy. As in the insurgents' army, the new tactics emphasized mobility and surprise. Breaking into small units—the battalion became the largest maneuver force—the Americans gradually spread over the islands until each of the larger towns was occupied by one or two rifle companies. From these bases American troops began platoon- and company-size operations to pressure local guerrilla bands.

Because of the difficult terrain, limited visibility, and requirement for mobility, artillery now saw limited use except as a defensive weapon. The infantry became the main offensive arm, with mounted riflemen used to pursue the fleeing enemy. Cavalry patrols were so valued for their mobility that American military leaders hired trusted Filipinos as mounted scouts and cavalrymen.

The Americans made other efforts to "Filipinize" the war—letting Asians fight Asians. (A similar tactic had been used in the American Indian campaigns twenty years before; it would resurface in Vietnam sixty years later as "Vietnamization.") In the Philippines the Americans recruited five thousand Macabebes, mercenaries from the central Luzon province of Pampanga, to form the American officered Philippine Scouts. The Macabebes

had for centuries fought in native battalions under the Spanish flag—even against their own countrymen when the revolution began in 1896.

Just as a later generation of American soldiers would react to the guerrilla war in Vietnam, American soldiers in the Philippines responded to insurgent terrorism terrorism in kind, matching cruelty with cruelty. Such actions vented their frustration at being unable to find and destroy the enemy. An increasing number of Americans viewed all Filipinos as enemies.

"We make everyone get into his house by 7 P.M. and we only tell a man once," Corporal Sam Gillis of the 1st California Volunteer Regiment wrote to his family. "If he refuses, we shoot him. We killed over 300 natives the first night. . . . If they fire a shot from a house, we burn the house and every house near it."

Another infantryman frankly admitted that "with an enemy like this to fight, it is not surprising that the boys should soon adopt 'no quarter' as a motto and fill the blacks full of lead before finding out whether they are friends or enemies."

That attitude should not have been too surprising. The army's campaigns against the Plains Indians were reference points for the generation of Americans that took the Philippines. Many of the senior officers and noncommissioned officers—often veterans of the Indian wars—considered Filipinos to be "as full of treachery as our Arizona Apache." "The country won't be pacified," one soldier told a reporter, "until the niggers are killed off like the Indians." A popular soldiers' refrain, sung to the tune of "Tramp, tramp, tramp, the boys are marching," began, "Damn, damn, damn the Filipinos," and again spoke of "civilizing 'em with a Krag."

Reprisals against civilians by Americans as well as insurgents became common. General Lloyd Wheaton, leading a U.S. offensive southeast of Manila, found his men impaled on the bamboo prongs of booby traps and with throats slit while they slept. After two of his companies were ambushed, Wheaton ordered that every town and village within twelve miles be burned.

The Americans developed their own terrorist methods, many of which would be used in later Southeast

Asian wars. One was torturing suspected guerrillas or insurgent sympathizers to force them to reveal locations of other guerrillas and their supplies. An often-utilized form of persuasion was the "water cure," placing a bamboo reed in the victim's mouth and pouring water (some used salt water or dirty water) down his throat, thus painfully distending the victim's stomach. The subject, allowed to void this, would, under threat of repetition, usually talk freely. Another method of torture, the "rope cure," consisted of wrapping a rope around the victim's neck and torso until it formed a sort of girdle. A stick (or Krag rifle), placed between the ropes and twisted, then effectively created a combination of smothering and garroting.

The anti-imperialist press reported such American brutality in lurid detail. As a result, a number of officers and soldiers were court-martialed for torturing and other cruelties. Their punishments, however, seemed remarkably lenient. Of ten officers tried for "looting, torture, and murder," three were acquitted; of the seven convicted, five were reprimanded, one was reprimanded and fined $300, and one lost thirty-five places in the army's seniority list and forfeited half his pay for nine months.

Officers and soldiers, fighting a cruel, determined, and dangerous enemy, could not understand public condemnation of the brutality they felt was necessary to win. They had not experienced such criticism during the Indian wars, where total extermination of the enemy was condoned by the press and the American public, and they failed to grasp the difference now. Press reports, loss of public support, and the soldiers' feeling of betrayal—features of an insurgent war—would resurface decades later during the Vietnam conflict.

SUCCESS

Although U.S. military leaders were frustrated by the guerrillas' determination on the one hand and by eroding American support for the war on the other, most believed that the insurgents could be subdued.

Especially optimistic was General Arthur MacArthur, who in 1900 assumed command of the seventy thousand American troops in the Philippines. MacArthur adopted a strategy like that successfully used by General Zachary Taylor in the Second Seminole War in 1835; he believed that success depended upon the Americans' ability to isolate the guerrillas from their support in the villages. Thus were born "strategic hamlets," "free-fire zones," and "search and destroy" missions, concepts the American army would revive decades later in Vietnam.

MacArthur strengthened the more than five hundred small strong points held by Americans throughout the Philippine Islands. Each post was garrisoned by at least one company of American infantrymen. The natives around each base were driven from their homes, which were then destroyed. Soldiers herded the displaced natives into *reconcentrado* camps, where they could be "protected" by the nearby garrisons. Crops, food stores, and houses outside the camps were destroyed to deny them to the guerrillas. Surrounding each camp was a "dead line," within which anyone appearing would be shot on sight.

Operating from these small garrisons, the Americans pressured the guerrillas, allowing them no rest. Kept off balance, short of supplies, and constantly pursued by the American army, the Filipino guerrillas, suffering from sickness, hunger, and dwindling popular support, began to lose their will to fight. Many insurgent leaders surrendered, signaling that the tide at last had turned in the Americans' favor.

In March 1901, a group of Macabebe Scouts, commanded by American Colonel Frederick "Fighting Fred" Funston, captured Aguinaldo. Aguinaldo's subsequent proclamation that he would fight no more, and his pledge of loyalty to the United States, sped the collapse of the insurrection.

As in the past, and as would happen again during the Vietnam conflict of the 1960s and '70s, American optimism was premature. Although a civilian commission headed by William H. Taft took control of the colonial government from the American army in July 1901, the army faced more bitter fighting in its "pacification" of the islands.

As the war sputtered, the insurgents' massacre of fifty-nine American soldiers at Balangiga on the island of Samar caused Brigadier General Jacob W. "Hell-Roaring Jake" Smith, veteran of the Wounded Knee massacre of the Sioux in 1890, to order his officers to turn Samar into a "howling wilderness." His orders to a battalion of three hundred Marines headed for Samar were precise: "I want no prisoners. I wish you to kill and burn, the more you kill and burn the better it will please me. I want all persons killed who are capable of bearing arms against the United States." Fortunately, the Marines did not take Smith's orders literally and, later, Smith would be court-martialed.

On July 4, 1902, the Philippine Insurrection officially ended. Although it took the American army another eleven years to crush the fierce Moros of the southern Philippines, the civil government's security force (the Philippine Constabulary), aided by the army's Philippine Scouts, maintained a fitful peace throughout the islands. The army's campaign to secure the Philippines as an American colony had succeeded.

American commanders would have experienced vastly greater difficulties except for two distinct advantages: 1) the enemy had to operate in a restricted area, in isolated islands, and was prevented by the U.S. Navy from importing weapons and other needed supplies; and 2) though the insurgents attempted to enlist help from Japan, no outside power intervened. These conditions would not prevail in some subsequent guerrilla conflicts in Asia.

In addition to the many tactical lessons the army learned from fighting a guerrilla war in a tropical climate, other problems experienced during this campaign validated the need for several military reforms that were subsequently carried out, including improved logistics, tropical medicine, and communications.

The combination of harsh and unrelenting military force against the guerrillas, complemented by the exercise of fair and equitable civil government and civic action toward those who cooperated, proved to be the Americans' most effective tactic for dealing with the insurgency. This probably was the most significant lesson to be learned from the Philippine Insurrection.

LESSONS FOR THE FUTURE

Vietnam veterans reading this account might nod in recollection of a personal, perhaps painful experience from their own war.

Many similarities exist between America's three-year struggle with the Filipino *insurrectos* and the decade-long campaign against the Communists in Vietnam. Both wars, modestly begun, went far beyond what anyone had foreseen in time, money, equipment, manpower, casualties, and suffering.

Both wars featured small-unit infantry actions. Young infantrymen, if they had any initial enthusiasm, usually lost it once they saw the war's true nature; they nevertheless learned to endure their allotted time while adopting personal self-survival measures as months "in-country" lengthened and casualty lists grew.

Both wars were harsh, brutal, cruel. Both had their Samar Islands and their My Lais. Human nature being what it is, both conflicts also included acts of great heroism, kindness, compassion, and self-sacrifice.

Both wars saw an increasingly disenchanted American public withdrawing its support (and even disavowing its servicemen) as the campaigns dragged on, casualties mounted, and news accounts vividly described the horror of the battlefields.

Some useful lessons might be gleaned from a comparison of the two conflicts. Human nature really does not change—war will bring out the best and the worst in the tired, wet, hungry, and fearful men who are doing the fighting. Guerrilla campaigns—particularly where local military and civic reforms cannot be effected to separate the guerrilla from his base of popular support—will be long and difficult, and will demand tremendous commitments in resources and national will. Finally, before America commits its armed forces to similar ventures in the future, it would do well to recall the lessons learned from previous campaigns. For, as the Spanish-born American educator, poet, and philosopher George Santayana reminded us, those who do not learn from the past are doomed to repeat it.

QUESTIONS TO CONSIDER

1 How and why did the United States initially become involved in the Philippines? What, according to the authors, were the fundamental mistakes committed by the Americans in making that decision?

2 Why did the Americans decide to take over the Philippines? What were the different categories of American public opinion in reaction to this development? How were they different, and what attitudes did they share?

3 What military advantages did the Philippine insurgents have? What were American military tactics and goals, and how did they change in response to the conditions of the Philippine conflict?

4 How does the conflict in the Philippines compare with the Indian wars that preceded it? In particular, how did the American public and American soldiers differ in comparing the Philippine conflict with the Indian wars, and what were the results and significance of this difference?

5 What, according to the authors, are the lessons to be learned from our involvement in the Philippines? Have they been learned?

PART FIVE

Currents of the Progressive Era

10 Theodore Roosevelt, President

EDMUND MORRIS

Despite a long, enervating depression, American industry continued to expand and consolidate throughout the 1890s, and the rate of expansion was even faster in the first decade of the twentieth century. By then, economic concentration had resulted in a handful of giant combinations that were dominating each area of industrial activity. In 1909, 1 percent of American business enterprises produced 44 percent of the nation's manufactured goods. Money and property were so maldistributed that 1 percent of the United States population—the corporate magnates and their families—owned seven-eighths of the country's wealth. Middle-class families were getting by, although precariously. And the rest—industrial workers in America's teeming, dilapidated cities and debtor farmers in the South and West—lived in poverty.

The new Populist party, a third-party reform movement, posed the first serious challenge to the new industrial order and the corporate bosses who controlled it. The Populist insurgents made thousands aware of the need for reform—the need to correct the abuses of industrial monopolies and to protect the mass of the nation's people. So did liberal intellectuals and crusading journalists—the celebrated muckrakers who exposed glaring malpractices in business and in municipal governments. Thanks to these men and women, thanks to tensions caused by rapid and unmanaged industrial growth, and thanks to a genuine desire to revive humanitarian democracy, there emerged the complex Progressive movement, which lasted from the late 1890s through the First World War. For the most part, those who joined the ranks of progressivism were victims of monopolies and were anxious to dismantle the biggest of them and control the rest.

Progressivism transcended party labels, as Democrats and Republicans alike took up the banners of reform. In the Democratic party, William Jennings Bryan crusaded against the conservative Republican–big business alliance that ran the country; later Bryan passed the leadership of Democratic progressivism to Woodrow Wilson, the subject of selection 13. In the Republican party, "Fighting Bob" La Follette, governor of Wisconsin, made his state a model of progressivism. But the best-known Progressive Republican was the man who found himself elevated to the White House when an assassin murdered William McKinley in 1901. "Now look!" exclaimed a horrified Republican. "That damned cowboy is president of the United States."

That damned cowboy, of course, was Theodore Roosevelt, a whirlwind of a man whose motto was "Get action, do things; be sane, don't fritter away your time; create, act, take a place wherever you are and be somebody: get action." Get action he did, as he hunted big game on three continents, sparred with prizefighters, rode with cowboys, dashed off voluminous histories, knocked down a tough in a western saloon, led the celebrated Rough Riders during the Spanish-American War, terrorized a police force, ran the Empire State as governor, and rose to the nation's highest office. Never mind that he was an accidental president. Once in the presidency, he put on a performance—for surely that is the word for it—that held the nation spellbound.

What president since the Civil War had had such uninhibited gusto, such a sense of the dramatic? He conducted a vigorous foreign policy that made the United States a major presence in the world. He dispatched a fleet of white battleships around the globe and won a Nobel Peace Prize for mediating the Russo-Japanese War. In this hemisphere, he rattled the Monroe Doctrine, ordered American troops to Santo Domingo, stationed marines in Cuba, encouraged a revolution against the Republic of Colombia that established the new nation of Panama, and then acquired the rights to build a canal there that would furnish America with a lifeline to the Pacific. Roosevelt's actions in Panama were provocative, even unethical, but he didn't care. As he said later, "If I had followed traditional conservative methods I would have submitted a dignified state paper of probably two hundred pages to the Congress and the debate would be going on yet, but I took the Canal Zone and let the Congress debate, and while the debate goes on, the canal does also."

He was just as vigorous in his domestic policy. He trumpeted the cause of conservation, sent troops to protect strikers in the Pennsylvania coal mines, and thundered so violently against "the malefactors of great wealth" and "the criminal rich" that conservative Republicans were appalled. The first post–Civil War president to recognize the threat of monopolies and trusts to America's economic life, TR shook his fist in the face of banker J. Pierpont Morgan, and his attorney general initiated more antitrust suits than all previous attorneys general combined. As a result, TR won a reputation as a crusading "trust buster." In point of fact, he accepted business consolidation as an economic reality in America and, instead of crushing all business combinations, established a policy of government scrutiny and control. Thus, he attacked only "bad" or "evil" trusts and left the "good" ones alone. Indeed, as one scholar put it, "the first great wave of business consolidation" actually came to a climax during Roosevelt's presidency.

Behind Roosevelt's actions was a volatile personality that kept his legions of followers enthralled. And that personality, full of contradiction, of great charm and physical exuberance, of egotistical moralizing and militarism, fairly explodes off the pages that follow. In them, TR's Pulitzer Prize–winning biographer, Edmund Morris, makes us aware of the importance of personal qualities in shaping the conduct and careers of historical figures. As you read this spirited portrait, you may not always like Theodore Roosevelt, but you will never find him boring.

GLOSSARY

HANNA, MARK Chairman of the Republican National Committee who aspired to take over the White House after TR had finished his "caretaker" term.

LIVINGSTONE, ROBERT Journalist who praised TR's great "gift of personal magnetism."

ROOSEVELT, ALICE LEE TR's first wife, who died of Bright's disease (kidney inflammation) on the same day that TR's mother died of typhoid fever.

ROOSEVELT, MARTHA BULLOCH "MITTIE" TR's mother.

TEEDIE TR's boyhood nickname.

WASHINGTON, BOOKER T. The head of Alabama's all-black Tuskegee Institute whom TR invited to dine at the White House; "it was the first time that a president had ever entertained a black man in the first house of the land," and it enraged southern white supremacists.

Let us dispose, in short order, with Theodore Roosevelt's faults. He was an incorrigible preacher of platitudes. . . . He significantly reduced the wildlife population of some three continents. He piled his dessert plate with so many peaches that the cream spilled over the sides. And he used to make rude faces out of the presidential carriage at small boys in the streets of Washington.

Now those last two faults are forgivable if we accept British diplomat Cecil Spring-Rice's advice, "You must always remember the President is about six." The first fault—his preachiness—is excused by the fact that the American electorate dearly loves a moralist. As to the second and most significant fault—Theodore Roosevelt's genuine blood-lust and desire to destroy his adversaries, whether they be rhinoceroses or members of the United States Senate—it is paradoxically so much a part of his virtues, both as a man and a politician, that I will come back to it in more detail later.

One of the minor irritations I have to contend with as a biographer is that whenever I go to the library to look for books about Roosevelt, Theodore, they infallibly are mixed up with books about Roosevelt, Franklin—and I guess FDR scholars have the same problem in reverse. Time was when the single word "Roosevelt" meant only Theodore; FDR

himself frequently had to insist, in the early thirties, that he was not TR's son. He was merely a fifth cousin, and what was even more distant, a Democrat to boot. In time, of course, Franklin succeeded in preempting the early meaning of the word "Roosevelt," to the point that TR's public image, which once loomed as large as Washington's and Lincoln's, began to fade like a Cheshire cat from popular memory. By the time of FDR's own death in 1945, little was left but the ghost of a toothy grin.

Only a few veterans of the earlier Roosevelt era survived to testify that if Franklin was the greater politician, it was only by a hairsbreadth, and as far as sheer personality was concerned, Theodore's superiority could be measured in spades. They pointed out that FDR himself declared, late in life, that his "cousin Ted" was the greatest man he ever knew.

Presently the veterans too died. But that ghostly grin continued to float in the national consciousness, as if to indicate that its owner was meditating a reappearance. I first became aware of the power behind the grin in Washington, in February of 1976. The National Theater was trying out an ill-fated musical by Alan Lerner and Leonard Bernstein, *1600 Pennsylvania Avenue.* For two and a half hours Ken Howard worked his way through a chronological series of impersonations of historic Presidents. The audience sat on its hands, stiff with boredom, until the very end, when Mr. Howard clamped on a pair of pince-nez and a false mustache, and bared all his teeth in a grin. The entire theater burst into delighted applause.

From Edmund Morris, "Theodore Roosevelt, President," *American Heritage,* June/July 1981, Vol. 32, No. 4. Reprinted by permission of American Heritage, Inc. Copyright © Forbes, Inc., 1981.

What intrigued me was the fact that few people there could have known much about TR beyond the obvious clichés of San Juan Hill and the Big Stick. Yet somehow, subconsciously, they realized that here for once was a positive President, warm and tough and authoritative and funny, who believed in America and who, to quote Owen Wister, "grasped his optimism tight lest it escape him."

In [recent times] Theodore Roosevelt has made his long-promised comeback. He has been the subject of a *Newsweek* cover story on American heroes; Russell Baker has called him a cinch to carry all fifty states if he were running for the White House today; he's starring on Broadway in *Tintypes,* on television in *Bully,* and you'll . . . see him on the big screen in *Ragtime.* Every season brings a new crop of reassessments in the university presses, and as for the pulp mills, he figures largely in the latest installment of John Jakes's Kent Chronicles. No time like the present, therefore, to study that giant personality in color and fine detail.

When referring to Theodore Roosevelt I do not use the word "giant" loosely. "Every inch of him," said William Allen White, "was overengined." Lyman Gage likened him, mentally and physically, to two strong men combined; Gifford Pinchot said that his normal appetite was enough for four people, Charles J. Bonaparte estimated that his mind moved ten times faster than average, and TR himself, not wanting to get into double figures, modestly remarked, "I have enjoyed as much of life as any nine men I know." John Morley made a famous comparison in 1904 between Theodore Roosevelt and the Niagara Falls, "both great wonders of nature." John Burroughs wrote that TR's mere proximity made him nervous. "There was always something imminent about him, like an avalanche that the sound of your voice might loosen." Ida Tarbell, sitting next to him at a musicale, had a sudden hallucination that the President was about to burst. "I felt his clothes might not contain him, he was so steamed up, so ready to go, to attack anything, anywhere."

Reading all these remarks it comes as a surprise to discover that TR's chest measured a normal forty-two inches, and that he stood only five feet nine in his size seven shoes. Yet unquestionably his initial impact was physical, and it was overwhelming. I have amused myself over the years with collecting the metaphors that contemporaries used to describe this Rooseveltian "presence." Here's a random selection. [Novelist] Edith Wharton thought him radioactive; Archie Butt and others used phrases to do with electricity, high-voltage wires, generators, and dynamos; Lawrence Abbott compared him to an electromagnetic nimbus; John Burroughs to "a kind of electric bombshell, if there can be such a thing"; James E. Watson was reminded of TNT; and Senator Joseph Foraker, in an excess of imagination, called TR "a steam-engine in trousers." There are countless other steam-engine metaphors, from Henry Adams' "swift and awful Chicago express" to Henry James's "verily, a wonderful little machine: destined to be overstrained, perhaps, but not as yet, truly, betraying the least creak." Lastly we have [western writer] Owen Wister comparing TR to a solar conflagration that cast no shadow, only radiance.

These metaphors sound fulsome, but they refer only to TR's physical effect, which was felt with equal power by friends and enemies. People actually tingled in his company; there was something sensually stimulating about it. They came out of the presidential office flushed, short-breathed, energized, as if they had been treated to a sniff of white powder. He had, as Oscar Straus once said, "the quality of vitalizing things." His youthfulness (he was not yet forty-three at the beginning of his first term, and barely fifty at the end of his second), his air of glossy good health, his powerful handshake—all these things combined to give an impression of irresistible force and personal impetus.

But TR was not just a physical phenomenon. In many ways the quality of his personality was more remarkable than its quantity. Here again, I have discovered recurrences of the same words in contemporary descriptions. One of the more frequent images is that of sweetness. "He was as sweet a man," wrote Henry Watterson, "as ever scuttled a ship or cut a throat." But most comments are kinder than that.

"There is a sweetness about him that is very compelling," sighed Woodrow Wilson. "You can't resist the man." Robert Livingstone, a journalist, wrote after TR's death: "He had the double gifts of a sweet nature that came out in every handtouch and tone . . . and a sincerely powerful personality that left the uneffaceable impression that whatever he said was right. Such a combination was simply irresistible." Livingstone's final verdict was that Theodore Roosevelt had "unquestionably the greatest gift of personal magnetism ever possessed by an American."

That may or may not be true, but certainly there are very few recorded examples of anybody, even TR's bitterest political critics, being able to resist him in person. Brand Whitlock, Mark Twain, John Jay Chapman, William Jennings Bryan, and Henry James were all seduced by his charm, if only temporarily. Peevish little Henry Adams spent much of the period from 1901 to 1909 penning a series of magnificent insults to the President's reputation. But this did not prevent him from accepting frequent invitations to dine at the White House and basking gloomily in TR's effulgence. By the time the Roosevelt era came to an end, Adams was inconsolable. "My last vision of fun and gaiety will vanish when my Theodore goes . . . never can we replace him."

It's a pity that the two men never had a public slanging match over the table, because when it came to personal invective, TR could give as good as he got. There was the rather slow British ambassador whom he accused of having "a mind that functions at six guinea-pig power." There was the State Supreme Court Justice he called "an amiable old fuzzy-wuzzy with sweetbread brains." There was that "unspeakable villainous little monkey," President Castro of Venezuela, and President Marroquin of Colombia, whom he described in one word as a "Pithecanthropoid." Woodrow Wilson was "a Byzantine logothete" (even Wilson had to go to the dictionary for that one); [retail magnate] John Wanamaker was "an ill-constitutioned creature, oily, with bristles sticking up through the oil," and poor Senator Warren Pfeffer never quite recovered from being called "a pinheaded anarchistic crank, of hirsute and slabsided

aspect." TR did not use bad language—the nearest to it I've found is his description of [jurist and statesman] Charles Evans Hughes as "a psalm-singing son of a bitch," but then Charles Evans Hughes tended to invite such descriptions. Moreover, TR usually took the sting out of his insults by collapsing into laughter as he uttered them. Booth Tarkington detected "an undertone of Homeric chuckling" even when Roosevelt seemed to be seriously castigating someone—"as if, after all, he loved the fun of hating, rather than the hating itself."

Humor, indeed, was always TR's saving grace. A reporter who spent a week with him in the White House calculated that he laughed, on average, a hundred times a day—and what was more, laughed heartily. "He laughs like an irresponsible schoolboy on a lark, his face flushing ruddy, his eyes nearly closed, his utterance choked with merriment, his speech abandoned for a weird falsetto. . . . The President is a joker, and (what many jokers are not) a humorist as well."

If there were nothing more to Theodore Roosevelt's personality than physical exuberance, humor, and charm, he would indeed have been what he sometimes is misperceived to be: a simple-minded, amiable bully. Actually he was an exceedingly complex man, a polygon (to use Brander Matthews' word) of so many political, intellectual, and social facets that the closer one gets to him, the less one is able to see him in the round. Consider merely this random list of attributes and achievements:

He graduated *magna cum laude* from Harvard University. He was the author of a four-volume history of the winning of the West which was considered definitive in his lifetime, and a history of the naval war of 1812 which remains definitive to this day. He also wrote biographies of Thomas Hart Benton, Gouverneur Morris, and Oliver Cromwell, and some fourteen other volumes of history, natural history, literary criticism, autobiography, political philosophy, and military memoirs, not to mention countless articles and approximately seventy-five thousand letters. He spent nearly three years of his life in Europe and the Levant, and had a wide circle of intellectual correspondents on both sides of the Atlantic. He habitually read one to three books a day, on subjects ranging from architecture to zoology, averaging two or three pages a minute and effortlessly memorizing the paragraphs that interested him. He could recite poetry by the hour in English, German, and French. He married two women and fathered six children. He was a boxing championship finalist, a Fifth Avenue socialite, a New York State Assemblyman, a Dakota cowboy, a deputy sheriff, a president of the Little Missouri Stockmen's Association, United States Civil Service Commissioner, Police Commissioner of New York City, Assistant Secretary of the Navy, Colonel of the Rough Riders, Governor of New York, Vice-President, and finally President of the United States. He was a founding member of the National Institute of Arts and Letters and a fellow of the American Historical Society. He was accepted by Washington's scientific community as a skilled ornithologist, paleontologist, and taxidermist (during the White House years, specimens that confused experts at the Smithsonian were occasionally sent to TR for identification), and he was recognized as the world authority on the big-game mammals of North America.

Now all these achievements *predate* his assumption of the Presidency—in other words, he packed them into his first forty-three years. I will spare you another list of the things he packed into his last ten, after leaving the White House in 1909, except to say that the total of books rose to thirty-eight, the total of letters to 150,000, and the catalogue of careers expanded to include world statesman, big game collector for the Smithsonian, magazine columnist, and South American explorer.

If it were possible to take a cross section of TR's personality, as geologists, say, ponder a chunk of continent, you would be presented with a picture of seismic richness and confusion. The most order I have been able to make of it is to isolate four major character seams. They might be traced back to childhood. Each seam stood out bright and clear in youth and early middle age, but they began to merge about the time he was forty. Indeed the white heat of the

Theodore Roosevelt, proudly displaying his specially-made Brooks Brothers cavalry uniform, prepares for battle. Morris describes the future president as a "militarist" who enjoyed "blood sports." In his Pulitzer-Prize winning biography, Morris quotes the toast Roosevelt gave to his Rough Riders before they departed for Cuba: "To the Officers—may they get killed, wounded, or promoted!" (Library of Congress)

Presidency soon fused them all into solid metal. But so long as they were distinct they may be identified as aggression, righteousness, pride, and militarism. Before suggesting how they affected his performance as President, I'd like to explain how they originated.

The most fundamental characteristic of Theodore Roosevelt was his aggression—conquest being, to him, synonymous with growth. From the moment he first dragged breath into his asthmatic lungs, the sickly little boy fought for a larger share of the world. He could never get enough air; disease had to be destroyed; he had to fight his way through big, heavy books to gain a man's knowledge. Just as the struggle for wind made him stretch his chest, so did the difficulty of relating to abnormally contrasting parents extend his imagination. Theodore Senior was the epitome of hard, thrusting Northern manhood; Mittie Roosevelt was the quintessence of soft, yielding Southern femininity. The Civil War—the first political phenomenon little Teedie was ever aware of—symbolically opposed one to the other. There was no question as to which side, and which parent, the child preferred. He naughtily prayed God, in Mittie's presence, to "grind the Southern troops to powder," and the victory of Union arms reinforced his belief in the superiority of Strength over Weakness, Right over Wrong, Realism over Romance.

Teedie's youthful "ofserv-a-tions" in natural history gave him further proof of the laws of natural selection, long before he fully understood [Charles] Darwin and Herbert Spencer. For weeks he watched in fascination while a tiny shrew successively devoured a mass of beetles, then a mouse twice her size, then a snake so large it whipped her from side to side of the cage as she was gnawing through its neck. From then on the rule of tooth and claw, aided by superior intelligence, was a persistent theme in Theodore Roosevelt's writings.

Blood sports, which he took up as a result of his shooting for specimens, enabled him to feel the "strong eager pleasure" of the shrew in vanquishing ever larger foes; his exuberant dancing and whooping after killing a particularly dangerous animal struck more than one observer as macabre. From among his own kind, at college, he selected the fairest and most unobtainable mate—"See that girl? I'm going to marry her. She won't have me, but I am going to have *her!*"—and he ferociously hunted her down. That was Alice Lee Roosevelt, mother of the late Alice Longworth.

During his first years in politics, in the New York State Assembly, he won power through constant attack. The death of Alice Lee, coming as it did just after the birth of his first child—at the moment of fruition of his manhood—only intensified his will to fight. He hurried West, to where the battle for life was fiercest. The West did not welcome him; it had

to be won, like everything else he lusted for. Win it he did, by dint of the greatest physical and mental stretchings-out he had yet made. In doing so he built up the magnificent body that became such an inspiration to the American people (one frail little boy who vowed to follow the President's example was the future world heavyweight champion, Gene Tunney). And by living on equal terms with the likes of Hashknife Simpson, Bat Masterson, Modesty Carter, Bronco Charlie Miller, and Hell-Roaring Bill Jones, he added another mental frontier to those he already had inherited at birth. Theodore Roosevelt, Eastern son of a Northern father and a Southern mother, could now call himself a Westerner also.

TR's second governing impulse was his personal righteousness. As one reviewer of his books remarked, "He seems to have been born with his mind made up." No violent shocks disturbed his tranquil, prosperous childhood in New York City. Privately educated, he suffered none of the traumas of school. Thanks to the security of his home, the strong leadership of his father, and the adoration of his brother and sisters, Teedie entered adolescence with no sexual or psychological doubts whatsoever. Or if he had any, he simply reasoned them out, according to the Judeo-Christian principles Theodore Senior had taught him, reached the proper moral decision, and that was that. "Thank heaven!" he wrote in his diary after falling in love with Alice Lee, "I am perfectly pure."

His three great bereavements (the death of his father in 1878, and the deaths of his mother and wife in the same house and on the same day in 1884) came too late in his development to do him any permanent emotional damage. They only served to convince him more that he must be strong, honest, clean-living, and industrious. "At least I can live," he wrote, "so as not to dishonor the memory of the dead whom I so loved," and never was a cliché more heartfelt. Experiment after experiment proved the correctness of his instincts—in graduating *magna cum laude* from Harvard, in marrying successfully, in defying the doctors who ordered him to live a sedentary life, in winning international acclaim as writer and politician long before he was thirty. (He received his first nomination for the Presidency, by the Baltimore *American,* when he was only twenty-eight; it had to be pointed out to the newspaper's editor that he was constitutionally debarred from that honor for the next seven years.)

In wild Dakota Territory, he proceeded to knock down insolent cowboys, establish the foundations of federal government, pursue boat thieves in the name of the law, and preach the gospel of responsible citizenship. One of the first things he did after Benjamin Harrison appointed him Civil Service Commissioner was call for the prosecution of Postmaster General William Wallace of Indianapolis—who just happened to be the President's best friend. "That young man," Harrison growled, "wants to put the whole world right between sunrise and sunset."

TR's egotistic moralizing as a reform Police Commissioner of New York City was so insufferable that the *Herald* published a transcript of one of his speeches with the personal pronoun emphasized in heavy type. The effect, in a column of gray newsprint, was of buckshot at close range. This did not stop TR from using the personal pronoun thirteen times in the first four sentences of his account of the Spanish-American War. In fact, a story went around that halfway through the typesetting, Scribner's had to send for an extra supply of capital *I's.*

The third characteristic of Theodore Roosevelt's personality was his sense of pride, both as an aristocrat and as an American. From birth, servants and tradespeople deferred to him. Men and women of high quality came to visit his parents and treated him as one of their number. He accepted his status without question, as he did the charitable responsibilities it entailed. At a very early age he was required to accompany his father on Sunday excursions to a lodging house for Irish newsboys and a night school for little Italians. It cannot have escaped his attention that certain immigrant groups lacked the intellectual and social graces of others. Extended tours of Europe and the Levant as a child, teen-ager, and young man soon taught him that this was not due to ethnic inferiority so much as to centuries of economic and political deprivation. Prosperous, independent countries

like England and Germany were relatively free of slums and disease; but in Italy women and children scrabbled like chickens for scraps of his cake, and in Ireland people lay down in the road from sheer hunger. From what he read, things were no better in the Slavic countries.

Only in America, with its limitless economic opportunities and freedom from political bondage, might these peasants begin to improve their stock. And only in America could they revitalize their racial characteristics. His own extremely mixed ancestry proved that a generation or two of life in the New World was enough to blend all kinds of European blood into a new, dynamic American breed. (As President, he had a habit when shaking hands with ethnic groups of saying, "Congratulations, I'm German too!" and "Dee-lighted! I'm also Scotch-Irish, you know!" Newspapermen privately referred to him as "Old Fifty-seven Varieties.")

TR knew the value of an ethnic vote as well as the next man. There is a famous—alas, probably apocryphal—story of his appointment of Oscar Straus as the first Jewish Cabinet officer in American history. At a banquet to celebrate the appointment, TR made a passionate speech full of phrases like "regardless of race, color, or creed" and then turned to Jacob Schiff, the New York Jewish leader, and said, "Isn't that so, Mr. Schiff?" But Schiff, who was very deaf and had heard little of the speech, replied, "Dot's right, Mr. President, you came to me and said, 'Chake, who is der best Choo I can put in de Cabinet?'"

TR realized, of course, that the gap between himself and Joe Murray—the Irish ward-heeler who got him into the New York Assembly—was unbridgeable outside of politics. But in America a low-born man had the opportunity—the *duty*—to fight his way up from the gutter, as Joe had done. He might then merit an invitation to lunch at Sagamore Hill, or at least tea, assuming he wore a clean shirt and observed decent proprieties.

Here I must emphasize that TR was not a snob in the trivial sense. He had nothing but contempt for the [aristocratic] Newport set and the more languid members of the Four Hundred. When he said, at twenty-one, that he wanted to be a member of "the governing class," he was aware that it was socially beneath his own. At Albany, and in the [Dakota] Bad Lands, and as Colonel of the Rough Riders, he preferred to work with men who were coarse but efficient, rather than those who were polished and weak. He believed, he said, in "the aristocracy of worth," and cherished the revolution that had allowed such an elite to rise to the top in government. On the other hand (to use his favorite phrase) the historian John Blum has noted that he rarely appointed impoverished or unlettered men to responsible positions. He made great political capital, as President, of the fact that his sons attended the village school at Oyster Bay, along with the sons of his servants, of whom at least one was black; but as soon as the boys reached puberty he whisked them off to Groton.

Only the very young or very old dared call him "Teddy" to his face. Roosevelt was a patrician to the tips of his tapering fingers, yet he maintained till death what one correspondent called an "almost unnatural" identity with the masses. "I don't see how you understand the common people so well, Theodore," complained Henry Cabot Lodge. "No, Cabot, you never will," said TR, grinning triumphantly, "because I am one of them, and you are not." TR deluded himself. His plebeian strength was due to understanding, not empathy.

The fourth and final major trait of Theodore Roosevelt's character was his militarism. I will not deal with it in much detail because it is a familiar aspect of him, and in any case did not manifest itself much during his Presidency. There is no doubt that in youth, and again in old age, he was in love with war; but oddly enough, of all our great Presidents, he remains the only one not primarily associated with war (indeed, he won the Nobel Peace Prize in 1906).

He did not lack for military influences as a child; four of his Georgian ancestors had been military men, and stories of their exploits were told him by his mother. Two of his uncles served with distinction in the Confederate navy—a fact of which he

proudly boasts in his *Autobiography,* while making no reference to his father's civilian status. . . .

When TR learned to read, he reveled in stories "about the soldiers of Valley Forge, and Morgan's riflemen," and confessed, "I had a great desire to be like them." In his senior year at Harvard, he suddenly developed an interest in strategy and tactics and began to write *The Naval War of 1812;* within eighteen months he was the world expert on that subject. As soon as he left college he joined the National Guard and quickly became a captain, which stood him in good stead when he was called upon to lead a cavalry regiment in 1898. Throughout his literary years he made a study of classical and modern campaigns, and he would wage the great battles of history with knives and forks and spoons on his tablecloth. No doubt much of this fascination with things military related to his natural aggression, but there was an intellectual attraction too: he read abstract tomes on armaments, navigation, ballistics, strategy, and service administration as greedily as swashbuckling memoirs. Nothing is more remarkable about *The Naval War of 1812* than its cold impartiality, its use of figures and diagrams to destroy patriotic myths. Roosevelt understood that great battles are fought by thinking men, that mental courage is superior to physical bravado. Nobody thrilled more to the tramp of marching boots than he, but he believed that men must march for honorable reasons, in obedience to the written orders of a democratically elected Commander in Chief. In that respect, at least, the pen was mightier than the sword.

Now how much did these four character traits—aggression, righteousness, pride, and militarism—affect TR's performance as President of the United States? The answer is, strongly, as befits a strong character and a strong Chief Executive. The way he arrived at this "personal equation" is interesting, because he was actually in a weak position at the beginning of his first administration.

When TR took the oath of office on September 14, 1901, he was the youngest man ever to do so—a Vice President, elevated by assassination, confronted by a nervous Cabinet and a hostile Senate. Yet from the moment he raised his hand in that little parlor in Buffalo, it was apparent that he intended to translate his personal power into presidential power. The hand did not stop at the shoulder; he raised it high above his head, and held it there, "steady as if carved out of marble." His right foot pawed the floor. *Aggression.* He repeated the words of the oath confidently, adding an extra phrase, not called for in the Constitution, at the end: "And so I swear." *Righteousness.* His two senior Cabinet officers, [Secretary of State] John Hay and [Secretary of the Treasury] Lyman Gage, were not present at the ceremony, but TR announced that they had telegraphed promises of loyalty to him. Actually they had not; they were both considering resignation, but TR knew any such resignations would be construed as votes of no confidence in him, and he was determined to forestall them. By announcing that Hay and Gage would stay, out of loyalty to the memory of the dead President, he made it morally impossible for them to quit. *Pride.*

As for *militarism,* TR was seen much in the company of the New York State Adjutant General the next few days, and an armed escort of cavalrymen accompanied him wherever he went. This was perhaps understandable, in view of the fact that a President had just been assassinated, but it is a matter of record that more and more uniforms were seen glittering around TR as the months and years went on. Toward the end of his second administration, *Harper's Weekly* complained that "there has been witnessed under President Roosevelt an exclusiveness, a rigor of etiquette, and a display of swords and gold braid such as none of his predecessors ever dreamed of."

As the theatrical gestures at TR's Inauguration make plain, he was one of the most flagrant showmen ever to tread the Washington boards. He had a genius for dramatic entrances—and always was sure the spotlight was trained his way before he made one. The first thing he asked at Buffalo was, "Where are all the newspapermen?" Only three reporters were present. His secretary explained that there was no room for more. Ignoring him, TR sent out for the rest of the press corps. Two dozen

scribes came joyfully crowding in, and the subsequent proceedings were reported to the nation with a wealth of detail.

Here again we see a pattern of presidential performance developing. The exaggerated concern for the rights of reporters, the carefully staged gestures (so easy to write up, such fun to read about!)—it was as if he sensed right away that a tame press, and an infatuated public, were his surest guarantees of political security. To win election in his own right in 1904—his overriding ambition for the next three years—he would have to awake these two sleeping giants and enlist their aid in moral warfare against his political opponents, notably Senator Mark Hanna. (Hanna was chairman of the Republican National Committee and the obvious choice to take over McKinley's government after "that damned cowboy," as he called TR, had filled in as interim caretaker.)

The new President accordingly took his case straight to the press and the public. Both instantly fell in love with him. Neither seemed to notice that administratively and legislatively he accomplished virtually nothing in his first year in office. As David S. Barry of the *Sun* wrote, "Roosevelt's personality was so fascinating, so appealing to the popular fancy, so overpowering, so alive, and altogether so unique that . . . it overshadowed his public acts; that is, the public was more interested in him, and the way he did things . . . than they were about what he did."

This does not mean that TR managed, or even tried, to please all the people all the time. He was quite ready to antagonize a large minority in order to win the approval of a small majority. The swords had hardly stopped rattling on the top of McKinley's coffin when the following press release was issued: "Mr. Booker T. Washington of Tuskegee, Alabama, dined with the President last evening." Now this release, arguably the shortest and most explosive ever put out by the White House, has always been assumed to be a reluctant confirmation of the discovery of a reporter combing TR's guest book. Actually the President himself issued it, at two o'clock in the morning—that is, just in time for maximum exposure in the first edition of the newspapers. By breakfast time white

This famous photograph of Theodore Roosevelt was taken in 1912. The mustache and toothy grin, the laughing eyes crinkled shut behind wire-rimmed glasses, have become caricature symbols of TR that we recognize easily in our own day. Yet they are equally evidence of the personal charm and self-confidence that were the key to TR's enormous popularity, a popularity that, when combined with his aggression, his pride, and his patriotism, made him a successful president. (Brown Brothers)

sent his invitation to Washington, another motive was simply to stamp a bright, clear, first impression of himself upon the public imagination. "I," he seemed to be saying, "am a man *aggressive* enough to challenge a hundred-year prejudice, *righteous* enough to do so for moral reasons, and *proud* enough to advertise the fact."

Again and again during the next seven years, he reinforced these perceptions of his personality. He aggressively prosecuted J. P. Morgan, Edward H. Harriman, and John D. Rockefeller (the holy trinity of American capitalism) in the Northern Securities antitrust case, threw the Monroe Doctrine at Kaiser Wilhelm's feet like a token of war in the Caribbean, rooted out corruption in his own administration, and crushed Hanna's 1904 presidential challenge by publicly humiliating the Senator when he was running for reelection in 1903. He righteously took the side of the American worker and the American consumer against big business in the great anthracite [coal] strike [in Pennsylvania], proclaimed the vanity of muckrake journalists, forced higher ethical standards upon the food and drug industry, ordered the dishonorable discharge of 160 Negro soldiers [charged with rioting and shooting in "the Brownsville Affair" in Texas], and to quote Mark Twain, "dug so many tunnels under the Constitution that the transportation facilities enjoyed by that document are rivalled only by the City of New York."

For example, when the anthracite strike began to drag into the freezing fall of 1902, TR's obvious sympathy for the miners, and for millions of Americans who could not afford the rise in fuel prices, began to worry conservative members of Congress. One day Representative James E. Watson was horrified to hear that the President had decided to send federal troops in to reopen the anthracite mines on grounds of general hardship. Watson rushed round to the White House. "What about the Constitution of the United States?" he pleaded. "What about seizing private property for public purposes without the due processes of law?"

TR wheeled around, shook Watson by the shoulder, and roared, "*To hell with the Constitution when the*

supremacists all over the South were gagging over their grits at such headlines as ROOSEVELT DINES A NIGGER, and PRESIDENT PROPOSES TO CODDLE THE SONS OF HAM. This was the first time that a President had ever entertained a black man in the first house of the land. The public outcry was deafening—horror in the South, acclamation in the North—but overnight 9,000,000 Negroes, hitherto loyal to Senator Hanna, trooped into the Rooseveltian camp. TR never felt the need to dine a black man again.

Although we may have no doubt he had the redistribution of Southern patronage in mind when he *people want coal!*" Remarks like that caused old Joe Cannon to sigh, "Roosevelt's got no more respect for the Constitution than a tomcat has for a marriage license."

Pride, both in himself and his office, was particularly noticeable in TR's second term, the so-called imperial years, when Henry James complained, "Theodore Rex is distinctly tending—or trying to make a court." But this accusation was not true. Although the Roosevelts entertained much more elaborately than any of their predecessors, they confined their pomp and protocol to occasions of state. At times, indeed, they were remarkable for the all-American variety of their guests. On any given day one might find a Rough Rider, a poet, a British viscount, a wolf hunter, and a Roman Catholic cardinal at the White House table, each being treated with the gentlemanly naturalness which was one of TR's most endearing traits. His pride manifested itself in things like his refusal to address foreign monarchs as "Your Majesty," in his offer to mediate the Russo-Japanese War (no American President had yet had such global presumptions), and, when he won the Nobel Peace Prize for successfully bringing the war to a conclusion, in refusing to keep a penny of the forty-thousand-dollar prize money. This was by no means an easy decision, because TR could have used the funds: he spent all his presidential salary on official functions and was not himself a wealthy man. He confessed he was tempted to put the Nobel money into a trust for his children, but decided it belonged to the United States.

Pride and patriotism were inseparable in Theodore Roosevelt's character; indeed, if we accept Lord Morely's axiom that he "was" America, they may be considered as complementary characteristics. And neither of them was false. Just as he was always willing to lose a political battle in order to win a political war, so in diplomatic negotiations was he sedulous to allow his opponents the chance to save face—take all the glory of settlement if need be—as long as the essential victory was his.

As I have noted earlier, TR's militarism did not loom large during his Presidency. The organizational structure of the U.S. Army was revamped in such a way as to strengthen the powers of the Commander in Chief, but Secretary of war Elihu Root takes credit for that. TR can certainly take the credit for expanding the American Navy from fifth to second place in the world during his seven and a half years of power—an amazing achievement, but quite in keeping with his policy, inherited from Washington, that "to be prepared for war is the most effectual means to promote peace." The gunboat TR sent to Panama in 1903 was the only example of him shaking a naked mailed fist in the face of a weaker power; for the rest of the time he kept that fist sheathed in a velvet glove. The metaphor of velvet on iron, incidentally, was TR's own; it makes a refreshing change from the Big Stick.

If I may be permitted a final metaphor of my own, I would like to quote one from *The Rise of Theodore Roosevelt* in an attempt to explain why, on the whole, TR's character shows to better advantage as President than in his years out of power. "The man's personality was cyclonic, in that he tended to become unstable in times of low pressure." The slightest rise in the barometer outside, and his turbulence smoothed into a whir of coordinated activity, while a core of stillness developed within. Under maximum pressure Roosevelt was sunny, calm, and unnaturally clear. This explains why the first Roosevelt era was a period of fair weather. Power became Theodore Roosevelt, and absolute power became him best of all. He loved being President and was so good at his job that the American people loved him for loving it. TR genuinely dreaded having to leave the White House, and let us remember that a third term was his for the asking in 1908. But his knowledge that power corrupts even the man who most deserves it, his reverence for the Washingtonian principle that power must punctually revert to those whose gift it is, persuaded him to make this supreme sacrifice in his prime. The time would come, not many years hence, when fatal insolence tempted him to renege on his decision. That is another story. But the self denial that he exercised in 1908 gives us one more reason to admire Old Fifty-seven Varieties.

QUESTIONS TO CONSIDER

1 How would you describe Theodore Roosevelt's character and personality? To what extent was he shaped by the era in which he lived? What is your impression of his intellectual capabilities?

2 Morris suggests that TR's presidency was stamped by his four most salient character traits or governing impulses: aggression, self-righteousness, pride, and militarism. What does Morris see as the sources of each of these characteristics? How did each characteristic affect TR's presidency? How much did TR's charm influence his presidency and his effect on Americans?

3 What does Morris mean when he says that Theodore Roosevelt's presidency was a performance?

Do you think it was a successful or unsuccessful show, by and large? Was TR any the less sincere for all his showmanship?

4 In what ways do you think TR's was a potentially dangerous or risky personality for a president? How, for example, did he regard the Constitution when it got in the way of things he thought were important?

5 Can you think of any presidents to compare with Theodore Roosevelt? Could a Theodore Roosevelt be elected in the political climate of the twenty-first century? How would a modern-day electorate feel about a president with such an impenetrable ego or one who behaved with such highhandedness as Roosevelt exhibited in his gunboat diplomacy off Colombia? You may want to keep Theodore Roosevelt in mind when you read about Ronald Reagan in selection 29.

11 African Americans and the Quest for Civil Rights

SEAN DENNIS CASHMAN

During the Progressive era, African Americans launched a protest movement against legally enforced segregation and the whole philosophy of white supremacy and black inferiority that underlay it. Segregation was worse in the South, because that was where most African Americans lived. Indeed, by the beginning of the twentieth century, southern whites had turned their region into a bastion of white supremacy and racial discrimination. A farrago of state constitutional amendments, Jim Crow laws, and local ordinances shackled African Americans to the bottom of the South's racist social order. African Americans could not vote or run for political office; they had to attend separate and inferior "colored" schools, sit in segregated waiting rooms in southern depots, ride in segregated trains and streetcars, drink from separate water fountains, relieve themselves in separate restrooms, lodge only in "colored" hotels, and face humiliating "Whites Only" signs at public swimming pools, golf courses, and libraries. In Jackson, Mississippi, they were buried in a separate cemetery. Woe to African Americans who tried to cross the color line: they could expect a gunshot, incineration, or a lynching. Indeed, lynchings multiplied at an alarming rate in the Deep South. Meanwhile, in Plessy v. Ferguson (1896) the United States Supreme Court upheld "separate but equal" accommodations in Dixie. Never mind that facilities for African Americans were almost never equal to those for whites; the Court ruled that no discrimination was involved. Justice John Marshall Harlan, however, issued a ringing dissent, arguing that "our Constitution is color-blind, and neither knows nor tolerates classes among citizens."

Initially, especially in the South, African Americans submitted to living as third-class citizens in a white-dominated country. In that period of reaction, there was little else they could do. Most followed the advice of Booker T. Washington, the head of all-black Tuskegee Institute in Alabama, who had been born a slave. In 1895, in Atlanta, Washington urged African Americans to forget about political and social equality for now and to learn skills and trades to support themselves. By imitating white standards and values, perhaps they could earn white people's friendship and preserve racial peace. But as Martin Luther King Jr. noted later, it was "an obnoxious negative peace" in which "the Negro's mind and soul were enslaved."

In the following selection, historian Sean Dennis Cashman describes in lucid and eloquent detail what black Americans faced in this period of racial reaction. He offers trenchant insights, based on the best of modern scholarship, into the origins of segregation, and explains the two very different reactions to it by Booker T. Washington, a southern black, and W. E. B. Du Bois, a northern African American, who became Washington's ideological adversary. Du Bois exhorted the blacks' "Talented Tenth" to take the lead and find solutions to the misery of the black masses. In 1905, against a backdrop of spiraling racial violence, Du Bois met with a small band of well-educated, bold, and unhappy African American professionals and businessmen in the city of Niagara Falls, Canada (the blacks could not stay in a hotel on the American side of the falls). They drafted a blazing manifesto demanding justice and equality for African Americans. The Niagara platform became the blueprint for the National Association for the Advancement of Colored People (NAACP), established in 1909 in the centennial of Abraham Lincoln's birth. Du Bois and seven other Niagara leaders joined nineteen white racial progressives on the NAACP's original board (the racial imbalance reflected the paternalistic attitudes of the white founders). The first nationwide organization dedicated to gaining African Americans their rights as citizens, the NAACP concentrated on legal action and court battles. It won its first victory in 1915—the same year the twentieth-century Ku Klux Klan was founded on Stone Mountain in Georgia—when the United States Supreme Court outlawed the grandfather clause to the state constitutions of Oklahoma and Maryland. Those clauses had prohibited African Americans from voting unless their grandfathers had voted in 1860.

In Cashman's stirring pages, you will meet Du Bois and other significant figures who launched the "Negro rebellion" in Progressive America.

GLOSSARY

ACCOMMODATION Doctrine preached by Booker T. Washington calling for southern blacks to forget about racial equality, to accommodate themselves to the South's racist social order, and to learn skills and trades to support themselves.

ATLANTA COMPROMISE Speaking in Atlanta in 1895, Washington propounded the doctrine of accommodation, which later became known as the "Atlanta Compromise."

BROWN, HENRY BILLINGS Justice of the Supreme Court in the case of *Plessy* v. *Ferguson* (1896), who spoke for the majority in ruling that "if one race be inferior to the other socially, the Constitution of the United States cannot put them upon the same plane."

BROWNSVILLE "RIOT" Three companies of the black Twenty-Fifth Regiment of the U.S. Army allegedly rioted in Brownsville, Texas, in 1906 after some of the soldiers had retaliated against whites for racial insults. The charges were unproved, but President Theodore Roosevelt "arbitrarily" discharged the three companies in question.

***BUCHANAN* v. *WARLEY* (1917)** The United States Supreme Court unanimously held that "all citizens of the United States shall have the same right in every state and territory, as is enjoyed by white citizens thereof, to inherit, purchase, lease, sell, hold and convey real and personal property." See also *Corrigan* v. *Buckley*.

CORRIGAN v. BUCKLEY (1926)   The *Buchanan* v. *Warley* decision resulted in "a spate of private restrictive covenants under which residents agreed to sell or rent their property to individuals of one race only." The court upheld the practice in *Corrigan* v. *Buckley*.

DU BOIS, W. E. B.   Reclusive professor of economics and sociology at Atlanta University who emerged as the leader of the African American elite, created the "myth of the Talented Tenth," helped found the NAACP, and served as first editor of the NAACP's official publication, *Crisis;* by his own reckoning, he was "the main factor in revolutionizing the attitude of the American Negro toward caste" between 1910 and 1930.

GRADUALISM   Another name for Booker T. Washington's doctrine of accommodation to the racial status quo; it stressed "patience, proposed submission, and emphasized material progress."

GREAT MIGRATION   During the 1910s and 1920s, blacks by the tens of thousands migrated from the South to the North. "The exodus," writes Cashman, "was mainly spontaneous and largely unorganized; whatever the personal motives for individual moves, the collective motive was bad treatment in the South."

HARLAN, JOHN MARSHALL   Justice of the United States Supreme Court who dissented from the majority decision in *Plessy* v. *Ferguson,* arguing that "our Constitution is color-blind, and neither knows nor tolerates classes among citizens."

JEFFERIES, JAMES J.   When black boxer Jack Johnson won the heavyweight title in 1908, white racists persuaded former world champion James J. Jefferies to come out of retirement and fight Johnson for the title. Johnson whipped this "great white hope" in Reno, Nevada, in 1912.

JIM CROW LAWS   Southern state and local laws that enforced segregation and discrimination against African Americans. They were called Jim Crow laws from the name of a song sung by Thomas Rice in a black minstrel show before the Civil War.

JOHNSON, JACK   An African American from Galveston, Texas, who won the heavyweight boxing title in 1908 and by doing so "aroused deep consternation throughout the white community." An excellent film about his life, *The Great White Hope* (1970) stars James Earl Jones as the legendary black boxer who was "the greatest heavyweight of his time."

NIAGARA MOVEMENT   In 1905, Du Bois and a cadre of other angry and unhappy black leaders met on the Canadian side of Niagara Falls and drafted a searing manifesto demanding justice and equality for African Americans. The Niagara platform became a blueprint for the National Association for the Advancement of Colored People (NAACP), established in 1909. It was the first nationwide organization dedicated to gaining African Americans their rights as citizens.

PLESSY v. FERGUSON (1896)   Decision of the United States Supreme Court that upheld "separate but equal" accommodations for whites and African Americans.

POLL TAX   A southern state tax on the right to vote, aimed at proscribing the poorer Negroes.

THE SOULS OF BLACK FOLK (1903)   Du Bois's brilliant collection of essays that summoned African Americans to resist Booker T. Washington's doctrine of accommodation.

TILLMAN, BEN "PITCHFORK"   Rabidly white supremacist governor of South Carolina and U. S. Senator.

TROTTER, WILLIAM   African American real-estate broker who in 1901 founded the *Boston Guardian* and devoted himself to destroying the teachings of Booker T. Washington.

VILLARD, OSWALD GARRISON   Grandson of William Lloyd Garrison, the great nineteenth-century abolitionist, Villard was a white journalist and pacifist who helped found the NAACP and served as chairman of its board.

WASHINGTON, BOOKER T.   Between 1903 and 1915, the champion of accommodation, who had once dined with President Theodore Roosevelt, found himself under a zealous ideological attack by Du Bois, Trotter, and other members of the radical African American elite.

WILLARD, JESS   Another "great white hope" chosen to defeat black heavyweight champion Jack Johnson, Willard was a former cowboy known for his strength. In a title fight in Havana, Cuba, in 1915, Willard knocked out a poorly conditioned Johnson, winning the title for the white race.

WILSON, WOODROW   President of the United States (1913–1921); his was "the most racist administration since the Civil War." Encouraged by his first wife and his postmaster general, Wilson "allowed systematic segregation in government offices, shops, restrooms, and lunchrooms. African Americans were even removed from appointments they had previously held."

The story of African-Americans and their quest for civil rights in the twentieth century . . . is a story with deep resonances. It is about nothing less than the transformation of African-American citizens' place in American society—constitutional, social and cultural—and it tells us something of the transformations white society had to ask of itself.

In a century where one of the primary themes of art has been the relationship of the individual and society, the continuously shifting fortunes of African-American citizens in American society have proved fertile subjects for argument and discussion. Moreover, the experience of African-Americans makes a stark comment on a central paradox of American history—how a nation composed of such diverse ethnic groups and beliefs could endure and survive. Thus novelist James Baldwin declared, "The story of the Negro in America is the story of America, or, more precisely, it is the story of Americans." His most fundamental point seems to have been that, as the African-American experience moved from slavery to incarceration to freedom and citizenship, African-Americans were, ironically enough, especially privileged to articulate the problems and preoccupations of men and women in modern society. . . .

The original circumstances for the development of a civil rights movement to restore their due dignity to African-American citizens had not been promising at the turn of the century and for several decades thereafter. Of the total American population of 76,094,000 in 1900, 8,833,000 were African-Americans—about 11.5 percent of the whole. Over 85 percent of them lived in the South—the eleven states of the old Confederacy and five others, Oklahoma and Kentucky to the west and Delaware, Maryland, West Virginia, and the District of Columbia to the north. Of the total population of 24,524,000 of this "Census South," 7,923,000 were African-Americans. Thus, whereas the ratio of African-Americans to whites

across the country as a whole was, approximately, one in nine, in the South it was one in three. In two states, Mississippi and South Carolina, they predominated.

The abolition of slavery and the destruction of the rebel Confederacy in the Civil War (1861–1865) had led to the granting of equal social and political rights to African-Americans i the period of Reconstruction (1865–1877). The Thirteenth Amendment (1865) proscribed slavery. The first section of the Fourteenth Amendment (1866) defined American citizens as all those born or naturalized in the United States. It enjoined states from abridging their rights to life, liberty, property, and process of law. The second section of the amendment threatened to reduce proportionately the representation in Congress of any state denying the suffrage to adult males. Congress determined to protect African-American suffrage in the South by the Fifteenth Amendment (1869–1870), according to which the right to vote was not to be denied "on account of race, color, or previous condition of servitude." Yet forty years later these rights had been assailed or eroded by white racists. The abject position of African-Americans was such that historian Rayford Logan in *The Betrayal of the Negro* (1954; 1969) described the turn of the century as "the nadir" of African-American history, notwithstanding the existence of slavery up to 1865.

THE TYRANT CUSTOM—RACE RELATIONS AT THEIR NADIR

The regular intimacy of contact under slavery was being superseded by a caste system with next to no sustained contact, which resulted in an inexorable gulf between African-Americans and whites. Although African-Americans were the largest of America's ethnic minorities, they were segregated in schooling, housing, and places of public accommodation, such as parks, theaters, hospitals, schools, libraries, courts, and even cemeteries. The variety and fluidity of access of the late nineteenth century were abandoned as state

Sean Dennis Cashman, "African Americans and the Quest for Civil Rights," from *African Americans and the Quest for Civil Rights, 1900–1990* (New York: New York University Press, 1991). Reprinted by permission of the New York University Press.

after state adopted rigid segregation in a series of so-called Jim Crow laws. ("Jim Crow" was the title of a minstrel song in 1830 that presented African-Americans as childlike and inferior.)

In *The Strange Career of Jim Crow* (1955) historian C. Vann Woodward argues that cast-iron segregation was a product of the late nineteenth and early twentieth centuries and that the avalanche of Jim Crow laws began when poor white farmers came to power. Moreover, a new generation of African-Americans had grown up who had never known slavery. Previously, aristocratic southerners had shown a paternalistic attitude to African-Americans, protecting them from some overt racist attacks by poor whites. They knew that they did not need segregation laws to confirm their own privileged social position. Nevertheless, none of the states passed a single comprehensive segregation law. Instead, they proceeded piecemeal over a period of thirty to fifty years. Thus South Carolina segregated the races in successive stages, beginning with trains (1898) and moving to streetcars (1905), train depots and restaurants (1906), textile plants (1915 and 1916), circuses (1917), pool halls (1924), and beaches and recreation centers (1934). Georgia began with railroads and prisons (1891) and moved to sleeping cars (1899) and, finally, pool halls (1925), but refused to segregate places of public accommodation until 1954.

Another factor in turning the tide of white resentment was the move of African-Americans to new mining and industrial communities where, for the first time, white hillbillies were not only thrown into daily contact with them but also into competition for the same low-caste jobs at rockbottom wages. For low-class whites, social segregation was a means of asserting their superiority. As C. Vann Woodward puts it in his *The Origins of the New South* (1951), "It took a lot of ritual and Jim Crow to bolster the creed of white supremacy in the bosom of a white man working for a black man's wages." The South had made sure that African-Americans were socially and academically inferior by denying them a decent education. Southern legislatures starved African-American schools of adequate funds, thereby making it impossible

for them to approach anywhere near the same standards. In 1910 the eleven southern states spent an average of $9.45 on each white pupil but only $2.90 on each African-American pupil.

The South reacted against the natural tide of resentment by African-Americans to its new restrictive policies with more repression. Mississippi was the first state effectively to disfranchise African-American citizens by a constitutional convention in 1890. It was followed by South Carolina in 1895, Louisiana in 1898, North Carolina (by an amendment) in 1900, Alabama in 1901, Virginia in 1901 and 1902, Georgia (by amendment) in 1908, and the new state of Oklahoma in 1910. Four more states achieved the same ends without amending their constitutions: Tennessee, Florida, Arkansas, and Texas. Three pernicious and sophistical arguments were advanced by the proponents of disfranchisement. The removal of the African-American vote, they said, would end corruption at elections. It would prevent African-Americans from holding the balance of power in contests between rival factions of whites. Moreover, it would oblige African-Americans to abandon their false hopes of betterment and, instead, make them accept their true social place. As a result, race relations would steadily improve.

The Mississippi Constitution of 1890 set the pattern. It required a poll tax of two dollars from prospective voters at registration. Those who intended to vote at elections had to present their receipt at the polls. Thus anyone who mislaid his receipt forfeited his vote. More insidious was the requirement that, in order to register, prospective voters had to be "able to read the Constitution, or to understand the Constitution when read." It also excluded those convicted of bribery, burglary, theft, and bigamy. Racist officials used the various ordinances to discriminate in favor of poor, illiterate whites and against African-Americans.

The ruling elites in other states approved of the new Mississippi plan and several states borrowed from one another. In so doing they improved on previous attempts to disfranchise African-Americans. For example, Louisiana believed that the understanding clause was so obviously suspect that it could be invalidated in a court case. Thus it hit on the grandfather clause as being, legally, more secure. Only those who had had a grandfather on the electoral roll of 1867 could vote.

These devices were nothing if not effective. In Louisiana, 130,344 African-Americans were registered to vote in 1890; in 1900 there were 5,320. In 1909 there were only 1,342. In Alabama there were 181,000 African-American voters in 1890; in 1900 there were three thousand. In the South as a whole African-American participation fell by 62 percent. In 1900 Ben ("Pitchfork") Tillman of South Carolina boasted on the floor of the Senate, "We have done our best. We have scratched our heads to find out how we could eliminate the last one of them. We stuffed ballot boxes. We shot them. We are not ashamed of it." Despite concessions to poor whites, white participation in elections also declined—by 26 percent. Thus while, on average, 73 percent of men voted in the 1890s, only 30 percent did so in the early 1900s. Opposition parties dwindled away and the Democrats were left undisputed champions of the South.

Social segregation was also upheld by the Supreme Court. Its most notorious decision came in *Plessy* v. *Ferguson* in 1896. Louisiana state law required "separate but equal" accommodations for African-American and white passengers on public carriers and provided a penalty for passengers sitting in the wrong car. Homer Plessy was an octoroon so pale that he usually passed for white, but when he sat in a white car he was arrested. He argued that the state law of Louisiana violated the Fourteenth and Fifteenth Amendments. Justice John Marshall Harlan of Kentucky agreed with him, maintaining. "Our constitution is color-blind and neither knows nor tolerates classes among citizens." Moreover, "What can more certainly arouse race hate, what more certainly create and perpetuate a feeling of distrust between these races, than state enactments which in fact proceed on the ground that colored citizens are so inferior and degraded that they cannot be allowed to sit in public coaches occupied by white citizens?" However, he

was overruled by the other eight justices, who approved of the doctrine of "separate but equal." Justice Henry Billings Brown of Michigan, speaking for the majority on May 18, 1896, ruled with corrosive racial candor, "If one race be inferior to the other socially, the Constitution of the United States cannot put them upon the same plane." In *Williams* v. *Mississippi* on April 25, 1898, the Court went further and approved the Mississippi plan for disfranchising African-Americans. The Court unanimously upheld the opinion of Justice Joseph McKenna that "a state does not violate the equal protection clause of the fourteenth amendment when it requires eligible voters to be able to read, write, interpret, or understand any part of the Constitution."

Edgar Gardner Murphy, a humanitarian journalist, reported in *The Basis of Ascendancy* (1909) how extremists had moved "from an undiscriminating attack upon the Negro's ballot to a like attack upon his schools, his labor, his life—from the contention that no Negro shall vote to the contention that no Negro shall learn, that no Negro shall labor, and [by implication] that no Negro shall live." The result was an "all-absorbing autocracy of race," an "absolute identification of the stronger race with the very being of the state." In 1903 analyst Charles W. Chestnutt said that "the rights of the Negroes are at a lower ebb than at any time during the thirty-five years of their freedom, and the race prejudice more intense and uncompromising."

Racist scientists tried to prove that African-Americans were inferior to whites. In 1929 Lawrence Fick in the *South African Journal of Science* declared that Africans showed "a marked inferiority" to European whites and that the number who could benefit from education was limited. Americans measured intelligence on the basis of a test first developed by Frenchman Alfred Binet in 1905 and based on the skills expected of, and acquired by, educated children from the middle class. Not surprisingly, such a test found undereducated children, whether poor white, immigrant, or African-American, less intelligent. The final, conclusive "proof" of the inferiority of African-Americans came when

African-American soldiers scored worse than whites in intelligence tests given in World War I. Subsequent investigation showed that African-Americans from the North scored higher than southern whites. Here was disturbing proof of the inferiority of southern education as a whole. . . .

BOOKER T. WASHINGTON AND W. E. B. DU BOIS

Since African-Americans were being displaced from their traditional trades and confined to menial jobs in the towns, those who did succeed in entering the worlds of business and the professions were obliged by white society to adopt its attitudes in order to retain their hard-won position. Their undeclared leader was Booker T. Washington, head of Tuskegee Industrial Institute, Alabama.

Booker Taliaferro Washington was born at Hale's Ford, Franklin County, Virginia, in 1856, the son of a white father and an African-American mother who was enslaved. At the end of the Civil War he worked in a coal mine and salt furnace at Malden, West Virginia, while he attended school. From 1872 to 1875 he studied at Hampton Institute, the Negro vocational school in Virginia, where he earned his keep by working as a janitor. He also taught school at Malden (1875–1877) and subsequently studied at Wayland Seminary, Washington, D.C. In 1879 he returned to Hampton Institute, where he was in charge of the Indian dormitory and night school. In 1881 he was selected to organize an African-American normal school at Tuskegee chartered by the Alabama legislature.

Thereafter, his name was practically synonymous with African-American education. In fact, Booker T. Washington created three major institutions: the Normal and Industrial Institute for Negroes, the college in rural Alabama devoted primarily to agricultural and technical education; the Tuskegee Machine, a lobby of African-American intellectuals, politicos, and educators and white philanthropists who supported Washington's political and economic aims; and the National Negro Business League, committed to establishing and consolidating a system of African-American entrepreneurs within the existing framework of white capitalism. Washington believed that the optimum strategy for the rural masses of African-Americans was to concentrate as much as possible on economic independence by thrift and the acquisition of property. For the time being they were to disregard disfranchisement and Jim Crow social segregation. The encouragement Washington and his school of thought gave to a new generation of African-American entrepreneurs and their clients to "buy black" and to think in terms of black nationalism allowed them to rise commercially at the expense of a different group of artisans, caterers, and porters who were essentially integrationists and who had had the lion's share of the market among African-Americans in the 1870s and 1880s.

Washington was as well known as a propagandist and polemicist as he was as an educational leader. He was invited to speak at the opening of the Cotton States and International Exposition in Atlanta on September 18, 1895, by businessmen who recognized his remarkable powers of expression. His address was one of the most effective political speeches of the Gilded Age, a model fusion of substance and style.

In what was later called the Atlanta Compromise he abandoned the postwar ideal of racial equality in favor of increased economic opportunity for African-Americans. "The wisest among my race understand that the agitation of questions of social equality is the extremist folly and that progress in the enjoyment of all the privileges that will come to us must be the result of severe and constant struggle rather than of artificial forcing." He preached patience, proposed submission, and emphasized material progress. Those African-Americans who rejected the Atlanta Compromise, such as rising activist W. E. B. Du Bois, considered his stance a capitulation to blatant racism. But Washington was telling white society exactly what it wanted to hear—that African-Americans accepted the Protestant work ethic. His most widely reported remark was a subtle metaphor about racial harmony: "In all things social we can be as separate as the fingers, yet one as the hand in all things essential to mutual progress."

Washington's emphasis on racial pride, economic progress, and industrial education encouraged white politicians and businessmen, such as steel tycoon Andrew Carnegie, to subsidize the institutions for African-Americans that he recommended. Through his close connections with business he was able to raise the funds necessary to create the National Negro Business League in 1900. Moreover, he used money not to advance acquiescence by African-Americans but to fight segregation. Others sought a more open insistence on racial pride. In 1890 T. Thomas Fortune, a journalist of New York, persuaded forty African-American protection leagues in cities across the country to join in a national body, the Afro-American League. Historian C. Vann Woodward assesses Washington's work thus: "Washington's life mission was to find a pragmatic compromise that would resolve the antagonisms, suspicions, and aspirations of 'all three classes directly concerned—the Southern white man, the northern white man, and the Negro.' It proved, he admitted 'a difficult and at times a puzzling task.' But he moved with consummate diplomacy, trading renunciation for concession and playing sentiment against interest."

Five weeks into his presidency (1901–1909), Theodore Roosevelt invited Booker T. Washington to the White House on October 18, 1901. Roosevelt was also committed to trying to reconcile the South to the Republican party. His invitation was intended as a symbolic gesture to African-Americans and was widely interpreted as such. There was terrible logic in the subsequent outrage of racist southerners when the story broke. The New Orleans *Times-Democrat* thought Roosevelt's action mischievous: "When Mr. Roosevelt sits down to dinner with a negro, he declares that the negro is the social equal of the White Man." Senator Benjamin ("Pitchfork") Tillman, declared, "The action of President Roosevelt in entertaining that nigger will necessitate our killing a thousand niggers in the South before they will learn their place again."

Despite Washington's insistence on patience, some African-Americans began to agitate fo desegregation on trains, a prime target of the protest movement that was the forerunner of civil rights. They reckoned that railroads would realize that it was more expensive to have segregated seating and would thus yield, if only for the sake of economy. In 1898 the Afro-American League called for a boycott of trains in protest of Jim Crow laws. In 1904 the Maryland Suffrage League began campaigning against the new Jim Crow law there and financed a successful lawsuit against segregated travel in 1905. Also in 1905, the Georgia Equal Rights League declared that African-Americans should be able "to travel in comfort and decency and receive a just equivalent for our money, and yet we are the victims of the most unreasonable sort of caste legislation." In 1909 the National Negro Conference denounced segregation and the oppression of African-Americans. Whites were taken aback by the effectiveness of boycotts when African-Americans either simply stopped using white-owned transport or established small companies of their own. White streetcar companies either ended segregation or went out of business, such as the streetcar company in Richmond, Virginia. However, the wave of protests was short lived.

Washington's approach of so-called gradualism could be justified as a necessary complement to the fearful atmosphere of prejudice and violence in the South. However, African-American intellectuals in the North grew impatient with his time-serving and ambiguity. William Trotter, son of Cleveland's recorder of deeds and a graduate of Harvard, founded the most vehemently critical paper, the *Boston Guardian,* in 1901, and roundly abused Washington for his association with Roosevelt, calling him a "self seeker" and a "skulking coward." Trotter criticized Washington at the 1903 annual convention of the Afro-American Council and created uproar at a meeting of the Boston Business League later the same year when he heckled Washington as he tried to speak. The uproar resulted in "the Boston riot" that ended with the imprisonment of Trotter for thirty days for having disturbed the peace. Nevertheless, Trotter and his creations were radical, vocal forces in the struggle for civil rights.

The publication of *The Souls of Black Folk* by W. E. B. Du Bois in 1903 solidified protest around a new spokesman. William Edward Burghardt Du Bois was born in Great Barrington, Massachusetts, in 1868, graduated from Fisk and Harvard, and attended the University of Berlin. After returning to America in 1894, he taught at Wilberforce University, Ohio, and Pennsylvania University before becoming professor of sociology at Atlanta. A handsome and invariably immaculately dressed man, Du Bois was also a creative writer who produced two novels, *The Quest of the Silver Fleece* (1911) and *The Dark Princess* (1928), and two volumes of essays and poems, *Dark Water* (1920) and *The Gift of Black Folk* (1924). One of Du Bois's early supporters, James Weldon Johnson, said of *The Souls of Black Folk* that "it had a greater effect upon and within the Negro race than any single book published in the country since *Uncle Tom's Cabin*." One of the essays was a withering attack on what Du Bois considered Washington's acceptance of the heinous doctrine of racial inferiority. Du Bois insisted on an end to accommodation: "By every civilized and peaceful method we must strive for the rights which the world accords to men."

Deeply angered by Washington's counterrevolutionary tactics and intensely hostile to the strategy of accommodation, Du Bois invited like-minded activists to a national conference at Fort Erie in July 1905 that established the Niagara Movement. This was an elite cadre of about four hundred college-educated professional people. The Niagara Movement committed itself to continuing vocal protest against "the abridgment of political and civil rights and against inequality of educational opportunity." Du Bois and others published the *Moon* and, later, the *Horizon* as unofficial journals of the movement. Nevertheless, the Niagara Movement failed to establish itself as a distinctive national voice.

Moreover, it was becoming obvious to increasing numbers of African-Americans and sympathetic whites that a policy of accommodation was futile in the face of outright racist hostility. Despite Washington's supposed influence with Roosevelt, the president arbitrarily discharged three companies of African-Americans

W. E. B. Du Bois was the foremost member of a gifted group of African American leaders during the early years of the twentieth century. A "child of the black elite" and highly educated, with a bachelor's degree from Fisk and a Ph.D. from Harvard, he played a major role in the founding of the National Association for the Advancement of Colored People and raised the "black protest movement" to a new level of effectiveness. (Schomburg Center for Research in Black Culture, The New York Public Library; Astor, Lenox and Tilden Foundations)

of the Twenty-fifth Regiment on an unproven charge of rioting in Brownsville, Texas, on August 14, 1906, after some soldiers had retaliated against racial insults. For their part, Roosevelt and his successor, William Howard Taft, (1909–1913), had to hold together a diverse coalition of Republicans that included a section of gross racial bigots, the lily-whites, who wanted to establish an all-white Republican party in the South. To appease this faction both presidents limited the number of federal appointments of African-Americans, thereby contributing to racial prejudice.

JACK JOHNSON AND THE GREAT WHITE HOPE

White southerners came to accept without question the racist orthodoxy of such men as educator Thomas Pearce Bailey, as expressed in his article "Race Orthodoxy in the South" for *Neale's Monthly Magazine* (1903). He set forth a creed of fifteen points, including such statements as "the white race must dominate"; "The Teutonic peoples stand for race purity"; "The Negro is inferior and will remain so"; "Let there be such industrial education of the Negro as will best fit him to serve the white man"; and "Let the lowest white man count for more than the highest Negro." Even environmentalists who argued that nurture, rather than nature, determined human behavior were reluctant to challenge popular stereotypes. Progressive intellectual John R. Commons expressed the dominant reformist view in 1907. He claimed that African-Americans had opportunities "not only on equal terms, but actually on terms of preference over the whites." Their failure to rise "is recognized even by their partisans as something that was inevitable in the nature of the race at that stage of its development."

However, arguments about genetic inferiority were silenced when boxer Jack Johnson, an African-American and former stevedore from Galveston, Texas, won the world heavyweight boxing title from Canadian Tommy Burns in Sydney, Australia, on Boxing Day, December 26, 1908. Johnson's victory aroused deep consternation throughout the white community. Racists in Congress were so disturbed by the defeat of a white man by an African-American that they proposed, and had passed, a law forbidding the interstate transportation of motion picture films showing prize fights. Immediately after Johnson's sensational victory, former world champion James J. Jeffries, then living in retirement on a farm in California, was urged to come out of retirement to regain the title for the white race. He was eventually persuaded to do so and was defeated in a fifteen-round match at Reno, Nevada, on July 4, 1912.

Johnson was the greatest heavyweight of his time, standing over six feet tall and weighing over two hundred pounds. He moved with the swiftness and grace of a panther. He was widely known for his good nature, his "golden smile," which revealed numerous crowned teeth, and his badinage while in the ring. During the bout with Jefferies, Johnson stopped briefly to lean on the shoulders of his weary opponent and jeered at another, former fighter, Jim Corbett, at the ringside, saying, "Jim this big bum can't fight any better than you could." However, when a blow reached Johnson that really told, his veneer of good nature vanished and his killer instinct surfaced. He gloried in adulation and enjoyed provoking his numerous white critics. Johnson's prowess was a symbol of strength to African-Americans and his success could make him a rallying point for solidarity among them. In fact, he was inaugurating a mighty tradition of powerful African-American heavyweight champions extending through Joe Louis in the 1930s to Muhammad Ali in the 1960s and 1970s and then to Mike Tyson in the 1980s.

In the 1910s Jack Johnson's numerous white enemies determined to find a white challenger who could defeat him and restore the myth of white supremacy. The great white hope turned out to be Jess Willard of Kansas, a former cowpuncher who was known for feats of strength such as bending a silver dollar between his fingers. However, he was a mediocre fighter. Eventually Johnson, sated with European night life and adulation, became homesick and was keen to accept the suggestion of promoters that he should return and fight Willard. The venue would be Havana, Cuba. When Johnson arrived in poor condition, he disappointed his backers by doing next to no training and spending his days driving about the city with his white wife. The fight was held on April 5, 1915, with soldiers surrounding the stadium in order to prevent racial violence. The first twenty-two rounds were dull but in the twenty-third Johnson sank to the floor—though whether from a blow by Willard or from sunstroke, opinions differ. Thus fell the first of the great African-American stars of the worlds of entertainment and sports. Johnson returned to Chicago, attended subsequent boxing contests in which champions won millions, and in the 1930s became conductor of his own jazz orchestra.

THE NAACP AND THE EARLY CIVIL RIGHTS MOVEMENT

Not surprisingly, given the prevailing atmosphere of hysteria stroked by institutional racism and the pseudoscientific jargon of prejudiced scientists, African-Americans became helpless victims of race riots instigated by malicious, scared whites, such as the one in Atlanta, Georgia, in 1906, in which ten African-Americans were killed before martial law restored order. In 1908, after a white women claimed she had been raped, whites invaded the African-American section of Springfield, Illinois, lynched two African-Americans, and flogged several others. The white assailants escaped without punishment. However, on this occasion the North was influenced by an article denouncing the outrage, "Race War in the North," written by a southern socialist, William English Walling. Together with settlement workers Mary White Ovington and Dr. Henry Moskowitz, Walling persuaded Oswald Garrison Villard, editor of the *New York Evening Post* and grandson of the abolitionist leader [William Lloyd Garrison], to call a conference on race in 1909, the centenary of the birth of Abraham Lincoln.

At a meeting in New York on May 31 and June 1, 1909, African-American and white American radicals proposed a new national organization to protect the rights of African-Americans and a similar conference in 1910 established the National Association for the Advancement of Colored People (NAACP), with its declared goal of "equal rights and opportunities for all." Under its first president, Moorfield Storey, the NAACP formed several hundred branches. Under the editorship of W. E. B. Du Bois, The NAACP journal, the *Crisis,* reached a circulation of one hundred thousand. Du Bois's own column, "As

the Crow Flies," attacked white racism. Together with the *Chicago Defender,* the *Pittsburgh Courier,* and the *Baltimore African-American,* the *Crisis* made an ever-increasing spectrum of literate African-Americans aware of their national responsibilities and what the nation owed them.

The NAACP's distinctive strategy was litigation to challenge racist laws. For example, in 1917 the NAACP challenged a statute of Louisville, Kentucky, requiring "the use of separate blocks for residence, places of abode, and places of assembly by white and colored people respectively." Moorfield Storey took the case to the Supreme Court at a time when it was, in the terms of analyst Richard Kluger, peopled by men of Paleolithic perspective, notable Justices Willis van Devanter and James Clark McReynolds. Nevertheless, in the case of *Buchanan* v. *Warley* the Court unanimously, and surprisingly, decided on November 5, 1917, that "all citizens of the United States shall have the same right in every state and territory, as is enjoyed by white citizens thereof, to inherit, purchase, lease, sell, hold and convey real and personal property." However, the *Buchanan* decision resulted in a spate of private restrictive covenants under which residents agreed to sell or rent their property to individuals of one race only. The Court subsequently upheld this pernicious practice in *Corrigan* v. *Buckley* in 1926, maintaining that civil rights were not protected against discrimination by individuals.

Another sequence of NAACP cases tested the constitutionality of disfranchisement. In 1910 Oklahoma introduced its own grandfather clause to prevent African-Americans from voting. Two of its election officials, Guinn and Beal, were prosecuted by the NAACP for carrying out the new state law. When the officials were found guilty of violating the Fifteenth Amendment by a district court, they appealed to the Supreme Court. However, in the case of *Guinn* v. *United States* (1915), the Court unanimously declared that the grandfather clause was "an unconstitutional evasion of the 15th Amendment guarantee that states would not deny citizens the right to vote because of their

The 369th infantry regiment proudly displays the Croix de Guerre *medals won for bravery in World War I. A grateful French government had bestowed this honor on them. Fighting in* segregated units *"to make the world safe for democracy," African American troops returned home only to face continued racial prejudice and discrimination. (National Archives)*

race." On the same day the Court ruled by seven votes to one in the case of *United States* v. *Mosely* that it "upheld congressional power to relegate elections tainted with fraud and corruption." It seemed the law was on the side of civil rights for African-Americans.

Oklahoma reacted quickly. It passed a new election law, providing permanent registration for those entitled to vote according to the unconstitutional law and allowing African-Americans only twelve days to register or to be disqualified from voting for life. The new law was not contested in the Supreme Court for another twenty-two years. . . .

THE GREAT MIGRATION

The way racist whites openly flouted the basic rights of African-American citizens was now so flagrant as to be scarcely credible in a society moving through a phase of self-styled progressivism. For African-Americans, the notion of progressive reform was a joke in very bad taste. Ironically, the African-American community, like the white, was stronger economically than ever. In 1913 African-Americans owned 550,000 houses, worked 937 farms, ran forty thousand businesses, and attended forty thousand African-American churches. There were thirty-five thousand African-American teachers, and 1.7 million African-American students attended public schools.

The accession of Woodrow Wilson to the presidency (1913–1921) resulted in the most racist administration since the Civil War. Southern Democrats were dominant in Congress, the White House, and the Supreme Court. African-American needs were peripheral to Wilson's interests. Inasmuch as he had views on the subject, they were in the tradition of southern paternalism. As a result, and spurred on by his first wife, Ellen Axson Wilson, he acquiesced in the unrest of segregation. His postmaster general, Albert S. Burleson, introduced the subject of segregation at an early cabinet meeting, suggesting separation to reduce friction between white and African-American railway clerks. Convinced by this argument, Wilson and the cabinet allowed systematic segregation in government offices, shops, rest rooms, and lunchrooms. African-Americans were even removed from appointments they had previously held. The sum total of the Wilson policies was that only eight African-Americans out of thirty working in the federal government in Washington retained their appointments.

Emboldened, racists began to demand that Congress legislate for segregation throughout the civil service, forbid interracial marriages, and even repeal the Fourteenth and Fifteenth Amendments. The South extended its segregation to public transport. Thus, African-Americans were prevented from using taxis reserved for whites in the state of Mississippi in 1922 and in the cities of Jacksonville in 1929 and Birmingham in 1930.

Such discrimination, important in itself, had more momentous consequences because of the contemporary exodus of African-Americans [to the North from the South, where 85 percent of African-Americans lived]. For the 1910s and 1920s were also years of the Great Migration. The immediate reason for the exodus was the industrial requirements of World War I. Whites were being drawn increasingly into the armed services and newly created war industries. However, the war prevented European immigrants from coming

to America and taking their place as laborers. Thus, in 1915 agents for northern employers began recruiting African-American labor from the South. However, at least four times as many African-Americans went north on word of mouth than did so at the prompting of labor agents. The exodus was mainly spontaneous and largely unorganized; whatever the personal motives for individual moves, the collective motive was bad treatment in the South. The Great Migration was facilitated by railroad transportation and continued after the war was over. In sum, the South lost 323,000 African-Americans in the 1910s and 615,000 in the 1920s—about 8.2 percent of its African-American population. At the outset white attitudes in both the North and the South to the migration were somewhat ambivalent. As time went on, they became alarmist: northerners resented another ethnic disruption following in the wake of the new immigration; southerners did not want to lose their ready supply of cheap labor. Some southern communities passed laws to prevent African-Americans from leaving. This happened in Montgomery, Savannah, Greenville, and elsewhere. Charleston editor William Watts Ball commented ruefully in 1925, "We have plenty of Southerners whose disposition is identical with that of the ancient Egyptians—they would chase the Negroes to the Red Sea to bring them back." However, nothing could reverse the tide.

Whereas the Great Migration is often interpreted as part of the inevitable progress of African-Americans to full citizenship because they were less likely to encounter political disfranchisement in the North than the South, some, such as playwright August Wilson, believe that it represented an incorrect cultural choice for African-Americans intent on capturing their legacy. In April 1990 he told the *New York Times,* "We were land-based agrarian people from Africa. We were uprooted from Africa, and we spend over 200 years developing our culture as Black Americans. Then we left the South. We uprooted ourselves and attempted to transplant this culture to the pavements of the industrialized North. And it was a transplant that did not take. I think if we had stayed in the South, we would have been a stronger people. And because the connection between the South of the '20s, '30s and '40s has been broken, it's very difficult to understand who we are."

Southern blacks who migrated North found to their dismay that the North was hardly the promised land, and migrants found themselves herded into city ghettos and kept there by a host of real estate and municipal codes. Thereafter when African Americans went north, as James Baldwin observed, they did not go to New York City, they went to Harlem; they did not go to Chicago, they went to the South Side; they did not go to Los Angeles, they went to Watts. As historian Leronne Bennett Jr. wrote, "Real estate became the principal dynamic in the ensemble of northern race relations," and the walls of segregation erected across the urban North in turn produced a new anger and militancy, indeed "a new and different black world." Black Muslim leaders Malcolm X and Louis Farrakhan (Louis X), among others, would be furious products of the northern black ghetto.

QUESTIONS TO CONSIDER

1 What were the basic principles and ideals of W. E. B. Du Bois, and how did they contrast with the program called for by Booker T. Washington?

To which segments of the black and white population did each of them direct his concern, and to whom did it appeal?

2 What were the fundamental goals of the Niagara Movement? What did the movement accomplish, and what undermined it?

3 Why was Jack Johnson an important figure for black Americans? Why did he cause great consternation among white supremacists?

4 What is the NAACP? Who were its founders and what were their intentions? What methods did the NAACP use to gain advances for African-Americans?

5 What was the Great Migration? Do you think it was beneficial for black Americans to move north? What is the legacy of the Great Migration for the northern cities?

6 Consider America's social problems concerning race. What positive changes have there been since the Progressive era? What problems remain? Why do you think the issue of race continues to be a major problem in America? Can the problem be solved?

PART SIX

The Struggle for Justice at Home and Abroad (1914–1920)

12 Suffragists' Storm Over Washington

WILLIAM LAVENDER AND MARY LAVENDER

The women's rights movement actually began back in the Jacksonian period, when American women first organized to break the shackles of strict domesticity and to expand their rights and opportunities. Led by two brilliant crusaders, Elizabeth Cady Stanton and Susan B. Anthony, the early feminists rejected the notion of female inferiority and advocated full sexual equality with men. They demanded equal access to education, the trades, and the professions, and an end to the sexual double standard. They wanted the right to vote, too, not as an end in itself, but as a means of achieving their broader aim—to make women self-sufficient, equal partners with men in all areas of human enterprise.

A few feminists like Victoria Woodhull went even further than that to champion free love and licensed prostitution. That, of course, enraged the enemies of the movement, who charged that feminists were members of the lunatic fringe, out to destroy the nuclear family and wreck the moral fiber of America. As the nineteenth century drew to a close, most feminists rejected radical ideas like Woodhull's and became conspicuously conservative, placing renewed emphasis on feminine virtue, motherhood, and community service.

By 1900, a new generation of feminists had narrowed the vision of their predecessors mainly to one goal: the winning of the elective franchise. In the following selection, William and Mary Lavender recount the struggles of the indefatigable suffragists, who faced an uphill battle to gain the right to vote for women. When Woodrow Wilson, a Progressive Democrat, was elected president in 1912, the future seemed bleak indeed for the suffragists. Most Progressive reformers were male, white, and upper-middle-class and had little sympathy for equal rights for women or African Americans. The suffragists realized that they had to pressure Wilson and the other Progressives if the women's movement was ever to achieve more than token gestures. After the start of the Great War in 1914, the suffragists also faced a disapproving public, which viewed any form of protest as unpatriotic. Even so, suffragists Alice Paul and Lucy Burns continued the sisterhood of leadership that Stanton, Woodhull, and Susan B. Anthony had begun in the previous century. When Paul and Burns were unjustly imprisoned for picketing the White House, they had to endure scathing ridicule and horrible prison conditions. Still, they and their followers persevered. And they won in the end. They did so by identifying their movement with Progressivism and winning President Wilson and the entire nation to their cause. It is an inspiring story, and the Lavenders tell it brilliantly in "Suffragists' Storm Over Washington."

GLOSSARY

ANTHONY, SUSAN B.   An eloquent champion of women's rights, Anthony helped found and lead the nineteenth century women's movement. She opposed the Fifteenth Amendment to the Constitution because it did not extend the elective franchise to women. Later, Anthony received a $100 fine (which she refused to pay) for attempting to vote in the 1872 presidential election. Because of her contributions to the women's movement, the proposed constitutional amendment that would grant women the right to vote was called the Susan B. Anthony Amendment.

BURNS, LUCY   Like Alice Paul, Burns lived in England and observed the successful strategy employed by the British suffragists. Burns was more outgoing than Paul and felt comfortable participating in the street demonstrations that helped advance the women's movement in America. The notoriety associated with her imprisonment pressured the Wilson administration to support the Nineteenth Amendment.

MALONE, DUDLEY FIELD   A friend of President Wilson and counsel to the National Woman's Party, Malone resigned his position as collector of the Port of New York because of the government's harsh treatment and imprisonment of suffragists. Along with fellow attorney Matthew O'Brien, Malone defended those women who peacefully protested for the right to vote.

NATIONAL AMERICAN WOMAN SUFFRAGE ASSOCIATION (NAWSA)   Formed in 1890, NAWSA consisted mainly of middle-class women, with Susan B. Anthony and Elizabeth Cady Stanton among its early presidents. NAWSA helped influence Progressive leaders to include woman's suffrage on their agenda of reform. After the Nineteenth Amendment was ratified, NAWSA became the League of Women Voters.

NATIONAL WOMAN'S PARTY (NWP)   This organization opposed the slow and generally unsuccessful strategy of pressuring individual states to support woman's suffrage through legislative initiatives and referenda. NWP's membership was more youthful and radical than the membership of NAWSA. In later years, the NWP championed the end to all forms of legal discrimination against women, and supported the Equal Rights Amendment to the United States Constitution.

NINETEENTH AMENDMENT   Ratified in 1920, this Amendment guaranteed American women the right to vote, stating that "the right of citizens of the United States to vote shall not be denied or abridged by the United States or by any State on account of sex."

WHITTAKER, WILLIAM   Superintendent of the Workhouse for Women in Occoquan, Virginia, Whittaker was responsible for the cruel treatment of the suffragists under his care.

ZINKHAN, LOUIS   The warden in charge of the jail in Washington, D.C., Zinkhan was responsible for the inhumane conditions that suffragist prisoners had to endure.

Six well-bred women stood before a judge in the Washington, D.C., Police Court on June 27, 1917. Not thieves, drunks or prostitutes like the usual defendants there, they included a university student, an author of nursing books, a prominent campaign organizer and two former schoolteachers. All were educated, accomplished and unacquainted with criminal activity. But today they stood accused in a court of law. Their alleged offense: "obstructing traffic."

What they had actually done was to stand quietly outside the White House carrying banners urging President Woodrow Wilson to support their decades-long struggle to add one sentence to the Constitution: "The right of citizens of the United States to vote shall not be denied or abridged by the United States or by any State on account of sex."

The Susan B. Anthony Amendment was introduced in Congress in 1878. There it lay, regarded with fear and loathing, for almost 40 years. Some saw no point in women voting; with no understanding of politics, they would only vote as their menfolk told them. Others argued that after getting the vote, women would take over the government. With such opposition, the Anthony Amendment seemed doomed to lie dormant forever. The six accused of obstructing traffic that summer day in 1917 denied all charges, insisting that the crowd outside the White House had gathered only because police had announced that arrests would be made. Moreover, picketing had gone on since January without obstructing anything, and with no interference. It was, after all, entirely legal. Why the sudden crackdown now?

But the judge declared the ladies outside the White House were the "proximate cause" of the curious crowd, and must take the consequences. Besides, he added, "there are certain . . . people . . . who believe you ladies ought not have the vote."

Excerpts from this article, "Suffragists Storm Over Washington," by William Lavender and Mary Lavender are reproduced from the October 2003 issue of *American History Magazine* with the permission of PRIMEDIA Enthusiast Publications (History Group), copyright *American History Magazine.*

Unimpressed by the prisoners' spirited defense, the judge found them guilty as charged, and imposed a $25 fine or three days' imprisonment on each. Refusing to pay, which they saw as admitting guilt, they were led off unrepentant to the Washington jail.

Those six made a bit of history that day. All were members of the National Woman's Party (NWP). They were the first of a long procession of women jailed on trumped-up charges solely for demonstrating for their right to vote. NWP members came from all across the country and all levels of society, with little in common except dedication to obtaining that right. This was the exclusive goal of the NWP, whose driving force was a determined young woman named Alice Paul.

At 32, Paul was widely admired as one of the most daring and imaginative leaders the women's movement had ever seen—and just as widely denounced as a dangerous radical. The daughter of Quakers in Moorestown, N.J., she was petite, frail and soft-spoken—hardly a radical image. She never married, nor displayed romantic interest in any man or woman. All her energy was concentrated on her one obsessive passion: women's political rights. Even her closest associates never claimed to know her well, yet her magnetism inspired in them idolizing loyalty. Campaign strategy was her forte, and she planned with such military precision that some likened her to a general.

Paul arrived in Washington in December 1912 to take over the local office of the National American Woman Suffrage Association (NAWSA), headquartered in New York. Committed to a state-by-state approach, NAWSA considered the nation's capital so unimportant that the Washington office's budget for 1912 was $10. Paul was expected to raise her own operating funds.

With her came her chief assistant Lucy Burns. Tall, robust and flame-haired, at 38 the Brooklyn-born Burns was Paul's temperamental opposite, yet they complemented each other perfectly: Paul directing strategy from the background, while Burns was leading public demonstrations.

This banner-carrying woman was photographed at the gates of the White House in 1917. Later that year, forty-one women from fifteen states were arrested outside the White House for demanding the right to vote. In 1919, after women had rallied in support of President Wilson's wartime policies, he finally threw his support behind the Nineteenth Amendment. (© Bettmann/CORBIS)

In March 1913, Woodrow Wilson began his first term as president. Paul considered his support essential to the cause—but women's suffrage, it turned out, was not on this president's agenda. Repeated appeals for his support of the Anthony Amendment were just as repeatedly evaded, Wilson claiming that a president should not try to influence Congress, but should follow the dictates of his party (the Democratic Party, then dominated by arch-conservative Southerners). Women scoffed at this, since Wilson was known as an autocratic president, constantly exerting influence on

Congress even in trivial matters. But the more they pressed him, the more he resisted, and the standoff lasted throughout his first term in office.

Meanwhile, Alice Paul's Washington-based group split from NAWSA in a fundamental dispute over strategy. NAWSA's conservative leadership, committed to patient, state-by-state campaigning, disdained action on the federal level and deplored Paul's tactics as far too aggressive. Paul insisted that the snail-paced, state-by-state approach was futile; victory could come only by passage of the Anthony Amendment, and the weak-kneed Congress would never pass it without the president's support. After the rupture, the indignant parent organization distanced itself from its unruly offspring as much as possible.

Headquarters for the Washington group was the handsome Cameron House, overlooking Lafayette Square, conveniently near the White House. There, on January 9, 1917, a fateful decision was made. Hours earlier President Wilson, recently elected for a second term, had walked out on a visiting suffrage delegation after angrily repeating his refusal to endorse their cause. This most brusque dismissal yet was the last straw. After years of polite appeals, it was time for direct action.

The next morning, 12 women carrying banners on long poles left Cameron House and took up positions outside the White House gates. In their movement's traditional colors—purple, white and gold—their banners demanded: "MR. PRESIDENT, HOW LONG MUST WOMEN WAIT FOR LIBERTY?"

They returned every day, in good weather and bad, silently directing this pointed question at the grand house behind them. No one quite knew what to think. Political picketing was uncommon in those days, and by women unheard of. Some passersby gawked, some hurled angry taunts, others were merely amused. The press was sharply divided. The president said nothing. Seemingly unperturbed, he sometimes smiled and tipped his hat at the pickets as his limousine drove through the White House gates. For long grueling weeks the women's severest challenge was a winter so bitingly cold that hands ached and feet felt like blocks of ice.

In March 1917, Alice Paul's organization joined an allied western group to form the National Woman's Party, and Paul, overwhelmingly elected chairwoman, became nationally prominent. A month later the United States entered World War I—and the NWP faced a major crisis.

At the outbreak of the Civil War, it was the nearly unanimous opinion of the leaders of the women's movement that they should suspend their work until peace was restored. Only Susan B. Anthony disagreed, fearing that what little progress they had made up until then would be lost. As Alice Paul

knew, Anthony had been right, and she was determined that the mistake made in that earlier time must not be repeated.

"We shall fight for the things we have always carried next to our hearts," President Wilson said in his war message to Congress. "For . . . the right of those who submit to authority to have a voice in their own governments." So shall we, declared the women of the NWP, hearing in Wilson's words an exact description of what they were striving for. The demonstrations would continue.

Public hostility toward the picketers dramatically increased. Rather than merely foolish and undignified, they were now branded as unpatriotic—even traitors. Some dropped out under the pressure. But the NWP's courage in the face of vilification also inspired a steady flow of eager recruits. The demonstrators became a peculiar kind of tourist attraction in Washington, objects of admiration, curiosity—or outrage. They were so quiet and orderly that the newspapers called them the "silent sentinels." But they were attracting attention—entirely the point in the eyes of master strategist Alice Paul.

For five months the White House siege continued, while Congress, controlled by the Democrats, refused to act without word from the president. Still Wilson remained silent. Finally, in late June, the stalemate broke. Public anger erupted and the administration's patience snapped when NWP pickets raised a banner highly critical of Wilson as a Russian delegation visited the White House. A hostile crowd ripped down the banner, and next morning Lucy Burns and another woman became the first picketers to be hustled away in a police patrol wagon. They were scolded for their behavior and released pending trial; four more later received the same treatment. Within a few days, those six women were convicted on the traffic obstruction charges and spent three days in jail—the first suffragists imprisoned for their cause. It was only the beginning. Early in July, 11 women—including Lucy Burns—were sent to jail. Two weeks later 16 women were stunned to get 60-day sentences, and not in the D.C. jail, but the more dreaded Work-house for Women at Occoquan, Va.

But the picketers had their legal champions, attorneys who were well aware that demonstrating was entirely within the rights of any citizen, and that the arrests were blatantly illegal. One of these, Dudley Field Malone, collector of the Port of New York, was a friend of the president's. As counsel for the NWP, Malone argued with Wilson against the Occoquan sentences, threatening to resign his own position in protest. He believed, like many others, that Wilson was directing the crackdown from behind the scenes. Wilson professed to know nothing, but a few days later, all suffragists at Occoquan were suddenly pardoned. Partially mollified, Malone returned to New York—but he would be heard from again.

More troubles arose in mid-August, when picketers unfurled a banner referring to the president as "Kaiser Wilson." Congressmen often called the autocratic Wilson that, or worse, but doing so publicly, in the midst of rabid, wartime anti-German sentiment, ignited mob violence. For two days, the women could not set foot outside Cameron House without being physically assaulted. Attackers climbed to the second-floor balcony, grappling with defenders and ripping down banners. A shot was fired through one window, narrowly missing one of the women inside. After passively watching the melee for two days, police finally restored order. The next day, arrests of the picketers resumed. Six more women received 30 days in Occoquan—and this time there would be no pardons.

For six more tension-filled weeks, arrests and convictions on the transparently false obstructing traffic charge continued, with the luckless prisoners receiving 30 to 60 days in Occoquan. Yet women kept picketing, and in early September, Lucy Burns and 11 others drew 60-day sentences there. It was her second time behind bars.

Dudley Field Malone now carried out his threat to resign over the administration's use of such oppressive methods, making headlines and ending his already strained friendship with Wilson. Thereafter, Malone and Washington attorney Matthew O'Brien

would comprise a formidable legal team for the embattled NWP.

Despite its quiet, rural setting, the workhouse at Occoquan was run like a concentration camp by its superintendent, William Whittaker. His name struck terror in all inmates, but the suffragist picketers aroused his special animosity—here were educated women, deliberately engaging in what he considered treasonable behavior.

Soon, in defiance of Whittaker's policy of suppressing his prisoners' contact with the outside world, horror stories began to leak out of Occoquan, mainly in the form of scribbled messages, cleverly smuggled to friends on the outside. "The worst misery was the food," one prisoner wrote, describing rancid meat, corn bread green with mold, grits containing worms, rat droppings and dead flies. "We tried to make sport of the worm hunt," reported another, but "when one prisoner reached fifteen worms during one meal, it spoiled our zest for the game." There was no sanitation, and the women were forced into intimate contact with regular inmates who, though obviously suffering from contagious diseases, received no medical attention. To many the worst punishment was the almost total isolation. Even their lawyers rarely got in, and then only under tight restrictions.

Armed with affidavits from former inmates and employees, attorney Malone demanded an investigation to expose "the rotten, filthy, depraved conditions at Occoquan under its present superintendent." But the investigative board only exonerated Whittaker, blaming all complaints on unruly prisoners. Whittaker was triumphant—for the time being.

Once, during a police court trial, a government attorney shook his finger at Alice Paul and said, "We'll get you yet." Although she had been directing battle strategy from behind the scenes until then, he was sure that sooner or later the general would go out to lead her troops—and be captured. It happened in October 1917, when Paul was hauled off the picket line twice in two weeks and hit with the heaviest sentence to date—seven months in the D.C. jail.

There she and her companions encountered hardships rivaling Occoquan's—no privacy; stifling, overcrowded vermin-infested cells; a near-starvation diet that left them almost too weak to stand; close to total isolation. Privileges enjoyed by regular inmates were denied the suffragists. Washington's Warden Louis Zinkhan was apparently competing with Occoquan's Whittaker for the title of "Most Ferocious."

Already detested by their jailers as troublemakers and traitors, the suffragists infuriated them further by demanding political prisoner status. Their claim contemptuously dismissed, they soon devised a form of resistance not so easily ignored. The moment of decision came, as Alice Paul told it:

> At the end of two weeks of solitary confinement . . . without any exercise, without going outside of our cells, some of the prisoners were released, having finished their terms. . . . With our number thus diminished to seven . . . the doors were unlocked and we were permitted to take exercise. Rose Winslow fainted as soon as she got into the yard. . . . I was too weak to move from my bed. Rose and I were taken on stretchers that night to the hospital. . . . Here we decided upon . . . the ultimate form of protest left us—the strongest weapon left with which to continue . . . our battle. . . .

Their ultimate form of protest was the hunger strike. Having worked with English suffragists some years before, Paul knew from painful experience what terrors lay in that direction: "From the moment we undertook the hunger strike, a policy of unremitting intimidation began. 'You will be taken to a very unpleasant place if you don't stop this,' was a favorite threat of prison officials, as they would hint vaguely of the psychiatric ward, and the government insane asylum." Particularly frightening was examination by the "alienist" (a specialist in mental disorders), whose word was enough to commit anyone to the asylum.

Seriously weakened after three days of refusing food, Paul was taken to the psychiatric ward and subjected, along with some of her companions, to force-feeding three times daily. Between those feedings she endured solitary confinement in a tiny cell

with boarded-up windows. This frail woman was, after all, the power behind the suffrage demonstrations. To crush them required breaking her spirit—and clearly, the authorities meant to break it.

But the government's heavy-handed tactics only made matters worse. As reports of the prisoners' experiences emerged, angry women flocked to Washington from across the country to join the fight and continue the picketing. In mid-November, 30 more demonstrators, drawing sentences ranging from six days to six months, were shipped to Occoquan. Grimly awaiting them was Superintendent Whittaker. Once, accused by a suffragist prisoner of practicing cruelty, he readily admitted, "Very well, I am willing to practice cruelty." His November 14 welcome for his latest group of picketers would live in NWP memory as the infamous "Night of Terror."

On Whittaker's order, one woman wrote later, "I was immediately seized by two heavy guards, dragged across the room, scattering chairs and furniture as I went . . . so fast that my feet could not touch the ground . . . to the punishment cells, where I was flung into a concrete cell with an iron-barred door."

"I saw Dorothy Day brought in," wrote Mary Nolan, at 73 the oldest of the suffragist prisoners. "The two men handling her were twisting her arms above her head. Then suddenly they lifted her up and banged her down over the arm of an iron bench—twice . . . and we heard one of them yell, 'The damned suffrager!'"

The feisty Lucy Burns, returning for the third time, got special treatment. Disobeying Whittaker's order to keep silent, she was handcuffed to the bars of her cell. Finally released from this torturous position, she was left handcuffed all night. But all this, and a near-sleepless night shivering on thin straw mattresses, only made the "suffragers" more defiant. They launched their own hunger strike. Undertaking Alice Paul's "ultimate form of protest" took courage. One faster described nausea and headaches, fever and dizziness, dry, peeling skin and swollen lips, and eventually, aphasia. "I could remember no names," she wrote, "and it was quite impossible to read." Many hallucinated and often fainted.

To crush the strike, prison officials tried everything from dire threats to tempting the strikers with fried chicken, mashed potatoes and all the trimmings. Nothing worked. After seven days, the fasters were dangerously weak. There was no escaping it—forced feeding was next. And facing that took the last ounce of courage they had left. One prisoner reported, "I was seized and laid on my back, where five people held me, [one] leaping upon my knees. . . . Dr. Gannon then forced the tube through my lips and down my throat, I was gasping and suffocating from the agony of it. I didn't know where to breathe from, and everything turned black. . . ."

A Washington prisoner later recalled:

Three times a day for fourteen days Alice Paul and Rose Winslow have been going through the torture of forcible feeding. I know what that torture is. The horrible griping and gagging of swallowing six inches of stiff rubber tubing—[it] is not to be imagined. That over, there is the ordeal of waiting while the liquids are poured through—then the withdrawal of that tube! With streaming eyes and parched, burning throat, one wonders how the people of this nation already tasting blood and pain can let this be done. . . .

The prisoners endured their punishment with unwavering resolve, but they were near collapse. If they meant to win or die, it seemed increasingly likely that dying would be their fate. But far away, the tide of their desperate war was turning, thanks to the NWP lawyers working overtime for the prisoners. Dudley Malone concentrated on the Washington jail, while Matthew O'Brien took on Occoquan, and their labors were producing results. Forcing their way into the prisons with court orders, both were outraged at what they found. In Washington, Alice Paul languished in a hellhole on the psychiatric ward, despite a clean bill of mental health from the alienist. The irate Malone demanded, and got, her prompt removal to the main jail. At Occoquan, O'Brien obtained a writ of habeas corpus ordering Superintendent Whittaker to produce all his suffragist prisoners for a hearing before the U.S. Court of Appeals in Alexandria, Va. Whittaker tried frantically

to evade the writ—even hiding out in his own home in vain. The hearing was held November 23 and 24 before a packed house, including newspaper reporters from far and wide.

Both attorneys argued eloquently for justice for Americans who, as O'Brien declared, "were railroaded to Occoquan, where unspeakable brutalities occurred, for the sole purpose of terrorizing them and compelling them to desist from doing what . . . they have every legal right to do."

The sympathetic judge called the testimony given on the prisoners' behalf "blood-curdling." But more compelling than any evidence was the appearance of the prisoners themselves. Haggard, pale and disoriented, many with ugly bruises sustained during the Night of Terror, some barely able to walk or sit upright, their condition sent a wave of shocked disbelief throughout the courtroom. The sight of those mistreated women, vividly reported in newspapers, clinched their case. The judge ordered the prisoners' immediate transfer to the Washington jail pending further review—and the grim conflict took a startling turn.

For months the government had gone to extremes—even breaking the law—to suppress the picketing. But the movement only grew stronger as public opinion shifted toward the women. Clearly, the policy was not working. Perhaps in recognition of this, three days after the Alexandria hearing—and with no explanations—all suffragist prisoners were abruptly released.

On November 27, emerging from the jail to blink in the sunlight after five weeks of living death, Alice Paul could not stand without assistance. But her indomitable will was intact as she declared, "We were put out of jail as we were put in—at the whim of the government." She hoped that "no more demonstrations will be necessary, that the Federal Amendment is well on its way," but added, "What we do depends on what the Government does."

Things were peaceful along the White House sidewalks that Christmas season. The picketers were gone, the former prisoners having retreated to heal their wounds. It was only a truce: They would be back soon to continue the fight.

Several developments that took place in early 1918 were morale boosters. On January 10—40 years to the day since it was introduced into Congress—the Anthony Amendment was passed by the House of Representatives. In March the District Court of Appeals overturned as illegal all the arrests and jailings of the suffragists. And soon afterward—going almost unnoticed except by his former victims—William Whittaker's tenure as superintendent of the Occoquan workhouse was abruptly terminated.

Nevertheless, a long road lay ahead before the ultimate victory on August 26, 1920, when the Anthony Amendment finally took effect as the 19th Amendment to the Constitution. But for many who lived through it, the climatic battle took place in the fall of 1917, when Alice Paul and her courageous, half-starved band laid their lives on the line to defy a repressive government—and the government backed down.

QUESTIONS TO CONSIDER

1 What was the goal of the Susan B. Anthony Amendment to the Constitution? Why did it foment so much opposition that it took forty years to get the Amendment added to the Constitution?

2 How did the personalities of Alice Paul and Lucy Burns differ? What strengths did each of these women bring to the suffrage movement? Why would the author conclude that those two women "complemented each other perfectly"?

3 Explain President Wilson's position on the woman's suffrage issue at the start of his first administration? How did Alice Paul pressure him to recognize the importance of her cause?

4 After the start of the Great War of 1914–1918, what change took place in the public reaction to the suffragist demonstrations? Explain how growing patriotism and calls for unity during the Great War helped the federal government justify its harsh treatment of the White House picketers? Think of other wars where civil liberties have been sacrificed for the sake of national unity.

5 Describe the conditions endured by the suffragists in the Washington, D.C., jail and the Workhouse for Women at Occoquan, Virginia. How did Alice Paul and her fellow prisoners protest such harsh treatment?

6 Why did the Progressive reform movement need pressure before it supported women's suffrage? Do the personalities of Theodore Roosevelt (selection 10) and Woodrow Wilson (selection 13) offer clues as to why such pressure was necessary? Do those selections also help you better understand why the Progressives did not advocate equal rights for African Americans (see selection 11)?

13 "A Tragedy of Disappointment": Woodrow Wilson and the Treaty of Versailles

MARGARET MacMILLAN

The Great War of 1914–1918 was the most savage conflict ever fought up to that time. It was called the Great War then because nobody knew that an even more monstrous war lay in the future. The Great War began when Austria-Hungary declared war on a small Balkan country named Serbia, whose staunch ally was Russia. Because of entangling alliances among Europe's great powers, the war quickly spread until it engulfed much of Europe, with the Central Powers (Austria-Hungary,

Germany, and Turkey) *fighting the Allied Powers (Russia, France, Britain, and Italy). It was the world's first "total war," in which whole societies battled one another. Before it was over, Russia had suffered almost 2 million casualties and collapsed in a Communist takeover; Germany had lost 2 million soldiers, France 1.5 million, and Britain almost 1 million.*

The United States officially entered the war in April 1917, on the side of the Allies. The United States did so, in part, because the Germans had resorted to submarine war, torpedoing Allied warships without warning; to Americans, this seemed barbaric. The Allied blockade of the German coast, calculated to starve Germany into submission, did not strike most Americans the same way, because of their anti-German sentiment and sympathies for the Allies. When a German U-boat sank a British passenger ship, the Lusitania, *with 128 Americans on board, the United States was enraged. President Woodrow Wilson warned the Germans that if they continued to commit such outrages, the United States would take the necessary action to protect its citizens traveling on non-military vessels. At first the Germans agreed not to sink any more enemy ships with Americans on board, but later withdrew the pledge on the grounds that Germany was already fighting American economic might—the United States was selling war materiel to the Allies—and had nothing to lose by attacking American merchant ships taking war supplies to Britain. "This means war," said Wilson. "The break that we have tried to prevent now seems inevitable." When the United States intercepted a secret telegram in which Germany invited Mexico to join the Central Powers, Wilson asked Congress to delcare war, and Congress did so with thunderous applause and cheering. "My message today," said Wilson, "was a message of death for our young men. How strange it seems to applaud that."*

As that remark suggests, Woodrow Wilson had a horror of violence and war. Why, then, would he lead the United States into a savage conflict like the Great War? The answer lies in Wilson's complex and contradictory character. A former college professor and president of Princeton with a Ph.D. in political economy, Wilson was a conservative Democrat before he won the presidency. Once in office, however, he became a Progressive reformer who championed a program called the New Freedom that included substantial reforms in currency, anti-trust, and tariff legislation. Working well with Congress, Wilson went on to support women's political rights and engineered the most sweeping legislative program since the days of Alexander Hamilton. Despite his spectacular achievements, Wilson was a sensitive, lonely man who wanted "the people to love me." And yet he felt a powerful need, he said, to guard his emotions "from painful overflow." Although his intellectual tradition was British (he extolled the British system of parliamentary government and admired English leaders such as Edmund Burke and William Gladstone), his politics were rooted in his southern heritage. A learned, eloquent champion of democracy, he nevertheless shared the racial prejudice that prevailed among white Americans of his generation, and as president he began a policy of discrimination against African Americans in federal employment.

In many ways, Wilson's foreign policy was even more paradoxical. He abhorred violence, yet he was inclined to use moralistic, gunboat diplomacy in dealing with Latin America: he transformed Nicaragua into a veritable United States protectorate, twice sent American forces into Mexico, and ordered full-scale military occupation of Haiti and the Dominican Republic. Although Wilson convinced himself that high moral purpose justified such intervention, it left a legacy of bitterness and distrust in Latin America.

Finally, despite the pacific liberalism he had learned from British intellectuals, Wilson led the United States into the Great War on a messianic crusade to make that conflict "a war to end all wars." To achieve that goal, he devised the League of Nations, a kind of world parliament, which was the sanest blueprint for world peace anyone had yet contrived. But Wilson's noble dream ended in a crushing defeat when the United States Senate rejected the League of Nations and America turned away from the idealism that had produced it.

In the following selection, excerpted from her prize-winning book, Paris 1919, *Margaret MacMillan tells the story of Wilson and the League of Nations in an elegant narrative filled with trenchant insights. She not only describes Wilson's complex and contradictory personality, but also tells the rollicking story of his second marriage, to Edith Galt, while he was president. MacMillan goes on to explain how Wilson's ill health and inability to compromise, combined with the tenacity of his adversaries and the sentiment of the times, brought about America's rejection of the League of Nations. In the end, the United States was not prepared for the responsibilities of world leadership that Wilson had thrust upon it. Desperately ill from crippling strokes, Wilson viewed the rejection as a personal defeat. As historian Richard Hofstadter observed, the president's "sense of guilt hung over him like a cloud." Steeped in gloom, Wilson summarized his presidency with these words: "What I seem to see, with all my heart I hope that I am wrong, is a tragedy of disappointment."*

GLOSSARY

ARTICLE X   The most controversial part of the League of Nations covenant, Article X committed nations that were members of the League to defend any member nation when another power threatened its "territorial integrity" by "external aggression."

BAKER, RAY STANNARD   Wilson's press officer, friend, and admirer, Baker accompanied the president to Paris.

BLISS, TASKER   Bliss was America's representative on the Supreme War Council in Paris. He later became one of the commissioners to the peace conference at Versailles.

BULLITT, WILLIAM   Bullitt was an advisor to the American delegation that helped negotiate the Treaty of Versailles. He later served as the United States ambassador to Russia and then to France.

BURKE, EDMUND   President Wilson greatly admired this British statesman and political writer, who lived from 1729 to 1797. A thoroughgoing Anglophile, Wilson adopted a foreign policy that favored Great Britain and finally led the United States to enter the Great War on the side of Britain and the other Allies.

CLEMENCEAU, GEORGES   The French prime minister who wanted a peace treaty that would guarantee Germany could never again be a threat to France. An imperialist, he rejected President Wilson's idealism, saying: "God gave us the Ten Commandments, and we broke them. Wilson gave us the Fourteen Points. We shall see" about breaking them.

CREEL, GEORGE   Creel headed the Committee on Public Information (CPI) that publicized and, at times, propagandized American involvement in the Great War. Creel's committee issued pamphlets, posters, and speeches that addressed such issues as "Why We Are Fighting" and that portrayed the Germans as bloodthirsty aggressors; CPI funds produced a film entitled *The Kaiser, the Beast of Berlin.*

FOURTEEN POINTS   Wilson's idealistic blueprint for world peace that was generous to defeated Germany, but failed to satisfy the wartime goals of the allied nations. The last and most important point called for a League of Nations, a kind of parliament of humankind, which would resolve international conflicts and thus avoid future wars.

GALT, EDITH BOLLING   Wilson married this southern woman, seventeen years his junior, less than two years after the death of his first wife. Edith Galt was totally devoted to her husband. After the stroke that disabled him, she protected Wilson from perceived tormentors during his struggle with the Senate over the Treaty of Versailles.

GRAYSON, CARY TRAVERS   Wilson's personal physician and friend, Grayson opposed the President's final speaking tour in 1919, which caused a further deterioration of his health. A naval officer, Grayson had also served as a physician to Presidents Theodore Roosevelt and William Howard Taft.

HANKEY, SIR MAURICE   Secretary to the British cabinet and later to the Paris Peace Conference, Hankey fervently believed that Wilson's Fourteen Points were the "moral background" that would establish a new world order.

HITCHCOCK, GILBERT   A Democratic senator from Nebraska who led his party in the losing struggle to preserve

Wilson's League of Nations against those who wanted to alter or destroy it.

HOUSE, COLONEL EDWARD M. House was a close friend to Wilson, who called him "my alter ego." The Colonel was one of the President's most important advisors until his second wife, Edith Galt Wilson, persuaded her husband to disregard his counsel.

IRRECONCILABLES A group of about a dozen senators who opposed the League of Nations in any form.

LANSING, ROBERT Wilson's secretary of state, Lansing had doubts about the League of Nations that caused the President to lose confidence in him.

LEAGUE OF NATIONS An international organization of nations designed to prevent future wars. Without American participation, the League of Nations was largely ineffectual in the years following the Great War

LLOYD GEORGE, DAVID The British prime minister who pushed for a harsher peace treaty with defeated Germany and the other Central Powers. He once threatened that the Allies would squeeze Germany "until the pipes squeak."

LODGE, HENRY CABOT Lodge was the senior Republican member on the Senate Foreign Relations Committee who led the fight against Wilson's League of Nations.

RESERVATIONS Amendments to the League of Nations charter. Many United States senators believed them necessary to protect American sovereignty and to make the peace treaty consistent with the United States Constitution. Wilson adamantly opposed such changes to his cherished League. As a result, the Senate refused to ratify the Treaty of Versailles and thus rejected United States participation in the League, which proved too weak to preserve global peace and collapsed soon after the outbreak of World War II.

TAFT, WILLIAM HOWARD Rotund Republican president from 1909 to 1913, he lost to Wilson in the election of 1912. Taft believed that Wilson had slighted his party in the treaty negotiations that ended the Great War, and he subsequently opposed the League of Nations.

TREATY OF VERSAILLES (1919) Formally ended the Great War; only about four of the Fourteen Points found their way into the treaty. When Wilson refused to compromise on the League of Nations covenant, the Senate rejected United States participation in the world organization. As a result, America signed a separate treaty with Germany and the other Central Powers and never joined the international organization that Wilson had hoped would end all future wars and preserve democracy the world over.

WHITE, HENRY A retired diplomat, White was the only Republican member of the peace commission that accompanied Wilson to Paris.

On December 4, 1918, the *George Washington* sailed out of New York with the American delegation to the Peace Conference on board. Guns fired salutes, crowds along the waterfront cheered, tugboats hooted and Army planes and dirigibles circled overhead. Robert Lansing, the American secretary of state, released carrier pigeons with messages to his relatives about his deep hope for a lasting peace. The ship, a former German passenger liner, slid out past the Statue of Liberty to the Atlantic, where an escort of destroyers and battleships stood by to accompany it and its cargo of heavy expectations to Europe.

On board were the best available experts, combed out of the universities and the government; crates of reference materials and special studies; the French and Italian ambassadors to the United States; and Woodrow Wilson. No other American president had ever gone to Europe while in office. His opponents accused him of breaking the Constitution; even his supporters felt he might be unwise. Would he lose his great moral authority by getting down to the hurly-burly of negotiations? Wilson's own view was clear: the making of the peace was as important as the winning of the war. He owed it to the peoples of Europe, who were crying out for a better world. He owed it to the American servicemen. "It is now my duty," he told a pensive Congress just before he left, "to play my full part in making good what they gave their life's blood to obtain." A British diplomat was more

From *Paris 1919: Six Months that Changed the World* by Margaret MacMillan, copyright © 2001 by Margaret MacMillan. Used by permission of Random House, Inc.

cynical; Wilson, he said, was drawn to Paris "as a debutante is entranced by the prospect of her first ball."

Wilson expected, he wrote to his great friend Edward House, who was already in Europe, that he would stay only to arrange the main outlines of the peace settlements. It was not likely that he would remain for the formal Peace Conference with the enemy. He was wrong. The preliminary conference turned, without anyone's intending it, into the final one, and Wilson stayed for most of the crucial six months between January and June 1919. The question of whether or not he should have gone to Paris, which exercised so many of his contemporaries, now seems unimportant. From Franklin Roosevelt at Yalta to Jimmy Carter or Bill Clinton at Camp David, American presidents have sat down to draw borders and hammer out peace agreements. Wilson had set the conditions for the armistices which ended the Great War. Why should he not make the peace as well?

Although he had not started out in 1912 as a foreign policy president, circumstances and his own progressive political principles had drawn him outward. Like many of his compatriots, he had come to see the Great War as a struggle between the forces of democracy, however imperfectly represented by Britain and France, and those of reaction and militarism, represented all too well by Germany and Austria-Hungary. Germany's sack of Belgium, its unrestricted submarine warfare and its audacity in attempting to entice Mexico into waging war on the United States had pushed Wilson and American public opinion toward the Allies. When Russia had a democratic revolution in February 1917, one of the last reservations—that the Allies included an autocracy—vanished. Although he had campaigned in 1916 on a platform of keeping the country neutral, Wilson brought the United States into the war in April 1917. He was convinced that he was doing the right thing. This was important to the son of a Presbyterian minister, who shared his father's deep religious conviction, if not his calling.

Wilson was born in Virginia in 1856, just before the Civil War. Although he remained a Southerner in some ways all his life—in his insistence on honor and his paternalistic attitudes toward women and blacks—he also accepted the war's outcome. Abraham Lincoln was one of his great heroes, along with Edmund Burke and William Gladstone. The young Wilson was at once highly idealistic and intensely ambitious. After four very happy years at Princeton and an unhappy stint as a lawyer, he found his first career in teaching and writing. By 1890 he was back at Princeton, a star member of the faculty. In 1902 he became its president, supported virtually unanimously by the trustees, faculty and students.

In the next eight years Wilson transformed Princeton from a sleepy college for gentlemen into a great university. He reworked the curriculum, raised significant amounts of money and brought into the faculty the brightest and the best young men from across the country. By 1910, he was a national figure and the Democratic party in New Jersey, under the control of conservative bosses, invited him to run for governor. Wilson agreed, but insisted on running on a progressive platform of controlling big business and extending democracy. He swept the state and by 1911 "Wilson for President" clubs were springing up. He spoke for the dispossessed, the disenfranchised and all those who had been left behind by the rapid economic growth of the late nineteenth century. In 1912, at a long and hard-fought convention, Wilson got the Democratic nomination for president. That November, with the Republicans split by Teddy Roosevelt's decision to run as a progressive against William Howard Taft, Wilson was elected. In 1916, he was reelected, with an even greater share of the popular vote.

Wilson's career was a series of triumphs, but there were darker moments, both personal and political, fits of depression and sudden and baffling illnesses. Moreover, he had left behind him a trail of enemies, many of them former friends. "An ingrate and a liar," said a Democratic boss in New Jersey in a toast. Wilson never forgave those who disagreed with him. "He is a good hater," said his press officer and devoted admirer Ray Stannard Baker. He was also stubborn. As House said, with admiration: "Whenever a question is presented he keeps an absolutely open mind and welcomes all suggestion or advice which will lead to a correct decision. But he is receptive only during the period that he is weighing the question and preparing to make his decision. Once the decision is made it is final and there is an absolute end to all advice and suggestion. There is no moving him after that." What was admirable to some was a dangerous egotism to others. The French ambassador in Washington saw "a man who, had he lived a couple of centuries ago, would have been the greatest tyrant in the world, because he does not seem to have the slightest conception that he can ever be wrong.

This side of Wilson's character was in evidence when he chose his fellow commissioners—or plenipotentiaries, as the chief delegates were known—to the Peace Conference. He was himself one. House, "my alter ego," as he was fond of saying, was another. Reluctantly he selected Lansing, his secretary of state, as a third, mainly because it would have been awkward to leave him behind. Where Wilson had once rather admired Lansing's vast store of knowledge, his meticulous legal mind and his apparent readiness to take a back seat, by 1919 that early liking had turned to irritation and contempt. Lansing, it turned out, did have views, often strong ones which contradicted the president's. "He has," Wilson complained to House, who noted it down with delight, "no imagination, no constructive ability, and but little real ability of any kind." The fourth plenipotentiary, General Tasker Bliss, was already in France as the American military representative on the Supreme War Council. A thoughtful and intelligent man who loved to lie in bed with a hip flask reading Thucydides in the original Greek, he was also, many of the junior members of the American delegation believed, well past his prime. Since Wilson was to speak to him on only five occasions during the Peace Conference, perhaps that did not matter.

The president's final selection, Henry White, was a charming, affable retired diplomat, the high point of whose career had been well before the war. Mrs. Wilson was to find him useful in Paris on questions of etiquette.

Wilson's selection caused an uproar in the United States at the time and has caused controversy ever since. "A lot of cheapskates," said William Taft. "I would swear if it would do any good." Wilson had deliberately slighted the Republicans, most of whom had supported the war enthusiastically and many of whom now shared his vision of a League of Nations. "I tell you what," the humorist Will Rogers had him saying to the Republicans, "we will split 50–50—I will go and you fellows can stay." Even his most partisan supporters had urged him to appoint men such as Taft or the senior Republican senator on the important Committee on Foreign Relations, Henry Cabot Lodge. Wilson refused, with a variety of unconvincing excuses. The real reason was that he did not like or trust Republicans. His decision was costly, because it undercut his position in Paris and damaged his dream of a new world order with the United States at its heart.

Wilson remains puzzling in a way that Lloyd George and Clemenceau, his close colleagues in Paris, do not. What is one to make of a leader who drew on the most noble language of the Bible yet was so ruthless with those who crossed him? Who loved democracy but despised most of his fellow politicians? Who wanted to serve humanity but had so few personal relationships? Was he, as Teddy Roosevelt thought, "as insincere and cold-blooded an opportunist as we have ever had in the Presidency"? Or was he, as Baker believed, one of those rare idealists like Calvin or Cromwell, "who from time to time have appeared upon the earth & for a moment, in burst of strange power, have temporarily lifted erring mankind to a higher pitch of contentment than it was quite equal to"?

Wilson wanted power and he wanted to do great works. What brought the two sides of his character together was his ability, self-deception perhaps, to frame his decisions so that they became not merely necessary, but morally right. Just as American neutrality in the first years of the war had been right for Americans, and indeed for humanity, so the United States' eventual entry into the war became a crusade, against human greed and folly, against Germany and for justice, peace and civilization. This conviction, however, without which he could never have attempted what he did in Paris, made Wilson intolerant of differences and blind to the legitimate concerns of others. Those who opposed him were not just wrong but wicked.

Like the Germans. The decision to go to war had been agony for Wilson. He had worked for a peace of compromise between the Allies and the Central Powers. Even when they had rejected his offer to mediate, when German submarines had sunk American ships, when opponents such as Roosevelt had attacked his cowardice and when his own cabinet had been unanimous for war, he had waited. In the end he decided to intervene because, as he saw it, Germany left him no alternative. "It is a fearful thing," he told Congress in April 1917, when he went before it to ask for a declaration of war, "to lead this great peaceful people into war, into the most terrible and disastrous of all wars, civilization itself seeming to be in the balance." In Wilson's view Germany, or at the very least its leaders, bore a heavy burden of guilt. The Germans might be redeemed, but they also must be chastised.

The photographs taken in 1919 make him look like an undertaker, but in the flesh Wilson was a handsome man, with fine, straight features and a spare, upright frame. In his manner he had something of the preacher and of the university professor. He placed great faith in reason and facts, but he saw it as auspicious that he landed in Europe on Friday, December 13. Thirteen was his lucky number. A deeply emotional man, he mistrusted emotion in others. It was good when it brought people to desire the best, dangerous when, like nationalism, it intoxicated them. Lloyd George, who never entirely got his measure, listed his good qualities to a friend—"kindly, sincere, straightforward"—and then added in the next breath "tactless, obstinate and vain."

In public, Wilson was stiff and formal, but with his intimates he was charming and even playful. He was particularly at ease with women. He was usually in perfect control of himself, but during the Peace Conference he frequently lost his temper. (It is possible he

suffered a stroke while he was in Paris.) He loved puns and limericks and he liked to illustrate his points with folksy stories. He enjoyed doing accents: Scottish or Irish, like his ancestors, or Southern black, like the people who worked for him in Washington. He was abstemious in his habits; at most he would drink a small glass of whisky in an evening. He loved gadgets and liked the new moving pictures. On the voyage to Europe he generally went to the after-dinner picture shows. To general consternation the feature one evening was a melodrama called *The Second Wife*.

Wilson's relations with women had always caused a certain amount of gossip. During his first marriage he had close, possibly even romantic, friendships with several women. His first wife, whom he had loved deeply if not passionately, had died in 1914; by the end of 1915, he was married again, to a wealthy Washington widow some seventeen years his junior. That this caused gossip bewildered and infuriated him. He never forgave a British diplomat for a joke that went around Washington: "What did the new Mrs. Wilson do when the President proposed? She fell out of bed with surprise." Wilson's own family and friends were more charitable. "Isn't it wonderful to see Father so happy," exclaimed a daughter. House, who was later to become Mrs. Wilson's bitter enemy, wrote in his diary that it was a relief that Wilson had someone to share his burdens: "his loneliness is pathetic."

Edith Bolling, the new Mrs. Wilson, accompanied the president to Europe, a privilege not allowed lesser wives. She was warm and lively and laughed a great deal. She loved golf, shopping, orchids and parties. She had, everyone agreed, wonderful eyes, but some found her a bit plump and her mouth too large. She wore, they thought in Paris, her clothes a little too tight, the necks too low, the skirts too short. Wilson thought she was beautiful. Like him, she came from the South. She did not want to spoil her maid by taking her to London, she told a fellow American, because the British treated blacks too well. Although she had the easy flirtatious ways of a Southern woman, she was a shrewd businesswoman. After her first husband's death she had run the family

Woodrow Wilson and his wife Edith in 1920, when the President was recuperating from his near fatal stroke. Sheltering her husband from the outside world, Edith controlled most of the visitors and correspondence that Wilson saw. Gravely ill and clinging to his foreign policy goals, Wilson witnessed the Republican controlled Senate defeat his cherished League of Nations. (Library of Congress)

jewelry store. When she married Wilson, he made it clear that he expected her to share his work. She took up the offer with enthusiasm. No intellectual, she was quick and determined. She was also ferociously loyal to her new husband. Wilson adored her.

On board the *George Washington*, the Wilsons kept to themselves, eating most of their meals in their stateroom and strolling on the deck arm in arm. The American experts worked away on their maps and their papers, asking each other, with some disquiet, what their country's policies were to be. Wilson had said much about general principles but had mentioned

few specifics. A young man called William Bullitt boldly went up to the president and told him that they were all confused by his silence. Wilson was surprised but agreed pleasantly to meet with a dozen of the leading experts. "It is absolutely the first time," said one afterward, "the president has let anyone know what his ideas are and what his policy is." There were to be few other such occasions. The experts left the meeting heartened and impressed. Wilson was informal and friendly. He spoke about the heavy task ahead and how he was going to rely on them to provide him with the best information. They must feel free to come to him at any time. "You tell me what's right and I'll fight for it." He apologized for talking about his own ideas: "they weren't very good but he thought them better than anything else he had heard."

When it came to making peace, Wilson said, their country would rightly hold the position of arbiter. They must live up to the great American traditions of justice and generosity. They would be, after all, "the only disinterested people at the Peace Conference." What was more, he warned, "the men whom we were about to deal with did not represent their own people." This was one of Wilson's deep convictions, curious in a man whose own Congress was now dominated by his political opponents. Throughout the Peace Conference he clung to the belief that he spoke for the masses and that, if only he could reach them—whether French, Italian or even Russian—they would rally to his views.

He touched on another favorite theme: the United States, he assured his audience, had not entered the war for selfish reasons. In this, as in so much else, it was unlike other nations, for it did not want territory, tribute or even revenge. (As a sign that American participation in the war was different from that of the Europeans, Wilson had always insisted on the United States being an Associate and not an Ally.) . . .

In that meeting on the *George Washington*, Wilson also talked briefly about the difficulties that lay ahead with the nations emerging from the wreckage of central Europe: Poland, Czechoslovakia, Yugoslavia and many more. They could have whatever form of government they wanted, but they must include in their new states only those who wanted to be there. "Criterion not who are intellectual or social or economic leaders but who form mass of people," a member of his audience wrote down. "Must have liberty—that is the kind of government they want."

Of all the ideas Wilson brought to Europe, this concept of self-determination was, and has remained, one of the most controversial and opaque. During the Peace Conference, the head of the American mission in Vienna sent repeated requests to Paris and Washington for an explanation of the term. No answer ever came. It has never been easy to determine

what Wilson meant. "Autonomous development," "the right of those who submit to authority to have a voice in their own governments," "the rights and liberties of small nations," a world made safe "for every peace-loving nation which, like our own, wishes to live its own life, determine its own institutions": the phrases had poured out from the White House, an inspiration to peoples around the world. But what did they add up to? Did Wilson merely mean, as sometimes appeared, an extension of democratic self-government? Did he really intend that any people who called themselves a nation should have their own state? In a statement he drafted, but never used, to persuade the American people to support the peace settlements, he stated, "We say now that all these people have the right to live their own lives under governments which they themselves choose to set up. That is the American principle." Yet he had no sympathy for Irish nationalists and their struggle to free themselves from British rule. During the Peace Conference he insisted that the Irish question was a domestic matter for the British. When a delegation of nationalist Irish asked him for support, he felt, he told his legal adviser, like telling them to go to hell. His view was that the Irish lived in a democratic country and they could sort it out through democratic means.

The more Wilson's concept of self-determination is examined, the more difficulties appear. Lansing asked himself: "When the President talks of 'self-determination' what unit has he in mind? Does he mean a race, a territorial area, or a community?" It was a calamity, Lansing thought, that Wilson had ever hit on the phrase. "It will raise hopes which can never be realized. It will, I fear, cost thousands of lives. In the end it is bound to be discredited, to be called the dream of an idealist who failed to realize the danger until it was too late to check those who attempt to put the principle into force.". . .

Wilson spent most of his time in the meeting with his experts on the matter closest to his heart: the need to find a new way of managing international relations. This did not come as a surprise to his audience. In his famous Fourteen Points of January 1918, and in subsequent speeches, he had sketched out his ideas. The balance of power, he told the U.S. Congress in his "Four Principles" speech of February 1918, was forever discredited as a way to keep peace. There would be no more secret diplomacy of the sort that had led Europe into calculating deals, rash promises and entangling alliances, and so on down the slope to war. The peace settlements must not leave the way open to future wars. There must be no retribution, no unjust claims and no huge fines—indemnities—paid by the losers to the winners. That was what had been wrong after Prussia defeated France in 1870. The French had never forgiven Germany for the monies paid over and for the loss of their provinces of Alsace and Lorraine. War itself must become more difficult. There must be controls on armaments—general disarmament, even. Ships must sail freely across the world's seas. (That meant, as the British well knew, the end of their traditional weapon of strangling enemy economies by blockading their ports and seizing their shipping; it had brought Napoleon down, and, so they thought, hastened the Allied victory over Germany.) Trade barriers must be lowered so the nations of the world would become more interdependent.

At the heart of Wilson's vision was a League of Nations to provide the collective security that, in a well-run civil society, was provided by the government, its laws, its courts and its police. "Old system of powers, balance of powers, had failed too often," one expert jotted down, as the president spoke. The League was to have a council that could "butt in" in case of disputes. "If unsuccessful the offending nation is to be outlawed—'And outlaws are not popular now.'"

Wilson's was a liberal and a Christian vision. It challenged the view that the best way to preserve the peace was to balance nations against each other, through alliances if necessary, and that strength, not collective security, was the way to deter attack. Wilson was also offering a riposte to the alternative being put out by the Russian Bolsheviks, that revolution would bring one world, where conflict would no longer exist. He believed in separate nations and in democracy, both as the best form of government

and as a force for good in the world. When governments were chosen by their people, they would not, indeed they could not, fight each other. "These are American principles," he told the Senate in 1917. "We could stand for no others. And they are also the principles and policies of forward looking men and women everywhere, of every modern nation, of every enlightened community. They are the principles of mankind and they must prevail." He was speaking, he thought, for humanity. Americans tended to see their values as universal ones, and their government and society as a model for all others. The United States, after all, had been founded by those who wanted to leave an old world behind, and its revolution was, in part, about creating a new one. American democracy, the American constitution, even American ways of doing business, were examples that others should follow for their own good. As one of the younger Americans said in Paris: "Before we get through with these fellows over here we will teach them how to do things and how to do them quickly."

The Americans had a complicated attitude toward the Europeans: a mixture of admiration for their past accomplishments, a conviction that the Allies would have been lost without the United States and a suspicion that, if the Americans were not careful, the wily Europeans would pull them into their toils again. As they prepared for the Peace Conference, the American delegates suspected that the French and the British were already preparing their traps. . . .

American exceptionalism has always had two sides: the one eager to set the world to rights, the other ready to turn its back with contempt if its message should be ignored. The peace settlement, Wilson told his fellow passengers, must be based on the new principles: "If it doesn't work right, the world will raise hell." He himself, he added half-jokingly, would go somewhere to "hide my head, perhaps to Guam." Faith in their own exceptionalism has sometimes led to a certain obtuseness on the part of Americans, a tendency to preach at other nations rather than listen to them, a tendency as well to assume that American motives are pure where those of others are not. And Wilson was very American. He came to the Peace Conference, said Lloyd George, like a missionary to rescue the heathen Europeans, with his "little sermonettes" full of rather obvious remarks.

It was easy to mock Wilson, and many did. It is also easy to forget how important his principles were in 1919 and how many people, and not just in the United States, wanted to believe in his great dream of a better world. They had, after all, a terrible reference point in the ruin left by the Great War. Wilson kept alive the hope that human society, despite the evidence, was getting better, that nations would one day live in harmony. In 1919, before disillusionment had set in, the world was more than ready to listen to him.

What Wilson had to say struck a chord, not just with liberals or pacifists but also among Europe's political and diplomatic élites. Sir Maurice Hankey, secretary to the British War Cabinet and then the Peace Conference itself, always carried a copy of the Fourteen Points in the box he kept for crucial reference material. They were, he said, the "moral background." Across Europe there were squares, streets, railway stations and parks bearing Wilson's name. Wall posters cried, "We Want a Wilson Peace." In Italy, soldiers knelt in front of his picture; in France, the left-wing paper *L'Humanité* brought out a special issue in which the leading lights of the French left vied with each other to praise Wilson's name. The leaders of the Arab revolt in the desert, Polish nationalists in Warsaw, rebels in the Greek islands, students in Peking, Koreans trying to shake off Japan's control, all took the Fourteen Points as their inspiration. Wilson himself found it exhilarating but also terrifying. "I am wondering," he said to George Creel, his brilliant propaganda chief, who was on board the *George Washington*, "whether you have not unconsciously spun a net for me from which there is no escape." The whole world was turning to the United States but, he went on, they both knew that such great problems could not be fixed at once. "What I seem to see—with all my heart I hope that I am wrong—is a tragedy of disappointment."

The *George Washington* reached the French port of Brest on December 13, 1918. The war had been over for just a month. While the president stood on the bridge, his ship steamed slowly in through a great avenue of battleships from the British, French and American navies. For the first time in days, the sun was shining. The streets were lined with laurel wreaths and flags. On the walls, posters paid tribute to Wilson, those from right-wingers for saving them from Germany and those from the left for the new world he promised. Huge numbers of people, many resplendent in their traditional Breton costumes, covered every inch of pavement, every roof, every tree. Even the lampposts were taken. The air filled with the skirl of Breton bagpipes and repeated shouts of "Vive l'Amérique! Vive Wilson!" The French foreign minister, Stéphen Pichon, welcomed him, saying, "We are so thankful that you have come over to give us the right kind of peace." Wilson made a noncommittal reply and the American party boarded the night train for Paris. At three in the morning, Wilson's doctor happened to look out the window of his compartment. "I saw not only men and women but little children standing with uncovered head to cheer the passage of the special train."

Wilson's reception in Paris was an even greater triumph, with even greater crowds: "the most remarkable demonstration," said an American who lived in Paris, "of enthusiasm and affection on the part of the Parisians that I have ever heard of, let alone seen." His train pulled into the Luxembourg station, which had been festooned with bunting and flags and filled with great masses of flowers. Clemenceau, the French prime minister, was there with his government and his longtime antagonist, the president Raymond Poincaré. As guns boomed across Paris to announce Wilson's arrival, the crowds started to press against the soldiers who lined the route. The president and his wife drove in an open carriage through the Place de la Concorde and on up the Champs-Elysées to their residence, to the sound of wild cheers. That night, at a quiet family dinner, Wilson said he was very pleased with his reception. "He had carefully watched the attitude of the crowd," he reportedly told the table, "and he was satisfied that they were most friendly." . . .

The Peace Conference continued until January 1920, but it was like a theatrical production whose stars had gone. The foreign ministers and the diplomats took over again but they never regained their old grip on foreign relations. The important decisions were always referred back to their political superiors in Rome or London or Washington and the difficult issues were hammered out in special conferences, of which Lloyd George alone attended thirty-three between 1919 and 1922.

Between January and June 1919, the peacemakers had accomplished an enormous amount: a League of Nations and an International Labour Organization, mandates handed out, the Germany treaty finished, the treaties with Austria, Hungary, Bulgaria and Ottoman Turkey nearly done—but there were many loose ends. . . .

The peacemakers in 1919 felt that they had done their best, but they had no illusions that they had solved the world's problems. As he left Paris on June 28, Wilson said to his wife, "Well, little girl, it is finished, and, as no one is satisfied, it makes me hope we have made a just peace; but it is all in the lap of the gods." It was also in the laps of those who came next to lead the world, some of whom had been in Paris—such as Prince Konoe of Japan and Franklin Delano Roosevelt—some of whom had been watching from afar. In Italy, Mussolini was rising fast in nationalist politics, as the old liberal order crumbled. . . . The young Adolf Hitler was in Munich that June, taking congenial courses on the glories of German history and the evils of international Jewish capital. Already he was discovering his own talents as an ideologue and an orator. . . .

Wilson's end was the saddest. Exhausted by the Peace Conference, he plunged into a wrenching and debilitating fight with the Senate over ratification of the Treaty of Versailles and, more specifically, the League of Nations. His supporters and his opponents had both been busy while he was away. The League

to Enforce the Peace was energetically lobbying for ratification. Wilson, unfortunately, did not much care for them, dismissing them as "butters-in" and "wool-gatherers." The League for the Preservation of American Independence, inspired, so it frequently said, by George Washington's and Thomas Jefferson's repeated warnings against permanent or entangling alliances, did its best to thwart the president. As for the ninety-six members of the Senate, it became apparent that they were dividing into roughly four groups. At least six Republicans would not have the League in any form—they came to be known as the Irreconcilables. A few Democrat mavericks would probably vote with them. Some nine Republicans were Mild Reservationists who would have accepted the League so long as their reservations to protect American sovereignty were registered. (Reservations were the well-established diplomatic practice of accepting an international agreement with qualifications; so long as all parties to the treaty agreed, the reservations stood.) This left three dozen Republicans who were not yet fully committed. Most Democrats still followed their president, although many privately hoped he would come to terms with the Mild Reservationists. If Wilson did compromise, there was a good chance that there would be enough votes to get the treaty passed. Would the European powers accept reservations? Lloyd George claimed in his memoirs that they had always expected they might have to. But they were never put to the test.

Wilson could have built his own coalition. The Republicans only had a majority of two in the Senate and he could have won over the moderates among them by accepting some reservations. When Lansing urged him to compromise, the president was unmoved: "His face took on that stubborn and pugnacious expression which comes when anyone tells him a fact which interferes with his plans." His opponents, Wilson told an intimate, were moved by the basest instincts. "They are going to have the most conspicuously contemptible names in history."

The president arrived back in Washington at midnight on July 8, 1919. A crowd of 100,000, enormous

The Council of Four included from left to right: Vittorio Orlando of Italy, David Lloyd George of England, Georges Clemenceau of France, and Woodrow Wilson. During the negotiation of the Treaty of Versailles, Wilson lost all but four of his Fourteen Points. The victorious European leaders were never committed to Wilson's noble goal of "a peace without victory." As Clemenceau sneered: "God gave us the ten commandments and we broke them. Wilson gave us the Fourteen Points—we shall see." (© Bettmann/CORBIS)

for those days, waited at the train station. Two days later he presented the Treaty of Versailles, with the League covenant at its start, to the Senate in person. "Dare we reject it," he asked them, "and break the heart of the world?" His speech, it was generally agreed, was poor. Unusually, he read parts of it and he lost his thread in places. Washington, and the country, readied themselves for the next step—the Senate's consideration of the treaty.

At first Wilson chose to work largely behind the scenes, meeting with Republican senators in an effort to persuade them that American independence was not compromised by membership in the League or by Article X, in particular, which was the heart of collective security. (Signatories promised "to respect and preserve as against external aggression the territorial integrity and existing political independence of all Members of the League.") He was confident, he told a British diplomat, that the treaty would go through the Senate. He was not prepared, he reiterated, to accept any changes; the treaty must be ratified as they had written it in Paris.

At the end of his first week in Washington, Wilson escaped the summer heat with a cruise on the Potomac on the presidential yacht. He was already looking tired. The impending treaty fight was not the only problem facing his administration that summer. Food prices were going up sharply; racial tensions were exploding into race riots; key unions threatened strikes. The weather broke, with violent thunderstorms, and the president took to his bed for several days. A touch of dysentery, was Admiral Grayson's explanation. There has been much speculation since that it was in fact a minor stroke. Whatever the case, and we will never know for certain, Wilson was clearly not the man he had been. He was easily confused and forgot things he should have known. He lost his temper frequently, often over small matters. Wilson's deteriorating mental and physical health contributed, perhaps, to his refusal to face the reality that he did not have the votes to get the treaty as it stood through the Senate and also to making his well-known stubbornness something more like blind obstinacy. Grayson and Mrs. Wilson, loyal and protective to a fault, did their best to persuade him to rest. They also downplayed the problems with his health.

On July 14 a Democrat who supported the treaty made the first of what were to be five months of speeches in the Senate. On July 31 the Senate Foreign Relations Committee under Lodge's chairmanship started six weeks of hearings. Not surprisingly, the questioning from the Republican majority focused on the League's covenant, especially the by now notorious Article X. On August 19, in an extraordinary breach with convention, Wilson appeared before the committee. He gave no indication that he was prepared to compromise. Four days later, the committee voted on the first of what were to be numerous amendments and reservations to the treaty. The issue they chose was Shantung—to reverse its award to Japan and hand it back to China.

An angry Wilson decided the time had come to reach beyond the senators to the American people.

On September 2, 1919, he left Washington for a trip across the country. His closest advisers begged him not to go. Wilson was adamant. The treaty must be saved, even if he had to give his life for it. "In the presence of the great tragedy which now faces the world," he told them, "no decent man can count his personal fortunes in the reckoning." Grayson heard the decision with dread: "There was nothing I could do except to go with him and take such care of him as I could." As Wilson boarded his special train, he complained about the dreadful headaches that he had been having. For almost a month Wilson made speech after speech, sometimes two, even three a day. He hammered at the same themes. The treaty was a great document for peace and for humanity, dearly bought with the sacrifice of the young American men who had gone over to fight in Europe. Those who opposed it back in Washington were partisan, shortsighted, selfish, ignorant, perhaps something worse. "When at last in the annals of mankind they are gibbeted, they will regret that the gibbet is so high." He was glad, he told an audience in St. Louis, that he was away from the capital. "The real voices of the great people of America sometimes sound faint and distant in that strange city!" The crowds grew larger and more enthusiastic as he headed west. Supporters of the treaty grew moderately confident that it might get through if only Wilson would accept some of the milder reservations.

Wilson's headaches grew worse and he looked more and more exhausted. Bad news came in from Washington. Sentiment was growing in favor of reservations. . . . Grayson noticed with alarm that the president turned pale and saliva appeared in the corners of his mouth. In San Francisco, Wilson told an old friend, a woman whom he had once been close to, that the attacks on the treaty were simply personal. "If *I* had nothing to do with the League of Nations, it would go through just like that!"

On September 25 Wilson was in Colorado. By now he was having repeated coughing attacks which

Grayson attributed to asthma. He had to sit propped up at nights and could not sleep for more than two hours at a time. He spoke in Pueblo that afternoon, his fortieth speech in twenty-one days. "Disloyalty," he said of the League's opponents. There would be no compromise with them, no reservations to the covenant: "We have got to adopt it or reject it."

Wilson never spoke in public again. At two the next morning, Mrs. Wilson woke Grayson. He found the president in a pitiable state, ill, gasping for air, the muscles in his face twitching. Wilson feebly insisted that he must carry on. His wife and doctor overruled him. "The doctor is right," Wilson told his secretary with tears in his eyes. "I have never been in a condition like this, and I just feel as if I am going to pieces." The president was suffering, Grayson said in a public statement, from physical exhaustion and a nervous reaction affecting his stomach. The rest of the tour was canceled and the president's train headed back to Washington.

On October 2, at the White House, Wilson had a massive stroke that left him partly paralyzed on his left side. Although he would make a limited recovery over time, he was not physically or mentally the man he had been. He never effectively functioned as president again, although he continued to influence the battle over the treaty from his sickroom. Mrs. Wilson and Grayson took it upon themselves to conceal the full extent of his illness and to carry out his wishes. In the first weeks after the stroke, when it was not clear that Wilson would survive, they kept everyone except Wilson's daughters and the essential nurses and doctors from seeing the president. The leader of the Senate Democrats, Gilbert Hitchcock of Nebraska, was shocked when he finally saw Wilson on November 7. "As he lay in bed slightly propped up by pillows with the useless arm concealed beneath the covers I beheld an emaciated old man with a thin white beard which had been permitted to grow."

The treaty continued to make its way through the Senate for the rest of October and part of November 1919. Amendments, twelve in all, were defeated by a combination of Democrats and moderate Republicans.

Lodge managed, however, to hold most of the Republicans together, and their votes, along with those of the few Democrats who crossed party lines, were sufficient to attach a number of reservations to the treaty. The most crucial reservation involved Article X; the United States would not act to protect the territorial integrity or independence of any League member unless Congress approved. Lodge put forward a motion of ratification incorporating the reservation. When Hitchcock went to Wilson's bedside for a second time on November 17 to discuss this, he found the president significantly more alert—but also more determined than ever. Wilson adamantly opposed the reservation in any form. "That cuts the very heart out of the treaty." He told Hitchcock to let the Republicans take the responsibility for defeating the treaty; they would have to answer to the people of the United States. The following day Mrs. Wilson sent Hitchcock a letter she had written at her husband's dictation. The reservations of Senator Lodge and his cronies amounted to a nullification of the treaty. "I sincerely hope," Wilson said unequivocally, "that the friends and supporters of the League will vote against the Lodge resolution of ratification." The next day the Senate voted on Lodge's motion. It was defeated by a combination of those Democrats, the majority, who still followed Wilson's bidding and Republican Irreconcilables. Four weeks later, Wilson learned that he had won the Nobel Peace Prize.

Moderate Republicans and Democrats made a last-ditch effort to find a compromise. From the White House an embittered Wilson did his best to block them. Even so the moderates came close; when the Senate voted for the final time on March 19, 1920, on a fresh resolution to ratify the treaty, with slightly modified reservations, the new resolution passed. Twenty-three Democrats defied their president to vote in favor. The necessary two-thirds majority, however, remained just out of reach so the Senate failed to give its consent to the treaty. "Doctor," Wilson said to Grayson that night, "the devil is a busy man."

He never changed his view that he had been right to reject compromise. The United States later signed separate treaties with Germany, Austria and Hungary, but it never joined the League. Wilson, who had briefly contemplated running for president again, lingered on until 1924. Mrs. Wilson survived to go to John F. Kennedy's inauguration in 1961.

Wilson's efforts, and those of the many other peacemakers who shared his ideals, were not completely wasted. The Treaty of Versailles, and the other treaties with the defeated that used it as a model, certainly contained provisions about territory and reparations that could have been written in earlier centuries, but they were also imbued with a new spirit. . . . The provisions for an International Labour Organization, for treaties to protect minorities, to set up a permanent court of justice or to try men such as the kaiser for offenses against international morality, underlined the idea that there were certain things that all humanity had in common and that there could be international standards beyond those of mere national interest. And when those treaties were attacked in the interwar years it was generally because they had failed to match those standards.

Later it became commonplace to blame everything that went wrong in the 1920s and 1930s on the peacemakers and the settlements they made in Paris in 1919, just as it became easy to despair of democracy. Pointing the finger and shrugging helplessly are effective ways of avoiding responsibility. Eighty years later the old charges about the Paris Peace Conference still have a wide circulation. "The final crime," declared *The Economist* in its special millennium issue, was "the Treaty of Versailles, whose harsh terms would ensure a second war." That is to ignore the actions of everyone—political leaders, diplomats, soldiers, ordinary voters—for twenty years between 1919 and 1939.

Hitler did not wage war because of the Treaty of Versailles, although he found its existence a godsend for his propaganda. Even if Germany had been left with its old borders, even if it had been allowed whatever military forces it wanted, even if it had been permitted to join with Austria, he still would have wanted more: the destruction of Poland, control of Czechoslovakia, above all the conquest of the Soviet Union. He would have demanded room for the German people to expand and the destruction of their enemies, whether Jews or Bolsheviks. There was nothing in the Treaty of Versailles about that.

The peacemakers of 1919 made mistakes, of course. By their offhand treatment of the non-European world, they stirred up resentments for which the West is still paying today. They took pains over the borders in Europe, even if they did not draw them to everyone's satisfaction, but in Africa they carried on the old practice of handing out territory to suit the imperialist powers. In the Middle East, they threw together peoples, in Iraq most notably, who still have not managed to cohere into a civil society. If they could have done better, they certainly could have done much worse. They tried, even cynical old Clemenceau, to build a better order. They could not foresee the future and they certainly could not control it. That was up to their successors. When war came in 1939, it was a result of twenty years of decisions taken or not taken, not of arrangements made in 1919.

Of course things might have been different if Germany had been more thoroughly defeated. Or if the United States had been as powerful after the First World War as it was after the Second—and had been willing to use that power. If Britain and France had not been weakened by the war—or if they had been so weakened that the United States had felt obliged to step in. If Austria-Hungary had not disappeared. If its successor states had not quarreled with each other. If China had not been so weak. If Japan had been more sure of itself. If states had accepted a League of Nations with real powers. If the world had been so thoroughly devastated by war that it was willing to contemplate a new way of managing international relations. The peacemakers, however, had to deal with reality, not what might have been. They grappled with huge and difficult questions. How can the irrational passions of nationalism or religion be contained before they do more damage? How can we outlaw war? We are still asking those questions.

QUESTIONS TO CONSIDER

1 Explain MacMillan's conclusion that Wilson "remained a Southerner in some ways all his life." Describe how Wilson's background and character made it difficult for him to compromise.

2 Why did Woodrow Wilson personally lead the peace delegation to Paris? What risks did he take by leaving the United States when it was still recuperating from the war and was filled with anxieties about the upcoming peace settlement? Why did his peace delegation cause rancor among Republicans?

3 What role did women, especially Edith Bolling Galt, play in Wilson's life? How did the second Mrs. Wilson attempt to shield and protect her husband during those days when, gravely ill, he battled with the Senate over the League of Nations?

4 Why, at the peace negotiations at Versailles, was Wilson's goal of self-determination not consistently applied to all nations? For example, why did the Irish find unconvincing the President's appeal for self-determination? In what ways did the League of Nations challenge the old belief of world peace achieved through a balance of power? Explain the author's conclusion that Wilson's peace program incorporated the concept of "American exceptionalism."

5 When Wilson returned from France with the Treaty of Versailles, what dissension did he encounter in the United States Senate? Why was the President in no mood to compromise on any changes in the League covenant? How might Wilson's health problems have contributed to his intransigence on the peace treaty?

6 Why does MacMillan assert that the failures of the 1919 peacemakers did not cause the foreign policy problems of the next two decades or the outbreak of the Second World War? In what ways are twenty-first-century world leaders still trying to resolve threats to world peace that are similar to those faced by the diplomats of 1919?

PART SEVEN

The Twenties

14 Henry Ford: Symbol of an Age

RODERICK NASH

The election of Warren G. Harding as president reflected a massive popular reaction against the missionary idealism of Woodrow Wilson and the reformist zeal of the Progressive era. Harding would take the country back to "normalcy," so that Americans might continue their "normal, onward way." Essentially, this meant that federal regulation of industry would be reduced to a minimum, that the business of government, as Calvin Coolidge put it, would be big business.

The popular stereotype of the 1920s is that it was a decade of political corruption, speculative orgies, violence, and the last happy fling before the Great Depression crushed American innocence. But in reality this decade of "normalcy" was a good deal more complex than that. True, business consolidation under Republican rule continued throughout the decade. True, excessive and irresponsible speculation on the New York Stock Exchange culminated in the crash of 1929. True, organized crime was widespread, and gang wars rocked Chicago and New York. And true, a revolution in manners and morals challenged traditional standards and profoundly upset Americans who clung to the old morality.

Yet for many contemporaries, the 1920s were a time of exhilarating hope and high expectation for the United States. In fact, a number of intellectuals found much in American life to celebrate. Most optimistic of all were the businesspeople, who believed they were living in a new era—a time not only of conservative Republican leadership in Washington but of striking innovation and change in business itself. As industrial officials happily observed, corporate managers were bringing scientific procedures and efficient techniques to industry. This change, they contended, would raise production so high that poverty would soon be eliminated and the American dream of abundance for all would be attained at last. Their expectations, alas, perished in the crash of 1929 and the ensuing Depression, the worst the country had ever known.

During the 1920s, however, the United States seemed enormously prosperous, and the American businessperson enjoyed new preeminence in American life. One businessman became a leading figure of the decade. Indeed, his technological genius, love of country, and old-fashioned Americanism made him a folk hero to a large segment of American society. This was car maker Henry Ford, who introduced the first car built for the common person—the Model T—and whose technique of assembly-line production revolutionized American technology. What Ford wrought, as David Halberstam has said, also profoundly altered the way Americans lived: it made them far more mobile than they had been in the railroad age, and it created a culture of leisure in which people thought as much about recreation as they did about their jobs. The automobile dramatically changed American customs of courtship.

Ironically, Ford himself despised most of the social changes he helped bring about. A champion of the Protestant work ethic, he abhorred the very idea of leisure. "Work," he contended, "is the salvation of the race, morally, physically, socially. Work does more than get us our living; it gets us our life." He could be remarkably contradictory and unpredictable. He introduced the $5 wage for an eight-hour day (which revolutionized labor policy in industrial America) and yet opposed the union movement. He owned a fifty-six-room mansion and built the Ford Motor Company into what one author described as the biggest "family-owned industrial empire in the world," accumulating a total of $1 billion in profits, and yet he claimed to care little for material things and pleasures. "I have never known," he said, "what to do with money after my expenses were paid." In the end, he donated $40 million to philanthropic enterprises. He considered himself a pacifist, so much so that in 1915 he dispatched a "peace ship" to Europe in a futile if honorable attempt to stop the First World War. Yet this same man had what Roderick Nash calls a rural, "Bible-belt morality." He expatiated on the evils of jazz (it was all "monkey talk" and "jungle squeals") and blamed it and the new dances on a Jewish conspiracy. In fact, he published anti-Semitic diatribes in his Dearborn, Michigan, newspaper (he did retract his anti-Semitic statements in 1927).

The key to Ford's contradictory mind, as Nash says in the next selection, was ambivalence. He was both "old and new." He looked backward and forward at the same time, defending technology while extolling the old rural values and attitudes of a bygone era. In this respect, he symbolized the America of his age—a changing, industrial America that longed for the security of the old days as it struggled with the complexities of the new.

GLOSSARY

ALGER, HORATIO   Gilded Age author whose heroes rose from poverty to greatness and thus fulfilled the "American dream."

FORDISMUS   German word for Ford's "revolutionary mass-production techniques."

McGUFFEY READER   Its "moral-coated language lessons" in such stories as "The Hare and the Tortoise" were the staple of Ford's academic diet.

MODEL T   Ford's first automobile, introduced in 1908 and built for the masses.

Few names were better known to Americans from 1917 to 1930 than that of Henry Ford. Whether one read his publications,[1] or followed his headline-making public life, or merely drove the car his company manufactured, Ford was inescapable in the twenties. Indeed it is possible to think of these years as the automobile age and Henry Ford as its czar. The flivver, along with the flask and the flapper, seemed to represent the 1920s in the minds of its people as well as its historians.

Cars symbolized change. They upset familiar patterns of living, working, recreating, even thinking. Much of the roar of the twenties came from the internal combustion engine. While providing portable bedrooms in which to enjoy the decade's alleged sexual freedom, cars also assisted gangsters and bootleggers in getting away. The image of two of them in every garage helped elect a President in 1928. The rise of widespread use of the automobile, in a word, contributed significantly to setting the twenties apart. And Henry Ford, calling machinery the "new Messiah" (as he did in 1929), seemed to herald the new era.

Beneath the surface, however, such generalizations ring hollow. Neither Ford nor the twenties merited the clichés with which each has been so frequently discussed. In the case of the man, both old and new mingled in his mind. On the one hand Ford was a builder and bulwark of the modern, mechanized nation; on the other he devoted a remarkable amount of effort and expense to sustaining old-fashioned America. In fact, the nostalgic, backward-looking Henry Ford repeatedly deplored the very conditions that Ford the revolutionary industrialist did so much

Henry Ford at the peak of his power, about 1914. As Nash observed, Henry Ford was a "plain, honest, old-fashioned billionaire" and "technological genius" who fretted about the new morality of the Jazz Age, ridiculing jazz itself as "monkey talk" and "jungle squeals" and blaming illicit liquor on a Jewish conspiracy. Still, despite his rural outlook and biblical virtues, Ford was one of the most popular Americans of the Roaring Twenties. (Collection of Greenfield Village and Henry Ford Museum, Dearborn, Michigan)

to bring about. This ambivalence did not signify a lack of values so much as a superfluity. His faith was strong if bigoted and contradictory. His prescriptions for America were clear if simple-minded. He seemed to the masses to demonstrate that there could be change without disruption, and in so doing he eased the twenties' tensions. "The average citizen," editorialized the *New Republic* in 1923, "sees Ford as a sort of enlarged crayon portrait of himself; the man able to fulfill his own suppressed desires, who has achieved enormous riches, fame and power without departing

---

From pp. 154–163 of *The Nervous Generation: American Thought, 1917–1930* by Roderick Nash. Published by Rand-McNally Publishing Company, Chicago. © 1970 by Roderick Nash. Reprinted by permission of Roderick Nash.

[1]In all probability Henry Ford did not actually write the numerous books, pamphlets, and articles associated with his name and attributed to him in this chapter. He was not a literary man; his critics even alleged he could not read! But Ford could pay people to express his opinions for him, and there is no reason to think that the ideas these writers recorded were not those of their employer.

from the pioneer-and-homespun tradition." In this nervous clinging to old values even while undermining them Ford was indeed a "crayon portrait" of his age.

But was Ford typical of the twenties? Can he really be said to symbolize the age? He was, after all, in his middle fifties when the decade began. However, a great many Americans were also middle-aged in the 1920s, far more in fact than the twenty-year-old collegians who have hitherto characterized these years. And at one point even a group of college students ranked Ford as the third greatest figure of all time, behind Napoleon and Jesus Christ.

The Dearborn, Michigan, into which Henry Ford was born in 1863 was a small farming community only a generation removed from the frontier. Both sides of the Ford family had agrarian backgrounds, and the children grew up on the farm. Henry's formal education began and ended in the Scotch Settlement School which he attended for eight years. The staple of his academic diet was the McGuffey reader with its moral-coated language lessons. When Ford left school to become an apprentice mechanic in Detroit, he also left the farm. But the farm never left Henry. Agrarian ideas and values shaped his thought even as he became an industrial king.

The 1880s for Ford were a time of aimlessness, his only real interest being in tinkering with watches and other engines. In 1892 he joined the Edison Company in Detroit as an engineer. During his spare time he struggled with the problem of building a gasoline engine compact enough to power a moving vehicle. By 1896 Ford had his automobile. Soon he had it doing ninety miles per hour! It required seven years more, however, for him to secure the necessary financial and administrative backing to launch the Ford Motor Company. The rest was pure Horatio Alger.

The first Model T appeared in 1908, and it soon made good Ford's boast that he could build a car for the masses. Six thousand sold the first year. Six years later, after the introduction of assembly line production, the figure was 248,000. From May to December 1920 almost 700,000 Model Ts rolled out of the Ford plants. The total for 1921 was one million.

In 1923, 57 percent of all cars manufactured in the United States were Fords. Three years later the Ford Motor Company produced its thirteen millionth car. From the perspective of efficient production the Ford organization was also something of a miracle. In 1913 it required twelve hours to make a car. The following year, after the introduction of the assembly line techniques, the figure dropped to ninety-three minutes. In 1920 Ford achieved his long-time dream of building one car for every minute of the working day. And still he was unsatisfied. On October 31, 1925, the Ford Motor Company manufactured 9,109 Model Ts, one every ten seconds. This was the high point, and competition was rising to challenge Ford's preeminence, but by the end of the twenties Henry Ford was a legend, a folk hero, and reputedly the richest man who ever lived. Transcending the role of automobile manufacturer, he had become an international symbol of the new industrialism. The Germans coined a word to describe the revolutionary mass production techniques: *Fordismus*. At home Ford's popularity reached the point where he could be seriously considered a presidential possibility for the election of 1924.

Fortunately for the historian of his thought, if not always for himself, Henry Ford had a propensity for forthrightly stating his opinions on a wide variety of subjects outside his field of competence. He also had the money to publish and otherwise implement his ideas. The resulting intellectual portrait was that of a mind steeped in traditional Americanism. For Ford agrarian simplicity, McGuffey morality, and Algerian determination were sacred objects. Nationalism was writ large over all Ford did, and America was great because of its heritage of freedom, fairness, and hard, honest work. Ford's confidence in the beneficence of old-fashioned virtues verged on the fanatical. The "spirit of '76," equal opportunity democracy, rugged individualism, the home, and motherhood were Ford's touchstones of reality. He deified pioneer ethics and values. "More men are beaten than fail," he declared in 1928. "It is not wisdom they need, or money, or brilliance, or pull, but just plain gristle and bone." A decade earlier "Mr. Ford's Page" in the

Dearborn Independent stated that "one of the great things about the American people is that they are pioneers." This idea led easily to American messianism. "No one can contemplate the nation to which we belong," the editorial continued, "without realizing the distinctive prophetic character of its obvious mission to the world. We are pioneers. We are pathfinders. We are the roadbuilders. We are the guides, the vanguards of Humanity." Theodore Roosevelt and Woodrow Wilson had said as much, but Ford was writing *after* the war that allegedly ended the nation's innocence and mocked its mission.

Ford's intense commitment to the traditional American faith led him to suspect and ultimately to detest whatever was un-American. The same loyalties compelled him to search for explanations for the unpleasant aspects of the American 1920s that exonerated the old-time, "native" citizen. The immigrant, and particularly the Jew, were primary targets of Ford's fire. In editorial after editorial in the *Dearborn Independent* and in several books Ford argued that aliens who had no knowledge of "the principles which have made our civilization" were responsible for its "marked deterioration" in the 1920s. They were, moreover, determined to take over the country if not the world. Spurred by such fears, Ford became a subscriber to the tired legend of an international Jewish conspiracy. When he couldn't find sufficient evidence for such a plot, Ford dispatched a number of special detectives to probe the affairs of prominent Jews and collect documentation. The search resulted in the "discovery" of the so-called "Protocols of the Learned Elders of Zion," an alleged exposition of the scheme by which the Jews planned to overthrow Gentile domination. Although the "Protocols" was exposed as a forgery in 1921, Ford continued to use the spurious document to substantiate his anti-Semitism until late in the decade. Everything wrong with modern American civilization, from the corruption of music to the corruption of baseball, was attributed to Jewish influence. Unable to admit that America as a whole might be blamed for its problems, unwilling to question the beneficence of time-honored ways, Ford searched for a scapegoat. He found it in the newcomers who, he believed, had no conception of or appreciation for American ideals.

The tension in Henry Ford's thought between old and new, between a belief in progress and a tendency to nostalgia, is dramatically illustrated in his attitude toward farming and farmers. On the one hand he believed farm life to be a ceaseless round of inefficient drudgery. Indeed, he had abundant personal evidence, remarking at one point, "I have traveled ten thousand miles behind a plow. I hated the grueling grind of farm work." With the incentive of sparing others this painful experience, Ford addressed himself to the problem of industrializing agriculture. The farmer, in Ford's opinion, should become a technician and a businessman. Tractors (Ford's, of course) should replace horses. Mechanization would make it possible to produce in twenty-five working days what formerly required an entire year. Fences would come down and vast economies of scale take place. Ford's modern farmer would not even need to live on his farm but instead could commute from a city home. To give substance to these ideals Ford bought and operated with astonishing success a nine-thousand-acre farm near Dearborn.

Still Ford, the "Father of Modern Agriculture," as he has been dubbed, was only part of the man. He also retained a strong streak of old-fashioned, horse-and-buggy agrarianism. Farming, from this standpoint, was more than a challenge in production; it was a moral act. Constantly in the twenties, even while he was helping make it possible, Ford branded the modern city a "pestiferous growth." He delighted in contrasting the "unnatural," "twisted," and "cooped up" lives of city-dwellers with the "wholesome" life of "independence" and "sterling honesty" that the farm environment offered. In Ford's view the importance of cities in the nation's development had been greatly exaggerated. Early in the 1920s the *Dearborn Independent* editorialized: "when we all stand up and sing, 'My Country 'Tis of Thee,' we seldom think of the cities. Indeed, in that old national hymn there are no references to the city at all. It sings of rocks and rivers and hills—the great American Out-of-Doors.

And that is really The Country. That is, the country is THE Country. The real United States lies outside the cities."

As such a manifesto suggests, a bias toward nature and rural conditions was an important element in Henry Ford's thought. "What children and adults need," he told one reporter, "is a chance to breathe God's fresh air and to stretch their legs and have a little garden in the soil." This ideal led Ford to choose small towns instead of cities as the sites of his factories. "Turning back to village industry," as Ford put it in 1926, would enable people to reestablish a sense of community—with nature and with men—that urbanization had destroyed. Ford believed that cities were doomed as Americans discovered the advantages of country life.

Ford's enthusiasm for nature did not stop with ruralism. From 1914 to 1924 he sought a more complete escape from civilization on a series of camping trips with Thomas A. Edison. John Burroughs, the naturalist, and Harvey Firestone, the tire king, also participated. Although the equipment these self-styled vagabonds took into the woods was far from primitive, they apparently shared a genuine love of the outdoors. In the words of Burroughs, they "cheerfully endured wet, cold, smoke, mosquitoes, black flies, and sleepless nights, just to touch naked reality once more." Ford had a special fondness for birds. With typical exuberance he had five hundred birdhouses built on his Michigan farm, including one with seventy-six apartments which he called, appropriately, a "bird hotel." There were also electric heaters and electric brooders for Ford's fortunate birds. The whole production mixed technology and nature in a way that symbolized Ford's ambivalence. When he could not camp or visit his aviary, Ford liked to read about the natural world. Indeed he preferred the works of Emerson, Thoreau, and Burroughs to the Bible. Ford so admired Burroughs' variety of natural history that even before becoming acquainted with him he sent him a new Ford car.

As for roads and automobiles, Ford saw them not as a threat to natural conditions but rather as a way for the average American to come into contact with nature. The machine and the garden were not incompatible. "I will build a motor car for the great multitude . . . ," Ford boasted, "so low in price that no man . . . will be unable to own one—and enjoy with his family the blessings of hours of pleasure in God's great open spaces." In *My Life and Work* of 1923 Ford again confronted the tension between nature and modern civilization. He declared that he did not agree with those who saw mechanization leading to a "cold, metallic sort of world in which great factories will drive away the trees, the flowers, the birds and the green fields." According to Ford, "unless we know more about machines and their use . . . we cannot have the time to enjoy the trees and the birds, and the flowers, and the green fields." Such reconciliations only partially covered Ford's nervousness about the mechanized, urbanized future. Contradictions persisted in his thinking. The same man who envisaged fenceless bonanza farms could say, "I love to walk across country and jump fences." The lover of trees could state in utmost seriousness, "better wood can be made than is grown."

Ford's attitude toward history has been subject to wide misunderstanding. The principal source of confusion is a statement Ford made in 1919 at the trial resulting from his libel suit against the *Chicago Tribune*. "History," he declared, "is more or less the bunk. It is tradition. We don't want tradition. We want to live in the present, and the only history that is worth a tinker's dam is the history we make today." On another occasion he admitted that he "wouldn't give a nickel for all the history in the world." Complementing this sentiment is Ford's reputation as a forward-looking inventor and revolutionary industrialist unsatisfied with the old processes. Here seems a man fully at home in the alleged new era of the 1920s. But in fact Ford idolized the past. His "history . . . is bunk" remark came in response to a question about ancient history and Napoleon Bonaparte and had reference to written history. For history itself—what actually happened in his nation's past and its tangible evidence—Ford had only praise.

The most obvious evidence of Ford's enthusiasm for history was his collector's instinct. He began with the bastion of his own youth, the McGuffey readers. Sending agents out to scour the countryside and putting aside considerations of cost, Ford owned by 1925 one of the few complete collections of the many McGuffey editions. Hoping to share his treasures with his contemporaries, Ford had five thousand copies of *Old Favorites from the McGuffey Readers* printed in 1926. The book contained such classic stories as "Try, Try Again" and "The Hare and the Tortoise." It dispensed an ideal of individualism and self-reliance at the same time that Ford's assembly lines were making men cogs in an impersonal machine.

From books Ford turned to things, and during the 1920s amassed a remarkable collection of American antiques. He bought so widely and so aggressively that he became a major factor in prices in the antique market. Everything was fair game. Lamps and dolls, bells and grandfather clocks made their way to Dearborn. Size was no problem. Ford gathered enough machines to show the evolution of the threshing operation from 1849 to the 1920s. Another exhibit traced the development of wagons in America. Eventually the entire heterogeneous collection went into the Edison Museum at Dearborn, a pretentious building designed to resemble, simultaneously, Independence Hall, Congress Hall, and the old City Hall of Philadelphia. Ford delighted in showing visitors around the five-acre layout. Asked on one occasion why he collected, Ford replied, "so that they will not be lost to America." Later, on the same tour, Ford played a few bars on an antique organ and observed, "that takes me back to my boyhood days. They were beautiful days."

This sentiment undoubtedly figured in Ford's 1920 decision to restore his boyhood home. Everything had to be exactly as he remembered it. Furniture, china, and rugs were rehabilitated or reconstructed. Ford even used archaeological techniques to recover artifacts around the family homestead. The ground was dug to a depth of six feet and the silverware, wheels, and other equipment used by his parents in the 1860s were recovered. In 1922 Ford purchased the Wayside Inn at Sudbury, Massachusetts, to preserve it from destruction. Celebrated by the poet

Henry Wadsworth Longfellow, the old inn appealed to Ford as a symbol of pioneer days. He opened it for the public's edification in 1924. But a new highway ran too near. Roaring cars disturbed the horse-and-buggy atmosphere. So, turning against the age he helped create, Ford had the state highway rerouted around the shrine at a cost of $250,000. He also bought and restored the schoolhouse in Sudbury alleged to be the site where Mary and her little lamb gamboled. Naturally the shop of the "Village Blacksmith," also in Sudbury, had to be included in Ford's antique empire.

Beginning in 1926 with the construction of Greenfield Village near Dearborn, Ford embarked on a career of large-scale historical restoration. This time not a building but a whole community was the object of his attention. Greenfield, named after the Michigan hamlet in which Ford's mother grew up, was a monument to his agrarianism as well as his reverence for the past. "I am trying in a small way," Ford explained with unwarranted modesty, "to help America take a step . . . toward the saner and sweeter idea of life that prevailed in pre-war days." Greenfield Village had gravel roads, gas street lamps, a grassy common, and an old-fashioned country store. The automobile mogul permitted only horse-drawn vehicles on the premises. The genius of assembly line mass production engaged a glass blower, blacksmith, and cobbler to practice their obsolete crafts in the traditional manner. Ford dispatched his agents to seek out, purchase, and transport to Greenfield the cottages of Walt Whitman, Noah Webster, and Patrick Henry. In time they even secured the crowning glory: the log cabin in which William Holmes McGuffey had been born and raised.

History, then, was not "bunk" to Henry Ford. The speed of change seemed to increase proportionately to his desire to retain contact with the past. As Ford declared in 1928, a year before completing Greenfield Village, "improvements have been coming so quickly that the past is being lost to the rising generation." To counter this tendency Ford labored to put history into a form "where it may be seen and felt." But values and attitudes were also on display.

Ford looked back with nostalgia to the pioneer ethic. With it, he believed, the nation had been sound, wholesome, happy, and secure. "The Old Ways," as the *Dearborn Independent* declared, "Were Good."

Ford's opinion of the new morality of the jazz age was, not surprisingly, low. He deplored the use of tobacco and even went so far as to publish for mass circulation a tract, entitled *The Case Against the Little White Slaver,* which excoriated cigarettes. When Ford had the power he went beyond exhortation. "No one smokes in the Ford industries," their leader proclaimed in 1929. As for alcohol, Ford was equally unyielding. Twice he threatened to make his international labor force teetotalers at the risk of their jobs. In his American plants Ford enforced a policy of abstinence. Any workman detected drinking publicly or even keeping liquor at home was subject to dismissal. The prohibition policy of the 1920s, in Ford's estimation, was a great triumph. "There are a million boys growing up in the United States," he exulted in 1929, "who have never seen a saloon and who will never know the handicap of liquor." When confronted with evidence of widespread violation of the Eighteenth Amendment, Ford had a ready explanation. A Jewish conspiracy was to blame for illicit booze. The mass of real Americans, Ford believed, were, like himself, dry by moral conviction as well as by law.

Sex was too delicate a matter to be addressed directly, but Ford conveyed his opinions through a discussion of music and dancing. Few aspects of the American 1920s worried him more than the evils of jazz. The new music clashed squarely with his ruralism and Bible-belt morality. In 1921 Ford struck out in anger at "the waves upon waves of musical slush that invaded decent parlors and set the young people of this generation imitating the drivel of morons." Organized Jewry, once again, was blamed for the musical degeneracy. "The mush, the slush, the sly suggestion, the abandoned sensuousness of sliding notes," declared the Dearborn Independent, "are of Jewish origin." The problem, obviously, was not only musical but sexual as well. The loosening of morals in the 1920s appalled Ford. He expressed his feelings in reference to jazz: "monkey talk, jungle squeals, grunts and squeaks and gasps suggestive of cave love are camouflaged by a few feverish notes." What Ford could only bring himself to call "the thing" appeared also in song titles such as *In Room 202* and *Sugar Baby.* Pointing to the Jewish origin of these tunes (Irving Berlin was a frequent target of attacks), Ford called on his countrymen to crush the serpent in their midst.

The reform of dancing fitted nicely into Ford's campaign to elevate the nation's morals to old-time standards. His interest began with the collection of traditional folk dances. Not only the scores but the backwoods fiddlers themselves were invited to Dearborn to play *Old Zip Coon* and *Arkansas Traveler.* To Ford's delight, here was something both wholesome and historical. He also manifested concern over social dancing, publishing in 1926 a guidebook entitled *"Good Morning": After a Sleep of Twenty-five Years Old-Fashioned Dancing is Being Revived by Mr. and Mrs. Henry Ford.* The book also endeavored to revive old-fashioned morality. It began by condemning as promiscuous the newer dances such as the Charleston and the whole flapper syndrome. "A gentleman," the book explained, "should be able to guide his partner through a dance without embracing her as if he were her lover." Proper deportment, according to Ford, minimized physical contact. "[The gentleman's] right hand should be placed at his partner's waist, thumb and forefinger alone touching her—that is, the hand being in the position of holding a pencil." There were also rules regarding gloves, handkerchiefs, and the way to request a partner for a dance. Ford's dance manual, in short, was a monument to the old conceptions of morality, decorum, and order, and the dances he and his wife hosted at Dearborn were implementations. Precisely at nine Ford's guests convened in evening dress in a lavish ballroom for a paean to Victorianism.

Ambivalence is the key to the mind of Henry Ford. He was both old and new; he looked both forward and backward. Confidently progressive as he was in some respects, he remained nervous about the new ways. The more conditions changed, the more the nostalgic Ford groped for the security of traditional values and institutions. He was not lost; on the contrary, he had too many gods, at least for consistency. Neither was he dissipated and roaring. And he hated jazz. But Ford was popular, indeed a national deity, in the twenties even if his senatorial and presidential bids fell short. As a plain, honest, old-fashioned billionaire, a technological genius who loved to camp out, he seemed to his contemporaries to resolve the moral dilemmas of the age. Like Charles A. Lindbergh, another god of the age, Ford testified to the nation's ability to move into the future without losing the values of the past.

QUESTIONS TO CONSIDER

1 Compare Henry Ford with "robber baron" Andrew Carnegie in selection 5. In what ways did each man symbolize the America of his age?

2 Analyze the sources of Ford's tremendous popularity in the 1920s. Was it true, as Nash argues, that despite the revolutionary social changes Ford's cars brought to American society, Ford's commitment to old-fashioned values comforted Americans who felt anxious about the effects of modernization?

3 Henry Ford was the symbol of the new industrial order of the 1920s, but he also reflected the urban-rural tensions of that decade, especially in his attitudes toward the "revolution in manners and morals" of the Jazz Age. Discuss Ford's attitudes toward alcohol, sex, music, and dancing and how they reflected the changes taking place in America in the 1920s.

4 In addition to being a technological genius, Ford was both an anti-Semite and a Victorian prude, but the American people loved him. Why do you think that was so?

15 Justice Denied: The Trial of Sacco and Vanzetti

JAMES WEST DAVIDSON AND MARK HAMILTON LYTLE

In the following selection, historians James West Davidson and Mark Hamilton Lytle examine the conflicting currents of the 1920s that produced "two nations" in this country. One "nation" consisted mainly of native-born white American Protestants. The other "nation" comprised the immigrants, most of them Jews and Catholics, who flooded into the country from Italy, Russia, and the rest of eastern Europe. Focusing on the nation of immigrants, the authors examine the notorious case of Nicola Sacco and Bartolomeo Vanzetti, "two Italian immigrants living on the fringe of American society." In 1921, a Massachusetts court convicted Sacco and Vanzetti of killing a paymaster and his guard and sentenced them to be executed. The jury had taken only five hours to find the two immigrants guilty. The trial provoked bitter national and international controversy. This was hardly the first execution in an American society that had long used the death penalty. So, the authors ask, "Why all the fuss?"

The answer, they believe, lies in the conflict between America's "two nations," which the trial of Sacco and Vanzetti symbolized. The "nation" of native-born white Anglo-Saxon Protestants was worried about the dark forces in the twenties that threatened their beloved country. Among these was a sexual revolution against the old Victorian moral code. This "revolution in manners and morals," as Frederick Lewis Allen described it, derived in part from the new consumer age, which afforded middle and upper-class Americans unbelievable luxuries and the time to indulge in them. One of those indulgences was Henry Ford's motor car, the topic of the previous selection, which proved to be more than an inexpensive means of transportation. When parked, the automobile allowed dating couples unprecedented privacy in sexual matters. As a result, new words like "petting" and "necking" entered the vocabulary. One disapproving journal called the automobile nothing more "than a house of prostitution on wheels." The twenties also witnessed the appearance of the legendary "flapper": an uninhibited young woman who wore her hair bobbed, dabbled rouge on her cheeks, wore shorter skirts, smoked in public, danced the Charleston, and dedicated herself generally to having fun and doing as she pleased. For a large percentage of native-born white Protestants, particularly those in the countryside, the youth-oriented sexual revolution posed a grave threat to traditional American values. So, too, did the teaching of Charles Darwin's theory of evolution in the nation's schools. Who was to blame for the dangerous moral threats to the traditional "American way of life"?

For many native-born Americans, the Catholic and Jewish immigrants from southern and eastern Europe were to blame. A new wave of anti-Semitic and anti-Catholic prejudice swept the land. Such prejudice prompted the federal government to set discriminatory immigration quotas. Worse still was the emergence of a new, more vicious, and more widespread Ku Klux Klan, which hated immigrants, Jews, and Catholics as well as African Americans.

For Attorney General A. Mitchell Palmer and millions of other native-born Protestant Americans, the increasing number of immigrants from eastern Europe posed a dangerous threat to the old values. Palmer declared that "out of the sly and crafty eyes of many of them, leap cupidity, cruelty, insanity, and crime; from their lopsided faces, sloping brows, and misshapen features may be recognized the unmistakable criminal types." In a flagrant violation of civil liberties, Palmer deported as many of these undesirables as he could. Few people protested. Indeed, as the authors point out, native-born Americans across the land were "alarmed that immigration threatened their cherished institutions."

It was their alarm, the authors believe, that brought about the trial and execution of Sacco and Vanzetti. As you read their sad and disquieting story, bear in mind that the courtroom has often served as a battleground between people with contrasting values. Do the have-nots of society still face discrimination under the American system of justice? Do people of Middle Eastern extraction in our day face some of the same prejudices that plagued Italian and eastern European immigrants in the 1920s? Do the ghosts of Sacco and Vanzetti still haunt us?

GLOSSARY

ANARCHISTS   Seeking to create a society where individuals voluntarily cooperate with each other, anarchists are against any form of imposed authority by the state. In the 1920s, class tensions and an opposition to capitalism produced a group of radicals who sought to overthrow the American government through a violent social upheaval. Many Americans believed that anarchists had infiltrated the labor movement and were among the wave of new immigrants who, following the Great War, came to American shores from southern and eastern Europe.

BOLSHEVIKS   In November, 1917, this group of Communist revolutionaries, led by V. I. Lenin, seized control of Russia. The new Bolshevik government made peace with

Germany and trumpeted an anticapitalist ideology that frightened many Americans.

COLLECTIVE BARGAINING   A process that permits negotiations between labor unions and employers on issues such as wages, hours, benefits, and working conditions. In 1935, the Wagner Act created a National Labor Relations Board that gave unions the support of the federal government in negotiating collective bargaining agreements.

DOS PASSOS, JOHN   In *Three Soldiers* (1921), novelist Dos Passos reflected the disillusionment of American writers that followed the Great War. Dos Passos was distressed by the executions of Sacco and Vanzetti. The fate of those immigrants symbolized, in Dos Passos's words, the presence of the "two nations"—immigrants and native citizens—in the post-war United States. The "two nations" had dramatically different values.

FRANKFURTER, FELIX   A Harvard Law School professor, Frankfurter served as an advisor to Presidents Woodrow Wilson and Franklin Roosevelt. In 1939, FDR appointed Frankfurter to the Supreme Court, where he served until 1962.

HAYMARKET SQUARE RIOT   On May 4, 1886, about three thousand workers gathered in Haymarket Square in downtown Chicago. They were protesting the death of two colleagues shot by policemen as they dispersed a group of strikers. Someone tossed a bomb that killed seven policemen. In the minds of many Americans, the ensuing riot linked the labor movement with radicalism and violence.

HOOVER, J. EDGAR   During the "Red Scare" that followed the Great War, Hoover was an assistant to attorney general A. Mitchell Palmer. Hoover later earned a reputation as an outspoken anti-Communist. In 1924, he became the director of the Bureau of Investigations (renamed the Federal Bureau of Investigations in 1935). Hoover remained that agency's imperious director until his death in 1972.

IMMIGRATION ACTS OF 1921 AND 1924   A reaction to the immigrants who came to America following the Great War, these acts established a quota system. The quotas discriminated against Jews and Catholics in southern and eastern Europe who sought sanctuary in the United States. The 1924 legislation was blatantly racist against such immigrants and against migrants from Asia as well. By contrast, the acts set liberal quotas for immigrants from western Europe.

KATZMANN, FREDERICK   The Massachusetts district attorney who prosecuted Sacco and Vanzetti, Katzmann based his case, not on solid legal evidence, but on character assassination and ethnic prejudice.

KU KLUX KLAN   On Thanksgiving night in 1915, on Stone Mountain in Georgia, the twentieth-century Klan was born. Unlike the violent night riders of the post–Civil War years, the modern Klan had support outside the South, in urban as well as rural communities. Even more vicious than its nineteenth-century predecessor, the new Ku Klux Klan hated immigrants, Jews, and Catholics, as well as African Americans.

MOORE, FRED   A Californian with an unorthodox style of life and radical sympathies, Moore served as the defense counsel for Sacco and Vanzetti until 1924. His casual dress and long hair alienated the judge and jury.

NATIVISM   A "defensive nationalism," nativism was rooted in the Protestant Anglo-Saxon value system that defined American culture for most of the nineteenth century. "Native-born" Americans believed that the religion, language, and perceived radicalism of the immigrants from southern and eastern Europe represented a threat to the established values of the native-born.

PALMER, A. MITCHELL   A Quaker and a progressive reformer, Palmer served as Woodrow Wilson's attorney general from 1919–1921. Following the Great War, Palmer launched a massive roundup of those immigrants he believed were foreign-born radicals. The government deported thousands of innocent people without hearings or trials. This was an unprecedented violation of civil liberties.

SINCLAIR, UPTON   A muckraking author and socialist, Sinclair wrote *The Jungle* (1906) that exposed the Chicago meat packing industry's unsanitary practices and its harsh treatment of immigrant workers. He would later denounce the executions of Sacco and Vanzetti. In 1934, Sinclair ran for governor of California.

THAYER, WEBSTER   The judge during the trial of Sacco and Vanzetti, Thayer later denied eight appeals of the convicted immigrants. On April 9, 1927, Thayer sentenced them to die. Thayer reflected the ethnic biases of his day and seemed predisposed to find the two defendants guilty. On August 22, 1927, Sacco and Vanzetti died in the electric chair.

In the years after World War I, crime statistics curved sharply upward. Armed robberies rose at an alarming rate, and anyone handling large sums of money had reason to exercise caution. On most paydays Frederick Parmenter, paymaster for the Slater and Morrill Shoe Company of South Braintree, Massachusetts, would have used a truck to deliver his money boxes to the lower factory building. Only a few months earlier, in December 1919, a brazen gang of bandits had attempted a daylight payroll heist in nearby Bridgewater. The bandits had fled empty-handed, and no one was hurt in the gunfight. Still, area businesses were uneasy. On the morning of April 15, 1920, however, the robbery attempt must have been far from Parmenter's mind. It was a mild spring day, and he set out on foot for the lower factory building with his assistant, Alessandro Berardelli, walking ahead.

Halfway to their destination, a man approached Berardelli from the side of the road, spoke to him briefly, and then suddenly shot him dead. As Parmenter turned to flee, the bandits fired again, mortally wounding him. A blue Buick pulled from its parking place. The two assailants and their lookout jumped into the car and fled toward Bridgewater. To discourage pursuers, the bandits threw tacks onto the streets. Two miles from Braintree they abandoned the Buick and escaped in another car.

Bridgewater Police Chief Michael Stewart thought he recognized a pattern in the Braintree crime. The same foreigners who bungled the December heist, he guessed, had probably pulled off the Braintree job. Stewart's investigation put him on the trail of Mike Boda, an Italian anarchist. Unable to locate Boda, Stewart kept watch on a car Boda had left at Simon Johnson's garage for repairs. Whoever came to get the car would, according to Stewart's theory, become a prime suspect in both crimes.

His expectations were soon rewarded. On May 5, 1920, Boda and three other Italians called for the car. Mrs. Johnson immediately slipped next door to alert the police, but the four men did not wait for her return. Boda and one friend, Riccardo Orciani, left on a motorcycle while their companions walked to a nearby streetcar stop. Apparently nervous, they moved on to another stop a half mile away. There they boarded the trolley for Brockton. As the trolley car moved down Main Street, Police Officer Michael Connolly climbed on. Having spotted the two foreigners, he arrested them. When they asked why, he replied curtly, "suspicious characters."

Thus began the epic story of Nicola Sacco and Bartolomeo Vanzetti, two obscure Italian aliens who became the focal point of one of the most controversial episodes in American history. Within little more than a year after their arrest a jury deliberated for just five hours before convicting both men of robbery and murder. Such a quick decision came as a surprise, particularly in a trial that had lasted seven weeks, heard more than 160 witnesses, and gained national attention.

Nor did the controversy end with the jury's decision. Six years of appeals turned a small-town incident of robbery and murder into a major international uproar. The Italian government indicated that it was following the case with interest. Thousands of liberals, criminal lawyers, legal scholars, civil libertarians, radicals, labor leaders, prominent socialites, and spokespersons for immigrant groups rallied to Sacco and Vanzetti's cause. Arrayed against them was an equally imposing collection of the nation's legal, social, academic, and political elite.

The case climaxed on April 9, 1927. Having denied some eight appeals, trial judge Webster Thayer sentenced Sacco and Vanzetti to die in the electric chair. His action triggered months of protests and political activities. Around Charleston Prison (where the two men were held) and the State House in Boston, Sacco and Vanzetti's supporters marched, collected petitions, and walked picket lines. Occasionally violence erupted between protesters and authorities, as mounted police attacked crowds in Boston and clubbed them off the streets in New York. On August 22, the morning

Edited excerpt from James West Davidson and Mark Hamilton Lytle. *After the Fact: The Art of Historical Detection,* 5th ed. (McGraw-Hill, 2005), pp. 262–279, 281–282, 284–286. Reproduced with permission of the McGraw-Hill Companies.

Nicola Sacco and Bartolomeo Vanzetti were two obscure Italian immigrants who were accused of committing murder during a payroll robbery. Immigration laws were controversial and their prosecution was tinged with ethnic prejudice. During a police line-up, Sacco and Vanzetti were forced to pose as bandits, alone in the middle of a room. (© Bettmann/CORBIS)

before Sacco and Vanzetti were scheduled to die, Charleston Prison appeared like an embattled fortress. Ropes circled the prison grounds to keep protesters at bay as eight hundred armed guards walked the walls. In New York's Union Square, 15,000 people gathered to stand in silent vigil. Similar crowds congregated in major European cities. All awaited the news of the fate of "a good shoemaker and a poor fish peddler."

The historian confronting that extraordinary event faces some perplexing questions. How did a case of robbery and murder become an international cause célèbre? How was it that two Italian immigrants living on the fringe of American society had become the focus of a debate that brought the nation's cherished legal institutions under attack? Or as one eminent law professor rhetorically posed the question:

Why all this fuss over a couple of "wops," who after years in this country had not even made application to become citizens; who had not learned to use our language even modestly well; who did not believe in our form of government; . . . who were confessed slackers and claimed to be pacifists but went armed with deadly weapons for the professed purpose of defending their individual personal property in violation of all the principles they preached?

THE QUESTION OF LEGAL EVIDENCE

Lawyers reviewing events might answer those questions by arguing that the Sacco and Vanzetti case raised serious doubts about the tradition of Anglo-Saxon justice so venerated in the United States. More specifically, many legal scholars then and since have asserted that the trial and appeals process failed to meet minimum standards of fairness, particularly for a criminal case in which the defendants' lives hung in the balance.

In the first flush of Sacco and Vanzetti's arrest, prosecutors seemed to have good reason to label the two men "suspicious characters." Both Sacco and Vanzetti were carrying loaded revolvers. Not only that, Sacco had twenty-three extra cartridges in his pockets, while Vanzetti carried several shotgun shells. When questioned, both men lied about their activities. They claimed not to know Mike Boda or to have been at the garage to pick up Boda's car. But suspicious behavior was one matter; proof that Sacco and Vanzetti had committed the Braintree murders was another. As the police and prosecutors went about making their case, they followed distinctly irregular procedures.

To be sure, in 1920 the police were allowed to conduct an investigation with far greater latitude than the law permits today. The Supreme Court decisions in *Miranda* (1966) and *Escobedo* (1964) established that criminal suspects have the right to remain silent, to be informed of their rights, and to stand in an impartial lineup for identification. None of those guarantees existed in 1920. Even so, District Attorney Frederick Katzmann and Chief Stewart showed unusual zeal in constructing a case against Sacco and Vanzetti. At no time during the first two days of questioning did they tell either suspect why they had been arrested. Chief Stewart repeatedly asked them not about the robbery, but about their political beliefs and associates. The district attorney did obliquely inquire about their activities on April 15, though he never mentioned the Braintree crimes. Furthermore, when the police asked witnesses to identify the suspects, they did not use a lineup. Instead, they forced Sacco and Vanzetti to stand alone in the middle of a room posing as bandits.

As the investigation continued, the case came close to collapsing for lack of evidence. Of the five suspected gang members, all but Vanzetti could prove they had not been in Bridgewater during the December holdup attempt. Despite an intensive search of the suspects' belongings, including a trunk sent to Italy, Katzmann was never able to trace the money, even among radical political groups with whom the suspects were associated. Fingerprint experts found no matches between prints lifted from the abandoned Buick and those taken from the suspects.

Faced with those gaps in the evidence, Katzmann still decided, first, to prosecute Vanzetti for the December Bridgewater holdup and, second, to charge both Sacco and Vanzetti with the Braintree murders in April. Arguing the Bridgewater case in June 1920 before Judge Webster Thayer, Katzmann presented a weak case against Vanzetti on the charge of assault with intent to rob. Still, he did manage to make the jury aware of Vanzetti's anarchist views and persuade them to convict. Judge Thayer then meted out an unusually severe sentence (twelve to fifteen years) to a defendant with no criminal record for a crime in which no one was hurt and nothing was stolen.

That conviction allowed Katzmann to proceed with the second trial, to be held in the suburban town of Dedham. Since this trial would be a special session of the superior court, a judge had to be appointed to hear the case. Judge Thayer asked his old college friend, Chief Justice John Aiken, for the assignment, even though he had presided over Vanzetti's earlier trial and could scarely consider himself impartial. Thus the second trial opened with a judge who already believed unequivocally in the defendants' guilt.

At Dedham, District Attorney Katzmann built his case around three major categories of evidence: (1) eyewitness identification of Sacco and Vanzetti at the scene, (2) expert ballistics testimony establishing Sacco's gun as the weapon that fired the fatal shot at Berardelli and Vanzetti's gun as one taken from Berardelli during the robbery, (3) the defendants' evasive behavior both before and after arrest as evidence of what is legally termed "consciousness of guilt."

The prosecution, however, had a difficult time making its case. Of the "eyewitnesses" claiming to place Sacco and Vanzetti at the scene, one, Mary Splaine, claimed to have observed the shooting from a window in the Slater and Morrill factory for no longer than three seconds at a distance of about 60 feet. In that time she watched an unknown man in a car traveling about 18 miles an hour. Immediately after the crime Splaine had difficulty describing any of the bandits, but one year later she picked out Sacco, vividly recalling such details as his "good-sized" left hand. She refused to recant her testimony even after the defense demonstrated that Sacco had relatively small hands.

Louis Pelzer testified for the prosecution that upon hearing shots, he had observed the crime from a window for at least a minute. He pointed to Sacco as the "dead image" of the man who shot Berardelli. Two defense witnesses, however, controverted Pelzer's story. Upon hearing the shots, they recalled, the intrepid Pelzer had immediately hidden under his workbench—hardly a vantage point from which to make a clear identification.

Lola Andrews, a third witness, claimed that on the morning of the crime she had stopped near the factory to ask directions from a dark-haired man working under a car. She later identified Sacco as that man. But a companion, Julia Campbell, denied that Andrews had ever spoken to the man under the car. Instead, Campbell testified, Andrews had approached a pale, sickly young man who was standing nearby. Other witnesses had recalled the same pale person. A second friend swore that he had heard Andrews say after she returned from police headquarters that "the government took me down and wanted me to recognize those men and I don't know a thing about them." Nor did Andrews's reputation as a streetwalker enhance her credibility. Yet in his summation, prosecutor Katzmann told the jury that in eleven years as district attorney he had not "ever before . . . laid eye or given ear to so convincing a witness as Lola Andrews."

Against Katzmann's dubious cast, the defense produced seventeen witnesses who provided the defendants with alibis for the day or who had seen the crime, but not Sacco or Vanzetti. One, an official of the Italian Consulate in Boston, confirmed Sacco's claim that he had been in Boston on April 15 acquiring a passport. The official remembered Sacco because he had tried to use a picture over 10 inches square for his passport photo. "Since such a large photograph had never been presented before," the official recalled, "I took it in and showed it to the Secretary of the Consulate. We laughed and talked over the incident. I remember observing the date . . . on a large pad calendar." Others said they had met Sacco at a luncheon banquet that day. Witnesses for Vanzetti claimed to have bought fish from him. Katzmann could only try to persuade the jury that the witnesses had little reason to connect such a mundane event with a specific date.

In the face of contradictory eyewitness testimony, the ballistics evidence might have decided the case. To prove murder, Katzmann wished to show that the fatal shot striking Berardelli had come from Sacco's gun. Ballistics specialists can often identify the gun that fired a bullet by characteristic marks, as distinct as fingerprints, that the barrel and hammer make on the projectile and casing. Two experts, Captains William Proctor and Charles Van Amburgh, connected the fatal bullet to a Colt pistol similar to and possibly the same as Sacco's. But neither of Katzmann's witnesses made a definitive link. "It is consistent with being fired by that pistol," Proctor replied to Katzmann. Van Amburgh also indicated some ambiguity: "I am inclined to believe that it was fired . . . from this pistol."

For unknown reasons defense attorneys never pursued the equivocation of those testimonies. Instead, they called their own ballistics specialists who stated with absolute certainty that the fatal bullet could not have come from Sacco's gun. In addition, they controverted the prosecutor's claim that Vanzetti had taken Berardelli's gun during the holdup. Shortly before his murder, Berardelli had left his pistol at a repair shop to have the hammer fixed. Shop records, though imprecise, indicated that the gun was .32 caliber, not a .38 such as Vanzetti was carrying. The records also supported Mrs. Berardellis's sworn testimony that her husband had never reclaimed his pistol. The defense then argued that the hammer on Vanzetti's gun had never been repaired.

Since the defense had weakened the ballistics evidence, Katzmann based his case primarily on "consciousness of guilt." To convict on those grounds, he had to convince the jury that Sacco and Vanzetti had behaved like men guilty of the crime, both before and after arrest. Here, Katzmann made his case with telling effect. Why had the defendants been carrying guns when they were arrested? They had gone hunting that morning, they claimed. But if that were the case, why were they still carrying hunting weapons and extra ammunition at night, when they set out to pick up Mike Boda's car? They were in such a hurry, Sacco and Vanzetti replied, that they forgot to leave their revolvers at home. But Katzmann continued his onslaught. Why did the two men lie at first about knowing Mike Boda or having visited the garage? Surely this evasion indicated a clear consciousness of guilt.

To explain such evasive behavior, defense lawyers were forced to introduce the inflammatory issue of Sacco and Vanzetti's political beliefs. For indeed, both men proudly proclaimed themselves to be anarchists, rejecting the authority of any government. Capitalism, they believed, was little more than an organized system of banditry under which the rich and powerful extorted the poor. Sacco and Vanzetti had both been active in the strikes and labor unrest of the era. As a result, they had been alarmed by the government crackdown on radicals that began in 1919. When Officer Connolly arrested them, the two men assumed that they, too, had been snared in the government's dragnet. They acted evasively, defense lawyers argued, not because they were criminals but because radicals were being persecuted and deported. Once arrested, Sacco and Vanzetti's fears were only confirmed by the police's constant questions about their political beliefs.

Similar worries accounted for their peculiar actions at Johnson's garage, the defense argued. Shortly before his arrest, Vanzetti had conferred with the Italian Defense Committee of New York, then inquiring into the fate of a fellow anarchist, Andrea Salsedo. The committee knew only that Salsedo was being held by Justice Department agents; members warned Vanzetti that he and his friends might be in danger of being jailed or deported. Only a week later, newspapers across the nation reported that Salsedo had fallen to his death from a twelfth-floor window. The police insisted the case had been a suicide, but many anarchists thought Salsedo had been pushed. Before he died, had he provided the government with the names of other anarchists? If so, Vanzetti and Sacco were at risk. Anyone found with anarchist literature could be arrested and deported. It was for that reason, Sacco and Vanzetti told the court, that they had gone to retrieve Mike Boda's car: they needed it to carry away the radical pamphlets stored in their homes—something they hardly wished to admit to police questioning them about radical activities.

The revelations of the defendants' radical politics could hardly have raised the jury's opinion of the two men. And their explanations did not stop Katzmann from focusing on consciousness of guilt in his final summation. Nor did Judge Thayer take into account their explanations in his charge to jury. In theory, a judge's charge guides the jury as it interprets conflicting evidence: in separating the relevant from the irrelevant and in establishing the grounds for an objective verdict. But Thayer made his sympathies all too clear. In discussing the ballistics testimony, he wrongly assumed that Katzmann's expert witnesses had unequivocally identified Sacco's gun as having fired the fatal shot. And he spent no time weighing the defense's argument that prosecution eyewitnesses had been unreliable. Only when he discussed consciousness of guilt did the judge become expansive and specific. He lingered over the evidence offered by the police and the garage owner while ignoring Sacco and Vanzetti's explanations.

Lawyers and legal historians have raised other telling criticisms—excesses in the trial procedures, prejudice on the part of both judge and prosecutor, bungling by the defense lawyer. Inevitably, these criticisms have influenced the way historians have approached the controversy. Most of them have centered on the issue of *proof* of guilt. Contrary to popular opinion, the courts do not determine whether a person is guilty or innocent of a crime. They decide merely whether the prosecutor has assembled sufficient evidence to establish guilt. The judge may even suspect a defendant is guilty, but if the evidence does not meet minimum standards of legal proof, the court must set the accused free. As one court concluded, "the commonwealth demands no victims . . . and it is as much the duty of the district attorney to see that no innocent man suffers, as it is to see that no guilty man escapes."

Thus lawyers tend to focus on narrow, yet admittedly important, questions. They are all the more crucial when human lives are at stake, as was the case with Sacco and Vanzetti. Believing that the legal system maintains vital safeguards of individual rights, lawyers in general seek to ensure that proper legal procedures have been followed, that evidence is submitted according to established rules, and, in accordance with those procedures, that guilt has been adequately determined. A lawyer answering the question, "Why all the fuss over the Sacco and Vanzetti case?" would most likely reply, "Because the trial, by failing to prove guilt beyond reasonable doubt, perpetrated a serious miscarriage of justice."

BEYOND GUILT OR INNOCENCE

. . . [H]istory affords far more latitude in weighing and collecting evidence than does the legal system. The law attempts to limit the flow of evidence in a trial to what can reasonably be construed as fact. A judge will generally exclude hearsay testimony, speculation about states of mind or motives, conjecture, and vague questions leading witnesses to conclusions. But those same elements are sources of information upon which historians can and do draw in their research. Historians can afford to speculate more freely, because their conclusions will not send innocent people to jail or let the guilty go free. In one instance, for example, appeals judges refused to act on defense claims that Judge Thayer had allowed his prejudices against Sacco and Vanzetti to influence his conduct of the trial. They ruled that remarks made outside the courtroom, no matter how inappropriate, had no bearing on what occurred inside. By contrast, the historian can accept the fact of Judge Thayer's prejudice regardless of where he revealed it.

Given their broader canons of evidence, historians might be tempted to go the lawyers one step further by establishing whether Sacco and Vanzetti actually did commit the robbery and murders at Braintree. To succeed in such an investigation would at least lay the controversy to its final rest. Yet that approach does not take us beyond the lawyers' questions. We are still dealing with only two men—Sacco and Vanzetti—and one central question—guilty or innocent?

We must remember, however, that when historians confront such either-or questions, their overriding obligation is to construct an interpretation that gives full play to *all* aspects of the subject being investigated, not just the question of guilt or innocence. They must look beyond Sacco and Vanzetti to the actions of the people and society around them. What political currents led the prosecutor to bring those two men to trial? How much were Judge Thayer, District Attorney Katzmann, and the men in the jury box representative of Massachusetts or of American society in general? Of just what crime did the jury actually convict the defendants? In answering those questions, historians must lift their drama out of the Dedham courtroom and into a larger theater of action. In short, we cannot answer our original question, "Why all the fuss?" merely by proving the defendants guilty or innocent. Historians want to know why this case provoked such sharp controversy for so many years.

Any historian who studies the climate of opinion in the early 1920s cannot help suspecting that those who persecuted Sacco and Vanzetti were far more concerned with who the defendants were and what they believed than with what they might have done. Throughout the nation's history, Americans have periodically expressed hostility toward immigrants and foreign political ideas that were perceived as a threat to the "American way of life." Nativism, as such defensive nationalism has been called, has been a problem at least since the first waves of Irish immigrants came ashore in the first half of the nineteenth century. Until then, the United States had been a society dominated by white Protestants with a common English heritage. The influx of the Catholic Irish and then political refugees from the 1848 German revolution diversified the nation's population. Native-born Americans became alarmed that immigration threatened their cherished institutions. Successive waves of newcomers from Asia, the Mediterranean, and eastern Europe deepened their fears.

In analyzing nativist ideology, historian John Higham has identified three major attitudes: anti-Catholicism, antiradicalism, and Anglo-Saxon nationalism. Anti-Catholicism reflected northern European Protestants' distrust of the Catholic Church, a rejection of its hierarchical and undemocratic structure, and a fear of the pope as a religious despot. Nativists often viewed Catholic immigrants as papal agents sent to bring the United States under the tyranny of Rome. Antiradicalism stemmed in part from an increasing rejection of America's own revolutionary tradition and in part from the American tendency to associate violence and criminal subversion with Europe's radical political creeds such as Marxism, socialism, and anarchism. Anglo-Saxon nationalism was a more amorphous blend of notions about the racial superiority of the northern European people and pride in the Anglo-Saxon heritage of legal, political, and economic institutions, one of the most cherished being the Anglo-Saxon belief in the rule of law.

The tides of nativism tend to rise and fall with the fortunes of the nation. During periods of prosperity,

Americans often welcome immigrants as a vital source of new labor. In the 1860s, for example, many Californians cheered the arrival of the strange Chinese coolies, without whom the transcontinental railroad could not have been so quickly completed. In the 1870s, as the nation struggled through a severe industrial depression, nativism became a virulent social disease. The same Californians who once welcomed the Chinese now organized vigilante groups to harass them and clamored for laws to restrict the number of Asian immigrants.

The period following World War I, which Higham labeled the "Tribal Twenties," marked the high tide of nativism. No group more fully embodied the nativist impulse than the reborn Ku Klux Klan. By 1924 it claimed large chapters not only in its traditional southern strongholds but also in major cities, in Oregon and in the states of the upper Midwest— Indiana, Ohio, and Illinois in particular. The Klan's constitution unabashedly advertised the organization's commitment to all three nativist traditions:

to unite white, male persons, native born gentile citizens of the United States of America, who owe no allegiance of any nature to any foreign government, nation, institution, sect, ruler, person or people; whose morals are good, whose reputations and vocations are exemplary . . . ; to shield the sanctity of white womanhood; to maintain forever white supremacy.

Loyalty to the church, the pope, a motherland, Old World culture, or any other tie outside the United States eliminated almost all immigrants from possible Klan membership.

Several factors accounted for the resurgence of nativism. World War I had temporarily interrupted the flow of immigrants who, since the 1880s, had increasingly included a preponderance of Catholics and Jews from countries with strong radical traditions. In 1914 alone, more than 138,000 of a total of 1.2 million immigrants to the United States were Jews. During the war, the number fell to just 3,672 newcomers in 1918 (out of a total of 110,000), but then rose to 119,000 (out of 805,000) in 1921, the

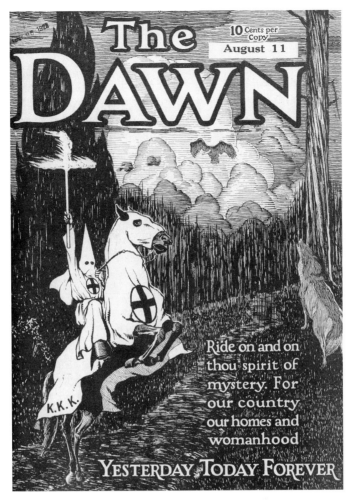

If Sacco and Vanzetti represented one of the "two nations" of the 1920s, the Ku Klux Klan was the symbol of the other. The new KKK expanded its list of enemies to include blacks, Jews, and Catholics. Its prejudices reached into urban areas of the East and Midwest, where immigrants and African Americans competed for jobs and housing with native-born white Anglo-Saxon Protestants. (The New York Public Library, Astor, Lenox and Tilden Foundations)

last year of unrestricted immigration. A similar pattern occurred among Italians. In the entire decade of the 1870s fewer than 50,000 Italians came to the United States. In the first fifteen years of the twentieth century almost 3 million made the crossing. That torrent, which slowed to a trickle during the war years, swelled again with the return of peace. The approximately 221,000 Italians who immigrated in 1921 made up, with the Jews, more than 42 percent of the total immigrants. More than ever, nativists protested

that these undesirable foreigners threatened to destroy cherished institutions, weaken the genetic pool, or in other ways undermine the American way of life.

The rocky transition to a peacetime economy only aggravated resentment toward immigrants. Returning veterans expected jobs from a grateful nation; instead, they found crowds of unemployed workers around factory gates. The army had discharged millions of soldiers almost overnight. The government dismissed hundreds of thousands of temporary wartime employees and canceled millions of dollars' worth of contracts with private businesses. As the economy plunged downward, native-born Americans once again looked on new immigrants as a threat to their livelihoods. Organized labor joined other traditional nativist groups in demanding new restriction laws.

Union leaders called for relief on another front. During the war they had cooperated with the government to control inflation by minimizing wage increases. At the same time, high wartime employment had attracted millions of new recruits to the union movement. The government had orchestrated labor-management harmony to ensure uninterrupted production schedules. Once the war ended, labor set out to consolidate its gains. Union leaders asked for higher wages, improved working conditions, and the recognition of collective bargaining.

Most business leaders were in no mood to compromise. They resented the assistance the government had given organized labor during the war. Now, they not only rejected even the mildest union demands but also sought to cripple the labor movement. Conservatives launched a national campaign to brand all organized labor as Bolsheviks, Reds, and anarchists. They called strikes "crimes against society," "conspiracies against the government," and "plots to establish communism." As the market for manufactures declined, employers had little reason to avoid a showdown. Strikes saved them the problem of laying off unneeded workers.

In 1919 American industry lost more labor hours to strikes than ever before in history. March brought 175 significant strikes, followed by 248 in April, 388 in May, 303 in June, 360 in July, and 373 in August. By September, strikes in the coal and steel industries alone had idled more than 700,000 workers and led to repeated violence. The average strike lasted thirty-four days, while some exceeded four months. Even employers who made minor concessions on wages or hours refused to yield on the question of collective bargaining.

Radicals played a minor role in the postwar labor unrest. Most union leaders were as archly conservative as the employers they confronted. Still, the constant

barrage of anti-Red propaganda turned public opinion against the unions. And American radicals fed that hostility by adopting highly visible tactics. The success of a small band of Bolsheviks in capturing Russia's tottering government in October 1917 had rekindled waning hopes and at the same time startled most Americans. Two years later, the Bolsheviks boldly organized the Third Communist International to carry the revolution to other countries. Communist-led worker uprisings in Hungary and Germany increased conservative anxiety that a similar revolutionary fever might infect American workers, especially after a Comintern official bragged that the money spent in Germany "was as nothing compared to the funds transmitted to New York for the purpose of spreading Bolshevism in the United States."

Only a few shocks were needed to inflame the fears of Americans caught in the midst of economic distress, labor unrest, and renewed immigration from southern and eastern Europe. Those shocks were provided by a series of anarchist bombings inspired by Luigi Galleani, an Italian immigrant who had settled in New England. Although authorities at the time did not know it, members of Galleani's circle were the source of a series of thirty parcels mailed in April 1919 to eminent officials, including Attorney General A. Mitchell Palmer, Supreme Court Justice Oliver Wendell Holmes, members of Congress, mayors, as well as the industrial magnates John D. Rockefeller and J. P. Morgan. Only one of the deadly packages detonated (blowing off the hands of the unsuspecting servant who opened it), but in June a series of even more lethal explosions rocked seven cities. The most spectacular explosion demolished the entire front wall of Attorney General Palmer's home. The device exploded prematurely, blowing to bits the man who was crouching by the front steps.

The American public had already learned to associate such deeds with anarchists: the Haymarket Square explosion of 1886 as well as the assassination of President William McKinley in 1901 by radical Leon Czolgosz. ("The anarchist is the enemy of humanity, the enemy of all mankind," proclaimed McKinley's successor, Teddy Roosevelt.) Following the bombings of 1919 Attorney General Palmer reacted swiftly, launching a roundup of as many radicals as he could find, branding each "a potential murderer or a potential thief." That the majority were only philosophical anarchists who had never undertaken any violent acts toward the government did not deter Palmer. That the majority were foreign-born served only to raise his patriotic bile: "Out of the sly and crafty eyes of many of them leap cupidity, cruelty, insanity, and crime; from their lopsided faces, sloping brows, and misshapen features may be recognized the unmistakable criminal types."

For more than a year, Palmer and his young, Red-hunting assistant J. Edgar Hoover organized government raids on homes, offices, union halls, and alien organizations. Seldom did the raiders pay even passing attention to civil liberties or constitutional prohibitions against illegal search and seizure. One particularly spectacular outing netted more than 4,000 alleged subversives in some thirty-three cities. Most of those arrested, though innocent of any crime, were detained illegally by state authorities either for trial or Labor Department deportation hearings. Police jammed suspects in cramped rooms with inadequate food and sanitation. They refused to honor the suspects' rights to post bail or obtain a writ of habeas corpus.

The public quickly wearied of Palmer and the exaggerated stories of grand revolutionary conspiracies. Not one incident had produced any evidence of a serious plot. Palmer predicted that on May 1, 1920, radicals would launch a massive attempt to overthrow the government. Alerted by the Justice Department, local police and militia girded for the assault. But May Day passed without incident. The heightened surveillance did, however, have profound consequences for Nicola Sacco and Bartolomeo Vanzetti. Both men were on a list of suspects the Justice Department had sent to District Attorney Katzmann and Chief Stewart. Just four days after the May Day scare, Officer Connolly arrested the two aliens.

Sacco and Vanzetti fit the stereotypes that nativists held of foreigners. Sacco arrived in the United States in 1908 at the age of seventeen. Like so many other Italians, he had fled the oppressive poverty of his homeland with no intention of making a permanent home in America. Most of the young men planned to stay only until they had saved enough money to return home and improve their family fortunes. Although born into a modestly well-to-do family, Sacco was no stranger to hard labor. Shortly after his arrival he found steady work in the shoe factories around Milford, Massachusetts.

Sacco's resourcefulness and industry marked him as the kind of foreign worker whose competition American labor feared. Although he lacked formal schooling, Sacco understood that skilled labor commanded steadier work and higher wages, so he paid $50 out of his earnings to learn the specialized trade of edge trimming. His wages soon reached as high as $80 per week. By 1917 he had a wife and child, his own home, and $1,500 in savings. His employer at the "3 K" shoe factory described him as an excellent worker and recalled that Sacco often found time, despite his long workdays, to put in a few hours each morning and evening in his vegetable garden.

Vanzetti conformed more to the nativist stereotype of shiftless foreigners who drifted from one job to the next. Born in 1888 in the northern Italian village of Villafalletto, he had come to America in 1908 where, like many other immigrants, he found a limited range of jobs open to him. He took a job as a dishwasher in hot, stinking kitchens. "We worked twelve hours one day and fourteen the next, with five hours off every other Sunday," he recalled. "Damp food hardly fit for a dog and five or six dollars a week was the pay." Fearing an attack of consumption, Vanzetti migrated to the countryside in search of open-air work. "I worked on farms, cut trees, made bricks, dug ditches, and quarried rocks. I worked in a fruit, candy and ice cream store and for a telephone company," he wrote his sister in Italy. By 1914 he had wandered to Plymouth, where he took a job in a cordage factory.

If that sketch captured the essence of Sacco and Vanzetti's lives, they would most likely never have come to the attention of Justice Department agents. But because they were aliens and anarchists, they embodied the kind of foreign menace American nativists

A. Mitchell Palmer was Woodrow Wilson's Attorney General. He suspected that many of the new immigrants were importing radical ideas that threatened American democracy, and he deported as many of them as he could. Authorities even denied numerous immigrants the right to a hearing. This was a deliberate violation of their civil liberties. (© CORBIS)

most feared. Although not a student of politics like Vanzetti, Sacco was a rebel. He identified closely with the workers' struggle for better wages and the right to organize. In 1912 he and Vanzetti had independently participated in a violent textile strike at Lawrence, Massachusetts. Three years later plant owners around Plymouth had blacklisted Vanzetti for his role in a local strike. Sacco had walked off his job to express sympathy for the cordage workers. Soon after a local labor leader organized a sympathy strike to support workers in Minnesota, authorities arrested Sacco and convicted him of disturbing the peace. All this time, he and his wife regularly joined street-theater productions performed to raise money for labor and radical groups.

American entry into World War I created a crisis for both men. Their anarchist beliefs led them to oppose any war that did not work to overthrow capitalism. Sacco even refused the patriotic pressures to buy war bonds. He quit his job rather than compromise his principles. Both began to dread the law requiring them to register (though in fact as aliens they were ineligible for military service). They decided to join a group of pacifists who in May 1917 fled to

Mexico, where the two first became personal friends. The hard life and absence from his family finally drove Sacco to return home under an alias, though he did resume his name and former job after the war. Vanzetti returned to Plymouth and soon outfitted himself as a fish peddler.

So in the eyes of many Americans, Sacco and Vanzetti were guilty in at least one important sense. As self-proclaimed enemies of the capitalist system, they had opposed "the American way of life" that nativists cherished. Their suspicious behavior, which Katzmann successfully portrayed as consciousness of guilt, was all too real, for they knew that their radical beliefs might subject them to arrest and deportation, the fate hundreds of other friends and political associates had already faced.

Certainly, the trial record shows that nativism influenced the way judge and jury viewed the defendants. Almost all the eyewitnesses who identified Sacco and Vanzetti were native-born Americans. That they saw a resemblance between the Italian suspects and the foreign-looking criminals proved only, as Harvard law professor Felix Frankfurter remarked, that there was much truth in the popular racist song "All Coons Look Alike to Me." On the other hand, almost all the witnesses substantiating the defendants' alibis were Italians who answered through an interpreter. The jury, also all native-born Americans, would likely accept Katzmann's imputation that foreigners stuck together to protect each other from the authorities.

The choice of Fred Moore as chief defense counsel guaranteed that radicalism would become a central issue in the trial. . . . He spent the bulk of defense funds to orchestrate a propaganda campaign dramatizing the plight of his clients and the persecution of radicals. He gave far less attention to planning defense strategy, left largely in the hands of two local cocounsels, Thomas and Jeremiah McAnarney.

Yet in the courtroom Moore insisted on playing the major role. The McAnarneys soon despaired of making a favorable impression on the jury. An outsider from California, Moore wore his hair long and sometimes shocked the court by parading around in his shirtsleeves and socks. Rumors abounded about

his unorthodox sex life. And at critical moments he sometimes disappeared for several days. Judge Thayer once became so outraged at Moore that he told a friend, "I'll show them that no long-haired anarchist from California can run this court." Not until 1924 did Moore finally withdraw in favor of William Thompson, a respected Massachusetts criminal lawyer.

Nativism, particularly antiradicalism, obviously prejudiced Judge Thayer and District Attorney Katzmann. We have already seen how Thayer used his charge to the jury to underscore Katzmann's construction of the evidence in the trial. Outside the courtroom, Thayer consistently violated the canons of judicial discretion by discussing his views of the case. George Crocker, who sometimes lunched with Thayer, testified that on many occasions the judge "conveyed to me by his words and manner that he was bound to convict these men because they were 'reds.'" Veteran court reporter Frank Silbey had been forced to stop lunching at the Dedham Inn to avoid Thayer and his indiscreet remarks. Silbey later recalled, "In my thirty-five years I never saw anything like it. . . . His whole attitude seemed to be that the jurors were there to convict these men."

From the moment the trial opened, Thayer and Katzmann missed few opportunities to strike a patriotic pose or to remind the jury that both defendants were draft dodgers. Thayer told the prospective jurors at the outset, "I call upon you to render this service . . . with the same patriotism as was exhibited by our soldier boys across the sea." Katzmann opened his cross-examination of Vanzetti with a cutting statement dressed up as a question: "So you left Plymouth, Mr. Vanzetti, in May 1917 to dodge the draft did you?" Since Vanzetti was charged with murder, not draft evasion, the question served to arouse the jury's patriotic indignation.

Katzmann struck hardest in his questioning of Sacco, whose poor command of English often left him confused or under a misapprehension. Judge Thayer never intervened to restrain the overzealous prosecutor, even when it became clear that Sacco could neither follow a question nor express his thoughts clearly. Playing again upon the residual patriotic war fervor,

Katzmann hammered away at the defendant's evident disloyalty:

KATZMANN: And in order to show your love for this United States of America when she was about to call upon you to become a soldier you ran away to Mexico. Did you run away to Mexico to avoid being a soldier for the country that you loved?

SACCO: Yes.

KATZMANN: And would it be your idea of showing love for your wife that when she needed you, you ran away from her?

SACCO: I did not run away from her.

When the defense objected, Thayer ruled that this line of questioning would help establish Sacco's character. But instead of showing Sacco's philosophical opposition to war, Katzmann made the defendant appear, as one critic expressed it, "an ingrate and a slacker" who invited the jury's contempt. With such skillful cross-examination Katzmann twisted Sacco's professed love of "a free country" into a preference for high wages, pleasant work, and good food.

The prosecutor summed up his strategy in his final appeal to the jury: "Men of Norfolk do your duty. Do it like men. Stand together you men of Norfolk." There was the case in a nutshell—native American solidarity against alien people and their values. Whether he had proved Sacco and Vanzetti guilty of murder mattered little, for he had revealed their disloyalty. In case the point was lost, Judge Thayer reiterated it in his charge:

Although you knew such service would be arduous, painful, and tiresome, yet you, like the true soldier, responded to the call in the spirit of supreme American loyalty. There is no better word in the English language than "loyalty."

And just who were those "men of Norfolk" to whom the judge and prosecutor appealed? Could they put aside inflammatory rhetoric and render a just verdict? Not a single foreign name, much less an Italian one, appeared on the juror's list. Because Fred Moore had rejected any "capitalists" during jury selection, a few prospective jurors whom the McAnarneys knew to be fair-minded were kept off the jury. Those jurors selected were drawn from the tradespeople and other respectable Protestants of the town. None would share the defendants' antipathy to capitalism; few would have had any compassion for the plight of Italian immigrants or union members. Even worse, the jury foreman, Harry Ripley, was a former police chief who outdid himself in persuading his fellow jurors to convict. He violated basic rules of evidence in a capital case by bringing into the jury room cartridges similar to those placed in evidence. A short time before, he had told his friend William Daly that he would be on the jury in "the case of the two 'ginneys' charged with murder at South Braintree." When Daly suggested that they might be innocent, Ripley replied, "Damn them, they ought to hang anyway."

By using the concept of nativism to gain a broader perspective, the historian has come to understand the answer to a question lawyers need not even ask: what factors accounted for the conviction of Sacco and Vanzetti where legitimate evidence was so clearly lacking? Nativism explains many prejudices exhibited in the trial record. It also explains why those attitudes were so widespread in 1920–1921. We must accept the truth of law professor Edmund M. Morgan's assertion that it was "almost impossible to secure a verdict which runs counter to the settled convictions of the community." Sacco and Vanzetti symbolized for a majority of Americans and the "men of Norfolk" alien forces that threatened their way of life.

Yet, having answered one important question, the historian still faces another. Granted that a jury convicted two alien radicals of robbery and murder in 1921, but "why all the fuss," as we asked earlier, in the years that followed? After all, Sacco and Vanzetti were not sentenced until 1927, long after the virulent nativist mood had passed. Corruption and scandal had by then killed the Klan. Prohibition had closed that infernal den of immigrant iniquity, the saloon. The Immigration Acts of 1921 and 1924 had severely curbed the flow of newcomers from Italy and eastern Europe. The damage from unsuccessful strikes, management opposition, and government hostility had sent organized labor into a decline from which it would not recover until the New Deal years. The historian must still explain how a local case extended its impact beyond Norfolk County to the nation and even the international community.

No single answer, even one so broad as nativism, can account for the notoriety. Certainly, from the beginning the case had sent ripples across the nation. Socially prominent individuals, intellectuals, the American Federation of Labor, immigrant groups, and radicals had all contributed to the defense fund for the Dedham trial. Those people represented a small minority without great political influence. But by tracing out the appeals process, the historian discovers a series of events that enlarged the significance of the case, heightened the public's awareness of the crucial issues involved, and raised the stakes many groups risked on the judicial outcome.

A Nation Stirred

In the American legal system, the right of appeal is designed to protect defendants against any miscarriage of justice rising out of the original trial. But in 1920 the appeals process in Massachusetts contained a provision that ultimately proved fatal to Sacco and Vanzetti. Any motion for a retrial based on new evidence had to be granted by the original trial judge. On each of eight motions made by the defense, including substantial evidence of prejudice on the part of the judge, the person who heard that appeal was none other than Webster Thayer! . . .

A mounting body of evidence seemed to indicate that the two men were innocent. Yet, as the courts remained deaf to the defense appeals, more and more reasonable people came to suspect that, indeed, powerful men and institutions were conspiring to destroy two people perceived as a threat to the social order. Thayer's sentence of death by electrocution seemed but a final thread in a web of legal intrigue to commit an injustice.

Sacco and Vanzetti played an important part in winning broad popular support for their cause. Steadfastly, in the face of repeated disappointments, they maintained their innocence. Sacco, the more simple and direct of the two, suffered deeply as a result of separation from his family. During the first trying years, he went on a hunger strike and suffered a nervous breakdown. From that point on, he stoically awaited the end, more preoccupied with saving his wife further anguish than with saving himself. To assist the defense effort, however, he had begun in 1923 to study English, though with little success. A letter written to his teacher in 1926 conveys his energetic, simple idealism. Sacco had wanted to explain to his teacher why he had been unable to master the language:

No, it isn't, because I have try with all my passion for the success of this beautiful language, not only for the sake of my family and the promise I have made to you—but for my own individual satisfaction, to know and to be able to read and write correct English. But woe is me! It wasn't so; no, because the sadness of these close and cold walls, the idea to be away from my dear family, for all the beauty and joy of liberty—had more than once exhaust my passion.

Vanzetti's articulate, often eloquent speeches and letters won him the respect of fellow prisoners, defenders, and literary figures drawn to the case, including Upton Sinclair, whose reformist instincts had not deserted him since writing *The Jungle* twenty years earlier. (Vanzetti was "one of the wisest and kindest persons I ever knew," Sinclair wrote, "and I thought him as incapable of murder as I was.") . . .

By the time all appeals were exhausted, the Sacco and Vanzetti case had brought to public attention not only issues of guilt and innocence, but more fundamental tensions in American society. On one side were arrayed immigrants, workers, and the poor for whom Sacco and Vanzetti stood as powerful symbols. On the other stood Thayer, the "men of Norfolk," the Protestant establishment, and those who believed that America should tolerate only certain peoples and ideas.

On the night of August 22, 1927, John Dos Passos, a young writer, stood with the crowd outside Charleston Prison waiting for news of Sacco and Vanzetti's fate. Shortly after midnight word came— the "good shoemaker and poor fish peddler" were dead. Grief and anger raked the crowd. Some wept, others cried out in the name of justice, and many tore their clothes in anguish. The scene outside the prison was repeated in New York and other cities around the world. Years later, Dos Passos expressed the outrage he felt against those who had persecuted Sacco and Vanzetti:

> they have clubbed us off the streets they are stronger they are rich they hire and fire the politicians the news-papereditors the old judges the small men with reputations the collegepresidents the ward heelers (listen collegepresidents judges America will not forget her betrayers). . . .
>
> all right you have won you will kill the brave men our friends tonight
> there is nothing left to do we are beaten. . . .
>
> America our nation has been beaten by strangers who have turned our language inside out who have taken the clean words our Fathers spoke and made them slimy and foul. . . .
>
> they have built the electricchair and hired the executioner to throw the switch
> all right we are two nations

Two nations—that was the reason for "all the fuss."

Will the real truth of the case ever be known? Perhaps not—at least not "beyond a reasonable doubt," to borrow the language of the courts. Yet historians have unearthed enough additional information to provide, if not the certainties of fact, at least a few ironies of probability. After Sacco and Vanzetti's execution, Upton Sinclair began to collect material for a novel about the case. As a socialist who had staunchly defended the two men during their years in prison, he was able to interview scores of friends and associates. While Sinclair remained convinced that Sacco and Vanzetti were innocent of the Bridgewater and Braintree robberies, he became less sure

whether the two men were merely philosophical anarchists. Both had "believed in and taught violence," he discovered. "I became convinced from many different sources that Vanzetti was not the pacifist he was reported to be under the necessity of defense propaganda. He was, like many fanatics, a dual personality, and when he was roused by the social conflict he was a very dangerous man."

Historian Paul Avrich, investigating the anarchist community of which the two men were a part, noted that Vanzetti was indeed a close friend of Luigi Galleani, the firebrand whose associates had launched the letter bombs of 1919 and dynamited Attorney General Palmer's home. "We mean to speak for [the proletariat through] the voice of dynamite, through the mouth of guns," announced the anarchist leaflet found nearby. Carlo Valdinoci, the man who was blown up carrying out his mission, had been a good friend of both Sacco and Vanzetti. Indeed, after Valdinoci's death, his sister Assunta moved in with Sacco and his family. Then, too, rumors within the anarchist community suggested that Vanzetti himself had assembled the bomb that demolished a judge's home in Boston the night Valdinoci had done his work in Washington.

"But my conviction is that I have suffered for things I am guilty of," Vanzetti told Thayer at the end. Perhaps there was pride as well as indignation in this response. What, in the end, was the guilt of which Sacco and Vanzetti were so conscious during the trial? Was it merely the knowledge that their radical pamphlets, if found, would get them deported? But both men had been preparing to flee the country anyway, before being arrested. (Recall Sacco's outsized passport photo.) Could their evasive behavior have resulted from the fact that they had more to conceal at home than a few pamphlets?

Upton Sinclair came to believe so. After the execution, Fred Moore confided to him that Sacco and Vanzetti had admitted "they were hiding dynamite on the night of their arrest, and that that was the real reason why they told lies and stuck to them." If true, Sacco and Vanzetti, like Valdinoci, had been willing to commit acts of anarchism that, by the laws of

American society, would have been punishable by death. Sacco made clear his own distinction between being tried for his beliefs and being arrested for mere bank robbery. "If I was arrested because of the Idea I am glad to suffer. If I must I will die for it. But they have arrested me for a gunman job."

Is the final irony that Sacco and Vanzetti were willing to die—perhaps even to kill others—for their Idea? Just as the "men of Norfolk" and the officials of Massachusetts were willing to execute Sacco and Vanzetti on behalf of *their* idea of what America should be? ("Damn them, they ought to hang anyway," remarked juror Ripley.) The historian must suspect that on that August night in 1927, citizens were not merely fighting over a matter of guilt or innocence, but (as Dos Passos put it) over the meaning of those "clean words our Fathers spoke." Sacco and Vanzetti had forced the nation to ask who in their own times best embodied the principles of freedom and equality inherited from 1776. Perhaps neither historians nor lawyers can resolve that question to the satisfaction of a divided nation.

QUESTIONS TO CONSIDER

1 Describe the crimes allegedly committed by Sacco and Vanzetti. When you consider the amount of evidence and the number of witnesses in their seven-week trial, explain why the jury came back with a guilty verdict in only five hours. Why did this trial of two lowly Italian immigrants generate such bitter controversy?

2 Why did the police label Sacco and Vanzetti as "suspicious characters"? Describe the unconventional investigation that attempted to link them to the Braintree murders. Given the lack of hard evidence (fingerprints, confiscated money), explain how the district attorney conducted his prosecution. Why would such a case have no credibility in the twenty-first-century American judicial system?

3 Why do the authors conclude "that those who prosecuted Sacco and Vanzetti were far more concerned with who the defendants were and what they believed than with what they might have done"? Define "nativism" and how it affected attitudes toward immigrants who came to America immediately after the Great War.

4 Who was A. Mitchell Palmer, and how did his actions reflect the ethnic prejudices of his day? How did Palmer violate the civil liberties of the people he suspected of radicalism? Following the Great War, what problems did the labor movement face? In what ways did labor unrest create an atmosphere in America that tolerated most of Palmer's excesses?

5 What factors transformed the trial of Sacco and Vanzetti into a national and international controversy? Explain why novelist John Dos Passos contended that the America of the 1920s consisted of "two nations."

6 What do the authors of this selection mean when they repeatedly contrast the rules of evidence that guide historians with the rules of evidence followed by judges and juries? How do these rules differ? How can historians explain why there was such acrimonious controversy over the trial of Sacco and Vanzetti?

PART EIGHT

Long Dark Night of the Depression

16 Under Hoover, the Shame and Misery Deepened

T. H. WATKINS

By the beginning of 1929, the nation seemed to have reached a permanent state of prosperity. Business and foreign trade both were expanding, the stock market was rising at a phenomenal rate, and national leadership appeared to be in expert hands. Republican Herbert Hoover had won the presidency the previous November, having easily defeated his Democratic opponent. "For the first time in our history," wrote two economists, "we have a President who, by technical training, engineering achievement, cabinet experience, and grasp of economic fundamentals, is qualified for business leadership."

"We in America today," Hoover himself had said, "are nearer to the final triumph over poverty than ever before in the history of any land. The poorhouse is vanishing from among us." Hoover was equally optimistic in his inaugural address in March 1929: "I have no fears for the future of our country," he proclaimed. "It is bright with hope."

Eight months later, the country plummeted into the most severe and protracted economic depression in American history. It started with the stock market crash in October 1929 and deepened slowly and inexorably until the entire economy and perhaps even the nation itself approached total collapse. It was the worst disaster the United States had faced since the Civil War, and there were voices of doubt everywhere. How had it happened? What would become of the American dream? Would the nation disintegrate? And who was to blame—President Hoover, the Republican party, or capitalism itself?

We now know that several factors caused economic collapse—chief among them underconsumption and overproduction, as consumer buying power lagged behind the quantity of goods being turned out. As factories and other businesses found themselves overextended, they began laying off workers, *which decreased consumer buying power, which in turn caused more layoffs and resulted in a vicious cycle. By 1932, some 12 million Americans were unemployed. At the same time, factories and businesses themselves shuttered their windows and closed their doors, and banks, unable to call in their loans, began failing at an alarming rate, taking people's savings down with them. In 1930 and 1931, a total of 3,646 banks failed, representing more than $2.5 billion in deposits. Never, in all the previous depressions and "panics," had the country been confronted with such statistics.*

The prosperity of the 1920s had turned into a nightmare. Unemployed men roamed the country in search of work, succumbing to feelings of guilt and worthlessness when they found nothing at all. In the following selection, excerpted from his prize-winning history of the Great Depression, a companion to the popular PBS series on that calamity, distinguished historian T. H. Watkins captures the human misery and the failure of early relief efforts through vignettes of common folk—whites, African Americans, and Mexican Americans. Watkins also offers an insightful discussion of President Hoover's approach to the crisis and why that failed.

As you read the next two selections, bear in mind that the Depression was a worldwide calamity that rocked industrial Europe and Japan as well as the United States. As historian John A. Garraty says, "While there were differences in its impact and in the way it was dealt with from one country to another, the course of events nearly everywhere ran something like this: By 1925, most countries had recovered from the economic disruptions caused by the Great War of 1914–18. There followed a few years of rapid growth, but in 1929 and 1930 the prosperity ended. Then came a precipitous plunge that lasted until early 1933. This dark period was followed by a gradual, if spotty, recovery. The revival, however, was aborted by the steep recession of 1937–38. It took a still more cataclysmic event, the outbreak of World War II, to end the Great Depression."

GLOSSARY

BLACK THURSDAY The day the stock market crashed, October 24, 1929, causing a panic in the business world that presaged the Great Depression.

DEPRESSION Called a "panic" in the nineteenth century, this was a severe downturn in the business cycle characterized by low business activity, bank and business failures, high unemployment, and want in the midst of plenty.

HOOVER, HERBERT President of the United States, 1929–1933, who was widely blamed for the stock-market crash and the onset of the Great Depression.

HOOVERVILLES Derogatory name for shantytowns, made of box crates, loose timber, and whatever else could be found that sprang up around many cities; unemployed families lived in them and called them Hoovervilles because they blamed a seemingly cold and remote president for their misery.

JIM CROW LAWS State and local laws enacted in the South after Reconstruction, they denied African Americans the right to vote, hold political office, and sit on juries; relegated them to menial labor; restricted them to black sections of towns and cities; and excluded them from public accommodations. The laws took their name from a song, "Jim Crow," sung by Thomas Rice in a pre–Civil War black minstrel show.

MINEHAN, THOMAS A sociologist who studied tramps and hoboes, roaming men and women who were unemployed.

RECONSTRUCTION FINANCE CORPORATION Federal agency established by President Hoover that in 1932 started handing out federal funds to support agriculture and industry; later it was a powerful agency of the New Deal.

RED CROSS International philanthropic organization that provided relief in war; national disasters like floods, pestilence, fires, storms; and other calamities like the Great Depression.

UNIVERSAL FEAR

Gordon Parks was sixteen years old in 1929, a young black man trying to work his way through high school in St. Paul, Minnesota, as a bellboy at a downtown club for white businessmen. One Wednesday afternoon, a notice was tacked to the employee bulletin board: "Because of unforeseen circumstances, some personnel will be laid off the first of next month. Those directly affected will be notified in due time." This puzzled Parks until the next day, Thursday, October 24, when the evening papers broke the news of the crash. "I read everything I could get my hands on," he recalled,

gathering in the full meaning of such terms as Black Thursday, deflation and depression. I couldn't imagine such financial disaster touching my small world; it surely concerned only the rich. But by the first week of November I . . . knew differently; along with millions of others across the nation, I was without a job. . . . Finally, on the seventh of November I went to school and cleaned out my locker, knowing it was impossible to stay on. A piercing chill was in the air as I walked back to the rooming house. The hawk had come. I could already feel his wings shadowing me.

While only a small percentage of the public was directly affected by the collapse of the stock market in October, 1929, it was still a moment of history shared by nearly every American. Like the Japanese attack of Pearl Harbor or the assassinations of John F. Kennedy, Martin Luther King, Jr., and Robert Kennedy in our own time, the crash was a point of reference for those of that time. People took the measure of their era by using the crash as an emotional baseline, and it became the one event on which tens of millions could fix their worry as the full dimensions of the debacle slowly began to be discerned. Gordon Parks was not the only one who felt the shadow of the hawk.

President Herbert Clark Hoover, though, apparently remained oblivious to that shadow—or if he felt it, did not want to acknowledge it. Unemployment had grown from about 1.5 million to at least 3.2 million in the five months since the crash, but on March 7, 1930, Hoover gave the American public the results of his own analysis of the situation. "All the evidences," he said, "indicate that the worst effects of the crash upon unemployment will have passed during the next sixty days."

A more accurate measure could have been found in an unnamed southern city that Sherwood Anderson visited that same month. The writer spent some time standing outside a big basement soup kitchen, where on a single day he watched seven hundred people go inside to get fed. He was struck by the number of those who did not want him to know their hunger. The man, for example, who approached the soup kitchen three times before swallowing his pride and going down the steps. "I am not here for soup," he told Anderson, who had not said a word. "I came here to meet a friend." Or the young woman who asked him where the soup kitchen was. "I do not want any soup," she assured him when he obliged. She just wanted to say hello to some of the women who were serving the needy. "They are friends of mine."

"They were Americans, such people as you and I," Anderson wrote. "I stood watching them. I was ashamed of my warm overcoat, my stout shoes.

"I made men ashamed standing there."

Most of those who were still coming to the soup kitchen six months later, as the first anniversary of the crash approached, probably would have put little or no faith in anything Herbert Hoover said on the subject of what was now being called, openly and increasingly, a depression. Unemployment had not declined; it had risen, implacably, and in another six months would hit at least 7.5 million. And they would have found plainly incomprehensible the confidence of Rome C. Stephenson, vice president of the American Bankers' Association, if they had heard the pep talk he gave his fellow bankers in downtown Cleveland on September 30. The bankers

Unemployment reached staggering levels during the long dark night of the Depression. To raise a little money, this man is forced to sell apples on West Street in New York City, 1932. In back of him is a "Hooverville," a collection of wrecked and abandoned buildings that became "home" for unemployed New Yorkers and their families. (Culver Pictures)

should not worry, Stephenson said, because business was about to get better. The slump, he insisted, was largely a matter of misperception:

The depression of the stock market impressed the general public with the idea that it would depress general business. Because of a psychological consequence, it did, but it should not have. There are 120,000,000 persons in the country and at the maximum not more than 10,000,000 were involved in stock-market transactions. The remaining 110,000,000 persons suffered no loss.

The bulk of the American population may not have suffered the loss of stock investments, but there were plenty of other ways to calculate loss, and by the end of 1929, with unemployment rising, with

shops and factories suddenly ornamented by Closed or Out of Business signs, and, perhaps most terrifying of all, with scores of banks failing and taking with them millions of dollars in deposits (which were at that time uninsured), the "general public's" confidence in the financial health of the country and the wisdom of its leaders was shaky at best. Confidence fell even further when 256 banks failed in the single month of November, 1930, and further yet on December 11, when the United States Bank, with deposits of more than $200 million, went under. It was the largest single bank failure in American history up to that time, and contributed no little portion to an economic hangover in which, in the words of banker J. M. Barker, "cupidity turned into unreasoning, emotional, universal fear."

FIGHTING FOR THE SCRAPS

There was reason enough for fear. The 1,352 banks that failed in 1930 represented more than $853 million in deposits. In 1931, 2,294 banks went under, with deposits of nearly $1.7 billion. In 1930, 26,355 businesses failed, and the rate of 122 failures per 10,000 was the highest ever recorded up to that time. Both numbers were surpassed in 1931 with 28,285 failures and a rate of 133. The 451,800 corporations still in business in 1932 had a combined deficit of $5.64 billion. The value of all farm property declined from $57.7 billion in 1929 (itself down from a high of $78.3 billion in 1920) to $51.8 billion in 1931. By the end of 1931 unemployment had climbed to 8 million and in a few months would be approaching 12 million.

There had never been such statistics in our history, and there have been none like them since. Their truest meaning, the effect they had on individual human lives, could be seen everywhere, as people struggled blindly and bravely to survive. Which is not to say that everyone was willing to see them for what they were. Like those who attempt to dismiss the homeless of our own day as aberrations, not indications, of the nation's economic condition, many of the pundits of the depression years spent a lot of time explaining away the presence of the poor and the hungry. These were temporary phenomena, it was said, transient indications of a momentary lapse in economic health. Many of the people were not even victims—they were just beggars too lazy or too ignorant to work. But the deprived of the depression years were even more difficult to ignore than the doorway sleepers and street-corner panhandlers of modern America. They could not be explained away, because they would not go away—and their numbers grew day by day, week by week. Like a plague, the disease of deprivation spread with such speed and across so many lines that there were few families in the United States who did not either experience or witness its pain.

When neighbors you had known all your life were found one morning with all their furniture stacked on the sidewalk, nowhere to go, no hope in sight, it did not take much imagination to see yourself standing there with them.

You did not even have to be especially vulnerable to feel the power of deprivation. Daniel Willard, president of the Baltimore & Ohio Railroad and in no danger of having his furniture stacked on anybody's sidewalk, for instance, received an honorary doctorate at the University of Pennsylvania in June, 1931, but instead of mouthing the usual platitudes on this happy occasion, burst out with a jeremiad against the very economic system that had made him rich:

A system—call it what you will—under which it is possible for 5,000,000 or 6,000,000 of willing and able-bodied men to be out of work and unable to secure work for months at a time, and with no other source of income, cannot be said to be perfect or even satisfactory. . . . I would be less than candid if I did not say in such circumstances I would steal before I would starve.

"No one is going hungry and no one need go hungry or cold," President Hoover still insisted in the winter of 1931. Willard would have disagreed. So would Louise V. Armstrong. "We saw the city at its worst," she wrote in *We, Too, Are the People* (1941). "One vivid, gruesome moment of those dark days we shall never forget. We saw a crowd of some fifty men fighting over a barrel of garbage which had been set outside the back door of a restaurant. American citizens fighting for scraps of food like animals!"

"Why does Every Thing have exceptional Value Except the Human being," one destitute person wrote the president, "—why are we reduced to poverty and starving and anxiety and Sorrow So quickly under your administration as Chief Executor. Can you not find a quicker way of Executing us than to starve us to death."

On Chicago's South Side, wandering reporter Edmund Wilson took a look at the old Angelus Building, a tottering, stinking wreck of a place whose owner would have demolished it if he had found the money to do so. It was now stuffed with black people who could afford to live nowhere else. The place, Wilson said, was

seven stories, thick with dark windows, caged in a dingy mess of fire-escapes like mattress-springs on a junk-heap, hunched up, hunchback-proportioned, jam-crammed in its dumbness and darkness with miserable wriggling life. . . . There is darkness in the hundred cells: the tenants cannot pay for light; and cold: the heating system no longer works. . . . And now, since it is no good for anything else, its owner had turned it over to the Negroes, who flock into the tight-packed apartments and get along there as best they can.

In an Appalachian Mountains school, a child who looked sick was told by her teacher to go home and get something to eat. "I can't," the girl replied. "It's my sister's turn to eat."

The city fathers over in Muncie, Indiana, did not like to think of people being that hungry in their all-American town. Muncie, after all, was the "Middle-town" of the famous 1929 study of Robert S. and Helen Merrell Lynd, and was generally proud of it, too. But by the spring of 1932, the layer of confidence with which the city had consistently blanketed the depression began to grow a little tattered. That year, a Muncie businessman later told the Lynds, "people would go around saying in low tones, 'Have you heard that they're boarding up the so-and-so plant?' And a few days later, 'Have you heard that so-and-so-many trucks of machinery were moved out of town today? They say that half the floor at the plant is stripped already.' It got on our nerves as this went on!" The plant in question was a General Motors assembly plant, and by the end of the summer it had indeed stripped its floors of machinery, closed down, and left Muncie.

New Orleans did its best to keep reality from the door, too. Unemployment was greatly exaggerated, a writer to the letters column of the *Times-Picayune* said in February, 1930, a rumor spread by a "host of fly-speckers, calamity howlers and woe-be-tiders [who] are barnacles on prosperity," but a week later

an estimated three to four hundred men showed up to answer a single classified advertisement for work available in Texas. When the advertisement turned out to be a fraud, the crowd started a small-scale riot and the police had to be brought in to put it down.

Out in Yavapai County, Arizona, depression was even harder to ignore for long. Hundreds of men who had been laid off from the copper mines in the southern part of the state wandered north to the vicinity of Prescott. During the summer of 1932, they spread "out into the hills and mountains in the hope of placer mining and getting a few cents a day out of the gravel-bars that were worked fifty years ago," Prescott poet Sharlot Hall wrote a friend in June. "Sometimes they really do pan out a few cents—or once in a while get a dollar or more—but the old diggings are very lean of gold. . . ." Others were trying the same thing up in Nevada, where in one lonely canyon a reporter found a man shoveling dirt into a primitive riffle chute to wash out gold. "Me a minin' man?" he replied when asked. "Yes, I'm a miner—all of ten weeks now. Before that, I'd been a sailor all my life. Now it's a simple case of 'root, hog, or die, so I'm rootin'.'"

Hundreds of thousands of people were on the move by then. The Southern Pacific Railroad estimated that its "railroad bulls" had thrown as many as 683,000 transients off its boxcars in a single year. At least 200,000 of the transients were adolescents, most of them male but with no small number of females among them. In the summer of 1932 sociologist Thomas Minehan began a study that took him on the road with young tramps and hoboes. Most of them, he noted, traveled in gangs for safety, an especially important consideration for the young women among them. "Girls in box cars," he wrote, "are not entirely at the mercy of any man on the road whatever their relations with the boys may be. In event of loneliness or illness, the boys and girls have friends to comfort and care for them."

One of the tramps with whom he traveled for a time was a Pennsylvania Dutch boy nicknamed Blink—so named because he had lost an eye when a live cinder blew into his face while he was riding an open car on the Santa Fe railroad. "A bloody socket forms a small and ever-weeping cave on the left side of his face," Minehan wrote. "Tears streak his cheek, furrowing the dirt and coal soot, leaving a strange moist scar alongside his nose." The boy showed Minehan a diary he had been keeping since August, 1932, when he had run away from an abusive father. The entry for September 10 was eloquently typical:

Slept in paper box. Bummed swell breakfast three eggs and four pieces meat. Hit guy in big car in front of garage. Cop told me to scram. Rode freight to Roessville. Small burg, but got dinner. Walked Bronson. N. G. Couple a houses. Rode to Sidell. N. G. Hit homes for meals and turned down. Had to buy supper 20 cents. Raining.

Young and old, male and female, the transient army drifted in a dark caravan of desperation from hobo jungle to hobo jungle, city mission to city mission, begging for leftovers at the back doors of homes, panhandling for pennies on city sidewalks, stealing chickens where chickens could be found, cooking up "mulligan" stews out of whatever could be boiled into edibility, being seduced and raped, thrown into jail, beaten by yard bulls. Those homeless who did not drift—and there were thousands in every city of any size at all—slept in lice-ridden and rat-infested flophouses when they could afford the ten or fifteen cents for a urine-stained mattress on the floor, and on park benches, under park shrubbery and bridge abutments, in doorways, packing crates, concrete pipes, culverts, construction sites, and abandoned automobiles when they could not afford it. The more ambitious among them contrived fragile shelters from scraps of wood and cardboard, old beer signs and fence posts, anything they could find that would keep off the wind and rain of winter and the direct sun of summer. They built them anywhere they could, but most of the time on the outskirts of cities and towns big enough to have outskirts, where outlandish villages began to coalesce like ramshackle suburbs. Everyone called them Hoovervilles; it was not a term of endearment.

THE LIMITS OF CHARITY

Like most of his contemporaries—and, indeed, most of the American middle class—if President Hoover believed in anything more profoundly than the virtues of self-reliance and individual initiative, it has not been recorded. This was, after all, the very ethos of a white, Protestant culture, the image that Hoover and his kind held up as the ideal of Americanism. Hard work, honesty, and independence, they believed utterly, had brought this country to the forefront of nations, had built a breed of men (and women, too, some conceded, though not often) who had taken the institutions of the founding fathers and made them the wonder of the world. Anything that might weaken the strength of that tradition would weaken the very character of America and was, by definition, evil. Government charity, especially, by robbing people of initiative, would be the very embodiment of error. The national government should stay out of the personal lives of its citizens, even if they were in trouble. For Hoover and for the millions of Americans who shared his convictions, the idea that people would turn to Washington, D.C., to help them out of a bad spot was nearly unthinkable.

It was a hard theory, but part of the accepted wisdom of the time and difficult for Hoover to abandon even in the face of the present situation. Still, when the dimensions of the crisis reached proportions that simply could not be ignored, he did not, as is often supposed, coldheartedly refuse to do anything about it. What he did do, for the most part, was call upon the natural generosity of the American people and the paternalism of local governments. Throughout his term he held to the firm belief that direct aid to the individual was not the business of the federal government—unless there were no other course, in which case he made it clear he would act, though almost certainly in great fear of permanently crippling the national character. "This is not an issue as to whether people shall go hungry or cold in the United States," he said in a statement to the press in the winter of 1931.

It is solely a question of the best method by which hunger and cold shall be prevented. . . . I am willing to pledge myself that if the time should ever come that the voluntary agencies of the country, together with the local and State governments, are unable to find resources with which to prevent hunger and suffering in my country, I will ask the aid of every resource of the Federal Government. . . . I have faith in the American people that such a day will not come.

In the meantime, Hoover authorized the expenditure of about $700 million on various public works projects. He also set up the Reconstruction Finance Corporation, which in early 1932 began doling out the $2 billion that Congress had appropriated to stimulate and prop up industry and agriculture in their time of need. The RFC was one of the few such efforts that amounted to much (it would survive to become one of the most powerful agencies in New Deal Washington). The National Business Survey Conference, for instance, was designed to "market" an optimistic feeling in the business community and as part of this goal its members took a solemn vow not to cut wages. Defections were almost immediate. The National Credit Corporation, for another example, was designed to set up a system whereby healthy banks would assist unhealthy banks; few did, and the NCC virtually collapsed in two years. The Federal Farm Board, created before the depression, was designed to stabilize farm prices through the temporary purchase of surplus farm produce; it managed to lose some $345 million and satisfied no one. The President's Emergency Committee for Employment (PECE) and its successor, the President's Organization for Unemployment Relief (POUR), were largely designed to promote the belief that things were not as bad as they appeared to be and even if they were they would soon get better; neither managed to get the message across with any great success—though the POUR was useful in helping local agencies and private charities raise money by getting pro bono advertisements placed in newspapers and magazines.

It must be said that many Americans tried to sustain self-reliance, as Hoover advised. Probably the best-known examples were the apple sellers who for a time appeared on the sidewalks of nearly every major city. In the fall of 1930, the hard-pressed International Apple Shippers Association came up with the idea of selling apples to the unemployed on credit at $1.75 a crate. The apples would retail on the street at a nickel apiece and if a seller got rid of all the apples in his or her crate, the net could be as much as $1.85. By the end of November, 1930, there were six thousand apple sellers on the streets of New York City alone, crouching, in the words of newspaperman Gene Fowler, "like half-remembered sins sitting upon the conscience of the town." Down in New Orleans, the same device was tried with Louisiana oranges—"Health for You—Help for the Needy," the *Times-Picayune* declared. While people at first responded with sympathy to these peddlers, they were altogether too visible a reminder of the nation's troubles; sales fell off drastically in a few months—not aided in the slightest by Hoover's peculiar public assertion at one point that "many persons left their jobs for the more profitable one of selling apples."

Many people tried to "maintain the spirit of charity" and the dogma of self-reliance in other ways, and many local governments struggled valiantly to meet the crisis themselves, as Hoover so fervently wished. Nothing worked for very long, even in the most successful instances. In Seattle, for example, a few Socialists got together and formed the Unemployed Citizens' League in July, 1931. The organization swiftly grew to a membership of somewhere between forty and fifty thousand. The UCL organized numerous self-help projects—cutting wood on donated land, picking unwanted fruit crops, fishing in Puget Sound, setting up commissaries for the distribution of food and wood, negotiating with landlords to prevent evictions, and putting together a kind of barter economy in which members exchanged services and goods. In response, Seattle mayor Robert Harlin formed the Mayor's Commission on Improved Employment to work with the UCL, and when a million-dollar bond issue was raised to finance it, put the leaders of the UCL in charge of the District Relief Organization. The UCL remained the principal distributor of food and work to the city's estimated forty-five thousand unemployed until the money began to run out.

In Philadelphia, it was the rich who organized, and for a time it seemed that the city would stand as the perfect model for Hoover's vision of private-public cooperation at the local level. On November 7, 1930, the Committee of One Hundred of the city's most influential people met for lunch at the Bellevue-Stratford Hotel and formed the Committee for Unemployment Relief, with Horatio Gates Lloyd, a partner in Drexel and Company, the Philadelphia branch of the House of Morgan, as its chairman. In order to "tide over the temporary distress" of the depression, the committee immediately raised $4 million, which Lloyd parceled out to various private charities. The committee also persuaded the Pennsylvania General Assembly to authorize the city to borrow $3 million for public relief. A municipal Bureau of Unemployment was established and Lloyd himself was put in charge of the distribution of its public funds. Like that of the Socialists in Seattle, the philanthropists' effort in Philadelphia was a great success—for as long as the money held out. The $7 million in private and public money was exhausted by November, 1931. A "United Campaign" raised another $10 million in cash and pledges; Lloyd's committee got $5 million of that, and in three months it, too, was gone, as was the remaining $5 million that had gone to other agencies. In April, 1932, the city got another $2.5 million in direct aid from the state; that was gone in two months. The Lloyd Committee, the *Philadelphia Record* reported on June 20, "is through. For fifty-seven thousand families to whom the Committee has meant life itself, it added, playing on the Hoover administration's assurances that "prosperity is just around the corner," "STARVATION is 'just around the corner.'"

Volunteerism had not worked in Philadelphia, and neither it nor self-reliance would be enough anywhere they were tried. They certainly were not enough in those states in which one of the worst droughts in history gave the overall economic calamity an almost biblical character. The hardest hit

was Arkansas, which in July and August, 1930, received only 4.19 inches of rain—35 percent of what it had gotten during the same two months the previous year—but rainfall in another twenty-two states in the Midwest, Great Plains, and South also dropped by an average of nearly 40 percent in those two months. "The families that are suffering now, or on the verge of it," the Red Cross representative for Arkansas wrote national headquarters in August,

are not singled out as by flood or tornado or fire, but are just in their homes, with gardens ruined, sweet potatoes not making a crop, the prospect of being in debt to the landlord when the pitiable cotton crop is gathered instead of having money with which to buy food and clothing for the winter.

Hoover immediately formed another committee—several committees, in fact. At a conference of governors from the affected states on August 14, he told them that they should establish local and state drought committees to handle the problem. For the most part, he insisted, local communities were going to have to carry the burden alone. Furthermore, he believed that the Red Cross should provide the lion's share of any help beyond that. During the terrible floods in the southern Mississippi River Valley in 1927, the Red Cross had stepped in and brought relief to hundreds of thousands of people whose homes and lives had been devastated. The organization had sheltered the homeless, fed the hungry, had helped thousands of people to survive the disaster. Surely, it could do so again.

But the drought of these years was not a single, isolated event like a flood; it had gone on for a long time already and would go on for some time to come, and its disruptive effect was magnified by the larger economic situation which the Red Cross would not have been in a position to do anything about in any event. The organization's institutional inadequacy to accomplish what Hoover expected of it was compounded by the philosophy of its leader, national chairman Judge John Barton Payne. Payne was a close friend of Hoover's and shared the president's reverence for self-reliance. He made it clear from the start that the local and state Red Cross chapters would depend on volunteers and money from the local and state regions, and only under the most extreme circumstances would the national organization step in to help.

The system thus established was more efficient at withholding aid than in furnishing it. The state and local Red Cross chapters, like the state and local drought committees, usually were headed up by the "best people" who had been part of the oppressive plantation system for generations, and were prepared to think the worst of those who sought direct help. Many people worried that if food were distributed, workers might refuse to pick cotton at the wages plantation farmers were willing to pay. "Some, you know," the Red Cross chairman for Monroe County, Arkansas, wrote in early September,

are ready to let the Red Cross do it all, we think after the cotton is out we can raise some money, and as the worst is to come in the cold winter months, we think it best to postpone doing only what is absolutely necessary at this time, knowing that a person can get along on very little during warm weather.

By November even the planters were calling for direct aid, because they could not feed the families of their workers. Still, most local chapters continued to tell the national headquarters what it wanted to hear and people at headquarters ignored the streams of letters from the desperate, like that from an African-American farmer in Jefferson County, Arkansas:

There is thousands of collard farmers in Jefferson and Lincoln counties that has not bread. They are Bairfooted and thin closed many has went to the County Judge and to the local Red Cross they Both say that they has no Funds We are planning on sending a Collard men to Washington to lay our Trubles more clearly before you.

Stubbornly holding to his principles, Hoover himself continued to insist that the burden of relief should be carried by the Red Cross, not the government, and he did not even support legislation that would

have provided $60 million for feed and seed loans from the Department of Agriculture. And Judge John Barton Payne continued to hold back the distribution of funds from the national Red Cross. But by January the situation was so terrible that even the local chapters had abandoned the pretense that local and state resources could provide sufficient relief, and national headquarters finally responded with a fund-raising drive that began on January 10 and ultimately raised a little over $10 million. Between then and the end of the program in the spring, 2,765,000 people had been fed just enough to get them through the winter. It was pinch-penny charity at best, and no one will ever know how many suffered how much during all the months in which virtually nothing had been handed out. And since records were as carelessly managed as the relief program itself, no one will know how many died.

Some "relief" efforts did not even pretend to charity. Chief among these was the attempted deportation of Mexican Americans, which managed to combine racism with selfishness and desperation in one of the least edifying episodes in American history. By the beginning of the thirties, there was a Mexican-American, or Chicano, population in the United States of about 1.5 million, much of it the result of immigration—some legal, some not (slovenly kept records and conflicting estimates between Mexican and U.S. officials made it impossible to say how many belonged in either category). Thousands of the immigrants had gone north to work the sugar-beet fields of Michigan and the other Great Lakes states, while others had refused stoop labor as a career, moving to Chicago, East Chicago, Gary, and Detroit to look for work in steel mills, automobile plants, and other industries. By 1930 there were 19,362 Mexican Americans living in Chicago, some 9,000 in East Chicago and Gary, and another 8,000 in Detroit, where the allure of the Ford Motor Company had reached into the towns of northern Mexico to call young workers to the "wonderful city of the magic motor."

Most of the immigrants, however, had spilled into the sugar-beet and cotton fields of Texas, Colorado, and Arizona, or on into the huge agribusiness farms of the Imperial and San Joaquin valleys of California. Those who had not joined the stream of migrant labor had gravitated toward the growing Mexican-American settlements in the larger cities. The biggest of these settlements was in Los Angeles, where the Chicano population had increased from 33,644 in 1920 to 97,116 in 1930, making the city the "Mexican capital" of the United States, exhausting the bounds of the older Chicano settlements and spreading out into the neighborhoods of East Los Angeles, where it would remain the largest single segment of the city's minority population.

The bigotry exercised against these people rivaled that endured by African Americans, and when the weight of the depression began to fall upon cities with large Chicano populations, unabashed racism was buttressed by the theory that unemployment among Anglo workers could be blamed on the presence of a labor force willing to work cheap and under conditions that "real" American workers would not tolerate—the Mexican Americans. The answer, some concluded, was deportation—or repatriation, as it was described more benignly. In Gary, Detroit, and other industrial centers, open discrimination, physical threats, racist propaganda campaigns, and free transportation helped to persuade thousands of Chicanos to return to Mexico.

Nowhere was the movement more vigorous than in Los Angeles, however, where the first consignment of 6,024 *repatriados* (songwriter-activist Woody Guthrie would call them "deportees" in one of his most famous songs) left Union Station aboard the cars of the Southern Pacific Railroad in February, 1931. At $14.70 a head, it cost the city and county of Los Angeles $77,249.29 to ship them out, but the savings in relief payments for that year amounted to $347,468.41—a net gain of $270,219.12. "In the last analysis," historian Rudolfo Acuña writes, "President Coolidge's maxim— 'the business of America is business'—was applicable, and repatriation proved profitable, at least in dollars and cents." Over the next three years, Los Angeles County would do a pretty good business, deporting 12,688 Chicanos back to Mexico—though Carey McWilliams, who had been

on hand to watch the first trainload leave Los Angeles in February, 1931, later pointed out, "Repatriation was a tragicomic affair: tragic in the hardships occasioned; comic because most of the Mexicans eventually returned to Los Angeles, having had a trip to Mexico at the expense of the county."

Elsewhere, there was little comedy, even dark comedy, to be found. In New York City, the apple sellers had vanished by the end of 1931 and by April, 1932, 750,000 people were living on city relief efforts that averaged $8.20 a month per person—about one-fifth of what it took to keep one human being decently—while an estimated 160,000 more waited to get on the rolls as soon as the money became available. In 1930, $6 million had gone for relief in New York; in 1931, $25 million; in 1932, it was estimated, the cost would be closer to $75 million. In Atlanta, the cost of relief for only thirty weeks was estimated at $1.2 million, but by December, 1931, only $590,000 had been raised and no more was forthcoming; in June, 1932, 20,000 people in Atlanta and Fulton County were simply removed from the relief rolls, most of them African Americans. In St. Louis, relief agencies were going through a quarter of a million dollars a month, and in July, 1932, the city had to drop 13,000 families off the rolls. In Fort Wayne, Indiana, the Allen County Emergency Unemployment Committee, formed in December, 1930, managed to raise enough money in its first two years to stay more or less even with the relief load. But in 1932, fund-raising targets were not met and the city's own relief expenditures began to slide. Like those in many other regions, Fort Wayne and other Allen County cities began printing their own scrip and using that as currency for goods and services within their own confines.

In Detroit, the Ford Motor Company was forced to shut down production lines on its spectacularly successful Model A. Introduced to a clamorous public in December, 1927, the Model A had taken the lead in sales away from Chevrolet, and even in 1930 the company had sold 1.4 million cars. But by August, 1931, sales were running at rates only half those of 1930, and Ford simply stopped production. Up to then, Detroit had been carrying a welfare budget of $14 million; it now was cut to $7 million, while the number of those in need of relief swelled. Similarly, a $17 million public works program was slashed to $6 million. Michigan Senator James Couzens offered to start a private relief fund with a personal donation of $1 million if Detroit's other rich people would come up with an additional $9 million; no one appeared interested.

A PRIVATE KIND OF SHAME

However desperate the measures taken against it by private and public agencies alike, nothing seemed powerful enough to lift the weight of the depression. For those in the middle class or those who might have hoped to work and save their way into the middle class, much of the weight was psychological. "What is surprising is the passive resignation with which the blow has been accepted," newsman Marquis Childs wrote, "this awful pretense that seeks to conceal the mortal wound, to carry on as though it were still the best possible of all possible worlds." Louis Adamic said of American workers, "I have a definite feeling that millions of them, now that they are unemployed, are licked," and many did seem to be finished, burdened beyond the bearing of it by a terrible load of guilt. They had been taught all their lives that hard work and thrift and honesty would be rewarded with at least security, if not wealth. That hope had failed them, and the fault must be in themselves; millions, Studs Terkel remembered, "experienced a private kind of shame when the pink slip came."

The architecture of despair could be seen everywhere, even among those, like most African Americans, who had been at the bottom so long that it might have seemed that nothing could possibly get any worse. But the hopes and psychic toughness of many black people, too, were tried as they had never been tried before—in the black working-class ghetto of Detroit's "Inkster," for example, where Ford Motor Company worker Odie Stallings scratched to keep his family alive.

Stallings, whose story was told in *American Odyssey,* Robert Conot's history of Detroit, had come to Detroit from Virginia after serving in World War I, joining an internal migration that had changed the face of urban America. If World War I had offered the wheat farmer of the Midwest the dream of avarice, it had given the African American of the South the dream of escape. Wartime America had needed bodies, and blacks had responded. Half a million had departed the rural South between 1916 and 1919 alone, and another million or more had migrated during the twenties. Most had found the promised land close to home—in such cities as Birmingham, Alabama, where the black population had nearly doubled in twenty years; or Memphis, Tennessee, where it had more than doubled; or Houston, Texas, where it had nearly tripled. But many of those who joined the Great Migration also had found opportunity winking at them from the Northeast and Midwest. "I'm tired of this Jim Crow," they sang, "gonna leave this Jim Crow town,/Doggone my black soul, I'm sweet Chicago bound," then had boarded trains by the carloads and headed north for Chicago, Detroit, Pittsburgh, Philadelphia, New York. "I should have been here 20 years ago," one transplant had written from Chicago to the folks back home in Hattiesburg, Mississippi.

I just begin to feel like a man. It's a great deal of pleasure in knowing that you got some privileges. My children are going to the same school with the whites and I don't have to umble to no one. I have registered—will vote the next election and there ain't any 'yes sir'—it's all yes and no and Sam and Bill.

Odie Stallings had been seduced by the same dream, settling in Inkster after finding work in the "black department" at the Ford Plant in River Rouge. He married, and he and his wife, Freda, soon produced two sons. She was pregnant with their third when Ford shut down operations in August, 1931. Shortly afterward, Freda gave birth to another boy. With no income, the Stallings family, like most of those in Inkster, lived on a diet that often was reduced to nothing but starches and water, and Odie dropped from 160 to 125 pounds. His wife was even more wasted, and her breasts were nearly dry; she fed the baby from a bottle filled with flour and water when she could not nurse him herself. Odie trudged the city streets and country roads all over Wayne County in search of any kind of work until his shoes were worn to less than shreds and he could no longer walk long distances. He patched his lightless and heatless shack with newspapers to keep out the cold, but when winter closed down on the ghetto like a fist, the children hacked and coughed incessantly, including the baby, who grew increasingly sick. The parents slept with the infant between them on a narrow bed to keep him warm, but nothing helped, and one morning when they woke he was dead. They put the tiny body in a cardboard box and walking close together under a gray morning sky the family carried their burden up the rutted muddy street and buried it in the makeshift cemetery next to the little community church.

So much, then, for belief in a system whose inherent strengths were supposed to prevent such misery from ever taking place—or if it could not guarantee that, would at least move swiftly and purposefully to repair the damage that had been done. That faith had been tested and had failed—in Detroit, in New York, Chicago, Philadelphia, Seattle, in the farm fields of the Midwest, the cotton plantations of the South, everywhere, resoundingly. What was left, then? Despair, certainly, the bleak anguish of a psychological depression whose dimensions matched the somber statistical dirge of the economic slump. But in human terms, depression often is just another form of anger. And in the end it would be anger, not despair, that would question conventional wisdom, dismantle comfortable assumptions about American society, challenge the machinery of government itself, and bring the first light to the long darkness of the Great Depression.

People everywhere protested their lot. In Arkansas, angry farmers invaded the town of England and demanded food for their hungry families. With reassurances from the Red Cross that they would be reimbursed, merchants distributed bread and other food to the farmers. In Oklahoma City, a mob of hungry men and women invaded a grocery store and seized what they needed. Despite tear gas fired by police, hundreds of workers staged a hunger march on Ford Motor Company at Dearborn, Michigan. In 1932, 20,000 veterans of the Great War marched on Washington after Hoover withheld bonuses promised them for their service in that savage conflict. Hoover sent in the army and six tanks to disperse these "dangerous radicals." That same year an angry and fearful electorate voted Hoover out of office, replacing him with a patrician Democrat who assured Americans that they had "nothing to fear but fear itself."

QUESTIONS TO CONSIDER

1 What economic conditions characterized the crash and the beginning of the Great Depression? The author cites a set of harrowing statistics to illustrate the gravity of the crisis. To what did they refer?

2 How did the Depression affect ordinary Americans, both economically and psychologically? Give examples from the text. What happened to Mexican Americans? Who was Odie Stallings? What does his story illustrate?

3 What was President Hoover's approach to the crisis? What were the beliefs that guided him in his attempt to solve it? What did he tell Americans they must do? What agencies did he rely on to provide relief? Did his approach succeed or fail?

4 What role did the Red Cross play in the early years of the Depression? If charity and volunteerism failed to solve the crisis, what do you think was needed?

5 Given the poverty, frustration, anger, and disillusionment of millions of Americans during the Depression, how can you explain the relative lack of violence or popular demands for radical change?

17 Government in Action: FDR and the Early New Deal

JAMES MacGREGOR BURNS

Franklin Roosevelt swept to power in 1932, carrying every state but six in the electoral college and gathering 23 million popular votes in contrast to Hoover's 16 million. It was a bitter defeat for the Republicans. But the election was even more disappointing for Norman Thomas and William Z. Foster, candidates for the Socialist and Communist parties, respectively. In this year of distress, with some 16 million people unemployed, Thomas collected 882,000 votes and Foster only 103,000.

Roosevelt was perhaps the most controversial president the United States ever had. For millions of Americans, he was a folk hero: a courageous statesman who saved a crippled nation from almost certain collapse and whose New Deal salvaged the best features of democratic capitalism while establishing unprecedented welfare programs for the nation. For others, he was a tyrant, a demagogue who used the Depression to consolidate his political power, whereupon he dragged the country zealously down the road to socialism. In spite of his immense popular appeal, Roosevelt became the hated enemy of much of the nation's business and political community. Conservatives denounced him as a Communist. Liberals said he was too conservative. Communists castigated him as a tool of Wall Street. And Socialists dismissed him as a reactionary. "He caught hell from all sides," recorded one observer, because few knew how to classify his political philosophy or his approach to reform. Where, after all, did he fit ideologically? Was he for capitalism or against it? Was his New Deal revolutionary or reactionary? Was it "creeping socialism" or a bulwark against socialism? Did it lift the country out of the Depression, or did it make the disaster worse?

In fact, as Roosevelt scholar James MacGregor Burns points out in the following selection, FDR was essentially nonideological. He rejected absolutes in favor of bold and practical experimentation. And the New Deal itself, as one scholar explained, was not a coherent, far-sighted program of reform, but "a series of improvisations" that reflected Roosevelt's empirical temper. He compared himself to a quarterback in a football game, "calling a new play after he saw how the last one turned out." There may not have been an ideology or philosophy behind FDR's New Deal. But "there was a loose collection of values," Burns says. These consisted of "Roosevelt's warm humanitarianism, his belief that the needy must be helped, that [the federal] government must step in when private institutions could not do the job."

And both private institutions and impoverished state governments were totally incapable of dealing with the Depression, the greatest economic disaster in American history, which threatened the very survival of the nation. As the winter of 1932–1933 approached, the crisis deepened. As Burns says elsewhere, "Business activity dropped to between a quarter and a third of 'normalcy' and one worker out of five—perhaps one out of four—was jobless." Those who had jobs were scarcely better off. In Manhattan sweatshops, women who lined slippers earned just over one dollar in a nine-hour day. Young women who sewed aprons made only twenty cents a day. "There is not a garbage-dump in Chicago which is not diligently haunted by the hungry," journalist and critic Edmund Wilson observed.

Out in the farmlands, rural families were also poverty-stricken and desperate. To stay warm, they burned their corn, which was cheaper than coal. When banks attempted to foreclose on farms, desperate rural folk brandished shotguns and hangman's nooses to drive the deputy sheriffs away. When a farm was auctioned, a neighbor would bid a dime and give the farm back to its owner. Farm leaders in Nebraska threatened to march thousands of protestors to the state capitol and destroy it if relief was denied. In Washington, D.C., officials warned that a revolution was building in the countryside.

Against this frightening background, fifty-one-year-old Franklin Delano Roosevelt prepared to speak to the nation in his inaugural address. Stricken by polio in 1921, the president-elect was unable to walk. He wore iron braces on his legs and gripped the arms of his sons in order to stand erect. This sets the scene for the gripping story Burns has to tell about the early New Deal, 1933–1934. It is the story of a crippled president who tried to save his crippled nation by bold and brilliant improvisations.

GLOSSARY

AGRICULTURAL ADJUSTMENT ADMINISTRATION (AAA)   A New Deal agency designed to relieve Depression-wracked farmers, who suffered from falling prices and mounting crop surpluses. Established in 1933, the AAA subsidized farm prices until they reached a point of "parity." The AAA also sought to reduce agricultural surpluses by telling farmers how much to plant (acreage allotments) and paying them for what they did not grow. Declared unconstitutional by the Supreme Court in 1935, the AAA was superceded by the Soil Conservation and Domestic Allotment Act.

BERLE, JR., ADOLF A.   A clergyman's son, Berle was a valuable member of FDR's Brain Trust. Berle was the author of *The Modern Corporation and Private Property* (1932) and worked to win the support of the business community for the New Deal.

BRAIN TRUST   Special group of advisers led by eminent political economists Raymond Moley, Rexford Guy Tugwell, and Adolf A. Berle, Jr.

BYRD, HARRY F.   Conservative Democratic senator from Virginia, Byrd often opposed the New Deal and advocated a return to a balanced budget and greater states' rights.

CIVILIAN CONSERVATION CORPS (CCC)   Created in 1933, the CCC employed over two million young people, who came mainly from urban families on relief, to work in the nation's parks and recreational facilities. CCC employees received thirty dollars per month to plant trees, build trails, and work on soil conservation.

CIVIL WORKS ADMINISTRATION (CWA)   Created in 1933, with Harry Hopkins at its head, the CWA put over four million people to work on "light" projects such as building roads and playgrounds. In its one-year existence, the CWA provided money for many unskilled workers who, because of the Depression, were unemployed and desperate.

CHURCHILL, WINSTON   In the spring of 1940, when World War II in Europe was only seven months old, Churchill replaced the disgraced Neville Chamberlain as the United Kingdom's prime minister. Churchill's courage bolstered Great Britain during its darkest hours when the bombing of the German *Luftwaffe* almost destroyed the country.

GARNER, JOHN NANCE   Former speaker of the House of Representatives, this Texan served as FDR's vice president from 1933 to 1941. Garner split with Roosevelt over the administration's failure to balance the budget and its refusal to oppose the labor movement's sit-down strikes.

GLASS, CARTER   Conservative Democratic senator from Virginia, Glass frequently opposed FDR's monetary policies. Glass was a tenacious foe of the NRA, which he believed promoted monopolies and kept consumer prices high.

GREEN, WILLIAM   President of the American Federation of Labor, Green was a respected leader of the organized labor movement in the 1930s.

HOPKINS, HARRY   Director of the Works Progress Administration (WPA) and later secretary of commerce, Hopkins was one of Roosevelt's closest and most trusted advisors. Although weakened by cancer, Hopkins vigorously organized the Cabinet to prepare the nation for war.

HUGHES, CHARLES EVANS   A former governor of New York and moderate Supreme Court justice, Hughes was the nominee of the Republican party in the presidential election of 1916. He later became President Harding's secretary of state and served as Chief Justice to the Supreme Court from 1930 to 1941.

ICKES, HAROLD "Honest Harold" served as Roosevelt's secretary of the interior and head of the Public Works Administration (PWA).

JOHNSON, HUGH Director of the National Recovery Administration (NRA), Johnson helped devise voluntary codes of fair competition and used public relations and propaganda to persuade employers to adhere to them.

LEWIS, JOHN L. Head of the United Mine Workers, Lewis was the driving force behind the creation of the Committee for Industrial Organization (CIO). Although a lifelong Republican, he campaigned for Roosevelt in 1936 and brought most of the labor movement into the Democratic camp. Lewis argued that "capitalism need not be uprooted, but its fruits must be more equally distributed."

MOLEY, RAYMOND A former Columbia University college professor, Moley was a shrewd and valuable member of FDR's Brain Trust. He also served as assistant secretary of state. Moley admired Roosevelt's courageous efforts to end the Depression, the greatest economic crisis in American history. Moley said FDR "was like the fairy-story prince who didn't know how to shudder."

NATIONAL RECOVERY ADMINISTRATION (NRA) Established in 1933, this New Deal agency sought to end unemployment by devising "industrial fair practice codes." It often impeded competition by authorizing production quotas and price fixing. In 1935, the Supreme Court declared the NRA unconstitutional.

PERKINS, FRANCES The first woman to serve in a presidential cabinet, Perkins was Roosevelt's secretary of labor from 1933 to 1945. She mediated bitter labor disputes and helped write the Social Security Act of 1935, the National Labor Relations Act of 1935, and other important New Deal legislation.

PUBLIC WORKS ADMINISTRATION (PWA) Created in 1933, with Harold Ickes at its head, the PWA focused on "heavy" projects such as building bridges and schools.

ROGERS, WILL This popular humorist was an astute observer of the American way of life. His sardonic assessments of political leaders made him into a legend.

TENNESSEE VALLEY AUTHORITY (TVA) In 1933, Congress created this public corporation, which focused on regional planning. The TVA completed a dam at Muscle Shoals, Alabama, on the Tennessee River, and improved or built many other dams, which all but ended flooding in the region. The TVA also generated and sold inexpensive electricity to thousands of rural Americans who had never had it before.

TUGWELL, REXFORD GUY A valuable member of Roosevelt's Brain Trust, Tugwell was an expert on agriculture.

---

*W*ashington, D.C., March 4, 1933: Perched on the icy branches of the gaunt trees overlooking the Capitol's east front, they waited for the ceremony to which they had no tickets: an old man in ancient, patched-up green tweeds; a pretty young redhead in a skimpy coat; an older woman in rags, her face lined with worry and pain; a college boy whose father was jobless. They watched the crowd below as rumors drifted through that Roosevelt had been shot, that the whole area was covered by army machine guns. The older woman prayed

From *The Crosswinds of Freedom*, by James MacGregor Burns, copyright © 1989 by James MacGregor Burns. Used by permission of Alfred A. Knopf, a division of Random House, Inc.

on her tree limb: "No more trouble, please, God. No more trouble."

They watched as dignitaries straggled down the Capitol steps: Herbert Hoover, morose and stony-faced; Chief Justice Charles Evans Hughes, his white beard fluttering a bit in the cold wind; Vice President [John Nance] Garner, shivering without an overcoat; finally Franklin D. Roosevelt, moving down the steps with agonizing slowness on the arm of his son James. They watched as the new President took the oath of office, his hand lying on the 300-year-old Roosevelt family Bible, open at Paul's First Epistle to the Corinthians: "though I have faith . . . and have not charity, I am nothing." And they watched as, still unsmiling, he gripped the rostrum firmly and looked out at the crowd.

"I am certain that my fellow Americans expect that on my induction into the Presidency I will address them with a candor and a decision which the present situation of our Nation impels." The cold wind riffled the pages of his text.

"This great nation will endure as it has endured, will revive and will prosper." The President's words rang out across the plaza. "So, first of all, let me assert my firm belief that the only thing we have to fear is fear itself—nameless, unreasoning, unjustified terror which paralyzes needed efforts to convert retreat into advance."

The great crowd stood in almost dead silence. Chin outthrust, face grave, Roosevelt went on: "In every dark hour of our national life a leadership of frankness and vigor has met with that understanding and support of the people themselves which is essential to victory."

The crowd began to respond as it caught the cadence of the phrases: "The money changers have fled from their high seats in the temple of our civilization. . . .

"This Nation asks for action, and action now. Our greatest primary task is to put people to work." The throng stirred to these words. The President gave the core of what would become the first New Deal programs. He touched on foreign policy only vaguely and briefly.

"In the field of world policy I would dedicate this Nation to the policy of the good neighbor—the neighbor who resolutely respects himself and, because he does so, respects the rights of others. . . ."

He hoped that the Constitution, with its normal balance of presidential and congressional power, would be adequate to the crisis. But if Congress did not respond to his proposals or act on its own, and if the national emergency continued, "I shall ask the Congress for the one remaining instrument to meet the crisis—broad Executive power to wage a war against the emergency, as great as the power that would be given to me if we were in fact invaded by a foreign foe." The American people wanted direct, vigorous action.

"They have asked for discipline and direction under leadership. They have made me the present instrument of their wishes. . . ."

As Roosevelt ended, he was still grim; but his face lighted up when the crowd seemed to come to life. The old man in the tree had broken into tears. "It was very, very solemn, and a little terrifying," Eleanor Roosevelt said later to reporters in the White House. "The crowds were so tremendous, and you felt that they would do anything—if only someone would tell them what to do."

Someone would. The new President had no sooner reviewed the inaugural parade and hosted a White House reception for a thousand guests than he swore in his cabinet en masse upstairs in the Oval Room. Washington had come alive with rumor and hope. Even while couples waltzed gaily at the inaugural balls, haggard men conferred hour after hour in the huge marble buildings along Pennsylvania Avenue. Republican holdovers and Democrats newly arrived in Washington sat side by side, telephoning anxious bankers, drawing up emergency orders, all the while feeling the financial pulse of the nation and world. . . .

At the center of the action sat Franklin Roosevelt, presiding, instructing, wheedling, persuading, enticing, pressuring, negotiating, manipulating, conceding, horse-trading, placating, mediating—leading and following, leading and misleading. People marveled how the President, his cigarette holder deployed more jauntily than ever, appeared to bounce and skip through the day, despite his inability to walk, as he punctuated solemn conferences with jests, long and somewhat imaginary stories, and great booming laughter. While still in bed in the morning, his large torso looming over legs that hardly ribbed the sheets, he spouted ideas, questions, instructions to his aides. Wheeled over to the west wing, he swung into his office chair for long hours of visitors, letters, telephone calls, emergency sessions.

Calvin Coolidge had allegedly disposed of visitors by a simple formula: "Don't talk back to 'em." Roosevelt used talk as a tool of influence, outtalking his advisers, outtalking department heads, even outtalking visiting senators.

The President soon proved himself an artist in government—in his fine sense of timing, his adroit application of pressure, his face-to-face persuasiveness, his craft in playing not only foes but friends off against one another. Like a creative artist, Frances Perkins said, he would begin his picture "without a clear idea of what he intends to paint or how it shall be laid out upon the canvas, and then, as he paints, his plan evolves out of the material he is painting." He could think and feel his way into political situations with imagination, intuition, insight.

These traits dominated his policy thinking as well as his political calculating—and with less success. People close to Roosevelt were dismayed by his casual and disorderly intellectual habits. To Adolf Berle his judgments of people and ideas were "primarily instinctive and not rational," his learning came not from books but from people. He read not books but newspapers, perhaps half a dozen before breakfast—devoured them "like a combine eating up grain," a friend noted. He was not so much a creator of ideas as a broker of them. He did not assemble his ideas into a comprehensive and ordered program, with priorities and interconnections. Just as he lived each day for itself, as he liked to tell friends, so he appeared to flirt with each idea as it came along.

Everything seemed to conspire to fortify these intellectual habits of the new President—his eclectic education and reading, the ideologically divided party he led, the factionalized Congress he confronted, above all the advisers he had chosen and who had chosen him. His chief brain truster during 1933 was Ray Moley. Prickly and hard-driving, the former Columbia professor—now Assistant Secretary of State—shared some of his boss's political shrewdness and opportunism, intuitive judgment, and keenness in evaluating friend and foe. But Roosevelt also talked at length with Berle about banking, railroad, and monetary problems, and Berle's ideas for raising business to a higher level of efficiency and responsibility; with Tugwell about conservation, agriculture, and industrial discipline, and Tugwell's notions of democratic planning of the economy. . . .

Most remarkable of all was that one-woman brain trust, Eleanor Roosevelt—and all the more influential for not being viewed in that role. Through quick visits to her husband while he was still breakfasting in bed, little chits and memos, thick reports infiltrated into the executive offices, the visitors she invited to the White House, and her own influence on public opinion and Washington attitudes, she soon became a penetrating voice for the humanitarian liberal-left. Through a wide correspondence—she received 300,000 pieces of mail the first year—her press conferences and newspaper columns, her speeches and magazine articles, her widely advertised (and criticized) trips to CCC camps and coal mines, she began to build up a potentially powerful constituency of her own. Historian Mary Beard wrote admiringly of her ability to give "inspiration to the married, solace to the lovelorn, assistance to the homemaker, menus to the cook, and help to the educator, direction to the employer, caution to the warrior, and deeper awareness of its primordial force to the 'weaker sex.'" The First Lady also served as a model for other women in Washington government. Her close friend Frances Perkins, with her labor and urban concerns and constituencies, had special access to both Roosevelts, and women . . . learned that they could be, all at the same time, competent, caring, and controversial.

Such was the flux and flow of advice to the President that no one really knew which advisers were influential or why or when. Who was having the President's ear at the moment provoked jealousies worthy of the royal courts of old. The President's mind seemed awesomely accessible—to the kitchen cabinet, to department heads like Ickes and Perkins, to experts coming through Washington. The President would be seen talking animatedly with men regarded by the orthodox—though not necessarily by history—as quacks.

Roosevelt was following no set course, left, right, or center. He was leading by guess and by God. He not only admitted to playing by ear but boasted of it. He was a football quarterback, he told reporters, calling a new play after he saw how the last one turned out. Snap judgments had to be made. But Washington wondered what lay back of the snap judgments—some ideology or philosophy?

Neither of these, but rather a loose collection of values—Roosevelt's warm humanitarianism, his belief

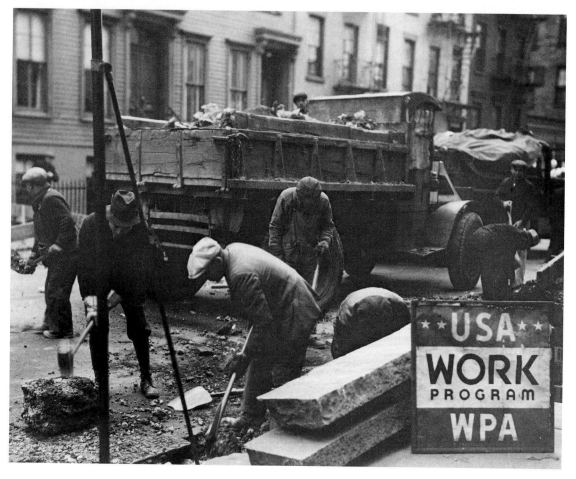

Through the Works Progress Administration, the New Deal put unemployed men like these to work on a variety of projects, from building bridges in the cities to blazing nature trails in the wilderness.

The workers shown here are widening a street. This creative agency also employed writers to do guidebooks to the states and artists to draw murals for government buildings. (The Bettmann Archive)

that the needy must be helped, that government must step in when private institutions could not do the job, and that now—in 1933—this meant the federal government. The President also had a fine grasp of political and governmental nuts and bolts. But between the two levels of grand philosophy and policy specifics he would be experimental, eclectic, nonprogrammatic, nondoctrinaire. He would be a broker of ideas as well as of interests and individuals.

As a master broker Roosevelt presided over a grand concert of interests. Labor, farmers, businessmen, investors, unemployed youth, some of the poor—all got a slice of the first New Deal, at least

on paper. FDR assumed the role of bipartisan leader, "president of all the people," virtually the national father. He happily cited a Nebraska congressman's definition of the New Deal as an effort "to cement our society, rich and poor, manual worker and brain worker, into a voluntary brotherhood of freemen, standing together, striving together, for the common good of all." Government, he told a convention of bankers, was "essentially the outward expression of the unity and the leadership of all groups." All this seemed a long cry from the "discipline and direction under leadership" he had promised in his inaugural address.

Congress, though more responsive to regional and special interests, quickened to the energy that radiated from the President. Even some Republicans fell over themselves to express support for the Democratic Roosevelt. In many respects the Chief Executive was Chief Legislator. Congress was by no means supine. Conservative Democratic senators like Carter Glass and Harry F. Byrd of Virginia usually opposed the President's bills. Congress as a whole, however, was more positive than even Roosevelt toward the New Deal. Many congressmen wanted more inflation than Roosevelt, ampler spending for people's needs, greater generosity to veterans and farmers, bigger public works, tougher policies toward Wall Street. The President skillfully brokered with the congressional left. For the conservative Democrats in the Senate he had growing hostility. Byrd opposed the AAA, FDR told Tugwell, because, as an apple grower, "he's afraid you'll force him to pay more than ten cents an hour for his apple pickers."

As master broker Roosevelt for a time could stay above the political and ideological battles raging around him. In the distribution of good things—whether government money or patronage jobs or social policy or his smile of approval—he could act as transactional leader within the existing system. He might give TVA to the left and economy to the right, but as a compromising broker rather than ideological leader he would not move decisively left or right. Social justice, he said, "ought not to consist of robbing Peter to pay Paul."

It all seemed to work beautifully for a time. Employment, prices, income all soared in the weeks after the Hundred Days. The industrial production index nearly doubled from March to July. Unemployment fell off from around 15 million at the time of Roosevelt's inaugural to about 11 million in October, a drop in the jobless rate from about 30 to about 22 percent.

Roosevelt's popularity floated high on this first gust of recovery. "If he burned down the capitol," said Will Rogers, "we would cheer and say, 'well, we at least got a fire started anyhow.'"

He won praise from Bertie McCormick's Republican Chicago *Tribune* and William Randolph Hearst's New York *American*. Daily, White House mailmen hauled in sacks of mail, most of it laudatory, some of it fulsome. An adviser found the President happily leafing through a sheaf of this mail. He was sorting letters he had received from British subjects addressing him as "Your Majesty" or "Lord Roosevelt" or in other monarchical terms. Why? He wanted to send them to King George V for his "amusement." History has not recorded that His Majesty was amused.

Psychology overwhelmed economics. In sad reality at least 10 million Americans remained jobless in 1933, and industrial production was still far below that of the prosperity years and even the first year of the depression. In October 3 million families—at least 12 million people—still depended on unemployment relief of about $23 a month, which covered food but left little or nothing for rent and utilities. But people *felt* better—and this was largely Roosevelt's doing. He exuded cheerfulness. He raised hopes and expectations. Above all, he *acted;* for several months he simply dominated the front pages of the nation's newspapers with his speeches, bill-signings, trips, executive orders, pronunciamentos.

His fireside chats carried his buoyant presence directly into home and hearth. "I want to talk for a few minutes with the people of the United States about banking," he said at the start of his first fireside chat in mid-March. "I want to tell you what has been done in the last few days, why it was done, and what the next steps are going to be." And he proceeded to do just that, in simple, human terms. Read later in cold print, the chats seemed a bit limp and pedestrian. Read by Roosevelt over the radio, they sounded warm, intimate, homely. Watching him deliver a fireside chat, Frances Perkins sensed that he could actually see the families listening at the other end. "His face would smile and light up as though he were actually sitting on the front porch or in the parlor with them." The President took care not to overuse this device, giving only four chats the first year, at two- or three-month intervals.

Nor did he overstrain the press conference as a way of reaching people. He held these twice a week, to the joy of the White House press corps, but the

FDR was the first president to effectively use mass communication. His radio "fireside chats" comforted Americans during the darkest moments of the Depression. Frances Perkins observed that Roosevelt's "face would smile and light up" when he delivered these broadcasts to the American people. It was "as though he were actually sitting on the front porch or in the parlor with them," Perkins said. (Bettmann/CORBIS)

sessions were often more frustrating than rewarding to the reporters. Roosevelt was a master at withholding information. He spent much of the half hour jovially fencing and parrying with the reporters, or offering them tidbits, or lecturing them. Crowding around the President's gadget-covered desk, the correspondents pressed him hard, with mixed results. Roosevelt wanted to control the flow of information, to create his own sensations, to set his own timing. He was not the first or the last President to do all this; he was simply more effective than most.

Nothing epitomized the New Deal in action better than the National Recovery Act and Administration—epitomized Roosevelt's Concert of Interests, his role of broker, the psychological impact of the Hundred Days, the fundamental problems of the "broker state" at work. As boss of NRA, Roosevelt chose General Hugh Johnson, who was a mass of contradictions himself—outwardly a tough old cavalryman with a leathery face, squint eyes, and a rough bark of a voice, inwardly an amalgam of public commitment, touchy ego, maudlin sentimentality, business savvy, and as clamorous and picturesque as a sideshow barker. The general's first job was to persuade employers to draw up codes of fair competition, a task he attacked like a cavalry charge. Once approved by the President and given the force of law, the codes were designed to discourage wasteful, junglelike competition by setting more orderly pricing and marketing policies, and to benefit workers by establishing higher wages, shorter hours, better working conditions, and the end of child labor. As part of the deal, anti-trust policies would be softened so that businessmen could cooperate in setting up the codes. Code signers could affix the "Blue Eagle" label to products and shopwindows.

With Johnson as bugler, the NRA galvanized the American people like a national call to arms. Suddenly the Blue Eagle was everywhere—on magazine covers, in the movies, on girls in chorus lines. (But not on Ford cars; Henry Ford perversely refused to sign the automobile code, then lived up to it anyway.) Rushing from city to city in an army plane, dishing out Boy Scout–style enthusiasm, biting criticism, and wisecracks at every stop, Johnson pressured and coaxed businessmen to endorse the codes, then gathered them in Washington for the signing and orating. As the very personification of recovery, the general staged a monster Blue Eagle parade on New York's Fifth Avenue. For hours he reviewed the parade of a quarter million persons, with another million and a half cheering from the sidewalks. Not since 1917 had Americans savored such a throbbing sense of marching unity.

As the months passed, though, the questions became more and more urgent: Unity for what? Marching to where? Under pressure for quick results, Johnson dealt with the business and labor leaders closest at hand, those who were most vocal, best organized, most skillful in dealing with bureaucrats and politicians. Inevitably he delegated crucial pricing and production decisions to the dominant interests, which often turned out to be the biggest corporations. . . .

Union labor, being organized, fared better under NRA. Section 7(a) of the act boldly proclaimed that employees "shall have the right to organize and bargain collectively through representatives of their own choosing, and shall be free from the interference, restraint, or coercion of employers" in choosing their representatives. No one seeking or holding a job "shall be required as a condition of employment to join any company union or to refrain from joining, organizing, or assisting a labor organization of his own choosing." Union leaders greeted this as labor's Magna Carta—comparable to Lincoln's Emancipation Proclamation, said John L. Lewis—and the message was clear: Organize. "THE PRESIDENT WANTS YOU TO JOIN A UNION," placards read. "Forget about injunctions, yellow dog contracts, black lists and the fear of dismissal." But there were complications. President William Green and the American Federation of Labor old guard wanted to organize workers into separate craft unions, even in huge auto plants, while Lewis and the rising young militants around him wanted to organize all the workers in a plant or company or industry into big, solid industrial unions.

Employers bridled at 7(a). Many set up company unions—or "employee representation plans"—which came to be run by company stooges. Labor responded with a rash of strikes during the summer of 1933; by September nearly 300,000 workers had walked out. The "concert of interests" seemed to be emitting discordant noises. "N.R.A. means National Run Around," read a sign hoisted on a picket line. The President set up special boards, trimmed NRA's power, eased Johnson out, and put in more domesticated chiefs, but to little avail; during 1934 the NRA eagle fluttered through heavy weather.

In the end the significance of the National Recovery Administration was not its impact on economic recovery, which was mixed, but its curbing of child labor, sweatshops, and unfair trade practices, its big boost to unionization and its modest protection to consumers. Why then was the NRA finally dismissed as a failure, even privately by Roosevelt himself? Largely because it failed in its highly touted supreme aim of bringing capital, labor, and other interests into a happy concert under the "Broker State," and by artificially raising prices and restricting production, it only marginally helped produce recovery.

If the Concert of Interests did not work, what would? Public works, the companion piece to the NRA, was launched with little of the drama of the Blue Eagle, under the leadership of one of the most committed and stout-hearted New Dealers, Secretary of the Interior Harold Ickes. Touchy and cantankerous, suspicious of friend and foe—and especially of government contractors— "Honest Harold" did not hesitate to use government snoopers to check on suspect PWA employees and their financial connections. Ickes was in no great hurry; his big projects needed careful planning and budgeting as well as laborious scrutiny by the secretary himself. When the public works program finally got underway it built gas and electric power plants, jails and hospitals, sewage and water systems, bridges, docks, and tunnels—and aircraft carriers, cruisers, destroyers, army and navy airplanes. But the $9 billion that PWA ultimately spent were not central to recovery during Roosevelt's first two years.

Much quicker to get underway was the federal relief program under a lanky young ex-director of private welfare programs named Harry Hopkins, who acted almost as fast as he talked. Appointed Federal Emergency Relief Administrator with a grant of half a billion dollars, Hopkins began authorizing millions of dollars in relief even while he was waiting in a hallway to be moved into his office. Since he could give money only to the state and local public relief agencies, which in turn administered relief programs, he could do little more than monitor the levels of compassion and competence with which programs were carried out. Behind his cynical, wisecracking façade Hopkins was deeply concerned with guarding the dignity, pride, and self-esteem of people on relief. Hence he was eager that the unemployed be given jobs and not merely handouts, but job programs cost more money. Late in 1933 Hopkins persuaded Roosevelt to launch a massive crash program to employ 4 million. In its brief existence, the Civil Works Administration undertook the building or rebuilding of vast numbers of roads, parks, schools, playgrounds, swimming pools, and other "light," short-term projects, in contrast to the PWA's "heavy" jobs.

It was this massive spending on work relief, supplemented by that of the PWA, the TVA, the CCC, the AAA, and other programs, that in 1933 and 1934 provided the central thrust of the early New Deal. It was not really planned that way; Roosevelt was responding not to grand ideology or to grand economics but to sheer human needs that he recognized and that Eleanor Roosevelt, Hopkins, Perkins, and the others brought to him. . . .

The public . . . saw a President who was doing his damnedest, quick to confront specific problems, brilliant at explaining his deeds and hopes, always positive, exuberant, seemingly on top of things. The public saw a leader.

For that public the ultimate test was economic recovery, and the flush of prosperity felt strong by fall 1934, compared to the miseries of March 1933. Could "bucks" be converted to ballots? A third of the senators and all the representatives were up for reelection. Roosevelt's tactic was to stand above the party battle, in line with his bipartisan posture of "leader of all the people." But he helped friendly candidates indirectly, and he posed the campaign issue by asking in a fireside chat, "Are you better off than you were last year? Are your debts less burdensome? Is your bank account more secure? Are your working conditions better? Is your faith in your own individual future more firmly grounded?"

The result was a resounding verdict for the President and his New Deal. Typically Presidents lost ground in midterm congressional elections, but in 1934 Democratic strength rose from 313 to 322 in the House and—incredibly—from 59 to 69 in the Senate. A clutch of highly conservative Republican senators was sacked. "Some of our friends think the majority top-heavy," Garner wrote the President, "but if properly handled, the House and Senate will be all right and I am sure you can arrange that."

Next month a late vote came in from Britain. "The courage, the power and the scale" of Roosevelt's effort, wrote Winston Churchill, "must enlist the ardent sympathy of every country, and his success could not fail to lift the whole world forward into the sunlight of an easier and more genial age." The British Conservative was seeking to place Roosevelt in the broadest sweep of history.

"Roosevelt is an explorer who has embarked on a voyage as uncertain as that of Columbus, and upon a quest which might conceivably be as important as the discovery of the New World."

With the early New Deal behind him, Roosevelt continued his bold experimentation throughout the 1930s. But the treacherous Depression continued to plague Americans. Too many teachers saw hungry children in their classrooms. Too many unemployed men committed "altruistic suicides" because they felt guilty about failing to feed their families. A man who had not had a steady job in over two years lamented: "Sometimes I feel like a murderer. What's wrong with me, that I can't protect my children?" In sum, the New Deal failed to end the Depression—America's entry into World War II would finally do that. Roosevelt had failed to devise a coherent strategy for dealing with the country's economic woes and to restore consumer purchasing power—the key to successful economic recovery.

Nevertheless, the New Deal accomplished many things. It provided relief for millions of Americans, protected the organizing and bargaining rights of labor, and saved the farmers through a system of price supports and acreage allotments. To those who were hurting, the New Deal represented a government that cared. And it made people feel better. Recall what Burns said: "This was largely Roosevelt's doing. He exuded cheerfulness. He raised hopes and expectations. Above all, he acted." And common Americans loved him for it. "He was my friend," said a man in Denver. Comparing Roosevelt's reforms to the relative inaction of the Hoover administration, historian William Manchester concluded that if FDR had "been another Hoover, the United States would have followed seven Latin American countries whose governments had been overthrown by Depression victims."

QUESTIONS TO CONSIDER

1 As FDR's inauguration day approached, what was the plight of the unemployed in American cities and the destitute farmers in the countryside? Why was Roosevelt's inaugural address, on that cold March day in 1933, one of the most important presidential speeches in American history?

2 Describe FDR's work habits and his approach toward problem solving. Why was Eleanor called FDR's "one woman brain trust"? Does the author believe that the early New Deal had an ideological focus? Or does he view it as emergency legislation designed to help those people who were hurting the most? Explain your answer by providing specific examples.

3 In describing America's mood in Roosevelt's first Hundred Days, Burns states that "psychology overwhelmed economics." Explain what his assessment means. What methods did FDR use to influence public opinion?

4 What were the goals of the NRA? What leadership qualities did Hugh Johnson bring to that New Deal agency? Describe the impact of the NRA, Section 7(a), on the labor movement.

5 Contrast the personalities and leadership styles of Harold Ickes and Harry Hopkins. What "heavy" jobs did the PWA undertake and what "light" tasks did the CWA initiate?

6 Describe how FDR was able to convert "bucks" into "ballots." How did most of the American people respond to the New Deal's first Hundred Days? How did Roosevelt's approach to solving the Depression compare to that of Herbert Hoover (selection 16)?

PART NINE

A World at War (1937–1945)

18 Franklin and Eleanor: The Early Wartime White House

DORIS KEARNS GOODWIN

For the first thirty-nine years of his life, success came easily to Franklin Delano Roosevelt. Born into a wealthy and prominent family in upstate New York (Theodore Roosevelt was a distant cousin), Franklin was a pampered only child who grew into a gregarious, handsome, and athletic young man. Educated at the finest private schools and graduated from Harvard, he chose politics for a career. With wealth and privilege, a famous name, powerful family connections, and a winning personality, he had every reason to believe that he would go far in politics, perhaps all the way to the White House. In 1905 he married his fifth cousin, Eleanor Roosevelt, a remarkably intelligent young woman who would prove to be as politically astute as her affable husband.

But in 1921 Roosevelt's world collapsed. He was stricken with polio, which left both legs paralyzed. He had to wear heavy metal braces on them and could get about only in a wheel chair or on crutches. For a man who had never had to struggle for success, Roosevelt could easily have submitted to his disability, left politics, and lived the rest of his life in the beautiful Roosevelt manor overlooking the Hudson River. Instead, his great inner strength enabled him not only to survive his "trial by fire," but also to continue and succeed brilliantly in politics. What is more, as Eleanor put it, his "great suffering" gave him "a greater sympathy and understanding of the problems of mankind."

In the following selection, prize-winning historian Doris Kearns Goodwin agrees with Eleanor's assessment. After his ordeal with polio, Franklin now "seemed less arrogant, less smug, less superficial, more focused, more complex, more interesting." Yet, as Goodwin reminds us, Roosevelt had his share of human frailties, which led him into an extramarital affair with his wife's social secretary, Lucy Mercer. If polio was the great test of Franklin's life, the discovery of his infidelity was

Eleanor's. Drawing on her own inner strength, Eleanor not only survived her husband's betrayal, but grew stronger from it and went on to become his indispensable political ally and the most influential first lady in American history.

Goodwin helps us understand the remarkable Roosevelt partnership against the backdrop of the early stages of the Second World War. That war began in Europe when powerful German forces invaded Poland in 1939. The United States, although theoretically neutral, was clearly sympathetic with the Allies, led by Britain and France. Indeed, Roosevelt was more preoccupied with the Nazi threat in Europe than with Japanese aggression in Asia. Time and again, he predicted that Hitler would eventually make war on the United States, and out of that belief flowed much of his European diplomacy: the destroyers-for-bases deal with Britain, Lend-Lease, and the Atlantic Charter. Still, through 1940 and 1941, as German planes bombed Britain and German armies swept into the Soviet Union, the Roosevelt administration often seemed adrift, as though the president and his advisers were confused, helplessly caught in a vortex of events over which they had no control.

Japanese intentions in the Pacific were especially perplexing. Since 1937, Japan had been laying waste to China, seizing its coastal territory and murdering its civilians—200,000 of them in Nanking alone. Did Japan's aggression against China constitute an immediate threat to United States security? Was a showdown with Japan inevitable, as American military leaders insisted? While the United States watched Japanese movements in Asia, Congress declared economic war against Germany with the controversial Lend-Lease program, which gave $7 billion in military aid to embattled Britain. Soon American convoys were carrying supplies across the Atlantic. When German submarines, called U-boats, torpedoed several American vessels, many observers contended that war with Hitler was only a matter of time.

Meanwhile, the Japanese question had become increasingly confusing. In Tokyo, a party led by General Hideki Tojo and the military demanded that the United States be driven from the Pacific so that Japan could establish an Asian empire free of Western influence. But Prime Minister Fumimaro, a moderate, wanted to negotiate with the United States and directed his ambassador in America to present Washington with a set of proposals that might avoid war. At the same time, the war party proceeded with a top-secret plan to attack the United States Pacific Fleet at Pearl Harbor if negotiations failed. By early December 1941, United States analysts knew that the Japanese were preparing to strike, but almost no one thought them capable of launching an air attack from aircraft carriers against distant Hawaii. When Japanese planes did exactly that, in a day that would "live in infamy," Americans from Pearl Harbor to Washington were caught completely by surprise.

Like the assassination of President John F. Kennedy and the terrorist attacks against the World Trade Center and the Pentagon, Pearl Harbor was one of those crises that mark the people who experience them for the rest of their lives. Americans of the war generation would recall exactly what they were doing when they first heard the news on that fateful Sunday. Roosevelt himself, Goodwin states, felt "great bitterness and anger toward Japan for the treachery involved in carrying out this surprise attack while the envoys of the two countries were still talking."

For years, Roosevelt detractors have charged that the president deliberately sent the Pacific fleet to Pearl Harbor so that the Japanese could attack it and give him an excuse to involve the United States in the war. There are those who still make this argument. But Gordon W. Prange's studies At Dawn We Slept *(1981) and* Pearl Harbor: The Verdict of History *(1985) and the bulk of modern scholarship exonerate Roosevelt of such a monstrous accusation. Goodwin concurs, "It is inconceivable that Roosevelt, who loved the navy with a passion, would have intentionally sacrificed the heart of the fleet, much less the lives of thirty-five hundred American sailors and soldiers, without lifting a finger to reduce the risk."*

On the Monday after Pearl Harbor, December 8, 1941, the United States declared war on the Japanese Empire. Three days later, Germany and Italy—Japan's Axis allies—declared war on the United States. Roosevelt and Congress reciprocated at once, thus placing America on the side of the Allied powers—Great Britain, the Soviet Union, and China. Franklin told Eleanor: "I never wanted to fight this war on two fronts." But now there was no choice. Fortunately for Franklin, the political partnership he had formed with Eleanor would serve him well in the terrible years ahead.

GLOSSARY

BULLITT, WILLIAM   Roosevelt's pessimistic ambassador to France who sent the president dramatic descriptions of the German invasion. On May 30, 1940, he wrote Roosevelt that he might "get blown up before I see you again."

CHAMBERLAIN, NEVILLE   British prime minister who resigned in the spring of 1940, shamed by his attempts to "appease" Hitler and by England's lack of military preparedness when the German military rolled through the Low Countries and France.

CHURCHILL, WINSTON   See glossary in previous selection.

CUDAHY, JOHN   Roosevelt's ambassador to Belgium who, in May of 1940, informed the president of Hitler's assault on the Low Countries. Goodwin writes that Cudahy "had almost been knocked down by the force of a bomb which fell three hundred feet from the embassy."

EARLY, STEPHEN   Roosevelt's press secretary from the South who helped manage the president's crowded schedule. He frequently disagreed with Eleanor's outspoken advocacy of civil rights and believed the first lady would harm the president among southern white voters, who traditionally voted for the Democratic ticket.

HOPKINS, HARRY   See glossary in previous selection.

HOWE, LOUIS   In the years that FDR struggled with polio, he was Roosevelt's closest political adviser and confidant. Howe eventually helped Roosevelt make a dramatic reentry into the political arena. He also encouraged Eleanor to become more actively involved in politics. The former newspaperman died in 1936.

KENNEDY, JOSEPH P.   A successful and ruthless businessman, ambassador to Great Britain, and father of a future president. Roosevelt eventually lost faith in Kennedy because of the diplomat's pessimism over the ability of England to resist Nazi aggression.

KNOX, FRANK   In 1940, Roosevelt appointed him secretary of the navy even though Knox was a Republican and a critic of the New Deal. One of Knox's fondest memories was charging up San Juan Hill with Theodore Roosevelt.

LeHAND, MARGUERITE "MISSY"   Roosevelt's personal secretary, who grew very close to the president after Eleanor's discovery of her husband's extramarital affair with Lucy Mercer. Missy shared FDR's private moments and became, in Goodwin's words, "his other wife."

MARSHALL, GEORGE   Roosevelt's army chief of staff and later, under Harry Truman, an influential and important secretary of state in the postwar years. When Hitler began his aggression against Germany's neighbors, this blunt, honest solider realized how unprepared the United States was to fight another world war.

McDUFFIE, IRVIN   Roosevelt's valet who lived in the White House and helped dress the president and prepare him for bed. He was friendly and talkative but was plagued with a drinking problem, and Eleanor worried that he would fail the president. The disabled chief executive, however, could not find it in his heart to dismiss him.

MERCER, LUCY PAGE   Eleanor's social secretary who had a love affair with Franklin. When Eleanor discovered their love letters, she gave her husband an opportunity for a divorce. Faced with disgrace and a lost inheritance, he refused, but their marriage was forever changed.

MORGENTHAU, HENRY   Roosevelt's secretary of the treasury who acted quickly to freeze the assets of those countries that Hitler's forces had overrun, making certain that those funds would not fall into the hands of the Nazis.

NEUTRALITY LAWS   In the isolationist 1930s, Congress passed this legislation designed to avoid the mistakes of the Great War and keep the United States out of future foreign conflicts. These measures prohibited loans and shipments of arms to belligerents and hampered Roosevelt's efforts to help England and France as those nations struggled against Nazi aggression.

PERKINS, FRANCES   See glossary in previous selection.

PHONY WAR   Many Americans used this term to describe the first part of World War II when little fighting was done. From the German attack on Poland in September of 1939 to the march of the German army through western Europe in May of 1940, the United States remained isolationist and hopeful that Nazi aggression would not threaten American national security.

RIBBENTROP, JOACHIM VON   Hitler's foreign minister who weakly argued that Nazi aggression against the Low Countries and France was a response to a threatened attack against Germany.

STIMSON, HENRY L.   In 1940, Roosevelt appointed this Republican as the secretary of war to give his cabinet a bipartisan direction as America prepared for global combat. This extremely intelligent head of the eastern establishment had served every president since William McKinley.

TULLY, GRACE   The White House secretary who, when Missy LeHand suffered a stroke, became a valued aide to Roosevelt. Nonetheless, in Goodwin's words, "she never enjoyed the intimacy, playfulness, and absolute trust Missy had."

WATSON, EDWIN "PA"   Roosevelt's secretary and military aide. He came to know the president's temperaments and did his best to channel FDR's busy schedule into productive directions.

WOODRING, HENRY   Roosevelt's first secretary of war. An isolationist from Kansas, he did not understand the need to strengthen the armed forces in response to increased aggression in Europe and Asia. Tension built when Louis Johnson, an internationalist, became assistant secretary of war.

On nights filled with tension and concern, Franklin Roosevelt performed a ritual that helped him to fall asleep. He would close his eyes and imagine himself at Hyde Park as a boy, standing with his sled in the snow atop the steep hill that stretched from the south porch of his home to the wooded bluffs of the Hudson River far below. As he accelerated down the hill, he maneuvered each familiar curve with perfect skill until he reached the bottom, whereupon, pulling his sled behind him, he started slowly back up until he reached the top, where he would once more begin his descent. Again and again he replayed this remembered scene in his mind, obliterating his awareness of the shrunken legs inert beneath the sheets, undoing the knowledge that he would never climb a hill or even walk on his own power again. Thus liberating himself from his paralysis through an act of imaginative will, the president of the United States would fall asleep.

Reprinted with the permission of Simon & Schuster Adult Publishing Group and Sll/Sterling Lord Litenstic, Inc., from *No Ordinary Time: Franklin and Eleanor Roosevelt: The Home Front in World War II* by Doris Kearns Goodwin. Copyright © 1994 by Doris Kearns Goodwin. All rights reserved.

The evening of May 9, 1940, was one of these nights. At 11 p.m., as Roosevelt sat in his comfortable study on the second floor of the White House, the long-apprehended phone call had come. Resting against the high back of his favorite red leather chair, a precise reproduction of one Thomas Jefferson had designed for work, the president listened as his ambassador to Belgium, John Cudahy, told him that Hitler's armies were simultaneously attacking Holland, Luxembourg, Belgium, and France. The period of relative calm—the "phony war" that had settled over Europe since the German attack on Poland in September of 1939—was over.

For days, rumors of a planned Nazi invasion had spread through the capitals of Western Europe. Now, listening to Ambassador Cudahy's frantic report that German planes were in the air over the Low Countries and France, Roosevelt knew that the all-out war he feared had finally begun. In a single night, the tacit agreement that, for eight months, had kept the belligerents from attacking each other's territory had been shattered.

As he summoned his military aide and appointments secretary, General Edwin "Pa" Watson, on this spring evening of the last year of his second term, Franklin

Roosevelt looked younger than his fifty-eight years. Though his hair was threaded with gray, the skin on his handsome face was clear, and the blue eyes, beneath his pince-nez glasses, were those of a man at the peak of his vitality. His chest was so broad, his neck so thick, that when seated he appeared larger than he was. Only when he was moved from his chair would the eye be drawn to the withered legs, paralyzed by polio almost two decades earlier.

At 12:40 a.m., the president's press secretary, Stephen Early, arrived to monitor incoming messages. Bombs had begun to fall on Brussels, Amsterdam, and Rotterdam, killing hundreds of civilians and destroying thousands of homes. In dozens of old European neighborhoods, fires illuminated the night sky. Stunned Belgians stood in their nightclothes in the streets of Brussels, watching bursts of anti-aircraft fire as military cars and motorcycles dashed through the streets. A thirteen-year-old schoolboy, Guy de Liederkirche, was Brussels' first child to die. His body would later be carried to his school for a memorial service with his classmates. On every radio station throughout Belgium, broadcasts summoned all soldiers to join their units at once.

In Amsterdam the roads leading out of the city were crowded with people and automobiles as residents fled in fear of the bombing. Bombs were also falling at Dunkirk, Calais, and Metz in France, and at Chilham, near Canterbury, in England. The initial reports were confusing—border clashes had begun, parachute troops were being dropped to seize Dutch and Belgian airports, the government of Luxembourg had already fled to France, and there was some reason to believe the Germans were also landing troops by sea.

After speaking again to Ambassador Cudahy and scanning the incoming news reports, Roosevelt called his secretary of the Treasury, Henry Morgenthau, Jr., and ordered him to freeze all assets held by Belgium, the Netherlands, and Luxembourg before the market opened in the morning, to keep any resources of the invaded countries from falling into German hands.

The official German explanation for the sweeping invasion of the neutral lowlands was given by Germany's foreign minister, Joachim von Ribbentrop.

Germany, he claimed, had received "proof" that the Allies were engineering an imminent attack through the Low Countries into the German Ruhr district. In a belligerent tone, von Ribbentrop said the time had come for settling the final account with the French and British leaders. Just before midnight, Adolf Hitler, having boarded a special train to the front, had issued the fateful order to his troops: "The decisive hour has come for the fight today decides the fate of the German nation for the next 1000 years."

There was little that could be done that night—phone calls to Paris and Brussels could rarely be completed, and the Hague wire was barely working—but, as one State Department official said, "in times of crisis the key men should be at hand and the public should know it." Finally, at 2:40 a.m., Roosevelt decided to go to bed. After shifting his body to his armless wheelchair, he rolled through a door near his desk into his bedroom.

As usual when the president's day came to an end, he called for his valet, Irvin McDuffie, to lift him into his bed. McDuffie, a Southern Negro, born the same year as his boss, had been a barber by trade when Roosevelt met him in Warm Springs, Georgia, in 1927. Roosevelt quickly developed a liking for the talkative man and offered him the job of valet. Now he and his wife lived in a room on the third floor of the White House. In recent months, McDuffie's hard drinking had become a problem: on several occasions Eleanor had found him so drunk that "he couldn't help Franklin to bed." Fearing that her husband might be abandoned at a bad time, Eleanor urged him to fire McDuffie, but the president was unable to bring himself to let his old friend go, even though he shared Eleanor's fear.

McDuffie was at his post in the early hours of May 10 when the president called for help. He lifted the president from his wheelchair onto the narrow bed, reminiscent of the kind used in a boy's boarding school, straightened his legs to their full length, and then undressed him and put on his pajamas. Beside the bed was a white-painted table; on its top, a jumble of pencils, notepaper, a glass of water, a package of cigarettes, a couple of phones, a bottle of nose drops. On the floor beside the table stood a small basket—the Eleanor basket—in which the first lady regularly left memoranda, communications, and reports for the president to read—a sort of private post office between husband and wife. In the corner sat an old-fashioned rocking chair, and next to it a heavy wardrobe filled with the president's clothes. On the marble mantelpiece above the fireplace was an assortment of family photos and a collection of miniature pigs. "Like every room in any Roosevelt house," historian Arthur Schlesinger has written, "the presidential bedroom was hopelessly Victorian—old-fashioned and indiscriminate in its furnishings, cluttered in its decor, ugly and comfortable."

Outside Roosevelt's door, which he refused to lock at night as previous presidents had done, Secret Service men patrolled the corridor, alerting the guardroom to the slightest hint of movement. The refusal to lock his door was related to the president's dread of fire, which surpassed his fear of assassination or of anything else. The fear seems to have been rooted in his childhood, when, as a small boy, he had seen his young aunt, Laura, race down the stairs, screaming, her body and clothes aflame from an accident with an alcohol lamp. Her life was ended at nineteen. The fear grew when he became a paraplegic, to the point where, for hours at a time, he would practice dropping from his bed or chair to the floor and then crawling to the door so that he could escape from a fire on his own. "We assured him he would never be alone," his eldest son, Jimmy, recalled, "but he could not be sure, and furthermore found the idea depressing that he could not be left alone, as if he were an infant."

Roosevelt's nightly rituals tell us something about his deepest feelings—the desire for freedom, the quest for movement, and the significance, despite all his attempts to downplay it, of the paralysis in his life. In 1940, Roosevelt had been president of the United States for seven years, but he had been paralyzed from the waist down for nearly three times that long. Before he was stricken at thirty-nine, Roosevelt was a man who flourished on activity. He had served in the New York legislature for two years, been assistant secretary of the navy for seven years, and his party's candidate for vice-president in 1920. He loved to swim and to sail, to play tennis and golf; to run in the woods and ride horseback in the fields. To his daughter, Anna, he was always "very active physically," "a wonderful playmate who took long walks with you, sailed with you, could out-jump you and do a lot of things," while Jimmy saw him quite simply as "the handsomest, strongest, most glamorous, vigorous physical father in the world."

All that vigor and athleticism ended in August 1921 at Campobello, his family's summer home in New Brunswick, Canada, when he returned home from swimming in the pond with his children and felt too tired even to remove his wet bathing suit. The morning after his swim, his temperature was 102 degrees and he had trouble moving his left leg. By afternoon, the power to move his right leg was also gone, and soon he was paralyzed from the waist down. The paralysis had set in so swiftly that no one understood at first that it was polio. But once the diagnosis was made, the battle was joined. For years he fought to walk on his own power, practicing for hours at a time, drenched with sweat, as he tried unsuccessfully to move one leg in front of the other without the aid of a pair of crutches or a helping hand. That consuming and futile effort had to be abandoned once he became governor of New York in 1929 and then president in 1933. He was permanently crippled.

Yet the paralysis that crippled his body expanded his mind and his sensibilities. After what Eleanor called his "trial by fire," he seemed less arrogant, less smug, less superficial, more focused, more complex, more interesting. He returned from his ordeal with greater powers of concentration and greater self-knowledge. "There had been a plowing up of his nature," Labor Secretary Frances Perkins observed. "The man emerged completely warmhearted, with new humility of spirit and a firmer understanding of profound philosophical concepts."

He had always taken great pleasure in people. But now they became what one historian has called "his vital links with life." Far more intensely than before, he reached out to know them, to understand them, to pick up their emotions, to put himself into their shoes. No longer belonging to his old world in the same way, he came to empathize with the poor and underprivileged, with people to whom fate had dealt a difficult hand. Once, after a lecture in Akron, Ohio, Eleanor was asked how her husband's illness had affected him. "Anyone who has gone through great suffering," she said, "is bound to have a greater sympathy and understanding of the problems of mankind."

Through his presidency, the mere act of standing up with his heavy metal leg-braces locked into place was an ordeal. The journalist Eliot Janeway remembers being behind Roosevelt once when he was in his chair in the Oval Office. "He was smiling as he talked. His face and hand muscles were totally relaxed. But then, when he had to stand up, his jaws went absolutely rigid. The effort of getting what was left of his body up was so great his face changed dramatically. It was as if he braced his body for a bullet."

Little wonder, then, that, in falling asleep at night, Roosevelt took comfort in the thought of physical freedom.

The morning sun of Washington's belated spring was streaming through the president's windows on May 10, 1940. Despite the tumult of the night before, which had kept him up until nearly 3 a.m., he awoke at his usual hour of eight o'clock. Pivoting to the edge of the bed, he pressed the button for his valet, who helped him into the bathroom. Then, as he had done every morning for the past seven years, he threw his old blue cape over his pajamas and started his day with breakfast in bed—orange juice, eggs, coffee, and buttered toast—and the morning papers: *The New York Times* and the *Herald Tribune,* the *Baltimore Sun,* the *Washington Post* and the *Washington Herald.*

Headlines recounted the grim events he had heard at 11 p.m. the evening before. From Paris, Ambassador William Bullitt confirmed that the Germans had launched violent attacks on a half-dozen French military bases. Bombs had also fallen on the main railway connections between Paris and the border in an attempt to stop troop movements.

Before finishing the morning papers, the president held a meeting with Steve Early and "Pa" Watson, to review his crowded schedule. He instructed them to convene an emergency meeting at ten-thirty with the chiefs of the army and the navy, the secretaries of state and Treasury, and the attorney general. In addition, Roosevelt was scheduled to meet the press in the morning and the Cabinet in the afternoon, as he had done every Friday morning and afternoon for seven years. Later that night, he was supposed to deliver a keynote address at the Pan American Scientific Congress. After asking Early to delay the press conference an hour and to have the State Department draft a new speech, Roosevelt called his valet to help him dress.

While Franklin Roosevelt was being dressed in his bedroom, Eleanor was in New York, having spent the past few days in the apartment she kept in Greenwich Village, in a small house owned by her friends Esther Lape and Elizabeth Read. The Village apartment on East 11th Street, five blocks north of Washington Square, provided Eleanor with a welcome escape from the demands of the White House, a secret refuge whenever her crowded calendar brought her to New York. For decades, the Village, with its winding streets, modest brick houses, bookshops, tearooms, little theaters, and cheap rents, had been home to political, artistic, and literary rebels, giving it a colorful Old World character. . . .

The week before, at the Astor Hotel, Eleanor had been honored by *The Nation* magazine for her work in behalf of civil rights and poverty. More than a thousand people had filled the tables and the balcony of the cavernous ballroom to watch her receive a bronze plaque for "distinguished service in the cause of American social progress." Among the many speakers that night, Stuart Chase lauded the first lady's concentrated focus on the problems at home. "I suppose she worries about Europe like the rest of us," he began, "but she does not allow this worry to divert her attention from the homefront. She goes around America, looking at America, thinking about America . . . helping day and night with the problems

Crippled by polio in 1921, Roosevelt had to wear heavy metal braces on his legs and could not walk on his own. But in public, as this photograph shows, the president gave the impression that he was walking. He did this by using a cane with his right hand, clasping the arm of a supporter with his left arm, and then shifting his weight back and forth as he moved. In the White House, away from the public, he got about in a wheelchair.
(UPI/Franklin D. Roosevelt Library)

of America." For, he concluded, "the New Deal is supposed to be fighting a war, too, a war against depression."

"What is an institution?" author John Gunther had asked when his turn to speak came. "An institution," he asserted, is "something that had fixity, permanence, and importance . . . something that people like to depend on, something benevolent as a rule, something we like." And by that definition, he concluded, the woman being honored that night was as great an institution as her husband, who was already being talked about for an unprecedented third term. Echoing Gunther's sentiments, NAACP head Walter

White turned to Mrs. Roosevelt and said: "My dear, I don't care if the President runs for the third or fourth term as long as he lets you run the bases, keep the score and win the game."

For her part, Eleanor was slightly embarrassed by all the fuss. "It never seems quite real to me to sit at a table and have people whom I have always looked upon with respect . . . explain why they are granting me an honor," she wrote in her column describing the evening. "Somehow I always feel they ought to be talking about someone else." Yet, as she stood to speak that night at the Astor ballroom, rising nearly six feet, her wavy brown hair slightly touched by gray, her wide mouth marred by large buck teeth, her brilliant blue eyes offset by an unfortunate chin, she dominated the room as no one before her had done. . . .

It was this tireless commitment to democracy's unfinished agenda that led Americans in a Gallup poll taken that spring to rate Mrs. Roosevelt even higher than her husband, with 67 percent of those interviewed well disposed toward her activities. "Mrs. Roosevelt's incessant goings and comings," the survey suggested, "have been accepted as a rather welcome part of the national life. Women especially feel this way. But even men betray relatively small masculine impatience with the work and opinions of a very articulate lady. . . . The rich, who generally disapprove of Mrs. Roosevelt's husband, seem just as friendly toward her as the poor. . . . Even among those extremely anti-Roosevelt citizens who would regard a third term as a national disaster there is a generous minority . . . who want Mrs. Roosevelt to remain in the public eye."

The path to this position of independent power and respect had not been easy. Eleanor's distinguished career had been forged from a painful discovery when she was thirty-four. After a period of suspicion, she realized that her husband, who was then assistant secretary of the navy, had fallen in love with another woman, Lucy Page Mercer.

Tall, beautiful, and well bred, with a low throaty voice and an incomparably winning smile, Lucy Mercer was working as Eleanor's social secretary when the love affair began. For months, perhaps even years,

Franklin kept his romance a secret from Eleanor. Her shattering discovery took place in September 1918. Franklin had just returned from a visit to the European front. Unpacking his suitcase, she discovered a packet of love letters from Lucy. At this moment, Eleanor later admitted, "the bottom dropped out of my own particular world & I faced myself, my surroundings, my world, honestly for the first time."

Eleanor told her husband that she would grant him a divorce. But this was not what he wanted, or at least not what he was able to put himself through, particularly when his mother, Sara, was said to have threatened him with disinheritance if he left his marriage. If her son insisted on leaving his wife and five children for another woman, visiting scandal upon the Roosevelt name, she could not stop him. But he should know that she would not give him another dollar and he could no longer expect to inherit the family estate at Hyde Park. Franklin's trusted political adviser, Louis Howe, weighed in as well, warning Franklin that divorce would bring his political career to an abrupt end. There was also the problem of Lucy's Catholicism, which would prevent her from marrying a divorced man.

Franklin promised never to see Lucy again and agreed, so the Roosevelt children suggest, to Eleanor's demand for separate bedrooms, bringing their marital relations to an end. Eleanor would later admit to her daughter, Anna, that sex was "an ordeal to be borne." Something in her childhood had locked her up, she said, making her fear the loss of control that comes with abandoning oneself to one's passions, giving her "an exaggerated idea of the necessity of keeping all one's desires under complete subjugation." Now, supposedly, she was free of her "ordeal."

The marriage resumed. But for Eleanor, a path had opened, a possibility of standing apart from Franklin. No longer did she need to define herself solely in terms of his wants and his needs. Before the crisis, though marriage had never fulfilled her prodigious energies, she had no way of breaking through the habits and expectations of a proper young woman's role. To explore her independent needs, to journey outside her home for happiness, was perceived as dangerous and wrong.

With the discovery of the affair, however, she was free to define a new and different partnership with her husband, free to seek new avenues of fulfillment. It was a gradual process, a gradual casting away, a gradual gaining of confidence—and it was by no means complete—but the fifty-six-year-old woman who was being fêted in New York was a different person from the shy, betrayed wife of 1918.

Above the president's bedroom, in a snug third-floor suite, his personal secretary, Marguerite "Missy" LeHand, was already dressed, though she, too, had stayed up late the night before.

A tall, handsome woman of forty-one with large blue eyes and prematurely gray, once luxuriant black hair fastened by hairpins to the nape of her neck, Missy was in love with her boss and regarded herself as his other wife. Nor was she alone in her imaginings. "There's no doubt," White House aide Raymond Moley said, "that Missy was as close to being a wife as he ever had—or could have." White House maid Lillian Parks agreed. "When Missy gave an order, we responded as if it had come from the First Lady. We knew that FDR would always back up Missy." . . .

When Franklin contracted polio, Missy's duties expanded. Both Franklin and Eleanor understood that it was critical for Franklin to keep active in politics even as he struggled unsuccessfully day after day, month after month, to walk again. To that end, Eleanor adhered to a rigorous daily schedule as the stand-in for her husband, journeying from one political meeting to the next to ensure that the Roosevelt name was not forgotten. With Eleanor busily occupied away from home, Missy did all the chores a housewife might do, writing Franklin's personal checks, paying the monthly bills, giving the children their allowances, supervising the menus, sending the rugs and draperies for cleaning. . . .

By the time Roosevelt was president, she had become totally absorbed in his life—learning his favorite games, sharing his hobbies, reading the same books, even adopting his characteristic accent and patterns of speech. Whereas Eleanor was so opposed to gambling that she refused to play poker with Franklin's friends if even the smallest amount of money changed hands, Missy became an avid player, challenging Roosevelt at every turn, always ready to raise the ante. Whereas Eleanor never evinced any interest in her husband's treasured stamp collection, Missy was an enthusiastic partner, spending hours by his side as he organized and reorganized his stamps into one or another of his thick leather books. "In terms of companionship," Eliot Janeway observed, "Missy was the real wife. She understood his nature perfectly, as they would say in a nineteenth-century novel."

At 10:30 a.m., May 10, 1940, pushed along in his wheelchair by Mr. Crim, the usher on duty, and accompanied by his usual detail of Secret Service men, the president headed for the Oval Office. A bell announced his arrival to the small crowd already assembled in the Cabinet Room—Army Chief of Staff George Marshall, Navy Chief Admiral Harold Stark, Attorney General Robert Jackson, Secretary of Treasury Henry Morgenthau, Secretary of State Cordell Hull, and Undersecretary Sumner Welles. But first, as he did every day, the president poked his head into Missy's office, giving her a wave and a smile which, Missy told a friend, was all she needed to replenish the energies lost from too little sleep.

Of all the men assembled in the big white-walled Cabinet Room that morning, General George Catlett Marshall possessed the clearest awareness of how woefully unprepared America was to fight a major war against Nazi Germany. The fifty-nine-year-old Marshall, chief of operations of the First Army in World War I, had been elevated to the position of army chief of staff the previous year. The story is told of a meeting in the president's office not long before the appointment during which the president outlined a pet proposal. Everyone nodded in approval except Marshall. "Don't you think so, George?" the president asked. Marshall replied: "I am sorry, Mr. President, but I don't agree with that at all." The president looked stunned, the conference was stopped, and Marshall's friends predicted that his tour of duty would soon come to an end. A few months later, reaching thirty-four names down the list of senior generals, the president asked the straight-speaking Marshall to be chief of staff of the U.S. Army. . . .

In 1940, the U.S. Army stood only eighteenth in the world, trailing not only Germany, France, Britain, Russia, Italy, Japan, and China but also Belgium, the Netherlands, Portugal, Spain, Sweden, and Switzerland. With the fall of Holland, the United States would rise to seventeenth! And, in contrast to Germany, where after years of compulsory military training nearly 10 percent of the population (6.8 million) were trained and ready for war, less than .5 percent of the American population (504,000) were on active duty or in the trained reserves. The offensive Germany had launched the morning of May 10 along the Western front was supported by 136 divisions; the United States could, if necessary, muster merely five fully equipped divisions.

In the spring of 1940, the United States possessed almost no munitions industry at all. So strong had been the recoil from war after 1918 that both the government and the private sector had backed away from making weapons. The result was that, while the United States led the world in the mass production of automobiles, washing machines, and other household appliances, the techniques of producing weapons of war had badly atrophied.

All through the winter and spring, Marshall had been trying to get Secretary of War Henry Woodring to understand the dire nature of this unpreparedness. But the former governor of Kansas was an isolationist who refused to contemplate even the possibility of American involvement in the European war. Woodring had been named assistant secretary of war in 1933 and then promoted to the top job three years later, when the price of corn and the high unemployment rate worried Washington far more than foreign affairs. As the European situation heated up, Roosevelt recognized that Woodring was the wrong man to head the War Department. But, try as he might, he could not bring himself to fire his secretary of war—or anyone else, for that matter.

Roosevelt's inability to get rid of anybody, even the hopelessly incompetent, was a chief source of the disorderliness of his administration, of his double-dealing and his tendency to procrastinate. "His real weakness," Eleanor Roosevelt observed, "was that—it came out of the strength really, or out of a quality—he had great sympathy for people and great understanding, and he couldn't bear to be disagreeable to someone he liked . . . and he just couldn't bring himself to really do the unkind thing that had to be done unless he got angry." . . .

The confusion multiplied when Roosevelt selected a staunch interventionist, Louis Johnson, the former national commander of the American Legion, as assistant secretary of war. Outspoken, bold, and ambitious, Johnson fought openly with Woodring, bringing relations to the sorry point where neither man spoke to the other. Paralyzed and frustrated, General Marshall found it incomprehensible that Roosevelt had allowed such a mess to develop simply because he disliked firing anyone. Years earlier, when Marshall had been told by his aide that a friend whom he had ordered overseas had said he could not leave because his wife was away and his furniture was not packed, Marshall had called the man himself. The friend explained that he was sorry. "I'm sorry, too," Marshall replied, "but you will be retired tomorrow."

Marshall failed to understand that there was a method behind the president's disorderly style. Though divided authority and built-in competition created insecurity and confusion within the administration, it gave Roosevelt the benefit of conflicting opinions. "I think he knew exactly what he was doing all the time," administrative assistant James Rowe observed. "He liked conflict, and he was a believer in resolving problems through conflict." With different administrators telling him different things, he got a better feel for what his problems were.

Their attitude toward subordinates was not the only point of dissimilarity between Roosevelt and Marshall. Roosevelt loved to laugh and play, closing the space between people by familiarity, calling everyone, even Winston Churchill, by his first name. In contrast, Marshall was rarely seen to smile or laugh on the job and was never familiar with anyone. . . .

As the officials sat in the Cabinet Room, at the great mahogany table under the stern, pinch-lipped stare of Woodrow Wilson, whose portrait hung above the fireplace, their primary reason for gathering together was to share the incoming information from Europe and to plan the American response. Ambassador John Cudahy in Brussels wired that he had almost been knocked down by the force of a bomb which fell three hundred feet from the embassy. From London, Ambassador Joseph P. Kennedy reported that the British had called off their Whitsun holiday, the long weekend on which Londoners traditionally acquired the tan that had to last until their August vacation—"tangible evidence," Kennedy concluded, "that the situation is serious."

Plans were set in motion for the army and navy to submit new estimates to the White House of what they would need to accomplish the seemingly insurmountable task of catching up with Germany's modern war machine. For, as Marshall had recently explained to the Congress, Germany was in a unique position. "After the World War practically everything was taken away from Germany in the way of materiel. So when Germany rearmed, it was necessary to produce a complete set of materiel for all the troops. As a result, Germany has an Army equipped throughout with the most modern weapons that could be turned out and that is a situation that has never occurred before in the history of the world." . . .

Seated at his desk with his back to the windows, Roosevelt faced the crowd that was now spilling into the Oval Office for his largest press conference ever. Behind him, set in standards, were the blue presidential flag and the American flag. "Like an opera singer about to go on the stage," Roosevelt invariably appeared nervous before a conference began, fidgeting with his cigarette holder, fingering the trinkets on his desk, exchanging self-conscious jokes with the reporters in the front row. Once the action started, however, with the doorkeeper's shout of "all-in," the president seemed to relax, conducting the flow of questions and conversation with such professional skill that the columnist Heywood Broun once called him "the best newspaperman who has ever been President of the United States."

For seven years, twice a week, the president had sat down with these reporters, explaining legislation, announcing appointments, establishing friendly contact, calling them by their first names, teasing them about their hangovers, exuding warmth and accessibility. Once, when a correspondent narrowly missed getting on Roosevelt's train, the president covered for him by writing his copy until he could catch up. Another time, when the mother of a bachelor correspondent died, Eleanor Roosevelt attended the funeral services, and then she and the president invited him for their Sunday family supper of scrambled eggs. These acts of friendship—repeated many times over—helped to explain the paradox that, though 80 to 85 percent of the newspaper publishers regularly opposed Roosevelt, the president maintained excellent relations with the working reporters, and his coverage was generally full and fair. "By the brilliant but simple trick of making news and *being* news," historian Arthur Schlesinger observed, "Roosevelt outwitted the open hostility of the publishers and converted the press into one of the most effective channels of his public leadership."

"History will like to say the scene [on May 10] was tense," Mark Sullivan wrote. "It was not. . . . On the President's part there was consciousness of high events, yet also complete coolness. . . . The whole atmosphere was one of serious matter-of-factness."

"Good morning," the president said, and then paused as still more reporters filed in. "I hope you had more sleep than I did," he joked, drawing them into the shared experience of the crisis. "I guess most of you were pretty busy all night." . . .

Asked if he would say what he thought the chances were that the United States could stay out of the war, the president replied as he had been replying for months to similar questions. "I think that would be speculative. In other words, don't for heaven's sake, say that means we may get in. That would be again writing yourself off on the limb and sawing it off." Asked if his speech that night would touch on the international situation, Roosevelt evoked a round of laughter by responding: "I do not know because I have not written it."

On and on he went, his tone in the course of fifteen minutes shifting from weariness to feistiness to

playfulness. Yet, in the end, preserving his options in this delicate moment, he *said* almost nothing, skillfully deflecting every question about America's future actions. Asked at one point to compare Japanese aggression with German aggression, he said he counted seven ifs in the question, which meant he could not provide an answer. Still, by the time the senior wire-service man brought the conference to an early close, "partly in consideration of the tired newspaper men and partly in consideration of the President," the reporters went away with the stories they needed for the next day's news. . . .

[While Franklin was in his press conference, Eleanor was in the country.] Franklin called Eleanor his "will o' the wisp" wife. But it was Franklin who had encouraged her to become his "eyes and ears," to gather the grass-roots knowledge he needed to understand the people he governed. Unable to travel easily on his own because of his paralysis, he had started by teaching Eleanor how to inspect state institutions in 1929, during his first term as governor.

"It was the best education I ever had," she later said. Traveling across the state to inspect institutions for the insane, the blind, and the aged, visiting state prisons and reform schools, she had learned, slowly and painfully, through Franklin's tough, detailed questions upon her return, how to become an investigative reporter.

Her first inspection was an insane asylum. "All right," Franklin told her, "go in and look around and let me know what's going on there. Tell me how the inmates are being treated." When Eleanor returned, she brought with her a printed copy of the day's menu. "Did you look to see whether they were actually getting this food?" Franklin asked. "Did you lift a pot cover on the stove to check whether the contents corresponded with this menu?" Eleanor shook her head. Her untrained mind had taken in a general picture of the place but missed all the human details that would have brought it to life. "But these are what I need," Franklin said. "I never remembered things until Franklin taught me," Eleanor told a reporter. "His memory is really prodigious. Once he has checked something he never needs to look at it again."

"One time," she recalled, "he asked me to go and look at the state's tree shelter-belt plantings. I noticed there were five rows of graduated size. . . . When I came back and described it, Franklin said: 'Tell me exactly what was in the first five rows. What did they plant first?' And he was so desperately disappointed when I couldn't tell him, that I put my best efforts after that into missing nothing and remembering everything."

In time, Eleanor became so thorough in her inspections, observing the attitudes of patients toward the staff, judging facial expressions as well as the words, looking in closets and behind doors, that Franklin set great value on her reports. "She saw many things the President could never see," Labor Secretary Frances Perkins said. "Much of what she learned and what she understood about the life of the people of this country rubbed off onto FDR. It could not have helped to do so because she had a poignant understanding. . . . Her mere reporting of the facts was full of a sensitive quality that could never be escaped. . . . Much of his seemingly intuitive understanding—about labor situations . . . about girls who worked in sweatshops—came from his recollections of what she had told him."

During Eleanor's first summer as first lady, Franklin had asked her to investigate the economic situation in Appalachia. The Quakers had reported terrible conditions of poverty there, and the president wanted to check these reports. "Watch the people's faces," he told her. "Look at the conditions of the clothes on the wash lines. You can tell a lot from that." Going even further, Eleanor descended the mine shafts, dressed in a miner's outfit, to absorb for herself the physical conditions in which the miners worked. It was this journey that later provoked the celebrated cartoon showing two miners in a shaft looking up: "Here Comes Mrs. Roosevelt!"

At Scott's Run, near Morgantown, West Virginia, Eleanor had seen children who "did not know what it was to sit down at a table and eat a proper meal." In one shack, she found a boy clutching his pet rabbit,

which his sister had just told him was all there was left to eat. So moved was the president by his wife's report that he acted at once to create an Appalachian resettlement project.

The following year, Franklin had sent Eleanor to Puerto Rico to investigate reports that a great portion of the fancy embroidered linens that were coming into the United States from Puerto Rico were being made under terrible conditions. To the fury of the rich American colony in San Juan, Eleanor took reporters and photographers through muddy alleys and swamps to hundreds of foul-smelling hovels with no plumbing and no electricity, where women sat in the midst of filth embroidering cloth for minimal wages. Publicizing these findings, Eleanor called for American women to stop purchasing Puerto Rico's embroidered goods.

Later, Eleanor journeyed to the deep South and the "Dustbowl." Before long, her inspection trips had become as important to her as to her husband. "I realized," she said in a radio interview, "that if I remained in the White House all the time I would lose touch with the rest of the world. . . . I might have had a less crowded life, but I would begin to think that my life in Washington was representative of the rest of the country and that is a dangerous point of view." So much did Eleanor travel, in fact, that the *Washington Star* once printed a humorous headline: "Mrs. Roosevelt Spends Night at White House." . . .

When [Franklin] met with his Cabinet at two that afternoon, his concerns as he looked at the familiar faces around the table were . . . how to get a new and expanded military budget through the Congress, how to provide aid to the Allies as quickly as possible, how to stock up on strategic materials; in other words, how to start the complex process of mobilizing for war. . . .

Labor Secretary Frances Perkins, the only woman in the Cabinet, tended to talk a great deal at these meetings, "as though she had swallowed a press release." But on this occasion she remained silent as the conversation was carried by Harry Hopkins, the secretary of commerce, who was present at his first Cabinet meeting in months.

For the past year and a half, Hopkins had been in and out of hospitals while doctors tried to fix his body's lethal inability to absorb proteins and fats. His health had begun to deteriorate in the summer of 1939, when, at the height of his power as director of the Works Progress Administration, he was told that he had stomach cancer. A ghastly operation followed which removed the cancer along with three-quarters of his stomach, leaving him with a severe form of malnutrition. Told in the fall of 1939 that Hopkins had only four weeks to live, Roosevelt took control of the case himself and flew in a team of experts, whose experiments with plasma transfusions arrested the fatal decline. Then, to give Hopkins breathing space from the turbulence of the WPA, Roosevelt appointed him secretary of commerce. Even that job had proved too much, however: Hopkins had been able to work only one or two days in the past ten months.

Yet, on this critical day, the fifty-year-old Hopkins was sitting in the Cabinet meeting in the midst of the unfolding crisis. "He was to all intents and purposes," Hopkins' biographer Robert Sherwood wrote, "a finished man who might drag out his life for a few years of relative inactivity or who might collapse and die at any time." His face was sallow and heavy-lined; journalist George Creel once likened his weary, melancholy look to that of "an ill-fed horse at the end of a hard day," while Churchill's former daughter-in-law, Pamela Churchill Harriman, compared him to "a very sad dog." Given his appearance—smoking one cigarette after another, his brown hair thinning, his shoulders sagging, his frayed suit baggy at the knees—"you wouldn't think," a contemporary reporter wrote, "he could possibly be important to a President."

But when he spoke, as he did at length this day on the subject of the raw materials needed for war, his sickly face vanished and a very different face appeared, intelligent, good-humored, animated. His eyes, which seconds before had seemed beady and suspicious, now gleamed with light. Sensing the urgency of the situation, Hopkins spoke so rapidly that he did not finish half of his words, as though, after being long held back, he wanted to make up for lost time. It was as if the crisis had given him a renewed reason for living; it seemed, in reporter Marquis Childs' judgment at the time, "to galvanize him into life." From then on, Childs observed, "while he would still be an ailing man, he was to ignore his health." The curative impact of Hopkins' increasingly crucial role in the war effort was to postpone the sentence of death the doctors had given him for five more years.

Even Hopkins' old nemesis, Harold Ickes, felt compelled to pay attention when Hopkins reported that the United States had "only a five or six months supply of both rubber and tin, both of which are absolutely essential for purposes of defense." The shortage of rubber was particularly worrisome, since rubber was indispensable to modern warfare if armies were to march, ships sail, and planes fly. Hitler's armies were rolling along on rubber-tired trucks and rubber-tracked tanks; they were flying in rubber-lined high-altitude suits in planes equipped with rubber de-icers, rubber tires, and rubber life-preserver rafts. From stethoscopes and blood-plasma tubing to gas masks and adhesive tape, the demand for rubber was endless. And with Holland under attack and 90 percent of America's supply of rubber coming from the Dutch East Indies, something had to be done.

Becoming more and more spirited as he went on, Hopkins outlined a plan of action, starting with the creation of a new corporation, to be financed by the Reconstruction Finance Corporation, whose purpose would be to go into the market and buy at least a year's supply of rubber and tin. This step would be only the first, followed by the building of synthetic-rubber plants and an effort to bring into production new sources of natural rubber in South America. Hopkins' plan of action met with hearty approval.

While Hopkins was speaking, word came from London that Neville Chamberlain had resigned his post as prime minister. This dramatic event had its source in the tumultuous debate in the Parliament over the shameful retreat of the British Expeditionary Force from Norway three weeks earlier. . . .

The seventy-one-year-old prime minister had little choice but to step down. Then, when the king's first choice, Lord Halifax, refused to consider the post on the grounds that his position as a peer would make it difficult to discharge his duties, the door was opened for Winston Churchill, the complex Edwardian man with his fat cigars, his gold-knobbed cane, and his vital understanding of what risks should be taken and what kind of adversary the Allies were up against. For nearly four decades, Churchill had been a major figure in public life. The son of a lord, he had been elected to Parliament in 1900 and had served in an astonishing array of Cabinet posts, including undersecretary for the colonies, privy councillor, home secretary, first lord of the admiralty, minister of munitions, and chancellor of the Exchequer. He had survived financial embarrassment, prolonged fits of depression, and political defeat to become the most eloquent spokesman against Nazi Germany. From the time Hitler first came to power, he had repeatedly warned against British efforts to appease him, but no one had listened. Now, finally, his voice would be heard. "Looking backward," a British writer observed, "it almost seems as though the transition from peace to war began on that day when Churchill became Prime Minister."

Responding warmly to the news of Churchill's appointment, Roosevelt told his Cabinet he believed "Churchill was the best man that England had." From a distance, the two leaders had come to admire each other: for years, Churchill had applauded Roosevelt's "valiant efforts" to end the depression, while Roosevelt had listened with increasing respect to Churchill's lonely warnings against the menace of Adolf Hitler. In September 1939, soon after the outbreak of the war, when Churchill was brought into the government as head of the admiralty, Roosevelt had initiated the first in what would become an extraordinary series of wartime letters between the two men. Writing in a friendly but respectful tone, Roosevelt had told Churchill: "I shall at all times welcome it if you will keep me in touch personally with everything you want me to know about. You can always send sealed letters through your pouch or my pouch." Though relatively few messages had been exchanged in the first nine months of the war, the

seeds had been planted of an exuberant friendship, which would flourish in the years to come.

Once the Cabinet adjourned, Roosevelt had a short meeting with the minister of Belgium, who was left with only $35 since an order to freeze all credit held by Belgium, the Netherlands, and Luxembourg had gone into effect, earlier that morning. After arrangements were made to help him out, there began a working session on the speech Roosevelt was to deliver that night to a scientific meeting.

Then Roosevelt, not departing from his regular routine, went into his study for the cocktail hour, the most relaxed time of his day. The second-floor study, crowded with maritime pictures, models of ships, and stacks of paper, was the president's favorite room in the White House. It was here that he read, played poker, sorted his beloved stamps, and conducted most of the important business of his presidency. The tall mahogany bookcases were stuffed with books, and the leather sofas and chairs had acquired a rich glow. Any room Roosevelt spent time in, Frances Perkins observed, "invariably got that lived-in and overcrowded look which indicated the complexity and variety of his interests and intentions." Missy and Harry Hopkins were there, along with Pa Watson and Eleanor's houseguest, the beautiful actress Helen Gahagan Douglas. The cocktail hour, begun during Roosevelt's years in Albany, had become an institution in Roosevelt's official family, a time for reviewing events in an informal atmosphere, a time for swapping the day's best laughs. The president always mixed the drinks himself, experimenting with strange concoctions of gin and rum, vermouth and fruit juice.

During the cocktail hour, no more was said of politics or war; instead the conversation turned to subjects of lighter weight—to gossip, funny stories, and reminiscences. With Missy generally presiding as hostess, distributing the drinks to the guests, Roosevelt seemed to find complete relaxation in telling his favorite stories over and over again. Some of these stories Missy must have heard more than twenty or thirty times, but, like the "good wife," she never let her face betray boredom, only delight at the knowledge that her boss was having such a good time. And with his instinct for the dramatic and his fine ability to mimic, Roosevelt managed to tell each story a little differently each time, adding new details or insights.

On this evening, there was a delicious story to tell. In the Congress there was a Republican representative from Auburn, New York, John Taber, who tended to get into shouting fits whenever the subject of the hated New Deal came up. In a recent debate on the Wage and Hour amendments, he had bellowed so loudly that he nearly swallowed the microphone. On the floor at the time was Representative Leonard Schultz of Chicago, who had been deaf in his left ear since birth. As Mr. Taber's shriek was amplified through the loudspeakers, something happened to Mr. Schultz. Shaking convulsively, he staggered to the cloakroom, where he collapsed onto a couch, thinking he'd been hit in an air raid. He suddenly realized that he could hear with his left ear—for the first time in his life—and better than with his right. When doctors confirmed that Mr. Schultz's hearing was excellent, Mr. Taber claimed it was proof from God that the New Deal should be shouted down! . . .

While Franklin was mixing cocktails, Eleanor was on a train back to Washington from New York. For many of her fellow riders, the time on the train was a time to ease up, to gaze through the windows at the passing countryside, to close their eyes and unwind. But for Eleanor, who considered train rides her best working hours, there was little time to relax. The pile of mail, still unanswered, was huge, and there was a column to be written for the following day. Franklin's cousin Margaret "Daisy" Suckley recalls traveling with Eleanor once on the New York–to–Washington train. "She was working away the whole time with Malvina, and I was sitting there like a dumbbell looking out the window, and suddenly Mrs. Roosevelt said to Malvina, 'Now I'm going to sleep for fifteen minutes,' and she put her head back on the seat. I looked at my watch, and just as it hit fifteen minutes, she woke up and said, 'Now Tommy, let's go on.' It was amazing. I was stunned."

Even if Eleanor had reached the White House that evening in time for the cocktail hour, she would probably not have joined. Try as she might over the years, Eleanor had never felt comfortable at these relaxed gatherings. Part of her discomfort was toward alcohol itself, the legacy of an alcoholic father who continually failed to live up to the expectations and trust of his adoring daughter. One Christmas, Eleanor's daughter, Anna, and her good friend Lorena Hickok had chipped in to buy some cocktail glasses for Eleanor's Greenwich Village apartment in the hopes she would begin inviting friends in for drinks. "In a funny way," Anna wrote "Hick," as Miss Hickok was called, "I think she has always wanted to feel included in such parties, but so many old inhibitions have kept her from it."

But, despite Anna's best hopes, Eleanor's discomfort at the cocktail hour persisted, suggesting that beyond her fear of alcohol lay a deeper fear of letting herself go, of slackening off the work that had become so central to her sense of self. "Work had become for Eleanor almost as addictive as alcohol," her niece Eleanor Wotkyns once observed. "Even when she thought she was relaxing she was really working. Small talk horrified her. Even at New Year's, when everyone else relaxed with drinks, she would work until ten minutes of twelve, come in for a round of toasts, and then disappear to her room to work until two or three a.m. Always at the back of her mind were the letters she had to write, the things she had to do."

"She could be a crashing bore," Anna's son Curtis Dall Roosevelt admitted. "She was very judgmental even when she tried not to be. The human irregularities, the off-color jokes he loved, she couldn't take. He would tell his stories, many of them made to fit a point, and she would say, 'No, no, Franklin, that's not how it happened.'"

"If only Mother could have learned to ease up," her son Elliott observed, "things would have been so different with Father, for he needed relaxation more than anything in the world. But since she simply could not bring herself to unwind, he turned instead to Missy, building with her an exuberant, laughing relationship, full of jokes, silliness, and gossip."

"Stay for dinner. I'm lonely," Roosevelt urged Harry Hopkins when the cocktail hour came to an end. There were few others at this stage of his life that the president enjoyed as much as Hopkins. With the death in 1936 of Louis Howe, the shriveled ex-newspaperman who had fastened his star to Roosevelt in the early Albany days, helped him conquer his polio, and guided him through the political storms to the White House, the president had turned to Hopkins for companionship. "There was a temperamental sympathy between Roosevelt and Hopkins," Frances Perkins observed. Though widely different in birth and breeding, they both possessed unconquerable confidence, great courage, and good humor; they both enjoyed the society of the rich, the gay, and the well-born, while sharing an abiding concern for the average man. Hopkins had an almost "feminine sensitivity" to Roosevelt's moods, Sherwood observed. Like Missy, he seemed to know when the president wanted to consider affairs of state and when he wanted to escape from business; he had an uncanny instinct for knowing when to introduce a serious subject and when to tell a joke, when to talk and when to listen. He was, in short, a great dinner companion.

As soon as dinner was finished, Roosevelt had to return to work. In less than an hour, he was due to deliver a speech, and he knew that every word he said would be scrutinized for the light it might shed on the crisis at hand. Taking leave of Hopkins, Roosevelt noticed that his friend looked even more sallow and miserable now than he had looked earlier in the day. "Stay the night," the President insisted. So Hopkins borrowed a pair of pajamas and settled into a bedroom suite on the second floor. There he remained, not simply for one night but for the next three and a half years, as Roosevelt, exhibiting his genius for using people in new and unexpected ways, converted him from the number-one relief worker to the number-one adviser on the war. Later, Missy liked to tease: "It was Harry Hopkins who gave George S. Kaufman and Moss Hart the idea for that play of theirs, 'The Man Who Came to Dinner.'"

As the president was preparing to leave for Constitution Hall, he remembered something he had meant to ask Helen Gahagan Douglas during the cocktail hour. There was no time to discuss it now, but, stopping by her room, he told her he had an important question for her and asked if she would meet him in his study when he returned. "Certainly," she replied, and he left to address several thousand scientists and scholars at the Pan American Scientific Congress.

"We come here tonight with heavy hearts," he began, looking out at the packed auditorium. "This very day, the tenth of May, three more independent nations have been cruelly invaded by force of arms. . . . I am glad that we are shocked and angered by the tragic news." Declaring that it was no accident that this scientific meeting was taking place in the New World, since elsewhere war and politics had compelled teachers and scholars to leave their callings and become the agents of destruction, Roosevelt warned against an undue sense of security based on the false teachings of geography: in terms of the moving of men and guns and planes and bombs, he argued, every acre of American territory was closer to Europe than was ever the case before. "In modern times it is a shorter distance from Europe to San Francisco, California than it was for the ships and legions of Julius Caesar to move from Rome to Spain or Rome to Britain."

"I am a pacifist," he concluded, winding up with a pledge that was greeted by a great burst of cheers and applause, "but I believe that by overwhelming majorities . . . you and I, in the long run if it be necessary, will act together to protect and defend by every means at our command our science, our culture, our American freedom and our civilization."

Buoyed by his thunderous reception, Roosevelt was in excellent humor when he returned to his study to find Helen Gahagan Douglas waiting for him. Just as he was settling in, however, word came that Winston Churchill was on the telephone. Earlier that evening, Churchill had driven to Buckingham Palace, where King George VI had asked him to form a government. Even as Churchill agreed to accept the seals of office, British troops were pouring into Belgium, wildly cheered by smiling Belgians, who welcomed them with flowers. The change was made official at 9 p.m., when Chamberlain, his voice breaking with emotion, resigned. It had been a long and fateful day for Britain, but now, though it was nearly 3 a.m. in London, Churchill apparently wanted to touch base with his old letter-writing companion before going to sleep.

Though there is no record of the content of this first conversation between the new prime minister of England and the president of the United States, Churchill did reveal that when he went to bed that night, after the extraordinary events of an extraordinary day, he was conscious of "a profound sense of relief. At last I had the authority to give directions over the whole scene. I felt as if I were walking with Destiny, and that all my past life had been but a preparation for this hour and this trial."

"Therefore," Churchill concluded, "although impatient for morning, I slept soundly and had no need for cheering dreams. Facts are better than dreams." He had achieved the very position he had imagined for himself for so many years.

While Roosevelt was talking with Churchill, Helen Douglas tried to prepare herself for the important question the president wanted to ask her. Perhaps, she thought, it was related to her work with the farm-security program, or the National Youth Administration. Both Helen and her husband, fellow actor Melvyn Douglas, were ardent New Dealers, members of the National Advisory Commission for the Works Progress Administration and the California Advisory Commission for the NYA. Earlier that year, they had hosted Mrs. Roosevelt's visit to Los Angeles, accompanying her to the migrant-labor camps in the San Joaquin Valley.

"The day was unforgettable," Helen later recalled. "Soon after we started, Mrs. Roosevelt spotted a cluster of makeshift shacks constructed of old boards, tarpaper and tin cans pounded flat, one of the ditch bank communities that were commonplace in California then." She asked to stop the car and walked across the field toward some migrants. "One of the

bent figures straightened to see who was approaching and recognized her at once. 'Oh, Mrs. Roosevelt, you've come to see us,' he said. He seemed to accept as a natural event of American life that the wife of the President of the United States would be standing in a mucky field chatting with him."

Perhaps the president's question related to something his wife had told him about her journey. To be sure, Helen knew that Roosevelt loved movies and movie people, but not even that knowledge prepared her for the whimsical nature of the question the president posed to her that night.

"OK, Helen," Roosevelt began, his eyes flashing with good humor. "Now, I want you to tell me exactly what happened under the table at Ciro's between Paulette Goddard and Anatole Litvak." The juicy gossip Roosevelt wanted to hear involved the Russian-born director Anatole Litvak and Paulette Goddard, the vivacious brunette actress who was married first to the filmmaker Hal Roach and then to Charlie Chaplin. As Helen Douglas told the story, Goddard and Litvak were having dinner at the elegant nightclub, where the men had to wear tuxedos and the women long dresses, when the urge to make love became so strong that they eased themselves onto the floor under the table. As the moans were heard across the restaurant floor, waiters rushed to the scene with extra tablecloths to cover the sides of the table. Or so the story was told. "I love it, I love it," Roosevelt responded.

Returning to the White House from Union Station just as Helen was finishing her tale, Eleanor heard her husband's laughter and assumed that, as usual, he was with Missy, relaxing at the end of the day. At such times, she later admitted to her son Elliott, she felt terribly left out, wishing that she could let herself go and simply join in the frivolity. But as it was, she knew that if she opened the door she would be driven to talk business, to share the information and insights she had gleaned from her recent trip. Then, if her husband was tired and unresponsive, she would feel hurt and rejected. It had happened this way before. Better to go to her own bedroom and wait until morning to see her husband.

"All her life," her niece Eleanor Wotkyns observed, "Eleanor yearned to be more spontaneous, to relax more readily, but in the end how can one force oneself to be spontaneous?"

At ten after eleven that evening, according to the White House usher diary, both Eleanor and Franklin went to bed—Franklin settling into his small bedroom off his study, Eleanor into her own suite of rooms, next to her husband's, in the southwest corner of the mansion. But the separation by night belied the partnership by day—a partnership that would help change the face of the country in the years ahead.

At 1 p.m. on May 16, 1940, President Roosevelt was scheduled to address a joint session of Congress. It was the president's first appearance in the House Chamber since the war in Western Europe had begun. Despite the blinding rain falling steadily since early morning, a huge audience had gathered to hear him.

Here, on the floor of the House of Representatives, all the contending forces of American life had gathered over the years to argue their causes—abolitionists versus slaveowners, liberals versus conservatives, unions versus management, farmers versus city-dwellers. On a number of occasions, particularly in the nineteenth century, the debates had descended into physical violence as members brandished pistols, smashed one another's heads with tongs, canes, and brass spittoons, and pummeled each other with fists. The very size of the House Chamber, with large numbers of legislators, clerks, and page boys running from place to place, conspired to produce confusion and chaos.

As one o'clock neared, there was a stir among the audience, an air of expectation. Every face, not knowing for sure where the country was going, wore a look of nervousness. In the Congress in 1940, there were 526 men and five women, nearly three hundred lawyers, two dozen schoolteachers, sixty merchants, twenty bankers and insurance agents, nine newspaper publishers, five dentists, a half-dozen preachers, the owner of the largest cattle ranch in the world, an amateur magician, and a half-dozen or more aspirants to the presidency. There was one Negro.

At 12:59 p.m. the assistant doorkeeper announced the members of the Cabinet. The spectators responded with warm applause. But when the audience caught sight of the president himself, his right hand holding a cane, his left hand grasping the forearm of a Secret Service man, they jumped to their feet, applauding and cheering him as he had never been cheered in the Capitol before, a bipartisan ovation that could only be interpreted as a demonstration of national unity in a time of crisis.

It had been a week no one in the Western world would forget. After only five days of fighting, Holland, with tens of thousands of her citizens said to be dead, had surrendered; the Belgian army was almost totally destroyed, and France, reputed to possess the best army in all of Europe, was being overrun. The Germans seemed to have discovered a radically new style of air-ground warfare that was somehow free from ordinary constraints of time and distance. The speed and destructiveness of Germany's powerful tanks—able to cross rivers and canals as if they were paved boulevards, resisting all fire at normal ranges—were almost incomprehensible. Against these metal mastodons, French Premier Paul Reynaud lamented, the French defenses were like "walls of sand that a child puts up against waves on the seashore." Equally hard to fathom was the effectiveness of Germany's air force, roaring in ahead of advancing columns, bombing communication lines, strafing and terrorizing ground troops to the point of an almost total Allied collapse.

For many in the audience, Roosevelt's dramatic journey to the Hill awakened memories of Woodrow Wilson's appearance before Congress in the spring of 1917, when America entered the Great War. Now, once again, Europe was engaged in an expanding war that threatened to engulf the entire world, and emotions were running high. As the applause continued to swell, the president slowly maneuvered his body up the long ramp from the well of the House to the rostrum.

Standing at the podium, his leg braces firmly locked into place, the president looked at his audience, and an uncharacteristic wave of nervousness came upon him. Absent were both his conspicuous smile and the swaggering way he usually held his head; in their place, a slight slump of the shoulders and a grim expression that matched the gray day. Reporters seated behind the podium detected anxiety in his trembling hands and in the faltering way he tried and failed, not once but twice, to put on his glasses. . . .

The president had cause to feel apprehensive. He knew that both Britain and France were looking to the United States for help. Alone among the democratic nations, the United States possessed the potential resources—the abundance of raw materials, the oil fields, the bauxite mines, the assembly lines, the production equipment, the idle manpower, the entrepreneurial skills, the engineering know-how— necessary to wage technological war on a scale equal to that of Nazi Germany. "I trust you realize, Mr. President," Churchill had written earlier that week, "that the voice and force of the United States may count for nothing if they are withheld too long."

But when all was said and done, there was nothing "the most productive nation in the world" could do to save France. At dawn on the morning of June 14, German troops entered Paris. . . . A week later, Hitler laid down his terms for an armistice, and, in the same railroad car in a clearing in the woods at Compiègne where the Germans had capitulated to the Allies in 1918, a defeated and humiliated France concluded a truce. After the signing, Hitler ordered that the historic carriage and the monument celebrating the original French victory be conveyed to Berlin. Then, in an attempt to obliterate even the slightest physical memory of Germany's earlier defeat, he ordered that the pedestal of the carriage and the stones marking the site be destroyed. With the French surrender, Adolf Hitler was now the master of Austria, Czechoslovakia, Poland, Luxembourg, Belgium, Denmark, the Netherlands, Norway, and France. . . .

[Through 1940 and 1941 the European war intensified, with Germany fighting a mighty air war over Britain to clear the way for an invasion. But when the British won that war, Hitler turned to the East. In June 1941, he unleashed three million troops on the Soviet Union—the largest land invasion in the history of warfare. Meanwhile, in the Far East, militaristic Japan was waging its own war of aggression against hapless China. While Japanese warplanes bombed China's cities to rubble, Japanese troops seized coastal territory and murdered Chinese civilians—200,000 in Nanking alone—with unspeakable savagery. When Japanese forces struck southward against French Indochina, President Roosevelt retaliated by declaring an oil embargo against Japan, thus cutting off U.S. shipments of oil desperately needed by the Japanese war machine. When negotiations between the two countries faltered, the Japanese navy made plans for a surprise attack against the United States Pacific Fleet at Pearl Harbor, Hawaii. Final plans called for the attack to take place on Sunday morning, December 7, 1941.]

Shortly after 7:30 a.m., local time, while sailors were sleeping, eating breakfast, and reading the Sunday papers, the first wave of 189 Japanese planes descended upon Pearl Harbor, dropping clusters of torpedo bombs on the unsuspecting fleet. Half the fleet, by fortunate coincidence, was elsewhere, including all three aircraft carriers, but the ships that remained were tied up to the docks so "snugly side by side," Harold Ickes later observed, "that they presented a target that none could miss. A bomber could be pretty sure that he would hit a ship even if not the one he aimed at." Within minutes—before any anti-aircraft fire could be activated, and before a single fighter plane could get up into the air—all eight of the American battleships in Pearl Harbor, including the *West Virginia,* the *Arizona,* and the *California,* had been hit, along with three destroyers and three light cruisers.

Bodies were everywhere—trapped in the holds of sinking ships, strewn in the burning waters, scattered on the smoke-covered ground. Before the third wave of Japanese planes completed its final run, thirty-five hundred sailors, soldiers, and civilians had lost their lives. It was the worst naval disaster in American history.

United States battleships anchored at Pearl Harbor were sitting ducks. A torpedo has just struck the Oklahoma, *kicking up a towering geyser. Struck by four additional torpedoes, the great battleship quickly capsized. (U.S. Navy Photo)*

Knox relayed the horrifying news to the president shortly after 1:30 p.m. Roosevelt was sitting in his study with Harry Hopkins when the call came. "Mr. President," Knox said, "it looks like the Japanese have attacked Pearl Harbor." Hopkins said there must be some mistake; the Japanese would never attack Pearl Harbor. But the president reckoned it was probably true—it was just the kind of thing the Japanese would do at the very moment they were discussing peace in the Pacific. All doubt was settled a few minutes later, when Admiral Stark called to confirm the attack. With bloody certainty, the United States had finally discovered the whereabouts of the Japanese fleet. . . .

The first thing Eleanor noticed when she went into her husband's study was his "deadly calm" composure. While his aides and Cabinet members were running in and out in a state of excitement, panic, and irritation, he was sitting quietly at his desk, absorbing the news from Hawaii as it continued to flow in—"each report more terrible than the last." Though he looked strained and tired, Eleanor observed, "he was completely calm. His reaction to any event was always to be calm. If it was something that was bad, he just became almost like an iceberg, and there was never the slightest emotion that was allowed to show." Sumner Welles agreed with Eleanor's assessment. In all the situations over the years in which he had seen the president, he "had never had such reason to admire him."

Beneath the president's imperturbable demeanor, however, Eleanor detected great bitterness and anger toward Japan for the treachery involved in carrying out the surprise attack while the envoys of the two countries were still talking. "I never wanted to have to fight this war on two fronts," Franklin told Eleanor. "We haven't got the Navy to fight in both the Atlantic and the Pacific . . . so we will have to build up the Navy and the Air Force and that will mean that we will have to take a good many defeats before we can have a victory." . . .

"Within the first hour," Grace Tully recalled, "it was evident that the Navy was dangerously crippled." And there was no way of knowing where the Japanese would stop. The president's butler Alonzo Fields recalls overhearing snatches of a remarkable conversation between Harry Hopkins and the president that afternoon in which they imagined the possibility of the invading Japanese armies' driving inland from the West Coast as far as Chicago. At that point, the president figured, since the United States was a country much like Russia in the vastness of its terrain, we could make the Japanese overextend their communication and supply lines and begin to force them back.

Meanwhile, a little bit at a time, the public at large was learning the news. "No American who lived through that Sunday will ever forget it," reporter Marquis Childs later wrote. "It seared deeply into the national consciousness," creating in all a permanent memory of where they were when they first heard the news.

Churchill was sitting at Chequers with envoy Averell Harriman and Ambassador John Winant when news of the Japanese attack came over the wireless. Unable to contain his excitement, he bounded to his feet and placed a call to the White House. "Mr. President, what's this about Japan?" "It's quite true," Roosevelt replied. "They have attacked us at Pearl Harbour. We are all in the same boat now."

"To have the United States at our side," Churchill later wrote, "was to me the greatest joy." After seventeen months of lonely fighting, he now believed the war would be won. "England would live; Britain would live; the Commonwealth of Nations and the Empire would live." The history of England would not come to an end. "Silly people—and

there were many . . . ," Churchill mused, "—might discount the force of the United States," believing the Americans were soft, divided, paralyzed, averse to bloodshed. He knew better; he had studied the Civil War, the bloodiest war in history, fought to the last inch. Saturated with emotion, Churchill thought of a remark British politician Sir Edward Grey had made to him more than 30 years before. The U.S. was like "a gigantic boiler. Once the fire is lighted under it there is no limit to the power it can generate."

Shortly before 5 p.m., the president called Grace Tully to his study. "He was alone," Tully recalled, with two or three neat piles of notes stacked on his desk containing all the information he had been receiving during the afternoon. "Sit down, Grace. I'm going before Congress tomorrow. I'd like to dictate my message. It will be short."

He began to speak in the same steady tone in which he dictated his mail, but the pace was slower than usual as he spoke each word incisively, specifying every punctuation mark. "Yesterday comma December 7th comma 1941 dash a day which will live in world history . . . "

At eight-thirty on Sunday night, the Cabinet began to gather in the president's study. A ring of extra chairs had been brought in to accommodate the overflow. The president, Perkins noted later, was sitting silently at his desk; he was preoccupied, seemed not to be seeing or hearing what was going on around him. "It was very interesting," Perkins observed, "because he was always a very friendly and outgoing man on the personal side. He never overlooked people. . . . But I don't think he spoke to anyone who came in that night. He was living off in another area. He wasn't noticing what went on on the other side of the desk. He was very serious. His face and lips were pulled down, looking quite gray. His complexion didn't have that pink and white look that it had when he was himself. It had a queer gray, drawn look."

Finally, he turned around and said, "I'm thankful you all got here." He went on to say this was probably the most serious crisis any Cabinet had confronted since the outbreak of the Civil War. Then he told them what he knew. "I remember," Perkins

On December 9, 1941, Roosevelt solemnly signed the declaration of war against Japan, which Congress approved with one dissenting vote. Germany and Italy, Japan's Axis allies, responded by declaring war on the United States. These acts plunged America into the greatest war in history. (Franklin D. Roosevelt Library)

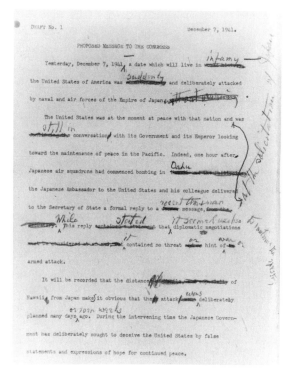

White House secretary Grace Tully was with the president just before 5 p.m. on the day the Japanese attacked Pearl Harbor. Roosevelt told her, "Sit down, Grace. I'm going before Congress tomorrow. I'd like to dictate my message. It will be short." The president made some handwritten changes to the original draft and the next day he received a thunderous ovation from a Congress now ready for war. (Franklin D. Roosevelt Library)

later said, "the President could hardly bring himself" to describe the devastation. "His pride in the Navy was so terrific that he was having actual physical difficulty in getting out the words that put him on record as knowing that the Navy was caught unawares. . . . I remember that he said twice to Knox, 'Find out, for God's sake, why the ships were tied up in rows.' Knox said, 'That's the way they berth them!' It was obvious to me that Roosevelt was having a dreadful time just accepting the idea that the Navy could be caught off guard."

By 10 p.m., congressional leaders had joined the Cabinet in the overcrowded study. The president told the gathering that he had prepared a short message to

be presented at a joint session of Congress the following day. The message called for a declaration by Congress that a state of war had existed between Japan and the United States from the moment of the attack Sunday morning. He then went on to describe the attack itself, repeating much of what he had told his Cabinet, including new information that Japanese bombs had also hit American airfields in Hawaii, destroying more than half the planes in the Pacific fleet. Apparently, the planes had been an easy mark, since they were grouped together on the ground, wing tip to wing tip, to guard against subversive action by Japanese agents. "On the ground, by God, on the ground," Roosevelt groaned.

"The effect on the Congressmen was tremendous," Stimson recorded. "They sat in dead silence and even after the recital was over they had very few words." Finally, Senator Tom Connally of Texas spoke up, voicing the question that was on everyone's mind. "How did it happen that our warships were caught like tame ducks in Pearl Harbor?" he shouted, banging the desk with his fist, his face purple. "How did they catch us with our pants down? Where were our patrols? They knew these negotiations were going on. They were all asleep."

"I don't know, Tom," the president muttered, his head bowed, "I just don't know."

Historians have focused substantial time and attention trying to determine who knew what and when before the 7th of December—on the theory that Roosevelt was aware of the Japanese plans to attack Pearl Harbor but deliberately concealed his knowledge from the commanders in Hawaii in order to bring the United States into hostilities through the back door. Unable to swing Congress and the public toward a declaration of war against Germany, critics contend, the president provoked Japan into firing the first shot and then watched with delight as the attack created a united America.

To be sure, Roosevelt was concerned that, if war came, the Japanese should be the ones to initiate hostilities. Stimson records a conversation on November 25 in which the president raised the possibility that Japan might attack without warning. The question Roosevelt asked "was how we should maneuver them into the position of firing the first shot without allowing too much danger to ourselves." But in the discussion, as in all others preceding Pearl Harbor, the reigning assumption was that Japan would attack from the south. Though Pearl Harbor was mentioned once, the previous January, in a report from the U.S. ambassador to Japan, Joseph Grew, to the State Department, it was assumed, again and again, right up to December 7, that the Philippines was the most likely target for Japanese aggression.

Moreover, "without allowing too much danger to ourselves," is the important phrase in the president's conversation with Stimson. Common sense suggests that, if the president had known beforehand about Pearl Harbor, he would have done everything he could to reposition the fleet and disperse the airplanes to ensure minimal damage. For the purposes of mobilizing the American people, one American ship torpedoed by the Japanese at Pearl Harbor would have sufficed. It is inconceivable that Roosevelt, who loved the navy with a passion, would have intentionally sacrificed the heart of its fleet, much less the lives of thirty-five hundred American sailors and soldiers, without lifting a finger to reduce the risk. It is an inquiry that obscures the more important question that Senator Connally posed: "How did it happen that our warships were caught like tame ducks in Pearl Harbor?"

It happened because the U.S. forces at Pearl Harbor were fatally unprepared for war on the morning of December 7. "Neither Army or Navy Commandants in Oahu regarded such an attack as at all likely," Secretary Knox explained to Roosevelt. "Both [General Walker Short and Admiral Husband Kimmel] felt certain that such an attack would take place nearer Japan's base of operations, that is, in the Far East." Lack of readiness characterized every aspect of the base—from the unmanned aircraft batteries to the radar station whose sentries went off duty at 7 a.m. that morning. . . .

Toward midnight, the meeting in the president's study drew to a close; and while every face wore an expression of regret and reproach, there was also relief. For Stimson, it was in the knowledge "that the indecision was over and that a crisis had come in a way which would unite our people." No matter how great the damage, at least, the matter was settled. "You know," Frank Knox whispered to Frances Perkins, "I think the boss must have a great load off his mind. I thought the load on his mind was just going to kill him, going to break him down. This must be a great sense of relief to him. At least we know what to do now."

"Monday was almost worse than Sunday," Marquis Childs observed. "A merciful kind of shock prevailed under the first impact and now as that wore off, the truth was inescapable." In Washington, the rumors of damage "hovered like a low-hanging gas, spreading the panic that seemed to infect the capital." On the same day as Pearl Harbor, the Japanese had attacked the Philippines, Malaya, Wake Island, Guam, and Hong Kong.

At noon, under heavy security, the president motored from the East Gate of the White House to the Capitol, where, to deafening applause, he delivered a brief but powerful speech. From his first words, commemorating the day that would "live in infamy," to his call upon Congress to declare that, since "the unprovoked and dastardly attack by Japan on Sunday, December 7th, a state of war has existed between the United States and the Japanese Empire," the president's anger and indignation burned through. His head held high, his chin thrust out, Roosevelt roused his audience to a standing ovation when he pledged that "this form of treachery shall never endanger us again. The American people in their righteous might will win through to absolute victory." The Congress responded unambiguously to the president's call; both chambers approved a declaration of war, with only one dissenting vote—that of white-haired Representative Jeanette Rankin of Montana.

Isolationism collapsed overnight. "American soil has been treacherously attacked by Japan," former President Herbert Hoover stated. "Our decision is clear. It is forced upon us. We must fight with everything we have." . . . After months of vacillation, confusion, and hesitation, the United States was committed at last to a common course of action.

QUESTIONS TO CONSIDER

1 Polio seemed to transform Roosevelt's life in many ways. What was his life like before crippling illness, and why would Goodwin conclude that FDR's disability "expanded his mind and his sensibilities"? Explain how Roosevelt's relationship with reporters provided him with favorable press coverage despite the opposition of most newspaper publishers? Would the media and the American people ignore a major political leader's disability today as they did then?

2 Goodwin's portrait of the Roosevelts is as complimentary to Eleanor as it is to Franklin. Why was this first lady so popular? What obstacles did she have to overcome in her personal life, including her marriage? How did her discovery of Franklin's infidelity free her to play a different role and become her husband's "eyes and ears" as she traveled around the country?

3 In the spring of 1940, was the United States militarily prepared to enter a major world war? In contrast, why were Germany's armed forces so modern? How did the Congress view aid to the struggling democracies of England and France?

4 Examine the personality of Franklin Roosevelt and how Missy LeHand and Harry Hopkins served his inner needs much better than Eleanor. How did the president relax and temporarily escape the overwhelming problems of the Depression and the foreign policy crisis abroad?

5 Describe the damage that the Japanese inflicted on the American fleet at Pearl Harbor. What was Churchill's reaction when he heard of the attack? Why does Goodwin believe that Roosevelt had no advance notice of the invasion, and why does she feel that our warships at Pearl Harbor were "like tame ducks"? Finally, how did Congress and the American people respond to the Japanese attack against Pearl Harbor?

19 America and the Holocaust

WILLIAM J. VANDEN HEUVEL

The Second World War was the deadliest conflict in human history. More than 53 million people perished, and whole towns and cities were annihilated in this roaring global inferno. The hardest hit was the Soviet Union, which felt the full fury of the invading Nazi war machine. Some 25 million Soviets were killed—by far the largest casualties of any other country. Compared to the destruction wrought in China, Japan, the Soviet Union, and Europe, the United States suffered relatively light casualties. There were no invasions of the American mainland, no bombing raids on American cities, no civilian massacres. Total American military deaths came to 408,000. By comparing statistics, we do not mean to slight those who died for our flag. Every American fighting man killed was a terrible sacrifice and a devastating blow to those who loved him.

As the next selection shows, the casualty rates of countries tell only part of the war's tragic story. The virulent anti-Semitism of Hitler and his Nazi henchmen led them to a "final solution" to the "Jewish question": the creation of hideous death camps, which systematically exterminated 6 million European Jews—men, women, and children alike. Winston Churchill called it "the most terrible crime ever committed in the whole history of the world."

How could the Allies have allowed this "terrible crime" to happen? Could the United States have stopped it? Did it even try? Many critics contend that American leaders did not do nearly enough to help the Jews of Europe, instead abandoning them to their fate. William J. vanden Heuvel disagrees. He points out that restrictive immigration laws limited the number of refugees America could accept before Hitler "put the lock on the most terrible dungeon in history." The author concedes that there were influential people in Congress and the State Department who were anti-Semitic. Even so, after anti-Semitic riots swept Germany in November 1938, more than half of all immigrants to the United States were Jewish.

Vanden Heuvel defends Roosevelt's Jewish policy, contending that the president and first lady were free of the prejudice that infected other Americans. Roosevelt knew about the death camps—he had read about them in a report from German refugee Gerhard Riegner, who warned that European Jews were being "exterminated in order to resolve, once and for all, the Jewish question in Europe." When a group of Jewish leaders called on Roosevelt, the president assured them: "We shall do all in our power to be of service to your people in this tragic moment." True, FDR refused to bomb railroad lines leading to the death camps, arguing that committing all military resources to defeating Germany as soon as possible would save more lives. Many Roosevelt critics question the validity of that argument, but not vanden Heuvel. He maintains that Roosevelt, given political realities and wartime priorities, did in fact do all he could to aid Europe's Jews. After reading this provocative essay, you will want to decide for yourselves if this argument is convincing and supported by the weight of evidence. For the opposing point of view, consult David S. Wyman's The Abandonment of the Jews: America and the Holocaust, 1941–1945 *(1984).*

GLOSSARY

AUSCHWITZ   The most notorious of the Nazi death camps. The Allies rejected any thought of bombing this concentration camp and the railroad tracks leading to it, and most mainstream Jewish groups agreed that the first victims of a bombing of Auschwitz would be the Jewish prisoners, who, if they survived the assault, would have no place to run. Moreover, the Germans could easily rebuild the railroad lines. The Allies believed that the best way to save Jewish lives was to end the war as soon as possible.

CHURCHILL, WINSTON   See glossary in selection 17.

DICKSTEIN, SAMUEL   Democrat who chaired the House subcommittee on immigration. Like Congressman Emanuel Celler of Brooklyn, he wanted to ease the quota restrictions to allow more Jewish immigrants to enter the United States, but he feared that such actions would provide reactionaries with an opportunity to further limit immigration.

EVIAN CONFERENCE   President Roosevelt helped organize this humanitarian effort "to facilitate the emigration from Germany and Austria of political refugees." It was largely a failure because of American immigration quotas and Hitler's refusal to permit refugees to keep some of their assets in order to start a new life.

GOEBBELS, JOSEF   Hitler's propaganda minister. Goebbels used radio and films to promote the Nazi cause at home, foment hatred toward European Jewry, and exaggerate German successes on the battlefield.

INTERNATIONAL RESCUE COMMITTEE   In 1933, Eleanor Roosevelt was one of the founders of this organization, which won sanctuary in America for many of the most prominent victims of Hitler's persecution.

KRISTALLNACHT   German word meaning "glass night," referring to the noise of breaking windows. In November 1938, anti-Semitic riots that resulted in looting and arson scarred much of Germany. Little was done to contain the senseless violence, which was a signal of much worse to come. In response, President Roosevelt extended the visas of twenty thousand Germans and Austrians in the United States so that they would not have to return home.

LONG, BRECKENRIDGE   Assistant secretary of state who allowed his biases to influence the restrictive immigration quotas established by Congress. These quotas limited the number of Jewish refugees who sought sanctuary in the United States.

MANN, THOMAS   Well-known humanist and German exile who believed that compromise was impossible in dealing with Hitler. He influenced policymakers in the United States to use the threat of force when negotiating with the Nazis.

NUREMBURG LAWS   In 1935, the Nazis severely restricted the rights of Jews through the Nuremburg Laws, a series of measures that limited the professions they could enter and barred marriage and sexual intercourse with gentiles. Hitler's purpose was to force German Jews to emigrate so that he could confiscate their property.

RIEGNER, GERHART   A representative of the World Jewish Congress whose telegram, in August of 1942, helped confirm the presence of Nazi death camps such as Auschwitz.

ST. LOUIS   In May of 1939, this ship carried 936 passengers, most of them Jewish, to Cuba, where all but 22 were refused sanctuary. Since the American government's strict immigration laws prevented their entry into the United States, American diplomats helped find temporary safety for them in other countries. However, most of those countries, like France and Belgium, eventually faced Nazi occupation and did not remain safe havens.

VICHY, FRANCE   After Hitler had overrun much of France, Marshal Pétain established a dictatorial government in the city of Vichy that collaborated with Germany. Pétain offered little resistance when the Nazis deported French Jews to extermination camps in eastern Europe.

WANNSEE CONFERENCE   In January 1942, the Nazi leadership formulated the "Final Solution" at this meeting in Berlin. Hitler's misguided belief in a pure master race of German "Aryans" resulted in a cruel plan to exterminate Europe's Jews.

WELLES, SUMNER   President Roosevelt's undersecretary of state who appreciated the plight of Jews trapped in Germany and the occupied countries. Welles urged the State Department to take more direct action to save them.

WISE, STEPHEN   A rabbi who was a friend of President Roosevelt and a respected leader of the American Jewish community. He spoke out against Hitler's atrocities, encouraged Jews to leave Germany, and pressured the American government to save as many lives as possible.

It was Winston Churchill's judgment that the Holocaust "was probably the greatest and most terrible crime ever committed in the whole history of the world." The Holocaust, of course, was part of a colossal struggle in which fifty-three million people were killed, where nations were decimated, where democracy's survival was in the balance. In his campaign to exterminate the Jews of Europe, Hitler and his Nazi followers murdered six million men, women, and children for no other reason than that they were Jewish. This crime is of such profound proportions that it can never be fully understood; it must continue to be analyzed from every aspect as to how and why it happened, and its memory must unite all of us.

Nine million non-Jewish civilians were also murdered by the Nazis, as were three million Soviet prisoners of war, yet the Holocaust remains a uniquely horrible crime, and there can be no greater indictment than to allege complicity in it. Such an accusation was made against America in general and its leader, Franklin D. Roosevelt, in particular by a recent PBS documentary entitled "America and the Holocaust: Deceit and Indifference." The show drew on a substantial and growing body of scholarship that has caused many young American Jews to criticize and even condemn their grandparents and parents for being so absorbed in the effort to become assimilated in American society that they chose silence rather than voice outrage at the Nazi crimes and gave their overwhelming support to a President who was indifferent to the fate of Europe's Jews. Why did not the United States let the *St. Louis,* a German ship carrying Jewish refugees to Cuba in 1939, land at an American port when Cuba refused them admission? Also, perhaps the most frequently asked question of the last decade, why did the Allies not bomb Auschwitz and the railways that fed it? The people who pose these questions believe they know the answers. As one eminent spokesman for this viewpoint has written, "The Nazis were the murderers but we"—here he includes the American government, its President, and its people, Christians and Jews alike—"were the all too passive accomplices."

How much truth is there in these painful assertions? As we ask ourselves what more might have been done to save the innocent, we must frame our response in the context of the realities of World War II and the events and values of the years that preceded it.

Five weeks after Adolf Hitler became chancellor of Germany, in 1933, Franklin Roosevelt became President of the United States. Roosevelt's loathing for the whole Nazi regime was known the moment he took office; alone among the leaders of the world, he stood in opposition to Hitler from the very beginning. In a book published in 1937, Winston Churchill—to whom free humanity everywhere must be eternally indebted and without whose courage and strength the defeat of Nazi Germany could never have been achieved—described Hitler's treatment of the Jews, stating that "concentration camps pock-mark the German soil . . ." and concluding his essay by writing that "the world lives on hopes that the worst is over and that we may live to see Hitler a gentler figure in a happier age." Roosevelt had no such hopes. Thomas Mann, the most famous of the non-Jewish refugees from the Nazis, met with FDR at the White House in 1935 and confided that for the first time he believed the Nazis would be beaten because in Roosevelt he had met someone who truly grasped the evil of Adolf Hitler.

To comprehend the situation of European Jewry during those years, we must differentiate between the German Jews who were the immediate and constant subjects of Hitler's persecution and the Jews of Central Europe who were the principal victims of the Holocaust. The German Jews numbered about 525,000 in 1933. They were the yeast of Germany's great culture—leaders in literature, music, medicine, science, and financial and intellectual life. For the most part they wanted to be thought of as Germans. They had been a proud part of Germany's army in World War I. Anti-Semitism shadowed their lives, but they thought of Germany as *their* country and

William J. vanden Heuvel, "America and the Holocaust," *American Heritage,* vol. 50, no. 4 (July/August, 1999), pp. 34–37, 40–43, 46, 48, 50–53. Reprinted by permission of *American Heritage* magazine, a division of Forbes, Inc. © Forbes, Inc., 1999.

Nazi troops turn their rifles on helpless women and children in Poland's Warsaw Ghetto. The victims were caught "in a vast prison from which there was no escape and no possible rescue." The young, elderly, weak, and disabled were of limited use to the Germans in the cruel labor camps and were among the first to perish in the hideous gas chambers. (Yivo Institute for Jewish Research)

were deeply rooted in its existence. In the face of Nazi persecution, those who left Germany did so reluctantly, many seeking refuge in neighboring countries, from which they expected to return once the Hitler madness subsided. In the early years many, if not most, believed Hitler and his regime could not survive.

When, in 1933, Rabbi Stephen Wise, one of the most powerful and respected leaders of the American Jewish community during that era and a personal friend and close adviser of President Roosevelt, organized a New York rally to protest Nazi treatment of Jews, he received a message from leading German rabbis urging him to cut out such meetings and which, insultingly, indicated that American Jews were doing this for their own purposes and in the process were destroying the Germany that German Jews loved. Rabbi Wise never wavered in his belief

that the only option for Jews was to leave Germany. As the Nazi persecution intensified, as the Nuremberg Laws further degraded the Jews as had nothing before, as Hitler strove to make them emigrate and confiscated their property, the prospect of escape and exile had to shadow every Jewish family. In 1933 thirty-seven thousand Jews fled Germany, but in the relative calm of the next year, sixteen thousand returned. Every Jewish group affirmed the right of Jews to be German, to live in and love their country; they affirmed the legal right, the moral necessity, and the religious imperative of not surrendering to their persecutors. As important as any barriers to immigration in Western countries was the desire not to leave Germany until absolutely necessary. It is crucial to our understanding of these years to remember that at the time no one inside or outside Germany anticipated that the Nazi persecution would lead to the Holocaust. The actions of the German government were generally understood by both victims and by-standers as a return to the sorts of persecutions of prior centuries, not as steps on the road toward genocide.

Kristallnacht in November 1938 changed the situation dramatically. The assassination of a German diplomat in Paris by a seventeen-year-old Jewish youth whose father had been among the thousands of Polish Jews expelled from Germany and dumped across the Polish border just weeks before sparked a frenzy of arson and looting by Nazi thugs in almost every town and city. Huge, silent crowds looked on. The police did nothing to contain the violence. Many German Jews for the first time understood the hopelessness of their situation, and some looked west across the Atlantic.

The America that elected Franklin Delano Roosevelt its President in 1932 was a deeply troubled country. Twenty-five percent of its work force was unemployed—this at a time when practically every member of that work force was the principal support of a family. The economy was paralyzed, while disillusion after the sacrifices of the First World War fomented profound isolationist sentiments.

The nation's immigration laws had been established by legislation in 1921 and 1924 under Presidents Harding and Coolidge and by a Congress that had rejected the League of Nations. A formula assigned a specific quota to countries based on the population origins of Americans living in the United States in 1890. The law was aimed at Eastern Europe, particularly Russia and Poland, which were seen as seedbeds of bolshevism. Italians were targeted, and Asians practically excluded. The total number of immigrants who could be admitted annually was set at 153,774; the two countries of origin given the highest quotas were Great Britain (65,721) and Germany (25,957). The deepening Depression encouraged an unusual coalition of liberal and conservative forces, labor unions and business leaders, to oppose any enlargement of the immigration quotas. Because of the relatively large German quota, Jewish refugees from Germany had an easier time than anticommunist refugees from the Soviet Union, not to mention Chinese victims of Japan's aggression, or

Armenians. The Spanish who wanted to escape a civil war that between 1936 and 1939 killed half a million people faced an annual quota of 252.

The President and Mrs. Roosevelt were leaders in the effort to help those fleeing Nazi persecution. Eleanor Roosevelt was a founder, in 1933, of the International Rescue Committee, which brought intellectuals, labor leaders, and political figures to sanctuary in the United States. President Roosevelt made a public point of inviting many of them to the White House. In 1936, in response to the Nazi confiscation of personal assets as a precondition to Jewish emigration, Roosevelt greatly modified President Hoover's strict interpretation of the refugee laws, thereby allowing a greater number of visas to be issued. As a result the United States accepted twice as many Jewish refugees as did all other countries put together. As the historian Gerhard L. Weinberg has shown, Roosevelt acted in the face of strong and politically damaging criticism for what was generally considered a pro-Jewish attitude.

When, in March 1938, the Anschluss put Austria's 185,000 Jews in jeopardy, Roosevelt called for an international conference "to facilitate the emigration from Germany and Austria of political refugees." There was no political advantage to FDR in this; no other major leader in any country matched his concern and involvement. The conference, which met in Evian, France, tried to open new doors in the Western Hemisphere. At first things went well; the Dominican Republic, for example, offered to give sanctuary to 100,000 refugees. Then came a devastating blow: The Polish and Romanian governments announced that they expected the same right as the Germans to expel their Jewish populations. There were fewer than 475,000 Jews left in Germany and Austria at this point—a number manageable in an emigration plan that the twenty-nine participating nations could prepare—but with the possibility of 3.5 million more from Eastern Europe, the concern now was that any offer of help would only encourage authoritarian governments to brutalize any unwanted portion of their populations, expecting their criminal acts against their own citizens to force the democracies to give them haven. National attitudes then were not very different from today's; no country allows any and every refugee to enter without limitations. Quotas are thought even now to deter unscrupulous and impoverished regimes from forcing their unwanted people on other countries.

The Evian Conference failed to accomplish anything except organization of the Inter-Governmental Committee (IGC), which was to pressure the Germans to allow Jewish refugees to leave with enough resources to begin their new lives. It led to direct negotiations between Hjalmar Schacht, head of the Reichsbank, and George Rublee, a distinguished Washington lawyer personally designated by FDR. Schacht proposed that 150,000 Jews be allowed to emigrate, taking 25 percent of their assets with them, the rest to be impounded in a trust fund that would serve as collateral on bonds to be issued by the German state. Schacht was trying to resolve Germany's foreign exchange crisis, but Hitler ordered an end to the discussions. The negotiations, like all barter negotiations in the years ahead, failed because the Führer never allowed them to succeed.

America's reaction to *Kristallnacht* was stronger than that of any of the other democracies. Roosevelt recalled his ambassador from Germany and at his next press conference said, "I myself can scarcely believe that such things could occur in a twentieth-century civilization." He extended the visitors' visas of twenty thousand Germans and Austrians in the United States so they would not have to return. Americans in opinion polls showed anger and disgust with the Nazis and sympathy for the Jews; nevertheless, Roosevelt remained the target of the hard-core anti-Semites in America. He fought them shrewdly and effectively, managing to isolate them from mainstream America and essentially equating their anti-Semitism with treason destructive to both the national interest and national defense. Recognizing the inertia at the State Department, he entrusted Sumner Welles, the Undersecretary of State and a man wholly sympathetic to Jewish needs, to be his instrument of action.

Immigration procedures were complicated and sometimes harshly administered. The laws and quotas were jealously guarded by Congress, supported by a strong, broad cross section of Americans who were against all immigrants, not just Jews. Of course, there were racists and anti-Semites in the Congress and in the country, as there are today, only now they dare not speak their true attitudes. The State Department, deeply protective of its administrative authority in the granting of visas, was frequently more concerned with congressional attitudes and criticisms than with reflecting American decency and generosity in helping people in despair and panic. Roosevelt undoubtedly made a mistake in appointing as Assistant Secretary of State Breckenridge Long, who many allege was an anti-Semite. His presence at State was an assurance to Congress that the immigration laws would be strictly enforced. On the other hand there were countless Foreign Service officers who did everything possible to help persecuted, innocent people, just as they would today. There was an attitude that many sanctuaries besides the United States existed in the world, so the department, controlled by a career elite, conservative and in large part anti–New Deal and anti-FDR, was quite prepared to make congressional attitudes rather than those of the White House the guide for their administration of immigration procedures. Yet, between 1933 and 1941, 35 percent of all immigrants to America under quota guidelines were Jewish. After *Kristallnacht,* Jewish immigrants were more than half of all immigrants admitted to the United States. . . .

For his part, Roosevelt, knowing that he did not have the power to change the quota system of his own country, was constantly seeking havens for the refugees in other countries. His critics severely underestimate limitations on presidential power; clearly, the President could not unilaterally command an increase in quotas. In fact, the Democratic congressional leaders, including Rep. Samuel Dickstein, who chaired the House subcommittee on immigration, warned him that reactionary forces in Congress might well use any attempt to increase the quotas as an opportunity to reduce them. In 1939 Congressman

Emanuel Celler of Brooklyn, an outspoken defender of Jewish interests, gave a speech in which he warned that "it would be dangerous at this time because of public opinion in the South and West to press for the passage in Congress of [his own] bills to give asylum in the United States to refugees and to reallot for refugees the unused quotas of various countries." Congressman Celler said he had been warned by representatives from other parts of the country that if he pressed his proposals, other bills "to cut the quotas in half or to stop all immigration would be introduced and probably passed." Nor were the Jews the only refugees Congress was determined to bar. A few days later the Reverend Joseph Ostermann, executive director of the Committeee for Catholic Refugees from Germany, said that there were five hundred thousand actual or potential Catholic refugees whom "Goebbels and Rosenberg in Germany have attempted to identify with communism."

By the time the war made further emigration impossible, 72 percent of all German Jews had left the country—and 83 percent of all those under twenty-one. There are many reasons why the others did not get out: Some were too old to leave; some, like the brave chief rabbi of Berlin, Leo Baeck, believed it their religious duty to stay; some were in concentration camps and prisons; some just did not know what to do. Even after *Kristallnacht* nobody could foresee the events that became the Holocaust. Louis de Jong, an eminent Dutch historian and Holocaust survivor, said in his Erasmus lectures at Harvard University in 1989: "[There is] an aspect of the Holocaust which is of cardinal importance and which can never be sufficiently underlined: that the Holocaust, when it took place, was beyond the belief and the comprehension of almost all people living at the time, Jews included. Everyone knew that human history had been scarred by endless cruelties. But that thousands, nay millions, of human beings— men, women and children, the old and the young, the healthy and the infirm—would be killed, finished off, mechanically, industrially so to speak, would be exterminated like vermin—that was a notion so alien to the human mind, an event so gruesome, so *new,* that the instinctive, indeed the natural, reaction of most people was: it can't be true."

Given the reality of the Holocaust, all of us in every country—and certainly in America—can only wish that we had done more, that our immigration barriers had been lower, that our Congress had had a broader world view, that every public servant had shared the beliefs of Franklin and Eleanor Roosevelt. If anyone had foreseen the Holocaust, perhaps, possibly, maybe . . . but no one did. Nevertheless, the United States, a nation remote from Europe in a way our children can hardly understand, took in double the number of Jewish refugees accepted by the rest of the world.

Among the anguishing events we read about is the fate of the ship *St. Louis* of the Hamburg-America Line, which left Germany and arrived in Cuba with 936 passengers, all but 6 of them Jewish refugees, on May 27, 1939. This was three months before the outbreak of the war and three years before the establishment of the death camps. Other ships had made the same journey, and their passengers had disembarked successfully, but on May 5 the Cuban government had issued a decree curtailing the power of the corrupt director general of immigration to issue landing certificates. New regulations requiring five-hundred-dollar bonds from each approved immigrant had been transmitted to the shipping line, but only 22 passengers of the *St. Louis* had fulfilled the requirements before leaving Hamburg on May 13. Those 22 were allowed to land; intense negotiations with the Cuban government regarding the other passengers—negotiations in which American Jewish agencies participated—broke down despite pressure from our government. It was not an unreported event. Tremendous international attention focused on the *St. Louis,* later made famous as the "Voyage of the Damned." Secretary of State Cordell Hull, Secretary of the Treasury Henry Morgenthau, Jr., and others, including Eleanor Roosevelt, worked to evade the immigration laws—for example, by attempting to land the passengers as "tourists" in the Virgin Islands. One survivor of the *St. Louis* whom I interviewed—a retired professor of human genetics at the University of Washington in Seattle—described its commander, Capt. Gustav Schroeder, as a compassionate man who ordered decent treatment for his Jewish passengers and who told them that he would run his ship aground off England rather than return them to Germany if Cuba refused admission. In the end, despite the legal inability of the United States to accept the passengers as immigrants, our diplomats were significantly helpful in resettling them. Not one was returned to Nazi Germany. They all went to democratic countries—288 in the United Kingdom, the rest in France, the Netherlands, Belgium, and Denmark. And who, in that spring of 1939, was prescient enough to foretell that in little more than a year all but one of those countries would be held by Nazi troops?

What were FDR's own attitudes toward Hitler and the Jews? Did he reflect the social anti-Semitism that was endemic in the America of that era? Contemporary Jews certainly didn't think so. Roosevelt opened the offices of government as never before to Jews. Henry Morgenthau, Jr., Samuel Rosenman, Felix Frankfurter, Benjamin Cohen, David Niles, Anna Rosenberg, Sidney Hillman, and David Dubinsky were among his closest advisers in politics and government. Rabbi Stephen Wise, the pre-eminent spokesman for American Zionism, said, "No one was more genuinely free from religious prejudice and racial bigotry."

Nazi policy changed radically after the outbreak of war. The Holocaust took place between 1941 and 1945. Hitler's conquest of the European continent let loose the full force of his psychopathic obsession about Jews. With the start of the war, on September 1, 1939, emigration from Germany was prohibited. Nevertheless, hundreds, perhaps thousands, of German Jews managed to escape across borders into Holland, Belgium, and Switzerland. But by June 1940, with the fall of France, Europe became a prison for Jews. Unoccupied France still offered an escape route, and despite intense criticism from the political left, FDR maintained diplomatic relations with Vichy, France, allowing that route to remain open. The International Rescue Committee, a group of which Eleanor Roosevelt remained very supportive, sent a team headed by Varian Fry that helped countless refugees find sanctuary in Spain and Portugal. But the vise was tightening. The invasion of Russia in June 1941 put the lock on the most terrible dungeon in history. Special squads of the German SS—the *Einsatzgruppen*—began the slaughter of 1.5 million Jews behind the German lines in Russia. The Wannsee Conference, which structured the "Final Solution," was held in a Berlin suburb in January 1942.

The Jews of Central Europe, the Jews from the occupied nations of Western Europe, the Jews of the Soviet Union—the principal victims of the Holocaust—were not refugees; they were prisoners in a vast prison from which there was no escape and no possible rescue. . . .

The doors had been closed not by the United States or its allies but by Hitler. On January 30, 1942, Hitler, speaking to the Reichstag, said, "This war can end in two ways—either the extermination of the Aryan peoples or the disappearance of Jewry from Europe." Since the mid-1920s Hitler had never voluntarily spoken to a Jew. He was the most determined ideologue of racial superiority and racial conflict who ever led a country. Nothing diminished his mission—not the defeat of his armies, not the destruction of his country. As Germany lay in ruins, as its dictator prepared to end his life in his bunker in Berlin, his Nazi acolytes continued his campaign, diverting even urgently needed reinforcements for his retreating armies in order to complete the Final Solution.

The prisoners of Hitler could be saved only by the total, unconditional surrender of Nazi Germany, and that was a task that required four years and the unprecedented mobilization of all the resources, human and material, of Great Britain, the Soviet Union, and the United States.

Some critics of American policy during these years maintain that the news of the annihilation of Europe's Jews was deliberately kept secret so that our people would not know about it and that if Americans had been aware of the Final Solution, they would have insisted on doing more than was done. The facts are otherwise. President Roosevelt, Winston Churchill, General Eisenhower, General Marshall, the intelligence services of the Allied nations, every Jewish leader, the Jewish communities in America, in Britain, in Palestine, and yes, anyone who had a radio or newspaper in 1942 knew that Jews in colossal numbers were being murdered. They may have received the news with disbelief; there was, after all, no precedent for it in human history. But the general information of the genocide was broadly available to anyone who would read or listen. The famous telegram from Gerhart Riegner, a representative of the World Jewish Congress, in Switzerland in August 1942, was not even the first knowledge of a death camp later to become known as Auschwitz when its gas chambers and crematoria had been built. Auschwitz, like every extermination camp, was treated as a top-secret project by the Nazis. The details and even the name of Auschwitz were not confirmed until the escape of two prisoners in April 1944, two years after its murderous processes had begun. But though the names, locations, and procedures of the death camps may not have been known—some not until the end of the war—the fact of the genocide and the Nazi determination to carry it out were not in doubt.

When Rabbi Wise was given the Riegner telegram, Sumner Welles asked him not to publicize it until its information could be confirmed by sources available to the Czech and Polish governments-in-exile. There was no video of this original version of "ethnic cleansing" such as we had available to us in Bosnia; there were no enterprising reporters who could photograph the Nazi butchery as there were in Rwanda. The experience of the First World War, in which atrocities attributed to the Germans turned out to be grossly inflated or Allied propaganda, caused many to wonder if the incredible reports coming from the continent of Europe would ultimately prove false as well.

When Sumner Welles confirmed the truth of the Riegner telegram to Rabbi Wise, the rabbi wept, as countless Jews and non-Jews would do in those terrible years when the Nazis lay beyond the reach of the armies that would defeat them. Encouraged by

Welles to hold a press conference to announce the news, Rabbi Wise did so, on November 28, 1942. Then he and his colleagues met with FDR and asked the President to warn Hitler and the Germans that they would be held individually responsible for what they were doing to the Jews. Roosevelt agreed immediately. An announcement to that effect in the name of the United Nations was made in Congress and in Britain's Parliament on December 17, 1942. It was repeated many times throughout the war. Parliament stood in silence for the first time in its history to mourn what was happening to the Jews and to pray for the strength needed to destroy their persecutors. In America the labor unions led the nation in a ten-minute period of mourning for the Jews of Europe. It is difficult to argue that there was a conspiracy of silence regarding the fate of Europe's Jews when the American broadcaster Edward R. Murrow, listened to throughout the nation, reported on December 13, 1942: "Millions of human beings, most of them Jews, are being gathered up with ruthless efficiency and murdered. . . . It is a picture of mass murder and moral depravity unequaled in the history of the world. It is a horror beyond what imagination can grasp. . . . The Jews are being systematically exterminated throughout all Poland. . . . There are no longer 'concentration camps'—we must speak now only of 'extermination camps.'"

American Jewry was no passive observer of these events. Despite issues that bitterly divided them, primarily relating to Palestine, the Jewish community in America spoke the same words in pleading to do whatever was possible for Europe's Jews. Jewish leaders lobbied Congress. Mass rallies were held across the country with overflow crowds throughout those years, praying, pleading for action to stop the genocide. The unremitting massacre continued because no one, no nation, no alliance of nations could do anything to close down the death camps—save, as Roosevelt said over and over again, by winning the war.

Had FDR followed the national will, Japan would have been our military priority, but understanding the Nazi threat to civilization, he ordered Germany to be the focus of our efforts. Had Roosevelt listened to General Marshall and his other military advisers, he would not have sent the few tanks we had in 1942 to help General Montgomery win at El Alamein, thereby probably saving Palestine from the same fate as Poland. Roosevelt gave frequent audience to Jewish leaders; he sent messages to rallies of Jews across the country; he listened to every plea and proposal for rescue that came to him. But he knew that the diversion of resources from the purpose of defeating the Nazi armies might palliate the anguish felt by so many, would rescue no one, and in all likelihood would kill the would-be rescuers. As Richard Lichtheim, a representative of the World Jewish Congress in Switzerland and a hero in informing the world of the genocide, said in December 1942, "You cannot divert a tiger from devouring his prey by adopting resolutions or sending cables. You have to take your gun and shoot him."

The historian Gerhard Weinberg answers those who question America's policy by suggesting that they consider how many more Jews would have survived had the war ended even a week or ten days earlier—and how many more would have died had it lasted an additional week or ten days. Given that the slaughter of the Jews went on into the final moments of the Third Reich, that every day until the surrender there were thousands of deaths by murder, starvation, and disease, the number of Jews saved by winning the war as quickly as possible was vastly greater than the total number who could have been saved by any rescue efforts proposed by anyone between 1941 and 1945. . . .

The proposal to bomb Auschwitz in 1944 has become the symbol for those who argue American indifference and complicity in the Holocaust. Some would have us believe that many American Jewish groups petitioned our government to bomb Auschwitz; in fact, there was considerable Jewish opposition in both the United States and Palestine. The focal center of the Holocaust Museum's exhibit on bombing Auschwitz is a letter from Leon Kubowitzki, head of the Rescue Department of the World Jewish Congress, in which he forwarded, without endorsement, a request from

the Czech State Council (in exile in London) to the War Department, in August 1944, to bomb the camp. Much is made of the Assistant Secretary John Mc-Cloy's response to Kubowitzki explaining the War Department's decision not to undertake such a mission. What is not on display and rarely mentioned is a letter dated July 1, 1944, from the same Leon Kubowitzki to the executive director of the War Refugee Board, arguing *against* bombing Auschwitz because "the first victims would be the Jews" and because the Allied air assault would serve as "a welcome pretext for the Germans to assert that their Jewish victims have been massacred not by their killers, but by Allied bombing."

Mainstream Jewish opinion was against the whole idea. The very thought of the Allied forces' deliberately killing Jews—to open the gates of Auschwitz so the survivors could run where?—was as abhorrent then as it is now. The Rescue Committee of the Jewish Agency in Jerusalem voted, at a meeting with the future Israeli prime minister David Ben-Gurion presiding, against even making the bombing request. Although only President Roosevelt or General Eisenhower could have ordered the bombing of Auschwitz, there is no record of any kind that indicates that either one ever heard of the proposal— even though Jewish leaders of all persuasions had clear access to both men.

A seemingly more reasonable proposal to bomb the railways to Auschwitz was made to Anthony Eden, the foreign minister of Great Britain, on July 6, 1944. Eden, with Churchill's immediate support, asked the RAF to examine the feasibility of doing so. The secretary of state for air, Sir Archibald Sinclair, replied several days later: "I entirely agree that it is our duty to consider every possible plan [to stop the murder of the Jews] but I am advised that interrupting the railways is out of our power. It is only by an enormous concentration of bomber forces that we have been able to interrupt communications in Normandy; the distance of Silesia from our bases entirely rules out doing anything of the kind." John McCloy had replied to a similar suggestion weeks earlier: "The War Department is of the opinion that the suggested air operation is impracticable for the reason that it could be executed only with the diversion of considerable air support essential to the success of our forces now engaged in decisive operations." Even the severest critics of America's response to the Nazi murder of the Jews acknowledge that successful interruption of railways required close observation of the severed lines and frequent rebombing, since repairs would take only a few days. Even bridges, which were costly to hit, were often back in operation in three or four days. Postwar studies of railway bombing totally vindicated the conclusion of the military authorities. Professor Istvan Deak of Columbia University asks in a recent article: "And if the rail lines had been bombed? The inmates of the cattle cars and those at the departure points would have been allowed to die of thirst, or of the heat, or of the cold, while the lines were being repaired."

It is often noted that American bombers were carrying out raids in the summer of 1944 on industrial targets only a few miles away from Auschwitz, suggesting how easy it would have been to bomb the gas chambers. They do not mention that preparation for the D-day invasion left only 12 percent of the U.S. Army Air Force available for the destruction of German fuel supplies, the primary mission as defined by Gen. Carl Spaatz. They point to the huge blowups of reconnaissance photographs at the Holocaust Museum that show not only the Farben synthetic-fuel plant, the target of the raids, but the outlines of Auschwitz and columns of prisoners. Yet the aerial photographs of Auschwitz on display were not developed until 1978, and their details were readable then only because advanced technology, developed by the CIA more than twenty years after the end of World War II, made it possible. *All* such strategic raids on military-industrial bases proceeded only after months of preparatory intelligence work, entailing the creation of a target folder with specific information about the size, hardness, structure placement, and defenses of the target and detailed aerial photography. These were costly, dangerous raids against heavily protected, frequently remote targets; the losses in men and planes were tragically heavy. The Allied air forces simply lacked the intelligence base necessary to plan and execute a bombing raid against the Auschwitz extermination camp. It would have been a nonmilitary mission. Only Roosevelt or Eisenhower could have ordered it, and as we have seen, no one proposed it to them.

Yet many insist that anti-Semitism alone spared Auschwitz the wrath of the Army Air Force. With this in mind, it is worth considering the plight of northern Holland, where during the last seven months of the war more than eighty thousand citizens starved to death because the German occupiers wanted to punish the Dutch for insurrection and strikes following the failed assault on Arnhem. The Allies knew what was happening. Allied armies were everywhere around this occupied segment of the Netherlands; air rescue, or at least the capacity for organizing food drops, was minutes away. Still, eighty thousand men, women, and children died while the forces that could have saved them remained intent on their objective of a military engagement with the Germans that would lead to victory in the shortest possible time. Perhaps these military decisions were wrong, but they were not made because of any bias against the Dutch—or, regarding Auschwitz, because of anti-Semitism.

And what of those who managed to escape the Nazis once the war had started? President Roosevelt created the War Refugee Board in January 1944, immediately upon Henry Morgenthau's presenting the case for doing so. There were thousands of refugees stranded on the outer peripheries of Nazi Europe. With the invasion of Italy in 1943, thousands more had sought safety in camps in the south. Tito's success in Yugoslavia had enabled many to escape from Croat fascism and Serb hatred. But those were refugees who were already saved. They were not escapees from the death camps. Under pressure from Roosevelt and Churchill, Spain kept open its frontiers, stating as its policy that "all refugees without exception would be allowed to enter and remain." Probably more than forty thousand, many of them Jewish, found safe sanctuary in Spain. Makeshift transit camps there and in

This blowup of a reconnaissance photograph, taken in September 1944, shows Auschwitz and columns of condemned prisoners. The Holocaust Museum displays similar pictures with captions that read "thousands were gassed daily in this industrial killing center, but the Allies decided to ignore it." Vanden Heuvel maintains that it was not until 1978 that the CIA developed the technology to decipher the details in these arial photographs.
(National Archives)

Portugal, Italy, and North Africa housed them in abysmal conditions. Those who fought for these people to come to America were right to do so; then, as now, refugees are generally powerless and voiceless. Governments have to be reminded constantly of their humanitarian responsibilities. But perhaps the Allied nations can be forgiven, in the midst of a war for survival, for not doing more for refugees whose lives had already been saved. . . .

Roosevelt's intervention with the government of Hungary, which by then understood that Nazi defeat was inevitable; the actions if the War Refugee Board,

such as retaining the heroic Raoul Wallenberg; the bombing of the Budapest area—all played a role in the rescue of half the Jewish community in Hungary. President Roosevelt was deeply and personally involved in this effort. Here is his statement to the nation on March 24, 1944: "In one of the blackest crimes of all history—begun by the Nazis in the day of peace and multiplied by them a hundred times in time of war—the wholesale systematic murder of the Jews of Europe goes on unabated every hour. As a result of the events of the last few days hundreds of thousands of Jews who, while living under persecution, have at least found a haven from death in Hungary and the Balkans, are now threatened with annihilation as Hitler's forces descend more heavily upon these lands. That these innocent people, who have already survived a decade of Hitler's fury, should perish on the very eve of triumph over the barbarism which their persecution symbolizes, would be a major tragedy. It is therefore fitting that we should again proclaim our determination that none who participate in these acts of savagery shall go unpunished. The United Nations have made it clear that they will pursue the guilty and deliver them up in order that justice be done. That warning applies not only to the leaders but also to their functionaries and subordinates in Germany and in the satellite countries. All who knowingly take part in the deportation of Jews to their death in Poland or Norwegians and French to their death in Germany are equally guilty with the executioner. All who share the guilt shall share the punishment." . . .

In December 1944 Anne O'Hare McCormick, a renowned foreign affairs reporter for *The New York Times,* wrote of a visit by a congressional delegation to the front in Italy. The congressmen expressed shock at the rigors of the campaign; they complained that this was one of the toughest battles of the war— and Americans were not being told about it. McCormick wrote: "The stories have been written and have been printed. They have even been overwritten and printed so many times that readers don't see the mud or blood anymore. They don't hear the screams of the shells or the thunder of the rockets. Congress either didn't read the accounts of the war in Italy or they couldn't take in the meaning of what they read. They had to see it. It is not their fault. It is because the thing is indescribable." How much more true is this insight regarding the death camps.

On April 12, 1945, General Eisenhower visited Ohrdruf Nord, the first concentration camp liberated by the American Army. "The things I saw beggar description," he wrote General Marshall. According to his biographer Stephen Ambrose, "Eisenhower had heard ominous rumors about the camps, of course, but never in his worst nightmares had he dreamed they could be so bad." He sent immediately for a delegation of congressional leaders and newspaper editors; he wanted to make sure Americans would never forget this. Five months later he dismissed his close friend and brilliant army commander Gen. George Patton for using former Nazi officials in his occupation structure and publicly likening "the Nazi thing" to differences between the Republicans and Democrats. (Patton had visited the Ohrdruf camp with Eisenhower and become physically ill from what he saw.)

Eisenhower got his first glimpse into the worst horrors at the heart of the Third Reich on the day death claimed the American who had done more than any other to bring them to an end. How ironic that Franklin Roosevelt—the man Hitler hated most, the leader constantly attacked by the isolationist press and derided by the anti-Semites, vilified by Goebbels as a "mentally ill cripple" and as "that Jew Rosenfeld"—should be faulted for being indifferent to the genocide. For all of us the shadow of doubt that enough was not done will always remain, even if there was little more that could have been done. But to say that "we are all guilty" allows the truly guilty to avoid that responsibility. It was Hitler who imagined the Holocaust and the Nazis who carried it out. We were not their accomplices. We destroyed them.

QUESTIONS TO CONSIDER

1 Would you agree with Winston Churchill that the Holocaust "was probably the greatest and most terrible crime ever committed in the whole history of the world"? After reading this selection, do you believe that the American government did all within its power to prevent it?

2 Why does vanden Heuvel argue that most German Jews, in spite of the anti-Semitism that they faced in their daily lives, were reluctant to abandon their homeland? When did emigration from Germany become virtually impossible?

3 Explain how immigration laws dictated the number of refugees who could enter the United States. Why did labor organizers, business leaders, and many members of Congress want to maintain those quotas? After *Kristallnacht,* about what percentage of immigrants who came to the United States were Jewish?

4 Why did both Cuba and the United States refuse to accept most of the Jewish passengers on the *St. Louis?* What did the future hold for most of those desperate travelers? Are you satisfied with vanden Heuvel's explanation that the United States did all it could given its restrictive immigration laws?

5 How do we know that, during the war years, President Roosevelt and the American people in general had knowledge of the senseless slaughter of Jews in the concentration camps? Why was there no attempt to bomb Auschwitz or the railroad lines leading to that death camp? What did Roosevelt believe was the most effective strategy to end the Holocaust?

6 What was the reaction of Generals Eisenhower and Patton when they liberated the death camps? In an age before instantaneous television film coverage, could the American people, Jews and gentiles, envision the horror of the Holocaust? Do you view this selection as an apology for American actions or a realistic appraisal of the response the United States adopted toward the Holocaust?

PART TEN

The Bomb

20 The Biggest Decision: Why We Had to Drop the Atomic Bomb

ROBERT JAMES MADDOX

Perhaps the most controversial episode of the Second World War was the decision of the American civil and military leadership to drop atomic bombs on Japan in order to win the Pacific war. To place the debate in proper context, let us review what had transpired in the Pacific theater. In November 1943, American forces moved from a holding action to an aggressive, two-pronged island-hopping campaign, with Admiral Chester Nimitz's forces attacking at Tarawa and Kwajalein and General Douglas MacArthur's command breaking through the Japanese barrier on the Bismarck Archipelago, islands in the South Pacific. Eventually, MacArthur recaptured the Philippines while Nimitz pushed toward Japan itself from the central Pacific.

Japan fought back desperately, sending out kamikaze planes to slow the American advance with suicidal dives against United States warships. The kamikazes took a terrible toll: 34 American ships sunk and 288 damaged. But the "Divine Wind" vengeance that the kamikazes represented also cost the Japanese heavily: their losses were estimated at 1,288 to 4,000 planes and pilots. Moreover, they could not stop American army and naval forces, which moved on relentlessly, capturing Iwo Jima and then Okinawa, located just south of the Japanese home islands.

From Okinawa, the United States planned to launch an all-out invasion of the Japanese home islands, to begin sometime in November 1945. Army and naval leaders thought initial casualties would run from 31,000 to 50,000. But ultimately the losses could be staggering if it took a year to break Japanese resistance, as some experts predicted.

The invasion, however, never took place, because the United States soon had an awesome and terrible alternative. On July 16, 1945, after three years of top-secret development and production,

American scientists successfully detonated an atomic bomb in the New Mexico desert. Some scientists involved in the project urged privately that a demonstration bomb be dropped on an uninhabited island. But an advisory committee of scientists opposed any such demonstration and recommended that the bomb be used against Japan at once. Secretary of War Henry L. Stimson emphatically agreed: while the bomb would kill thousands of civilians, he said, it would shock Japan into surrendering and save thousands of American lives. Had the soldiers and marines in America's Pacific forces known about the bomb, they would have agreed, emphatically.

The final decision lay with Harry Truman, who became president after Roosevelt had died of a brain hemorrhage in April 1945. "I regarded the bomb as a military weapon and never had any doubt that it should be used," Truman later wrote. "The top military advisers to the president recommended its use, and when I talked to [British Prime Minister Winston] Churchill he unhesitatingly told me that he favored the use of the atomic bomb if it might aid to end the war." On July 25, Truman ordered that atomic bombs be dropped on or about August 3, unless Japan surrendered before that date. Then the United States, Great Britain, and China sent the Japanese an ultimatum that demanded unconditional surrender. The Japanese made an ambiguous reply. When August 3 passed and Japan fought on, Truman's orders went into effect, and American B-29s unleashed two of the "superhuman fireballs of destruction"—the first on Hiroshima, the other on Nagasaki—that forced Japan to surrender. Thus, the Pacific war ended as it had begun—with a devastating air raid. You may find it profitable to compare the Pearl Harbor air raid, a sneak attack against military targets (described in selection 18) with the nuclear blast at Hiroshima (covered in the following selection), which annihilated an entire city, including civilians and military installations.

Ever since, the use of the bomb has generated extraordinarily heated debate. Those against the bomb argue passionately that the monstrous weapon was not the only alternative open to Truman and his advisers in July and August. They point out that the invasion of Japan was not scheduled until November, so Truman had plenty of time "to seek and use alternatives." He could have sought a Russian declaration of war against Japan, or he could have ignored the advisory committee of scientists and dropped a demonstration bomb to show Japan what an apocalyptic weapon it was. He had another bomb to drop if the Japanese remained unimpressed. But Truman, in a remarkable display of "moral insensitivity," used the bomb because it was there to be used, and he never questioned his decision. To these critics, it is almost unthinkable that Truman and his advisers should ignore the entire moral question of dropping the bombs on civilians and ushering in a frightening and unpredictable atomic age. To this day, they point out with despair, America remains the only nation that has ever dropped an atomic bomb on another.

Other critics contend that Truman employed the bomb with an eye toward postwar politics. In their view, the president wanted to end the war in a hurry, before the Soviet Union could enter the conflict against Japan, seize territory, and threaten America's role in the postwar balance of power. Still others argue that the United States could have offered the Japanese conditional surrender, or found other ways to demonstrate the bomb, and so could have ended the war before the Soviets entered it.

Many analysts, however, defend Truman as passionately as his critics denounce him. Those for the bomb insist that his decision was a wise one that avoided a protracted land invasion in which hundreds of thousands of soldiers and civilians would have died. Sure, the bomb killed civilians, these critics say; it was unavoidable because the Japanese established military installations in residential areas of Hiroshima and Nagasaki. Besides, the Japanese could not complain: in their aggressions in Asia, the Japanese military had left 8 million civilians dead. "Did we have to drop the bomb?" asked a physicist who helped develop it. "You bet your life we did." He referred to a recent demonstration in the United States in memory of Hiroshima. "No one seems to realize," he said, "that without Pearl Harbor there wouldn't have been a Hiroshima."

In the following selection, historian Robert James Maddox of Pennsylvania State University presents the case for the bomb. Drawing on all available facts, he demolishes the "myths" of the anti-bomb school, one of which holds that several leading military advisers beseeched Truman not to use the bomb. As Maddox says, there is no evidence that a single one of them did so. After the war, Truman and others maintained that half a million American soldiers would have fallen if the United States had been forced to invade the Japanese home islands. Truman's critics have dismissed such claims as "gross exaggerations designed to forestall scrutiny of Truman's real motives." They point out that a war-plans committee estimated "only" 193,500 casualties. Maddox lampoons "the notion that 193,500 anticipated casualties were too insignificant to have caused Truman to resort to atomic bombs" and concludes that they were indeed necessary to end the war: the Japanese army, which ran the country, was preparing to fight to the last man, and the bomb was the only way to bring Japanese leaders to their senses and force them to surrender.

GLOSSARY

BOCK'S CAR   Nickname of the B-29 that dropped a second atomic bomb, called Fat Man, on Nagasaki.

ENOLA GAY   Nickname of the B-29 that dropped the first atomic bomb, called Little Boy, on Hiroshima.

GREW, JOSEPH   Truman's undersecretary of state; he had spent ten years in Japan as an ambassador and believed that the Japanese in the summer of 1945 were not even close to surrendering. Their "peace feelers," he claimed, were "familiar weapons of psychological warfare" whose purpose was to "divide the Allies."

HIROHITO   Emperor of Japan; the Japanese believed that the very soul of their nation resided in him.

JOINT WAR PLANS COMMITTEE (JWPC)   A report from this committee estimated that an American invasion of the Japanese home islands of Kyushu and Honshu would result in 193,500 total casualties in dead, wounded, and missing.

KAMIKAZES   Nickname for the Japanese pilots who flew suicide missions against United States naval forces toward the end of the Pacific war; the objective of the kamikazes was to crash their bomb-laden planes into American warships. The term *kamikaze* means "Divine Wind" in Japanese.

KONOYE, PRINCE FUMINARO   Sent to Moscow as a personal envoy of Emperor Hirohito. Prince Konoye sought to open negotiations that would lead to an end to the Pacific war.

MacARTHUR, GENERAL DOUGLAS   Commander of the army's half of the island-hopping campaign in the Pacific; it ran through the Carolinas and Solomons to the Philippines.

MARSHALL, GENERAL GEORGE C.   Army chief of staff during the Second World War and a close adviser to both Roosevelt and Truman. Warning that it was difficult to estimate battle casualties in advance, Marshall nevertheless thought that initial American losses from an invasion of Japan would be around 31,000 men. A subsequent medical report estimated that "total battle and non-battle casualties might run as high as 394,859" for the invasion of the southernmost Japanese island alone. Marshall not only supported Truman's decision to drop the atomic bomb on Japan, but considered using such bombs as tactical weapons during the land invasion.

NIMITZ, ADMIRAL CHESTER W.   Commander of the Pacific Ocean area; he headed the United States Navy's island-hopping campaign that led to the costly Battle of Okinawa; he believed that an invasion of Kyushu, the southernmost Japanese home island, ought to follow the operation at Okinawa.

OLYMPIC   Code name for the first phase of an American invasion of Japan, to commence at Kyushu, the southernmost home island, on November 1, 1945.

OPERATION CORNET   Code name for the United States invasion of Honshu, the main Japanese home island, on March 1, 1946.

SATO, NAOTAKI   Japanese ambassador to the Soviet Union in 1945.

TOGO, SHIGENORI   Japanese foreign minister in 1945; he made an overture to the Soviets asking that they initiate peace talks between Japan and the United States.

On the morning of August 6, 1945, the American B-29 *Enola Gay* dropped an atomic bomb on the Japanese city of Hiroshima. Three days later another B-29, *Bock's Car,* released one over Nagasaki. Both caused enormous casualties and physical destruction. These two cataclysmic events have preyed upon the American conscience ever since. The furor over the Smithsonian Institution's *Enola Gay* exhibit and over the mushroom-cloud postage stamp in the autumn of 1994 are merely the most obvious examples. Harry S Truman and other officials claimed that the bombs caused Japan to surrender, thereby avoiding a bloody invasion. Critics have accused them of at best failing to explore alternatives, at worst of using the bombs primarily to make the Soviet Union "more manageable" rather than to defeat a Japan they knew already was on the verge of capitulation.

By any rational calculation Japan was a beaten nation by the summer of 1945. Conventional bombing had reduced many of its cities to rubble, blockade had strangled its importation of vitally needed materials, and its navy had sustained such heavy losses as to be powerless to interfere with the invasion everyone knew was coming. By late June advancing American forces had completed the conquest of Okinawa, which lay only 350 miles from the southernmost Japanese home island of Kyushu. They now stood poised for the final onslaught.

Rational calculations did not determine Japan's position. Although a peace faction within the government wished to end the war—provided certain conditions were met—militants were prepared to fight on regardless of consequences. They claimed to welcome an invasion of the home islands, promising to inflict such hideous casualties that the United States would retreat from its announced policy of unconditional surrender. The militarists held effective power over the government and were capable of defying the emperor, as they had in the past, on the ground that his civilian advisers were misleading him.

Okinawa provided a preview of what invasion of the home islands would entail. Since April 1 the Japanese had fought with a ferocity that mocked any notion that their will to resist was eroding. They had inflicted nearly 50,000 casualties on the invaders, many resulting from the first large-scale use of kamikazes. They also had dispatched the superbattleship *Yamato* on a suicide mission to Okinawa, where, after attacking American ships offshore, it was to plunge ashore to become a huge, doomed steel fortress. *Yamato* was sunk shortly after leaving port, but its mission symbolized Japan's willingness to sacrifice everything in an apparently hopeless cause.

The Japanese could be expected to defend their sacred homeland with even greater fervor, and kamikazes flying at short range promised to be even more devastating than at Okinawa. The Japanese had more than 2,000,000 troops in the home islands, were training millions of irregulars, and for some time had been conserving aircraft that might have been used to protect Japanese cities against American bombers.

Reports from Tokyo indicated that Japan meant to fight the war to a finish. On June 8 an imperial conference adopted "The Fundamental Policy to Be Followed Henceforth in the Conduct of the War," which pledged to "prosecute the war to the bitter end in order to uphold the national polity, protect the imperial land, and accomplish the objectives for which we went to war." Truman had no reason to believe that the proclamation meant anything other than what it said.

Against this background, while fighting on Okinawa still continued, the President had his naval chief

Robert James Maddox, "The Biggest Decision: Why We Had to Drop the Atomic Bomb," *American Heritage,* vol. 46, no. 3 (May/June 1995), pp. 71–74, 76–77. Reprinted by permission of *American Heritage* magazine, a division of Forbes, Inc. © Forbes, Inc., 1995.

of staff, Adm. William D. Leahy, notify the Joint Chiefs of Staff (JCS) and the Secretaries of War and Navy that a meeting would be held at the White House on June 18. The night before the conference Truman wrote in his diary that "I have to decide Japanese strategy—shall we invade Japan proper or shall we bomb and blockade? That is my hardest decision to date. But I'll make it when I have all the facts."

Truman met with the chiefs at three-thirty in the afternoon. Present were Army Chief of Staff Gen. George C. Marshall, Army Air Force's Gen. Ira C. Eaker (sitting in for the Army Air Force's chief of staff, Henry H. Arnold, who was on an inspection tour of installations in the Pacific), Navy Chief of Staff Adm. Ernest J. King, Leahy (also a member of the JCS), Secretary of the Navy James Forrestal, Secretary of War Henry L. Stimson, and Assistant Secretary of War John J. McCloy. Truman opened the meeting, then asked Marshall for his views. Marshall was the dominant figure on the JCS. He was Truman's most trusted military adviser, as he had been President Franklin D. Roosevelt's.

Marshall reported that the chiefs, supported by the Pacific commanders Gen. Douglas MacArthur and Adm. Chester W. Nimitz, agreed that an invasion of Kyushu "appears to be the least costly worthwhile operation following Okinawa." Lodgment in Kyushu, he said, was necessary to make blockade and bombardment more effective and to serve as a staging area for the invasion of Japan's main island of Honshu. The chiefs recommended a target date of November 1 for the first phase, code-named Olympic, because delay would give the Japanese more time to prepare and because bad weather might postpone the invasion "and hence the end of the war" for up to six months. Marshall said that in his opinion, Olympic was "the only course to pursue." The chiefs also proposed that Operation Cornet be launched against Honshu on March 1, 1946.

Leahy's memorandum calling the meeting had asked for casualty projections which that invasion might be expected to produce. Marshall stated that

campaigns in the Pacific had been so diverse "it is considered wrong" to make total estimates. All he would say was the casualties during the first thirty days on Kyushu should not exceed those sustained taking Luzon in the Philippines—31,000 men killed, wounded, or missing in action. "It is a grim fact," Marshall said, "that there is not an easy, bloodless way to victory in war." Leahy estimated a higher casualty rate similar to Okinawa, and King guessed somewhere in between.

King and Eaker, speaking for the Navy and the Army Air Forces respectively, endorsed Marshall's proposals. King said that he had become convinced that Kyushu was "the key to success of any siege operations." He recommended that "we should do Kyushu now" and begin preparations for invading Honshu. Eaker "agreed completely" with Marshall. He said he had just received a message from Arnold also expressing "complete agreement." Air Force plans called for the use of forty groups of heavy bombers, which "could not be deployed without the use of airfields on Kyushu." Stimson and Forrestal concurred.

Truman summed up. He considered "the Kyushu plan all right from the military standpoint" and directed the chiefs to "go ahead with it." He said he "had hoped that there was a possibility of preventing an Okinawa from one end of Japan to the other," but "he was clear on the situation now" and was "quite sure" the chiefs should proceed with the plan. Just before the meeting adjourned, McCloy raised the possibility of avoiding an invasion by warning the Japanese that the United States would employ atomic weapons if there were no surrender. The ensuing discussion was inconclusive because the first test was a month away and no one could be sure the weapons would work.

In his memoirs Truman claimed that using atomic bombs prevented an invasion that would have cost 500,000 American lives. Other officials mentioned the same or even higher figures. Critics have assailed such statements as gross exaggerations designed to forestall scrutiny of Truman's real motives. They have given wide publicity to the report prepared by the Joint War Plans Committee (JWPC) for the chiefs'

A Japanese soldier surrendering on Okinawa in May 1945. This was unusual. Most Japanese soldiers refused to surrender—it violated their sacred code of honor—and fought to the death. Robert James Maddox points out that "Okinawa provided a preview of what invasion of the [Japanese] home islands would entail. Since

April 1 the Japanese had fought with a ferocity that mocked any notion that their will to resist was eroding. . . . The Japanese could be expected to defend their sacred homeland with even greater fervor." (UPI/Corbis-Bettmann)

meeting with Truman. The committee estimated that the invasion of Kyushu, followed by that of Honshu, as the chiefs proposed, would cost approximately 40,000 dead, 150,000 wounded, and 3,500 missing in action for a total of 193,500 casualties.

That those responsible for a decision should exaggerate the consequences of alternatives is common-place. Some who cite the JWPC report profess to see more sinister motives, insisting that such "low" casualty projections call into question the very idea that atomic bombs were used to avoid heavy losses. By discrediting that justification as a cover-up, they seek to bolster their contention that the bombs really were used to permit the employment of "atomic diplomacy" against the Soviet Union.

The notion that 193,500 anticipated casualties were too insignificant to have caused Truman to resort to atomic bombs might seem bizarre to anyone other than an academic, but let it pass. Those who have cited the JWPC report in countless op-ed pieces in newspapers and in magazine articles have created a myth by omitting key considerations: First, the report itself is studded with qualifications that casualties "are not subject to accurate estimate" and that the projection "is admittedly only an educated guess." Second, the figures never were conveyed to Truman. They were excised at high military echelons, which is why Marshall cited only estimates for the first thirty days on Kyushu. And indeed, subsequent Japanese troop buildups on Kyushu rendered the

JWPC estimates totally irrelevant by the time the first atomic bomb was dropped.

Another myth that has attained wide attention is that at least several of Truman's top military advisers later informed him that using atomic bombs against Japan would be militarily unnecessary or immoral, or both. There is no persuasive evidence that any of them did so. None of the Joint Chiefs ever made such a claim, although one inventive author has tried to make it appear that Leahy did by braiding together several unrelated passages from the admiral's memoirs. Actually, two days after Hiroshima, Truman told aides that Leahy had "said up to the last that it wouldn't go off."

Neither MacArthur nor Nimitz ever communicated to Truman any change of mind about the need for invasion or expressed reservations about using the bombs. When first informed about their imminent use only days before Hiroshima, MacArthur responded with a lecture on the future of atomic warfare and even after Hiroshima strongly recommended that the invasion go forward. Nimitz, from whose jurisdiction the atomic strikes would be launched, was notified in early 1945. "This sounds fine," he told the courier, "but this is only February. Can't we get one sooner?" Nimitz later would join Air Force generals Carl D. Spaatz, Nathan Twining, and Curtis LeMay in recommending that a third bomb be dropped on Tokyo.

Only Dwight D. Eisenhower later claimed to have remonstrated against the use of the bomb. In his *Crusade in Europe*, published in 1948, he wrote that when Secretary Stimson informed him during the Potsdam Conference of plans to use the bomb, he replied that he hoped "we would never have to use such a thing against any enemy," because he did not want the United States to be the first to use such a weapon. He added, "My views were merely personal and immediate reactions; they were not based on any analysis of the subject."

Eisenhower's recollections grew more colorful as the years went on. A later account of his meeting with Stimson had it taking place at Ike's headquarters in Frankfurt on the very day news arrived on the successful atomic test in New Mexico. "We'd had a nice evening at headquarters in Germany," he remembered. Then, after dinner, "Stimson got this cable saying that the bomb had been perfected and was ready to be dropped. The cable was in code . . . 'the lamb is born' or some damn thing like that." In this version Eisenhower claimed to have protested vehemently that "the Japanese were ready to surrender and it wasn't necessary to hit them with that awful thing." "Well," Eisenhower concluded, "the old gentleman got furious."

The best that can be said about Eisenhower's memory is that it had become flawed by the passage of time. Stimson was in Potsdam and Eisenhower in Frankfurt on July 16, when word came of the successful test. Aside from a brief conversation at a flag-raising ceremony in Berlin on July 20, the only other time they met was at Ike's headquarters on July 27. By then orders already had been sent to the Pacific to use the bombs if Japan had not yet surrendered. Notes made by one of Stimson's aides indicate that there was a discussion of atomic bombs, but there is no mention of any protest on Eisenhower's part. Even if there had been, two factors must be kept in mind. Eisenhower had commanded Allied forces in Europe, and his opinion on how close Japan was to surrender would have carried no special weight. More important, Stimson left for home immediately after the meeting and could not have personally conveyed Ike's sentiments to the President, who did not return to Washington until after Hiroshima.

On July 8 the Combined Intelligence Committee submitted to the American and British Combined Chiefs of Staff a report entitled "Estimate of the Enemy Situation." The committee predicted that as Japan's position continued to deteriorate, it might "make a serious effort to use the USSR [then a neutral] as a mediator in ending the war." Tokyo also would put out "intermittent peace feelers" to "weaken the determination of the United Nations to fight to the bitter end, or to create inter-allied dissension." While the Japanese people would be willing to make large concessions to end the war, "For a surrender to be acceptable to the Japanese army, it would be necessary for the military leaders to believe that it would not entail discrediting warrior tradition and that it would permit the ultimate resurgence of a military Japan."

Small wonder that American officials remained unimpressed when Japan proceeded to do exactly what the committee predicted. On July 12 Japanese Foreign Minister Shigenori Togo instructed Ambassador Naotaki Sato in Moscow to inform the Soviets that the emperor wished to send a personal envoy, Prince Fuminaro Konoye, in an attempt "to restore peace with all possible speed." Although he realized Konoye could not reach Moscow before the Soviet leader Joseph Stalin and Foreign Minister V. M. Molotov left to attend a Big Three meeting scheduled to begin in Potsdam on the fifteenth, Togo sought to have negotiations begin as soon as they returned.

American officials had long since been able to read Japanese diplomatic traffic through a process known as the MAGIC intercepts. Army intelligence (G-2) prepared for General Marshall its interpretation of Togo's message the next day. The report listed several possible constructions, the most probable being that the Japanese "governing clique" was making a coordinated effort to "stave off defeat" through Soviet intervention and an "appeal to war weariness in the United States." The report added that Undersecretary of State Joseph C. Grew, who had spent ten years in Japan as ambassador, "agrees with these conclusions."

Some have claimed that Togo's overture to the Soviet Union, together with attempts by some minor Japanese officials in Switzerland and other neutral countries to get peace talks started through the Office of Strategic Services (OSS), constituted clear evidence that the Japanese were near surrender. Their sole prerequisite was retention of their sacred emperor, whose unique cultural/religious status within the Japanese polity they would not compromise. If only the United States had extended assurances about the emperor, according to this view, much bloodshed and the atomic bombs would have been unnecessary.

A careful reading of the MAGIC intercepts of subsequent exchanges between Togo and Sato provides no evidence that retention of the emperor was the sole obstacle to peace. What they show instead is that the Japanese Foreign Office was trying to cut a deal through the Soviet Union that would have permitted Japan to retain its political system and its prewar empire intact. Even the most lenient American official could not have countenanced such a settlement.

Togo on July 17 informed Sato that "we are not asking the Russians' mediation in *anything like unconditional surrender* [emphasis added]." During the following weeks Sato pleaded with his superiors to abandon hope of Soviet intercession and to approach the United States directly to find out what peace terms would be offered. "There is . . . no alternative but immediate unconditional surrender," he cabled on July 31, and he bluntly informed Togo that "your way of looking at things and the actual situation in the Eastern Area may be seen to be absolutely contradictory." The Foreign Ministry ignored his pleas and continued to seek Soviet help even after Hiroshima.

"Peace feelers" by Japanese officials abroad seemed no more promising from the American point of view. Although several of the consular personnel and military attachés engaged in these activities claimed important connections at home, none produced verification. Had the Japanese government sought only an assurance about the emperor, all it had to do was grant one of these men authority to begin talks through the OSS. Its failure to do so led American officials to assume that those involved were either well-meaning individuals acting alone or that they were being orchestrated by Tokyo. Grew characterized such "peace feelers" as "familiar weapons of psychological warfare" designed to "divide the Allies."

Some American officials, such as Stimson and Grew, nonetheless wanted to signal the Japanese that they might retain the emperorship in the form of a constitutional monarchy. Such an assurance might remove the last stumbling block to surrender, if not when it was issued, then later. Only an imperial rescript would bring about an orderly surrender, they argued, without which Japanese forces would fight to the last man regardless of what the government in Tokyo did. Besides, the emperor could serve as a stabilizing factor during the transition to peacetime.

There were many arguments against an American initiative. Some opposed retaining such an undemocratic institution on principle and because they feared it might later serve as a rallying point for future militarism. Should that happen, as one assistant Secretary of State put it, "those lives already spent will have been sacrificed in vain, and lives will be lost again in the future." Japanese hard-liners were certain to exploit an overture as evidence that losses sustained at Okinawa had weakened American resolve and to argue that continued resistance would bring further concessions. Stalin, who earlier had told an American envoy that he favored abolishing the emperorship because the ineffectual Hirohito might be succeeded by "an energetic and vigorous figure who could cause trouble," was just as certain to interpret it as a treacherous effort to end the war before the Soviets could share in the spoils.

There were domestic considerations as well. Roosevelt had announced the unconditional surrender policy in early 1943, and it since had become a slogan of the war. He also had advocated that peoples everywhere should have the right to choose their own form of government, and Truman had publicly pledged to carry out his predecessor's legacies. For him to have formally *guaranteed* continuance of the emperorship, as opposed to merely accepting it on American terms pending free elections, as he later did, would have constituted a blatant repudiation of his own promises.

Nor was that all. Regardless of the emperor's actual role in Japanese aggression, which is still debated, much wartime propaganda had encouraged Americans to regard Hirohito as no less a war criminal than Adolf Hitler or Benito Mussolini. Although Truman said on several occasions that he had no objection to retaining the emperor, he understandably refused to make the first move. The ultimatum he issued from Potsdam on July 26 did not refer specifically to the emperorship. All it said was that occupation forces would be removed after "a peaceful and responsible" government had been established according to the "freely expressed will of the Japanese people." When the Japanese rejected the ultimatum rather than at least inquire whether they might retain the emperor, Truman permitted the plans for using the bombs to go forward.

Reliance on MAGIC intercepts and the "peace feelers" to gauge how near Japan was to surrender is misleading in any case. The army, not the Foreign Office, controlled the situation. Intercepts of Japanese military communication, designated ULTRA, provided no reason to believe the army was even considering surrender. Japanese Imperial Headquarters had correctly guessed that the next operation after Okinawa would be Kyushu and was making every effort to bolster its defenses there.

General Marshall reported on July 24 that there were "approximately 500,000 troops in Kyushu" and that more were on the way. ULTRA identified new units arriving almost daily. MacArthur's G-2 reported on July 29 that "this threatening development, if not checked, may grow to a point where we attack on a ratio of one (1) to one (1) which is not the recipe for victory." By the time the first atomic bomb fell, ULTRA indicated that there were 560,000 troops in southern Kyushu (the actual figure was closer to 900,000), and projections for November 1 placed the number at 680,000. A report, for medical purposes, of July 31 estimated that total battle and nonbattle casualties might run as high as 394,859 *for the Kyushu operation alone*. This figure did not include those men expected to be killed outright, for obviously they would require no medical attention. Marshall regarded Japanese defenses as so formidable that even after Hiroshima he asked MacArthur to consider alternate landing sites and began contemplating the use of atomic bombs as tactical weapons to support the invasion.

The thirty-day casualty projection of 31,000 Marshall had given Truman at the June 18 strategy meeting had become meaningless. It had been based on the assumption that the Japanese had about 350,000 defenders in Kyushu and that naval and air interdiction would preclude significant reinforcement. But the Japanese buildup since that time meant that the defenders would have nearly twice the number of troops available by "X-day" than earlier assumed. The assertion that apprehensions about casualties are insufficient to explain Truman's use of the bombs, therefore, cannot be taken seriously. On the contrary, as Winston Churchill wrote after a conversation with him at Potsdam, Truman was tormented by "the terrible responsibilities that rested upon him in regard to the unlimited effusion of American blood."

Some historians have argued that while the first bomb *might* have been required to achieve Japanese surrender, dropping the second constituted a needless barbarism. The record shows otherwise. American officials believed more than one bomb would be necessary because they assumed Japanese hard-liners would minimize the first explosion or attempt to explain it away as some sort of natural catastrophe, precisely what they did. The Japanese minister of war, for instance, at first refused even to admit that the Hiroshima bomb was atomic. A few hours after Nagasaki he told the cabinet that "the Americans appeared to have one hundred atomic bombs . . . they could drop three per day. The next target might well be Tokyo."

Even after both bombs had fallen and Russia entered the war, Japanese militants insisted on such lenient peace terms that moderates knew there was no sense even transmitting them to the United States. Hirohito had to intervene personally on two occasions during the next few days to induce hard-liners to abandon their conditions and to accept the American stipulation that the emperor's authority "shall be subject to the Supreme Commander of the Allied Powers." That the militarists would have accepted such a settlement before the bombs is farfetched, to say the least.

Some writers have argued that the cumulative effects of battlefield defeats, conventional bombing, and naval blockade already had defeated Japan. Even without extending assurances about the emperor, all the United States had to do was wait. The most frequently cited basis for this contention is the *United States Strategic Bombing Survey,* published in 1946, which stated that Japan would have surrendered by November 1 "even if the atomic bombs had not been dropped, even if Russia had not entered the war, and even if no invasion had been planned or contemplated." Recent scholarship by the historian Robert P. Newman and others has demonstrated that the survey was "cooked" by those who prepared it to arrive at such a conclusion. No matter. This or any other document based on information available only after the war ended is irrelevant with regard to what Truman could have known at the time.

What often goes unremarked is that when the bombs were dropped, fighting was still going on in the Philippines, China, and elsewhere. Every day that the war continued thousands of prisoners of war had to live and die in abysmal conditions, and there were rumors that the Japanese intended to slaughter them if the homeland was invaded. Truman was Commander in Chief of the American armed forces, and he had a duty to the men under his command not shared by those sitting in moral judgment decades later. Available evidence points to the conclusion that he acted for the reason he said he did: to end a bloody war that would have become far bloodier had invasion proved necessary. One can only imagine what would have happened if tens of thousands of American boys had died or been wounded on Japanese soil and then it had become known that Truman had chosen not to use weapons that might have ended the war months sooner.

QUESTIONS TO CONSIDER

1 What do you feel about Truman's decision to drop the atomic bomb on Japan? Do you think it was the right choice under the circumstances, or do you think it was wrong? What alternatives did he have? Would any of them have convinced the Japanese to accept America's terms of "unconditional surrender"?
2 Why did Truman and his advisers demand "unconditional surrender" by the Japanese? Why did

Japan's political and military leaders balk at accepting such terms? Why were they so determined to preserve the Emperor? What was the American view of him?

3 Much has been made of the estimated casualties the Americans would have suffered had they been forced to invade the Japanese homeland. To invade the first home island alone (this was Kyushu), Marshall came up with one casualty figure and Admiral Leahy with a somewhat higher figure for the first month of fighting. The Report of the Joint War Plans Committee estimated total losses from an invasion of the Japanese homeland at 193,500. After the war, Truman claimed that an invasion would have resulted in 500,000 American deaths. How do you explain such discrepancies? What does Professor Maddox say about them? Were Japanese forces on Kyushu and the main home island, Honshu, strong enough to inflict such losses? What is Maddox's opinion of critics who use the estimate of the Joint War Plans Committee to condemn Truman?

4 Why did the Japanese look to Stalin's regime in hopes of securing favorable peace terms? Why did the Soviet Union refuse to intercede in Japan's behalf in an effort to end the Pacific war? Had the Soviets approached the United States, asking for terms for Japan other than unconditional surrender, how do you think Truman and his advisers would have reacted?

5 What do you think might have happened had the Truman administration decided not to use its nuclear capacity against Japan?

21 Hiroshima: The Victims

FLETCHER KNEBEL AND CHARLES W. BAILEY II

One of our friends, who thinks that dropping the bomb was a necessity, believes nevertheless that the horrors it visited on Hiroshima and Nagasaki ought never to be forgotten. Indeed, perhaps the best argument against the bomb is what it did to its victims, which is the subject of the following selection. It and the previous selection ought to generate fiery discussions in every classroom in which Portrait of America *is read.*

For the people of Hiroshima and Nagasaki, the questions faced by Truman and his advisers did not matter. Nothing mattered to them but the searing flash of light that ultimately killed some 130,000 people in Hiroshima and 60,000 to 70,000 in Nagasaki and scarred and twisted thousands more. One scorched watch, found in the wreckage at Hiroshima, stopped at the exact moment of the atomic blast: 8:16 A.M. When the bomb exploded two thousand feet above the center of the city, thousands of people "were simply burned black and dead where they stood by the radiant heat that turned central Hiroshima into a gigantic oven." Some 60 percent of the city—roughly four square miles—was totally vaporized. "Beyond the zone of utter death and destruction," as one history puts it, "lightly built houses were knocked flat as far as three miles from ground zero, so that 80 percent of all buildings were destroyed and almost all the rest badly damaged." Nothing was left of Hiroshima but smoking, radioactive rubble. After the second bomb wrought similar destruction on Nagasaki, Emperor Hirohito spoke to his people by radio—the first time he had ever communicated with them. "The enemy," he said, "who has recently made use of an inhuman bomb, is incessantly subjecting innocent people to grievous wounds and massacre. The devastation is taking on incalculable proportions. To continue the war under these conditions would not only lead to the annihilation of Our Nation, but the destruction of human civilization as well."

Since then, a number of books have appeared about the atomic explosions at Hiroshima and Nagasaki. Among the best are J. Samuel Walker's Prompt and Utter Destruction *(1997), John Hersey's* Hiroshima *(1946), available in a new edition, and* No High Ground *(1960), by Fletcher Knebel and Charles W. Bailey II. The latter recounts the entire history of the first atomic bomb at Hiroshima, from Truman's decision to use it, to the flight of the* Enola Gay *(which dropped "Little Boy," as the bomb was called), up to the actual explosion and its cataclysmic results. In this selection, Knebel and Bailey describe that explosion with telling details, narrating the experiences of several people who somehow lived through that "fireball of destruction." Telling the personal side of Hiroshima is what makes this such a powerful account, with implicit lessons about the horror of nuclear war that have universal resonance. We can all identify with the people here, with Mr. Nukushina, Mrs. Susukida, and Dr. Imagawa, as the atomic blast swept over their city and changed the world forever.*

GLOSSARY

ENOLA GAY Nickname of the B-29 that dropped the atomic bomb called "Little Boy" on Hiroshima.

HIRANO, MAJOR TOSAKU Staff officer stationed in Hiroshima, he had gone up to Tokyo, and his decision to stay there a couple of extra nights saved his life; later, he persuaded Japan's leading nuclear scientist, who already suspected that the bomb dropped on Hiroshima was a nuclear weapon, to fly there and investigate.

DR. IMAGAWA Visiting a patient's home when the bomb burst, he found himself "standing on top of a five-foot pile of rubble" with his clothes shredded; he made for his home in a suburb, helping the wounded along the way.

KINOSHITA, HIDEO An officer at the monitoring station of the Japanese quasi-governmental news agency near Tokyo, he reported to his boss the news from America that an atomic bomb had been dropped on Hiroshima, and the boss relayed that report to the chief secretary of the Japanese cabinet.

NAKAMURA, BIN Subchief of the Hiroshima bureau of Japan's news agency, he was eating breakfast when the explosion "lifted him off the straw mat on which he was sitting and sent a wave of 'immense' heat washing over his face"; miraculously unhurt, he spent the day interviewing survivors and got a story out on a suburban radio station.

NUKUSHINA, MICHIYOSHI Fire-truck driver at the Hiroshima Army Ordnance Supply Depot, he had just returned home when the bomb exploded, flattening his home and blowing him into a corner where two safes prevented the falling roof from crushing him; he eventually found himself at an emergency aid station on Ninoshima Island.

OPPENHEIMER, J. ROBERT Scientist and director of the top-secret project at Los Alamos, New Mexico, that built the first atomic bomb.

SAKAMOTO, CHINAYO A mother who was mopping her kitchen floor when the *Enola Gay* droned by overhead, she and her family escaped "the blast and fire," because their home was situated behind a high protective hill.

SAKAMOTO, MIHO Chinayo Sakamoto's daughter-in-law, who, after learning that her husband and his entire military unit had been wiped out, slit her throat with a razor in front of a little altar.

SUSUKIDA, HAYANO Picking up salvaged roof tiles with other volunteers, she found herself suddenly slammed to the ground, her back severely burned, and her watch blown off; she made it to the emergency aid station on Ninoshima Island.

YAMAGUCHI, YUKO She lived with her children in a rented farmhouse in a suburb and was just cleaning up after breakfast when the walls exploded in a black cloud of soot; unhurt, she went into the wrecked city and found her father and mother, both dying, in a Red Cross hospital; she never did find her husband's parents.

The sounding of the all-clear signal in Hiroshima at 7:13 A.M. on August 6 made little change in the tempo of the city. Most people had been too busy, or too lazy, to pay much attention to the alert. The departure of the single, high-flying B-29 caused no more stir than its arrival over the city twenty-two minutes earlier.

As the plane flew out over the sea, Michiyoshi Nukushina, a thirty-eight-year-old fire-truck driver at the Hiroshima Army Ordnance Supply Depot, climbed onto his bicycle and headed for home. He had received special permission to quit his post half an hour before his shift ended. Wearing an official-duty armband to clear himself through the depot gates, and carrying a new pair of wooden clogs and a bag of fresh tomatoes drawn from the depot commissary, he headed home through the narrow streets of Hiroshima.

Nukushina crossed two of the seven river channels that divided the city into fingerlike islands and finally arrived at his home in Kakomachi precinct a little more than half an hour after leaving the firehouse. Propping his bicycle by an entrance to his small combination home and wineshop he walked inside and called to his wife to go get the tomatoes.

At this same instant, in a comfortable house behind the high hill that made Hijiyama Park a welcome variation in the otherwise flat terrain of Hiroshima, a mother named Chinayo Sakamoto was mopping her kitchen floor after breakfast. Her son Tsuneo, an Army captain fortunately stationed right in his home town, had left for duty with his unit. His wife Miho had gone upstairs. Tsuneo's father lay on the straw mat in the living room, reading his morning paper.

Off to the east and south of the city, a few men in air defense posts were watching the morning sky or listening to their sound-detection equipment. At the Matsunaga lookout station, in the hills east of Hiroshima, a watcher filed two reports with the air defense center. At 8:06, he sighted and reported two planes, headed northwest. At 8:09, he saw another, following some miles behind them, and corrected his report to include it.

At 8:14, the telephone talker at the Nakano searchlight battery also made a report. His sound equipment had picked up the noise of aircraft engines. Unidentified planes were coming from Saijo, about fifteen miles east of Hiroshima, and were heading toward the city.

The anti-aircraft gunners on Mukay-Shima Island in Hiroshima harbor could now see two planes, approaching the eastern edge of the city at very high altitude. As they watched, at precisely seventeen seconds after 8:15, the planes suddenly separated. The leading aircraft made a tight, diving turn to the right. The second plane performed an identical maneuver to the left, and from it fell three parachutes which opened and floated slowly down toward the city.

The few people in Hiroshima who caught sight of the two planes saw the parachutes blossom as the aircraft turned away from the city. Some cheered when they saw them, thinking the enemy planes must be in trouble and the crews were starting to bail out.

For three quarters of a minute there was nothing in the clear sky over the city except the parachutes and the diminishing whine of airplane engines as the B-29's retreated into the lovely blue morning.

Then suddenly, without a sound, there was no sky left over Hiroshima.

For those who were there and who survived to recall the moment when man first turned on himself the elemental forces of his own universe, the first instant was pure light, blinding, intense light, but light of an awesome beauty and variety.

In the pause between detonation and impact, a pause that for some was so short it could not register on the senses, but which for others was long enough for shock to give way to fear and for fear in turn to yield to instinctive efforts at self-preservation, the

Excerpt from pp. 175–201 of *No High Ground* by Fletcher Knebel and Charles W. Bailey II. Copyright © 1960 by Fletcher Knebel and Charles W. Bailey II, renewed © 1988 by Fletcher Knebel and Charles W. Bailey II. Reprinted by permission of HarperCollins, Publishers, Inc.

sole impression was visual. If there was sound, no one heard it.

To Nukushina, just inside his house, and to Mrs. Sakamoto, washing her kitchen floor, it was simply sudden and complete blackness.

For Nukushina's wife, reaching for the bag of tomatoes on her husband's bicycle, it was a blue flash streaking across her eyes.

For Dr. Imagawa, at his patient's city home, it again was darkness. For his wife, in the suburban hills to the west, it was a "rainbow-colored object," whirling horizontally across the sky over the city.

To Yuko Yamaguchi, cleaning up after breakfast in the rented farmhouse where she and her in-laws now lived, it was a sudden choking black cloud as the accumulated soot and grime of decades seemed to leap from the old walls.

Hayano Susukida, bent over to pick up a salvaged roof tile so she could pass it down the line of "volunteer" workers, did not see anything. She was merely crushed to the ground as if by some monstrous supernatural hand. But her son Junichiro, lounging outside his dormitory at Otake, saw a flash that turned from white to pink and then to blue as it rose and blossomed. Others, also at a distance of some miles, seemed to see "five or six bright colors." Some saw merely "flashes of gold" in a white light that reminded them—this was perhaps the most common description—of a huge photographic flashbulb exploding over the city.

The duration of this curiously detached spectacle varied with the distance of the viewer from the point in mid-air where the two lumps of U-235 were driven together inside the bomb. It did not last more than a few seconds at the most.

For thousands in Hiroshima it did not last even that long, if in fact there was any moment of grace at all. They were simply burned black and dead where they stood by the radiant heat that turned central Hiroshima into a gigantic oven. For thousands of others there was perhaps a second or two, certainly not long enough for wonder or terror or even recognition of things seen but not believed, before they were shredded by the thousands of pieces of shattered

This scorched watch, found in the rubble at Hiroshima, stopped at the exact moment of the atomic blast: 8:16 A.M. When the bomb exploded, thousands of people "were simply burned black and dead where they stood by the radiant heat that turned central Hiroshima into a gigantic oven." (John Launois/Black Star; Hiroshima: National Archives)

window glass that flew before the blast waves or were crushed underneath walls, beams, bricks, or any other solid object that stood in the way of the explosion.

For everyone else in history's first atomic target, the initial assault on the visual sense was followed by an instinctive assumption that a very large bomb had scored a direct hit on or near the spot where they were standing.

Old Mr. Sakamoto, who a moment before had been lounging on the living-room floor with his newspaper, found himself standing barefoot in his back yard, the paper still in his hand. Then his wife staggered out of the house, and perhaps half a minute later, his daughter-in-law Miho, who had been upstairs, groped her way out also.

Dr. Imagawa had just reached for his medical satchel to begin the examination of his patient. When the blackness lifted from his senses, he found himself standing on top of a five-foot pile of rubble that had been the sickroom. With him, surprisingly, were both the sick man and the patient's young son.

Mrs. Susukida, flat on the ground amid the pile of old roof tiles, was left all but naked, stripped of every piece of outer clothing and now wearing only her underwear, which itself was badly torn.

Mrs. Nukushina had just time to throw her hands over her eyes after she saw the blue flash. Then she was knocked insensible. When she recovered consciousness, she lay in what seemed to her to be utter darkness. All around her there was only rubble where a moment earlier there had been her home and her husband's bicycle and the bag of fresh tomatoes. She too was now without clothing except for her underwear. Her body was rapidly becoming covered with her own blood from dozens of cuts. She groped around until she found her four-year-old daughter Ikuko. She saw no trace of her husband. Dazed and terrified, she took the child's hand and fled.

But Michiyoshi Nukushina was there, and was still alive, though buried unconscious inside the wreckage of his home. His life had been saved because the blast blew him into a corner where two big, old-fashioned office safes, used in the family wine business, took the weight of the roof when it fell and thus spared him from being crushed. As he came to, raised his head and looked around, everything seemed strangely reddened. He discovered later that blood from cuts on his head had gushed down over his eyelids, forming a sort of red filter over his eyes. His first conscious thought was that the emergency water tank kept on hand for fire-bombing protection was only one-third full. As his head cleared, he called for his wife and daughter. There was no reply. Getting painfully to his feet— his left leg was badly broken—he found a stick for a crutch and hobbled out of the rubble.

Hold out your left hand, palm down, fingers spread, and you have a rough outline of the shape of Hiroshima. The sea is beyond the fingertips. The back of the hand is where the Ota River comes down from the hills to the north. The spot where the bomb exploded is about where a wedding ring would be worn, just south of the main military headquarters and in the center of the residential-commercial districts of the city. Major Ferebee's aim was nearly perfect. Little Boy was detonated little more than two hundred yards from the aiming point on his target chart, despite the fact that it was released from a fast-moving aircraft over three miles to the east and nearly six miles up in the air.

Dropped with such precision, the bomb performed better than its makers had predicted. Several factors combined by chance to produce even more devastation than had been expected.

First was the time of the explosion. All over Hiroshima, thousands of the charcoal braziers that were the stoves in most households were still full of hot coals after being used for breakfast cooking. Almost every stove was knocked over by the massive blast wave that followed the explosion, and each became an incendiary torch to set fire to the wood-and-paper houses. In addition, where [J. Robert] Oppenheimer had estimated casualties on the assumption that most people would be inside their air-raid shelters, almost no one in Hiroshima was sheltered when the bomb actually fell. The recent all-clear, the fact that it was a time when most people were on their way to work, the mischance by which there had been no new alert when the *Enola Gay* approached the city, the fact that small formations of planes had flown over many times before without dropping bombs, all combined to leave people exposed. Thus more than seventy thousand persons instead of Oppenheimer's estimate of twenty thousand were killed outright or so badly injured that they were dead in a matter of hours.

The initial flash spawned a succession of calamities.

First came heat. It lasted only an instant but was so intense that it melted roof tiles, fused the quartz crystals in granite blocks, charred the exposed sides of telephone poles for almost two miles, and incinerated nearby humans so thoroughly that nothing remained except their shadows, burned into asphalt pavements or stone walls. Of course the heat was most intense near the "ground zero" point, but for thousands of yards it had the power to burn deeply. Bare skin was burned up to two and a half miles away.

A printed page was exposed to the heat rays a mile and a half from the point of explosion, and the black letters were burned right out of the white paper. Hundreds of women learned a more personal lesson in the varying heat-absorption qualities of different colors when darker parts of their clothing burned out while lighter shades remained unscorched, leaving skin underneath etched in precise detail with the flower patterns of their kimonos. A dress with blue polka dots printed on white material came out of the heat with dark dots completely gone but the white background barely singed. A similar phenomenon occurred in men's shirts. Dark stripes were burned out while the alternate light stripes were undamaged. Another factor that affected injury was the thickness of clothing. Many people had their skin burned except where a double-thickness seam or a folded lapel had stood between them and the fireball. Men wearing caps emerged with sharp lines etched across their temples. Below the line, exposed skin was burned, while above it, under the cap, there was no injury. Laborers working in the open with only undershirts on had the looping pattern of shoulder straps and armholes printed on their chests. Sometimes clothing protected the wearer only if it hung loosely. One man standing with his arm bent, so that the sleeve was drawn tightly over his elbow, was burned only around that joint.

The heat struck only what stood in the direct path of its straight-line radiation from the fireball. A man sitting at his desk writing a letter had his hands deeply burned because the heat rays coming through his window fell directly on them, while his face, only eighteen inches away but outside the path of the rays, was unmarked. In countless cases the human body was burned or spared by the peculiarity of its position at the moment of flash. A walking man whose arm was swinging forward at the critical instant was burned all down the side of his torso. Another, whose moving arm happened to be next to his body, was left with an unburned streak where the limb had blocked out the radiation. In scores of cases

people were burned on one side of the face but not on the other because they had been standing or sitting in profile to the explosion. A shirtless laborer was burned all across his back—except for a narrow strip where the slight hollow down his spine left the skin in a "shadow" where the heat rays could not fall.

Some measure of the heat's intensity can be gained from the experience of the mayor of Kabe, a village ten miles outside the city. He was standing in his garden and even at that distance distinctly felt the heat on his face when the bomb exploded.

After the heat came the blast, sweeping outward from the fireball with the force of a five-hundred mile-an-hour wind. Only those objects that offered a minimum of surface resistance—handrails on bridges, pipes, utility poles—remained standing. The walls of a few office buildings, specially built to resist earthquakes, remained standing, but they now enclosed nothing but wreckage, as their roofs were driven down to the ground, carrying everything inside down under them. Otherwise, in a giant circle more than two miles across, everything was reduced to rubble. The blast drove all before it. The stone columns flanking the entrance to the Shima Surgical Hospital, directly underneath the explosion, were rammed straight down into the ground. Every hard object that was dislodged, every brick, every broken timber, every roof tile, became a potentially lethal missile. Every window in the city was suddenly a shower of sharp glass splinters, driven with such speed and force that in hundreds of buildings they were deeply imbedded in walls—or in people. Many people were picking tiny shards of glass from their eyes for weeks afterward as a result of the shattering of their spectacles, or trying to wash out bits of sand and grit driven under their eyelids. Even a blade of grass now became a weapon to injure the man who tended it. A group of boys working in an open field had their backs peppered with bits of grass and straw which hit them with such force that they were driven into the flesh.

Many were struck down by a combination of the heat and the blast. A group of schoolgirls was working on the roof of a building, removing tiles as the structure was being demolished for a firebreak. Thus completely exposed, they were doubly hurt, burned and then blown to the ground. So quickly did the blast follow the heat that for many they seemed to come together. One man, knocked sprawling when the blast blew in his window, looked up from the floor to see a wood-and-paper screen across the room burning briskly.

Heat and blast together started and fed fires in thousands of places within a few seconds, thus instantly rendering useless the painfully constructed firebreaks. In some spots the ground itself seemed to spout fire, so numerous were the flickering little jets of flame spontaneously ignited by the radiant heat. The city's fire stations were crushed or burned along with everything else, and two-thirds of Hiroshima's firemen were killed or wounded. Even if it had been left intact, the fire department could have done little or nothing to save the city. Not only were there too many fires, but the blast had broken open the city's water mains in seventy thousand places, so there was no pressure. Between them, blast and fire destroyed every single building within an area of almost five square miles around the zero point. Although the walls of thirty structures still stood, they were no more than empty shells.

After heat, blast, and fire, the people of Hiroshima had still other ordeals ahead of them. A few minutes after the explosion, a strange rain began to fall. The raindrops were as big as marbles—and they were black. This frightening phenomenon resulted from the vaporization of moisture in the fireball and condensation in the cloud that spouted up from it. As the cloud, carrying water vapor and the pulverized dust of Hiroshima, reached colder air at higher altitudes, the moisture condensed and fell out as rain. There was not enough to put out the fires, but there was enough of this "black rain" to heighten the bewilderment and panic of people already unnerved by what had hit them.

After the rain came a wind—the great "fire wind"— which blew back in toward the center of the catastrophe, increasing in force as the air over Hiroshima grew hotter and hotter because of the great fires.

The wind blew so hard that it uprooted huge trees in the parks where survivors were collecting. It whipped up high waves on the rivers of Hiroshima and drowned many who had gone into the water in an attempt to escape from the heat and flames around them. Some of those who drowned had been pushed into the rivers when the crush of fleeing people overflowed the bridges, making fatal bottlenecks of the only escape routes from the stricken islands. Thousands of people were simply fleeing, blindly and without an objective except to get out of the city. Some in the suburbs, seeing them come, thought at first they were Negroes, not Japanese, so blackened were their skins. The refugees could not explain what had burned them. "We saw the flash," they said, "and this is what happened."

One of those who struggled toward a bridge was Nukushina, the wine seller turned fireman whose life had been saved by the big office safes in his house just over a half mile from "zero," the point over which the bomb exploded. Leaning on his stick, he limped to the Sumiyoshi bridge a few hundred yards away, where, with unusual foresight, he kept a small boat tied up, loaded with fresh water and a little food, ready for any possible emergency.

"I found my boat intact," he recalled later, "but it was already filled with other desperate victims. As I stood on the bridge wondering what to do next, black drops of rain began to splatter down. The river itself and the river banks were teeming with horrible specimens of humans who had survived and come seeking safety to the river."

Fortunately for Nukushina, another boat came by, operated by a friend who offered to take him on board.

"With his assistance, I climbed into the boat. At that time, they pointed out to me that my intestines were dangling from my stomach but there was nothing I could do about it. My clothes, boots and everything were blown off my person, leaving me with only my loincloth. Survivors swimming in the river shouted for help, and as we leaned down to pull them aboard, the skin from their arms and hands literally peeled off into our hands.

Their homes destroyed, city dwellers huddle on the Miyuki Bridge near the heart of Hiroshima. After the heat of the explosion came the "black rain," with drops as big as marbles, and then the "fire wind." Swept with conflagration, Hiroshima grew hotter and hotter.

Many refugees, attempting to escape the heat, drowned in the rivers, and the "crush of fleeing people overflowed the bridges, making fatal bottlenecks of the only escape routes." (Culver Pictures)

"A fifteen- or sixteen-year-old girl suddenly popped up alongside our boat and as we offered her our hand to pull her on board, the front of her face suddenly dropped off as though it were a mask. The nose and other facial features suddenly dropped off with the mask, leaving only a pink, peachlike face front with holes where the eyes, nose and mouth used to be. As the head dropped under the surface, the girl's black hair left a swirling black eddy. . . ."

Here Nukushina mercifully lost consciousness. He came to five hours later as he was being transferred into a launch that carried him, with other wounded, to an emergency first-aid station set up on the island of Ninoshima in the harbor. There he found safety, but no medical care. Only twenty-eight doctors were left alive and able to work in a city of a quarter million people, fully half of whom were casualties.

When Hayano Susukida tried to get up off the ground onto which she and the other members of her tile-salvaging labor gang had been thrown, she thought she was going to die. Her whole back, bared by the blast, burned and stung when she moved. But the thought of her four-year-old daughter Kazuko, who had been evacuated from the city after Hayano's husband was sent overseas and the family home had been marked for destruction in the firebreak program, made her try again. This time she got to her feet and staggered home. The blast had not leveled her house, about a mile and a quarter from the zero point, and the fire had not yet reached it. Hurriedly she stuffed a few things—a bottle of vegetable oil, some mosquito netting, two quilts, a small radio—into an old baby carriage, and started wheeling it toward the nearest bomb shelter. After going a few feet, she had to carry the carriage, for the street was choked with debris. She reached the shelter and passed the oil around to those inside, using the last of it to salve her own burns, which had not blistered or peeled but were nevertheless strangely penetrating and painful. She wondered what time it was. Her wrist watch was gone, so she walked home again to get her alarm clock. It was still running; it showed a little after ten. Back at the shelter, she just sat and waited. At noon someone handed out a few rice balls. As the survivors ate, an Army truck miraculously appeared and carried them to the water front, just beyond the edge of the bomb's destruction. Then they were ferried over to the emergency hospital on Ninoshima Island.

Dr. Imagawa, a little further from the center of the blast, was not seriously injured, although he was cut by flying glass in a number of places. His first reaction was annoyance. His clothes were in tatters, and he wondered how he would find the new pair of shoes which he had left at his patient's front door. Helping the small boy down off the five-foot rubble pile that had been the sickroom, he asked the youngster to take him to the front door. Oddly enough, they could not even find where the front of the house had been. Imagawa, much to his disgust, was out a new pair of shoes. At an artesian well with a pump that was still operating, he washed as best he could and set out for suburban Furue where his wife and children should be. He stopped frequently in response to appeals for help from the injured. One was a woman who wandered aimlessly in the street holding her bare breast, which had been split open. She pleaded with him to tell her whether she would live. The doctor, although positive she could not survive, assured her that a mere breast injury would not be fatal. Later, he drew water for a score of wounded from another well pump. Down the street, a trolley car burned briskly. Finally he got clear of the city and climbed the hill to Furue, where he found his family safe and uninjured. The walls of the house had cracked, in some places fallen, but his wife and the two little children had escaped injury, while the

oldest girl had walked home from school without a scratch after the blast. The doctor ate, washed thoroughly, painted his cuts with iodine and worked till dark with his wife cleaning up their house. That evening the somewhat sybaritic physician sat down to dinner and then relaxed, as he had done the night before in Hiroshima—twenty-four hours and an age earlier—over a few cups of wine.

The doctor sipping his wine that night had one thing in common with Mrs. Susukida and Michiyoshi Nukushina, both lying injured and untended in the emergency hospital on Ninoshima Island. None of them knew what it was that had destroyed their city. Nor did they yet have either time or inclination to wonder.

But others, outside Hiroshima, were anxiously trying to find out what the *Enola Gay* had dropped on the city. The search for information was a frustrating one.

At first there had been no indication that anything unusual had happened in Hiroshima. A moment after 8:16 A.M., the Tokyo control operator of the Japanese Broadcasting Corporation noticed that his telephone line to the radio station in Hiroshima had gone dead. He tried to re-establish his connection, but found that he could not get a call through to the western city.

Twenty minutes later the men in the railroad signal center in Tokyo realized that the mainline telegraph had stopped working. The break seemed to be just north of Hiroshima. Reports began to come in from stations near Hiroshima that there had been some kind of an explosion in the city. The railroad signalmen forwarded the messages to Army General Headquarters.

It was almost ten o'clock when Ryugen Hosokawa, managing editor of the *Asahi* vernacular newspaper in Tokyo, received a telephone call at his home. It was the office, reporting that Hiroshima had "almost completely collapsed" as the result of bombing by enemy planes. Hosokawa hurried to the office and sifted through the reports collected by *Asahi*'s relay room. Every one of them sounded to him like something quite different from any previous bombing.

This must have been caused, he thought to himself, by very unusual bombs.

At about the same time Major Tosaku Hirano, a staff officer of the II Army Corps, was in General Headquarters in Tokyo. He had come up from Hiroshima a week earlier to report on the status of military supplies in the port city, and had been scheduled to fly back on Sunday. But he had put his departure off for a day or two and thus was still in the capital.

Now his telephone rang. It was a call from Central Command Headquarters in Osaka, an installation under the control of the II Army Corps in Hiroshima, reporting that its communications to Hiroshima and points west had failed.

Tokyo GHQ tried several times to raise the Hiroshima communications center, in the earth-and-concrete bunker next to the moat of the old castle, but could not get through. There was no explanation. The succession of reports from the radio network, from the railroad signal center, from *Asahi's* newsroom and from Osaka indicated that something serious had happened, but no one could find out what it was.

Then, shortly after 1 P.M., General Headquarters finally heard from the II Army Corps. The message was short but stunning: "Hiroshima has been annihilated by one bomb and fires are spreading."

This flash came not from Corps Headquarters but from the Army shipping depot on the Hiroshima water front, which was outside the blast area and was not reached by the fire that followed. There was considerable damage at the shipping depot, something in the neighborhood of 30 per cent, but officers there were able to get a message out as far as Kure, where the naval station relayed it to Tokyo. There was no word at all from the II Army Corps Headquarters at the old castle in the northern part of town.

Reports continued to trickle in. By the middle of the afternoon, the Army knew that only three enemy planes had been over Hiroshima when the bomb exploded. It had been told that two of these did not drop any bombs. This information supported the startling assertion in the first flash that there had been only one bomb exploded. Something very big, and very frightening, had hit Hiroshima.

In mid-afternoon the managing editors of the five big Tokyo newspapers, plus their counterpart in the Domei news agency, were called to the office of the government Information and Intelligence Agency, which had charge of press and radio censorship. An Army press officer addressed the little group of newsmen:

"We believe that the bomb dropped on Hiroshima is different from an ordinary one. However, we have inadequate information now, and we intend to make some announcement when proper information has been obtained. Until we issue such an announcement, run the news in an obscure place in your papers and as one no different from one reporting an ordinary air raid on a city."

In other words, the lid was on. The Army already had a strong suspicion that the Hiroshima bomb might be an atomic weapon. Japanese Naval intelligence had reported U.S. work on the bomb in late 1944, noting the interest of the American government in buying up all available pitchblende (uranium ore). Thus, although the best scientists in Japan had agreed that there was no chance of the United States producing a fission bomb in less than three to five years, there was now immediate suspicion that an atomic bomb had fallen. But the Army, anxious to keep the war going so it could fight a showdown hand-to-hand battle with the Americans on Japanese soil, was determined to withhold the news from the Japanese people as long as it could.

The editors protested mildly, but the decision stood. At six o'clock that evening, the radio gave the people of Japan their first hint that Hiroshima had been chosen for a place in history as the spot where man first proved he could tear apart the basic structure of his world. A listener, however, would have been hard put to deduce the true story from the first news item as it was read:

A few B-29s hit Hiroshima city at 8:20 A.M. August 6, and fled after dropping incendiaries and bombs. The extent of the damage is now under survey.

This cryptic item was repeated several times between six and nine o'clock without further explanation. On the nine o'clock program in Osaka, the sound of the musical chime that signaled the switch from national to local news was followed by this item:

An announcement by the Osaka railway bureau in regard to changes in various transportation organs and changes in handling of passenger baggage:

First of all, the government lines. Regarding the down train, trains from Osaka will turn back from Mihara on the Sanyo line. From Mihara to Kaitichi, the trains will take the route around Kure. . . .

Mihara was about halfway from Osaka to Hiroshima. Kaitichi was on the southeastern edge of Hiroshima. Trains headed there from Osaka on the main line ordinarily ran through the Hiroshima yards and station before swinging back to the smaller community.

The morning *Asahi* in Tokyo on August 7 carried a long front-page story with a sizable headline reporting "Small and Medium Cities Attacked by 400 B-29s." At the end of this story, there was a four-line item tacked on. It read:

Hiroshima Attacked by Incendiary Bombs

Hiroshima was attacked August 6th by two B-29 planes, which dropped incendiary bombs.

The planes invaded the city around 7:50 A.M. It seems that some damage was caused to the city and its vicinity.

Those who survived in Hiroshima still did not know what it was that had struck them so viciously the day before. They did not have much time for thinking about it. Merely keeping alive was a full-time job. Some thought, as they fled the burning city, that the Americans had deluged their homes with "Molotov flower baskets," as the unhappily familiar incendiary clusters were nicknamed. Others, sniffing the air and detecting a strong "electric smell," decided that some kind of poison gas had been dropped. Another explanation was that a magnesium powder had been sprayed on the city, exploding wherever it fell on trolley wires and other exposed electrical conductors.

The prefectural government did what it could to bring order in the city. Somehow almost two hundred policemen were found for duty on August 7. They set to work, with whatever help they could commandeer, to clear the streets of bodies and debris. Police stations became emergency food depots, doling out hastily gathered supplies of rice, salt, pickled radishes, matches, canned goods, candles, straw sandals, and toilet paper.

The governor of Hiroshima prefecture, Genshin Takano, issued a proclamation:

People of Hiroshima Prefecture: Although damage is great, we must remember that this is war. We must feel absolutely no fear. Already plans are being drawn up for relief and restoration measures. . . .

We must not rest a single day in our war effort. . . . We must bear in mind that the annihilation of the stubborn enemy is our road to revenge. We must subjugate all difficulties and pain, and go forward to battle for our Emperor.

But most people in Hiroshima, if they could overcome their pain on this second day of the atomic age, were more concerned with finding their loved ones than with battling for their Emperor.

Yuko Yamaguchi, waiting out the war in the rented suburban farmhouse while her husband served overseas in the Army, was unhurt. So were her three little children. But her father-in-law, who had driven into the city Sunday for the meeting of his gas company board of directors, and her mother-in-law, who had left early Monday morning to fetch more supplies from their requisitioned city house, had not been heard from since the bomb fell. Yuko had had no word, either, from her own parents.

So at 6:30 this Tuesday morning, she left her children and set out for the city, walking the whole way because the suburban rail lines were not running. It was a long walk. By the time she reached the Red Cross Hospital, where she thought her in-laws might have been taken, it was noon.

Yuko did not find her husband's parents there. But, by sheerest chance, she found her own father, lying untended on the floor with an ugly wound in the back of his head. He begged his grief-stricken daughter for some water. When she did her best and filled a broken cup with stagnant water from a nearby pond, the delirious eye specialist was furious, insisting that ice and a slice of lemon be added to make it more palatable. Somehow, she found both in the wrecked hospital kitchen and made him as comfortable as possible. Then she started through the littered, jammed wards and halls to search for her other relatives. Again she found no trace of her in-laws, but at five o'clock she came on her own mother, lying unconscious, her face smashed almost beyond recognition and her intestines bared by a savage stomach wound.

Daughter dragged mother through the corridors to her father's side so the two could at least be together. There was little enough time. Near dusk the mother died, and Yuko had to carry the body outside, build a crude pyre and cremate it herself. At about dawn her father also died. This time, there were enough other corpses on hand so the hospital arranged a makeshift mass cremation, and Yuko left. She spent the day searching again for her husband's parents, but there was no trace of them, and she finally walked home to the hills to join her children. It was to be more than a month before she found any trace of her in-laws. Then she got only the stub of a commutation ticket bearing her mother-in-law's name, recovered from the wreckage of the train she had been riding at 8:16 A.M. Monday. A few charred bones uncovered still later in the burned-out office of the gas company president were the only trace ever found of her father-in-law.

Some who survived seemed to accept with stoicism the death of their loved ones. Miho Sakamoto, who with her husband's parents had escaped the blast and fire because their home was protected by the city's only high hill, was told on August 7 that her husband's military unit had been completely wiped out. She shed no tears and showed no emotion. Four days later, she visited the ruins of the building in

which he had died, found a bent ash tray which she recognized as his and brought it home. That night, she seemed in good spirits when she went upstairs to the room she had shared with her Tsuneo. The next morning she did not come down to breakfast. Her mother-in-law found her lying in front of a little altar, the ash tray in front of her beside a photograph of her dead husband, the razor with which she had cut her throat still clutched in her hand. She left a note of apology to "My Honorable Father and Mother":

What I am about to do, I do not do on sudden impulse; nor is it due to temporary agitation. It is a mutual vow exchanged with my husband while he still lived. This is the road to our greatest happiness and we proceed thereon. Like a bird which has lost one wing, we are crippled birds who cannot go through life without one another. There is no other way. Please, do not bewail my fate. Somewhere both of us will again be living happily together as we have in the past. . . . My honorable Tsuneo must be anxiously awaiting me and I must rush to his side.

Sixteen-year-old Junichiro Susukida, at his factory-school dormitory in Otake, sixteen miles west of Hiroshima, had seen the fireball and the great cloud that rose over the city Monday morning. When the first refugees arrived with the news that the city had been badly hit, he was one of many students who demanded permission to go to their homes, and he was one of five finally allowed to go into the city to contact authorities at the main school building and seek news of the students' families.

By the time they reached Miya-jima, on the southwestern edge of the city, the students could see the fires still burning in the bright late afternoon. As they came closer, they began to realize the full extent of the calamity. It was dark before the boys reached their home neighborhood and began their search for relatives. Junichiro, though unable to find either his mother or younger brother, did at last encounter neighbors who told him his brother had survived, though wounded, and had been taken to the home of other relatives in Fuchu. He could learn nothing about his mother, however, and finally headed back to his dormitory in Otake. Dead tired when he arrived at 2 A.M., he was nevertheless too distraught to sleep. He sat in the school auditorium and incongruously played the piano until fatigue finally subdued his nerves just before dawn on Tuesday, August 7.

Junichiro was not the only one who did not sleep that night. In Tokyo, the truth about Hiroshima was beginning to be revealed in ways that made it clear that the facts could not be kept from the people of Japan much longer.

A little before midnight on the sixth, the Tokyo office of Domei, the quasi-governmental news agency that served the whole nation, much as the Associated Press or Reuters do in the West, received a bulletin from Okayama prefecture, just east of Hiroshima. It was followed by a longer dispatch: the first eye-witness account of the bombing by a professional newsman.

Bin Nakamura, subchief of Domei's Hiroshima bureau, had been eating breakfast in his suburban garden when the bomb's explosion lifted him off the straw mat on which he was sitting and sent a wave of "immense" heat washing over his face. Once Nakamura discovered that the concussion and heat had not been caused by the nearby explosion of a "blockbuster"—his first reaction had been the typical one—he went to work as a reporter. On his bicycle and on foot, he spent the day in the city and talking to the refugees who streamed through his suburb. Then, at 10 P.M., like the experienced press-association man he was, he found communications at the suburban Haramura radio station and dictated a story to Okayama, the only point he could reach. In his dispatch, he said there was no way to tell what kind of a bomb had caused such havoc.

But before the night was much older the editors of Domei, and the leaders of Japan, had a way of telling much more about the bomb. In Saitama prefecture outside Tokyo, Domei operated a big monitoring station where nearly fifty workers, many of them Nisei girls born in the United States, listened to broadcasts from American stations. About 1 A.M. on the 7th of August (noon on the 6th in Washington, D.C.), Hideo Kinoshita, chief of the monitoring room, was awakened by the Japanese youth who had charge of the operation that night. The boy reported that U.S. stations were all broadcasting a statement by President Truman, describing the weapon that had been dropped on Hiroshima as "an atomic bomb." Kinoshita listened to the account and the boy's explanation of what "atomic bomb" might mean. Then he quickly called his own superior, Saiji Hasegawa, Domei's foreign news chief. Hasegawa was asleep in his hotel. When he was told of an "atomic bomb," he had no idea what it was, but although he was irritated at being awakened he hustled to his office. When he saw the text transcripts that were beginning to come through from the Saitama monitors, he was glad he had come to work. He reached for his telephone and called Hisatsune Sakomizu, chief secretary of the cabinet.

Sakomizu sleepily answered his bedside telephone, then came suddenly wide awake as he listened to the Domei executive. He already knew, from the first confused reports on the 6th, that the Americans had used some kind of new weapon. Now, learning that it was an atomic bomb, something the cabinet had discussed briefly almost a year earlier, he knew it meant just one thing: the war was over.

Sakomizu quickly called Prime Minister Suzuki, with whom he had been working in the effort to arrange a peace settlement by negotiation. They knew immediately, he said later,

. . . that if the announcement were true, no country could carry on a war. Without the atomic bomb it would be impossible for any country to defend itself against a nation which had the weapon. The chance had come to end the war. It was not necessary to blame the military side, the manufacturing people, or anyone else—just the atomic bomb. It was a good excuse.

The Army, however, was unwilling to accept this attitude, despite the urgings of the peace group that the bomb gave military leaders a chance to save face by blaming the "backwardness of scientific research" for Japan's inability to counter the new American bomb. The generals, sitting in an emergency cabinet meeting on the seventh, pointedly recalled an old Japanese legend about an Army commander who became a laughingstock because he mistook the fluttering of a flight of birds for the sound of the approaching enemy and fled. They argued that the bomb was not atomic but was merely a huge conventional projectile. They flatly refused Foreign Minister Togo's proposal to take up for immediate consideration the possibility of surrender on the terms of the Potsdam ultimatum, and insisted on keeping the Truman atomic statement from the Japanese people until the Army could conduct an "investigation" on the ground at Hiroshima.

The military had already started such a check. Major Hirano, the staff officer from the Hiroshima headquarters whose desire to spend a couple of extra nights in Tokyo had saved his life, called Yoshio Nishina, the nation's ranking nuclear scientist. He told him of the Truman claims and asked him to ride down to Hiroshima in his little liaison plane to investigate the matter. Nishina agreed to make the trip. The scientist was already pretty well convinced, on the basis of Hirano's report and further excerpts from the Truman statement given him a few minutes later by a reporter, that the bomb had indeed been the fission weapon which he and his colleagues had believed the United States could not manufacture so quickly. Truman's claim of a destructive power equal to twenty thousand tons of TNT coincided exactly with theoretical calculations made recently by one of Nishina's laboratory associates on the yield of an atomic bomb.

But the Army high command was keeping the lid on tight. When the Tokyo managing editors met again with the Information Agency censors that afternoon, they all had seen the text of Truman's statement. But they got nowhere with requests for permission to print it. The Army grudgingly allowed use of the phrase "a new-type bomb," but not the word "atomic." The editors argued hard this time, but to no avail. The end result of the wrangle was

this communiqué from Imperial General Headquarters at 3:30 P.M. on Tuesday, August 7:

1 A considerable amount of damage was caused by a few B-29s which attacked Hiroshima August 6th.
2 It seems that the enemy used a new-type bomb in the raid. Investigation of the effects is under way.

By evening, the newsmen were stretching the Army embargo as far as they could. A home service broadcast at 7 P.M. amplified the cryptic communiqué by adding that "a considerable number of houses were reduced to ashes and fires broke out in various parts of the city . . . investigations are now being made with regard to the effectiveness of the bomb, which should not be regarded as light." The broadcast went on to attack the Americans for "inhuman and atrocious conduct" and to urge the Japanese not to be "misled" by "exaggerated propaganda" such as "an announcement regarding the use of a new-type bomb" by Truman.

One man who was not likely to be "misled" by any announcement that night was Major Hirano, who finally had started back to Hiroshima in his five-seater liaison plane late in the afternoon. He had arrived at the Tokyo airport with the hurriedly assembled team of investigators earlier in the day, but had been ordered to wait until afternoon to avoid the U.S. Navy fighter planes that were now operating over Japan daily. There was some top brass in the inspection group which apparently was not anxious to hasten the day of personal contact with American invaders. Thus it was almost seven in the evening when Hirano's plane came down over Hiroshima. It was still light, however, so he got the full picture with shocking suddenness:

Being a soldier, my eye had been inured to the effects of bombing by that time. But this was a different sight. *There were no roads in the wastes that spread below our eyes:* that was my first impression. In the case of a normal air raid, roads were still visible after it was over. But in Hiroshima, everything was flattened and all roads were undiscernibly covered with debris.

When Hirano stepped from his plane, the first person he saw was an Air Force officer who came out on the runway to meet the team from Tokyo. His face was marked by a sharp dividing line right down the middle. One side was smooth and unhurt. The other, the one that had been toward the explosion, was burned, blistered, blackened. The investigators picked their way through the city to the wreckage of II Army Corps headquarters. Nobody was there. They finally found what was left of the headquarters—a few officers holed up in a hillside cave. By the time they began their formal investigation the next morning, the men from Tokyo knew the truth anyway. Hirano, in fact, had known it the moment he caught sight of what was left of Hiroshima from his circling plane.

QUESTIONS TO CONSIDER

1 What chance factors at Hiroshima added to the inherent destructiveness of the atomic bomb and produced more deaths and devastation than American scientists had expected?

2 Describe the sequence of destruction caused by the bomb's explosion. What were the physical effects of the bomb on human beings?

3 What was the immediate reaction of the Japanese army and government to the news of what had happened at Hiroshima? Why was the true nature of the American attack kept from the Japanese people?

4 Discuss the responsibility of the Japanese high command for prolonging the war after the bombing of Hiroshima.

5 Given the present-day proliferation of atomic weapons, what lessons can we draw from the firsthand accounts of the Japanese who experienced the horrors at Hiroshima fifty years ago?

PART ELEVEN

Perils of the Cold War

22 Harry Truman: "One Tough Son-of-a-Bitch of a Man"

DAVID McCULLOUGH

When he learned that Roosevelt had died and that he was now president of the United States, Truman told a group of reporters: "Boys, if you ever pray, pray for me now. I don't know whether you fellows ever had a load of hay fall on you, but when they told me yesterday what had happened, I felt like the moon, the stars, and all the planets had fallen on me."

He did not want to be president, and he certainly did not look like one: though cheery and brisk and always dressed in a spotless suit "as if he had just stepped from a bandbox," as his wife said, he was short, slight, and plain looking, wore thick spectacles, spoke in a Missouri twang, and radiated ordinariness. But, as a friend said, behind that plain-looking façade was "one tough son-of-a-bitch." Though not privy to Roosevelt's war strategy and military secrets, Truman stepped into the job with alacrity and confidently made decisions that led the country to victory in the Second World War.

In the postwar world, he faced a vortex of difficulties that would have daunted a lesser man. At home, the United States had to demobilize its vast military forces and convert wartime industry back to peacetime production. Abroad, the Allied victory proved to be a victory without peace. For out of the muck and rubble of the Second World War emerged a Cold War between the Soviet Union and the West that threatened the very survival of humankind. The genesis of the Cold War, as Truman learned, went back to the early days of the Second World War and involved control of eastern Europe. Russia and the Western Allies clashed over that area, and their rival strategies for the domination of eastern Europe influenced most of the wartime conferences among the big three (the United States, Great Britain, and the Soviet Union). The West hoped to establish democratic regimes in eastern Europe, but it proved an impossible program, for the massive Red Army overran eastern

Europe, and Stalin vowed to maintain Russian supremacy there. He did so not to export world Communism but to ensure Soviet security from the West—to make certain no western army could ever sweep through Poland and invade Russia as the Germans had done. The Soviet Union had lost from 20 to 25 million people in the war against Germany; no other nation swept up in the war, not even Germany itself, had suffered such casualties. Dominating eastern Europe, Soviet leaders hoped, would prevent such a catastrophe from ever happening again.

Once the Red Army occupied eastern Europe, Roosevelt did the only thing he could do. At the Yalta Conference of February 1945, he acknowledged Soviet hegemony in the region but pressed Stalin to hold free elections in the countries he controlled. Mainly to hold the wartime alliance together, Stalin promised free elections for eastern Europe. But obsessed as he was with Russian security, the Soviet boss never kept his promise, instead setting up Soviet puppet states from the Baltic to the Adriatic.

The West felt betrayed. By the time Truman came to power, the United States and many of its allies increasingly saw Stalin as a mad and devious Marxist dictator out to spread Communism across the globe. In the United States especially, a profound suspicion of the Soviets and world Communism swept over Washington and the Truman White House. Unlike Roosevelt, who had tried to conciliate the Russians, Truman in 1947 adopted a get-tough containment policy designed to block Soviet expansion and save the "free world" from Communism. The purpose of containment was not to overthrow the Soviet regime or invade the Soviet sphere but to prevent the Soviets from expanding the influence of Communism. To do that, Washington poured billions of dollars in aid into Greece, Turkey, and western Europe and extended American military power around the globe. American aid to western Europe, called the Marshall Plan, rebuilt its war-torn countries and neutralized Communist parties there.

From 1947 on, containment formed the basis of United States foreign policy. When in 1948 the Soviets blockaded Allied-controlled West Berlin (Berlin was located in the Russian sector of occupied Germany), Truman ordered a massive airlift by B-29s that prevented West Berlin from falling to the Soviets. His containment policy dictated that the United States get tough with China, too, after the Communists took over there in 1949 and drove Chiang Kai-shek's Nationalist Chinese into exile on Formosa (now known as Taiwan). The fall of China whipped up a storm of outrage and fears of Communism in the United States. In this sinister turn of events, Americans once again saw the evil hand of Joseph Stalin. At home, a terrible Red scare swept the land, as Americans saw Communists everywhere, from Hollywood to Washington, D.C., plotting to overthrow the government and hand the country over to the Soviets. Truman himself contributed to the scare by instituting a sweeping loyalty oath program and beginning extensive security checks for federal employment.

The Red scare produced in 1950 a finger-pointing rabble-rouser named Joseph McCarthy, who claimed that the State Department itself was crawling with Reds. He even accused Truman and General George Marshall, secretary of state, of being Communists. His strident accusations, which the press published with relish under black headlines, destroyed the careers of many innocent Americans. Yet not once in his anti-Communist crusade did McCarthy expose a single bona fide Communist.

The year, 1950, brought another shock. China's neighbor, Korea, was divided at the 38th parallel between a Communist regime in the north and a pro-Western government in the south. That June, North Korean forces invaded South Korea in what Washington viewed as an act of naked Communist aggression instigated by the Kremlin. Under the auspices of the United Nations, Truman sent in American troops, who in a few months drove the North Koreans back across the 38th parallel. By September, however, Truman had changed the purpose of the war: instead of simply maintaining the integrity of South Korea, he resolved to invade North Korea and liberate it from Communist rule. When United Nations forces under General Douglas MacArthur drove to the Chinese borders, that was enough for the Red Chinese: 260,000 of them crossed the Yalu and inflicted on MacArthur one of the worst military defeats in American history, sending him in pell-mell retreat back toward the 38th parallel. With that, Truman again changed the purpose of the war: he gave up fighting to liberate North Korea and fell back on the original United States goal of simply ensuring the sovereignty of South Korea. At that point, the Korean War bogged down in stalemate. When a frustrated MacArthur issued public statements vehemently criticizing Truman's policies and went on to advocate an all-out war against China, the president relieved him of command on the grounds that the general was trying to force his policies on his civilian commander in chief, which violated the constitutional provision of civilian control of the military.

In the following selection, David McCullough, Truman's foremost biographer and winner of the Pulitzer Prize, brings the tough little man from Missouri brilliantly alive in a warm and sympathetic portrait. McCullough shows us how Truman's personality and character—his no-nonsense bluntness, honesty, determination, courage, sense of history, and love of people—affected his postwar decisions and made him an extremely effective president despite his flaws and mistakes.

GLOSSARY

ACHESON, DEAN Truman's third secretary of state (1949–1953); he was the principal force behind the creation of the North Atlantic Treaty Organization (NATO), which allied the western democracies against the Soviet Union and its eastern bloc. Acheson implemented Truman's decision to send United States troops to South Korea, which had been invaded by Communist North Korea. Though Acheson was a diehard anti-Communist, Republicans accused him of being soft on Communism and blamed him for the Communist takeover of China in 1949.

BYRNES, JIMMY A conservative Democrat and "avowed segregationist," he was Truman's friend and adviser and served as his secretary of state from 1945 to 1947. He was one of the most vigorous advocates of dropping the atomic bomb on Japan. After the war, he tried to reconcile the United States and the Soviet Union but then became a harsh critic of Soviet designs.

CLIFFORD, CLARK Truman's special adviser from 1945 to 1950, he helped to formulate Truman's policy of containment and to create the Department of Defense.

DEWEY, THOMAS E. Republican nominee for president in 1948; he was universally expected to defeat Truman, so much so that before all the votes were counted, one newspaper ran a front-page headline: "DEWEY DEFEATS TRUMAN." As it turned out, Truman won the election, defying the pollsters and the odds.

FORRESTAL, JAMES Served as secretary of the navy from 1944 to 1947 and became the first secretary of defense when the Truman administration established the Department of Defense in 1947. He advocated a powerful military to contain Soviet aggression and persuaded the federal government to institute a peacetime draft.

HARRIMAN, W. AVERELL American businessman turned statesman; he served as United States ambassador to the Soviet Union from 1943 to 1946 and as Truman's secretary of commerce from 1946 to 1948.

KENNAN, GEORGE Historian and diplomat who helped formulate Truman's policy of containment toward the Soviet Union; he served as United States ambassador to Moscow until the Soviets demanded his removal.

LILIENTHAL, DAVID A long-time director of the Tennessee Valley Authority, which provided hydroelectric power for the Tennessee Valley. In 1946, Truman appointed him to chair of the United States Atomic Energy Commission, which stressed "civilian control and government monopoly of atomic energy."

LOVETT, ROBERT Influential undersecretary of state during Truman's presidency.

MARSHALL PLAN Also known as the European Recovery Program, it was the brainchild of George C. Marshall, Truman's second secretary of state (1947–1949) and former army chief of staff. The program distributed $12 billion in American aid that helped rebuild war-ravaged western Europe.

McCARTHY, JOSEPH   Republican senator from Wisconsin who earned his reputation by making fantastic accusations of Communist infiltration into the federal government, particularly the State Department. The cartoonist Herbert Block coined the term *McCarthyism* to describe the senator's Cold War witch-hunt to ferret out alleged Communists.

MUNICH, LESSON OF   In 1938, in Munich, Germany, the British and the French reached an accord with Adolf Hitler allowing Germany to possess an area of Czechoslovakia called the Sudetenland in exchange for Hitler's promise not to seize any more European territory. British Prime Minister Neville Chamberlain flew home to London, where he proclaimed that the Munich Pact had achieved "peace in our time." It had done nothing of the kind. A year later, Hitler's mighty mechanized army invaded Poland, thus setting off the Second World War. The "lesson of Munich" was that aggressors must never be appeased.

PENDERGAST, TOM   Boss of Missouri's Democratic political machine, through which Truman rose from judge of a county court to the United States Senate.

VAUGHAN, HARRY   Lifelong friend of Harry Truman who furnished him "comic relief." He was "Truman's Falstaff"—Falstaff being the bawdy, brazen, good-natured rascal in Shakespeare's *Henry IV, Parts 1 and 2,* and *The Merry Wives of Windsor.*

Harry Truman was President of the United States for not quite eight years. Looking back now we see him standing there in the presidential line, all of five foot nine, in a double-breasted suit, between two heroic figures of the century, Franklin Delano Roosevelt and Dwight D. Eisenhower. It's hard to convey today the feeling Americans had about General Eisenhower, the aura of the man, after World War II. He was charismatic, truly, if anyone ever was. Truman was not like that, not glamorous, not photogenic. And from the April afternoon when Truman took office, following the death of Franklin Roosevelt, he would feel the long shadow of Roosevelt, the most colossal figure in the White House in this century. He had none of Roosevelt's gifts—no beautiful speaking voice, no inherited wealth or social standing, no connections. He is the only president of our century who never went to college, and along with his clipped Missouri twang and eyeglasses thick as the bottom of a Coke bottle, he had a middlewestern plainness of manner, that, at first glance, made him seem "ordinary."

He had arrived first in Washington in the 1930s as a senator notable mainly for his background in the notorious Pendergast machine of Kansas City. He was of Scotch-Irish descent, and like many of Scotch-Irish descent—and I know something of this from my own background—he could be narrow, clannish, short-tempered, stubborn to a fault. But he could also be intensely loyal and courageous. And deeply patriotic. He was one of us, Americans said, just as they also said, "To err is Truman."

He was back in the news again after the Republican sweep in November 1994, the first such Republican triumph since 1946, and so naturally comparisons were drawn. Like Bill Clinton, Truman had been humiliated in his mid-term election of 1946, treated with open scorn and belittlement by Republicans, and seldom defended by his fellow Democrats. He was written off.

But how Truman responded is extremely interesting and bears directly on our subject, character in the presidency. It was as if he had been liberated from the shadow of Roosevelt. "I'm doing as I damn please for the next two years and to hell with all of them," he told his wife, Bess. And what's so remarkable and fascinating is that the next two years were the best of Truman's presidency. The years 1947 and 1948 contained most of the landmark achievements of his time in office: the first civil rights message ever sent to Congress, his executive order to end segregation in the armed forces, the Truman Doctrine, the recognition of Israel, the Berlin Airlift, and the

---

David McCullough, "Harry Truman: One Tough Son-of-a-Bitch" originally titled "Harry S Truman: 1945–1953" from *Character Above All,* edited by Robert A. Wilson. Reprinted by permission of Robert A. Wilson, Wilson Associates, Dallas, TX.

President Harry Truman, the tough little man from Missouri who made the decision to use atomic bombs against Japan, put forth the Truman Doctrine to contain the spread of Communism and sent *American troops into the Korean War. Gruff and direct though he was, Truman also had "a resilient sense of humor" and particularly enjoyed "the good stories of politics." (Stock Montage)*

Marshall Plan, which saved Western Europe from economic and political ruin and stands today as one of the great American achievements of the century.

He showed again and again that he understood the office, how the government works, and that he understood himself. He knew who he was, he liked who he was. He liked Harry Truman. He enjoyed being Harry Truman. He was grounded, as is said. He stressed, "I tried never to forget who I was, where I came from, and where I would go back to." And again and again, as I hope I will be able to demonstrate, he could reach down inside himself and come up with something very good and strong. He is the seemingly ordinary American who when put to the test, rises to the occasion and does the extraordinary.

Now by saying he knew himself and understood himself and liked himself, I don't mean vanity or conceit. I'm talking about self-respect, self-understanding. To an exceptional degree, power never went to his head, nor did he ever grow cynical, for all the time he spent in Washington. He was never inclined to irony or to grappling with abstract thoughts. He read a great deal, enjoyed good bourbon—Wild Turkey preferably—he was a good listener. His physical, mental, and emotional stamina were phenomenal. . . . There's much to be seen about people in how they stand, how they walk. Look at the photographs of Harry Truman, the newsreels—backbone American.

In the spring of 1945, the new untested President of the United States sat in the Oval Office. Across the desk, in the visitor's chair, sat a grim-looking old friend, Sam Rayburn, the Speaker of the House. They were alone in the room, just the two of them, and they were, in many ways, two of a kind. Rayburn knew he could talk straight from the shoulder to Truman, who had been in office only a few days.

"You have got many great hazards and one of them is in this White House. I've been watching this thing a long time," Rayburn began. "I've seen people in the White House try to build a fence around the White House and keep the very people away from the president that he should see. That is one of your hazards, the special interests and the sycophants who will stand in the rain a week to see you and will treat you like a king. They'll come sliding in and tell you you're the greatest man alive. But you know, and I know, you ain't."

Truman knew he wasn't Hercules, he knew he wasn't a glamour boy, he knew he didn't have—and this is so important—the capacity to move the country with words, with eloquence. He had none of the inspirational magic of his predecessor. If Roosevelt was Prospero, Truman was Horatio.

. . . Character counts in the presidency more than any other single quality. It is more important than how much the President knows of foreign policy or economics, or even about politics. When the chips are down—and the chips are nearly always down in the presidency—how do you decide? Which way do you go? What kind of courage is called upon? Talking of his hero Andrew Jackson, Truman once said, it takes one kind of courage to face a duelist, but it's nothing like the courage it takes to tell a friend, no.

In making his decision to recognize Israel, Truman had to tell the man he admired above all others, no—but more on that shortly.

Truman had seen a lot of life long before he came to Washington. He was born in 1884. He was a full-grown, mature, nearly middle-aged man by the time of the Great War, as his generation called World War I, which was the real dividing line between the nineteenth and the twentieth centuries and the turning point in his life. Everything changed in the period after World War I, which in retrospect may be seen as the first, hideous installment of a two-part

world catastrophe. Even the same characters—Hitler, Churchill, Roosevelt, Truman, MacArthur, Marshall—reappear in World War II. Growing up in Victorian middle America, Truman came to maturity with much of the outlook, good and bad, of that very different time.

At heart he remained a nineteenth-century man. He never liked air-conditioning, hated talking by telephone. (And thank goodness, for he wrote letters instead, thousands as time went on, and as a result it is possible to get inside his life, to know what he thought and felt, in a way rarely possible with public figures, and presidents in particular.) He disliked Daylight Saving Time and time zones. (He liked wearing two watches, one set on Eastern Standard Time, the other on Missouri time "real time," as he called it.)

He was also a farmer, a real farmer let it be remembered, not a photo opportunity or a gentleman farmer like FDR or Tom Dewey. With his father, he *worked* on the farm, facing all the perils of bad weather, failing crops, insect plagues, and debt. Truman & Son, of Grandview, Missouri, were never out of debt. He was there for eleven years, until he went off to war in 1917, and as he used to say, "It takes a lot of pride to run a farm." Certainly on a family farm, you don't "do your own thing." Let down your end and the whole enterprise may fall. And every morning there's your father at the foot of the stairs at five-thirty, no matter the weather, no matter the season, telling you it's time to be up and at it.

There was no running water on the Truman farm, no electricity. When his mother had to have an emergency appendectomy, she was operated on by a country doctor on the kitchen table, and it was young Harry who stood beside her through all of it holding the lantern.

He was, as his pal Harry Vaughan, once said, "one tough son-of-a-bitch of a man. . . . And that," said Vaughan, "was part of the secret of understanding him." He could take it. He had been through so much. There's an old line, "Courage is having done it before."

It's been often said that Truman was poorly prepared for the presidency. He came to office not knowing any of the foreign policy establishment in Washington. He had no friends on Wall Street, no powerful financial backers, no intellectual "brain trust." When Winston Churchill came to Washington in the early 1940s and busied himself meeting everybody of known influence, no one suggested he look up the junior senator from Missouri.

But Truman had experienced as wide a range of American life as had any president, and in that sense he was well prepared. He had grown up in a small town when the small town was the essence of American life. He'd been on the farm all those years, and he'd gone to war. And the war was the crucible. Captain Harry Truman returned from France in 1919 having led an artillery battery through the horrific Battle of the Argonne and having discovered two vitally important things about himself. First, that he had courage, plain physical courage. Until then he had never been in a fight in his life. He was the little boy forbidden by his mother to play in roughhouse games because of his glasses. He was a bookworm—a sissy, as he said himself later on, using the dreaded word. But in France he'd found he could more than hold his own in the face of the horrors of battle and, second, that he was good at leading people. He liked it and he had learned that courage is contagious. If the leader shows courage, others get the idea.

Often he was scared to death. One of the most endearing of his many letters to Bess was written after his first time under fire in France, to tell her how terrified he was. It happened at night in the rain in the Vosges Mountains. The Germans had opened fire with a withering artillery barrage. Truman and his green troops thought it could be the start of a gas attack and rushed about trying frantically not only to get their own gas masks on, but to get masks on the horses as well. And then they panicked, ran. Truman, thrown by his horse, had been nearly crushed when the horse fell on him. Out from under, seeing the others all running, he just stood there, locked in place, and called them back using every form of profanity he'd ever heard. And back they came. This was no Douglas MacArthur strutting the edge of a trench to inspire the troops. This was a man who carried extra eyeglasses in every pocket because without glasses he was nearly blind. He had memorized the eye chart in order to get into the Army. And there he was in the sudden hell of artillery shells exploding all around, shouting, shaming his men back to do what they were supposed to do.

Now flash forward to a night thirty years later, in 1948, at the Democratic National Convention in Philadelphia, when Democrats on the left and Democrats on the right had been doing everything possible to get rid of President Harry Truman for another candidate. The Dixiecrats had marched out of the convention. The liberals, who had tried to draft General Eisenhower, were down in the dumps as never before, convinced, after Truman was nominated, that all was lost. Truman was kept waiting backstage hour after hour. It was not until nearly two in the morning that he came on stage to accept the nomination. That was the year when the conventions were covered by television for the first time and the huge lights made even worse the summer furnace of Philadelphia. The crowd was drenched in perspiration, exhausted. For all the speeches there had been, nobody had said a word about winning.

Truman, in a white linen suit, walked out into the floodlights and did just what he did in the Vosges Mountains. He gave them hell. He told them, in effect, to soldier up—and that they were going to win. It was astounding. He brought the whole hall to its feet. He brought them up cheering. Old-hand reporters, even the most diehard liberals who had so little hope for him, agreed it was one of the greatest moments they had ever witnessed in American politics.

So there we have it, courage, determination, call it as you will. Dean Acheson, his Secretary of State, much later, searching for a way to describe the effect Truman could have on those around him, and why they felt as they did about him, quoted the lines from Shakespeare's *Henry V,* when King

Henry—King Harry—walks among the terrified, dispirited troops the night before the Battle of Agincourt:

> . . . every wretch, pining and pale before,
> Beholding him, plucks comfort from his looks. . . .
> His liberal eye doth give to every one . . .
> A little touch of Harry in the night.

Acheson was remembering one of the darkest times of the Truman years, when unexpectedly 260,000 Chinese Communist troops came storming into the Korean War. Through it all, as Acheson and others saw at close hand, Truman never lost confidence, never lost his essential good cheer, never lost his fundamental civility and decency toward those who worked with him. He was never known to dress down a subordinate. "Give 'em hell, Harry" never gave anybody hell behind the scenes, on the job.

His decision to go into Korea in June 1950 was the most difficult of his presidency, he said. And he felt it was the most important decision of his presidency—more difficult and important than the decision to use the atomic bomb, because he feared he might be taking the country into another still more horrible world war, a nuclear war. Yet at the time, it was a very popular decision, a point often forgotten. The country was waiting for the President to say we would go to the rescue of the South Koreans, who were being overrun by the Communist North Korean blitzkrieg. The lesson of Munich weighed heavily on everyone. In Congress, the President had strong support on both sides of the aisle, at the start at least. He was applauded by the press across the country. It was only later that summer of 1950 when the war went so sour that it became "Truman's War."

But you see, there was no corollary between popularity and the ease or difficulty of the decision. His most popular decision was, for him, his most difficult decision, while his least popular decision was, he said, not difficult at all. That was the firing of General Douglas MacArthur, by far the most unpopular, controversial act of his presidency. Attacked by all sides, torn to shreds in editorials and by radio commentators, a potent force then as today, Truman went on with his

work as usual, just riding it out. He seemed to have a sort of inner gyroscope for such times. Those around him wondered how it was possible. He said he was sure that in the long run the country would judge him to have done the right thing. Besides, he had only done his duty. The Constitution stated clearly that there will be civilian control over the military and he had taken an oath to uphold the Constitution. "It wasn't difficult for me at all," he insisted.

Truman's profound sense of history was an important part of his makeup. He believed every president should know American history at the least, and world history, ideally. A president with a sense of history is less prone to hubris. He knows he is but one link in the long chain going all the way back to the first president and that presumably will extend far into the future. He knows he has only a limited time in office and that history will be the final judge of his performance. What he does must stand the test of time. If he is blasted by the press, if his polls are plummeting as Truman's did during the Korean War, these are not the first concerns. What matters—or ought to matter—is what's best for the country and the world in the long run.

Truman probably understood the history of the presidency as well as or better than any president of this century with the exception of Woodrow Wilson, and in his first years in the White House he felt acutely the presence of the predecessors. He was sure the White House was haunted. This was before restoration of the old place, when it creaked and groaned at night with the change of temperature. Sometimes doors would fly open on their own. Alone at night, his family back in Missouri, he would walk the upstairs halls, poke about in closets, wind the clocks. He imagined his predecessors arguing over how this fellow Truman was doing so far.

His reputation seems to grow and will, I believe, continue to grow for the reason that he not only faced difficult decisions and faced them squarely, if not always correctly, but that the decisions were so often unprecedented. There were no prior examples to go by. In his first months in office, he made more difficult and far-reaching decisions than any

In April 1951, President Truman sacked General Douglas MacArthur (shown in this photograph) as commander of United Nations forces in Korea. McCullough concedes that it was the most "unpopular" and "controversial act" of Truman's presidency. But the president was confident, McCullough says, "that in the long run the country would judge him to have done the right thing." Today most American historians agree that Truman, in his capacity as commander in chief, was justified in relieving the contentious and insubordinate general. (© Carl Mydans, Time & Life Pictures-Getty Images).

president in our history, including Franklin Roosevelt and Abraham Lincoln. This much belittled, supposed backwater political hack, who seemed to have none or certainly very few of the requisite qualities of high office, turned out to do an extremely good job. And it is quite mistaken to imagine that nobody saw this at the time. Many did, and the closer they were to him, the more clearly they saw. Churchill, Marshall, and especially, I would say, Acheson, who was about as

different from Harry Truman in background and manner as anyone could be. Acheson once remarked that he had great respect for Franklin Roosevelt, but that he reserved his love for another president, meaning Harry Truman. Acheson didn't much like Roosevelt, I suspect, because Roosevelt was condescending toward him. I imagine that if Acheson were to tolerate condescension, it would have to be Acheson being condescending toward someone else.

In the course of more than one hundred interviews for my biography of Truman, I found no one who had worked with him, no one who was on the White House staff, or the White House domestic staff, or his Secret Service detail, who did not like him. He knew everybody by name on the White House staff and in the mansion itself. He knew all the Secret Service people by name. He knew all about their families—and this wasn't just a politician's trick. If he could have picked his own father, one former Secret Service man told me, it would have been Truman.

John Gunther, in a wonderful interview with Truman when Truman was Vice President, asked him what he was most interested in. "People," Truman said without hesitation.

He had a further quality, also greatly needed in the presidency: a healthy, resilient sense of humor. He loved especially the intrinsic humor of politics, the good stories of politics. Campaigning in Texas by train in 1948, he had nothing but blue skies and huge, warm crowds everywhere he stopped. It was the first time a Democratic candidate for President had ever come to Texas to campaign. That had never been necessary before. The reason now was his civil rights program, which was anything but popular in Texas. There had been warnings even of serious trouble if ever he were to show his face in Texas. But his reception was good-natured and approving the whole way across the state and Truman loved every moment. It was probably his happiest time of the whole 1948 whistle-stop odyssey. On board the train were Sam Rayburn and young Lyndon Johnson, who was running for the Senate, as well as Governor Beaufort Jester, who had earlier called Truman's civil rights program a stab in the back.

But all that was forgotten in the warmth of the days and the warmth of the crowds, and at the last stop, Rayburn's home town of Bonham, Rayburn invited the President to come by his little house on the highway, outside of the town. When the motorcade arrived, hundreds of people were on the front lawn. Rayburn told them to form a line and he would see they met the President. The Secret Service immediately objected, saying they had no identifications for anyone. Rayburn was furious. He knew every man, woman, and child on that lawn, he said, and could vouch for each and every one. So the line started for the house where Governor Jester offered greetings at the door and the President, a surreptitious bourbon within reach, shook hands with "the customers," as he called them. All was going well until Rayburn, who never took his eye off the line, shouted, "Shut the door, Beaufort, they're coming through twice."

Yet for all that it is mistaken to picture Harry Truman as just a down-home politician of the old stamp. The Harry Truman of Merle Miller's *Plain Speaking,* or of the play *Give-em Hell, Harry,* is entertaining and picturesque, but that wasn't the man who was President of the United States. He wasn't just some kind of cosmic hick.

Now he did make mistakes. He was not without flaw. He could be intemperate, profane, touchy, too quick with simplistic answers. In private conversation, he could use racial and religious slurs, old habits of the mouth. In many ways his part of Missouri was more like the Old South than the Middle West, and he grew up among people who in so-called polite society commonly used words like "nigger" and "coon."

Yet here is the man who initiated the first civil rights message ever and ordered the armed services desegregated. And let's remember, that was in 1948, long before Martin Luther King, Jr., or *Brown* v. *Board of Education,* the landmark Supreme Court decision on the desegregation of schools, or the civil rights movement. When friends and advisers warned him that he was certain to lose the election in 1948

if he persisted with the civil rights program, he said if he lost for that, it would be for a good cause. Principle mattered more than his own political hide. His courage was the courage of his convictions.

Truman's greatest single mistake was the loyalty oath program, requiring a so-called loyalty check of every federal employee. It was uncalled for, expensive, it contributed substantially to the mounting bureaucracy of Washington and damaged the reputations and lives of numbers of people who should never have had any such thing happen to them. He did it on the advice that it was good politics. He let his better nature be overcome by that argument. It was thought such a move could head off the rising right-wing cry of Communists in government, the McCarthy craze then in its early stages. But it didn't work. It was shameful.

His Supreme Court appointments weren't particularly distinguished. His seizure of the steel industry during the Korean War to avert a nationwide strike was high-handed and rightly judged unconstitutional, though his motives were understandable. We were at war and a prolonged shutdown of the production of steel threatened the very lives of our fighting forces in Korea.

He himself thought one of his worst mistakes was to have allowed the pell-mell demobilization that followed World War II. Almost overnight American military might had all but vanished. When we intervened in Korea, we had little to fight with, except for the atomic bomb. That Truman refused to use the atomic bomb in Korea, despite tremendous pressure from General MacArthur and others, stands as one of his most important decisions and one for which he has been given little credit.

The idea that Harry Truman made the decision to use the bomb against Japan and then went upstairs and went to sleep is an unfortunate myth for which he is largely accountable. I think he gave that impression because he came from a time and place in America where you were not supposed to talk about your troubles. "How are you?" "I'm fine." You might be dying of some terrible disease—"I'm fine. And you?" He refused ever to talk of the weight of the decision except to say that he made it and that it was his responsibility. . . .

With the return of peace, Truman's political troubles began. The year 1946 was particularly rough. He seemed hopelessly ineffectual. He seemed to be trying to please everybody at once, willing to say to almost anybody whatever they most wanted to hear. He wasn't at all like the Harry Truman I've been describing. He had never wanted the job and for some time appeared willing to give it up as soon as possible. He tried twice to get General Eisenhower to agree to run as a Democrat in the next election, saying he would gladly step aside. According to one account, he even offered to run as Vice President with Ike at the head of the ticket. But then after the setback in the '46 congressional elections, he became a different man.

Fire-in-the-belly for presidential glory was never part of his nature. He wasn't in the job to enlarge his estimate of himself. He didn't need that. He didn't need the limelight or fawning people around him in order to feel good about being Harry Truman.

On that note, it is interesting to see whom he did choose to have around him, as a measure of his character. There were Omar Bradley and Matthew Ridgway at the Pentagon, Eisenhower at the head of NATO. George C. Marshall served as Secretary of State and later as Secretary of Defense. There were Dean Acheson, Averell Harriman, Robert Lovett, George Kennan, Chip Bohlen, David Lilienthal, James Forrestal, Sam Rosenman, Clark Clifford—the list is long and very impressive. That most of them had more distinguished backgrounds than he, if they were taller, handsomer, it seemed to bother him not at all. When it was suggested to him that General Marshall as Secretary of State might lead people to think Marshall would make a better president, Truman's response was that yes, of course, Marshall would make a better president, but that he, Harry Truman, was President and he wanted the best people possible around him.

As no president since Theodore Roosevelt, Truman had a way of saying things that was so much his own, and I would like to quote some of them:

"I wonder how far Moses would have gone, if he had taken a poll in Egypt."

"God doesn't give a damn about pomp and circumstance."

"There are more prima donnas in Washington than in all the opera companies."

He is also frequently quoted as having said, "If you want a friend in Washington, buy a dog," and, "If you want to live like a Republican, vote Democratic." I doubt he said the first, but the second does sound like him.

"The object and its accomplishment is my philosophy," he said. Let me say that again. "The object and its accomplishment is my philosophy." And no president ever worked harder in office. At times, a little discouraged, he would say, "All the President is, is a glorified public relations man who spends his time flattering, kissing and kicking people to get them to do what they are supposed to do anyway."

Where were his strengths and his weaknesses in conflict? In interviews with those who knew him, I would ask what they believed to have been the President's major flaw. Almost always they would say he was too loyal to too many people to whom he should not have been so loyal—not as President. They were thinking mainly of the cronies—people like Harry Vaughan. Or remembering when Boss Tom Pendergast died and Vice President Harry Truman commandeered an Air Force bomber and flew to Kansas City for the funeral. "You don't forget a friend," was Truman's answer to the press.

Tom Pendergast had made Truman, and the Pendergast machine, though colorful and not without redeeming virtues, was pretty unsavory altogether.

But Truman was also, let us understand, the product of the smoke-filled room in more than just the Kansas City way. He was picked at the 1944 Democratic Convention in Chicago in a room at the Blackstone Hotel thick with smoke. He was tapped as Roosevelt's running mate and almost certain successor by the party's big-city bosses, the professional polls, who didn't want Henry Wallace, then the Vice President, because Wallace was too left wing, and didn't want Jimmy Byrnes, another Roosevelt favorite, because Byrnes was too conservative, an avowed segregationist and a lapsed Roman Catholic. They wanted Harry Truman, so Truman it was. They knew their man. They knew what stuff he was made of. And remember, this was all in a tradition of long standing. Theodore Roosevelt had been picked by a Republican machine in New York, Woodrow Wilson by the Democratic machine in New Jersey. For Franklin Roosevelt, such "good friends" as Ed Kelly of Chicago, Boss Crump of Memphis, Ed Flynn of the Bronx were indispensable. And because a candidate had the endorsement of a machine, or as in Truman's case owed his rise in politics to a corrupt organization, it didn't necessarily follow that he himself was corrupt. John Hersey, who did one of the best of all pieces ever written about Harry Truman, for *The New Yorker,* said he found no trace of corruption in Truman's record. Nor did I. Nor did the FBI when it combed through Truman's past at the time Pendergast was convicted for an insurance fraud and sent to prison. Nor did all the Republicans who ran against him in all the elections in his long political career.

I think he was almost honest to a fault. Still he understood, and felt acutely, the bargain he made with loyalty to the likes of Pendergast, and he understood why he was so often taken to task by the Republicans or the press or just ordinary citizens who didn't care for the kind of political company he kept.

Harry Vaughan was for comic relief, Truman's Falstaff. Among the delights of Truman as a biographical subject is that he enjoyed both Vaughan and Mozart. He loved a night of poker with "the boys," and he loved the National Symphony, which he attended as often as possible. If the program included Mozart or Chopin, he would frequently take the score with him.

This same Harry Truman, who adored classical music, who read Shakespeare and Cicero and *Don Quixote,* comes out of a political background about as steamy and raw as they get. And at times, this would get to him and he would escape to the privacy of a downtown Kansas City hotel room. There he would pour himself out on paper, an innermost anguish in long memoranda to himself, and these amazing documents survive in the files of the Truman Library in Independence, Missouri, along with thousands of his letters and private diaries.

Here is a striking example written when Truman was a county judge (a county commissioner really) and one of his fellow commissioners had made off with $10,000 from the county till:

This sweet associate of mine, my friend, who was supposed to back me, had already made a deal with a former crooked contractor, a friend of the Boss's . . . I had to compromise in order to get the voted road system carried out . . . I had to let a former saloonkeeper and murderer, a friend of the Boss's, steal about $10,000 from the general revenues of the county to satisfy my ideal associate and keep the crooks from getting a million or more out of the bond issue.

He is not exaggerating with the million-dollar figure. When the Pendergast organization collapsed and its ways of operation were revealed, a million dollars was found to be about standard. But then, importantly, Truman goes on:

Was I right or did I compound a felony? I don't know. . . . Anyway I've got the $6,500,000 worth of roads on the ground and at a figure that makes the crooks tear their hair. The hospital is up at less cost than any similar institution in spite of my drunken brother-in-law [Fred Wallace], whom I'd had to employ on the job to keep peace in the family. I've had to run the hospital job myself and pay him for it. . . . Am I an administrator or not? Or am I just a crook to compromise in order to get the job done? You judge it, I can't.

This is all very painful for him. He writes of being raised at his mother's knee to believe in honor, ethics, and "right living." Not only is he disgusted by the immorality he sees behind the scenes, he doesn't understand it.

But let me return to 1948, where I think we see Truman, the President, at his best. Consider first the crisis over Berlin. That spring the Russians had suddenly clamped a blockade around the city, which was then under Allied control though within the Russian zone of East Germany. Overnight, without warning, Berlin was cut off. Other than by air, there was no way to supply it. Two and a half million people were going to be without food, fuel, medical supplies. Clearly Stalin was attempting to drive the Allies out. The situation was extremely dangerous.

At an emergency meeting in the Oval Office, it was proposed that the Allies break through with an armored convoy. It looked as though World War III might be about to start. It was suggested that Berlin be abandoned. Nobody knew quite what to do. Truman said, "We stay in Berlin, period." He didn't know how that could be done any more than anyone else, but he said, "We stay in Berlin." Backbone.

An airlift had already begun as a temporary measure. Truman ordered it stepped up to the maximum. It was said by experts, including the mayor of Berlin, that to supply the city by air would be impossible, given the size of the planes and the calculated number of landings possible per day. The whole world was on edge.

"We'll stay in Berlin," Truman said again, "come what may." The supposedly insoluble problem of the limit of the plane landings per day was nicely solved: they built another airport. The airlift worked. The Russians gave up the blockade. The crisis passed.

Among the most difficult and important concepts to convey in teaching or writing history is the simple fact that things never had to turn out as they did. Events past were never on a track. Nothing was foreordained any more then than now. Nobody knew at the start that the Berlin Airlift would work. It was a model, I think, of presidential decision making, and of presidential character proving decisive.

All this, I should also remind you, was taking place in an election year. Yet at no time did Truman include any of his political advisers in the discussions about Berlin. Nor did he ever play on the tension of the crisis for his own benefit in the speeches he made.

With the question of whether to recognize Israel, Truman faced an equally complex situation but one greatly compounded by emotion. Of particular difficulty for him, personally and politically, was the position of his then Secretary of State, George Marshall, who was gravely concerned about Middle Eastern oil supplies. If Arab anger over American support for a new Jewish state meant a cut-off of Arab oil, it would not only jeopardize the Marshall Plan and the recovery of Europe but could prove disastrous should the Berlin crisis indeed turn to war.

Marshall was thinking as a military man, determined to hold to a policy that was in the best interest of the United States. It was by no means a matter of anti-Semitism, as was sometimes charged, or any lack of sympathy for the idea of a Jewish homeland. But the fact that Marshall was against an immediate recognition put Truman in an extremely difficult position. No American of the time counted higher in Truman's estimate than Marshall. He saw Marshall as the modern-day equivalent of George Washington or Robert E. Lee and valued his judgment more than that of anyone in the cabinet. Further, Marshall was far and away the most widely respected member of the administration, and if Truman were to decide against him and Marshall were then to resign, it would almost certainly mean defeat for Truman in November. He could lose the respect of the man he most respected and lose the presidency.

Truman did recognize Israel—immediately, within minutes—and he never doubted he was doing the right thing. His interest in the history of the Middle East was long standing. He had been a strong supporter of a homeland for Jewish refugees from Europe from the time he had been in the Senate. But he also knew George Marshall and was sure Marshall would stand by him, as of course Marshall did.

I have spent a sizable part of my writing life trying to understand Harry Truman and his story. I don't think we can ever know enough about him. If his loyalty was a flaw, it was his great strength also, as shown by his steadfast loyalty to Dean Acheson when Joe McCarthy came after Acheson or the unflinching support he gave David Lilienthal when Lilienthal, Truman's choice to head the Atomic Energy Commission, was accused as a "pink," a Communist. Franklin Roosevelt had not been willing to stand up for Lilienthal. Truman did. And Lilienthal was approved by the Senate.

Perhaps Truman's greatest shortcoming was his unwillingness to let us know, to let the country know then, how much more there was to him than met the eye, how much more he was than just "Give 'em hell, Harry"—that he did have this love of books, this interest in history, his affection for people, his kindness, his thoughtfulness to subordinates, the love of music, the knowledge of music, his deep and abiding love for his wife, his bedrock belief in education and learning. Though he had never gone beyond Independence High School, this was a president who enjoyed Cicero in the original Latin. We should have known that. It's good to know now, too.

A few words about the '48 campaign, which will always be part of our political lore. It's a great American metaphor, a great American story. The fellow who hasn't got a chance comes from behind and wins. Nobody in either party, not a professional politician, not a reporter, not even his own mother-in-law doubted that Tom Dewey would be the next president. The result of a *Newsweek* poll of fifty top political commentators nationwide who were asked to predict the outcome was Dewey 50, Truman 0.

No president had ever campaigned so hard or so far. Truman was sixty-four years old. Younger men who were with him through it all would describe the time on the train as one of the worst ordeals of their lives. The roadbed was rough and Truman would get the train up to 80 miles an hour at night. The food was awful, the work unrelenting. One of them told me, "It's one thing to work that hard and to stay the course when you think you're going to win, but it's quite another thing when you *know* you're going to lose." The only reason they were there, they all said, was Harry Truman.

For Truman, I think, it was an act of faith—a heroic, memorable American act of faith. The poll takers, the political reporters, the pundits, all the sundry prognosticators, and professional politicians—it didn't matter what they said, what they thought. Only the people decide, Truman was reminding the country. "Here I am, here's what I stand for—here's what I'm going to do if you keep me in the job. You decide."

Was he a great president? Yes. One of the best. And a very great American. Can we ever have another Harry Truman? Yes, I would say so. Who knows, maybe somewhere in Texas she's growing up right now.

QUESTIONS TO CONSIDER

1 Describe Truman's character. How did his character affect his political career, especially his presidency? How was Truman's "profound sense of history" an important part of his makeup? Compare him as a man to Franklin D. Roosevelt, the subject of selection 18.

2 What was the most difficult decision Truman had to make as president? What did he fear his decision might lead to? What was "the lesson of Munich"? What controversial move did Truman make to uphold his oath to the Constitution? Why did he insist that the move was "not difficult" for him?

3 What was Truman's "greatest single mistake" as president? Why did he make it? Why did David McCullough say it was "shameful"? According to McCullough, what were some of President Truman's other mistakes?

4 What crisis showed Truman, as president, at his best? How did his character affect his decision to stand firm in that crisis?

5 How did Truman make evident America's resolve to maintain the global status quo and yet avoid precipitating a third world war? When during his presidency did nuclear war seem probable?

23 Eisenhower and Kennedy: Contrasting Presidencies in a Fearful World

MICHAEL R. BESCHLOSS

Dwight David Eisenhower, the supreme commander of Allied forces in Europe during 1944 and 1945, was America's greatest hero in the postwar years. In 1952, the Republicans chose this balding, avuncular, mild-mannered soldier to win the White House back for the GOP after twenty straight years of Democratic chief executives. No Republican had occupied the White House since Herbert Hoover, whom much of the country had blamed for the crash and Depression. In the 1952 election, Eisenhower soundly defeated liberal Democrat Adlai E. Stevenson and went on to serve two terms in the White House. He left such a mark that the 1950s became popularly known as the Eisenhower years, or "the Ike Age."

For some contemporary critics, his mark was entirely negative, for they thought him an inept president who spent more time on the golf course than in tending to affairs of state. When he did attend to his job, such critics contended, his policies only worsened Cold War tensions. He ended up adopting Truman's containment policy and even announced "the domino theory," which held that if the West allowed the Communists to take over one country, they would seize its neighbors, then their neighbors, and so on until they had conquered the world. Other contemporary critics, however, regarded Ike as a masterful statesman who ended the Korean War, opposed military intervention in the internal struggles of other nations, and presided over a period of domestic prosperity.

In the years after his presidency, historians tended to side with Eisenhower's hostile critics and rated him a poor chief executive. But more recently, with new evidence and new perspectives, scholars took another look at Eisenhower and liked what they saw. Their "revisionist" view has had a considerable influence on the current generation, so much so that a recent poll of historians and presidential scholars ranked Ike ninth on the list of presidents.

As for his young successor, John F. Kennedy, presidential scholars tend to place him in the bottom tier of chief executives. Such a low ranking probably reflects a negative scholarly reaction to the "myth of Camelot," created by First Lady Jacqueline Kennedy, which compared Kennedy and his men to legendary King Arthur and his Knights of the Round Table; the King's palace and court were known as Camelot. In sharp contrast to presidential scholars, the American public has had an ongoing love affair with the slain president. Public opinion polls have consistently ranked Kennedy as the best chief executive America has ever had.

In the following selection, presidential scholar Michael R. Beschloss eschews numerical ratings and assesses Eisenhower and Kennedy solely on the basis of their strengths and weaknesses, accomplishments and failures. He argues that Eisenhower, who wanted to be "a calm unifying national symbol," was "magnificently suited" to the 1950s. On the positive side, "Ike" accepted the New Deal and tried to administer it with typical Republican efficiency. For most of the fifties, "he balanced the budget, kept inflation low, and presided over a postwar boom." On the negative side, Beschloss gives Eisenhower demerits for his failure to grasp the importance of civil rights, for his refusal to speak out against McCarthyism, and for his inability to make the Republican party a moderate one. Even so, "with his impeccable reputation for character and integrity," Beschloss writes, "he was as much a national father figure as George Washington."

Assessing Kennedy, the youngest elected president in American history and the first born in the twentieth century, is a difficult task given the relatively brief period—"two years, ten months, and two days"—that he held office. Beschloss says nothing about Kennedy's notorious philandering, which deeply hurt his wife and threatened their marriage. But Beschloss does describe the young president's "embarrassing defeat" in the 1961 Bay of Pigs fiasco—the invasion of Cuba by CIA-trained Cuban exiles, which ended in disaster. On the positive side, Beschloss contends that Kennedy excelled at "crisis management—hour to hour to hour." The "paramount moment" of his presidency was the Cuban missile crisis of October 1962, when a nuclear war almost broke out between the United States and the Soviet Union. It was the closest the world has ever come to a nuclear holocaust. Kennedy's restrained and intelligent management of that crisis, Beschloss believes, "may have saved the world." Kennedy also gets high marks for the nuclear test ban treaty he negotiated with the Soviets in 1963. On the domestic front, the author praises Kennedy for sending a powerful new civil rights bill to Congress, where it met bitter southern white opposition.

One of the most vexing problems of Kennedy's presidency was the war in distant Vietnam. Some Kennedy scholars, on the basis of declassified government documents, believe that he planned to pull American military "advisers" out of Vietnam after the 1964 election. Beschloss, however, is skeptical of that contention. He concedes that JFK might have been more willing to withdraw from Vietnam than his successor, Lyndon Johnson. But "the fact is we will never know."

After reading this clear, concise, and well-argued essay, decide for yourselves who was the more effective president—the beloved Old Warrior with bad syntax and a passion for golf (Lyndon Johnson claimed that "Ike" often wore his golf shoes in the Oval Office, leaving cleat marks on the floor) or the handsome, articulate young statesman who suffered from Addison's disease and back pain and who spoke with a Boston accent, pronouncing Cuba as "Cuber" and party as "pahty."

GLOSSARY

BAY OF PIGS   In 1961, this represented Kennedy's greatest mistake in foreign policy. It was an ill-fated invasion of Fidel Castro's island that resulted in the death or capture of Cuban refugees whom the United States had inspired, trained, and armed. The young president learned a hard lesson and never again placed his full trust in the advice of the military and intelligence communities.

BROWN v. BOARD OF EDUCATION OF TOPEKA (1954)   Chief Justice Earl Warren stated in this landmark case that "separate educational facilities are inherently unequal" and that to segregate children by race "generates a feeling of inferiority as to their status in the community that may affect their hearts and minds in a way unlikely ever to be undone." Eisenhower did not put the moral weight of the presidency behind this decision and allowed southern governors to impede integration in the public schools.

CASTRO, FIDEL   In 1959, he led a successful revolution against the dictatorial government of Fulgencio Batista in Cuba. A Communist who developed close ties with the Soviet Union, Castro remained a threat to the United States and a potential exporter of subversive doctrines that might afflict other nations in the Caribbean and Latin America.

DIRKSEN, EVERETT   A Republican leader of the Senate from Illinois, he supported Lyndon Johnson's 1964 civil rights initiatives. Johnson, unlike Kennedy, was able to artfully manipulate key political leaders to accomplish his domestic goals.

DOMINO THEORY   First voiced by President Eisenhower, it became a reason for America's reluctance to leave Vietnam. It argued that if Vietnam fell to Communism so would its neighbors. The tumbling process would eventually threaten Japan and the Philippines and thus would endanger the national security of the United States.

EXECUTIVE COMMITTEE (EX COMM)   The group of Kennedy advisers who brainstormed possible solutions to the Cuban missile crisis. They were a diverse group of doves (Adlai Stevenson) and hawks (Curtis LeMay). Ultimately, they recommended a blockade or "quarantine" of Cuba that provided Khrushchev with a way to remove the Soviet missiles and still save face (the United States promised not to invade the tiny island and informally agreed to remove its missiles from Turkey and Italy).

GAGARIN, YURI   In the spring of 1961, this Russian was the first man in space. Kennedy, under pressure to win the space race, promised that the United Sates by the end of the decade would put a man on the moon and return him safely to earth.

GOLDWATER, BARRY   A leading Republican senator from Arizona, he was the presidential nominee of his party in 1964. Lyndon Johnson easily defeated him, mainly because many Americans feared that Goldwater might too hastily use nuclear weapons in a confrontation with the Soviet Union.

KENNEDY, ROBERT F.   The president's brother, attorney general, and closest adviser. As a member of Ex Comm, he argued against military action. He ran for president in 1968 but like his brother, was cruelly assassinated.

KHRUSHCHEV, NIKITA   The bellicose and emotional Soviet premier who frightened many Americans with his boast that "we will bury you." He would accelerate the space race with the first orbiting satellite *Sputnik* and bring the world to the brink of nuclear annihilation by placing offensive missiles in Cuba.

KOREAN WAR   It started during the Truman administration when North Korean forces invaded South Korea across the 38th parallel in June 1950. Sixteen member nations of the newly formed United Nations fought this aggression. Eisenhower pledged to end the war when he ran for president in 1952, and an armistice was signed soon after his election.

MANSFIELD, MIKE   The Senate majority leader and a Kennedy friend who felt that the president would withdraw from Vietnam after he won a mandate from the American people in the 1964 election.

McCARTHYISM   A political philosophy, named after a Wisconsin senator, that frightened Americans in the 1950s and destroyed the careers of many innocent people. The demagogue Joseph McCarthy argued that Communism had infiltrated the army, the State Department, and even Hollywood.

MORROW, E. FREDERICK   The only significant African American within the Eisenhower administration, he was repeatedly frustrated in his attempt to convince the president to adopt a vigorous and proactive position that would help his race achieve a measure of equality.

O'DONNELL, KENNETH   One of Kennedy's closest advisers who, along with David Powers, wrote a moving tribute to the president entitled *Johnny, We Hardly Knew Ye*. He argued that Kennedy would have withdrawn from Vietnam after winning the presidential election of 1964.

PT 109   Kennedy's boat that was rammed by a Japanese destroyer during World War II. The future president showed courage in bringing his crew to safety. He paid a heavy price for his heroism by incurring an injury to his back that caused him great pain for the rest of his life.

RESTON, JAMES   The *New York Times* columnist who was not certain that Kennedy had a grand vision of the presidency. Yet, when the young chief executive died in Dallas, Reston wrote that what was killed "was not only the president, but the promise."

SORENSEN, THEODORE   Kennedy's speech writer and friend who was responsible for some of the president's most memorable statements, such as "Ask not what your country can do for you, ask what you can do for your country." Soon after the tragic assassination, he wrote a first-hand book about the murdered president entitled *Kennedy*.

SPUTNIK   The first orbiting satellite that the Russians put into space in 1957. This panicked many Americans and resulted in educational initiatives in science and math so that the United States could catch up with the Soviets in the space race. The assumption was that the nation that controlled space would have an enormous advantage in a nuclear war.

STEVENSON, ADLAI   Eisenhower defeated this former Illinois governor in presidential elections in 1952 and 1956. A liberal and an idealist, he did not capture the imagination of the American people as much as the World War II hero, who represented stability and continued prosperity.

TAFT, ROBERT A.   Isolationist leader of the Republican party from Ohio who might have won the Republican nomination for president in 1952 had he assured Eisenhower that defeating the Soviets and maintaining a significant American presence in the world community was a high priority.

U-2   A high-altitude spy plane that was shot down over the Soviet Union in 1960. It accelerated Cold War tensions and ruined a summit meeting in Paris that Eisenhower had planned with Khrushchev.

For most of American history, the presidency has been a weak office—and that was very much in keeping with what the framers intended. They did not want another king of England; they didn't want a dictator. They made sure that there were checks against presidential power, one of them being impeachment, and they were very worried about the idea of a president who would do too much. So a lot of the power of the presidency comes not at all from what's in the Constitution but from two other factors.

The first is the president's ability to go to the American people and ask them for something—especially sacrifice. One very good example would be Franklin Roosevelt in 1940, saying, "You may not want to get prepared for a possible war in Europe and Asia, but this is something I've thought a lot about and this is a sacrifice that we may have to make." Another example would be a president's appeal for a painful tax increase to achieve a balanced budget.

The second source of presidential power is a president's ability to get things out of Congress. The founders hoped that presidents would have such moral authority and people would think they were so wise that members of Congress would be intimidated. If a president went to Congress and asked for something like civil rights, members would take heed. That's one reason why Lyndon Johnson was a much more powerful president in 1964, 1965, and 1966 than I think others might have been: Because of his experience as one of the most canny and powerful leaders in the history of Congress, he was extraordinarily effective at getting what he wanted.

For most of our lifetimes, we have been in a situation that is something of an aberration. When I was ten years old, hoping to be able to write history about presidents when I grew up, it seemed very

glamorous. I thought these people were, to crib a phrase from Leonardo DiCaprio, "kings of the world." The president was the centerpiece of the American political solar system, the center of our foreign and domestic policy, the most powerful person in the American government—and America was astride the world. That was the case from Franklin Roosevelt until the last year of George Bush.

In the 1930s Congress and the American people granted Roosevelt extraordinary influence over domestic affairs. In the wake of Pearl Harbor, they extended that power into foreign affairs. After 1945, Americans thought it was a good idea for power to flow to Washington. That enhanced the power of presidents. People liked federal action and federal programs. Congress was inclined to defer to the chief executive in foreign policy because we had to win the cold war. Then in the late 1960s and early 1970s, Americans grew more skeptical about Big Government. Power began to flow away from Washington. Then the cold war ended, and foreign policy seemed less urgent. The result is that now we are returning to a moment in which presidents don't have the kind of power that they had between the 1930s and the 1980s.

Dwight Eisenhower became president of the United States in 1953, at the apex of presidential power. But that power was enhanced by the man himself and the situation in which he found himself. It is hard to imagine a leader in a more commanding position. As the hero of World War II in Europe, Eisenhower enjoyed as august a national and world reputation as anyone who has ever entered the White House. With his impeccable reputation for character and integrity, he was as much a national father figure as George Washington.

Eisenhower had been elected by a landslide, and in that election he took both houses of Congress back from the Democrats. He could fairly argue that his ample coattails had made the difference. This was a new president with enormous reservoirs of political strength but also limited ambitions—much more limited than those of Woodrow Wilson, Franklin Roosevelt, or Lyndon Johnson.

Michael R. Beschloss, "Dwight D. Eisenhower and John F. Kennedy: A Study in Contrasts," from *Power and the Presidency* by Robert A. Wilson. Copyright © 1999 by Robert A. Wilson. Reprinted by permission of PublicAffairs, a member of Perseus Books, L.L.C.

Dwight David Eisenhower was the most popular Republican of his era. In the presidential elections of 1952 and 1956, huge cheering crowds chanted "We like Ike" and helped the World War II hero easily defeat Democratic candidate Adlai Stevenson. (© UPI/Bettmann/Corbis)

Although he would never have alienated conservatives in his party by saying so in public, Eisenhower had no desire to turn back the clock on the New Deal. Instead, he wanted to consolidate those reforms and do what Republicans do: administer the programs more efficiently and economically. Beyond that he saw himself—among the conflicting demands of labor, business, finance, and other engines of the American economy—as a balance wheel poised to let postwar prosperity roar ahead under a balanced budget.

He wanted to eliminate isolationism from the Republican Party and postwar America. We sometimes forget how close Republicans came to nominating the isolationist senator Robert Taft of Ohio in 1952. Ike had such deep convictions about this issue that in the winter of 1952 he went to Taft and said, "I feel so strongly about defending the Free World against the Soviets that I will make you a deal. If you renounce isolationism, I won't run against you for president."

Taft easily could have accepted, and Eisenhower never would have been president. It shows you how deeply he felt about this. He wanted to use his office to make sure that no postwar national leader could come to power without vowing to ensure that the United States would remain permanently engaged in the world. That comes about as close as anything Eisenhower had to a deep political conviction.

He hoped that by the end of his eight years in office he would be able somehow to reduce the harshness of the cold war. As a military man, he knew the danger of nuclear war. Once, sitting through a briefing by a civil defense official who was blithely describing how the federal government could survive underground after a Soviet nuclear attack, Ike told him to stop. "We won't be carrying on with government," he barked. "We'll be grubbing for worms!" He was disgusted that the United States had to spend billions of dollars on what he called "sterile" military programs, when it could have invested in schools and hospitals and roads.

To hold down the arms race as much as possible, he worked out a wonderful tacit agreement with Soviet premier Nikita Khrushchev. Khrushchev wanted to build up his economy. He didn't want to spend a lot of money on the Soviet military because he wanted to start feeding people and recover from the devastation of World War II. But he knew that to cover this he would have to give speeches in public that said quite the opposite. So Khrushchev would deliver himself of such memorable lines as, "We Soviets are cranking out missiles like sausages, and we will bury you because our defense structure is pulling ahead of the United States."

Eisenhower dealt with this much as an adult deals with a small boy who is lightly punching him in the stomach. He figured that leaving Khrushchev's boasts unanswered was a pretty small price to pay if it meant that Khrushchev would not spend much money building up his military.

The result was that the arms race was about as slow during the 1950s as it could have been, and Eisenhower was well on the way to creating an atmosphere of communication. Had the U-2 not fallen down in 1960 and had the presidential campaign taken place in a more peaceful atmosphere, I think you would have seen John Kennedy and Richard Nixon competing on the basis of who could increase

the opening to the Soviets that Eisenhower had created. Whether or not that would have sped the end of the cold war is open to argument.

In 1953 Eisenhower was disheartened by the bitterness and exhaustion in the American political climate. We had been through a stock market crash, a Great Depression, five years of global war, a growing Soviet threat, full-fledged cold war, the Korean War, McCarthyism and the backlash against it—all in the space of less than a generation. Our nerves were frayed. Ike wanted to be the calming, unifying national symbol who could give us a little bit of breathing space.

What personal qualities did Eisenhower bring to the Oval Office? The most obvious: He was the most popular human being in America and probably the most popular human being in the world. But he was also a much more intelligent man than people understood at the time. People who watched his press conferences—filled with those sentences that lacked verbs and never seemed to end—thought Ike was a wonderful guy but not too bright. Now, almost a half-century later, we have access to his letters and diaries and records of his private meetings. When you take Ike off the public platform and put him in a small room where he's talking candidly to his aides and friends, you find a leader much in command of complex issues—very different from the caricature of the time.

Harry Truman once predicted that when Ike became president he would be frustrated. Truman said that as a general, Eisenhower would shout, "Do this!" and "Do that!"—but that in the White House, when he did that, nothing would happen. Indeed, Ike had never been in domestic politics. But what people overlooked was that in the army for almost forty years he had been operating in large, bureaucratic organizations, not least the Allied Expeditionary Force in Europe. This was good experience for a president who had to deal with a rapidly growing CIA and Pentagon—and with ballooning domestic bureaucracies like the new Department of Health, Education, and Welfare.

What qualities did Eisenhower lack? Well, as an orator, he was no Franklin Roosevelt. He seemed to design his language to make sure that no one would remember—or in some cases, understand—what he said. Some scholars, like Fred Greenstein of Princeton, think that Eisenhower was often deliberately boring or opaque as a ploy, to keep from polarizing people. Maybe so, but the inability to use what Theodore Roosevelt called the "bully pulpit" is a big problem for a president. I think it robbed Eisenhower of considerable power that, used in the right way, could have been very important for this country.

Imagine if Eisenhower had been president in 1939. That was when FDR was making the case to the American people that we had to build our own defense forces because we might have to fight a war. His oratorical skills helped to move opinion in Congress and among the American people enough so that when war came, we were prepared. Had Roosevelt been mute, we would have lost World War II.

The ability to move a nation is essential if a president wants to ask Congress and the American people for something. It is just as essential if things are going bad. That's when a president needs to reassure the public. In 1958 America was plunging into recession. Eisenhower refused to improve things by unbalancing the budget. The Republicans lost badly in the 1958 midterm elections, largely because Ike could not or would not explain to Americans why it was necessary to stay the economic course. He allowed his critics to take the initiative, saying, "Eisenhower is tired and washed up and so obsessed with a balanced budget that he doesn't care about people who are suffering."

Another example came the previous year, with the Soviet launching of Sputnik, the first earth satellite. Eisenhower's foes said, "Ike is so lazy and asleep at the switch that he's allowed the Russians to be first to launch a satellite. Now the Russians can drop nuclear weapons on Chicago or Detroit—or Hanover, New Hampshire." In fact, sending up Sputnik was not the same thing as being able to drop a bomb precisely on a target by missile. The Soviets were still years away from being able to do that. But Eisenhower was unable to make that case to the American people. The result was near national hysteria.

Another of Ike's shortcomings was as a horse trader. He once said, "I don't know how to do what you have to do to get something out of a congressman." You wouldn't have heard Lyndon Johnson saying such a thing. Getting members of Congress to do things they don't want to do is a crucial part of being president.

On one of the tapes LBJ made of his private conversations as president, you hear Johnson in 1964. He knows that the key to getting his civil rights bill passed will be Everett Dirksen of Illinois, Republican leader of the Senate. He calls Dirksen, whom he's known for twenty years, and essentially says, "Ev, I know you have some doubts about this bill, but if you decide to support it, a hundred years from now every American schoolchild will know two names—Abraham Lincoln and Everett Dirksen." Dirksen liked the sound of that. He supported the bill, and the rest was history. You will never find an example of a conversation like that in the annals of Dwight Eisenhower. And his diffidence about Congress limited his ability to get things done.

If Eisenhower were president in a time requiring a leader standing in the epicenter of heroic change—like Roosevelt in the 1930s and 1940s, for example—he probably would have been a disaster because he lacked the ambitions and the skills that kind of presidential leadership requires. Yet Eisenhower was magnificently suited to the 1950s. He got people to accept Social Security and other controversial reforms as a permanent way of American life. For much of the decade, he balanced the budget, kept inflation low, and presided over a postwar boom. He fathered the interstate highway system. He was the very image of a chief of state. He made Americans feel happy about themselves and their country. He killed isolationism. He muted the U.S.–Soviet arms race as much as any president could have.

To use the parlance of West Point, I'd suggest three demerits in Ike's record as president. The first: Joseph McCarthy. Eisenhower was a civil libertarian. He knew what Senator McCarthy's reckless charges about internal communism were doing to this country. Imagine if Eisenhower had stood up in 1953 and said, "McCarthyism is a poison in this society. Believe me, of all people, I'll be the last to let this country be injured by communists within, but we can't tear this nation apart." That could have changed history. Instead, Ike was stunningly quiet, although some recent revisionists argue that he tried to tunnel against McCarthy behind the scenes.

The most coherent statement Ike made against McCarthy was at Dartmouth in June 1953. He had been chatting about the virtues of playing golf. He urged Dartmouth men to have fun in their lives. They didn't seem to need the advice. But toward the end of that speech, he got serious. He had been told how McCarthy's agents had tried to have certain "subversive" books removed from U.S. embassy libraries abroad. He told the Dartmouth graduates, "Don't join the book burners. Instead, go to the library and read books on communism so you'll know what you're fighting against." Nicely said, but these two paragraphs got little attention. They leave you feeling that Eisenhower could and should have said so much more.

Demerit two: civil rights. Ike never understood how vital it was to integrate American society after World War II. Imagine how he could have used that great moral authority and world reputation. He could have said in 1953, "I went to Europe and helped win the Second World War, but that was just part of the job. Now we have to finish what we fought for by bringing equal rights to all Americans." No other political figure would have carried so much weight.

But Ike had something of a blind spot on civil rights. He had spent a lot of his life in the South and, I think, overestimated the degree of resistance to a civil rights bill. We now know that in 1954, when the Supreme Court in *Brown* v. *Board of Education* ordered the desegregation of public schools, Eisenhower privately thought it a bad idea.

Ike had an aide named Frederic Morrow, who was the first African American to serve on a president's staff. Morrow would talk to the president about civil rights on occasion and would come away feeling that he had made some headway. Then Ike would fly to Georgia for a hunting weekend with southern friends. And when he came back, it was almost as if his conversation with Morrow had never occurred.

Civil rights was a case where Eisenhower's instincts of compromise and moderation served him badly. Segregation was a moral issue. I think that the president's foot-dragging caused the civil rights revolution, when it reached full force in the 1960s, to be more bitter and violent.

The final demerit: One test of leaders is how they make sure that their ideas and programs will live on after they're gone. One way they do that is by building a political movement like a political party. Eisenhower tried to recreate his party in the image of what he called "modern Republicanism." But he failed. Four years after he left office, Republicans scorned his moderation as a "dime-store New Deal" and nominated Barry Goldwater. The Republican Party we see today is far more the party of Goldwater than of Eisenhower.

Another way you make sure your policies survive is with your words. But so unable or unwilling was Eisenhower to use his powers of persuasion that some of the basic tenets of his political credo vanished almost as soon as he left the White House. Because Ike failed to make the case for a balanced budget, his Democratic successors were able to start the great inflation of the 1960s. Because Ike failed to make the case for a moderate arms race, John Kennedy started what was at that time the largest arms buildup in human history.

Another way is to make sure you are followed by leaders who will carry on your purposes. Here Eisenhower failed. He once said that one of the biggest disappointments of his life was that in the race to succeed him, John Kennedy defeated his vice president, Richard Nixon. He called that "a repudiation of everything I've stood for for eight years."

It is hard to imagine two more different men than Dwight Eisenhower and John F. Kennedy—and perhaps in no way more so than this: Eisenhower in 1953 had access to vast amounts of power; Kennedy in 1961 had access to little.

This 1962 photograph shows the Kennedy brothers at the height of the "Camelot" era. Robert, the attorney general, is on the left; Ted, the new senator from Massachusetts, is in the center; and John, the president, is on the right. They brought glamour, wealth, and the inimitable "Kennedy style" to the political arena. The Kennedys were also fortunate that the press corps, in the early 1960s, ignored the private indiscretions of public figures. (Cecil Stoughton, White House/John Fitzgerald Kennedy Library, Boston)

Kennedy had been elected president by a margin of only 100,000 votes. Congress remained Democratic, but since most members had run well ahead of the new president, they felt they owed him little. As Kennedy saw it, he was faced by a House and Senate dominated by hostile coalitions of conservative Republicans and southern Democrats. Many of those who had known him as a fellow congressman or senator found it hard to get out of the habit of thinking of him as a distracted, absentee backbencher.

The American people had voted for Kennedy—narrowly—but they didn't really know him. Unlike Eisenhower, from the moment he was elected, Kennedy had to work hard to make an impression. He was always worried that he looked too young for people to think of him as a president. And when you look at videotape and newsreels of the period, you notice how stiff and formal Kennedy is on the platform.

JFK came to the presidency devoid of executive experience. The biggest organizations he had ever run were his Senate office and the PT-109 he commanded during World War II. What's more, he had been seeking the presidency for so long that he had only vague instincts about where he wanted to take the country. He did want to do something in civil rights. In the 1960 campaign, he promised to end discrimination "with the stroke of a pen." On health care, education, the minimum wage, the other social issues, he was a mainstream Democrat. He hoped to get the country through eight years without a nuclear holocaust and to improve things with the Soviets, if possible. He wanted a nuclear test ban treaty.

But as he was riding to the inaugural ceremonies with Kennedy in 1961, James Reston, the great *New York Times* columnist, asked what kind of country Kennedy wanted to leave his successor. Kennedy looked at him quizzically, as if he were looking at the man in the moon. Kennedy's method was never the grand vision of a Wilson or Reagan. It was crisis management—hour to hour to hour.

Kennedy's vow to land a man on the moon before 1970 is a perfect example. When he became president, he had no intention of launching a crash moon program. Advisers told him it would be too expensive and would unbalance a space program that was divided among communications, military, weather, exploration, and other projects.

But in the spring of 1961, the Russians injured American pride by launching the first man, Yuri Gagarin, into space. Then Kennedy suffered an embarrassing defeat when he and the CIA tried to use Cuban exiles to invade Cuba at the Bay of Pigs and seize the country from Fidel Castro. In the wake of that botched invasion, he badgered his aides for some quick fix that would help to restore American prestige. The moon-landing program was rolled out of mothballs.

People at the time often said Eisenhower was responsible for the Bay of Pigs, since it was Eisenhower's plan to take Cuba back from Castro. I think that has a hard time surviving scrutiny. Eisenhower would not necessarily have approved the invasion's going forward, and he would not necessarily have run it the same way. His son once asked him, "Is there a possibility that if you had been president, the Bay of Pigs would have happened?" Ike reminded him of Normandy and said, "I don't run no bad invasions."

Unlike Eisenhower, who almost flaunted his affinity for paperback westerns, Kennedy was a voracious reader of high intelligence. And we also remember JFK as one of the great orators of American history, which is only half right. Extemporaneously, he tended to speak too fast and with language that did not last for long. The great utterances we think of as coming from Kennedy—"Ask not what your country can do for you"; "We choose to go to the moon";

"Ich bin ein Berliner"—were almost all in prepared speeches, usually written by his gifted speechwriter Theodore Sorensen. If you read Kennedy's speeches from his earliest days as a congressman in 1947, you can see the difference at the instant Sorensen signs on in 1953. It's almost like the moment in *The Wizard of Oz* when the film goes from black and white to color. Suddenly, Kennedy had found his voice.

And when he used that voice, he was amazingly successful in moving public opinion. Think of the impact of Kennedy's inaugural or his Oval Office speech in October 1962, announcing Soviet missiles in Cuba and what he planned to do about them, or his civil rights address in June 1963, when he finally declared—as no president had ever declared—that civil rights was a "moral issue" that was "as old as the Scriptures and as clear as the Constitution."

JFK may never have run a large bureaucratic organization, but he was terrific at managing small groups. Look at the paramount moment of the Kennedy presidency—the Cuban missile crisis. How did he deal with the problem? He formed a small group of trusted officials, the Ex Comm (Executive Committee), which met in the Cabinet Room under the close supervision of the president and his brother Robert. Robert Kennedy was probably the most powerful member of a presidential entourage that we've seen in this century. That cut both ways. On the one hand, John Kennedy had someone he could rely upon as absolutely loyal, someone who totally shared his purposes. But on the other hand, it was virtually impossible for the president to distance himself from anything his attorney general did, since people assumed that when Robert Kennedy spoke, the message came from his brother.

The tape recordings of the Ex Comm meetings over thirteen days make it clear how enormously important it was to have Kennedy and his brother massaging the discussion. During the first week, the group moved from an almost certain intention to bomb the missile sites and invade Cuba to what JFK finally did: throw a quarantine around the island and demand that Nikita Khrushchev haul the missiles out. We now know that had Kennedy bombed, it might have easily escalated to a third world war. If Eisenhower had been running those meetings, with his Olympian approach, they might have been not nearly so effective. Here, Kennedy's talent for crisis management may have saved the world.

He had less success in his day-to-day dealings with Congress. One senator observed that the president would call him and say, "I sure hope I can count on your help on this bill." And he'd reply, "Mr. President, I'd love to help you, but it would cause me big problems in my state." If Lyndon Johnson had been president, he would have said, "Tough luck!" and pulled every lever he could to get his bill, even if it meant phoning the senator's bank and having his mortgage called. But Kennedy would say, "I understand. Perhaps you'll be with me the next time."

A good example is civil rights. Whatever he had pledged in the 1960 campaign, he was too overwhelmed by the opposition on Capitol Hill to do much to integrate American society. Voters who remembered his promise to end racial separation with a stroke of his pen angrily sent bottles of ink to the White House. Privately, he kept saying, "Wait until 1965. I've got to get reelected in a big way. If I'm lucky enough to run against Barry Goldwater, I'll win in a landslide with a big margin in Congress. Then on all the legislation I want, I can let 'er rip."

But the "Negro revolution," as people called it then, would not wait. In June 1963, with the South erupting in flames, Kennedy sent Congress a civil rights bill that was radical for its time. It was late, and he was pushed into it by events, but this was genuinely a profile in courage. JFK's public approval ratings dropped about twenty points. Southern states that had helped him win the presidency in 1960 turned against him. When Kennedy went to Texas in November 1963, he was by no means a shoo-in for reelection, and the reason was civil rights.

Unlike Eisenhower, Kennedy never had the eight years he had hoped for. Only two years, ten months, two days. And he never got that landslide in 1964. That went to Lyndon Johnson, who did have the good luck to run against Barry Goldwater. Thus to understand JFK's use of power, we have to ask two final questions about what might have happened had he lived.

First, what would have happened to his civil rights bill? I think that there is a good chance the Senate would have defeated it. In the aftermath of Kennedy's murder, Johnson was able to say, "Pass this bill as the memorial to our beloved late president." As I've mentioned, the Johnson tapes show that he used his monumental abilities to squeeze members of Congress to get the bill passed. Had Kennedy lived, neither of those things would have been possible. If you have to pull something redeeming out of the tragedy of Dallas, then, it is fair to say that because JFK gave his life, 20 million African Americans gained their rights sooner than they might have.

The other question is what Kennedy would have done in Vietnam. Some of Kennedy's champions, like Senate majority leader Mike Mansfield and his aide Kenneth O'Donnell, quote him as having said privately that he couldn't pull out before the 1964 election because he would be vilified as soft on communism. According to them, he planned to keep the troops in until after he was safely reelected, get the Saigon government to ask us to leave, and then withdraw.

I tend to be skeptical of this. If true, it means that Kennedy cynically would have kept young Americans in harm's way for fourteen months or more merely to help himself through the next election, then surrendered the commitment for which they'd been fighting.

Nor am I convinced by the notion that a reelected Kennedy in 1965, suddenly would have thrown caution to the winds. He still would have to serve as president for four years, and if he seemed to cave in on Vietnam in those times in which most Americans believed in the domino theory, there would have been a national backlash that would have undercut his ability to get anything he wanted from Congress, foreign or domestic.

And there was always in his mind the possibility that Robert Kennedy, or other Kennedys, might run for president. I doubt that he would have done something that might so injure his family's durability in American politics.

A greater possibility is that if Kennedy had escalated the war for two years and found himself as frustrated as Lyndon Johnson was, he might have been more willing than LBJ to pull out. Throughout his political career, Kennedy was adept at cutting losses.

The fact is, we will never know.

QUESTIONS TO CONSIDER

1 Did the framers of the Constitution want an all-powerful presidency? What two factors from the 1930s through the 1980s have increased the power of the men who have occupied the Oval Office? What roles did Franklin Roosevelt and Lyndon Johnson play in increasing the power of the presidency?

2 What made Dwight David Eisenhower a man with a "national and world reputation" by the time he became president? What were his views on the continuation of the New Deal, the role that the United States should play in world affairs, and the handling of Nikita Khrushchev?

3 What personal qualities did Eisenhower have that made him an effective president, and what qualities did he lack that made his administration less notable than it might have been? Why does Beschloss conclude that Eisenhower was "magnificently suited to the 1950s" in the goals he accomplished?

4 What "three demerits" does Beschloss give Eisenhower's presidential record? Were these negative measures more important than Eisenhower's achievements? What did Eisenhower mean when he stated that the outcome of the 1960 presidential election was "a repudiation of everything I've stood for"?

5 Compare the impressions that the American people had of Eisenhower and Kennedy at the start of their presidential administrations. Why does Beschloss conclude that Kennedy's strength was "crisis management"? How did Kennedy display this talent during the Cuban missile crisis?

6 Compare Kennedy's dealings with Congress with those of Lyndon Johnson. Explain why Beschloss believes that Kennedy would not have been able to drive his civil rights legislation through Congress or remove American troops from Vietnam. Is it fair to evaluate a president who lived for only one thousand days in office?

24 Trapped: Lyndon Johnson and the Nightmare of Vietnam

LARRY L. KING

The Vietnam War was one of the most controversial episodes in United States history. American involvement in that conflict began with Truman and persisted through Democratic and Republican administrations alike, although the largest escalation took place under Lyndon Johnson—the subject of this selection.

To place Larry King's account in proper context, let us review what had gone on in Vietnam before the Johnson escalation. For more than twenty years, war had racked that distant Asian land. Initially, Communist and nationalist forces under Ho Chi Minh had battled to liberate their homeland from French colonial rule. The United States was suspicious of Ho, who was an avowed Communist trained in Moscow. But Ho was also an intense nationalist: he was determined to create a united and independent Vietnam and never wavered from that goal. Suspicious of Ho because of his Communist connections, the United States sided with the French against Ho and the Vietnamese; by 1954, when Dwight D. Eisenhower was president, the United States was footing 70 percent of the French cost of prosecuting a war that was highly unpopular in France. When Vietnamese forces surrounded and besieged twelve thousand French troops at Dien Bien Phu, Eisenhower's closest personal advisers urged armed American intervention to save the French position. Admiral Arthur Radford, chairman of the Joint Chiefs, even recommended dropping the atomic bomb on the Vietnamese. But Eisenhower would have none of it.

The Eisenhower administration, however, continued using American aid and influence to combat Communism in Indochina. In 1955, after suffering a humiliating defeat at Dien Bien Phu, the French withdrew from Vietnam, whereupon the United States acted to prevent Ho Chi Minh from gaining complete control there. Eisenhower and his secretary of state, John Foster Dulles, ignored an international agreement in Geneva that called for free elections and helped install a repressive, anti-Communist regime in South Vietnam, supplying it with money, weapons, and military advisers. From the outset, American policymakers viewed Ho Chi Minh's government in North Vietnam as part of a world Communist conspiracy directed by Moscow and Beijing. If Communism was not halted in Vietnam, they feared, then all Asia would ultimately succumb. Eisenhower himself repeated the analogy that it would be like a row of falling dominoes.

American intervention aroused Ho Chi Minh, who rushed help to nationalist guerrillas in South Vietnam and set out to unite all of Vietnam under his leadership. With civil war raging across South Vietnam, the Eisenhower administration stepped up the flow of American military aid to the government there, situated in the capital city of Saigon. Under President John F. Kennedy, an enthusiast for counterinsurgency (or counterguerrilla warfare), the number of American advisers rose from 650 to 23,000. But Kennedy became disillusioned with American involvement in Vietnam and devised a disengagement plan before he was assassinated in November 1963. Whether he would have implemented the plan cannot be stated with certainty. When Vice President Johnson succeeded Kennedy, he nullified the disengagement plan and (with the encouragement of Kennedy's own advisers) continued American assistance to South Vietnam. Then, in the Gulf of Tonkin Resolution in August 1964, Congress empowered the president to use armed force against "Communist aggression" in Vietnam. But Johnson repeatedly vowed, "We are not going to send American boys nine or ten thousand miles away from home to do what Asian boys ought to be doing for themselves."

Over the next winter, however, all that changed. In November and December 1964, South Vietnamese guerrillas of the National Liberation Front (or Vietcong) killed seven United States advisers and wounded more than a hundred others in mortar and bomb attacks. Johnson's Texas blood was up: he wasn't going to let them "shoot our boys" out there, fire on "our flag." He talked obsessively about Communist "aggression" in Vietnam, about Munich and the lesson of appeasement, about how his enemies would call him "a coward," "an unmanly man," if he let Ho Chi Minh run through the streets of Saigon. He couldn't depend on the United Nations to act—"It couldn't pour piss out of a boot if the instructions were printed on the heel." In February 1965, the administration became convinced that the coup-plagued Saigon government was about to collapse and that the United States had to do something drastic or South Vietnam would be lost and American international prestige and influence severely damaged. Accordingly, Johnson and his advisers moved to Americanize the war, sending waves of United States warplanes roaring over North Vietnam and 3,200 marines into the South.

The Americanization of the war took place with such stealth that people at home were hardly aware of the change. As reporter David Halberstam later wrote, United States decision makers "inched across the Rubicon without even admitting it," and the task of their press secretaries was "to misinform the public." The biggest misinformers were Johnson and his spokesmen, who lied about costs (which were staggering), casualties, victories, and build-ups. By June, more than 75,000 American soldiers were in Vietnam, and combat troops were fighting Vietcong and North Vietnamese regulars in an Asian land war that Johnson had sworn to avoid. Soon troops were pouring in, and the war reeled out of control as each American escalation stiffened Vietcong and North Vietnamese resistance, which in turn led to more American escalation. By 1968, more than 500,000 American troops were fighting in that fire-scarred land. In the eyes of the administration and the Pentagon, it was unthinkable that America's awesome military power could fail to crush tiny North Vietnam and the Vietcong.

But the unthinkable came true. America's military forces failed to smash their Vietnamese foe, and the war bogged down in stalemate. How Johnson trapped himself and his country in the quagmire of Vietnam is the subject of the following selection, written by Larry L. King, a native Texan and an eminent author, historian, and journalist. As a member of Johnson's political staff, King had occasion to observe his fellow Texan up close, and it shows in the stunning story he has to tell. To help us understand Johnson, King recounts the president's Texas background, personality, and political career in prose so stirring and full of insight and wit that you will not believe you are reading history. You will hear Johnson speak, see the world through his eyes, and feel his hurts and anger. You will think with Johnson as a combination of factors—his Cold War assumptions about a world Communist conspiracy and the domino theory, his belief in American invincibility, his emulation of mythical forebears, and his own deep-seated insecurities—drives him ever deeper into a war he never wanted to fight.

Finally, as King says, Johnson's manhood got tangled up in that horrendous conflict. To illustrate, King describes an episode that is shocking, hilarious, and sad all at the same time, an episode that captures perfectly Johnson's agony over Vietnam. This is surely one of the great portraits in literature.

GLOSSARY

ACHESON, DEAN   As Harry Truman's secretary of state, he was one of the principal architects of the policy of containing Communism that the United States developed in the early years of the Cold War.

ALAMO   The famous battle of the Texas revolution where 187 rebels held off a much larger force of Mexicans for more than a week. Lyndon Johnson saw this as a symbol of the willpower and macho determination that characterized the American spirit.

BUNDY, McGEORGE   The former dean of the arts and sciences faculty at Harvard, he was a "hawk" on the war in Vietnam when he served as national security adviser for both Kennedy and Johnson.

CHIANG KAI-SHEK   The leader of the Chinese Nationalists, who, despite American support, lost to the Communist forces under Mao Tse-tung. In 1949, the Nationalists

retreated to Formosa, where they hoped to mount an assault to regain control of the mainland.

CLIFFORD, CLARK   He replaced Robert McNamara as President Johnson's secretary of defense. Along with other trusted "wise men" (Dean Acheson and Omar Bradley among them), Clark recommended limiting the bombing of North Vietnam.

DIEM, NGO DINH   After the French left Vietnam in 1954, the United States provided economic and military support to Diem, who led the new government in South Vietnam. However, he was unable to unite his people or effectively fight the Communists. In November 1963, Diem died in a coup that had the approval of the American government.

DOMINO THEORY   First voiced by President Eisenhower, it became a reason for America's reluctance to leave Vietnam. It argued that if Vietnam fell to Communism so would its neighbors. The tumbling process would eventually threaten Japan and the Philippines and thus endanger the national security of the United States.

DULLES, JOHN FOSTER Eisenhower's secretary of state (1953–1959) and a militant cold warrior, he believed that threats of "massive nuclear retaliation" were the best way to deal with the Communist world.

FULBRIGHT, WILLIAM J. An Arkansas senator and chairman of the Foreign Relations Committee, he became an increasingly vocal critic of Johnson's escalation of the war in Vietnam. LBJ began referring to him as "Halfbright."

GOLDWATER, BARRY A conservative Republican senator from Arizona and a leading "hawk," Johnson easily defeated him in the presidential election of 1964.

GREAT SOCIETY Johnson's domestic reform agenda, which he saw as a fulfillment of FDR's New Deal. Many of the programs (civil rights, Medicaid, Medicare) were part of Kennedy's New Frontier. The war in Vietnam took both the focus and the funding of LBJ's administration away from the Great Society.

GULF OF TONKIN In August of 1964, the American destroyer *Maddox* opened fire on what it believed were enemy gunboats. When Johnson addressed Congress, he stated that the Communists had initiated an unprovoked attack. Since American ships had shelled the North Vietnamese coast and there was no evidence that Communist gunboats had attacked the *Maddox,* the president's statements were clearly misleading. Not knowing the true facts of the case, Congress empowered Johnson to use "all measures to repel any armed attack against the forces of the United States." The Gulf of Tonkin Resolution gave LBJ a virtual blank check to fight an undeclared war in Vietnam.

HALBERSTAM, DAVID A Pulitzer Prize–winning journalist who wrote a best-selling book entitled *The Best and the Brightest.* It examined the talented and intelligent advisers who made so many poor decisions while leading both Kennedy and Johnson into the war in Vietnam.

HO CHI MINH A Communist and a nationalist, he fought the French and then the Americans to establish a unified and independent Vietnam.

HUMPHREY, HUBERT LBJ's vice president who ran for president in 1968 only to lose to Richard Nixon. King concludes that Johnson abused Humphrey by publicly embarrassing him, and even kicking the proud Minnesotan.

KEARNS, DORIS (Now Doris Kearns Goodwin) As a White House fellow, she came to know Johnson on a personal basis. In the president's retirement years, she helped him with his memoirs, *Vantage Point,* and later wrote a biography entitled *Lyndon Johnson and the American Dream.*

McCARTHY, EUGENE A liberal senator from Minnesota who challenged LBJ for the presidential nomination of the Democratic party in 1968. McCarthy won almost half of the New Hampshire primary on a platform that called for American withdrawal from Vietnam. Johnson realized his vulnerability and how much the war had hurt his popularity. In March 1968, the president announced that he would not seek another term.

McCARTHY, JOSEPH R. The demagogic senator from Wisconsin who argued during the Cold War of the 1950s that the Communists had not only infiltrated the American government but also had gained power abroad. He blamed Truman's weak foreign policy based on containment. King argues that LBJ's "Texas was a particularly happy hunting ground" for McCarthyism.

McGOVERN, GEORGE A liberal Democratic senator from South Dakota who opposed the war in Vietnam, he lost the presidential election of 1972 to Richard Nixon.

McNAMARA, ROBERT He served as secretary of defense in the Kennedy and Johnson administrations. Near the end of Johnson's presidency, McNamara began to doubt whether America could win the war in Vietnam. He left the administration to head the World Bank.

MONOLITHIC COMMUNISM The belief that all Communists—Russian, Chinese, Vietnamese—were bent on world domination and cooperated with each other to achieve that goal.

MOYERS, BILL A former Peace Corps official and a close friend of Johnson whom the president treated like "a surrogate son." Moyers eventually left the administration to become an editor of *Newsday.*

PLEIKU In February of 1965, the North Vietnamese attacked Pleiku, killing nine Americans and destroying five aircraft. This resulted in an escalating program of air assaults against Communist targets above the 17th parallel.

PUEBLO An American warship seized by North Korea in 1968. There was also a crisis in Berlin that year. Johnson realized that Cold War tensions were not limited to Vietnam.

RAYBURN, SAM Powerful speaker of the House of Representatives and a Texan, he became one of LBJ's closest associates. When Johnson was a congressman, Rayburn assigned him to powerful committees that helped the future president learn about the importance of military preparedness.

RUSK, DEAN Secretary of state in the Kennedy and Johnson administrations, he was an ardent cold warrior and a "hawk" on the war in Vietnam.

TET OFFENSIVE Although Johnson continued to boast that "the enemy had been defeated in battle after battle" and that America was winning the war, the Vietcong on the last day of January 1968 launched the massive Tet Offensive. The Communists assaulted most of the major cities in South Vietnam and even temporarily occupied the American embassy in Saigon. This seemed undeniable proof that Johnson's military solution was a failure and that the claims of the president and his generals could not be believed.

WESTMORELAND, WILLIAM American commander in Vietnam who devised "search and destroy" missions that the general hoped would help the United States win a war of attrition where "body counts" meant more than territory taken from the enemy.

He was an old-fashioned man by the purest definition. Forget that he was enamored of twentieth-century artifacts—the telephone, television, supersonic airplanes, spacecraft—to which he adapted with a child's wondering glee. His values were the relics of an earlier time; he had been shaped by an America both rawer and more confident than it later would become; his generation may have been the last to believe that for every problem there existed a workable solution; that the ultimate answer, as in old-time mathematics texts, always reposed in the back of the book.

He bought the prevailing American myths without closely inspecting the merchandise for rips or snares. He often said that Americans inherently were "can-do" people capable of accomplishing anything they willed. It was part of his creed that Americans were God's chosen; why, otherwise, would they have become the richest, the strongest, the freest people in the history of man? His was a God, perhaps, who was a first cousin to Darwin; Lyndon B. Johnson believed in survival of the fittest, that the strong would conquer the weak, that almost always the big 'uns ate the little 'uns.

There was a certain pragmatism in his beliefs, a touch of fatalism, and often a goodly measure of common sense and true compassion. Yet, too, he could be wildly romantic or muddle-headed. Johnson

King's portrait of Lyndon Johnson, shown above, reveals a complex man with manifold contradictions. He could be crude yet caring, overbearing yet insecure, committed to a moral cause yet deceitful and mendacious. Like his mentor, Franklin Roosevelt, Johnson wanted to make "people's lives a little brighter." He was a skillful manipulator of Congress and a bold advocate of civil rights. But in the end, the war in Vietnam destroyed his dream of building the Great Society in America. (LBJ Library Photo by Franke Wolfe)

Larry L. King, "Trapped: Lyndon Johnson and the Nightmare of Vietnam," from *Outlaws, Con Men, Whores, Politicians, and Other Artists*, Viking Press, 1980. Reprinted by permission of Sterling Lord Literistic, Inc. Copyright © 1980 by Larry L. King.

truly believed that any boy could rise to become President, though only thirty-five had. Hadn't he—a shirt-tailed kid from the dusty hardscrabble of the

Texas outback—walked with royalty and strong men, while reigning over what he called, without blushing, the Free World? In his last days, though bitter and withering in retirement at his rural Elba, he astonished and puzzled a young black teenager by waving his arms in windmill motions and telling the youngster, during a random encounter, "Well, maybe someday all of us will be visiting *your* house in Waco, because *you'll* be President and your home will be a national museum just as mine is. It'll take a while, but it'll happen, you'll see. . . ." Then he turned to the black teenager's startled mother: "Now, you better get that home of yours cleaned up spick-and-span. There'll be hundreds of thousands coming through it, you know, wanting to see the bedroom and the kitchen and the living room. Now, I hope you get that dust rag of yours out the minute you get home. . . ."

Doris Kearns, the Harvard professor and latter-day LBJ confidante, who witnessed the performance, thought it a mock show: "almost a vaudeville act." Dr. Johnson peddling the same old snake oil. Perhaps. Whatever his motives that day, Lyndon Johnson chose his sermon from the text he most fervently believed throughout a lifetime; his catechism spoke to the heart of American opportunity, American responsibility, American good intentions, American superiority, American destiny, American infallibility. *Why, hell, boy*—he was saying to the black teenager—*this country's so goddamn great even a nigger's gonna be President! And you and others like you got to be ready!*

Despite a sly personal cynicism—a suspicion of others who might pull their dirks on him; the keen, cold eye of a man determined not to be victimized at the gaming tables—he was, in his institutional instincts, something of a Pollyanna in that, I think, he somehow believed people in the abstract to be somewhat better than they are. He expected they would *do* more, and more things could be done *for* them, than probably is true. There *was* such a thing as a free lunch; there *was* a Santa Claus; there *was*, somewhere, a Good Fairy, and probably it was made of the component parts of Franklin Roosevelt, Saint Francis, and Uncle Sam.

There were certain thoroughly American traits—as LBJ saw them—which constituted the foundation stone upon which the Republic, and his own dream castle, had been built; he found it impossible to abandon them even as the sands shifted and bogged him in the quagmire of Vietnam. If America was so wonderful (and it *was;* he had the evidence of himself to prove it), then he had the obligation to export its goodness and greatness to the less fortunate. It would not do to limit this healing ministry merely to domestic unfortunates—to the tattered blacks of Mississippi or to the bombed and strafed disadvantaged of the South Bronx—because man, *everywhere,* deserved the right to be just like us! Yessir! This good he would accomplish at any cost; it was why we had no choice but "to nail the coonskin to the wall." For if Lyndon B. Johnson believed in God and America and its goodness and greatness, he also believed in guts and gunpowder.

All the history he had read, and all he had personally witnessed, convinced him that the United States of America—if determined enough, if productive enough, if patriotic enough—simply could not lose a war. We have evidence from his mother that as a boy his favorite stories were of the Minutemen at Lexington and Concord, of the heroic defenders of the Alamo, of rugged frontiersmen who'd at once tamed the wild land and marauding Indians. He had a special affinity for a schoolboy poem proclaiming that the most beautiful sight his eyes had beheld was "the flag of my country in a foreign land." He so admired war heroes that he claimed to have been fired on "by a Japanese ace," though little evidence supported it; he invented an ancestor he carelessly claimed had been martyred at the Alamo; at the Democratic National Convention in 1956 he had cast his state's delegate votes for the vice presidential ambitions of young John F. Kennedy, "that fighting sailor who bears the scars of battle."

On a slow Saturday afternoon in the late 1950s, expansive and garrulous in his Capitol Hill office, Johnson discoursed to a half dozen young Texas staffers in the patois of their shared native place. Why—he said—you take that ragtag bunch at Valley

Forge; who'd have given them a cut dog's chance? There they were, barefoot in the snow and their asses hanging out, nothing to eat but moss and dead leaves and snakes, not half enough bullets for their guns, and facing the soldiers of the most powerful king of his time. Yet they sucked it up, wouldn't quit, went on to fight and win. Or take the Civil War, now; it had been so exceptionally bloody because you had aroused Americans fighting on *both* sides; it had been something like rock against rock, or two mean ol' pit bulldogs going at each other and both of 'em thinking only of taking hunks out of the other. He again invoked the Alamo: a mere handful of freedom-loving men, knowing they faced certain death; but they'd carved their names in history for all time, and before they got through with ol' General Santa Anna, he thought he'd stumbled into a swarm of bumblebees.

Fifteen years later Johnson would show irritation when Clark Clifford suggested that victory in Vietnam might require a sustaining commitment of twenty to thirty years. No—LBJ said—no, no, the thing to do was get in and out quickly, pour everything you had into the fight, land the knockout blow; hell, the North Vietnamese *had* to see the futility of facing all that American muscle! If you really poured it on 'em, you could clean up that mess within six months. We had the troops, the firepower, the bombs, the sophisticated weaponry, the oil—everything we needed to win. Did we have the resolve? Well, the Texas Rangers had a saying that you couldn't stop a man who just kept on a-coming. And that's what we'd do in Vietnam, Clark, just keep on a-coming. . . .

Always he talked of the necessity to be strong; he invoked his father's standing up to the Ku Klux Klan in the 1920s, Teddy Roosevelt's carrying that big stick, FDR's mobilizing the country to beat Hitler and Tojo. He had liked ol' Harry Truman—tough little bastard and his own man—but, listen, Harry and Dean Acheson had lost control when they failed to prosecute the Korean War properly. They lost the public's respect, lost control of General MacArthur,

lost the backing of Congress, lost the *war* or the next thing to it. Next thing you know, they got blamed for losing China, and then there was Joe McCarthy accusing them of being soft on communism and everybody believed it. Well, it wouldn't happen to him, no, sir. *He* hadn't started the Vietnam War—Jack Kennedy had made the first commitment of out-and-out combat troops in force, don't forget—but *he* wouldn't bug out no matter how much the Nervous Nellies brayed. Kennedy had proved during the Cuban missile crisis that if you stood firm, then the Reds would back down. They were bullies, and he didn't intend to be pushed around any more than Jack Kennedy had. When a bully ragged you, you didn't go whining to the teacher but gave him some of his own medicine.

Only later, in exile, when he spoke with unusual candor of his darker secretions, did it become clear how obsessed with failure Lyndon Johnson always had been. As a preschool youngster he walked a country lane to visit a grandfather, his head stuffed with answers he knew would be required ("How many head of cattle you got, Lyndon? How much do they eat? How many head can you graze to the acre?") and fearing he might forget them. If he forgot them, he got no bright-red apple but received, instead, a stern and disapproving gaze. LBJ's mother, who smothered him with affection and praise should he perform to her pleasure and expectations, refused to acknowledge his presence should he somehow displease or disappoint her. His father accused him of being a sleepyhead, a slow starter, and sometimes said every boy in town had a two-hour head start on him. Had we known those things from scratch, we might not have wondered why Lyndon Johnson seemed so blind for so long to the Asian realities. His personal history simply permitted him no retreats or failures in testings.

From childhood LBJ experienced bad dreams. As with much else, they would stay with him to the shadow of the grave. His nightmares were of being paralyzed and unable to act, of being chained inside a cage or to his desk, of being pursued by hostile forces. These and other disturbing dreams haunted his White House years; he could see himself stricken and ill on a cot, unable even to speak—like Woodrow Wilson—while, in an adjoining room, his trusted aides squabbled and quarreled in dividing his power. He translated the dreams to mean that should he for a moment show weakness, be indecisive, then history might judge him as the first American President who had failed to stand up and be counted. Johnson's was a benign translation; others might see a neurotic fear of losing power—*his* power—to subordinates he did not, at least subconsciously, trust.

These deep-rooted insecurities prompted Lyndon Johnson always to assert himself, to abuse staff members simply to prove that he held the upper hand; to test his power in small or mean ways. Sometimes, in sending Vice President Hubert Humphrey off on missions or errands with exhortations to "get going," he literally kicked him in the shins. "Hard," Humphrey later recalled, pulling up his trouser leg to exhibit the scars to columnist Robert Allen. Especially when drinking did he swagger and strut. Riding high as Senate Majority Leader, Johnson one night after a Texas State Society function, in the National Press Club in Washington—in the spring of 1958—repaired to a nearby bar with Texas Congressmen Homer Thornberry and Jack Brooks.

"I'm a powerful sumbitch, you know that?" he repeatedly said. "You boys realize how goddamn *powerful* I am?"

Yes, Lyndon, his companions uneasily chorused. Johnson pounded the table as if attempting to crack stout oak. "Do you know Ike couldn't pass the Lord's Prayer without me? You understand that? Hah?" Yes, Lyndon. "Hah? Do you? Hah?" Sitting in an adjoining booth, with another Capitol Hill aide, James Boren, I thought I never had seen a man more desperate for affirmations of himself.

Lyndon Johnson always was an enthusiastic Cold Warrior. He was not made uncomfortable by John Foster Dulles's brinkmanship rhetoric about "rolling back" communism or "unleashing" Chiang Kai-shek to "free" the Chinese mainland—from which the generalissimo earlier had been routed by the Reds.

LBJ was, indeed, one of the original soldiers of the Cold War, a volunteer rather than a draftee, just as he had been the first member of Congress to rush to the recruiting station following Japan's attack on Pearl Harbor. Immediately after World War II he so bedeviled Speaker Sam Rayburn about his fears of America's dismantling its military machine that Rayburn, in vexation, appointed him to the postwar Military Policy Committee and to the Joint Committee on Atomic Energy. Johnson early had a preference for military assignments in Congress; he successfully campaigned for a seat on the House Naval Affairs Committee in the 1930s and, a decade later, the Senate Armed Services Committee. He eventually chaired the Senate Preparedness Committee and the Senate Space Committee. Perhaps others saw the exploration of outer space in scientific or peaceful terms; Johnson, however, told Senate Democrats that outer space offered "the ultimate position from which total control of the earth may be exercised. Whoever gains that ultimate position gains control, total control, over the earth."

He was a nagger, a complainer, a man not always patient with those of lesser gifts or with those who somehow inconvenienced him. Sometimes he complained that the generals knew nothing but "spend and bomb"; almost always, however, he went along with bigger military spending and, in most cases, with more bombing or whatever tough military action the brass proposed. This was his consistent record in Congress, and he generally affirmed it as President. On November 12, 1951, Senator Johnson rattled his saber at the Russians:

We are tired of fighting your stooges. We will no longer sacrifice our young men on the altar of your conspiracies. The next aggression will be the last. . . . We will strike back, not just at your satellites, but at you. We will strike back with all the dreaded might that is within our control and it will be a crushing blow.

Even allowing for those rhetorical excesses peculiar to senatorial oratory, those were not the words of a man preoccupied with the doctrine of peaceful coexistence. Nor were they inconsistent with Johnson's mind-set when he made a public demand—at the outbreak of the Korean War, in June 1950—that President Truman order an all-out mobilization of all military reserve troops, National Guard units, draftees, and even civilian manpower and industry. He told intimates that this Korean thing could be the opening shot of World War III, and we had to be ready for that stark eventuality. In a Senate debate shortly thereafter, Senator Johnson scolded colleagues questioning the Pentagon's request for new and supplementary emergency billions: "Is this the hour of our nation's twilight, the last fading hour of light before an endless night shall envelop us and all the Western world?"

His ties with Texas—with its indigenous xenophobic instincts and general proclivities toward a raw yahooism—haunted him and, in a sense, may have made him a prisoner of grim political realities during the witch-hunting McCarthy era. "I'm damned tired," he said, "of being called a Dixiecrat in Washington and a communist in Texas"; it perfectly summed up those schizophrenic divisions uneasily compartmentalizing his national political life and the more restrictive parochial role dictated by conditions back home. He lived daily with a damned-if-I-do-and-damned-if-I-don't situation. Texas was a particularly happy hunting ground for Senator Joe McCarthy, whose self-proclaimed anticommunist crusade brought him invitation after invitation to speak there; the Texas legislature, in the 1950s controlled beyond belief by vested interests and showing the ideological instincts of the early primates, whooped through a resolution demanding that Senator McCarthy address it despite the suggestion of State Representative Maury Maverick, Jr., that the resolution be expanded to invite Mickey Mouse also. Both Johnson's powerful rightist adversaries and many of his wealthy Texas benefactors were enthusiastic contributors to the McCarthy cause and coffers.

Privately, LBJ groused of McCarthy's reckless showboat tactics and, particularly, of the Texas-directed pressures they brought him. Why—he said—Joe McCarthy was just a damn drunk, a blowhard, an incompetent who couldn't tie his own shoelaces, probably the biggest joke in the Senate. But—LBJ reminded those counseling him to attack McCarthy—people *believed* him; they were so afraid of the communists they would believe anything. There would come a time when the hysteria died down, and then McCarthy would be vulnerable; such a fellow was certain to hang himself in time. But right now anybody openly challenging McCarthy would come away with dirty hands and with his heart broken. "Touch pitch," he paraphrased the Bible, "and you'll be defiled."

By temperament a man who coveted the limelight and never was bashful about claiming credit for popular actions, Johnson uncharacteristically remained in the background when the U.S. Senate voted to censure McCarthy in late 1954. Though he was instrumental in selecting senators he believed would be effective and creditable members in leading the censure effort, Johnson's fine hand was visible only to insiders. A correspondent for Texas newspapers later would remember it as "the only time we had to hunt to find Johnson. He almost went into hiding."

Johnson believed, however—and probably more deeply than Joe McCarthy—in a worldwide, monolithic communist conspiracy. He believed it was directed from Moscow and that it was ready to blast America, or subvert it, at the drop of a fur hat. LBJ never surrendered that view. In retirement he suggested that the communists were everywhere, honeycombing the government, and he told astonished visitors that sometimes he hadn't known whether he could trust even his own staff; *that's* how widespread spying and subversion had become. The communists (it had been his first thought on hearing the gunshots in Dallas, and he never changed his mind) had killed Jack Kennedy; it had been their influence that turned people against the Vietnam War. One of LBJ's former aides, having been treated to that angry lecture, came away from the Texas ranch with the sad and reluctant conclusion that "the Old Man's absolutely paranoid on the communist thing."

In May 1961 President Kennedy dispatched his Vice President to Asia on a "fact-finding" diplomatic trip. Johnson, who believed it his duty to be a team player, to reinforce the prevailing wisdom, bought without qualification the optimistic briefings of military brass with their charts and slides "proving" the inevitable American victory. "I was sent out here to report on the *progress* of the war," he told an aide, as if daring anyone to bring him anything less than good news. Carried away, he publicly endowed South Vietnam's President Ngo Dinh Diem with the qualities of Winston Churchill, George Washington, Andrew Jackson, and FDR. Visiting refugee camps, he grew angry at communist aggressions "against decent people" and concluded: "There is no alternative to United States leadership in Southeast Asia. . . . We must decide whether to help to the best of our ability or throw in the towel [and] pull back our defenses to San Francisco and a 'Fortress America' concept." Yes, sir, the damned dirty Reds would chase us all the way to the Golden Gate! LBJ believed then—and always would believe—in the domino theory first stated by President Eisenhower. Even after announcing his abdication, he continued to sing the tired litany: If Vietnam fell, then the rest of Asia might go, and then Africa, and then the Philippines. . . .

When Lyndon Johnson suddenly ascended to the presidency, however, he did not enter the Oval Office eager to immediately take the measure of Ho Chi Minh. Although he told Ambassador Henry Cabot Lodge, "I am not going to be the President who saw Southeast Asia go the way China went," he wanted, for the moment, to keep the war—and, indeed, all foreign entanglements—at arm's length. His preoccupation was with his domestic program; here, he was confident, he knew what he was doing. He would emulate FDR in making people's lives a little brighter. To aides he talked eagerly of building schools and houses, of fighting poverty and attaining full employment, of heating the economy to record prosperity. The honeymoon with Congress—he said—couldn't last; he had seen Congress grow balky and obstinate, take its measure of many Presidents, and he had to assume it would happen again. Then he would lean forward, tapping a forefinger against someone's chest or squeezing a neighboring knee,

and say, "I'm like a sweetheart to Congress right now. They love me because I'm new and courting 'em, and it's kinda exciting, like that first kiss. But after a while the new will wear off. Then Congress will complain that I don't bring enough roses or candy and will accuse me of seeing other girls." The need was to push forward quickly, pass the civil rights bill in the name of the martyred John F. Kennedy, then hit Capitol Hill with a blizzard of domestic proposals and dazzle it before sentiment and enthusiasms cooled. Foreign affairs could wait. Even war could walk at mark-time speed.

Lyndon B. Johnson at that point had little experience in foreign affairs. Except for his showcase missions accomplished as Vice President, he had not traveled outside the United States save for excursions to Mexico and his brief World War II peregrinations. He probably had little confidence in himself in foreign affairs; neither did he have an excessive interest in the field. "Foreigners are not like the folks I am used to," he sometimes said—and though it passed as a joke, there was the feeling he might be kidding on the level.

Ambassadors waiting to present their credentials to the new President were miffed by repeated delays—and then angrily astonished when LBJ received them in groups and clumps, seemingly paying only perfunctory attention, squirming in his chair, scowling or muttering during the traditional ceremonies. He appeared oblivious to their feelings, to their offended senses of dignity. "Why do I have to see them?" the President demanded. "They're Dean Rusk's clients, not mine."

Defense Secretary Robert McNamara was selected to focus on Vietnam while LBJ concocted his Great Society. McNamara should send South Vietnam equipment and money as needed, a few more men, issue the necessary pronouncements. But don't splash it all over the front pages; don't let it get out of hand; don't give Barry Goldwater Vietnam as an issue for the 1964 campaign. Barry, hell, he was a hip shooter; he'd fight Canada or Mexico—or give that impression anyhow—so the thing to do was sit tight, keep the lid on, keep all Asian options open. Above all, "Don't let it turn into a Bay of Pigs." Hunker down; don't gamble.

The trouble—Johnson said to advisers—was that foreign nations didn't understand Americans or the American way: They saw us as "fat and fifty, like the country-club set"; they didn't think we had the steel to act when the going got rough. Well, in time they'd find out differently. They'd learn that Lyndon Johnson was not about to abandon what other Presidents had started; he wouldn't permit history to write that he'd been the only American President to cut and run; he wouldn't sponsor any damn Munich. But for right now—cool it. Put Vietnam on the back burner, and let it simmer.

But the communists—he later would say—wouldn't permit him to cool it. There had been that Gulf of Tonkin attack on the United States destroyer *Maddox,* in August of 19-and-64, and if he hadn't convinced Congress to get on record as backing him up in Vietnam, why, then, the Reds would have interpreted it as a sign of weakness and Barry Goldwater would have cut his heart out. And in February of 19-and-65, don't forget, the Vietcong had made that attack on the American garrison at Pleiku, and how could he be expected to ignore that? There they came, thousands of 'em, barefoot and howling in their black pajamas and throwing homemade bombs; it had been a damned insult, a calculated show of contempt. LBJ told the National Security Council: "The worst thing we could do would be to let this [Pleiku] thing go by. It would be a big mistake. It would open the door to a major misunderstanding."

Twelve hours later, American aircraft—for the first time—bombed in North Vietnam; three weeks later, Lyndon Johnson ordered continuing bombing raids in the north to "force the North Vietnamese into negotiations"; only 120 days after Pleiku, American ground forces were involved in a full-scale war and seeking new ways to take the offensive. Eight Americans died at Pleiku. Eight. Eventually 50,000-plus Americans would die in Asia.

Pleiku was the second major testing of American will, within a few months, in LBJ's view. In the

spring of 1965 rebels had attacked the ruling military junta in the Dominican Republic. Lives and property of U.S. citizens were endangered, as Johnson saw it, but—more—this might be a special tactic by the Reds, a dry run for bigger mischief later on in Vietnam. The world was watching to see how America would react. "It's just like the Alamo," he lectured the National Security Council. "Hell, it's like you were down at that gate, and you were surrounded, and you damn well needed somebody. Well, by God, I'm going to *go*—and I thank the Lord that I've got men who want to go with me, from McNamara right down to the littlest private who's carrying a gun."

Somewhat to his puzzlement, and certainly to his great vexation, Lyndon Johnson would learn that not everybody approved of his rushing the Marines into the Dominican Republic, and within days building up a 21,000-man force. Congress, editorials, and some formerly friendly foreign diplomats blasted him. Attempting to answer these critics, he would claim thousands of patriots "bleeding in the streets and with their heads cut off"; paint a false picture of the United States ambassador cringing under his desk "while bullets whizzed over his head"; speak of howling Red hordes descending on American citizens and American holdings; and, generally, open what later become known as the Credibility Gap.

By now he had given up on his original notion of walking easy in Vietnam until he could put across the Great Society. Even before the three major "testings" of Tonkin Gulf, the Dominican Republic, and Pleiku, he had said—almost idly—"Well, I guess we have to touch up those North Vietnamese a little bit." By December 1964 he had reversed earlier priorities: "We'll beat the communists first; then we can look around and maybe give something to the poor." Guns now ranked ahead of butter.

Not that he was happy about it. Though telling Congress, "This nation is mighty enough, its society is healthy enough, its people are strong enough, to pursue our goals in the rest of the world while still building a Great Society here at home," he knew, in his bones, that this was much too optimistic an outlook. He privately fretted that his domestic program would be victimized. He became touchy, irritable, impatient with those who even timorously questioned America's increasing commitment to the war. Why should *I* be blamed—he snapped—when the communists are the aggressors, when President Eisenhower committed us in Asia in 19-and-54, when Kennedy beefed up Ike's efforts? If he didn't prosecute the Vietnam War now, then later Congress would sour and want to hang him because he hadn't—and would gut his domestic programs in retaliation.

He claimed to have "pounded President Eisenhower's desk" in opposing Ike's sending 200 Air Force "technicians" to assist the French in Indochina (though those who were present in the Oval Office later recalled that only Senators Russell of Georgia and Stennis of Mississippi had raised major objections). Well, he'd been unable to stop Ike that time, though he *had* helped persuade him against dropping paratroopers into Dienbienphu to aid the doomed French garrison there. And after all *that,* everybody now called Vietnam "Lyndon Johnson's War"! It was unfair: "The only difference between the Kennedy assassination and mine is that I am alive and it is more torturous."

Very well, if it was his war in the public mind, then he would personally oversee its planning. "Never move up your artillery until you move up your ammunition," he told his generals—a thing he'd said as Senate Majority Leader when impatient liberals urged him to call for votes on issues he felt not yet ripe. Often he quizzed the military brass, sounding almost like a dove, in a way to resemble courtroom cross-examinations. He forced the admirals and generals to affirm and reaffirm their recommendations as vital to victory. Reading selected transcripts, one might make the judgment that Lyndon Johnson was a most reluctant warrior, one more cautious in Vietnam than not. The larger evidence of Johnson's deeds, however, suggests that he was being a crafty politician—making a record so that later he couldn't be made the sole scapegoat.

He trusted Robert McNamara's computers, perhaps more than he trusted men, and took satisfaction when their printouts predicted that X amount of bombing would be needed to damage the Vietcong by Y or that X number of troops would be required to capture Z. Planning was the key. You figured what you had to do, you did it, and eventually you'd nail the coonskin to the wall. Johnson devoutly believed that all problems had solutions; in his lifetime alone we'd beaten the Great Depression, won two world wars, hacked away at racial discrimination, made an industrial giant and world power of a former agrarian society, explored outer space. This belief in available solutions led him, time and again, to change tactics in Vietnam and discover fresh enthusiasm for each new move; he did not pause, apparently, to reflect on why given tactics, themselves once heralded as practical solutions, had failed and had been abandoned. If counterinsurgency failed, you bombed. If bombing wasn't wholly effective, then you tried the enclave theory. If *that* proved disappointing, you sent your ground troops on search-and-destroy missions. If, somehow, your troops couldn't find the phantom Vietcong in large numbers (and therefore couldn't destroy them), you began pacification programs in the areas you'd newly occupied. And if *this* bogged down, if the bastards still sneaked up to knife you in the night, you beefed up your firepower and sent in enough troops simply to outmuscle the rice-paddy ragtags: Napalm 'em bomb 'em, shoot 'em; burn 'em out, and flush 'em out. Sure it would work! It always had! Yes, surely, the answer was there somewhere in the back of the book, if only you looked long enough. . . .

He sought, and found, assurances. Maybe he had only a "cow-college" education; perhaps he'd not attended West Point; he might not have excessive experience in foreign affairs. But he was surrounded by the good men David Halberstam later, and ironically, would label "the best and the brightest," and certainly they were unanimous in their supportive conclusions. "He would look around him," Tom Wicker later said, "and see in Bob McNamara that [the war] was technologically feasible, in McGeorge

Bundy that it was intellectually respectable, and in Dean Rusk that it was historically necessary." It was especially easy to trust expertise when the experts in their calculations bolstered your own gut feelings—and when their computers and high-minded statements and mighty hardware all boiled down to reinforce your belief in American efficiency, American responsibility, American destiny. If so many good men agreed with him, then what might be wrong with those who didn't?

He considered the sources of dissatisfaction and dissent: the liberals—the "red-hots," he'd often sneeringly called them; the "pepper pots"—who were impractical dreamers, self-winding kamikazes intent on self-destruction. He often quoted an aphorism to put such people in perspective: "Any jackass can kick down a barn, but it takes a carpenter to build one." He fancied, however, that he knew all about those queer fellows. For years, down home, Ronnie Dugger and his *Texas Observer* crowd, in LBJ's opinion, had urged him to put his head in the noose by fighting impossible, profitless fights. They wanted him to take on Joe McCarthy, slap the oil powers down, kick Ike's tail, tell everybody who wasn't a red-hot to go to hell. Well, he'd learned a long time ago that just because you *told* a fellow to go to hell, he didn't necessarily have to go. The liberals just didn't understand the communists. Bill Fulbright and his bunch—the striped-pants boys over at the State Department; assorted outside red-hots, such as the goddamn Harvards—they thought you could *trust* the communists. They made the mistake of believing the Reds would deal with you honorably when—in truth—the communists didn't respect anything but force. You had to fight fire with fire; let them know who had the biggest guns and the toughest hide and heart.

Where once he had argued the injustice of Vietnam's being viewed as "his" war, Lyndon Johnson now brought to it a proprietary attitude. This should have been among the early warnings that LBJ would increasingly resist less than victory, no matter his periodic bombing halts or conciliatory statements inviting peace, because once he took a thing personally,

his pride and vanity and ego knew no bounds. Always a man to put his brand on everything (he wore monogrammed shirts, boots, cuff links; flew his private LBJ flag when in residence at the LBJ Ranch; saw to it that the names of Lynda Bird Johnson and Luci Baines Johnson and Lady Bird Johnson—not Claudia, as she had been named—had the magic LBJ; he even named a dog Little Beagle Johnson), he now personalized and internalized the war. Troops became "my" boys; those were "my" helicopters; it was "my" pilots he prayed might return from their bombing missions as he paid nocturnal calls to the White House situation room to learn the latest news from the battlefields; Walt Rostow became "my" intellectual because he was hawkish on LBJ's war.

His machismo was mixed up in it now, his manhood. After a Cabinet meeting in 1967 several staff aides and at least one Cabinet member—Stewart Udall, Secretary of the Interior—remained behind for informal discussions. Soon LBJ was waving his arms and fulminating about his war. Who the hell was Ho Chi Minh, anyway, that he thought he could push America around? Then the President of the United States did an astonishing thing: He unzipped his trousers, dangled a given appendage, and asked his shocked associates, "Has Ho Chi Minh got anything like that?"

By mid-1966 he had cooled toward many of his experts: not because they'd been wrong in their original optimistic calculations, no, so much as that some of them had recanted and now rejected *his* war. This Lyndon Johnson could not forgive; they'd cut and run on him. Nobody had deserted Roosevelt—he gloomed—when FDR had been fighting Hitler. McGeorge Bundy, deserting to head the Ford Foundation, was no longer the brilliant statesman but merely "a smart kid, that's all." Bill Moyers, quitting to become editor of *Newsday* and once almost a surrogate son to the President, suddenly became "a little puppy I rescued from sacking groceries"—a reference to a part-time job Moyers held while a high school student in the long ago. George Ball, too, was leaving? Well, George had always been a chronic bellyacher.

This photograph shows the anguish and exhaustion of a president worn down by a seemingly endless war and the chants of protesters: "Hey hey LBJ/How many kids did you kill today?" Johnson moaned: "The only difference between the Kennedy assassination and mine is that I am alive and it is more torturous." (LBJ Library Photo by Jack Kightlinger)

When Defense Secretary McNamara doubted too openly (stories of his anguish leaked to the newspapers), he found it difficult to claim the President's time; ultimately he rudely was shuttled to the World Bank. Vice President Hubert Humphrey, privately having second thoughts, was not welcomed back to high councils until he'd muffled his timid dissent and shamelessly flattered LBJ. Even then, Johnson didn't wholly accept his Vice President; Hubert, he said, wasn't a real man, he cried as easily as a woman, he didn't have the weight. When Lady Bird Johnson voiced doubts about the war, her husband growled that *of course* she had doubts; it was *like* a woman to be uncertain. *Has Ho Chi Minh got anything like that?*

Shortly after the Tet offensive began—during which Americans would be shocked when the Vietcong temporarily captured a wing of the American Embassy in Saigon—the President, at his press conference of February 2, 1968, made such patently false statements that even his most loyal friends and supporters were troubled. The sudden Tet offensive had been traumatic, convincing many Americans that our condition was desperate, if not doomed. For years the official line ran that the Vietcong could not hang on, would shrink by the attritions of battle and an ebbing of confidence in a hopeless cause. Stories were handed out that captured documents showed the enemy to be of low morale, underfed, ill-armed. The Vietcong could not survive superior American firepower; the kill ratio favored our side by 7 to 1, 8 to 1; more. These and other optimisms were repeated by the President, by General Westmoreland, by this ambassador and that fact-finding team. Now, however, it became apparent that the Vietcong had the capability to challenge even our main lair in Asia—and there to inflict serious damage as well as major embarrassments. It dawned on the nation that we were a long way from defanging those rice-paddy ragtags.

It was a time demanding utmost candor, and LBJ blew it. He took the ludicrous position that the Tet offensive—which would be felt for weeks or months to come—had abysmally failed. Why, we'd known about it all along—had, indeed, been in possession of Hanoi's order of battle. Incredible. To believe the President, one also had to believe that American authorities had simply failed to act on this vital intelligence, had wittingly and willingly invited disaster. The President was scoffed at and ridiculed; perhaps the thoughtful got goose bumps in realizing how far Lyndon Johnson now lived from reality. If there was a beginning of the end—of Lyndon Johnson, of hopes of anything remotely resembling victory, of a general public innocence of official razzmatazz—then Tet, and that Looney Tunes press conference, had to be it.

Even the stubborn President knew it. His presidency was shot, his party ruined and in tatters; his credibility was gone; he could speak only at military bases, where security guaranteed his safety against the possibility of mobs pursuing him through the streets as he had often dreamed. The old nightmares were real now. Street dissidents long had been chanting their cruel *"Hey Hey LBJ/How many kids did you kill today?";* Senator Eugene McCarthy soon would capture almost half the vote in the New Hampshire primary against the unpopular President. There was nothing to do but what he'd always sworn he would not do: quit.

On March 31, 1968, at the end of a televised speech ordering the end of attacks on North Vietnam in the hope of getting the enemy to the negotiating table, Johnson startled the nation by announcing: ". . . I do not believe that I should devote an hour or a day of my time to any personal partisan causes or to any duties other than the awesome duties of this office—the presidency of your country. Accordingly, I shall not seek, and I will not accept, the nomination of my party for another term. . . ."

"In the final months of his Presidency," a former White House aide, and Princeton professor, Eric Goldman, wrote, "Lyndon Johnson kept shifting in mood. At times he was bitter and petulant at his repudiation by the nation; at times philosophical, almost serene, confidently awaiting the verdict of the future." The serenity always was temporary; he grew angry with Hubert Humphrey for attempting to disengage himself from the Johnson war policy and, consequently, refused to make more than a token show of support for him. He saw Richard Nixon win on a pledge of having "a secret plan" to end the war—which, it developed, he did not have. LBJ never forgave George McGovern for opposing "his" war and let the world know it by a lukewarm endorsement of the South Dakota senator in 1972 which pointedly was announced only to LBJ's little hometown weekly newspaper.

In his final White House thrashings—and in retirement—Lyndon Johnson complained of unfinished business he had wanted to complete: Vietnam peace talks; free the crew of the *Pueblo;* begin talks with the Russians on halting the arms race; send a

man to the moon. But the war, the goddamned war, had ruined all that. The people hadn't rallied around him as they had around FDR and Woodrow Wilson and other wartime Presidents; he had been abandoned, by Congress, by Cabinet members, by old friends; no other President had tried so hard or suffered so much. He had a great capacity for self-pity and often indulged it, becoming reclusive and rarely issuing a public statement or making public appearances. Doris Kearns has said that she and others helping LBJ write his memoirs, *The Vantage Point,* would draft chapters and lay out the documentation—but even then Lyndon Johnson would say no, no, it wasn't like that; it was like *this.* And he would rattle on, waving his arms and attempting to justify himself, invoking the old absolutes, calling up memories of the Alamo, the Texas Rangers, the myths, and the legends. He never seemed to understand where or how he had gone wrong.

When President Nixon assumed command of the war, he seemed to take up where Johnson left off. Like his predecessors, Nixon worried about "American credibility," about what would happen to American prestige if the United States sold out its South Vietnamese ally, and in 1970 he sent American troops into contiguous Cambodia to exterminate Communist hideouts there. The Cambodian invasion brought antiwar protest to a tragic climax, as Ohio national guard troops opened fire on protesting students at Kent State University and killed four of them. With the campuses in turmoil and the country divided and adrift, Nixon gradually disengaged American ground troops in Vietnam and sought détente with both Russia and China.

Although the Nixon administration continued to speak of "peace with honor" in Indochina, and although it continued to bomb Hanoi, it was clear nevertheless that American involvement in the Vietnamese civil war was a tragic and costly mistake. Indeed, the signs were unmistakable that the original premise for American intervention in Indochina was erroneous. The domino theory, based as it was on the assumption of a worldwide monolithic Communist conspiracy directed by Moscow, appeared more and more implausible. For one thing, China and Russia developed an intense and bitter ideological feud that sharply divided the Communist world, and they almost went to war over their disputed boundary. The Sino-Soviet split exploded the notion of a Communist monolith out for world domin- ion, and so did the fierce independence of North Vietnam itself. Although Hanoi continued to receive aid from both Russia and China, North Vietnam apparently never asked China to intervene in the struggle (and apparently China never offered to do so). The truth was that North Vietnam was fighting to unite the country under Hanoi's leadership rather than under Beijing's or Moscow's.

At last, in top-secret negotiations in Paris, United States Secretary of State Henry Kissinger and North Viet- nam's Le Duc Tho worked out a peace agreement. Eventu- ally, the United States removed its combat forces, and in 1975 South Vietnam's regime fell to the North Viet- namese and the National Liberation Front. After almost two decades of bitter civil war and the loss of more than 1 million lives, Vietnam was united under Hanoi's Com- munist government, something that would probably have happened without further violence had general elections been held in 1956, according to the Geneva agreements of two years before.

QUESTIONS TO CONSIDER

1 Describe Johnson's background, personality, and vision of America. Do you think that LBJ, in retire- ment, was sincere when he called out to a young African American in Waco, Texas, that he and his mother better prepare for the day when the teenager would become president? Or, as Doris Kearns stated in her biography of Johnson, was it just "a vaude- ville act"?

2 Explain King's assessment that Johnson's "personal history simply permitted him no retreats or failures in testings." Were there other reasons why LBJ could not conceive of an American defeat in Viet- nam? Did the president generally support the mili- tary and its requests for manpower?

3 Why would King call Johnson an "enthusiastic Cold Warrior"? Why did Johnson view the space race as a vital element of America's national security? Although he despised Joseph McCarthy, why did LBJ fail to attack him?

4 When he first became president, did Johnson place more value in domestic or foreign policy goals? Had he much experience in dealing with foreign af- fairs or even much interest in the conduct of diplo- macy?

5 King concludes that Johnson usually overreacted when he perceived a foreign policy threat. Do the president's actions after Pleiku, the rebel attacks in the Dominican Republic, and the Gulf of Tonkin incident support that assessment? At about what point in his presidency did he start believing that "guns now ranked ahead of butter"?

6 Was Johnson correct in assuming that the Eisen- hower and Kennedy administrations committed him to the war in Vietnam? Explain how LBJ's character and background made it difficult for him to appreci- ate the position of his antiwar opponents or the sig- nificance of the Tet Offensive.

PART TWELVE

A New Birth of Freedom

25 Trumpet of Conscience: Martin Luther King Jr.

STEPHEN B. OATES

For most African Americans, the Depression had been an unmitigated calamity. An impoverished group to begin with, African Americans, especially southern sharecroppers, suffered worse than any other minority. World War II, however, offered African Americans relief, and they made considerable progress during the conflict. The war accelerated their exodus to the North, as southern blacks sought employment in war-related industry there. At first, white employers refused to hire African American workers, and the Roosevelt administration did little to stop such discrimination until A. Philip Randolph—the celebrated African American labor leader—threatened to lead a massive protest march. Roosevelt responded with an executive order that prohibited racial discrimination in defense plants and government agencies alike. By the close of 1944, two million African American men and women were working in shipyards, aircraft factories, steel mills, and other defense plants. At the same time, almost one million African Americans served in the United States armed forces— half of them overseas in segregated outfits. By war's end, however, some of the army bases at home were partly integrated, and African American sailors were serving on ships with whites.

Alas, African American soldiers and sailors who fought in a war against Nazi racists returned home to confront massive racial discrimination against them, especially in segregated Dixie. Many of those veterans joined the National Association for the Advancement of Colored People (NAACP), which now had chapters across the South, and became civil rights activists. In the postwar years, President Harry Truman proved to be sympathetic to the plight of African Americans and did much to help them: he established a special committee on civil rights, which worked out an agenda for attacking segregation that continued for two decades. Truman also issued an executive order that ended segregation in the armed forces. Ironically, the military would become the most integrated institution in the United States.

The NAACP, meanwhile, continued to battle segregation in case-by-case litigation in the federal courts and marked hard-earned victories against southern white primaries and segregated law schools in the border states. In May 1954, the NAACP Legal Defense Fund won its most spectacular triumph before the United States Supreme Court. In Brown *v.* Board of Education of Topeka, *the High Court outlawed segregation in public schools, thus reversing the doctrine of "separate but equal" that had prevailed since* Plessy *v.* Ferguson *fifty-eight years earlier. Said the Court: "Separate educational facilities are inherently unequal" and created "a feeling of inferiority" in African American students "that may affect their hearts and minds in a way unlikely ever to be undone." In one historic blow, the Supreme Court smashed the whole legal superstructure for the idea of racial separateness, knocking down a century and a half of devious rationalizations in defense of the doctrine that African Americans must be kept apart because they were inferior.*

But the white South obstructed the school decision at every turn. The Alabama legislature "nullified" the Court decision, vowing to preserve white supremacy come what may. Fiery crosses burned against Texas and Florida skies, and random Klan terrorism broke out against African Americans in many parts of Dixie. Faced with stiffening white resistance, the Supreme Court did not order immediate compliance with the Brown *decision and called instead for desegregation of public schools "with all deliberate speed." But the Court offered no guidelines and set no timetable. In 1956, more than one hundred southern members of Congress signed a "manifesto" that damned the Court decision and summoned the white South to defy it to the bitter end. Mustering its own legal forces, white officialdom promised to tie up the* Brown *decision in "a century of litigation."*

For African Americans, the road to freedom's land was elusive indeed. Most African Americans in the South languished in searing poverty and a rigid racial caste system that relegated them to the gutters of southern society and kept them away from the polls and out of politics.

How did African Americans feel about segregation? What did they say alone among themselves? "Lawd, man!" an elevator operator once told an African American writer. "Ef it wuzn't fer them polices n' them ol' lynch-mobs, there wouldn't be nothin' but uproar down here."

In 1955, African Americans in the South created an uproar despite the police and the lynchings. That was the year of the Montgomery bus boycott, an event that launched the nonviolent civil rights protest movement of the 1950s and 1960s. Many people rose to prominence in the movement, but Martin Luther King Jr. became its most popular and most eloquent spokesman. In this selection, you will walk with King from his birth in Atlanta and his intellectual odyssey in college to the great and impassioned days of the civil rights movement in the 1960s. As you ponder King's life and significance, consider what writer-historian Garry Wills said of King in The Kennedy Imprisonment *(1982), "While Washington's 'best and brightest' worked us into Vietnam," Wills wrote, "an obscure army of virtue arose in the South and took the longer spiritual trip inside a public bathroom or toward the front of a bus. King rallied the strength of broken [men and women], transmuting an imposed squalor into the beauty of chosen suffering. No one did it for his followers. They did it for themselves. Yet, in helping them, he exercised real power, achieved changes that dwarf the moon shot as an American achievement. The 'Kennedy era' was really the age of Dr. King."*

GLOSSARY

BLACK POWER   In 1966, angry, disaffected young militants in the Student Nonviolent Coordinating Committee (SNCC) and the Congress of Racial Equality (CORE) turned away from nonviolence and racial integration; inspired by the earlier teachings of Malcolm X, a famous Black Muslim, they started advocating Black Power—the need for African Americans to organize themselves and consolidate their economic and political resources—as well as black separatism and even violent resistance.

CIVIL RIGHTS ACT OF 1964   Outlawed segregated public accommodations—the goal of King's civil rights campaign in Birmingham.

CONGRESS OF RACIAL EQUALITY (CORE)   Founded in 1942, it staged sit-ins and applied Gandhian direct-action techniques to the American scene; in 1961, under the leadership of James Farmer, CORE sponsored the freedom rides to call attention to segregated busing facilities in the South, and the federal government responded by desegregating interstate bus stations.

CONNOR, EUGENE "BULL"   City police commissioner who gained worldwide notoriety when he turned firehoses and police dogs on King's followers during the Birmingham demonstrations in 1963.

GANDHI, MOHANDAS   The father of modern India whose teachings on nonviolent resistance and love for the oppressor profoundly influenced King.

MONTGOMERY BUS BOYCOTT (1955–1956)   King rose to prominence as leader of this protest demonstration against segregated seating on Montgomery city buses; the Supreme Court finally nullified the Alabama laws that enforced the practice.

RAY, JAMES EARL   King's assassin and a petty crook; subsequent evidence linked Ray to two white men in the St. Louis area who had offered "hit" money for King's life.

SOUTHERN CHRISTIAN LEADERSHIP CONFERENCE (SCLC)   King's civil rights organization, which worked through African American churches to effect social and political change.

STUDENT NONVIOLENT COORDINATING COMMITTEE (SNCC)   Established with King's help in 1960, SNCC organized sit-ins and voter-registration drives in segregated Dixie; many of its leaders were jealous of King, calling him "De Lawd."

VOTING RIGHTS ACT OF 1965   Passed in response to the Selma campaign, the measure outlawed barriers to voting by African Americans and authorized the attorney general to supervise federal elections in seven southern states where African Americans were kept off the voting rolls.

He was M.L. to his parents, Martin to his wife and friends, Doc to his aides, Reverend to his male parishioners, Little Lord Jesus to adoring churchwomen, De Lawd to his young critics in the Student Nonviolent Coordinating Committee, and Martin Luther King, Jr., to the world. At his pulpit or a public rostrum, he seemed too small for his incomparable oratory and international fame as a civil rights leader and spokesman for world peace. He stood only five feet seven, and had round cheeks, a trim mustache, and sad, glistening eyes—eyes that revealed both his inner strength and his vulnerability.

From "Trumpet of Conscience," by Stephen B. Oates. In *American History Illustrated* (April 1988), 18–27, 52. Reprinted through courtesy of Cowles Magazines, publisher of *American History Illustrated*.

He was born in Atlanta on January 15, 1929, and grew up in the relative comfort of the black middle class. Thus he never suffered the want and privation that plagued the majority of American blacks of his time. His father, a gruff, self-made man, was pastor of Ebenezer Baptist Church and an outspoken member of Atlanta's black leadership. M.L. joined his father's church when he was five and came to regard it as his second home. The church defined his world, gave it order and balance, taught him how to "get along with people." Here M.L. knew who he was—"Reverend King's boy," somebody special.

At home, his parents and maternal grandmother reinforced his self-esteem, praising him for his precocious ways, telling him repeatedly that he was *somebody*. By age five, he spoke like an adult and had such a prodigious memory that he could recite whole

Biblical passages and entire hymns without a mistake. He was acutely sensitive, too, so much so that he worried about all the blacks he saw in Atlanta's breadlines during the Depression, fearful that their children did not have enough to eat. When his maternal grandmother died, twelve-year-old M.L. thought it was his fault. Without telling anyone, he had slipped away from home to watch a parade, only to find out when he returned that she had died. He was terrified that God had taken her away as punishment for his "sin." Guilt-stricken, he tried to kill himself by leaping out of his second-story window.

He had a great deal of anger in him. Growing up a black in segregated Atlanta, he felt the full range of southern racial discrimination. He discovered that he had to attend separate, inferior schools, which he sailed through with a modicum of effort, skipping grades as he went. He found out that he—a preacher's boy—could not sit at lunch counters in Atlanta's downtown stores. He had to drink from a "colored" water fountain, relieve himself in a rancid "colored" restroom, and ride a rickety "colored" elevator. If he rode a city bus, he had to sit in the back as though he were contaminated. If he wanted to see a movie in a downtown theater, he had to enter through a side door and sit in the "colored" section in the balcony. He discovered that whites referred to blacks as "boys" and "girls" regardless of age. He saw "WHITES ONLY" signs staring back at him in the windows of barber shops and all the good restaurants and hotels, at the YMCA, the city parks, golf courses, swimming pools, and in the waiting rooms of the train and bus stations. He learned that there were even white and black sections of the city and that he resided in "nigger town."

Segregation caused a tension in the boy, a tension between his parents' injunction ("Remember, you are *somebody*") and a system that constantly demeaned and insulted him. He struggled with the pain and rage he felt when a white woman in a downtown store slapped him and called him "a little nigger" . . . when a bus driver called him "a black son-of-a-bitch" and made him surrender his seat to a white . . . when he stood on the very spot in Atlanta where whites had lynched

a black man . . . when he witnessed nightriding Klansmen beating blacks in the streets. How, he asked defiantly, could he heed the Christian injunction and love a race of people who hated him? In retaliation, he determined "to hate every white person."

Yes, he was angry. In sandlot games, he competed so fiercely that friends could not tell whether he was playing or fighting. He had his share of playground combat, too, and could outwrestle any of his peers. He even rebelled against his father, vowing never to become a preacher like him. Yet he liked the way Daddy King stood up to whites: he told them never to call him a boy and vowed to fight this system until he died.

Still, there was another side to M.L., a calmer, sensuous side. He played the violin, enjoyed opera, and relished soul food—fried chicken, cornbread, and collard greens with ham hocks and bacon drippings. By his mid-teens, his voice was the most memorable thing about him. It had changed into a rich and resonant baritone that commanded attention whenever he held forth. A natty dresser, nicknamed "Tweed" because of his fondness for tweed suits, he became a connoisseur of lovely young women. His little brother A.D. remembered how Martin "kept flitting from chick to chick" and was "just about the best jitterbug in town."

At age fifteen, he entered Morehouse College in Atlanta, wanting somehow to help his people. He thought about becoming a lawyer and even practiced giving trial speeches before a mirror in his room. But thanks largely to Morehouse President Benjamin Mays, who showed him that the ministry could be a respectable forum for ideas, even for social protest, King decided to become a Baptist preacher after all. By the time he was ordained in 1947, his resentment toward whites had softened some, thanks to positive contact with white students on an intercollegiate council. But he hated his segregated world more than ever.

Once he had his bachelor's degree, he went north to study at Crozer Seminary near Philadelphia. In this mostly white school, with its polished corridors and quiet solemnity, King continued to ponder the plight of blacks in America. How, by what method and means, were blacks to improve their lot in a white-dominated country? His study of history, especially of Nat Turner's slave insurrection, convinced him that it was suicidal for a minority to strike back against a heavily armed majority. For him, voluntary segregation was equally unacceptable, as was accommodation to the status quo. King shuddered at such negative approaches to the race problem. How indeed were blacks to combat discrimination in a country ruled by the white majority?

As some other blacks had done, he found his answer in the teachings of Mohandas Gandhi—for young King, the discovery had the force of a conversion experience. Nonviolent resistance, Gandhi taught, meant noncooperation with evil, an idea he got from Henry David Thoreau's essay "On Civil Disobedience." In India, Gandhi gave Thoreau's theory practical application in the form of strikes, boycotts, and protest marches, all conducted nonviolently and all predicated on love for the oppressor and a belief in divine justice. In gaining Indian independence, Gandhi sought not to defeat the British, but to redeem them through love, so as to avoid a legacy of bitterness. Gandhi's term for this—*Satyagraha*—reconciled love and force in a single, powerful concept.

As King discovered from his studies, Gandhi had embraced nonviolence in part to subdue his own violent nature. This was a profound revelation for King, who had felt much hatred in his life, especially toward whites. Now Gandhi showed him a means of harnessing his anger and channeling it into a positive and creative force for social change.

At this juncture, King found mostly theoretical satisfaction in Gandhian nonviolence; he had no plans to become a reformer in the segregated South. Indeed, he seemed destined to a life of the mind, not of social protest. In 1951, he graduated from Crozer and went on to earn a Ph.D. in theology from Boston University, where his adviser pronounced him "a scholar's scholar" of great intellectual potential. By 1955, a year after the school desegregation decision, King had married

A pensive King stands beside a portrait of Mohandas Gandhi, the Indian spiritual and political leader. "As King discovered from his studies, Gandhi had embraced nonviolence in part to subdue his own violent nature. This was a profound revelation for King, who had felt much hatred in his life, especially toward whites. Now Gandhi showed him a means of harnessing his anger and channeling it into a positive and creative force for social change." (Bob Fitch / Black Star)

comely Coretta Scott and assumed the pastorship of Dexter Avenue Baptist Church in Montgomery, Alabama. Immensely happy in the world of ideas, he hoped eventually to teach theology at a major university or seminary.

But, as King liked to say, the *Zeitgeist,* or spirit of the age, had other plans for him. In December 1955, Montgomery blacks launched a boycott of the city's segregated buses and chose the articulate twenty-six-year-old minister as their spokesman. As it turned out, he was unusually well prepared to assume the kind of leadership thrust on him. Drawing on Gandhi's teachings and example, plus the tenets of his own Christian faith, King directed a nonviolent boycott designed both to end an injustice and redeem his white adversaries through love. When he exhorted blacks to love their enemies, King did not mean to love them as friends or intimates. No, he said, he meant a disinterested love in all humankind, a love that saw the neighbor in everyone it met, a love that sought to restore the beloved community. Such love not only avoided the internal violence of the spirit, but severed the external chain of hatred that only produced more hatred in an endless spiral. If American blacks could break the chain of hatred, King said, true brotherhood could begin. Then posterity would have to say that there had lived a race of people, of black people, who "injected a new meaning into the veins of history and civilization."

During the boycott King imparted his philosophy at twice-weekly mass meetings in the black churches, where overflow crowds clapped and cried as his mellifluous voice swept over them. In these mass meetings King discovered his extraordinary power as an orator. His rich religious imagery reached deep into the black psyche, for religion had been the black people's main source of strength and survival since slavery days. His delivery was "like a narrative poem," said a woman journalist who heard him. His voice had such depths of sincerity and empathy that it could "charm your heart right out of your body." Because he appealed to the best in his people, articulating their deepest hurts and aspirations, black folk began to idolize him; he was their Gandhi.

Under his leadership, they stood up to white Montgomery in a remarkable display of solidarity. Pitted against an obdurate city government that blamed the boycott on Communist agitators and resorted to psychological and legal warfare to break it, the blacks stayed off the buses month after month, and walked or rode in a black-operated carpool. When an elderly woman refused the offer of a ride, King asked her, "But don't your feet hurt?" "Yes," she replied, "my feet is tired but my soul is rested." For King, her irrepressible spirit was proof that "a new Negro" was emerging in the South, a Negro with "a new sense of dignity and destiny."

That "new Negro" menaced white supremacists, especially the Ku Klux Klan, and they persecuted King with a vengeance. They made obscene phone calls to his home, sent him abusive, sickening letters, and once even dynamited the front of his house. Nobody was hurt, but King, fearing a race war, had to dissuade angry blacks from violent retaliation. Finally, on November 13, 1956, the U.S. Supreme Court nullified the Alabama laws that enforced segregated buses, and handed King and his boycotters a resounding moral victory. Their protest had captured the imagination of progressive people all over the world and marked the beginning of a southern black movement that would shake the segregated South to its foundations. At the forefront of that movement was a new organization, the Southern Christian Leadership Conference (SCLC), which King and other black ministers formed in 1957, with King serving as its president and guiding spirit. Operating through the southern black church, SCLC sought to enlist the black masses in the freedom struggle by expanding "the Montgomery way" across the South.

The "Miracle of Montgomery" changed King's life, catapulting him into international prominence as an inspiring new moral voice for civil rights. Across the country, blacks and whites alike wrote him letters of encouragement; *Time* magazine pictured him on its cover; the National Association for the Advancement of Colored People (NAACP) and scores of church and civic organizations vied for his services as a speaker. "I am really disturbed how fast all this has happened to me," King told his wife. "People will expect me to perform miracles for the rest of my life."

But fame had its evil side, too. When King visited New York in 1958, a deranged black woman stabbed him in the chest with a letter opener. The weapon was lodged so close to King's aorta, the main artery from the heart, that he would have died had he sneezed. To extract the blade, an interracial surgical team had to remove a rib and part of his breastbone; in a burst of inspiration, the lead surgeon made the incision over King's heart in the shape of a cross.

That he had not died convinced King that God was preparing him for some larger work in the segregated South. To gain perspective on what was happening there, he made a pilgrimage to India to visit

Gandhi's shrine and the sites of his "War for Independence." He returned home with an even deeper commitment to nonviolence and a vow to be more humble and ascetic like Gandhi. Yet he was a man of manifold contradictions, this American Gandhi. While renouncing material things and giving nearly all of his extensive honorariums to SCLC, he liked posh hotels and zesty meals with wine, and he was always immaculately dressed in a gray or black suit, white shirt, and tie. While caring passionately for the poor, the downtrodden, and the disinherited, he had a fascination with men of affluence and enjoyed the company of wealthy SCLC benefactors. While trumpeting the glories of nonviolence and redemptive love, he could feel the most terrible anger when whites murdered a black or bombed a black church; he could contemplate giving up, turning America over to the haters of both races, only to dedicate himself anew to his nonviolent faith and his determination to redeem his country.

In 1960, he moved his family to Atlanta so that he could devote himself fulltime to SCLC, which was trying to register black voters for the upcoming federal elections. That same year, southern black students launched the sit-in movement against segregated lunch counters, and King not only helped them form the Student Nonviolent Coordinating Committee (SNCC) but raised money on their behalf. In October he even joined a sit-in protest at an Atlanta department store and went to jail with several students on a trespassing charge. Like Thoreau, King considered jail "a badge of honor." To redeem the nation and arouse the conscience of the opponent, King explained, you go to jail and stay there. "You have broken a law which is out of line with the moral law and you are willing to suffer the consequences by serving the time."

He did not reckon, however, on the tyranny of racist officials, who clamped him in a malevolent state penitentiary, in a cell for hardened criminals. But state authorities released him when Democratic presidential nominee John F. Kennedy and his brother Robert interceded on King's behalf. According to many analysts, the episode won critical black votes for Kennedy and gave him the election in November. For King,

the election demonstrated what he had long said: that one of the most significant steps a black could take was the short walk to the voting booth.

The trouble was that most blacks in Dixie, especially in the Deep South, could not vote even if they so desired. For decades, state and local authorities had kept the mass of black folk off the voting rolls by a welter of devious obstacles and outright intimidation. Through 1961 and 1962, King exhorted President Kennedy to sponsor tough new civil rights legislation that would enfranchise southern blacks and end segregated public accommodations as well. When Kennedy shied away from a strong civil rights commitment, King and his lieutenants took matters into their own hands, orchestrating a series of southern demonstrations to show the world the brutality of segregation. At the same time, King stumped the country, drawing on all his powers of oratory to enlist the black masses and win white opinion to his cause.

Everywhere he went his message was the same. *The civil rights issue,* he said, *is an eternal moral issue that will determine the destiny of our nation and our world. As we seek our full rights, we hope to redeem the soul of our country. For it is our country, too, and we will win our freedom because the sacred heritage of America and the eternal will of God are embodied in our echoing demands. We do not intend to humiliate the white man, but to win him over through the strength of our love. Ultimately, we are trying to free all of us in America—Negroes from the bonds of segregation and shame, whites from the bonds of bigotry and fear.*

We stand today between two worlds—the dying old order and the emerging new. With men of ill-will greeting this change with cries of violence, of interposition and nullification, some of us may get beaten. Some of us may even get killed. But if you are cut down in a movement designed to save the soul of a nation, no other death could be more redemptive. We must realize that change does not roll in "on the wheels of inevitabilty," but comes through struggle. So "let us be those creative dissenters who will call our beloved nation to a higher destiny, to a new plateau of compassion, to a more noble expression of humaneness."

That message worked like magic among America's long-suffering blacks. Across the South, across

America, they rose in unprecedented numbers to march and demonstrate with Martin Luther King. His singular achievement was that he brought the black masses into the freedom struggle for the first time. He rallied the strength of broken men and women, helping them overcome a lifetime of fear and feelings of inferiority. After segregation had taught them all their lives that they were *nobody,* King taught them that they were *somebody.* Because he made them believe in themselves and in "the beauty of chosen suffering," he taught them how to straighten their backs ("a man can't ride you unless your back is bent") and confront those who oppressed them. Through the technique of nonviolent resistance, he furnished them something no previous black leader had been able to provide. He showed them a way of controlling their pent-up anger, as he had controlled his own, and using it to bring about constructive change.

The mass demonstrations King and SCLC choreographed in the South produced the strongest civil rights legislation in American history. This was the goal of King's major southern campaigns from 1963 to 1965. He would single out some notoriously segregated city with white officials prone to violence, mobilize the local blacks with songs, scripture readings, and rousing oratory in black churches, and then lead them on protest marches conspicuous for their grace and moral purpose. Then he and his aides would escalate the marches, increase their demands, even fill up the jails, until they brought about a moment of "creative tension," when whites would either agree to negotiate or resort to violence. If they did the latter, King would thus expose the brutality inherent in segregation and . . . stab the national conscience so [much] that the federal government would be forced to intervene with corrective measures.

The technique succeeded brilliantly in Birmingham, Alabama, in 1963. Here Police Commissioner Eugene "Bull" Connor, in full view of reporters and television cameras, turned firehoses and police dogs on the marching protesters. Revolted by such ghastly scenes, stricken by King's own searching eloquence

and the bravery of his unarmed followers, Washington eventually produced the 1964 Civil Rights Act, which desegregated public facilities—the thing King had demanded all along from Birmingham. Across the South, the "WHITES ONLY" signs that had hurt and enraged him since boyhood now came down.

Although SNCC and others complained that King had a Messiah complex and was trying to monopolize the civil rights movement, his technique worked with equal success in Selma, Alabama, in 1965. Building on a local movement there, King and his staff launched a drive to gain southern blacks the unobstructed right to vote. The violence he exposed in Selma—the beating of black marchers by state troopers and deputized possemen, the killing of a young black deacon and a white Unitarian minister—horrified the country. When King called for support, thousands of ministers, rabbis, priests, nuns, students, lay leaders, and ordinary people—black and white alike—rushed to Selma from all over the country and stood with King in the name of human liberty. Never in the history of the movement had so many people of all faiths and classes come to the southern battleground. The Selma campaign culminated in a dramatic march over the Jefferson Davis Highway to the state capital of Montgomery. Along the way, impoverished local blacks stared incredulously at the marching, singing, flag waving spectacle moving by. When the column reached one dusty crossroads, an elderly black woman ran out from a group of old folk, kissed King breathlessly, and ran back crying, "I done kissed him! The Martin Luther King! I done kissed the Martin Luther King!"

In Montgomery, first capital and much-heralded "cradle" of the Confederacy, King led an interracial throng of 25,000—the largest civil rights demonstration the South had ever witnessed—up Dexter Avenue with banners waving overhead. The pageant was as ironic as it was extraordinary, for it was up Dexter Avenue that Jefferson Davis's first inaugural parade had marched, and [it was] in the portico of the capitol [that] Davis had taken his oath of office as president of the slave-based Confederacy. Now, in the spring of 1965, Alabama blacks—most of them descendants of slaves—stood massed at the same statehouse, singing a new rendition of "We Shall Overcome," the anthem of the civil rights movement. They sang, "Deep in my heart, I do believe, We have overcome—*today*."

Then, watched by a cordon of state troopers and the statue of Jefferson Davis himself, King mounted a trailer. His vast audience listened, transfixed, as his words rolled and thundered over the loudspeaker: "My people, my people listen. The battle is in our hands. . . . We must come to see that the end we seek is a society at peace with itself, a society that can live with its conscience. That day will be a day not of the white man, not of the black man. That will be the day of man as man." And that day was not long in coming, King said, whereupon he launched into the immortal refrains of "The Battle Hymn of the Republic," crying out, "Our God is marching on! Glory, glory hallelujah!"

Aroused by the events in Alabama, Washington produced the 1965 Voting Rights Act, which outlawed impediments to black voting and empowered the attorney general to supervise federal elections in seven southern states where blacks were kept off the rolls. At the time, political analysts almost unanimously attributed the act to King's Selma campaign. Once federal examiners were supervising voter registration in all troublesome southern areas, blacks were able to get on the rolls and vote by the hundreds of thousands, permanently altering the pattern of southern and national politics.

In the end, the powerful civil rights legislation generated by King and his tramping legions wiped out statutory racism in America and realized at last the social and political promise of emancipation a century before. But King was under no illusion that legislation alone could bring on the brave new America he so ardently championed. Yes, he said, laws and their vigorous enforcement were necessary to regulate destructive habits and actions, and to protect blacks and their rights. But laws could not eliminate the "fears, prejudice, pride, and irrationality" that were barriers to a truly integrated society, to peaceful intergroup and interpersonal living. Such a society

could be achieved only when people accepted that inner, invisible law that etched on their hearts the conviction "that all men are brothers and that love is mankind's most potent weapon for personal and social transformation. True integration will be achieved by true neighbors who are willingly obedient to unenforceable obligations."

Even so, the Selma campaign was the movement's finest hour, and the Voting Rights Act the high point of a broad civil rights coalition that included the federal government, various white groups, and all the other civil rights organizations in addition to SCLC. King himself had best expressed the spirit and aspirations of that coalition when, on August 28, 1963, standing before the Lincoln Memorial, he electrified an interracial crowd of 250,000 with perhaps his greatest speech, "I Have a Dream," in which he described in rhythmic, hypnotic cadences his vision of an integrated America. Because of his achievements and moral vision, he won the 1964 Nobel Peace Prize, at thirty-four the youngest recipient in Nobel history.

Still, King paid a high price for his fame and his cause. He suffered from stomachaches and insomnia, and even felt guilty about all the tributes he received, all the popularity he enjoyed. Born in relative material comfort and given a superior education, he did not think he had earned the right to lead the impoverished black masses. He complained, too, that he no longer had a personal self and that sometimes he did not recognize the Martin Luther King people talked about. Lonely, away from home for protracted periods, beset with temptation, he slept with other women, for some of whom he had real feeling. His sexual transgressions only added to his guilt, for he knew he was imperiling his cause and hurting himself and those he loved.

Alas for King, FBI Director J. Edgar Hoover found out about the black leader's infidelities. The director already abhorred King, certain that Communist spies influenced him and masterminded his demonstrations. Hoover did not think blacks capable of organizing such things, so Communists had to be behind them and King as well. As it turned out, a lawyer in King's inner circle and a man in SCLC's New York office did have Communist backgrounds, a fact that only reinforced Hoover's suspicions about King. Under Hoover's orders, FBI agents conducted a ruthless crusade to destroy King's reputation and drive him broken and humiliated from public life. Hoover's men tapped King's phones and bugged his hotel rooms; they compiled a prurient monograph about his private life and showed it to various editors, public officials, and religious and civic leaders; they spread the word, Hoover's word, that King was not only a reprobate but a dangerous subversive with Communist associations.

King was scandalized and frightened by the FBI's revelations of his extramarital affairs. Luckily for him, no editor, not even a racist one in the South, would touch the FBI's salacious materials. Public officials such as Robert Kennedy were shocked, but argued that King's personal life did not affect his probity as a civil rights leader. Many blacks, too, declared that what he did in private was his own business. Even so, King vowed to refrain from further affairs—only to succumb again to his own human frailties.

As for the Communist charge, King retorted that he did not need any Russians to tell him when someone was standing on his neck; he could figure that out by himself. To mollify his political friends, however, King did banish from SCLC the two men with Communist backgrounds (later he resumed his ties with the lawyer, a loyal friend, and let Hoover be damned). He also denounced Communism in no uncertain terms. It was, he believed, profoundly and fundamentally evil, an atheistic doctrine no true Christian could ever embrace. He hated the dictatorial Soviet state, too, whose "crippling totalitarianism" subordinated everything—religion, art, music, science, and the individual—to its terrible yoke. True, Communism started with men like Karl Marx who were "aflame with a passion for social justice." Yet King faulted Marx for rejecting God and the spiritual in human life. "The great weakness in Karl Marx is right here," King once told his staff, and he went on to describe his ideal Christian commonwealth in Hegelian terms: "Capitalism fails to realize that life is social. Marxism fails to realize that life is

individual. Truth is found neither in the rugged individualism of capitalism nor in the impersonal collectivism of Communism. The kingdom of God is found in a synthesis that combines the truths of these two opposites. Now there is where I leave brother Marx and move on toward the kingdom."

But how to move on after Selma was a perplexing question King never successfully answered. After the devastating Watts riot in August 1965, he took his movement into the racially troubled urban North, seeking to help the suffering black poor in the ghettos. In 1966, over the fierce opposition of some of his own staff, he launched a campaign to end the black slums in Chicago and forestall rioting there. But the campaign foundered because King seemed unable to devise a coherent anti-slum strategy, because Mayor Richard Daley and his black acolytes opposed him bitterly, and because white America did not seem to care. King did lead open-housing marches into segregated neighborhoods in Chicago, only to encounter furious mobs who waved Nazi banners, threw bottles and bricks, and screamed, "We hate niggers!" "Kill the niggers!" "We want Martin Luther Coon!" King was shocked. "I've been in many demonstrations all across the South," he told reporters, "but I can say that I have never seen—even in Mississippi and Alabama—mobs as hostile and as hate-filled as I've seen in Chicago." Although King prevented a major riot there and wrung important concessions from City Hall, the slums remained, as wretched and seemingly unsolvable as ever.

That same year, angry young militants in SNCC and the Congress of Racial Equality (CORE) renounced King's teachings—they were sick and tired of "De Lawd" telling them to love white people and work for integration. Now they advocated "Black Power," black separatism, even violent resistance to liberate blacks in America. SNCC even banished whites from its ranks and went on to drop "nonviolent" from its name and to lobby against civil rights legislation.

Black Power repelled the older, more conservative black organizations such as the NAACP and the

Urban League, and fragmented the civil rights movement beyond repair. King, too, argued that black separatism was chimerical, even suicidal, and that nonviolence remained the only workable way for black people. "Darkness cannot drive out darkness," he reasoned: "only light can do that. Hate cannot drive out hate: only love can do that." If every other black in America turned to violence, King warned, then he would still remain the lone voice preaching that it was wrong. Nor was SCLC going to reject whites as SNCC had done. "There have been too many hymns of hope," King said, "too many anthems of expectation, too many deaths, too many dark days of standing over graves of those who fought for integration for us to turn back now. We must still sing 'Black and White Together, We Shall Overcome.'"

In 1967, King himself broke with the older black organizations over the ever-widening war in Vietnam. He had first objected to American escalation in the summer of 1965, arguing that the Nobel Peace Prize and his role as a Christian minister compelled him to speak out for peace. Two years later, with almost a half-million Americans—a disproportionate number of them poor blacks—fighting in Vietnam, King devoted whole speeches to America's "immoral" war against a tiny country on the other side of the globe. His stance provoked a fusillade of criticism from all directions—from the NAACP, the Urban League, white and black political leaders, *Newsweek, Life, Time,* and the *New York Times,* all telling him to stick to civil rights. Such criticism hurt him deeply. When he read the *Times*'s editorial against him, he broke down and cried. But he did not back down. "I've fought too long and too hard now against segregated accommodations to end up segregating my moral concerns," he told his critics. "Injustice *any*where is a threat to justice everywhere."

That summer, with the ghettos ablaze with riots, King warned that American cities would explode if funds used for war purposes were not diverted to emergency antipoverty programs. By then, the Johnson administration, determined to gain a military victory in Vietnam, had written King off as an antiwar agitator, and was now cooperating with the FBI in its efforts to defame him.

The fall of 1967 was a terrible time for King, the lowest ebb in his civil rights career. Everybody seemed to be attacking him—young black militants for his stubborn adherence to nonviolence, moderate and conservative blacks, labor leaders, liberal white politicians, the White House, and the FBI for his stand on Vietnam. Two years had passed since King had produced a nonviolent victory, and contributions to SCLC had fallen off sharply. Black spokesman Adam Clayton Powell, who had once called King the greatest Negro in America, now derided him as Martin Loser King. The incessant attacks began to irritate him, creating such anxiety and depression that his friends worried about his emotional health.

Worse still, the country seemed dangerously polarized. On one side, backlashing whites argued that the ghetto explosions had "cremated" nonviolence and that white people had better arm themselves against black rioters. On the other side, angry blacks urged their people to "kill the Honkies" and burn the cities down. All around King, the country was coming apart in a cacophony of hate and reaction. Had America lost the will and moral power to save itself? he wondered. There was such rage in the ghetto and such bigotry among whites that he feared a race war was about to break out. He felt he had to do something to pull America back from the brink. He and his staff had to mount a new campaign that would halt the drift to violence in the black world and combat stiffening white resistance, a nonviolent action that would "transmute the deep rage of the ghetto into a constructive and creative force."

Out of his deliberations sprang a bold and daring project called the poor people's campaign. The master plan, worked out by February 1968, called for SCLC to bring an interracial army of poor people to Washington, D.C., to dramatize poverty before the federal government. For King, just turned thirty-nine, the time had come to employ civil disobedience against the national government itself. Ultimately, he was projecting a genuine class movement that he hoped would bring about meaningful changes in American society—changes that would redistribute economic and political power and end poverty, racism, "the madness of militarism," and war.

In the midst of his preparations, King went to Memphis, Tennessee, to help black sanitation workers there who were striking for the right to unionize. On the night of April 3, with a storm thundering outside, he told a black audience that he had been to the mountaintop and had seen what lay ahead. "I may not get there with you. But I want you to know tonight that we as a people *will* get to the promised land."

The next afternoon, when King stepped out on the balcony of the Lorraine Motel, an escaped white convict named James Earl Ray, stationed in a nearby building, took aim with a high-powered rifle and blasted King into eternity. Subsequent evidence linked Ray to white men in the St. Louis area who had offered "hit" money for King's life.

For weeks after the shooting, King's stricken country convulsed in grief, contrition, and rage. While there were those who cheered his death, the *New York Times* called it a disaster to the nation, the *London Times* an enormous loss to the world. In Tanzania, Reverend Trevor Huddleston, expelled from South Africa for standing against apartheid, declared King's death the greatest single tragedy since the assassination of Gandhi in 1948, and said it challenged the complacency of the Christian Church all over the globe.

On April 9, with 120 million Americans watching on television, thousands of mourners—black and white alike—gathered in Atlanta for the funeral of a man who had never given up his dream of creating a symphony of brotherhood on these shores. As a black man born and raised in segregation, he had had every reason to hate America and to grow up preaching cynicism and retaliation. Instead, he had loved the country passionately and had sung of her promise and glory more eloquently than anyone of his generation.

They buried him in Atlanta's South View Cemetery, then blooming with dogwood and fresh green boughs of spring. On his crypt, hewn into the marble, were the words of an old Negro spiritual he had often quoted: "Free at Last, Free at Last, Thank God Almighty I'm Free at Last."

QUESTIONS TO CONSIDER

1 Martin Luther King Jr. was an angry young man who hated the segregated world of the American South and the injustices he saw inflicted on African Americans all over the nation. In adulthood, he came to feel that anger offered no solution to the problems that he and other African Americans faced. What made him change his mind? What were the roots of the philosophy that he adopted and used to lead the civil rights movement of the 1950s and 1960s? How did King give African Americans a sense of self-worth and the tools to achieve their aims?

2 What were SNCC and SCLC? How did these organizations differ from each other? In what ways were they alike? What changes took place in SNCC after the mid-1960s? How did Black Power differ from the civil rights movement under King?

3 What were the two major accomplishments of the civil rights movement in the mid-1960s? What specific actions did King and his followers undertake to influence public opinion and effect legislative change, and at what cost?

4 Describe the internal and external difficulties that beset King and the civil rights movement in the late 1960s. How did King defuse charges that he was a Communist? How did he react to the FBI crusade against him? To white and black backlashes? To the attacks on his policies that seemed to come from all sides? What did his support of the anti–Vietnam War movement cost him?

5 Why do you think Americans were receptive to King's pacifist message and nonviolent approach in the 1960s? Do you think similar tactics would be effective against oppression in a country such as the People's Republic of China?

26 Betty Friedan Destroys the Myth of the Happy Housewife

MARCIA COHEN

The Nineteenth Amendment, which gave American women the right to vote, did not bring them into the center of the nation's political life, and suffragists like Eleanor Roosevelt accepted a separate and subordinate "gender" role in their political work. During the Great Depression, as one feminist scholar has said, women "were partners in the struggle for survival." They also became involved in social and political activity; indeed, a "women's network" emerged within the New Deal and the Democratic party, allowing women for the first time to become a grassroots force. But women's achievements in the thirties proved to be short-lived, as historian Sara Evans has said, and women as a whole "were not empowered."

During the Second World War, women made significant economic advances as workers in America's defense plants. But after the war, as Marcia Cohen points out in this selection, the industrial establishment tended to push women back into the home because it recognized "the housewife's valuable role as the prime consumer of household products." At the same time, women's magazines such as Redbook *and* McCall's, *many of them published and edited by men, popularized the image of the happy housewife and stressed the old female virtues of passivity, marriage, and motherhood.*

The image of the happy homemaker and contented "auxiliary" troubled Betty Friedan, who in the mid-1950s was living in the suburb of Rockland County, New York, and trying to combine marriage and motherhood with freelance journalism. Back in the 1940s, she had been a brilliant student at Smith College and had done such outstanding work in psychology that she won a fellowship from the University of California at Berkeley. There she studied with the famous analyst Erik Erikson and won an even more prestigious grant that would have carried her into a professional career. But for some incredible reason—perhaps because a young man she was dating complained about the fellowship—she turned it down. Almost at once she suffered a protracted attack of asthma. Wheezing, gasping for breath, she left academe and the young man and fled to New York, where she sought relief in psychoanalysis.

When she felt better, she secured an editorial position at a small labor newspaper, married an amusing, ambitious man named Carl Friedan, and started raising a family. When she became pregnant with her second child, her employer decided that one pregnancy leave was enough; the paper fired her, ignoring the stipulation in her contract that guaranteed her maternity leave. She protested, but the Newspaper Guild refused to support her. Meanwhile, her marriage to Carl was becoming stormy; when they argued, she said, books and sugar bowls seemed to fly. Racked again by asthma, she resumed psychoanalysis.

Now living in a suburban Victorian house, Friedan did occasional freelance writing for women's magazines. She was increasingly attracted to stories about women who wanted the same things she did—an integrated life that used all of a woman's talents. She noted that prosperity offered the American woman an education and a living standard her grandmother would have envied, but it brought frustration too. By the 1950s, the American woman had been educated as never before, but to what end? When Friedan sent out a questionnaire for an article she was writing for McCall's, *she was astounded to learn that many women felt as unhappy as she did. Worse, their discontents were hidden behind the pervasive image of the happy housewife.*

In 1963, after years of struggling, Friedan published a book that demolished that image, The Feminine Mystique; *it galvanized millions of female readers, rocketed Friedan to national fame, and led to the modern feminist movement. Friedan's achievements were as important as those of many of the famous men we have studied thus far, and yet most of you would probably be hard pressed to identify her. You will get to know her well in the following selection, written by journalist Marcia Cohen, author of* The Sisterhood *(1988). Cohen recounts Friedan's extraordinary story, describing how she came to write* The Feminine Mystique *and to challenge a whole generation's assumptions and practices relating to women. An epilogue tells how Friedan initiated the "second wave" of organized feminism and founded and became the first president of the National Organization for Women, the first mainstream women's organization and the most successful one in history.*

GLOSSARY

BROCKWAY, GEORGE   Editor at W. W. Norton who signed Friedan on to write *The Feminine Mystique,* which grew out of her article "The Togetherness Woman."

BROWN, HELEN GURLEY   Author of *Sex and the Single Girl* (1962) and editor of *Cosmopolitan* who played a "pioneering role" in the sexual liberation of women in the 1960s and 1970s.

STEIN, BOB   Editor of *Redbook* who agreed to publish an article ("The Togetherness Woman") based on Friedan's Smith class questionnaire if she expanded it to include younger women; he rejected the completed article on the

ground that it would appeal only to "the most neurotic housewife."

"THE TOGETHERNESS WOMAN"   An article Friedan wrote for *McCall's* magazine that the male editor refused to publish. Based on a questionnaire Friedan had sent to her Smith College classmates, the article attacked woman's "homemaking role" as dull and unrewarding.

WOMEN'S WORLD (1952)   Motion picture that stressed how much the home was a "woman's world" in which women buried their ambitions and subordinated themselves to their husbands.

It was a strange stirring, a sense of dissatisfaction, a yearning that women suffered in the middle of the twentieth century in the United States. Each suburban wife struggled with it alone. As she made the beds, shopped for groceries, matched slipcover material, ate peanut butter sandwiches with her children, chauffeured Cub Scouts and Brownies, lay beside her husband at night, she was afraid to ask even of herself the silent question—"Is this all?"

BETTY FRIEDAN, *The Feminine Mystique,* 1963

Her so-called "brilliant career"! Not much had come of that, Betty thought miserably as she trudged back to her beloved Smith College for her fifteenth reunion. The great promise her professors had seen—that eager, whirling intellectual energy—had come to nothing more than a

couple of women's magazine articles. Hardly "brilliant." Hardly even worthy of the term "career."

Betty—the class of 1942's hortatory, patriotic, tough tomato, always ready to take on an argument and, more often than not, *win* it. That same plump little girl who was so determined, way back in Peoria, to make her snooty contemporaries "respect her," who had set out, in her younger brother Harry's words, "to be somebody important . . ."

She was now, in 1957, returning to the alma mater that had been for her, such a glory, an affirmation,

Marcia Cohen, "Betty Friedan Destroys the Myth of the Happy Housewife," from *The Sisterhood: The True Story of the Women Who Changed the World.* © 1988 by Marcia Cohen.

"that whole thing," as she would put it years later in her gruff, gravelly voice, "of the *passion* of the mind." And she was coming back not as the professional psychologist they must all have expected, but as, well, "just a housewife" with a few articles to her credit.

"It rankled me," she would remember, "because I hadn't lived up to my brilliant possibilities."

But the undergraduates on campus, she found, were not the slightest bit interested in such "possibilities," and she was shocked by their distracted answers to her questions. Questions about, naturally, their scholarly interests, what ideas or professors they were "passionately excited about."

"They looked at me," she would recall, "as if I were speaking a foreign language. 'We're not excited about things like that,' they said. 'All we want to do is to get married and have children and do things with them, like go ice skating . . .'"

But it was now, of course, the quiet Eisenhower era, the gritrock pit of what would be viewed in retrospect as the heavy-duty husband-hunting years. "I chased her until she caught me," was a standard husband's joke, though the truth probably lay as much in the male youth's intent on settling down as the female's. The house in the suburbs, the station wagon bursting with kids and collie dogs, the ability to provide for a family proved manhood as much as homemaking proved femininity, and testified as well to those most important virtues of the decade: "adjustment," "maturity."

By now psychology was a preoccupation. Freud's vaunted theory of "penis envy" and [Dr. Helene] Deutsch's interpretation of the achieving, intellectual woman as "masculinized . . . her warm, intuitive knowledge . . . [having] yielded to cold unproductive thinking," hinted of maladjustments to be avoided at all costs. The idea that woman's true nature, reflecting her anatomy, was passive and could be fulfilled only through renouncing her goals and "sublimating" to a male had taken firm root in the American ethic.

The women's magazines, growing ever more powerful as advertising pages and circulations mounted, had been pounding the message home for nearly a decade. Women, as [Ferdinand] Lundberg and

[Dr. Marynia F.] Farnham had written [in *Modern Woman: The Lost Sex*], needed propaganda to keep them *in* traditional homemaking tasks, such as cooking or decorating, and *out* of those "fields belonging to the male area"—that is, "law, mathematics, physics, business, industry and technology." And indeed, the magazines invariably portrayed women as, above and beyond all else, housewives and mothers. If an interview subject happened to be an actress or dancer (two acceptably feminine undertakings), the editors quickly clarified: She was merely dabbling, taking a breather from her real work—and life—at home.

Nor was this notion purely the province of the popular press. Great citadels of learning were equally convinced and convincing. In most eastern women's schools, "gracious living" was the order of the day. This meant, on the whole, little more than learning to pour tea from a silver-plated samovar. But to carry out this future mission, give or take a samovar, you had to have a life of gentility, with, of course, a husband. Most college women, even those who never stood their turn at the tea kettle, knew beyond a shadow of a doubt that marriage—not a career—was their primary goal in life. Running a close second was the psychological health of their children, who were likely to erupt into neurotic misfits, psychologists warned, should Mother attempt any serious work outside the home.

Admittedly, the female's focus on marriage had an extra edge. The birth rate was soaring and given their dependent condition, women needed to be supported financially. The status gap of the thirties—between the gracious, respected matron, cared for by her breadwinner husband, and the lonely, forlorn working girl—was revived and slickly refurbished. Rare indeed was the college counselor who, by discussing the job market, would damn a female graduate to the latter state.

Some women left college without graduating. (Might as well get on with it. What's the point of waiting, anyhow?) Most collected a "Mrs." after or with their undergraduate degrees. You understood that you were marrying not just a husband but "a life," and this wholesale effort seemed at the time to blur class distinctions. Women cooked pot roast everywhere.

The idealized housewife from 1955, shown here on the cover of the Saturday Evening Post *for May 21, was well dressed and fashionably coiffed, even at home. Surrounded by modern appliances in her impeccable kitchen, she looks just as discontented as Betty Friedan found her a few years later—although the problem was a great deal more complex than runny chocolate icing.*

That there were, in fact, differences—in both class and interests—would eventually create knotty problems for feminists of the future. Many women, not only working-class women but also those with less defined intellectual appetites, very much enjoyed their roles as homemakers, household decision makers, disciplinarians, or managers, preferences that would eventually set them at odds with the revolutionaries of the sixties.

At the moment, though, like it or not, most women were preparing for the esteemed role of "auxiliary."

If, for instance, a woman was married to a doctor, she would join the hospital "auxiliary," have dinner ready when the doctor got home, and subscribe to a magazine called *Doctor's Wife.*

It was a given, in those days, that a young woman with a burning interest in the law should marry a lawyer. She would help him develop his practice and live the life of a lawyer's wife, mother of a lawyer's children. Or an engineer's, or a writer's, or a pharmacist's, or a retailer's—or especially a corporate executive's. That the deportment of an executive's wife had a major influence on her husband's advancement was a lesson clearly delivered, not just in an announcement from Radcliffe College of an Institute for Executive Wives, but in Jean Negulesco's popular film pointedly entitled *Women's World.*

In this 1952 movie, Lauren Bacall—no longer the sultry siren of the forties—played a devoted wife who, along with two others, June Allyson and Arlene Dahl, was summoned to corporate headquarters in New York, where their husbands were about to audition for top honcho.

"The best couple for the job," the company owner frankly informed the men, "will win. Your wife is under observation. She must never compete with the company. If there is a choice between wife and work, it must be work."

As the husbands in this "women's world" proceeded with their unmemorable politicking, the motivations (and "qualifications") of the wives were quickly established. June was frightfully anxious to rush home to her kids in the Midwest. Lauren fretted that the job might exacerbate her husband's ulcer. Arlene, on the other hand, was so delighted by the prospect of life in New York that she overreached by flirting with the owner, thus proving that she had missed not just one, but several commandments dosed out in the dialogue.

I "What's important to him is important to me."

II "You must convince him that you're perfectly happy even if you feel like screaming."

III "The man who gets the job must have a wife who loves him very much."

IV (the overriding theme): "A man is working for the children, and they're your children so it's a *woman's world.*"

And if, in the end, it's Arlene's man who does win the job, this plot twist occurs only after her restrained, expressionless husband has impressed the owner by dispensing with his "handicap": his ambitious, brazen, childless (and therefore dispensable) wife.

Though heavy-handed, the movie accurately reflected a large segment of the women's world of the fifties, where back in the suburbs wives quickly buried ambitions of the sort (vicarious or not) that plagued the unfortunate Arlene.

Few could imagine, in the expanding economy of the post–Korean War years, that among these selfless wives would be many who would find themselves, twenty and thirty years hence, in the wake of defunct marriages or financial belt-tightening, pounding the pavements, or training for jobs that could bring in much-needed cash or restore flagging self-esteem.

There were, of course, exceptions. A few remarkable college graduates *did* pursue professional careers. Among them, ironically—though barely noticed at the time—was an assertive, achieving Illinois woman who, in 1952, ran for Congress. Phyllis Schlafly, who would eventually stand forth as the new feminism's most vocal enemy, who would sound the alarm for women's return to the home, was among those who were not, at the moment, at home.

For even then, in spite of the social propaganda, many women, including those from middle-income families, were quietly moving into the workforce—so many, in fact, that they soon accounted for 60 percent of its growth in that decade. Among them were many single women, including college graduates who, as they waited for Mr. Right, took jobs as "Gal Fridays" in ad agencies, or as researchers, "helping" a reporter on a news magazine. Many took speed-writing or shorthand courses so they could be secretaries and thus avoid the typing pool, jobs for which there was plenty of call under "Female" in the help-wanted columns. The men who ran America's industries knew better than to give their girls (as in "Call my girl, she'll make an appointment for you") dangerous notions about careers. "Gal Fridays," summa cum laude be damned, ran errands and made coffee. They were lucky, they were told, to be hired at all, since it was a given that they wouldn't be around for long. If they were

"normal," they would soon drop out to get married, have babies.

And if they were "normal," they were known to be emotionally delicate as well, not cut out for the rough-and-tumble of the business world. . . .

If, for example, a wife was working outside the home, she retained her auxiliary, ladylike status by referring to her job as unimportant and transitory, a diversion, never a "career." She was helping out—just for the moment—with the family finances. She was subdued and modest. She strolled, seldom ran, let alone worked up a sweat. She knew better than to enter one of those rare girls' track meets, where young men guffawed to each other on the sidelines: "Nice tits" or "Some ass." She aspired, if not to June Allyson's saccharine self-sacrifice, to the controlled charm of Doris Day, the elfin poise of Audrey Hepburn, the serene aristocracy of Grace Kelly.

Any sign of ambition was disaster. What would be known in the seventies as "abrasive" in the fifties was a "castrating bitch."

Simone de Beauvoir's *The Second Sex,* a brilliant feminist polemic, was published in this country in 1953, but nobody in America talked about it much. The revolutionary Kinsey Report on *Sexual Behavior in the Human Female,* documenting the fact that women enjoyed sex both emotionally and physically pretty much the same way men did, went barely noticed in America's heartland. As the lure of television swept the country, people watched "Ozzie and Harriet" and "Father Knows Best," images of the perfect American family. Blacks appeared on the screen almost solely as servants; women, as wives and mothers. It was the age of "conformity," or, as probably suited best, the "silent generation."

And yet . . .

Anyone with an ear to the quiet, frozen lake of the mid-fifties might have heard the rumble, the growl and surge of a riptide beneath the ice. In the late forties, Holden Caulfield, J. D. Salinger's sensitive hero of *Catcher in the Rye,* inspired thousands of young fans by limning the hypocrisy he saw around him. (No one yet used the term "drop out," but Holden seemed destined to do it.) In 1954, the Supreme Court ordered desegregation in all public schools, an act that would not only change the paper-white face of the country, but may well have precipitated the enormous upheavals to come. In 1955, the sensitive, introspective James Dean struck a chord of disaffection in *Rebel Without a Cause*. Elvis Presley had begun to heat up and transform the soul of pop music. Writers Jack Kerouac in *On the Road* and Allen Ginsberg in "Howl" were giving voice to a strange youthful ennui, a rough-timbered, off-balance sense of disillusionment.

In 1953, *Playboy* magazine—with a nude calendar photo of Marilyn Monroe—was launched. Being the "party organ," as feminist writer Barbara Ehrenreich would one day call it, of the male, hedonistic rebellion, it had nothing good to say about collie dogs, station wagons, church picnics, or the family. It was billed as Hugh Hefner's answer to conformity, to "home, family and all that jazz," as he put it, and to "togetherness"—the resoundingly successful advertising slogan of *McCall's* magazine, the symbol of the happy, glorified home with Daddy at work, Mommy in the kitchen, and 2.5 children as total fulfillment.

"The Togetherness Woman" was, in fact, the title of the article Betty had promised *McCall's*. She had taken the assignment simply to justify the months and months she had spent on a questionnaire that Smith had asked her to prepare for her class reunion.

Betty had labored mightily over the thing, even brought a couple of her friends in to hash over the questions. She had worked so hard, in fact, that her classmates at the reunion had giggled about how *long* the form was. How involved, how detailed the questions.

"What difficulties have you found in working out your role as a woman?" "What are the chief satisfactions and frustrations of your life today?" "How do you feel about getting older?" Leave it to Betty, the psychology buff, they joked, to dream up all that stuff!

Yet all she had been trying to do was prove one little point, just a corollary to the women's home-is-all psychology of the day, a sort of reassurance to her classmates and herself.

"All I was trying to do with that questionnaire," Betty would remember, "was to show that an education wasn't *bad* for a woman, it didn't make her *maladjusted* in her role as wife and mother." That academic learning was not, in short—as so many psychologists were then implying—an actual hindrance to femininity.

"I didn't realize it at the time," she would recall, "but I was asking the questions that were beginning to concern me." For indeed, skilled as she was in social science, and guiltily restless, Betty had designed the sort of query that took dead aim at the secrets of the heart—including her own.

"How have you changed inside?" she asked. "What do you wish you had done differently?"

And when, finally, she sat down to analyze the results for *McCall's*, she discovered that the responses raised more questions than they answered. Why was it, for example, that those of her classmates who were not active outside their homes were not especially happy at all? That they seemed, in fact, just as restless as she was?

They had written about a strange sense of emptiness—how like her own!—or a gnawing guilt, or shame, an uncertainty about who, exactly, they were: Jim's wife? Sally's mother? Betty found turmoils of indecision among these stay-at-home moms, and ennui, feelings of failure, despair, depression—even, for some, alcohol and drugs. And, most striking of all, from those isolated posts in suburbia, the uneasy sense that, because they had these feelings, they were unquestionably "neurotic."

So clearly Betty was not, as she had once thought, alone with these feelings. She was not, as she had also thought, a "freak."

But was education the villain, as all the psychologists and anthropologists and social scientists and magazine writers were more or less subtly suggesting?

That was, quite simply, a premise that the intense, verbal, thirty-six-year-old sometime writer, with her longings for intellectual achievement, could not accept. And as Betty read and reread and searched and analyzed, she discovered yet another piece to the puzzle.

"I found," she would remember at a later, much calmer time of her life, "that the women who seemed the strongest were not quite living this complete image of the housewife and feminine fulfillment. And that education had made them not willing to settle. . . ."

She was on to something!

Slowly but passionately, she began to write. Words and sentences began to fill the pages, words that bore no resemblance to "Millionaire's Wife," or "Two Are an Island," or anything she had ever written before. No panaceas, no hopeful methods of adjusting to the status quo, of finding total fulfillment in the home, poured forth from her pen. Instead of praising the homemaking role, she attacked the endless, monotonous, unrewarding housework it demanded. Instead of soothing her potential readers into the "feminine role" prescribed by the magazine she was writing for, she blasted the notion of vicarious living through husband and children. Rather than touting the "togetherness" so precious to *McCall's,* she indicted the slogan as a fraud.

She had to be kidding.

The male editor of *McCall's* summarily rejected "The Togetherness Woman."

A nasty shock for Betty Friedan. Never in her life had anything she had written been turned down. Quickly, she interviewed more women, then sent the piece to *Ladies' Home Journal.* There, sure enough, it was accepted, but . . .

"They rewrote it," she would remember years later, with the anger and dismay still in her voice, "to make the opposite point! That education *did* make women maladjusted in their role as women!"

Betty refused to allow the magazine to publish the article, retrieved it, and made one last try.

Bob Stein, then editor of *Redbook,* said he would indeed be interested in a piece based on Betty's Smith class questionnaire if it was greatly expanded to include younger women, and other, more extensive data.

Betty was already talking to younger married women and they weren't changing her view of the problem at all. In fact, she was beginning to think, the situation for women who graduated from college after 1942 seemed to be even worse than it was for her classmates. Given that domestic fantasy she had already seen among members of Smith's graduating class, even fewer women in their twenties and early thirties were active outside their homes; even *more* seemed vaguely unhappy.

She hadn't yet been paid for the article, of course, and she was violating that "enough-money-to-pay-the-maid" pact with herself. But still, since Bob Stein had asked—and since she was fascinated herself—she did more interviews. She rewrote the piece, integrating the new material, and shipped it off to the editor.

Who was, he would remember, stunned.

"I liked Betty a lot," Bob Stein would recall. "She was a solid, trustworthy writer, a bit argumentative maybe, but so were most writers worth their salt. I had been looking forward to 'The Togetherness Woman,' but when I read it, I could only wonder what in God's name had come over Betty Friedan. It was a very angry piece. I didn't think that our readers would identify with it at all."

The *Redbook* editor—like all successful editors of women's magazines—was fully aware of the link binding readers to *their* magazine, the great umbilical, as some called it, the trust which, if broken, could doom both magazine and its boss. And Betty was, Bob Stein would remember, "very sensitive about her writing. . . . Luckily, I'd never had to reject her work before." But this?

In years to come, Bob Stein would find himself on television and radio talk shows with Betty, defending her, if only because, as he would put it, "the opposition was so impossible," but admitting, too, that he hadn't realized "that the feelings dammed up out there were so strong." At the moment, though, he could only call Betty's agent and report regretfully: "Look, we can't print this. Only the most neurotic housewife would identify with this."

And that, perhaps, might have been the end of it.

Redbook had been Betty's last hope, and in the weeks that followed, she was very depressed. She wrote nothing and dropped out of an important writer's seminar because it met the same night of the week that she served as assistant den mother for her son's Cub Scout troop. She had already chastised herself, had an asthma attack, in fact, over missing some of those Scout meetings.

One night, though, just as a prop to her ego, just to make herself feel like a professional writer again, she made the trek in from Rockland County to hear the successful author Vance Packard talk about his book *The Hidden Persuaders,* an exposé of the sinister effects of advertising. Packard had written it, he said, after an article on the subject had been turned down by every major magazine.

And then—not long afterward, as Betty would remember it—she was riding the bus into Manhattan, taking the kids to the dentist, mulling it over . . . The juggernaut women's magazines, with their fingers on the commercial pulse, had been feeding the domestic palate to ever-rising profit margins . . .

"Damn it all," Betty suddenly realized, "I was right! Somehow what I was saying had gone against the grain of the women's magazines."

And now she knew she couldn't let it go.

In some deep place in the psyche of this impatient, demanding, worrisome, dedicated, prickly, volatile woman, a quiet vision was forming. Inside, as she would later write, she felt "this calm, strange sureness, as if in tune with something larger, more important than myself that had to be taken seriously."

It would be a book. Like *The Hidden Persuaders,* "The Togetherness Woman" could be a book. She would call that editor who had wanted her to expand "The Coming Ice Age," and this time she would tell him yes. Yes, she would write a book for W. W. Norton. But just as she had said before, it would not be about someone else's work. It would be hers. Her own research, her own social science, her own accomplishment in her field.

The Togetherness Woman.

And why not? said [Norton Editor] George Brockway, who immediately saw the potential.

The affluence of the fifties had permitted—even stimulated—critical examinations of contemporary life. *The Man in the Grey Flannel Suit, The Hucksters, Executive Suite, The View from the 40th Floor* had all been big sellers. *The Togetherness Woman,* the editor thought, would make a fine parallel to the latest sharp attack on the rage for conformity, William H. Whyte's *The Organization Man.*

And this woman had the fire in the belly.

"She was incredibly ambitious," Brockway would remember. "The most ambitious woman I had ever met. She said that she didn't know what to call the subject exactly, but that it had something to do with a lack of identity, that women weren't being told . . . they aren't being allowed . . ."

Betty talked on and on at that meeting, half her thoughts, as usual, dropping off mid-sentence, her mind going even faster than her tongue. She had been interviewing so many women. She didn't know quite how to put it, but . . .

There was *something* very wrong with the way women were feeling these days.

And, over the barrage, the furtive insights, the distress, George Brockway honed in.

"Ride it," he told Betty. "You've got the idea, now ride it, ride it!"

How long did she think it would take?

Well, she said, it took her about a month to do an article, so figure a chapter a month . . .

"A year," she said. "I'll have it done in a year." Oh, and yes, she supposed [an advance of] a thousand dollars now would be okay, with the rest of the $3,000 [advance] to come in installments.

It was years later—more research was required, a mysterious block arose—before Betty even *began* to write. She worked three days a week in the Frederick Lewis Allen Room of the New York Public Library and then, when her allotted time there ran out (and the maid quit), in her favorite spot at home, the beautiful dining room with windows on the garden.

"Neither my husband nor my publisher nor anyone else who knew about it thought I would ever finish it," she would write. "When the writing of it took me over completely . . . I wrote every day on the dining room table, while the children were in school, and after they went to bed at night. (It didn't do any good to have a desk of my own; they used it for their homework anyhow.)"

She worked against patronizing jokes about a "woman's book." Against guilt. Against fear. Given the resistance she had already encountered to her views, there must be *no* holes in her argument or her documentation, *no* room for attack.

But slowly, if not steadily, the chapters, scribbled on a legal pad, began to pile up in an old china cupboard in the corner of the dining room. In them, her thesis emerged.

At rock bottom, it was economics, if not to say greed. After World War II, women had been pushed back into the home as industrialists assessed the housewife's valuable role as the prime consumer of household products. The marketing of toasters, washing machines, cosmetics, and the like was the true purpose behind the hard sell of "femininity." Educators, sociologists, psychologists—and, of course, the women's magazines, with their hunger for the advertising dollar—followed suit.

One by one, Betty took them all on, both the current crop and their historical forebears.

Freud and his "sexual solipsism": "It is a Freudian idea . . . hardened into apparent fact, that has trapped so many American women today." Freud and his Victorian bias had perpetrated the greatest sin in psychotherapy; he had infantilized women, denied them their ability to grow, cut them off from "the zest that is characteristic of human health."

[Anthropologist] Margaret Mead: "The role of Margaret Mead as the professional spokesman of femininity would have been less important if American women had taken the example of her own life, instead of listening to what she said in her books."

Contemporary educators: They induced women into the superficial comfort of the home, thus depriving them of their function in society, consigning millions of women "to spend their days at work an eight-year-old could do."

As for the women's magazines, which offered that fraudulent home-as-religion editorial content: "I helped create this image. I have watched American women for fifteen years try to conform to it. But I can no longer deny its terrible implications. It is not a harmless image. There may be no psychological terms for the harm it is doing."

And, of course, "togetherness": "The big lie . . . the end of the road . . . where the woman has no independent self to hide even in guilt; she exists only for and through her husband and children."

It was this vicarious existence that caused educations to "fester," caused housewife's fatigue, ennui, depression. Not neurosis. It was society—not women—that was sick!

Like Lundberg and Farnham, Betty resurrected earlier feminists, but instead of damning them as sick souls, she sang their praises as heroines. Mary Wollstonecraft, Margaret Fuller, Elizabeth Cady Stanton, Lucy Stone, Susan B. Anthony. Anatomy, she agreed, with a somewhat cursory bow to Simone de Beauvoir's evocative phrasing in *The Second Sex,* is not destiny. Women were not simply their biology. They also had *minds.* And, "as if waking from a coma," they were beginning to ask, "Where am I? What am I doing here?"

She answered the hyperbole of Lundberg and Farnham with some of her own. The isolated suburban home, she wrote, was a "comfortable concentration camp," the women trapped within them cut off, like prisoners, from past adult interests and their own identities. It was a new neurosis, this modern ache, and you could read it in the hundreds of interviews and psychological tests she had accumulated—among them, one test that must have been reassuring, since it suggested that "the high-dominance woman was more psychologically free" than one who was "timid, shy, modest, neat, tactful, quiet, introverted, retiring, more feminine, more conventional." And perhaps, Betty herself speculated, only an "ugly duckling adolescence" or an unhappy marriage could fuel the ambition to resist the deadening, conformist pressure.

For "the problem lay buried, unspoken, for many years in the minds of American women." It was a problem, she wrote, "that had no name," a problem that was caused by the pervasive social pressure relegating women to the four walls of their homes, a pressure whose weapon was an image: "the feminine mystique."

Five years from the time Betty had signed the contract, four years late, *The Feminine Mystique* was published.

It was February 1963, and the New York newspapers, including the *Times,* were on strike. With no review in the *Times,* the chances that a book—even this thunderous polemic—would reach a substantial

The photographer has captured Betty Friedan in a moment of profound weariness. In the years after the publication of The Feminine Mystique, *Friedan worked zealously for women's rights: she organized demonstrations, lobbied for antidiscrimination legislation, and struggled to hold the women's movement together in the face of internal dissension. "In truth, she paid a high personal price for her cause." (Michael Ginsburg/Magnum Photos)*

public were practically nil. And there was plenty of competition. Morton Hunt had just published a gentle, affectionate paean to women's role *outside* as well as in the home. His book was called *Her Infinite Variety,* and it was moving off the bookstore shelves at a frighteningly rapid pace.

Betty was beside herself. And so, for that matter, was Carl. Never had the state of their marriage been worse, never stormier than during the last year she was writing, when, Carl would complain to friends, he would come home from work and "that bitch," instead of cooking dinner, was writing away at the dining-room table. Betty, friends would whisper, was writing out the problems of her marriage, writing a book instead of leaving Carl. His one-man advertising

and public relations firm was far from a booming success, and now this. Who would even hear of *The Feminine Mystique,* let alone buy it? Where, after all these years, was the payoff?

"Betty would come in with ideas to promote the book," George Brockway would recall. "You could tell Carl was behind them, saying, 'Tell 'em to do this, tell 'em to do that.'

"One day she told me that Carl wanted to know what could be done to make *The Feminine Mystique* as big a seller as *Gifts from the Sea.*" (This popular book was written by Anne Morrow Lindbergh, the wife of the heroic aviator.)

"'Tell Carl,' I told her, 'that he can fly the Atlantic solo.'"

Irascible Carl, George would call him—the low-key editor being far from charmed by what he regarded as Carl Friedan's "sharp and nasty" tongue.

But Betty thought her husband knew his business. She would always remember that it was Carl who had persuaded Norton to hire a publicist. Eventually, in fact, she would switch to another publishing house, leaving Brockway entirely.

"I remember him pleading with me," Betty would tell a reporter, "and I remember looking him right in the eye and saying, 'George, you made me feel Jewish for trying to sell that book. Go fuck yourself.'"

But, with the help of the publicist, excerpts from the book began to appear, and articles ran in major news magazines about Betty as an "angry battler for her sex." She began bouncing around the country for speaking engagements, crusaded enthusiastically on radio and that potent new vehicle, the television talk show.

After one of these appearances—outside Rockefeller Center—she met another author who had just taped a show herself. She was just about Betty's age, a former copywriter who had performed the remarkable feat of hitting the nonfiction best-seller list the year before.

The woman was Helen Gurley Brown, and her book, *Sex and the Single Girl,* aimed, obviously, at the burgeoning singles market, had actually set down in print the startling notion that it was perfectly all right to have "an affair." Even with a married man.

For those who would, in retrospect, regard the sexual revolution as either intrinsic to or actually the wellspring of the Golden Age of Feminism, it would be hard to ignore the pioneering role of Helen Brown. Most feminists, however, would manage to do just that.

It was a matter, in part, of philosophy. In even greater part, perhaps, of style.

Sex and the Single Girl was a typical how-to of the women's magazine genre. It offered advice on decorating your apartment, diet, clothes, and money—not, however, for the purpose of hooking a man into marriage, but for getting him into your bed.

Helen Brown didn't protest much of anything—least of all society's ills. She only wrote about, as she herself insisted, what was already going on anyhow. Single women having sex with men, married or not. She simply made them feel better about doing it. Like the women's magazines, and in a similarly blithe, not to say giddy style, she was reassuring and helpful. The major difference—the shocker—was that while the women's magazines were still righteously committed to the double standard, continually warning their readers of the dire consequences of sex without marriage, Helen Gurley Brown wrote that this was perfectly okay. "Nice single girls *do* have affairs and they don't necessarily die of them." *Sex and the Single Girl*—aimed, unlike underground erotica, at a mass audience—was undoubtedly something of a relief.

The single life the book touted was one of supreme independence, satisfying work, fashion and success and money—a life, in short, that most married women were bound to envy. The single woman was sexy, Helen had written, "because she lives by her wits." She was not "a parasite, a dependent, a scrounger, a sponger or a bum." And when, in 1965, Helen would take over the Hearst Corporation's ailing *Cosmopolitan,* the appeal of that view, and the skill of its pragmatic, meticulous editor, would eventually triple the magazine's circulation.

On television, Helen was, from the beginning, flirtatious, supremely tactful, frankly manipulative, an open disciple of male-flattering femininity. "Helen Gurley Girly," some viewers called her. She was a former secretary who had never gone to college and didn't plan to, a "girl" for whom *work* was the given, the man in one's life the pleasure to be sought. She had written her book at the suggestion of her husband, movie producer David Brown, and she had no hesitation about saying so.

And yet, in spite of Helen's flirtatiousness, and the focus on sex, which, Betty had written, was totally irrelevant, actually damaging to women's struggle for independence, the two women liked each other.

"We talked about business, promotion, all that," Helen would remember. "We became friends . . . and we've been friends ever since." They differed, but, in spite of her passionate nature, Betty would often differ with someone and still remain a loyal friend.

Unlike Helen Brown, however, Betty wasn't "cool"; her personality was not tailor-made for television. Often, in impatient, enthusiastic pursuit of an idea, she would talk so fast that hardly anyone could understand her. Or leave sentences dangling. Or angrily demand time. Her publicist would remember her screaming at hostess Virginia Graham on "Girl Talk": "If you don't let me have my say, I'm going to say orgasm ten times."

But Betty had been provoked.

Virginia Graham, Betty would one day explain, had coaxed the camera: "Girls, how many of us really need bylines? What better thing can we do with our lives than to do the dishes for those we love?"

"Well, I knew that her agent fought for every foot of the size of her byline on the television screen, and I wondered when the last time was she'd done the dishes for someone she loved. I turned to the camera and said, 'Women, don't listen to her. She needs you out there doing the dishes, or she wouldn't have the captive audience for this television program, whose byline she evidently doesn't want you to compete for.'"

Betty never was, never would be, any talk show host's favorite guest. She was confrontational, often tactless, and not—by any standard—a TV beauty.

But neither was she a phony. And there was something about this woman, who looked like everyone's . . . Aunt Minnie, something about what she proclaimed, in her hell-for-leather style, that made hundreds of viewers attend.

Scores of Americans, of course, including many women, were outraged. They could scarcely believe what they were hearing. A woman's career could be as important as a man's? A woman should go out in the world and compete with men?. . .

One Smith alumna, writing in *Reader's Digest* about "the feminine *mistake*," saluted the housewife's "small acts of domesticity" with the good Scout cheer: "Well, sure! That's what we signed up for!" And when the *New York Times* got around to reviewing the book—in a short blurb under "Digest"—Lucy Freeman, who had written a best-seller on her own conquest of mental illness, zapped it as "superficial. . . . The fault, dear Mrs. Friedan, is not in our culture, but in ourselves."

"*Where,*" wailed a letter writer in *Commonweal* magazine, "are all these women to go, having fled their homes? And *what* are they to do?"

In the midst of it all, Betty brought Carl and the kids back to Peoria for her twenty-fifth high school reunion. There, instead of praise, she found herself sitting alone at the banquet table. She stayed with a friend, and the next morning found the tree outside her door festooned with toilet paper.

Yet the sales of *The Feminine Mystique* were beginning to climb, and there was no stopping Betty now. Especially since hundreds of letters, expressing enormous gratitude, were starting to pour in. Letters from women who said they had no idea, until they read her book, that anyone else had such strange feelings. They had felt, they wrote, like sexual freaks, or like "appliances," insecure in their dependence, unable, much longer, to keep up the "act" of selflessness. She had given them courage, they wrote, to go back to school, to begin careers.

For threaded through the social criticism of *The Feminine Mystique* was also a message of Emersonian self-reliance and responsibility. This message was not, at bottom, altogether unlike Helen Brown's, but it was one that would set Betty at odds with many women who might have been her allies. Since, as Betty wrote, the women she was addressing were not

those beset by dire poverty or disease, they were not, therefore, *completely* at the mercy of an unjust society.

"In the last analysis," Betty had written, "millions of able women in this free land choose themselves not to use the door education could have opened for them. The choice—and the responsibility—for the race back [to the] home was finally their own."

The Feminine Mystique reached women very much like Friedan herself: white, educated wives and mothers mainly of the middle class. "Inspired and validated by finding their own truth presented as truth," as writer Marilyn French has said, "many of them changed their lives, returning to school, entering the work force." The Feminine Mystique also aroused professional and single women, both white and African American, for it exposed the attitudes and practices that blocked their own advancement. Along with Helen Gurley Brown and Gloria Steinem, Friedan helped liberate younger women, too, especially on the college campuses. Had Friedan done nothing more than write her book, she would be historically significant.

But for her, The Feminine Mystique was only the beginning. Thrust into national prominence as the voice of the new American woman, Friedan initiated the "second wave" of organized feminism, the first wave having ended with women's suffrage. In 1966, with the help of Dr. Kay Clarenbach, a Wisconsin women's leader, Friedan founded and became the first president of the National Organization for Women (NOW), the first mainstream women's organization and the most successful in history. "It is a mystery," Betty would say later, "the whole thing—why it happened, how it started. What gave any of us the courage to make that leap?" Under NOW's banners, the new women's movement sought equality for women through political means, for the 1960s civil rights movement had shown Friedan and her colleagues how effective antidiscrimination legislation could be. Employing the civil rights methods of picket lines, marches, political pressure, and media exposure, NOW set out to gain full citizenship for women: it challenged federal guidelines that sanctioned discrimination against them in employment, initiated lawsuits against companies refusing to hire women in positions traditionally occupied by men, sought legal abortion, and campaigned for the Equal Rights Amendment (ERA), which had languished since 1923. NOW helped to bring about a body of laws and rulings that prohibited sexual discrimination in education and in hiring and promotion; NOW was also instrumental in gaining congressional approval of the Equal Rights Amendment. In the 1980s, however, the ERA went down to defeat when it failed to be ratified by three fourths of the states. Even so, NOW was strong enough by 1984 to pressure the Democratic presidential candidate into selecting a woman as his running mate.

Meanwhile, the women's movement had splintered into various dissenting groups; one of them even advocated lesbianism as the ultimate expression of feminism and demanded that NOW affirm this by publicly avowing, "We are all lesbians." This shocked Friedan, who with other NOW leaders argued that such a stance would alienate men and would be a tactical blunder. Feminism, she said, regarded men not as eternal foes but also as victims of a repressive, dehumanizing society.

Struggling to hold the movement together wore Friedan out. In truth, she had paid a high personal price for her cause: she had lectured and traveled everywhere in its behalf, living out of suitcases in lonely motel rooms; she had missed her children fiercely and the warmth and intimacy of family life. Too, her marriage to Carl had failed—he had beaten her more than once. In 1970, divorced and exhausted, she resigned as NOW president and turned to writing, lecturing, and teaching. She remained faithful to feminism's larger vision, a vision of "human wholeness" that liberated men as well as women. It did so by repudiating the laws and customs that prevented men from expressing their own nurturing qualities and caused them to deny women their birthright as Americans—an equal opportunity to better themselves, to realize their full potential as their talent and industry allowed.

QUESTIONS TO CONSIDER

1 Describe the American cultural ideal of womanhood in the 1950s. What does Marcia Cohen think were some of the sources of our culture's "home-is-woman's-all" psychology? Explain the role that consumerism, the press, and the American educational system played in perpetuating prevailing assumptions about women. Was anyone rebelling against all this conformity?

2 Betty Friedan did not deliberately set out to start a feminist revolution. Describe the steps she took in raising her own consciousness and the series of revelations and reversals that led her to write *The Feminine Mystique*.

3 *The Feminine Mystique* was not a political book, but just a few years after its publication Friedan found herself at the head of a reform movement and president of NOW. At what point did the yearning for self-awareness and self-fulfillment that Friedan aroused in American women become transformed into political activity? Why did women feel they needed a political movement to achieve personal gains?

4 Discuss the basic thesis of *The Feminine Mystique*. Whose ideas did Betty Friedan attack? Specifically, how did she feel about Sigmund Freud and Margaret Mead? About "togetherness"? About suburbia? About women's magazines? How did Friedan's ideas differ from those of Helen Gurley Brown? What underlying message did the two writers have in common? Did Friedan feel the sexual revolution was compatible with the new feminism?

5 Friedan's book was addressed to educated, white, upper- and middle-class women. She herself was aware that she had not tackled the problems of uneducated or poor or African American or immigrant women. Is it possible to apply all or part of Friedan's analysis to this second group? What additional complications might issues of race and social class bring to women's lives?

6 What strides has feminism made since the publication of *The Feminine Mystique*? Has true equality been achieved? What do you see as the future of the historic "women's rights" movement as we enter the twenty-first century?

PART THIRTEEN

The Seventies

27 "I Have Never Been a Quitter": A Portrait of Richard Nixon

OTTO FRIEDRICH

As his biographer Stephen Ambrose has said, Richard Nixon wanted to be one of the great presidents, even a modern-day Lincoln. But the flaws in Nixon's character prevented him from leaving that kind of legacy. He did accomplish many positive things during his tenure in the White House (1969–1973): though an ardent and dedicated anti-Communist during his entire political career, he effected a rapprochement with Communist China, established détente with the Soviet Union, and finally ended America's disastrous involvement in the Vietnam War. These were spectacular achievements for "the world's No. 1 anti-Communist," as Ambrose describes him. But Nixon above all was a pragmatist: his objective was to strengthen the United States in world affairs by playing the Soviets and Chinese off against one another through "triangular diplomacy."

At home, he reduced military spending and signed the measure that lowered the voting age to eighteen, but he was not much interested in getting legislation enacted on Capitol Hill. What occupied most of his time and energy was the antiwar movement and other enemies of his administration; he was obsessed with them and with what he perceived to be a liberal, anti-Nixon slant among the nation's major newspapers. Before long, a bunker mentality pervaded the Nixon White House: it viewed domestic politics as a desperate battlefield between "them" and "us," with the Nixon administration increasingly identifying "them" as traitors and "us" as the only patriots and true saviors of America. In the name of "national security," the Nixon administration flagrantly violated the law and the Constitution in its zeal to suppress dissent, defeat opponents, and uphold administration politics. Nixon himself compiled a list of his "enemies" and not only had their phones tapped, but also ordered the Internal Revenue Service to audit them. Most frightening of all,

Nixon's "campaign of subversion" produced the Watergate scandal. It began in June 1972, when five men associated with the Committee to Re-Elect the President (CREEP) broke into the Democratic National Committee headquarters in Washington, D.C., and were arrested on a charge of burglary. For a time, Nixon successfully covered up his complicity in the break-in and the abuse of executive power it represented. When reporters Carl Bernstein and Bob Woodward of the Washington Post *exposed the Watergate scandal, it precipitated what one historian called "the greatest constitutional crisis the country had faced since the Civil War." The crisis shook Americans of every political persuasion and eventually brought down Nixon's presidency. In August 1973, he resigned his office—the first American President ever to do so—and flew back to California in disgrace.*

Some historians have linked Watergate to the growth of an "imperial presidency," which resulted in an imbalance of power, tilted to the executive branch. Lyndon Johnson had hastened the process by waging his undeclared war in Vietnam and pressuring Congress into endorsing and funding it. In the Watergate crisis, as historian William H. Chafe put it, the country rallied against the excesses of the imperial presidency, insisting on "a government of laws rather than personal whim."

Nixon's only crime was not, as many Americans still contend, that he simply got caught doing what other presidents have done. Historian C. Vann Woodward observes in Responses of the Presidents to Charges of Misconduct *(1974): "Heretofore, no president has been proved to be the chief coordinator of the crime and misdemeanor charged against his own administration. . . . Heretofore, no president has been held to be the chief personal beneficiary of misconduct in his administration or of measures taken to destroy or cover up evidence of it. Heretofore, the malfeasance and misdemeanor have had no confessed ideological purpose, no constitutionally subversive ends. Heretofore, no president has been accused of extensively subverting and secretly using established government agencies to defame or discredit political opponents and critics, to obstruct justice, to conceal misconduct and protect criminals, or to deprive citizens of their rights and liberties. Heretofore, no president has been accused of creating secret investigative units to engage in covert and unlawful activities against private citizens and their rights."*

In "a post-Watergate backlash," as one historian termed it, American voters in 1974 gave the Democrats the second-biggest congressional victory in their entire history. Two years later, they sent Democrat Jimmy Carter to the White House, ousting Republican Gerald Ford, whom Nixon had chosen as his successor.

In the following selection, Otto Friedrich describes Nixon's painful and impoverished early years, which did so much to shape the angry, ambitious man he became. Though highly intelligent and gifted, as Friedrich shows, Nixon made his reputation by smearing political opponents, accusing them of being soft on Communism. He rationalized such tactics on the grounds that he had to win. "Of course I knew Jerry Voorhis wasn't a communist," he said of one defeated opponent, "but I had to win. That's the thing you don't understand. The important thing is to win." Friedrich goes on to show how Nixon kept rising and falling, rising and falling, and finally rising again, in a political career that spanned more than a quarter of a century.

GLOSSARY

AGNEW, SPIRO Nixon's vice president (1969–1973); he resigned after being indicted for graft and corruption.

BREZHNEV, LEONID Soviet leader (first secretary of the Communist party) who with Nixon signed the 1972 SALT I treaty. In it, the United States and the Soviet Union agreed to limit antiballistic missiles and reached "an interim accord" on restricting offensive nuclear weapons.

BROWN, PAT Incumbent governor of California who defeated Nixon in the gubernatorial election of 1962. Afterward Nixon held his "final press conference," in which he told reporters: "Think of what you've lost. You won't have Nixon to kick around anymore."

CHECKERS SPEECH Nixon's maudlin speech on television during the presidential election of 1952; in that speech, Nixon sought to clear his name after news of his $18,000 slush fund donated by California businessmen had come to the surface. As he spoke, he told the story of the Nixon family dog, Checkers; hence the speech's name.

COX, ARCHIBALD Appointed special prosecutor in the Watergate case; he was fired during the "Saturday night massacre" for insisting that Nixon turn over the tapes he had made of his conversations in the Oval Office.

DEAN, JOHN Nixon's legal counsel; he was one of three top Nixon officials involved in the cover-up of the Watergate break-in. The other two officials were Attorney General John Mitchell and Mitchell's deputy, Jeb Stuart Magruder. Dean pleaded guilty when he was indicted for obstructing justice in the Watergate investigations.

DOUGLAS, HELEN GAHAGAN Nixon defeated this former movie actress in the 1950 election in California for a seat in the United States Senate. She gave him his pejorative nickname, "Tricky Dick." Nixon won this mud-slinging election by calling Douglas "the pink lady"—that is, a Communist—and insisting that she was "pink right down to her underwear."

EHRLICHMAN, JOHN Nixon's chief domestic adviser who was indicted by a grand jury for obstructing justice in the investigation of Watergate. He resigned his office, stood trial for his part in the Watergate scandal, and served time in a federal prison.

FORD, GERALD United States congressman and House minority leader from Michigan who in 1973 replaced Spiro Agnew as Nixon's vice president; Ford became president when Nixon resigned the office in 1974. One month later Ford pardoned Nixon for his crimes in the Watergate scandal.

HALDEMAN, H. R. Nixon's chief of staff. Like John Ehrlichman, Haldeman was indicted by a grand jury for obstructing justice in the Watergate investigations. He, too, resigned from the White House, stood trial for his role in the Watergate scandal, and was confined to a federal prison.

HISS, ALGER Served in the State Department from 1936 to 1947; in that capacity he helped coordinate United States foreign policy. In 1948, Whittaker Chambers, an editor and confessed Communist courier, charged that Hiss had passed on confidential government documents to the Soviets. HUAC, led by Nixon, accused Hiss of espionage; he vigorously denied the charges and found himself indicted by a grand jury for perjury. He was later found guilty of that charge and sentenced to forty-four months in prison. He was never found guilty of espionage. The Hiss case "made Nixon a national figure."

HOOVER, J. EDGAR Powerful head of the Federal Bureau of Investigation from 1924 to 1972. Hoover advised Nixon to order illegal wiretaps on his alleged enemies, as Lyndon Johnson had done.

HUAC Acronym for the House Un-American Activities Committee (its official name was the House Committee on Un-American Activities), originally established in 1938 to uncover "malign foreign influences in the United States." It was taken over by conservative Republicans who, in 1947, launched widely publicized investigations into the extent of Communist subversion in this country.

HUMPHREY, HUBERT Lyndon Johnson's vice president (1965–1969) and Democratic nominee for president in the 1968 election; Nixon defeated him by a narrow margin.

KISSINGER, HENRY Nixon's national security adviser and second secretary of state (1973–1974); he arranged Nixon's visit to Communist China in 1972 and negotiated with the North Vietnamese a cease-fire agreement in North Vietnam that called for an American withdrawal.

McGOVERN, GEORGE Democratic nominee for president in 1972; Nixon soundly defeated him.

MITCHELL, JOHN Nixon's attorney general (1969–1972), who was implicated in the cover-up of the Watergate break-in.

SALT I TREATY See *Leonid Brezhnev*.

SATURDAY NIGHT MASSACRE On the night of October 20, 1973, a Saturday, Nixon ordered Attorney General Elliot

Richardson to fire special prosecutor Archibald Cox, who was investigating the Watergate case. Richardson refused Nixon's order and resigned; so did Deputy Attorney General William Ruckelshaus. General Alexander Haig, Nixon's new chief of staff, then persuaded Solicitor General Robert Bork to fire Cox. The "massacre" left the Nixon administration "a shambles."

STEVENSON, ADLAI Democratic presidential nominee who lost to Eisenhower in the elections of 1952 and 1956. As Eisenhower's running mate, Nixon spent much of his time in the 1952 campaign accusing Stevenson of being soft on Communism.

TEAPOT DOME SCANDAL President Warren G. Harding (1921–1923), at the urging of Albert Fall, secretary of the interior, transferred control of the navy's oil reserves in Wyoming to Fall's Interior Department. Fall leased the oil reserves to a couple of wealthy businessmen in return for almost $500,000 in "loans." Tried and convicted of bribery, Fall served a year in prison.

VOORHIS, JERRY The liberal Democrat Nixon defeated in the congressional election of 1946 in the Twelfth Congressional District east of Los Angeles.

Richard Nixon's first conscious memory was of falling—falling and then running. He was three years old, and his mother had taken him and his brother out riding in a horse-drawn buggy, and the horse turned a corner too fast on the way home. The boy fell out. A buggy wheel ran over his head and inflicted a deep cut. "I must have been in shock," Nixon recalled later, "but I managed to get up and run after the buggy while my mother tried to make the horse stop." The only aftereffect, Nixon said, was a scar, and that was why he combed his hair straight back instead of parting it on the side.

In a sense, Nixon spent his whole life falling and running and falling again. A symbol of the politics of anger, he was one of the most hated figures of his time, and yet he was also the only man in U.S. history ever to be elected twice as Vice President and twice as President. In the White House, he achieved many major goals: the U.S. withdrawal from Vietnam, restored relations with China, the first major arms agreement with the Soviet Union and much more. But he will always be remembered . . . as the chief perpetrator—and chief victim—of the Watergate scandal, the only President ever to resign in disgrace.

Despite all his gifts—his shrewd intelligence, his dedication and sense of public service, his mastery

of political strategy—there was a quality of self-destructiveness that haunted Nixon. To an admiring aide he once acknowledged, "You continue to walk on the edge of the precipice because over the years you have become fascinated by how close to the edge you can walk without losing your balance."

He kept losing it, tumbling to great depths, then grimly climbing back. After being defeated in the presidential race of 1960 and then the California gubernatorial race of 1962, he bitterly told reporters, "You won't have Nixon to kick around anymore." Six years later, he fought his way to another Republican presidential nomination, which he spoke of as "the culmination of an impossible dream." But at his last meeting with his Cabinet in August 1974, after what seemed like the final defeat in a lifetime devoted to the idea of winning, he burst into tears. "Always remember," he said, "others may hate you, but those who hate you don't win unless you hate them—and then you destroy yourself."

From anyone else, that might have served as a public farewell, but the disgraced Nixon spent more than a dozen years in climbing once more out of the abyss and re-creating himself as an elder statesman. He wrote his memoirs in 1978, then eight more books largely devoted to international strategy. He moved to the wealthy suburb of Saddle River, New Jersey (where he stayed until 1990, moving a mile away to Park Ridge), and began giving discreet dinners for movers and shakers. President Reagan called to ask his advice. So did President Bush. In November 1989, he became the first important American to

---

Otto Friedrich, "I Have Never Been a Quitter," *Time*, May 2, 1994. Copyright © 1994 Time Inc. Reprinted by permission.

Richard Nixon (number 23), the second son of Frank and Hannah Nixon, was named after the English King Richard the Lion-Hearted. He attended Whittier College and wanted to play football, but was "too small and slow to make the starting team," writes Otto Friedrich, so "he showed up every day for practice in the line." (UPI/Corbis-Bettmann)

make a public visit to Beijing after the massacre at Tiananmen Square.

The hallmark of Nixon's youth had been poverty—poverty and family illness and endless work. His father Frank, who had dropped out of school and run away from home after the fourth grade, was a combative and quarrelsome Ohioan. After running through a string of jobs, Frank moved to California in 1907, built a house in the desert-edge town of Yorba Linda and tried to grow lemons. There Frank's pious Quaker wife Hannah gave birth on Jan. 9, 1913, to a second son. She named him Richard, after the English King Richard the Lion-Hearted, plus Milhous, her own family name. The newborn baby, an attendant nurse later recalled, had a "powerful, ringing voice."

His mother sent him to school every day in a starched white shirt and a black bow tie, and he worked hard for his good grades. He liked to recite long poems and play the piano. One of his favorite forms of competition was debating, which he did well. Another was football. Too small and slow to make the starting team in Fullerton or Whittier High School or at Whittier College, he showed up every day for practice in the line. "We used Nixon as a punching bag," one of his coaches recalled. "What starts the process, really," Nixon later said of his life-long passion for winning, "are the laughs and slights and snubs when you are a kid. But if . . . your anger is deep enough and strong enough, you learn that you can change those attitudes by excellence, personal gut performance."

Nixon grew up in Whittier because his father had given up on citrus farming and found a new job there as an oil-field worker, then started a gas station, then expanded it into a general store. Hannah Nixon liked Whittier because it was largely a Quaker town where nobody drank or smoked or carried on. But life was not easy. All through high school, Nixon had to get up at 4 every morning and drive to the Seventh Street markets in Los Angeles to buy fresh vegetables for the family store.

When Dick Nixon was 12, his younger brother Arthur, the fourth of the five boys, complained of a headache; a month later he was dead of meningitis. Nixon wrote later that he cried every day for weeks. When Harold, the eldest son, was stricken with tuberculosis, Hannah left the rest of the family to take him to the drier air in Prescott, Arizona. She could pay for this only by operating a clinic where other TB patients waited out their last weeks of life. In the summers Dick found jobs nearby as a janitor, a chicken plucker, a carnival barker. After five years, Harold died. "We all grew up rather fast in those years," Nixon recalled.

Harold's illness was also a great financial drain. Nixon had to turn down a scholarship offer from Harvard (Yale was also interested in him) and save money by attending tiny Whittier College. Duke University Law School was just starting when it offered Nixon one of the 25 scholarships available to a class of 44. At first he lived in a $5-a-month room. Later he shared a one-room shack that had no plumbing or electricity; he shaved in the men's room of the library. In three years at Duke, he never once went out on a date. He finished third in the class of 1937.

Nixon had shown an interest in politics since the age of six, when he began reading news of current events and talking about them with his father. When he was 11, the Teapot Dome scandal prompted him to announce to his mother, "I'll be a lawyer they can't bribe." The practice of law in Whittier was hardly so inspiring. Taken into the firm of a family friend, he spent his first day dusting the books in the office library, then bungled his first case, losing all his client's money in a real estate deal. But he persevered, began joining various clubs, making speeches. He even joined a local theater group, where he met a schoolteacher named Thelma ("Pat") Ryan.

Driving her home from the theater, he said, "I'd like to have a date with you."

"Oh, I'm too busy," she replied. An orphan, she was not only working but attending classes as well. The second time Nixon drove her home, he again asked for a date, again was shrugged off. The third time it happened, Nixon said, "Someday I'm going to marry you." It took two years of courtship before she agreed in 1940; she converted to the Quaker faith and used her own savings to buy the wedding ring.

Nixon probably would not have been content to stay in Whittier forever, but Pearl Harbor uprooted his whole generation. He knew that if he was ever to have a political career, he would have to join the armed forces. So despite the Quaker belief in pacifism, he won a commission in the Navy in June 1942. He served creditably as a supply officer in New Caledonia, then the Solomon Islands. His most remarkable activity, though, was to become a master at bluffing in stud poker. By the end of the war, he had won and saved a stake estimated at as much as $10,000. He invested half of it in the following year in launching his political career.

Jerry Voorhis, a popular liberal Democrat, had won five straight elections in the 12th Congressional District east of Los Angeles, but a group of local businessmen hoped to unseat him. Nixon promised them "an aggressive and vigorous campaign." He began working up to 20 hours a day, making speeches about his war experiences, denouncing the New Deal. When Pat gave birth to their first daughter Patricia (Tricia), Nixon was out campaigning. (Confident of re-election, he stayed home when Julie was born two years later.)

Nixon implied—falsely—that Voorhis was virtually a communist. "Remember," said one of Nixon's ads, "Voorhis is a former registered Socialist and his voting record in Congress is more socialistic and communistic than Democratic." This kind of smear was to become a Nixon trademark. To one of Voorhis' supporters, Nixon later offered a very personal rationale: "Of course I knew Jerry Voorhis wasn't a communist, but I had to win. That's the thing you don't understand. The important thing is to win."

Win he did, with 56% of the vote. This was part of the end-of-the-war landslide that gave the G.O.P. control of both houses for the first time since the election following the Great Crash of 1929. Nixon asked to be put on the Education and Labor Committee, which was going to rewrite the rules of labor relations through the Taft-Hartley Act. In return, he was asked to serve on an eccentric committee [the House Committee on Un-American Affairs] that devoted its time to noisy investigations of "un-American activities." It was to be the making of his career.

Nixon began looking for experts on communist influence in labor unions. This led him to a Maryknoll priest whose report on the subject included the fact that a *Time* senior editor named Whittaker Chambers had told the FBI that he had belonged to a communist cell in Washington, and that it included Alger Hiss. It seemed incredible. A lawyer who had once clerked for Justice Oliver Wendell Holmes, Hiss had served as a State Department adviser at the Yalta conference, had helped organize the United Nations and was being touted as perhaps its first Secretary-General.

Hiss, then president of the Carnegie Endowment, denied ever having met anyone named Whittaker Chambers. Nixon had both men summoned before the committee to confront each other. Hiss finally admitted knowing Chambers slightly under a different name. Chambers insisted that they had been "close friends . . . caught in a tragedy of history." But nothing could be proved until Chambers produced the "pumpkin papers," microfilms of State Department documents that he said Hiss had given him for transmission to Moscow. Hiss was convicted of perjury in January 1950, served 44 months in prison and has spent the rest of his long life denying guilt.

The Hiss case made Nixon a national figure and launched him into a run for the Senate in 1950 against Helen Gahagan Douglas, a former actress who had served six years in the House as an ardent New Dealer. Since red hunting was a national mania in these Korean War days, Douglas foolishly tried to accuse Nixon of being soft on communism, and invented the name that haunted him for the rest of his life: Tricky Dick. But when it came to mudslinging, she was up against a champion. He called her the "pink lady" and declared that she was "pink right down to her underwear." He won by the biggest plurality of any Senate candidate that year.

Nixon had hardly begun serving in the Senate before the Republican leadership started fighting over whether the 1952 presidential nomination should go to conservative Senator Robert Taft or to the immensely popular General Dwight Eisenhower. The convention was in danger of deadlocking, in which case it might turn to California Governor Earl Warren. That was certainly Warren's plan, and all the California delegates, including Nixon, were pledged to back him. In some complicated maneuvering, though, the Eisenhower forces put forward a resolution that would give them a number of disputed Southern delegations. Nixon, who had already been sounded out as a running mate for Eisenhower, persuaded the California delegates to back this resolution, and so Eisenhower won. Warren never forgave Nixon for what he considered a betrayal.

Once nominated as Vice President, Nixon was assigned to play hatchet man on "communism and corruption" while Eisenhower remained statesmanlike. Nixon was all too eager to comply. He described Democratic nominee Adlai Stevenson as one who "holds a Ph.D. from [Secretary of State Dean] Acheson's College of Cowardly Communist Containment."

The Democrats got their revenge when the press discovered and trumpeted that Nixon had a secret slush fund of $18,000 provided by California businessmen to help finance his activities. Nixon insisted that the fund was perfectly legal and was used solely for routine political expenses, but the smell of scandal thickened. At Eisenhower's urging, Nixon went before a TV audience estimated at 58 million with an impassioned defense of his honesty. "Pat and I have the satisfaction that every dime we've got is honestly

Nixon and Dwight Eisenhower. "Once nominated as Vice President," Friedrich points out, "Nixon was assigned to play hatchet man on 'communism and corruption' while Eisenhower"—the Republican nominee for President—"remained statesmanlike."

During the scandal over the secret slush fund provided for Nixon by California businessmen, Nixon gave his famous Checkers speech, after which Eisenhower proclaimed in public, "You're my boy!" (UPI/Corbis-Bettmann)

ours," he said. The only personal present he had received was "a little cocker spaniel dog in a crate. Black-and-white spotted. And our little girl—Tricia, the six-year-old—named it Checkers. And you know, the kids love that dog." Hundreds of thousands of listeners cabled or wrote their support of Nixon, and Eisenhower settled his future by saying publicly, "You're my boy!"

Eisenhower won 55% of the vote, and the freshman Senator from California, still only 39, found himself the second youngest Vice President. He also found that a President and Vice President rarely like each other very much, because the latter's only real job is to wait for the former's death. Nixon faced the

great test of this uneasy relationship when Eisenhower suffered a heart attack in September 1955. It was up to Nixon to chair Cabinet meetings and generally run the White House machinery without ever seeming to covet the power that lay just beyond his fingertips. He did the job tactfully and skillfully throughout the weeks of Eisenhower's recovery.

One major function of modern Vice Presidents is to travel, and Nixon turned himself into a latter-day Marco Polo: nine trips to 61 countries. Everywhere he went, he conferred, orated, debated, press-conferenced. In Moscow to open a U.S trade exhibit in 1959, Nixon got into a finger-pointing argument on communism with Soviet Party Secretary Nikita Khrushchev in the kitchen of an American model home.

To some extent, Vice Presidents' tasks are defined by their own skills and experiences. Nixon knew more about politics than almost anyone else in Eisenhower's Administration, so he became the G.O.P.'s chief campaigner. When Eisenhower's second term expired, Nixon was the inevitable successor; he was nominated to run against the Democrats' John F. Kennedy.

Eisenhower and others warned Nixon not to accept Kennedy's challenge to a televised debate—Nixon was the Vice President, after all, and far better known than the junior Senator from Massachusetts—but Nixon took pride in his long experience as a debater. He also ignored advice to rest up for the debate and went on campaigning strenuously until the last minute. So what a record 80 million Americans saw on their TV screens was a devastating contrast. Kennedy looked fresh, tanned, vibrant; Nixon looked unshaven, baggy-eyed, surly. The era of the politics of TV imagery had begun, and the debates were a major victory for Kennedy.

The vote was incredibly close, with Kennedy winning 50.4% of the popular vote and Nixon 49.6%. He accepted the bitter defeat and returned to California. Then Nixon's legendary political shrewdness abandoned him. He let himself be talked into running for Governor of California against the popular Edmund G. ("Pat") Brown, and tried to imply that Brown was a dangerous leftist. It was after his crushing defeat that Nixon blew up at reporters and announced that this was his "last press conference."

Still only 49, he decided to move to New York City and make some money by practicing corporate law. He joined a prosperous Wall Street firm, which thereupon became Nixon, Mudge, Rose, Guthrie and Alexander. But he never really retired from politics. He was just biding his time. He thought Jack Kennedy would be unbeatable in 1964, and Lyndon Johnson soon appeared almost as much so. Nixon played elder statesman, letting Barry Goldwater and Nelson Rockefeller fight for the G.O.P. nomination.

Nixon stumped loyally for Goldwater, and when that campaign ended in disaster, he became the logical man to reunite the splintered party in 1968.

Following the advice of a young advertising man named H. R. Haldeman, he finally learned how to make effective use of television: not in speeches or press conferences but answering questions from "typical voters" and then carefully editing the results. If that was artificial, so in a way was the whole 1968 campaign. Democratic candidate Hubert Humphrey dared not repudiate Johnson's doomed Vietnam policy and talked instead about "the politics of joy." Nixon, who had agreed with Johnson's escalation of the war and hoped to court segregationist votes in the South, spoke mainly in code words about "peace with honor" in Vietnam and "law and order" at home. In a year of assassinations and ghetto riots, Nixon sounded reassuring, or enough so to defeat Humphrey and the war-torn Democrats. But it was close: 43.4% for Nixon, 42.7% for Humphrey, 13.5% for George Wallace.

Nixon's first term included sweeping innovations, often surprisingly liberal. He was the first President in years to cut military spending; the first to tie Social Security increases to the cost of living. He instituted "revenue sharing" to funnel $6 billion a year in federal tax money back to the states and cities. He signed the act lowering the voting age to 18. And he benefited from Kennedy's decision to go to the moon. When Neil Armstrong landed there in 1969, Nixon somewhat vaingloriously declared that "this is the greatest week in the history of the world since the Creation."

His imaginative measures were shadowed, however, by Vietnam. Nixon, who had supported each previous escalation—and indeed repeatedly demanded more—had campaigned on a promise to end the war "with honor," meaning no surrender and no defeat. He called for a cease-fire and negotiations, but the communists showed no interest. And while U.S. casualties continued at a rate of about 400 a month, protests against the war grew in size and violence.

To quiet antiwar demonstrators, Nixon announced that he would gradually withdraw U.S. forces, starting with 25,000 in June 1969. From now on, the war would be increasingly fought by the Vietnamese themselves. When, from their sanctuaries in Cambodia, the North Vietnamese began harassing the retreating Americans in the spring of 1970, Nixon ordered bombing raids and made a temporary "incursion" into the country. The main effect of this expansion of the war was an explosion of new antiwar outcries on college campuses.

These were fiercely contentious times, and Nixon was partly to blame for that. He had always been the fighter rather than the conciliator, and though he had millions of supporters among what he liked to call "the Silent Majority" in "middle America," the increasing conflicts in American politics made it difficult to govern at all. Nixon, as the nation learned later when it heard the Watergate tapes, brought to the White House an extraordinarily permanent anger and resentment. His staff memos were filled with furious instructions to fire people, investigate leaks and "knock off this crap."

Together with this chronic anger, the mistrustful Nixon had a passion for secrecy. He repeatedly launched military operations without telling his own Defense Secretary, Melvin Laird, and major diplomatic initiatives without telling his Secretary of State, William Rogers. All major actions went through his White House staff members, particularly National Security Adviser Henry Kissinger and Nixon's two chief domestic aides, Bob Haldeman and John Ehrlichman.

Just as he loved secrecy, Nixon hated leaks to the press (though he himself was a dedicated leaker to favored reporters). And so when he first ordered an unannounced air raid against communist bases in Cambodia in April 1969, he was furious to read about it in a Washington dispatch in the New York Times. FBI chief J. Edgar Hoover told the President that the only way to find the leaker was to start tapping phones. When Nixon entered the White House and dismantled the elaborate taping system that Johnson had installed, Hoover told him that the FBI, on Johnson's orders, had bugged Nixon's campaign plane.

Now Nixon started down the same path, getting Attorney General John Mitchell to sign the orders for 17 taps.

When a series of secret Vietnam documents known as the Pentagon Papers began appearing in the New York Times in June 1971, Kissinger persuaded Nixon that the leaker, Daniel Ellsberg, "must be stopped at all costs." The FBI turned balky at extralegal activities, so Nixon told Ehrlichman, "Then by God, we'll do it ourselves. I want you to set up a little group right here in the White House."

Thus was born the team of "plumbers." Its only known job involving Ellsberg was to break into his psychiatrist's office that September in search of evidence against him. But once such a team is created, other uses for it tend to be found. The following June, seven plumbers (five of them wearing surgical rubber gloves) were arrested during a burglary of Democratic national headquarters in the Watergate office and apartment complex.

They admitted nothing, and nobody connected them with Nixon. The White House itself was already doing its best to block any FBI investigation, but it formally denied any involvement in what press secretary Ron Ziegler dismissed as "a third-rate burglary attempt." Nobody has ever disclosed exactly what the burglars were looking for or what they found, if anything.

The Watergate burglary quickly faded from the front pages. Nixon was campaigning hard for reelection, portraying himself as a global peacemaker. In February 1972 he had reversed nearly 30 years of American policy by flying to Beijing, ending restrictions on trade with China and supporting China's entry into the U.N. In May he had signed the first arms-control agreement with Soviet leader Leonid Brezhnev, placing sharp restrictions on antiballistic missiles. And although Kissinger's protracted secret negotiations with the Vietnamese communists had not yet brought a truce agreement, Nixon pulled out the last U.S. combat troops in August.

Nixon trounced Senator George McGovern that fall, capturing nearly 61% of the vote. Then, after one last spasm of belligerence in the carpet bombing of

Hanoi at Christmas, Nixon announced in January 1973, "We today have concluded an agreement to end the war and bring peace with honor to Vietnam."

But the Watergate mystery remained. In court, five of the burglars pleaded guilty in January 1973 (the other two were quickly convicted), but they still admitted nothing. Federal Judge John Sirica angrily sentenced them to long prison terms (up to 40 years) and indicated that he might reduce the punishment if they confessed more fully. One of the seven, James McCord, wrote Sirica on March 20 that "others involved in the Watergate operation were not identified during the trial." In two secret sessions with Watergate committee counsel Sam Dash, he later named three top Nixon officials: Attorney General Mitchell; Mitchell's deputy, Jeb Stuart Magruder; and White House counsel John Dean.

Caught lying—but still denying any wrongdoing—Nixon said he was ordering a new investigation of the situation. Two federal grand juries were also investigating. So was the press. Though a lot of this probing was only loosely connected to the burglary, the term Watergate began to apply to a whole series of misdeeds that seriously tainted Nixon's great election victory. Not only did more than $100,000 donated to Nixon's campaign end up in the bank account of one of the plumbers, but the entire fund-raising operation was marked by illegalities, irregularities and deceptions. Congress decided to investigate all this too. It chose a select committee to be headed by North Carolina's folksy Senator Sam Ervin.

Two and a half weeks before the committee was scheduled to open televised hearings in May 1973, Nixon made a stunning announcement: his two chief White House aides, Haldeman and Ehrlichman, were resigning, as were Attorney General Richard Kleindienst (who had succeeded Mitchell) and White House attorney Dean. "There can be no whitewash at the White House," Nixon said.

The Senate hearings soon showed otherwise. Magruder testified that Mitchell and Dean had been deeply involved. Then the dismissed Dean took the stand in June and testified that Nixon himself had been lying, that he had known about the White House cover-up attempts since at least September 1972. He also disclosed that the White House kept hundreds of names on an "enemies list" and used tax investigations and other methods to harass them. But how could anyone prove such charges? That question received an astonishing answer a month later when a former White House official named Alexander Butterfield almost offhandedly told the committee that Nixon had installed voice-activated recorders that secretly taped all his White House conversations.

When the senate committee promptly demanded the tapes, Nixon refused, claiming Executive privilege. The new Attorney General, Elliot Richardson, had appointed Harvard law professor Archibald Cox as a special prosecutor in the whole case, and Cox sent a subpoena for tapes he wanted to hear. Nixon refused him too. Judge Sirica upheld Cox's demand, so Nixon resisted him in the U.S. Court of Appeals, which backed Sirica.

Nixon then offered to produce an edited summary of the tapes. When Cox rejected that idea, Nixon on Oct. 20 angrily told Richardson to fire Cox. Richardson refused and resigned instead. Nixon told Deputy Attorney General William Ruckelshaus to fire Cox; he too refused and resigned. General Alexander Haig, Haldeman's successor as White House chief of staff, finally got Solicitor General Robert Bork to do the job, and so the "Saturday Night Massacre" ended, leaving the Nixon Administration a shambles. (In the midst of all this, it was almost incidental that Vice President Spiro Agnew resigned under fire for having taken graft and that he was replaced by Michigan Congressman Gerald Ford.)

The House began on Oct. 30 to look into the possibilities of impeachment. Inside the besieged White House, Nixon raged like a trapped animal. There were unconfirmed reports that he was drinking heavily, that he couldn't sleep, that he even wandered around late at night and spoke to the paintings on the walls. To a meeting of Associated Press editors, he piteously declared, "I am not a crook."

Special prosecutor Cox had by now been replaced by a conservative Texas attorney, Leon Jaworski, who

On August 9, 1974, having resigned the Presidency in the wake of Watergate, Nixon bade good-bye to his staff and Cabinet in the East Room of the White House. To his right is his son-in-law, David Eisenhower. (Gene Forte/Consolidated News Pictures/Getty)

appeared no less determined to get the tapes. Still resisting inch by inch, Nixon released 1,254 pages of edited transcript. They were a revelation of the inner workings of the Nixon White House, a sealed-off fortress where a character designated as P in the transcripts talked endlessly and obscenely about all his enemies. "I want the most comprehensive notes on all those who tried to do us in," P said to Haldeman at one point, for example. "We have not used . . . the Justice Department, but things are going to change now." The edited tapes still left uncertainties about Nixon's involvement in the Watergate cover-up, however, so Jaworski insisted on the unedited originals of 64 specific tapes, transcripts and other documents. Nixon refused. Jaworski filed suit. The Supreme Court ruled unanimously that a President cannot withhold evidence in a criminal case (Mitchell,

Haldeman, Ehrlichman and others were by now under indictment, and Nixon himself had been named by the grand jury as an "unindicted co-conspirator").

During all this, the House Judiciary Committee, headed by New Jersey's Democratic Congressman Peter Rodino, had been conducting hearings on impeachment. It soon decided to impeach Nixon on three counts: obstruction of justice, abuse of presidential powers and defiance of the committee's subpoenas.

Nixon meanwhile sat out in his beach house in San Clemente, California, reading a biography of Napoleon and staring at the ocean. But he had also been listening to some of the disputed tapes, and he had found one—the "smoking gun"—that threatened to destroy his whole case. It was a talk with Haldeman on June 23, 1972, a time when Nixon had long pretended to know virtually nothing about the Watergate break-in just six days earlier. This tape recorded Nixon talking with Haldeman about Mitchell's involvement, ordering a cover-up, planning to use the FBI and CIA to protect himself. For good measure, the tape also included presidential slurs on Jews, women, homosexuals, Italians and the press. The reaction to the new tape, when Nixon finally released it, was disastrous. Even conservatives like Ronald Reagan and Barry Goldwater demanded Nixon's resignation, as did G.O.P. chairman George Bush. A congressional delegation told the President he had no more than 15 votes in the Senate, about the same in the House. Shortly after, Nixon told his family, "We're going back to California." His daughters burst into tears; his wife did not.

Two days later, on Aug. 8, 1974, Nixon made his last televised statement from the White House: "I have never been a quitter. To leave office before my term is completed is abhorrent to every instinct in my body. But as President I must put the interest of America first . . . Therefore, I shall resign the presidency effective at noon tomorrow." There remained then only a series of farewells. He spoke once again of winning and losing. "We think that when we suffer a defeat, that all is ended. Not true. It is only a beginning, always."

And so it was, once again, for Nixon. When he left Washington, there was a chance he might yet be prosecuted. Gerald Ford fixed that a month later by issuing a presidential pardon protecting Nixon from legal penalties for anything he had done in connection with Watergate. But Nixon's health was poor, his psychic shock obvious. An attack of phlebitis nearly killed him. He later told friends that he heard voices calling, "Richard, pull yourself back." And so he did.

His first public appearance came in 1978, and then the long, slow process of self-rehabilitation. Perhaps, in his last years, having regained a certain amount of public respect and even some grudging admiration, having acquired four grandchildren and all the comforts of leisurely wealth, Nixon finally found a little peace, finally got over that mysterious anger that had fueled his ambition throughout his long life. Perhaps.

QUESTIONS TO CONSIDER

1 What in Richard Nixon's background shaped him into the angry, ambitious man he became? How did his character traits affect his political career? What did he tell a supporter of Jerry Voorhis the most important thing was? What does this tell you about Nixon's character?

2 What was Nixon's favorite issue in his campaign against Jerry Voorhis for a seat in the national House and his campaign against Helen Douglas for a seat in the United States Senate? Describe the political atmosphere at the time that made that issue such a successful one for Nixon. What was Nixon's role on HUAC? What famous case rocketed him to national prominence?

3 What were Nixon's greatest successes as president? Why was he able to achieve momentous diplomatic breakthroughs with Communist China and the Soviet Union when nobody else could do so? We saw in selection 24 that Lyndon Johnson's policies trapped the United States in a stalemated war in Vietnam. How was Nixon able to end American involvement there? Why did he do so?

4 Discuss the Watergate scandal. How was the Nixon White House involved? Why did Nixon lie about his knowledge of the Watergate break-in and with the help of his aides try to cover it up? Why didn't Nixon simply tell the public the truth? What finally brought down the Nixon presidency, causing him to become the first American president ever to resign his office? Do you think that Gerald Ford should have pardoned Nixon?

5 Nixon's political career has been described as one of rising and falling, rising and falling, rising and falling, and rising again. How do you account for his resiliency? Do you think the nickname, "Tricky Dick," was appropriate or inappropriate? How would you rate him as president compared with Roosevelt, Truman, and Eisenhower?

28 How the Seventies Changed America

NICHOLAS LEMANN

To many Americans, it was the "loser" decade, a ten-year hangover from the excesses of the sixties, a time of bitter disillusionment, what with Watergate and the withdrawal from Vietnam, the only war America ever lost. It was a plastic era, to use Norman Mailer's term, that featured polyester suits and disco music. Many Americans still regard the 1970s as a vague interim between the liberal idealism and social upheaval of the sixties and the conservative individualism of the eighties. But to journalist Nicholas Lemann, looking back from today's vantage point, the seventies can no longer be dismissed as "the runt decade" in which relatively nothing significant occurred. On the contrary, he finds profound importance in terms of several "sweeping historical trends" that began or were acceler-ated in the seventies and that went on to shape what American society has become in our time.

First, he says, it was the decade in which geopolitics started revolving less around ideology than around oil and religion. He cites the 1973–1974 oil embargo of the oil-producing Arab-Muslim states as the "epochal event" of the decade, one that dashed the 1960s assumption of endless eco-nomic growth and prosperity for all in the United States. The oil embargo spurred the growth of the Sun Belt, initiated a period of staggering inflation, and marked the end, maybe forever, of "the mass upward economic mobility of American society." And that in turn fragmented the country into squabbling interest groups that cared more about looking out for themselves than about sacrificing for the national good.

Second, the presidential electorate became conservative and Republican, a trend that would last throughout the eighties, ending in the election of Democrat Bill Clinton in 1992. In reaction to the seeming paralysis and weakness of Jimmy Carter's liberal Democratic administration, 1977–1981, American voters sent Republican Ronald Reagan to the White House because he preached "pure strength" in foreign affairs and promised to reduce taxes at home (the Reagan presidency is treated in selection 29). Thus, Reagan capitalized on a third sweeping trend of the seventies—the middle-class tax revolt, which Lemann describes as "an aftershock" of the Arab oil embargo. For the first time, he says, the American middle class, once considered uniquely fortunate, perceived itself as an op-pressed group, the victim of runaway inflation, and revolted against the use of federal funds to help the less privileged.

A reporter for the Washington Post *during the seventies, Lemann draws an arresting portrait of this oft-disparaged decade. Indeed, Lemann believes that the seventies witnessed "the working of the phenomena of the sixties into the mainstream of American life." Lemann also contends that the six-ties' obsession with self-discovery became "a mass phenomenon" in the seventies and that the ethic of individual freedom as the "highest good," converging with the end of the American economy as an "expanding pie," led Americans to look out mainly for themselves.*

GLOSSARY

DÉTENTE   Relaxing of international tensions.

EST (ERHARD SEMINARS TRAINING)   System of encounter groups designed to help people "get in touch with themselves."

ORGANIZATION OF PETROLEUM EXPORTING STATES (OPEC)   Bargaining unit for the oil-exporting states in the Middle East and Africa; OPEC's oil embargo of 1973 quadrupled the price of oil and caused soaring inflation.

PROPOSITION 13   Initiative on the California state ballot that called for a significant reduction in property taxes; it passed overwhelmingly and led to similar tax revolts across the country.

That's it," Daniel Patrick Moynihan, then U.S. ambassador to India, wrote to a colleague on the White House staff in 1973 on the subject of some issue of the moment. "Nothing will happen. But then nothing much is going to happen in the 1970s anyway."

Moynihan is a politician famous for his predictions, and this one seemed for a long time to be dead-on. The seventies, even while they were in progress, looked like an unimportant decade, a period of cooling down from the white-hot sixties. You had to go back to the teens to find another decade so lacking in crisp, epigrammatic definition. It only made matters worse for the seventies that the succeeding decade started with a bang. In 1980 the country elected the most conservative President in its history, and it was immediately clear that a new era had dawned. (In general the eighties, unlike the seventies, had a perfect dramatic arc. They peaked in the summer of 1984, with the Los Angeles Olympics and the Republican National Convention in Dallas, and began to peter out with the Iran–contra scandal in 1986 and the stock market crash in 1987.) It is nearly impossible to engage in magazine-writerly games like discovering "the day the seventies died" or "the spirit of the seventies"; and the style of the seventies—wide ties, sideburns, synthetic fabrics, white shoes, disco—is so far interesting largely as something to make fun of.

But somehow the seventies seem to be creeping out of the loser-decade category. Their claim to importance is in the realm of sweeping historical trends, rather than memorable events, though there were some of those too. In the United States today a few basic propositions shape everything: The presidential electorate is conservative and Republican. Geopolitics revolves around a commodity (oil) and a religion (Islam) more than around an ideology (Marxism-Leninism). The national economy is no longer one in which practically every class, region, and industry is upwardly mobile. American culture is essentially individualistic, rather than communitarian, which means that notions like deferred gratification, sacrifice, and sustained national effort are a very tough sell. Anyone seeking to understand the roots of this situation has to go back to the seventies.

The underestimation of the seventies' importance, especially during the early years of the decade, is easy to forgive because the character of the seventies was substantially shaped at first by spillover from the sixties. Such sixties events as the killings of student protesters at Kent State and Orangeburg, the original Earth Day, the invasion of Cambodia, and a large portion of the war in Vietnam took place in the seventies. Although sixties radicals (cultural and political) spent the early seventies loudly bemoaning the end of the revolution, what was in fact going on was the working of the phenomena of the sixties into the mainstream of American life. Thus the first Nixon

---

"How the Seventies Changed America" by Nicholas Lemann, *American Heritage*, XLII (July/August 1991), 39–42, 44, 46, 48–49. Reprinted by permission of *American Heritage* magazine, a division of Forbes, Inc. © Forbes, Inc., 1991.

administration, which was decried by liberals at the time for being nightmarishly right-wing, was actually more liberal than the Johnson administration in many ways—less hawkish in Vietnam, more free-spending on social programs. The reason wasn't that Richard Nixon was a liberal but that the country as a whole had continued to move steadily to the left throughout the late sixties and early seventies; the political climate of institutions like the U.S. Congress and the boards of directors of big corporations was probably more liberal in 1972 than in any year before or since, and the Democratic party nominated its most liberal presidential candidate ever. Nixon had to go along with the tide.

In New Orleans, my hometown, the hippie movement peaked in 1972 or 1973. Long hair, crash pads, head shops, psychedelic posters, underground newspapers, and other Summer of Love–inspired institutions had been unknown there during the real Summer of Love, which was in 1967. It took even longer, until the middle or late seventies, for those aspects of hippie life that have endured to catch on with the general public. All over the country the likelihood that an average citizen would wear longish hair, smoke marijuana, and openly live with a lover before marriage was probably greater in 1980 than it was in 1970. The sixties' preoccupation with self-discovery became a mass phenomenon only in the seventies, through home-brew psychological therapies like EST. In politics the impact of the black enfranchisement that took place in the 1960s barely began to be felt until the mid- to late 1970s. The tremendously influential feminist and gay-liberation movements were, at the dawn of the 1970s, barely under way in Manhattan, their headquarters, and certainly hadn't begun their spread across the whole country. The sixties took a long time for America to digest; the process went on throughout the seventies and even into the eighties.

The epochal event of the seventies as an era in its own right was the Organization of Petroleum Exporting Countries' oil embargo, which lasted for six months in the fall of 1973 and the spring of 1974.

Everything that happened in the sixties was predicated on the assumption of economic prosperity and growth; concerns like personal fulfillment and social justice tend to emerge in the middle class only at times when people take it for granted that they'll be able to make a living. For thirty years—ever since the effects of World War II on the economy had begun to kick in—the average American's standard of living had been rising, to a remarkable extent. As the economy grew, indices like home ownership, automobile ownership, and access to higher education got up to levels unknown anywhere else in the world, and the United States could plausibly claim to have provided a better life materially for its working class than any society ever had. That ended with the OPEC embargo.

While it was going on, the embargo didn't fully register in the national consciousness. The country was absorbed by a different story, the Watergate scandal, which was really another sixties spillover, the final series of battles in the long war between the antiwar liberals and the rough-playing anti-Communists. Richard Nixon, having engaged in dirty tricks against leftish politicians for his whole career, didn't stop doing so as President; he only found new targets, like Daniel Ellsberg and [Democratic Party chairman] Lawrence O'Brien. This time, however, he lost the Establishment, which was now far more kindly disposed to Nixon's enemies than it had been back in the 1950s. Therefore, the big-time press, the courts, and the Congress undertook the enthralling process of cranking up the deliberate, inexorable machinery of justice, and everybody was glued to the television for a year and a half. The embargo, on the other hand, was a non-video-friendly economic story and hence difficult to get hooked on. It pertained to two subcultures that were completely mysterious to most Americans—the oil industry and the Arab world—and it seemed at first to be merely an episode in the ongoing hostilities between Israel and its neighbors. But in retrospect it changed everything, much more than Watergate did.

By causing the price of oil to double, the embargo enriched—and therefore increased the wealth, power,

*"Steer clear of that one. Every day
is always the first day of the rest of his life."*

*Charles Saxon's spirited sketch is good social history. In 1972
this is what a lot of Americans looked like. (© The New Yorker*

*Collection 1972 Charles Saxon from cartoonbank.com. All rights
reserved.)*

and confidence of—oil-producing areas like Texas, while helping speed the decline of the automobile-producing upper Midwest; the rise of OPEC and the rise of the Sunbelt as a center of population and political influence went together. The embargo ushered in a long period of inflation, the reaction to which dominated the economics and politics of the rest of the decade. It demonstrated that America could now be "pushed around" by countries most of us had always thought of as minor powers.

Most important of all, the embargo now appears to have been the pivotal moment at which the mass upward economic mobility of American society ended, perhaps forever. Average weekly earnings, adjusted for inflation, peaked in 1973. Productivity—that is, economic output per man-hour—abruptly stopped growing. The nearly universal assumption in the post–World War II United States was that children would do better than their parents. Upward

mobility wasn't just a characteristic of the national culture; it was the defining characteristic. As it slowly began to sink in that everybody wasn't going to be moving forward together anymore, the country became more fragmented, more internally rivalrous, and less sure of its mythology.

Richard Nixon resigned as President in August 1974, and the country settled into what appeared to be a quiet, folksy drama of national recuperation. In the White House good old Gerald Ford was succeeded by rural, sincere Jimmy Carter, who was the only President elevated to the office by the voters during the 1970s and so was the decade's emblematic political figure. In hindsight, though, it's impossible to miss a gathering conservative stridency in the politics of the late seventies. In 1976 Ronald Reagan, the retired governor of California, challenged Ford for the Republican presidential nomination. Reagan lost the opening primaries and seemed to be about to drop out of the race when, apparently to the surprise even of his own staff, he won the North Carolina primary in late March.

It is quite clear what caused the Reagan campaign to catch on: He had begun to attack Ford from the right on foreign policy matters. The night before the primary he bought a half-hour of statewide television time to press his case. Reagan's main substantive criticism was of the policy of détente with the Soviet Union, but his two most crowd-pleasing points were his promise, if elected, to fire Henry Kissinger as Secretary of State and his lusty denunciation of the elaborately negotiated treaty to turn nominal control of the Panama Canal over to the Panamanians. Less than a year earlier Communist forces had finally captured the South Vietnamese capital city of Saigon, as the staff of the American Embassy escaped in a wild scramble into helicopters. The oil embargo had ended, but the price of gasoline had not retreated. The United States appeared to have descended from the pinnacle of power and respect it had occupied at the close of World War II to a small, hounded position, and Reagan had hit on a symbolic way of expressing rage over that change. Most journalistic and academic opinion at the time was fairly cheerful about the course of American foreign policy—we were finally out of Vietnam, and we were getting over our silly Cold War phobia about dealing with China and the Soviet Union—but in the general public obviously the rage Reagan expressed was widely shared.

A couple of years later a conservative political cause even more out of the blue than opposition to the Panama Canal Treaty appeared: the tax revolt. Howard Jarvis, a seventy-five-year-old retired businessman who had been attacking taxation in California pretty much continuously since 1962, got onto the state ballot in 1978 an initiative, Proposition 13, that would substantially cut property taxes. Despite bad press and the strong opposition of most politicians, it passed by a two to one margin.

Proposition 13 was to some extent another aftershock of the OPEC embargo. Inflation causes the value of hard assets to rise. The only substantial hard asset owned by most Americans is their home. As the prices of houses soared in the mid-seventies (causing people to dig deeper to buy housing, which sent the national savings rate plummeting and made real estate prices the great conversation starter in the social life of the middle class), so did property taxes, since they are based on the values of the houses. Hence, resentment over taxation became an issue in waiting.

The influence of Proposition 13 has been so great that it is now difficult to recall that taxes weren't a major concern in national politics before it. Conservative opposition to government focused on its activities, not on its revenue base, and this put conservatism at a disadvantage, because most government programs are popular. Even before Proposition 13, conservative economic writers like Jude Wanniski and Arthur Laffer were inventing supply-side economics, based on the idea that reducing taxes would bring prosperity. With Proposition 13 it was proved—as it has been proved over and over since—that tax cutting was one of the rare voguish policy ideas that turn out to be huge political winners. In switching from arguing against programs to arguing against taxes, conservatism had found another key element of its ascension to power.

The tax revolt wouldn't have worked if the middle class hadn't been receptive to the notion that it was oppressed. This was remarkable in itself, since it had been assumed for decades that the American middle class was, in a world-historical sense, almost uniquely lucky. The emergence of a self-pitying strain in the middle class was in a sense yet another sixties spillover. At the dawn of the sixties, the idea that *anybody* in the United States was oppressed might have seemed absurd. Then blacks, who really were oppressed, were able to make the country see the truth about their situation. But that opened Pandora's box. The eloquent language of group rights that the civil rights movement had invented proved to be quite adaptable, and eventually it was used by college students, feminists, Native Americans, Chicanos, urban blue-collar "white ethnics," and, finally, suburban homeowners.

With fleeting success, Jimmy Carter brings moral pressure to bear on a troubled world in a 1977 cartoon by Edward Sorel.   *(Courtesy of Edward Sorel)*

Meanwhile, the social programs started by Lyndon Johnson gave rise to another new, or long-quiescent, idea, which was that the government was wasting vast sums of money on harebrained schemes. In some ways the Great Society accomplished its goal of binding the country together, by making the federal government a nationwide provider of such favors as medical care and access to higher education; but in others it contributed to the seventies trend of each group's looking to government to provide it with benefits and being unconcerned with the general good. Especially after the economy turned sour, the middle class began to define its interests in terms of a rollback of government programs aimed at helping other groups.

As the country was becoming more fragmented, so was its essential social unit, the family. In 1965 only 14.9 percent of the population was single; by 1979 the figure had risen to 20 percent. The divorce rate went from 2.5 per thousand in 1965 to 5.3 per thousand in 1979. The percentage of births that were out of wedlock was 5.3 in 1960 and 16.3 in 1978. The likelihood that married women with young children would work doubled between the mid-sixties and the late seventies. These changes took place for a variety of reasons—feminism, improved birth control, the legalization of abortion, the spread across the country of the sixties youth culture's rejection of traditional mores—but what they added up to was that the nuclear family, consisting of a working husband and a nonworking wife, both in their first marriage, and their children, ceased to be the dominant type of American household during the seventies. Also, people became more likely to organize themselves into communities based on their family status, so that the unmarried often lived in singles apartment complexes and retirees in senior citizens' developments. The overall effect was one of much greater personal freedom, which meant, as it always does, less social cohesion. Tom Wolfe's moniker for the seventies, the Me Decade, caught on because it was probably true that the country had placed relatively more emphasis on individual happiness and relatively less on loyalty to family and nation.

Like a symphony, the seventies finally built up in a crescendo that pulled together all its main themes. This occurred during the second half of 1979. First OPEC engineered the "second oil shock," in which, by holding down production, it got the price for its crude oil (and the price of gasoline at American service stations) to rise by more than 50 percent during the first six months of that year. With the onset of the summer vacation season, the automotive equivalent of the Depression's bank runs began. Everybody considered the possibility of not being able to get gas, panicked, and went off to fill the tank; the result was hours-long lines at gas stations all over the country.

It was a small inconvenience compared with what people in the Communist world and Latin America live through all the time, but the psychological effect was enormous. The summer of 1979 was the only time I can remember when, at the level of ordinary life as opposed to public affairs, things seemed to be out of control. Inflation was well above 10 percent and rising, and suddenly what seemed like a quarter of every day was spent on getting gasoline or thinking about getting gasoline—a task that previously had been completely routine, as it is again now. Black markets sprang up; rumors flew about well-connected

people who had secret sources. One day that summer, after an hour's desperate and fruitless search, I ran out of gas on the Central Expressway in Dallas. I left my car sitting primly in the right lane and walked away in the hundred-degree heat; the people driving by looked at me without surprise, no doubt thinking, "Poor bastard, it could have happened to me just as easily."

In July President Carter scheduled a speech on the gas lines, then abruptly canceled it and repaired to Camp David to think deeply for ten days, which seemed like a pale substitute for somehow setting things aright. Aides, cabinet secretaries, intellectuals, religious leaders, tycoons, and other leading citizens were summoned to Carter's aerie to discuss with him what was wrong with the country's soul. On July 15 he made a television address to the nation, which has been enshrined in memory as the "malaise speech," although it didn't use that word. (Carter did, however, talk about "a crisis of confidence . . . that strikes at the very heart and soul and spirit of our national will.")

To reread the speech today is to be struck by its spectacular political ineptitude. Didn't Carter realize that Presidents are not supposed to express doubts publicly or to lecture the American people about their shortcomings? Why couldn't he have just temporarily imposed gas rationing, which would have ended the lines overnight, instead of outlining a vague and immediately forgotten six-point program to promote energy conservation?

His describing the country's loss of confidence did not cause the country to gain confidence, needless to say. And it didn't help matters that upon his return to Washington he demanded letters of resignation from all members of his cabinet and accepted five of them. Carter seemed to be anything but an FDR-like reassuring, ebullient presence; he communicated a sense of wild flailing about as he tried (unsuccessfully) to get the situation under control.

I remember being enormously impressed by Carter's speech at the time because it was a painfully honest and much thought-over attempt to grapple with the main problem of the decade. The American economy had ceased being an expanding pie, and by unfortunate coincidence this had happened just when an ethic of individual freedom as the highest good was spreading throughout the society, which meant people would respond to the changing economic conditions by looking out for themselves. Like most other members of the word-manipulating class whose leading figures had advised Carter at Camp David, I thought there *was* a malaise. What I didn't realize, and Carter obviously didn't either, was that there was a smarter way to play the situation politically. A President could maintain there was nothing wrong with America at all—that it hadn't become less powerful in the world, hadn't reached some kind of hard economic limit, and wasn't in crisis—and, instead of trying to reverse the powerful tide of individualism, ride along with it. At the same time, he could act more forcefully than Carter, especially against inflation, so that he didn't seem weak and ineffectual. All this is exactly what Carter's successor, Ronald Reagan, did.

Actually, Carter himself set in motion the process by which inflation was conquered a few months later, when he gave the chairmanship of the Federal Reserve Board to Paul Volcker, a man willing to put the economy into a severe recession to bring back price stability. But in November fate delivered the *coup de grâce* to Carter in the form of the taking hostage of the staff of the American Embassy in Teheran, as a protest against the United States' harboring of Iran's former shah.

As with the malaise speech, what is most difficult to convey today about the hostage crisis is why Carter made what now looks like a huge, obvious error: playing up the crisis so much that it became a national obsession for more than a year. The fundamental problem with hostage taking is that the one sure remedy—refusing to negotiate and thus allowing the hostages to be killed—is politically unacceptable in the democratic media society we live in, at least when the hostages are middle-class sympathetic figures, as they were in Iran.

There isn't any good solution to this problem, but Carter's two successors in the White House demonstrated that it is possible at least to negotiate for the release of hostages in a low-profile way that will cause the press to lose interest and prevent the course of the hostage negotiations from completely defining the Presidency. During the last year of the Carter administration, by contrast, the hostage story absolutely dominated the television news (recall that the ABC show *Nightline* began as a half-hour five-times-a-week update on the hostage situation), and several of the hostages and their families became temporary celebrities. In Carter's defense, even among the many voices criticizing him for appearing weak and vacillating, there was none that I remember willing to say, "Just cut off negotiations and walk away." It was a situation that everyone regarded as terrible but in which there was a strong national consensus supporting the course Carter had chosen.

So ended the seventies. There was still enough of the sixties spillover phenomenon going on so that Carter, who is now regarded (with some affection) as having been too much the good-hearted liberal to maintain a hold on the presidential electorate, could be challenged for renomination by Ted Kennedy on the grounds that he was too conservative. Inflation was raging on; the consumer price index rose by 14.4 percent between May 1979 and May 1980. We were being humiliated by fanatically bitter, premodern Muslims whom we had expected to regard us with gratitude because we had helped ease out their dictator even though he was reliably pro–United States. The Soviet empire appeared (probably for the last time ever) to be on the march, having invaded Afghanistan to Carter's evident surprise and disillusionment. We had lost our most recent war. We couldn't pull together as a people. The puissant, unified, prospering America of the late 1940s seemed to be just a fading memory.

I was a reporter for the *Washington Post* during the 1980 presidential campaign, and even on the *Post*'s national desk, that legendary nerve center of politics, the idea that the campaign might end with Reagan's being elected President seemed fantastic, right up to

Brian Basset saw Carter lying helpless while the 1980 election bore down; the polls never did let him loose. (© Brian Basset)

the weekend before the election. At first [Ted] Kennedy looked like a real threat to Carter; remember that up to that point no Kennedy had ever lost a campaign. While the Carter people were disposing of Kennedy, they were rooting for Reagan to win the Republican nomination because he would be such an easy mark.

He was too old, too unserious, and, most of all, too conservative. Look what had happened to Barry Goldwater (a sitting officeholder, at least) only sixteen years earlier, and Reagan was so divisive that a moderate from his own party, John Anderson, was running for President as a third-party candidate. It was not at all clear how much the related issues of inflation and national helplessness were dominating the public's mind. Kennedy, Carter, and Anderson were all, in their own way, selling national healing,

that great post-sixties obsession; Reagan, and only Reagan, was selling pure strength.

In a sense Reagan's election represents the country's rejection of the idea of a sixties-style solution to the great problems of the seventies—economic stagnation, social fragmentation, and the need for a new world order revolving around relations between the oil-producing Arab world and the West. The idea of a scaled-back America—husbanding its resources, living more modestly, renouncing its restless mobility, withdrawing from full engagement with the politics of every spot on the globe, focusing on issues of internal comity—evidently didn't appeal. Reagan, and the country, had in effect found a satisfying pose to strike in response to the problems of the seventies, but that's different from finding a solution.

Today some of the issues that dominated the seventies have faded away. Reagan and Volcker did beat inflation. The "crisis of confidence" now seems a long-ago memory. But it is striking how early we still seem to be in the process of working out the implications of the oil embargo. We have just fought and won [the Gulf War] against the twin evils of Middle East despotism and interruptions in the oil supply, which began to trouble us in the seventies. We still have not really even begun to figure out how to deal with the cessation of across-the-board income gains, and as a result our domestic politics are still dominated by squabbling over the proper distribution of government's benefits and burdens. During the seventies themselves the new issues that were arising seemed nowhere near as important as those sixties legacies, minority rights and Vietnam and Watergate. But the runt of decades has wound up casting a much longer shadow than anyone imagined.

QUESTIONS TO CONSIDER

1 What, according to Nicholas Lemann, is the long-term influence of the 1960s on American politics and culture? In what way were "the phenomena of the sixties" worked into the cultural mainstream?

2 Lemann sees the OPEC oil embargo of 1973–1974 as "the epochal event" of the 1970s. What were its economic and practical effects? What were the psychological effects on Americans' confidence in their country and their culture? How did the cultural trends of the 1970s make this reaction even more critical at the end of the decade?

3 According to Lemann, the 1970s were characterized by a "gathering conservative stridency." Discuss the events and developments underlying this trend. In what ways was it fed by trends from the 1960s, and in what ways was it a reaction against the sixties?

4 What is Lemann's judgment of Jimmy Carter and Ronald Reagan as men and as politicians? Does he find Reagan's presidency more successful than Carter's?

5 What to Lemann is the long-term importance of the 1970s? Do you see any signs of change, or do you think we are still working out the legacy of the 1970s?

PART FOURTEEN

The End of the Cold War

29 Reagan: His Place in History

RICHARD BROOKHISER

The collapse of the Soviet Union and the end of the Cold War came with such speed and surprise that the pace of events was almost too much to comprehend. It began in 1985 when Mikhail Gorbachev acceded to power as Soviet general secretary. To the utter astonishment of the West, he became "the most revolutionary figure in world politics in at least four decades," as one historian put it. Gorbachev not only launched glasnost, which ended many of the Soviet Union's most repressive practices, but started perestroika, or the restructuring of the Soviet Union, in order to end decades of economic stagnation and backwardness under Communism. Gorbachev sought to remake the Soviet economy by introducing such elements of capitalism as the profit motive and private ownership of property. His policies set the Soviet Union down the road toward a market economy; severely weakened the Soviet Communist party, which lost its monopoly of political power in 1990; and brought about détente with the West and the pioneering Intermediate Nuclear Forces Treaty (INF) with the United States, which led the two countries to jettison their intermediate-range missiles.

In 1989, meanwhile, world Communism itself appeared to collapse. Our television sets brought us the stunning spectacle of eastern Europeans, subjected to decades of violent repression, demonstrating in the street in favor of individual freedom and democratic government. Every nation in the eastern bloc—East Germany, Bulgaria, Romania, Hungary, Czechoslovakia, and Poland—overthrew its Communist regime or made that regime reform itself into a non-Communist government. Most dramatic of all was the dismantling of the Berlin Wall, long the preeminent symbol of Cold War between East and West, and the reunification of Germany itself. At long last, the troubled legacy of the Second World War appeared to be over, leaving our planet a safer place. For those of us who *lived through World War II and the entire length of the Cold War, the events of the late 1980s and early 1990s defied belief. Few thought we would ever live to see the downfall of the Soviet Communist state and the end of the Cold War at the same time.*

In the following selection, Richard Brookhiser gives Ronald Reagan much of the credit for these dramatic changes. This former governor of California, one-time movie actor, and New Deal Democrat turned conservative Republican was an eloquent and dedicated foe of Communism. He made international headlines when he called the Soviet Union "the Evil Empire." During his eight years as president (1981–1989), Reagan greatly increased defense spending, so much so, his supporters argue, that the Soviet Union collapsed in a desperate but futile effort to keep pace with the United States. As Professor Garry Wills has said, Reagan brought about the end of "the Evil Empire" by spending so much on America's military that the national debt more than doubled, to $2.3 trillion, the deficit almost tripled, and the trade deficit more than quadrupled. In addition to augmenting conventional weapons, Reagan embarked on the futuristic and inordinately expensive Strategic Defense Initiative (SDI, nicknamed Star Wars after George Lucas's phenomenally successful science-fiction movie). The Reagan administration claimed that SDI, "through the use of lasers and satellites, would provide an impenetrable shield against incoming missiles and thus make nuclear war obsolete." The SDI program provoked something close to hysteria among Soviet leaders because the U.S.S.R. lacked the financial resources and the technical expertise to keep up with the United States in an escalation of the arms race into space. Perhaps this was a major reason why Gorbachev sought détente with the West, agreed to a ban on intermediate-range missiles, and set about restructuring the Soviet system. But Brookhiser argues that Reagan was the lead player in bringing about these momentous events.

To help us understand Reagan and his place in history, Brookhiser examines the salient traits of his personality that helped shape his performance in office. Brookhiser stresses that Reagan was upbeat, witty, and supremely optimistic. Even when John Hinckley shot him in a failed assassination attempt, Brookhiser says, Reagan "reacted to actual gunfire with better humor than many politicians do to bad headlines." The story goes that when he met the physicians at George Washington University Hospital, he was cracking one-liners. "Please tell me you're all Republicans," the President said.

Because of his basic optimism, Reagan never doubted America's ultimate victory over the forces of evil symbolized by Communism and the Soviet Union. But, as Brookhiser reminds us, there was a "black velvet backdrop behind his cheerfulness," which reveals another of Reagan's "salient traits": his coldness. Behind his "bonhomie," he was inaccessible. Even people who worked closely with him for years believed that they never really knew him.

In Brookhiser's view, Reagan was a classic "hedgehog"—historian Isaiah Berlin's term for one who thinks only about the big picture and thus misses crucial details. Even so, Reagan lived to witness the collapse of the Berlin Wall, the relegation of Communism to "the ash-heap of history," and the end of the Cold War that had plagued the planet for almost a half century. Brookhiser gives Reagan the credit for ending that war. Bestselling novelist Tom Clancy agrees. He dedicated his novel, Executive Orders *(1996), "To Ronald Wilson Reagan, fortieth president of the United States: The man who won the war."*

GLOSSARY

BRADY, JAMES   Reagan's press secretary, Brady was shot in the spray of bullets when John Hinckley tried to assassinate the President with a handgun. Brady's wounds were so severe that he had to be confined to a wheelchair. Later, the Brady Bill, named in honor of Reagan's stricken aide, placed restrictions on the purchase of handguns and assault weapons.

BUCHANAN, PATRICK J.   Previously a speech writer for Richard Nixon, Buchanan was Reagan's communications director. He ran for president on a conservative third-party ticket in 1992, 1996, and 2000.

CHAMBERS, WHITTAKER   A repentant Communist, Chambers gained notoriety in 1948 when he accused State Department official Alger Hiss of spying for the Soviets.

GORBACHEV, MIKHAIL   When he became the Soviet general secretary in 1985, Gorbachev represented a younger generation of leaders who wanted to move the Soviet Union away from the repressive political practices of the past and toward a market economy that included the ownership of private property. Gorbachev embraced détente and signed a treaty with the United States that banned intermediate-range missiles.

HINCKLEY, JOHN   On March 30, 1981, Hinckley attempted to assassinate Reagan. The president had just finished a speech at a Washington, D.C., hotel. Hinckley's shots hit a police officer and press secretary James Brady. One bullet ricocheted and struck Reagan in the chest. Declared mentally incompetent, Hinckley was institutionalized at St. Elizabeth's Hospital in Washington, D.C.

LAFFER, ARTHUR   A proponent of the supply-side theory of economics, Laffer believed that lower taxes would stimulate the economy and increase federal government revenue.

MORAL MAJORITY   Paul Weyrich and the Reverend Jerry Falwell helped establish this organization whose base consisted of "born again" evangelical Christians. The Moral Majority championed a return to prayer in public schools and opposed abortion, homosexuality, and the Equal Rights Amendment to the Constitution.

MORRIS, EDMUND   While still in office, Reagan selected Morris, a white person born and educated in Kenya, to be his official biographer. The president was impressed with Morris's Pulitzer Prize–winning biography of Theodore Roosevelt. Morris went on to write *Dutch: A Memoir of Ronald Reagan* (1999), which was highly controversial.

NOONAN, PEGGY   A White House speech writer, Noonan is best known for crafting Reagan's address at Normandy Beach in 1984, in a ceremony commemorating the fortieth anniversary of the Allied invasion of German-occupied France during World War II.

NORTH, OLIVER   A marine lieutenant colonel, North was a central figure in the Iran-Contra affair. The trading of arms for American hostages in Iran resulted in funds that North secretly diverted to support the anti-Communist Contra forces in Nicaragua. North argued that he did this to defend democracy. In fact, his actions were illegal and unconstitutional, and they embarrassed the Reagan administration.

O'NEILL, THOMAS P. (TIP)   A politically astute Massachusetts congressman, O'Neill served as the Democratic majority leader from 1973 to 1977 and speaker of the House of Representatives from 1977 to 1987.

STRATEGIC DEFENSE INITIATIVE (SDI)   Also known as "Star Wars," SDI was Reagan's program of lasers and satellites in space that in theory would provide the United States with a protective shield against nuclear missiles.

Contemporary judgments of presidents are notoriously erratic. Consider the four who decorate Mount Rushmore, the stony seal of posterity's approval. Although Washington retired with almost universally good reviews, Benjamin Franklin's grandson did say he had "debauched" the nation. Jefferson left the White House with the joy of an escaping prisoner and a stress-induced migraine condition. The Senate was so angry with Theodore Roosevelt in his last days in office that it refused to accept his communications. Lincoln, who tops every historian's rating of Presidents, was murdered.

When Ronald Reagan left office in 1989, he truly retired, intending no Nixonian or Carteresque codas, and the onset of Alzheimer's was soon setting his agenda in any case. Journalists and historians could thus get an early start on their posthumous shiftings. But their work will go on for years. . . .

Whatever the writers finally come up with, all their labors, like all the events of their subject's career, will be distilled by the national memory into two or three facts or phrases, maybe only one. My childhood history of the Presidents, which had to find something important and moderately good to say about every Chief Executive, could at least say of Millard Fillmore that he sent Commodore Perry to Japan.

Here is a preliminary list of six aspects of Ronald Reagan—three personal, three political—from which those in the year 2075 may make their selection.

Like notable predecessors—Jefferson, FDR—Reagan had an optimistic view of things. Also like them, he had demons and enemies. But he was serenely confident that he would prevail. His political optimism came from a buoyant temperament. The command performance for his personality was the moment when, at the age of 70, one of John Hinckley's bullets lodged an inch from his heart. He spent his time, before and after the operation that saved his life, cracking jokes almost as old as himself. We often use military metaphors to describe normal political controversy—for instance, a "barrage" of criticism. Ronald Reagan reacted to actual gunfire with better humor than many politicians do to bad headlines.

In normal circumstances, Reagan's favorite story about his sunny worldview concerned two boys who were told to clean out a stable. The task proved so Augean that one of them gave up. The other kept going. With so much excrement, he reasoned, there had to be a pony in there somewhere.

That story conveyed a truth about Reagan's optimism: It was willed, sometimes contrary to all reason. Another story, which he told on the opening pages of his first memoir, the 1965 *Where's the Rest of Me?*, supplies the psychological background of his determined hopefulness. Reagan describes finding his father, Jack, a genial, but alcoholic, shoe salesman, collapsed on the front porch one night after a binge. The scene was pure Frank Capra, down to the weather conditions: Jack Reagan's "hair [was] soaked with melting snow." As in some Frank Capra movies, there was also a dark subtext beneath a sentimental gloss. Ronald remembered helping his father, pityingly, to bed: "I could feel no resentment." If he couldn't feel any, why does he mention it? Any drunk's child feels a host of negative emotions: resentment, anger, betrayal. Each child then deals with them in his own way. Ronald Reagan's way was to dismiss his pain and to focus on the bright side: "In a few days" his father "was the bluff, hearty man I knew and loved." In later life, Reagan would blot out both real problems and false obstacles, as well as bullets.

The black velvet backdrop behind his cheerfulness explains a second salient trait of Reagan's: his coldness. Yes, he had a funny story for everyone, including Tip O'Neill and Mikhail Gorbachev, and he laughed at other people's funny stories, not just his own. But behind the bonhomie, there was nothing accessible. "Even as a teenager," wrote Edmund Morris, "he had taken no personal interest in people. They were, and remained, a faceless audience to his

Excerpts from Richard Brookhiser, "Reagan, His Place in History," *American Heritage* (August/September, 2004), pp. 35–38. Reprinted by permission of the author.

Ronald Reagan and his wife Nancy as they appeared on inauguration day, January 20, 1981. The photographer captures Reagan's winning smile and movie-star appeal. Brookhiser praises him for *his "sunny worldview" and his unflinching confidence in America's future. (Courtesy Ronald Reagan Library)*

perpetual performance." Certainly Morris felt faceless in Reagan's presence, which seems to have driven the biographer to distraction. But he was not the only one. People who worked with Reagan closely for years felt they never penetrated. According to his speechwriter Peggy Noonan, White House staffers made jokes of his elusiveness: "Who was that masked man?"

Reagan's coldness allowed him to be stubborn. He used all the resources of public relations, from marks on the floor to theme-of-the-day spin control to movie-star looks, to make his case. But after he had done all that he could do, he did not care what

people thought of him. He had his message; when he became President, he had his programs; that was that. He often settled for less than he wanted, but he never stopped wanting it. His stubbornness helped him reach the White House despite one of the more discouraging pre-victory political records. Some politicians have won second contests after previously losing runs for the Presidency: Andrew Jackson, Richard Nixon. Some have won, after one failed attempt to secure their party's nomination: James Monroe, George H. W. Bush. Reagan failed twice to get the Republican nomination—in 1968 and 1976—before lightning struck. Repeat losers, from Henry

Clay to Bob Dole, usually go on losing. Only Reagan broke the pattern.

Reagan's third important personal trait was simplicity. The literature of management is filled with variations on the polarity between big-picture men and detail men; in the realm of philosophy, Isaiah Berlin taught us to think of hedgehogs (the thinkers who see in the universe one big thing) and foxes (the thinkers who see multiplicity). The characteristic mistake of big-picture hedgehogs is to ignore details that are in fact crucial; the characteristic mistake of detail foxes is to assume that hedgehogs see nothing at all. John Quincy Adams, the first Boylston Professor of Rhetoric at Harvard, called Andrew Jackson a "barbarian" who "hardly could spell his own name"; this was five years after Jackson had cleaned Adams's clock in the election of 1828.

Tip O'Neill, no Boylston Professor of Rhetoric but a Massachusetts politician, like Adams, said Reagan knew "less than any president I've ever known" (O'Neill, like Adams, also had his clock cleaned by his ignoramus enemy). Reagan indeed was about as far over in the direction of the big picture and hedgehog as it is possible to be. In his book *The Presidential Difference*, the political scientist Fred I. Greenstein made a useful movie-industry analogy to Reagan's intellectual and management style. Reagan obviously was the star of his own administration, but he was also its producer. The writing, even the directing, could always be left to someone else. He was responsible for Reaganism.

What was that? The most concentrated (Reaganesque?) summary of its leading heads was made by the journalist R. Emmett Tyrrell, Jr.: "The Evil Empire; cut taxes; the pieties." The economist Milton Friedman daydreams about an income tax return so simple it could be printed on a postcard. Reaganism could be jotted down on the back of a business card.

What fell off the card, Reagan believed, could safely be ignored. Pat Buchanan, another speechwriter, remembered sitting in on a cabinet-level debate between Secretary of State George Shultz and Secretary of Agriculture John Block on grain exports. While it raged, Reagan reached for a bowl of jellybeans, his favorite snack food, and began picking out his favorite colors. "My God," Buchanan thought, "what in heaven's name is with this guy?" Reagan, who caught Buchanan's eye, winked. Buchanan interpreted the wink to mean: "They're having an argument here, and I'm not getting into it." Maybe that is what the wink meant. Or maybe—the coldness kicking in—it was Reagan's way of averting an intrusive gaze. In either case, Mr. Shultz and Mr. Block were not attended to. That was safe enough when the subject was grain exports; less safe when it was the money shuffling of Lt. Col. Oliver North.

On the issues that constituted Reaganism, Reagan batted two for three. It became the fashion, after their collapse, to dismiss Communism and the Soviet Union as threats. It is easy to be wise after the fact. In the late seventies, Cuban soldiers patrolled the former Portuguese empire in Africa. The Soviets had acquired two new client states in the Western Hemisphere, Nicaragua and Grenada, and had invaded Afghanistan. Western Europe was rocked by a pro-Communist peace movement, terrified by the introduction of Soviet and American intermediate-range missiles on European soil.

Reagan's distrust of Communism was deep and long-standing. As a president of the Screen Actors Guild, he had seen Communist attempts to take over Hollywood crafts unions; when the guild's position on these turf wars shifted from neutral to anti-Communist, Reagan got an anonymous phone call on a movie set threatening that his face would be "fix[ed]." Early in the fifties, he read *Witness*, by the former Communist spy Whittaker Chambers. *Witness* was more than an espionage memoir; in one passage, Chambers recalled that the delicate folds of his baby daughter's ears persuaded him that the universe was divinely designed and that scientific socialism was false. Three decades later, Reagan cited the passage on the baby's ear to White House speechwriter Tony Dolan. Reagan was not well read, but what he read lodged in his mind.

Because of his optimism, he never adopted the defensive power-sharing strategy of longtime anti-Communists like Richard Nixon and Henry Kissinger.

He thought Communism was bad, and he thought it was doomed. When he became President, he confidently declared that freedom and the West would "transcend" Communism, that it would end "on the ash-heap of history," that the Berlin Wall should be torn down.

The steps he took to bring this about included rolling back Communist gains at the margins, invading Grenada, supporting a counterrevolution in Nicaragua, and sending Stinger missiles to the Afghan resistance. (As in all wars, there were unintended consequences, as the Taliban and Osama bin Laden demonstrate.) He announced that he would take advantage of America's lead in high tech by producing a missile defense system. Critics derided the Strategic Defense Initiative as a fantasy from *Star Wars;* Reagan embraced the pop-culture reference. He never deployed the system, and tests of its effectiveness continue to this day, as do arguments over the results. But the threat worried the Soviets; Gorbachev's foreign minister, Aleksandr Bessmertnykh, told a 1993 conference of Cold Warriors at the Woodrow Wilson School of Public and International Affairs that SDI caused a tug of war inside the Soviet bureaucracy that was reflected in the divided purposes of the Gorbachev regime. Former Defense Secretary Frank Carlucci said at the same press conference that he "never believed" in SDI, and his skepticism may prove to be justified. On the other hand, the Cold War postmortem at which Bessmertnykh and Carlucci spoke was hosted by the victors, in Princeton, New Jersey, not Leningrad.

No one thing wins a war by itself. But Reagan's appearance at the end of the Cold War was crucial. When he came into office, the Soviet Union was an aggressive hard-line state; when he left, it was a reforming, improvising one partly in response to his pressures. Less than a year after he retired, the Berlin Wall was torn down; two years after that, the Soviet Union was no more. It is hard to think of a comparably rapid collapse of a major power without major bloodletting. Woodrow Wilson helped beat the Central Powers in World War I, and Franklin Roosevelt played a far larger role in beating the

Axis in World War II. World War III—the Cold War—was less cataclysmic but longer, and the role of the United States was even more central. Ronald Reagan helped guarantee an American victory, without fighting a Second Battle of the Marne or a D-day.

When Reagan came into office, the American economy seemed as weak as the Yeltsin-era Russian army. The oil shock of the early seventies had hit it hard, and a combination of high inflation and high unemployment known as "stagflation"—which the reigning economists' paradigm of the Phillips curve declared to be impossible—seemed impervious to the best efforts of Presidents Nixon, Ford, and Carter to massage it.

Reagan's remedy was as theological as the passage on the baby's ear. A school of economists, called "supply-siders," had studied the economic impact of tax rates (Robert Mundell, the school's founder, was awarded the Nobel Prize in economics in 1999). They too had a curve, shaped like a croquet wicket and named after one of their number, Arthur Laffer, which they said showed the diminishing returns of revenue that resulted from ever-higher rates. If you cut tax rates, they argued, the economy would be stimulated, and the federal government would collect more money in tax revenues. Making use of a post-shooting wave of good feeling, Reagan was able to persuade Congress to implement something like their program.

In the event, the Laffer curve, like the Phillips curve, had some kinks in it. The great tax-rate cut was followed by two short, sharp recessions, one at the beginning of Reagan's first term, the other at the end of George H. W. Bush's only one. Both Bush and then Bill Clinton repudiated supply-side doctrine, though they did not in fact raise tax rates that much. The deficit, contrary to predictions, rose alarmingly, until the late nineties, when politicians began talking of surplus.

Still, the eighties and nineties were economically vastly different from the seventies. Americans worried less about OPEC or the potency of Asian models of capitalism and profited from their own. Success has many fathers. The Federal Reserve, which always goes its own way, deserves credit. So, more recently, does the computer economy, which was a spinoff of high-tech military spending. But Reagan was on the bridge when the twenty-year boom began.

On the third item of his agenda, "the pieties," more commonly known as the social issues, Reagan was completely defeated. After signing an expansive abortion-rights bill as governor of California, Reagan came to oppose the practice. When he was elected President, abortion opponents spoke hopefully of a constitutional amendment returning jurisdiction on abortion to the states or banning abortion outright or of a congressional act (per Article III, Section 2) removing the issue from the sway of the courts. Nothing happened. When Reagan addressed audiences of gun owners as a fellow NRA member, they helped him in Republican primaries. Gun-control supporters made little progress during his administration, but recently they have made lots, aided in no small part by the crippled presence of former press secretary James Brady, shot by one of John Hinckley's bullets. Sex continues to rock and roll through popular entertainment and, not so very long ago, even the Oval Office. Come to think of it, Reagan was the first divorced man to be elected President.

In 1979 the Washington political operative Paul Weyrich helped the Reverend Jerry Falwell found the Moral Majority, the organization's name confidently assuming that there was such a thing, as Weyrich and Falwell defined it. In 1999 Weyrich gloomily announced that religious and social conservatives should retreat to their families and communities since the political and cultural situation was hopeless. . . .

Perhaps the pieties fell victim to simplicity. It may be that a hedgehog's agenda maxes out at two big ideas. Abortion opponents were told during the early Reagan years to wait patiently while Communism and high tax rates were attended to; their turn would come. It never did.

Great generals and politicians often preside over social transformations they deplore. Washington's Farewell Address deplores the party spirit, yet partisan politics became an unshakable aspect of American life in his administration. Thomas Jefferson was the harbinger of the new era, yet as Henry Adams argued in stout volumes, that era was not the republican, country party ideal of Jefferson's youth. If posterity accords Reagan some measure of their success—a world war and a twenty-year boom—it will also accord him their failure.

Reagan's Presidency came at the end of the twentieth century—the actual one, not the calendrical one. The twentieth century, as many historians have noted, was a short century, running from 1914 to 1991. It was also an evil century, defined by tyranny and bloodshed. The United States came through it less badly scarred than any other major power and than many small ones. Ronald Reagan, who was born in 1911, before the Evil Century began, lived to see and understand its end—which he, as much as anyone else, assured would be relatively successful. Mount Rushmore is full, and that kind of pantheon should probably be reserved for those who speak to America's spirit (then what's TR doing there?). But when historians and children have to think of Ronald Reagan at the end of the twenty-first century, they won't have to scratch around for some Commodore Perry.

QUESTIONS TO CONSIDER

1 Describe how Ronald Reagan reacted to the assassination attempt. What does his reaction tell you about his temperament? How did Reagan view the episode in his youth when he had to help his alcoholic father to bed?

2 What is Brookhiser's evidence that there was a "coldness" beneath Reagan's cheerful demeanor? How does Reagan's political record before his presidency provide clues to his determination and tenacity?

3 Describe the difference between "hedgehogs" and "foxes." Why did Reagan fit perfectly into one of these categories? What were the three major goals of "Reaganism"? Why does Brookhiser conclude that

the President "batted two for three" with reference to the three goals?

4 Describe the origin of Reagan's "deep and long standing disdain" for Communism. Explain what Reagan did as president to place Communism "on the ash-heap of history." Why did Brookhiser conclude that Reagan "helped generate an American victory" in the Cold War without the bloodletting that ended the previous world wars? Do you agree with the author's conclusions?

5 Describe the economic theory of the "supply-siders." Why did Reagan believe that they would restore health to the American economy? Why does Brookhiser conclude that "the eighties and nineties were economically vastly different from the seventies"?

6 How does President Reagan's record on social issues measure up to the goals that he established at the start of his first administration? What grades would abortion opponents, NRA members, and the Moral Majority give to him?

30 Some Lessons from the Cold War

ARTHUR M. SCHLESINGER JR.

It is too soon to know what the demise of the Soviet Union and the end of the Cold War means for the future of humankind. But it is not too soon to reflect on some lessons of the Cold War, which on at least one occasion—the Cuban missile crisis of October 1962—almost exploded into a nuclear holocaust and the end of the world as we know it. How did humankind survive the Cold War? What caused and sustained it? The experts do not agree. Some see the Cold War as fundamentally an ideological struggle between the forces of freedom and the forces of autocracy. Still others view the Cold War as a geopolitical and military contest that involved not just a Soviet–United States confrontation but a western Europe–Soviet confrontation as well. While some specialists maintain that the Cold War strengthened hard-liners in the Soviet Union and sustained Communist rule there, others, such as Ronald Steel, believe that American policymakers exaggerated the military capacity of the Soviet Union throughout the Cold War, thus creating a bogus enemy that justified huge American defense build-ups.

In the selection that follows, Arthur M. Schlesinger Jr., one of our greatest historians, argues that it is irrelevant to allocate blame for the Cold War. It emerged, he says, from the efforts of the United States and the Soviet Union to fill the "power vacuum" left by World War II, and it developed into "a holy war" because of very real ideological differences between the two new superpowers and their allies. At bottom, Schlesinger believes, the Cold War was a "fundamental debate" between Communism and liberalism, including democratic socialism, and that debate charged the Cold War with its religious intensity.

Now that the holy war is over, Schlesinger suggests six fallacies that helped make it so long, so dark, and so dangerous. These fallacies, Schlesinger suggests, resulted from the perception of events by both sides. Yes, the perception of reality is the crucial element in understanding the past. How people perceive events and the motives of an alleged enemy determine how they act, and how they act in turn affects the course of subsequent events. When it comes to the Cold War, human error, exaggeration, misunderstanding, overinterpretation—all played a key role in shaping and sustaining tensions between East and West. Schlesinger hopes that his six fallacies, or errors of perception, judgment, and action, will benefit future policymakers, so that the world can avoid another Cold War, another "intimate brush with collective suicide." In the end, he argues, "Democracy won the political argument between East and West" and "the market won the economic argument." Yet in retrospect, Schlesinger says, the Cold War can only remind us "of the ultimate interdependence of nations and of peoples."

GLOSSARY

QUISLING   Someone who betrays his country by helping enemy invaders and going on to serve in a puppet government; named after pro-Nazi Norwegian Vidkun Quisling (1887–1945).

STALIN, JOSEPH   Soviet dictator from the 1920s until his death in 1953, he ruled the Soviet Union with a brutal hand, resorting to massive purges in the 1930s and again in the post–World War II years; he viewed the West as a devious menace (several times in its history Russia had been invaded by western European powers) and clamped an iron hand on eastern Europe, using it as a bulwark against Western "aggression."

WALLACE, HENRY A.   FDR's vice president, 1941–1945, and Truman's secretary of commerce, 1945–1946; Wallace was forced to resign as commerce secretary after he publicly attacked Truman's "get tough" policy toward the Soviets; in 1948, Wallace made an unsuccessful bid for the presidency as the candidate of the Progressive party.

ZERO-SUM GAME   Cold War notion that "a gain for one side was by definition a defeat for the other."

I n those faraway days when the Cold War was young, the English historian Sir Herbert Butterfield lectured at Notre Dame on "The Tragic Element in Modern International Conflict." Historians writing about modern wars, Butterfield said, characteristically start off with a "heroic" vision of things. They portray good men struggling against bad, virtue resisting evil. In this embattled mood, they see only the sins of the enemy and ignore the underlying structural dilemmas that so often provoke international clashes.

As time passes and emotions subside, history enters the "academic" phase. Now historians see "a terrible human predicament" at the heart of the story, "a certain situation that contains the element of conflict irrespective of any special wickedness in any of the parties concerned." Wickedness may deepen the predicament, but conflict would be there anyway.

Perspective, Butterfield proposed, teaches us "to be a little more sorry for both parties than they knew how to be for one another." History moves on from melodrama to tragedy.

Butterfield made a pretty good forecast of the way Cold War historiography has evolved in the more than forty years since he spoke. In the United States the "heroic" phase took two forms: the orthodox in the 1940s and 1950s, with the Russians cast as the villains, and the revisionist in the 1960s, with the Americans as the villains. By the 1980s, American Cold War historians discerned what one of the best of them, John Lewis Gaddis, called an "emerging post-revisionist synthesis." History began to pass from a weapon in the battle into a more analytical effort to define structural dilemmas and to understand adversary concerns. *Glasnost* permitted comparable historiographical evolution in the former Soviet Union.

Quite right: The more one contemplates the Cold War, the more irrelevant the allocation of blame seems. The Second World War left the international order in acute derangement. With the Axis states vanquished, the Western European allies spent, the colonial empires in tumult and dissolution, great gaping holes appeared in the structure of world power. Only two nations—the United States and the Soviet Union—had the military strength, the ideological conviction, and the political will to fill these vacuums.

But why did this old-fashioned geopolitical rivalry billow up into a holy war so intense and obsessive as to threaten the very existence of human life on the planet? The two nations were constructed on opposite and profoundly antagonistic principles. They were divided by the most significant and fundamental disagreements over human rights, individual liberties, cultural freedom, the role of civil society, the direction of history, and the destiny of man. Each state saw the other as irrevocably hostile to its own essence. Given the ideological conflict on top of the geopolitical confrontation, no one should be surprised at what ensued. Conspiratorial explanations are hardly required. The real surprise would have been if there had been no Cold War.

And why has humanity survived the Cold War? The reason that the Cold War never exploded into hot war was surely (and by providential irony) the invention of nuclear weapons. One is inclined to support the suggestion (Elspeth Rostow's, I think) that the Nobel Peace Prize should have gone to the atomic bomb.

At last this curious episode in modern history is over, and we must ask what lessons we may hope to learn from a long, costly, dark, dreary, and dangerous affair; what precautions humanity should take to prevent comparable episodes in the future. I would suggest half a dozen fallacies that the world might well forego in years to come.

The first might be called the fallacy of overinterpreting the enemy. In the glory days of the Cold War, each side attributed to the other a master plan for world domination joined with diabolical efficiency in executing the plan. Such melodramatic imagining of brilliant and demonic enemies was truer to, say, Sax Rohmer, the creator of Dr. Fu Manchu, than to shuffling historical reality.

No doubt Soviet leaders believed that the dialectic of history would one day bring about the victory of

In late 1988, Gorbachev announced that he would reduce Soviet military presence in the eastern bloc nations. Five months later, the first of the military units scheduled for withdrawal—thirty-one Soviet T.64 tanks—pulled out of Hungary and returned to the Soviet Union. (Jean Gaumy/Magnum)

communism. No doubt Western leaders believed that the nature of man and markets would one day bring about the victory of free society. But such generalized hopes were far removed from operational master plans.

"The superpowers," as Henry Kissinger well put it,

often behave like two heavily armed blind men feeling their way around a room, each believing himself in mortal peril from the other whom he assumes to have perfect vision. Each side should know that frequently uncertainty, compromise, and incoherence are the essence of policymaking. Yet each tends to ascribe to the other a consistency, foresight, and coherence that its own experience belies. Of course, over time, even two blind men can do enormous damage to each other, not to speak of the room.

The room has happily survived. But the blind men meanwhile escalated the geopolitical/ideological confrontation into a compulsively interlocked heightening of tension, spurred on by authentic differences in principle, by real and supposed clashes of interest, and by a wide range of misperception, misunderstanding, and demagoguery. Each superpower undertook for what it honestly saw as defensive reasons actions that the other honestly saw as unacceptably threatening and requiring stern countermeasures. Each persevered in corroborating the fears of the other. Each succumbed to the propensity to perceive local conflicts in global terms, political conflicts in moral terms, and relative differences in absolute terms. Together, in lockstep, they expanded the Cold War.

In overinterpreting the motives and actions of the other, each side forgot Emerson's invaluable precept: "In analysing history, do not be too profound, for often the causes are quite simple." Both superpowers should have known from their own experience that governments mostly live from day to day responding to events as they come, that decisions are more often the result of improvisation, ignorance, accident, fatigue, chance, blunder, and sometimes plain stupidity than of orchestrated master plans. One lesson to be drawn from the Cold War is that more things in life are to be explained by cock-up, to use the British term, than by conspiracy.

An accompanying phenomenon, at first a consequence and later a reinforcing cause of overinterpretation, was the embodiment of the Cold War in government institutions. Thus our second fallacy: The fallacy of overinstitutionalizing the policy. The Soviet Union, a police state committed to dogmas of class war and capitalist conspiracy and denied countervailing checks of free speech and press, had institutionalized the Cold War from the day Lenin arrived at the Finland Station. In later years the Cold War became for Stalin a convenient means of justifying his own arbitrary power and the awful sacrifices he demanded from the Soviet peoples. "Stalin needed the Cold War," observed Earl Browder, whom Stalin purged as chief of the American Communist party, "to keep up the sharp international tensions by which he alone could maintain such a regime in Russia."

In Washington by the 1950s the State Department, the Defense Department, the Central Intelligence Agency, the Federal Bureau of Investigation, and the National Security Council developed vested bureaucratic interests in the theory of a militarily expansionist Soviet Union. The Cold War conferred power, money, prestige, and public influence on these agencies and on the people who ran them. By the natural law of bureaucracies, their stake in the conflict steadily grew. Outside of government, arms manufacturers, politicians, professors, publicists, pontificators, and demagogues invested careers and fortunes in the Cold War.

In time, the adversary Cold War agencies evolved a sort of tacit collusion across the Iron Curtain. Probably the greatest racket in the Cold War was the charade periodically enacted by generals and admirals announcing the superiority of the other side in order to get bigger budgets for themselves. As President John F. Kennedy remarked to Norman Cousins, the editor of the *Saturday Review,* in the spring of 1963, "The hard-liners in the Soviet Union and the United States feed on one another."

Institutions, alas, do not fold their tents and silently steal away. Ideas crystallized in bureaucracies resist change. With the Cold War at last at an end, each side faces the problem of deconstructing entrenched Cold War agencies spawned and fortified by nearly half a century of mutually profitable competition. One has only to reflect on the forces behind the anti-Gorbachev conspiracy of August 1991 [which sought in vain to overthrow him].

A third fallacy may be called the fallacy of arrogant prediction. As a devotee of a cyclical approach to American political history, I would not wish to deny that history exhibits uniformities and recurrences. But it is essential to distinguish between those phenomena that are predictable and those that are not.

Useful historical generalizations are mostly statements about broad, deep-running, long-term changes: the life-cycle of revolutions, for example, or the impact of industrialization and urbanization, or the influence of climate or sea power or the frontier. The short term, however, contains too many variables, depends too much on accident and fortuity and personality, to permit exact and specific forecasts.

We have been living through extraordinary changes in the former Soviet Union and in Eastern Europe, in South Africa and in the Middle East. What is equally extraordinary is that *no one foresaw these changes.* All the statesmen, all the sages, all the savants, all the professors, all the prophets, all those bearded chaps on "Nightline"—all were caught unaware and taken by surprise; all were befuddled and impotent before the perpetual astonishments of the future. History has an abiding capacity to outwit our certitudes.

Just a few years back some among us were so absolutely sure of the consequences if we did not smash the Reds at once that they called for preventive nuclear war. Had they been able to persuade the U.S. government to drop the bomb on the Soviet Union in the 1950s or on China in the 1960s . . . but, thank heaven, they never did; and no one today, including those quondam preventive warriors themselves, regrets the American failure to do so.

The Almighty no doubt does know the future. But He has declined to confide such foresight to frail and erring mortals. In the early years of the Cold War, [theologian] Reinhold Niebuhr warned of "the depth of evil to which individuals and communities may sink . . . when they try to play the role of God to history." Let us not fall for people who tell us that we must take drastic action today because of their conjectures as to what some other fellow or nation may do five or ten or twenty years from now.

Playing God to history is the dangerous consequence of our fourth fallacy—the fallacy of national self-righteousness. "No government or social system is so evil," President Kennedy said in his American University speech in 1963, "that its people must be condemned as lacking in virtue," and he called on Americans as well as Russians to reexamine attitudes toward the Cold War, "for our attitude is as essential as theirs." This thought came as rather a shock to those who assumed that the American side was so manifestly right that self-examination was unnecessary.

Kennedy liked to quote a maxim from the British military pundit Liddell Hart: "Never corner an opponent, and always assist him to save his face. Put yourself in his shoes—so as to see things through his eyes. Avoid self-righteousness like the devil—nothing is so self-blinding." Perhaps Kennedy did not always live up to those standards himself, but he did on great occasions, like the Cuban missile crisis, and he retained a capacity for ironical objectivity that is rare among political leaders.

Objectivity—seeing ourselves as others see us—is a valuable adjunct to statesmanship. Can we be so sure that our emotional judgments of the moment represent the last word and the final truth? The angry ideological conflicts that so recently obsessed us may not greatly interest our posterity. Our great-grandchildren may well wonder what in heaven's name those disagreements could have been that drove the Soviet Union and the United States to the brink of blowing up the planet.

Men and women a century from now will very likely find the Cold War as obscure and incomprehensible as we today find the Thirty Years War—the terrible conflict that devastated much of Europe not too long ago. Looking back at the twentieth century, our descendants will very likely be astonished at the disproportion between the causes of the Cold War, which may well seem trivial, and the consequences, which could have meant the veritable end of history.

Russians and Americans alike came to see the Cold War as a duel between two superpowers, a Soviet-American duopoly. But the reduction of the Cold War to a bilateral game played by the Soviet Union and the United States is a fifth fallacy. The nations of Europe were not spectators at someone else's match. They were players too.

Revisionist historians, determined to blame the Cold War on an American drive for world economic hegemony, have studiously ignored the role of Europe. Washington, they contend, was compelled to demand an "open door" for American trade and investment everywhere on the planet because American capitalism had to expand in order to survive. The Soviet Union was the main obstacle to a world market controlled by the United States. So, by revisionist dogma, American leaders whipped up an unnecessary Cold War in order to save the capitalist system.

No matter that some fervent open door advocates, like Henry A. Wallace, were also fervent opponents of the Cold War. No matter that the republics of the former Soviet Union now want nothing more than American trade and investment and full integration into the world market. And no matter that most Western European nations in the 1940s had Socialist governments and that the democratic socialist leaders— Clement Attlee and Ernest Bevin in Britain, Leon Blum and Paul Ramadier in France, Paul-Henri Spaak in Belgium, Kurt Schumacher, Ernst Reuter, and Willy Brandt in West Germany—had powerful reasons of their own to fear the spread of Stalinist influence and Soviet power.

Such men could not have cared less about an open door for American capitalism. They cared deeply, however, about the future of democratic socialism. When I used to see Aneurin Bevan, the leader of the left wing of the British Labour party, in London in 1944, he doubted that the wartime alliance would last and saw the struggle for postwar Europe as between the democratic socialists and the Communists. "The Communist party," Bevan wrote in 1951, "is the sworn and inveterate enemy of the Socialist and Democratic parties. When it associates with them it does so as a preliminary to destroying them." Many in the Truman administration in the 1940s espoused this view and, dubbing themselves (in private) NCL, favored American support for the non-Communist Left.

The democratic socialists, moreover, were in advance of official Washington in organizing against the Stalinist threat. Despite his above-the-battle stance at Notre Dame, Herbert Butterfield himself wrote in 1969, "A new generation often does not know (and

does not credit the fact when informed) that Western Europe once wondered whether the United States could ever be awakened to the danger from Russia." The subsequent opening of British Foreign Office papers voluminously documents Sir Herbert's point.

Far from seeing President Truman in the revisionist mode as an anti-Soviet zealot hustling a reluctant Europe into a gratuitous Cold War, the Foreign Office saw him for a considerable period as an irresolute waffler distracted by the delusion that the United States could play mediator between Britain and the Soviet Union. Ernest Bevin, Britain's Socialist foreign secretary, thought Truman's policy was "to withdraw from Europe and in effect leave the British to get on with the Russians as best they could." A true history of the Cold War must add European actors to the cast and broaden both research nets and analytical perspectives.

The theory of the Cold War as a Soviet-American duopoly is sometimes defended on the ground that, after all, the United States and the Soviet Union were in full command of their respective alliances. But nationalism, the most potent political emotion of the age, challenged the reign of the superpowers almost from the start: Tito [of Yugoslavia], Mao, and others vs. Moscow; De Gaulle, Eden and others vs. Washington. Experience has adequately demonstrated how limited superpowers are in their ability to order their allies around and even to control client governments wholly dependent on them for economic and military support. Far from clients being the prisoners of the superpower, superpowers often end as prisoners of their clients.

These are lessons Washington has painfully learned (or at least was painfully taught; has the government finally learned them?) in Vietnam, El Salvador, Israel, Saudi Arabia, Kuwait. As for the Soviet Union, its brutal interventions and wretched Quislings in Eastern Europe only produced bitterness and hatred. The impact of clients on principals is another part of the unwritten history of the Cold War. The Cold War was *not* a bilateral game.

Nor was it—our sixth and final fallacy—a zero-sum game. For many years, Cold War theology decreed

The Berlin Wall, a symbol of the Cold War for nearly three decades, separated Communist East Berlin from West Berlin. With the easing of Cold War tensions, "the wall" was torn down in 1989 and Germany itself was reunited under western rule. (Guy Le Querrec/Magnum)

that a gain for one side was by definition a defeat for the other. This notion led logically not to an interest in negotiation but to a demand for capitulation. In retrospect the Cold War, humanity's most intimate brush with collective suicide, can only remind us of the ultimate interdependence of nations and of peoples.

After President Kennedy and Premier Khrushchev stared down the nuclear abyss together in October 1962, they came away determined to move as fast as they could toward détente. Had Kennedy lived, Khrushchev might have held on to power a little longer, and together they would have further subdued the excesses of the Cold War. They rejected the zero-sum approach and understood that intelligent negotiation brings mutual benefit. I am not an unlimited admirer of Ronald Reagan, but he deserves

his share of credit for taking Mikhail Gorbachev seriously, abandoning the zero-sum fallacy he had embraced for so long, and moving the Cold War toward its end.

And why indeed has it ended? If the ideological confrontation gave the geopolitical rivalry its religious intensity, so the collapse of the ideological debate took any apocalyptic point out of the Cold War. The proponents of liberal society were proven right. After seventy years of trial, communism turned out—by the confession of its own leaders—to be an economic, political, and moral disaster. Democracy won the political argument between East and West. The market won the economic argument. Difficulties lie ahead, but the fundamental debate that created the Cold War is finished.

QUESTIONS TO CONSIDER

1 What are the six fallacies of judgment and action that aggravated the tensions between East and West after World War II, according to Arthur Schlesinger, and why did the two sides fall into them? What are the overarching lessons Schlesinger would like nations and peoples to learn from the mistakes of the Cold War?

2 Schlesinger says that democracy and the market economy won the Cold War, but do we know for certain what the future holds for the former Soviet Union and for eastern Europe? What do you think are the lasting effects of the Cold War on the United States and our future?

3 What have been the general trends in Cold War historiography? How are historians influenced by the traditions from which they come and the times in which they live? Do you think they may in turn influence those times?

4 As you reflect on Schlesinger's selection, what do you think is the relative influence of general social and political factors and the actions of individuals on the course of history? How have people's perceptions affected subsequent events?

5 Arthur Schlesinger calls himself a "devotee of a cyclical approach to American political history." In your general experience in American history, do you see certain recurring historical themes, trends, or concerns? What might these tell you about the basic principles and character of the American experience?

PART FIFTEEN

From the Technological Revolution to Modern Terrorism

31 | Bill Gates: Enigmatic Genius of Microsoft

WALTER ISAACSON

We are living in the midst of a technological revolution whose historical significance has already eclipsed that of the Industrial Revolution. Such technological innovations as television, fax and photocopy machines, communications satellites, cell phones, teleconferencing, telecommuting, and computers with email and Internet capabilities have profoundly altered our lives. The advent of the computer is perhaps the most important technological achievement of all. The computer has made space programs and missile and air-defense systems possible; it has revolutionized the armed services and their weapons of war. It has completely transformed our methods of literary composition, book publishing, and filmmaking. It is the nerve center of governments, economies, educational institutions, and transportation and business operations the world over. The computer and the World Wide Web have helped convert our planet into a community of interconnected and interdependent nations. The computer has changed the way we work, play, think, and speak. Indeed, it has added a new nomenclature (megabyte, software, surf, browser, laptop, user-friendly, RAM) to our vocabulary.

In the last two decades, we have also witnessed a revolution in personal computers (PCs). The leading spirit of the PC revolution is William ("Bill") Henry Gates III, co-founder of Microsoft and the subject of the following selection by Time *writer Walter Isaacson. At age fourteen, Gates established his first company, Traf-o-Data, which sold systems that counted traffic flow; young Gates earned $20,000 from that venture. In 1973, he entered Harvard with plans to become a lawyer. Two years later he dropped out, moved to Albuquerque, New Mexico, and with Paul Allen* formed Microsoft (Allen soon left the company because of a personality clash with Gates). Microsoft's first important contract, negotiated with the Tandy Corporation, was to create software for its Radio Shack computers. In 1980, now relocated in Seattle, Washington, Microsoft began an association with International Business Machines (IBM), which was starting to build personal computers meant for home use. In the late 1980s, Gates's company introduced the Windows operating system, which provided a "user-friendly" method of operating IBM-compatible computers with a hand-operated "mouse." By the late 1990s, Bill Gates had thoroughly "thrashed competitors in the world of desktop operation systems and application software," so much so that Microsoft had a near monopoly in the field, with a market value of $160 billion. And Microsoft's ruling genius, Bill Gates, was earning $30 million a day, which made him "by far" the richest person and most famous businessman on earth. Says Ann Winblad, a friend and fellow software entrepreneur: "We share our thoughts about the world and ourselves. And we marvel about how, as two young overachievers, we began a great adventure on the fringes of a little-known industry and it landed us at the center of an amazing universe."

What follows is an intimate portrait of Bill Gates, described by Isaacson as "one of the most important minds and personalities of our era." A plump man in his mid-forties, Gates is something of an enigma. Isaacson says he possesses "an awesome and at times frightening blend of brilliance, drive, competitiveness and personal intensity." Associates describe him in the vocabulary of the computer age: he has "incredible processing power" and "unlimited bandwidth." He is agile at "parallel processing" and "multitasking." The richest person in the world often speaks in youthful slang: a good strategy is "really neat," "supercool," and "hardcore." A bad strategy is "really dumb" and "random to the max." Above all, Gates is fiercely competitive and has cutthroat instincts. Such traits helped him build Microsoft into "a media and Internet behemoth." In sum, Isaacson says, "He has become the Edison and Ford of our age. A technologist turned entrepreneur, he embodies the digital era."

For years, competitors have accused Gates of unfair and even illegal business practices: they claim that he has tried to eliminate competition in desktop operating systems, so that he can dominate everything "from word processing and spreadsheets to Web browsers and content." After investigating Microsoft's operations, the Federal Department of Justice agreed with Gates's critics and brought an antitrust suit against his Microsoft empire. In 2000, a federal court found Microsoft "liable for maintaining an illegal monopoly in personal computer operating systems." Two years later, after an appeal and several court hearings, the United States District Court for the District of Columbia ordered Gates's company to stop specific practices that destroyed competition in the desktop computer market. But the software giant successfully avoided a breakup and also avoided federal government interference in the company's efforts in product development. Insiders regarded this as "a big win" for Microsoft. Like Andrew Carnegie (selection 5) and John D. Rockefeller (selection 8), his innovative and cunning predecessors, Bill Gates continued to thrive, earning enormous profits for himself and giving much of it away in philanthropic donations.

GLOSSARY

ALLEN, PAUL   A boyhood friend of Gates. They met at the exclusive Lakeside School in Seattle and shared an enthusiasm for computers. In 1975, they formed Microsoft. Although the two men remain close, Allen left the new software company because, in Isaacson's words, the personalities of the youthful founders clashed; Allen was a "dreamy visionary" while Gates was the "workaholic code writer and competitor."

BALLMER, STEVE   A former Harvard classmate and friend of Gates who, in 1980, left Procter & Gamble to join the management team at Microsoft.

BUFFETT, WARREN   A multibillionaire Omaha, Nebraska, investor who became close friends with Gates. Although their business interests and areas of expertise are different, both men share an unpretentious style and enjoy each other's company.

MICROSOFT   In 1975, Gates and Allen formed this company to develop computer operating systems. Originally based in Albuquerque, New Mexico, its first big contract was with the Tandy Corporation to create software for Radio Shack computers. In 1980, with the company now in Seattle, Washington, Microsoft began a business relationship with IBM, which was starting to build personal computers. In the late 1980s, Gates introduced the "Windows" operating system, which provided a "user-friendly" way to operate IBM-compatible computers with a hand-held "mouse." By the late 1990s, the stock market valuation of Microsoft was $160 billion. Its dominance of the software market resulted in a federal antitrust suit.

MYHRVOLD, NATHAN   He earned a doctorate in physics from Princeton and managed Microsoft's advanced research group.

SOFTWARE   Computer operating systems such as BASIC, MS-DOS, and Windows. These systems became increasingly easier to understand and apply. Microsoft's versatile Windows product, with its on-screen symbols, dominated the market and overwhelmed competitors such as Apple Computer, with its more expensive Macintosh model.

He's the most famous businessman in the world. Reams have been written about how he dominated the revolution in personal computing and is now poised to turn Microsoft into a media and Internet behemoth. But we know little about him as a person. What beliefs and values drive this man who, as much as anyone, will determine the way we look not only at computers but at ourselves and our world? Here's an intimate look at one of the most important minds and personalities of our era.

When Bill Gates was in the sixth grade, his parents decided he needed counseling. He was at war with his mother Mary, an outgoing woman who harbored the belief that he should do what she told him. She would call him to dinner from his basement bedroom, which she had given up trying to make clean, and he wouldn't respond. "What are you doing?" she once demanded over the intercom.

"I'm thinking," he shouted back.

"You're thinking?"

"Yes, Mom, I'm thinking," he said fiercely. "Have you ever tried thinking?"

The psychologist they sent him to "was a really cool guy," Gates recalls. "He gave me books to read after each session, Freud stuff, and I really got into psychology theory." After a year of sessions and a battery of tests, the counselor reached his conclusion. "You're going to lose," he told Mary. "You had better just adjust to it because there's no use trying to beat him." Mary was strong-willed and intelligent herself, her husband recalls, "but she came around to accepting that it was futile trying to compete with him."

A lot of computer companies have concluded the same. In the 21 years since he dropped out of Harvard to start Microsoft, William Henry Gates III, [now 46], has thrashed competitors in the world of desktop operating systems and application software.

Walter Isaacson, "In Search of the Real Bill Gates," *Time,* vol. 149, no. 2 (January 13, 1997), pp. 44–52. © 1997 Time Inc. Reprinted by permission.

Now he is attempting the audacious feat of expanding Microsoft from a software company into a media and content company.

In the process he has amassed a fortune worth (as of last Friday) $23.9 billion. The 88 percent rise in Microsoft stock in 1996 meant he made on paper more than $10.9 billion, or about $30 million a day. That makes him the world's richest person, by far. But he's more than that. He has become the Edison and Ford of our age. A technologist turned entrepreneur, he embodies the digital era.

His success stems from his personality: an awesome and at times frightening blend of brilliance, drive, competitiveness and personal intensity. So too does Microsoft's. "The personality of Bill Gates determines the culture of Microsoft," says his intellectual sidekick Nathan Myhrvold. But though he has become the most famous business celebrity in the world, Gates remains personally elusive to all but a close circle of friends.

Part of what makes him so enigmatic is the nature of his intellect. Wander the Microsoft grounds, press the Bill button in conversation and hear it described in computer terms: he has "incredible processing power" and "unlimited bandwidth," an agility at "parallel processing" and "multitasking." Watch him at his desk, and you see what they mean. He works on two computers, one with four frames that sequence data streaming in from the Internet, the other handling the hundreds of E-mail messages and memos that extend his mind into a network. He can be so rigorous as he processes data that one can imagine his mind may indeed be digital: no sloppy emotions or analog fuzziness, just trillions of binary impulses coolly converting input into correct answers.

"I don't think there's anything unique about human intelligence," Gates says over dinner one night at a nearly deserted Indian restaurant in a strip mall near his office. Even while eating, he seems to be multitasking; ambidextrous, he switches his fork back and forth throughout the meal and uses whichever hand is free to gesture or scribble notes. "All the neurons in the brain that make up perceptions and emotions operate in a binary fashion," he

Bill Gates, shown in this photograph, built Microsoft into a corporate behemoth worth $160 billion. "His success," Isaacson says, "stems from his personality: an awesome and at times frightening blend of brilliance, drive, competitiveness, and personal intensity." His employees at Microsoft describe his intellect in computer terms: "he has 'incredible processing power'" and "unlimited bandwidth, an agility at 'parallel processing' and 'multitasking.'" (©Reuters NewMedia, Inc./Corbis)

explains. "We can someday replicate that on a machine." Earthly life is carbon based, he notes, and computers are silicon based, but that is not a major distinction. "Eventually we'll be able to sequence the human genome and replicate how nature did intelligence in a carbon-based system." The notion, he admits, is a bit frightening, but he jokes that it would also be cheating. "It's like reverse-engineering someone else's product in order to solve a challenge."

Might there be some greater meaning to the universe? When engaged or amused, he is voluble, waving his hands and speaking loudly enough to fill the restaurant. "It's possible, you can never know, that the universe exists only for me." It's a mix of Descartes' metaphysics and Tom Stoppard's humor. "If so," he jokes, "it's sure going well for me, I must admit." He laughs; his eyes sparkle. Here's something machines can't do (I don't think): giggle about their plight in the cosmos, crack themselves up, have fun.

Right? Isn't there something special, perhaps even divine, about the human soul? His face suddenly becomes expressionless, his squeaky voice turns toneless, and he folds his arms across his belly and vigorously rocks back and forth in a mannerism that has become so mimicked at Microsoft that a meeting there can resemble a round table of ecstatic rabbis. Finally, as if from an automaton, comes the answer: "I don't have any evidence on that." Rock, rock, rock. "I don't have any evidence on that."

The search for evidence about the soul that underlies Bill Gates' intellectual operating system is a task that even this boyish man might find a challenge.

"As a baby, he used to rock back and forth in his cradle himself," recalls Gates' father, a man as big and huggable as his son is small and tightly coiled. A retired lawyer, he still lives in the airy suburban Seattle house overlooking Lake Washington where Bill III—the boy he calls "Trey"—grew up. (The name comes from the card term for three, though the father is now resigned to being called Bill Sr.)

His mother Mary was "a remarkable woman." Bill Sr. says. A banker's daughter, she was adroit in both social and business settings, and served on numerous boards, including those of the University of Washington, the United Way, USWest and First Interstate Bancorp. After her death in 1994, the city council named the avenue leading into their neighborhood after her.

"Trey didn't have a lot of confidence in social settings," says his father. "I remember him fretting for two weeks before asking a girl to the prom, then getting turned down. But Mary did. She was a star at social intercourse. She could walk into a room . . ." He has the same toothy smile as his son, the same smudgy glasses covering twinkling eyes. But now, for just a moment, he is starting to tear up. His mind does not seem like a computer. He folds his arms across his stomach and starts to rock, gently.

He gets up to show some more pictures of Mary and of her mother. Both loved cards, and they would organize bridge games, as well as Password and trivia contests, after the big family dinners they held every Sunday. "The play was quite serious," Bill Sr. recalls. "Winning mattered."

As he wanders through the house, he points out more framed pictures of his son: Trey, the towheaded Cub Scout; Trey with sister Kristi, a year older, who now has the joy of being his tax accountant; and with Libby, nine years younger, who lives a few blocks away raising her two kids; with Bill Sr. and his new wife Mimi, the director of the Seattle Art Museum; and hugging his wife Melinda while listening to Willie Nelson play at their New Year's Day 1994 wedding in Hawaii.

"He's a busy guy," says Bill Sr., "so we don't see him a lot, but we spend holidays together." Thanksgiving was in Spokane, Washington, at Kristi's house, Christmas playing golf in Palm Springs, California, where Bill Sr. and Mimi have a place. They communicate mainly by E-mail. Just this morning he got one describing a photocopier Trey bought him for his birthday.

He lumbers over a table where he has gathered some pictures of summer vacations they used to take with friends at a cluster of rental cabins known as Cheerio on the Hood Canal, about two hours away. There were nightly campfires, family skits and the type of organized competitive games the Gates family loved. "On Saturdays there was a tennis tournament, and on Sundays our Olympics, which were a mixture of games and other activities," Bill Sr. recalls. "Trey was more into the individual sports, such as water skiing, than the team ones."

In 1986, after Microsoft became successful, Gates built a four-house vacation compound dubbed Gateaway for his family. There his parents would help him replicate his summer activities on a grander scale for dozens of friends and co-workers in what became known as the Microgames. "There were always a couple of mental games as well as performances and regular games," says Bill Sr. as he flips through a scrapbook. These were no ordinary picnics: one digital version of charades, for example, had teams competing to send numerical messages using smoke-signal machines, in which the winners devised their own 4-bit binary code.

"We became concerned about him when he was ready for junior high," says his father. "He was so small and shy, in need of protection, and his interests were so different from the typical sixth grader's." His intellectual drive and curiosity would not be satisfied in a big public school. So they decided to send him to an elite private school across town.

Walking across the rolling quad of the Lakeside School, Bill Sr. points out the chapel where his son played the lead in Peter Shaffer's Black Comedy. "He was very enthusiastic about acting. But what really entranced him was in there," he says, pointing to a New England-style steepled classroom building. With the proceeds from a rummage sale, the Mothers' Club had funded a clunky teletype computer terminal.

Learning BASIC language from a manual with his pal Paul Allen, Trey produced two programs in the eighth grade: one that converted a number in one mathematical base to a different base, and another (easier to explain) that played tic-tac-toe. Later, having read about Napoleon's military strategies, he devised a computer version of Risk, a board game he liked in which the goal is world domination.

Trey and Paul were soon spending their evenings at a local company that had bought a big computer and didn't have to pay for it until it was debugged. In exchange for computer time, the boys' job was to try (quite successfully) to find bugs that would crash it. "Trey got so into it," his father recalls, "that he would sneak out the basement door after we went to bed and spend most of the night there."

The combination of counseling and the computer helped transform him into a self-assured young businessman. By high school he and his friends had started a profitable company to analyze and graph traffic data for the city. "His confidence increased, and his sense of humor increased," his father says. "He became a great storyteller, who could mimic the voices of each person. And he made peace with his mother."

"In ninth grade," Gates recalls over dinner one night, "I came up with a new form of rebellion. I hadn't been getting good grades, but I decided to get all A's without taking a book home. I didn't go to math class, because I knew enough and had read ahead, and I placed within the top 10 people in the nation on an aptitude exam. That established my independence and taught me I didn't need to rebel anymore." By 10th grade he was teaching computers and writing a program that handled class scheduling, which had a secret function that placed him in classes with the right girls.

His best friend was Kent Evans, son of a Unitarian minister. "We read FORTUNE together; we were going to conquer the world," says Gates. "I still remember his phone number." Together with Paul Allen, they formed the official-sounding Lakeside Programmers Group and got a job writing a payroll system for a local firm. A furious argument, the first of many, ensued when Allen tried to take over the work himself. But he soon realized he needed the tireless Gates back to do the coding. "O.K., but I'm in charge," Gates told him, "and I'll get used to being in charge, and it'll be hard to deal with me from now on unless I'm in charge." He was right.

To relieve the pressures of programming, Evans took up mountain climbing. One day Gates got a call from the headmaster: Evans had been killed in a fall. "I had never thought of people dying," Gates says. There is a flicker of emotion. "At the service, I was supposed to speak, but I couldn't get up. For two weeks I couldn't do anything at all."

After that he became even closer to Paul Allen. They learned an artificial-intelligence language together and found odd jobs as programmers. "We were true partners," Gates says. "We'd talk for hours every day." After Gates went off to Harvard, Allen drove his rattletrap Chrysler cross-country to continue their collaboration. He eventually persuaded Gates to become that university's most famous modern dropout in order to start a software company, which they initially dubbed Micro-Soft (after considering the name Allen & Gates Inc.), to write versions of BASIC for the first personal computers. It was an intense relationship: Gates the workaholic code writer and competitor, Allen the dreamy visionary.

Over the years they would have ferocious fights, and Allen would, after a Hodgkin's disease scare, quit the company and become estranged. But Gates worked hard to repair the relationship and eventually lured Allen, who is now one of the country's biggest high-tech venture-capital investors (and owner of the Portland Trail Blazers), back onto the Microsoft board. "We like to talk about how the fantasies we had as kids actually came true," Gates says. Now, facing their old classroom building at Lakeside is the modern brick Allen/Gates Science Center. (Gates lost the coin toss.)

Steve Ballmer, big and balding, is bouncing around a Microsoft conference room with the spirit of the Harvard football-team manager he once was. "Bill lived down the hall from me at Harvard sophomore year," he says. "He'd play poker until 6 in the morning, then I'd run into him at breakfast and discuss applied mathematics." They took graduate-level math and economics courses together, but Gates had an odd approach toward his classes: he would skip the lectures of those he was taking and audit the lectures of those he wasn't, then spend the period before each exam cramming. "He's the smartest guy I've ever met," says Ballmer, 40, continuing the unbroken sequence of people who make that point early in an interview.

Ballmer nurtured the social side of Gates, getting him to join one of the college's eating clubs (at his initiation Gates gave a drunken disquisition on an artificial-intelligence machine), playing the video game Pong at hamburger joints and later wandering with him to places like the old Studio 54 during visits to New York City. "He was eccentric but charismatic," says Ballmer.

When Microsoft began to grow in 1980, Gates needed a smart nontechie to help run things, and he lured Ballmer, who had worked for Procter & Gamble, to Seattle as an equity partner. Though he can be coldly impersonal in making business decisions, Gates has an emotional loyalty to a few old friends. "I always knew I would have close business associates like Ballmer and several of the other top people at Microsoft, and that we would stick together and grow together no matter what happened," he says. "I didn't know that because of some analysis. I just decided early on that was part of who I was."

As with Allen, the relationship was sometimes stormy. "Our first major row came when I insisted it was time to hire 17 more people," Ballmer recalls. "He claimed I was trying to bankrupt him." Gates has a rule that Microsoft, rather than incurring debt, must always have enough money in the bank to run for a year even with no revenues. (It currently has $8 billion in cash and no long-term debt.) "I was living with him at the time, and I got so pissed off I moved out." The elder Gates smoothed things over, and soon the new employees were hired.

"Bill brings to the company the idea that conflict can be a good thing," says Ballmer. "The difference from P&G is striking. Politeness was at a premium there. Bill knows it's important to avoid that gentle civility that keeps you from getting to the heart of an issue quickly. He likes it when anyone, even a junior employee, challenges him, and you know he respects you when he starts shouting back." Around Microsoft, it's known as the "math camp" mentality: a lot of cocky geeks willing to wave their fingers and yell with the cute conviction that all problems have a right answer. Among Gates' favorite phrases is "That's the stupidest thing I've ever heard," and victims wear it as a badge of honor, bragging about it the way they do about getting a late-night E-mail from him.

The contentious atmosphere can promote flexibility. The Microsoft Network began as a proprietary online system like CompuServe or America Online. When the open standards of the Internet changed the game, Microsoft was initially caught flat-footed. Arguments ensued. Soon it became clear it was time to try a new strategy and raise the stakes. Gates turned his company around in just one year to disprove the maxim that a leader of one revolution will be left behind by the next.

During the bachelor years in the early '80s, the math-camp mentality was accomplished by a frat-boy

Bill Gates and his wife Melinda built this luxurious $97 million home with a 30-car garage on the shores of Lake Washington.

(© Reuters NewMedia, Inc./Corbis)

recreational style. Gates, Ballmer and friends would eat out at Denny's, go to movies and gather for intellectual games like advanced forms of trivia and Boggle. As friends started getting married, there were bachelor parties involving local strippers and skinny-dipping in Gates' pool. But eventually, after Gates wed, he took up more mature pursuits such as golf. "Bill got into golf in the same addictive way he gets into anything else," says Ballmer. "It gets his competitive juice flowing."

It's a rainy night, and Gates is bombing around in his dark blue Lexus. He loves fast cars. When Microsoft was based in Albuquerque, New Mexico, in its early years, he bought a Porsche 911 and used to race it in the desert; Paul Allen had to bail him out of jail after one midnight escapade. He got three speeding tickets—two from the same cop who was

trailing him—just on the drive from Albuquerque the weekend he moved Microsoft to Seattle. Later he bought a Porsche 930 Turbo he called the "rocket," then a Mercedes, a Jaguar XJ6, a $60,000 Carrera Cabriolet 964, a $380,000 Porsche 959 that ended up impounded in a customs shed because it couldn't meet import emission standards, and a Ferrari 348 that became known as the "dune buggy" after he spun it into the sand.

Despite this record, Gates is not wearing a seat belt. (A dilemma: Is it too uncool to use mine?) He rarely looks at you when he talks, which is disconcerting, but he does so when he's driving, which is doubly disconcerting. (I buckle up. As his mother and others have learned, it's not always prudent to compete.) . . .

Gates met Melinda French [his wife] 10 years ago at a Microsoft press event in Manhattan. She was working for the company and later became one of the executives in charge of interactive content. Their daughter Jennifer was born last April. Melinda, 32, is no longer at Microsoft, and she is active in charity work and on the board of Duke, where she studied computer science as an undergraduate and then got a graduate degree in business. Like Gates, she is smart and independent. Like his mother, she is also friendly and social, with an easy manner of organizing trips and activities. But she zealously guards her privacy and doesn't give interviews.

"I used to think I wouldn't be all that interested in the baby until she was two or so and could talk," says Gates as he shows off the more intimate family quarters. "But I'm totally into it now. She's just started to say 'ba-ba' and have a personality."

Melinda is Catholic, goes to church and wants to raise Jennifer that way. "But she offered me a deal," Gates says. "If I start going to church—my family was Congregationalist—then Jennifer could be raised in whatever religion I choose." Gates admits that he is tempted, because he would prefer she have a religion that "has less theology and all" than Catholicism, but he has not yet taken up the offer. "Just in terms of allocation of time resources, religion is not very efficient," he explains. "There's a lot more I could be doing on a Sunday morning."

If Ballmer is Gates' social goad, his intellectual one is Nathan Myhrvold (pronounced Meer-voll), 37, who likes to joke that he's got more degrees than a thermometer, including a doctorate in physics from Princeton. With a fast and exuberant laugh, he has a passion for subjects ranging from technology (he heads Microsoft's advanced-research group) to dinosaurs . . . to cooking. He sometimes moonlights as a chef at Rover's, a French restaurant in Seattle.

When he arrives there for dinner, owner Thierry Rautureau comes out to hug him and pour champagne. There follows a procession of a dozen courses, from black truffles and pureed celery root in smoked game consommé to venison with obscure types of mushrooms, each with different vintage wines. (The bill for two comes to $390, and picking it up assuages my discomfort that Gates had insisted on putting the previous evening's $37 tab at the Indian restaurant on his MasterCard.)

"There are two types of tech companies," Myhrvold says in between pauses to inhale the aroma of the food. "Those where the guy in charge knows how to surf, and those where he depends on experts on the beach to guide him." The key point about Gates is that he knows—indeed loves—the intricacies of creating software. "Every decision he makes is based on his knowledge of the merits. He doesn't need to rely on personal politics. It sets the tone."

Myhrvold describes a typical private session with Gates. Pacing around a room, they will talk for hours about future technologies such as voice recognition (they call their team working on it the "wreck a nice beach" group, because that's what invariably appears on the screen when someone speaks the phrase "recognize speech" into the system), then wander onto topics ranging from quantum physics to genetic engineering. "Bill is not threatened by smart people," he says, "only stupid ones."

Microsoft has long hired based on I.Q. and "intellectual bandwidth." Gates is the undisputed ideal: talking to most people is like sipping from a fountain, goes the saying at the company, but with Gates it's like drinking from a fire hose. Gates, Ballmer and Myhrvold believe it's better to get a brilliant but untrained young brain—they're called "Bill clones"—than someone with too much experience. The interview process tests not what the applicants know but how well they can process tricky questions: If you wanted to figure out how many times on average you would have to flip the pages of the Manhattan phone book to find a specific name, how would you approach the problem?

Gates' intellect is marked by an ability, as he puts it, to "drill down." On a visit to Time Inc.'s new-media facility, he answered questions from a collection of magazine editors as if by rote, but on his way out he asked to see the Internet servers and spent 45 minutes grilling the claque of awed techies there. Broad discussions bore him, he shows little curiosity about other people, and he becomes disengaged when people use small talk to try to establish a personal rapport.

Even after spending a lot of time with him, you get the feeling that he knows much about your thinking but nothing about such things as where you live or if you have a family. Or that he cares.

In that regard he is the opposite of, say, Bill Clinton, who brackets the other end of the baby boom: Gates analytically rigorous and emotionally reserved, the President equally smart but intellectually undisciplined and readily intimate. They played golf on Martha's Vineyard once, and the President, as usual, worked hard at bonding emotionally and being personally charming and intimate. He expressed sorrow about the death of Gates' mother, shared the pain of the recent death of his own mother and gave golfing tips to Melinda. But Gates noticed that Clinton never bore in or showed rigorous curiosity about technological issues. Though he vaguely considers himself a Democrat, Gates stayed neutral in the presidential election.

Warren Buffett, the Omaha, Nebraska, investor whom Gates demoted to being merely the second richest American, seems an unlikely person to be among his closest pals. A jovial, outgoing 66-year-old grandfather, Buffett only recently learned to use a computer. But as multibillionaires go, both are unpretentious, and they enjoy taking vacations together. Buffett's secretary apologetically explains that Buffett isn't giving interviews these days and at the moment is traveling, but she promises to pass along the request. Less than three hours later, Buffett calls to say he happens to be in the Time & Life Building with some free time between meetings in Manhattan, and he would be happy to come by to be interviewed. He likes to talk about Gates. . . .

When Gates decided to propose to Melinda in 1993, he secretly diverted the chartered plane they were taking home from Palm Springs one Sunday night to land in Omaha. There Buffett met them, arranged to open a jewelry store that he owned and helped them pick a ring. That year Gates made a movie for Buffett's birthday. It featured Gates pretending to wander the country in search of tales about Buffett and calling Melinda with them from pay phones. After each call, Gates is shown checking the coin slot for loose change. When she mentions that Buffett is only the country's second richest man, he informs her that on the new Forbes list Buffett had (at least that one year) regained the top spot. The phone suddenly goes dead. "Melinda, Melinda," Gates sputters, "you still there? Hello?"

Last October Gates brought Melinda and their new daughter to visit Buffett and his wife in San Francisco. They ended up playing bridge for nine hours straight. Another marathon session in Seattle started in the morning and lasted—with a break for Melinda to pick up lunch at Burger King—until guests started arriving for dinner. "He loves games that involve problem solving," Buffett says. "I showed him a set of four dice with numbers arranged in a complex way so that any one of them would on average beat one of the others. He was one of three people I ever showed them to who figured this out and saw the way to win was to make me choose first which one I'd roll." (For math buffs: the dice were nontransitive. One of the others who figured it out was the logician Saul Kripke.) . . .

Another of Gates' vacation companions is Ann Winblad, the software entrepreneur and venture capitalist he dated during the 1980s. They met in 1984 at a Ben Rosen–Esther Dyson computer conference and started going on "virtual dates" by driving to the same movie at the same time in different cities and discussing it on their cell phones. For a few years she even persuaded him to stop eating meat, an experiment he has since resolutely abandoned.

They were kindred minds as well as spirits. On a vacation to Brazil, he took James Watson's 1,100-page textbook, *Molecular Biology of the Gene,* and they studied bioengineering together. On another vacation, to a Santa Barbara, California, ranch, she took tapes of Richard Feynman's lectures at Cornell, and they studied physics. And on a larger excursion with friends to central Africa, which ended at some beach cottages on an island off Zanzibar, among their companions was anthropologist Donald Johanson, known for his work on the human ancestor Lucy, who helped teach them about human evolution. In the evenings on each trip they would go to the beach with four or five other couples for bonfires, Hood Canal-style games and a tradition they called the sing-down, where each team is given a word and has to come up with songs that feature it. Winblad remembers Gates disappearing on a dark beach after his group had been given the word *sea,* and then slowly emerging from the mist singing a high-pitched solo of *Puff, the Magic Dragon.*

They broke up in 1987, partly because Winblad, five years older, was more ready for marriage. But they remain close friends. "When I was off on my own thinking about marrying Melinda," Gates says, "I called Ann and asked for her approval." She gave it. "I said she'd be a good match for him because she had intellectual stamina." Even now, Gates has an arrangement with his wife that he and Winblad can keep one vacation tradition alive. Every spring, as they have for more than a decade, Gates spends a long weekend with Winblad at her beach cottage on the Outer Banks of North Carolina, where they ride dune buggies, hang-glide and walk on the beach. "We can play putt-putt while discussing biotechnology," Gates says. Winblad puts it more grandly. "We share our thoughts about the world and ourselves," she says. "And we marvel about how, as two young overachievers, we began a great adventure on the fringes of a little-known industry and it landed us at the center of an amazing universe."

After a recent whirl of travel that included a speech in Las Vegas and a meeting in Switzerland, Gates detoured to a secluded resort in New York's Adirondacks to spend a weekend with Melinda and Jennifer. There they played with 1,000-piece jigsaw puzzles from a craftsman in Vermont who makes them for customers like Gates. Melinda has helped broaden her husband. Instead of studying biotechnology together, they find time to take singing lessons.

Gates is ambivalent about his celebrity. Although he believes that fame tends to be "very corrupting," he is comfortable as a public figure and as the personification of the company he built. Like Buffett, he remains unaffected, wandering Manhattan and Seattle without an entourage or driver. Nestled into a banquette one Sunday night at 44, a fashionable Manhattan restaurant, he is talking volubly when another diner approaches. Gates pulls inward, used to people who want his autograph or to share some notion about computers. But the diner doesn't recognize him and instead asks him to keep his voice down. Gates apologizes sheepishly. He seems pleased to be regarded as a boyish cutup rather than a celebrity.

The phone in Gates' office almost never rings. Nor do phones seem to ring much anywhere on the suburban Microsoft "campus," a cluster of 35 low-rise buildings, lawns, white pines and courtyards that resemble those of a state polytechnic college. Gates runs his company mainly through three methods: he bats out a hundred or more E-mail messages a day (and night), often chuckling as he dispatches them; he meets every month or so with a top management group that is still informally known as the boop (Bill and the Office of the President); and most important, taking up 70 percent of his schedule by his own calculation, he holds two or three small review meetings a day with a procession of teams working on the company's various products.

There is a relaxed, nonhierarchical atmosphere as the seven young managers of the "WebDVD" group, all in the standard winter uniform of khakis and flannel shirts, gather in a windowless conference room near Gates' office. They have been working for almost a year on a digital videodisc intended to provide content along with Web browsing for television sets, and he wants to review their progress before leaving for Japan, where he will meet with such potential partners as Toshiba.

Craig Mundy, the veteran Microsoft exec who oversees all noncomputer consumer products, lets the younger team members lead the discussion. Gates quickly flips ahead through the deck of papers and within minutes has the gist of their report. He starts rocking, peppering them with questions that segue from the politics of their potential partners, the details of the technology, the potential competition and the broad strategy. The answers are crisp, even as Gates drills down into arcane details. No one seems to be showing off or competing for attention, but neither do any hesitate to speak up or challenge

Gates. To a man (and they all are), they rock when they think.

"Does this allow scripting in HTML?" he asks, referring to the authoring language used to create Websites. They explain how. He challenges them about why it requires four megabytes of memory. They explain; he drills down more; they finally prevail. There is an intense discussion of layers, sectors, modes, error corrections and mpeg-2 video-compression standards. "Our basic strategy must be processor agnostic," Gates decrees. Everyone nods. Then he shifts without missing a beat to corporate tactics. "Are we going to get Philips and other manufacturers and the moviemakers to agree on a standard?" We'll get to that in a minute, he's told. He wants to get to it now. There is a rapid discussion of the internal politics of Philips, Sony, Time Warner (the corporate parent of this magazine), Matsushita and Toshiba, along with their respective Hollywood alliances.

Gates doesn't address anyone by name, hand out praise or stoke any egos. But he listens intently, democratically. His famous temper is in check, even when he disagrees with someone's analysis of the DVD's capability to handle something called layering. "Educate me on that," he says in challenging the analysis, and after a minute or so cuts off the discussion by saying, "Send me the specs."

Gates does not hide his cutthroat instincts. "The competitive landscape here is strange, ranging from Navio to even WebTV," he says. He is particularly focused on Navio, a consumer-software consortium recently launched by Netscape and others designed to make sure that Windows and Windows CE (its consumer-electronics cousin) do not become the standard for interactive television and game machines. "I want to put something in our product that's hard for Navio to do. What are their plans?" The group admits that their intelligence on Navio is poor. Gates rocks harder. "You have to pick someone in your group," he tells Mundy, "whose task it is it to track Navio full time. They're the ones I worry about. Sega is an investor. They may be willing to feed us info." Then he moves on to other competitors. "What about the Planet TV guys?" Mundy explains that they are focusing on video games, "a platform we haven't prioritized." Gates counters: "We can work with them now, but they have other ambitions. So we'll be competitive with them down the line."

Though the videodisc is not at the core of Microsoft's business, this is a competition Gates plans to win. The group argues that the $10-per-unit royalty is too low. "Why charge more?" he asks. They explain that it will be hard to make a profit at $10, given what they are putting in. Gates turns stern. They are missing the big picture. "Our whole relationship with the consumer-electronic guys hangs in the balance," he declares. "We can get wiped." Only the paranoid survive. "The strategic goal here is getting Windows CE standards into every device we can. We don't have to make money over the next few years. We didn't make money on ms-dos in its first release. If you can get into this market at $10, take it." They nod.

His mother may have come to terms with this competitive intensity, but much of the computer world has not. There are Websites dedicated to reviling him, law firms focused on foiling him and former friends who sputter at the mention of his name. Companies such as Netscape, Oracle and Sun Microsystems publicly make thwarting his "plan for world domination" into a holy crusade.

The criticism is not just that he is successful but that he has tried to leverage, unfairly and perhaps illegally, Microsoft's near monopoly in desktop operating systems in ways that would let him dominate everything from word processing and spreadsheets to Web browsers and content. The company is integrating its Internet Explorer browser and Microsoft Network content into its Windows operating system, a process that will culminate with the "Active Desktop" planned for Windows 97, due out in a few months. Critics see a pattern of Microsoft's playing hardball to make life difficult for competing operating systems and applications: Microsoft Word has been buggy on Macintosh operating systems, users have found it tricky to make Netscape their default browser when going back and forth from Windows to the Microsoft Network, and application developers have complained that they don't get the full specs for new releases of Windows as quickly as Microsoft's own developers do.

"They are trying to use an existing monopoly to retard introduction of new technology," says Gary Reback, the Silicon Valley antitrust lawyer representing Netscape and other Microsoft competitors. The stakes are much higher than whose Web browser wins. Netscape is enhancing its browser to serve as a platform to run applications. "In other words," says Reback, "if Netscape is successful, you won't need Windows or a Microsoft operating system anymore." On the other hand, if Microsoft is allowed to embed its Web browser into its operating system in a manner that maintains its monopoly, Reback warns, "where will it stop? They'll go on to bundle in content, their Microsoft Network, financial transactions, travel services, everything. They have a game plan to monopolize every market they touch."

Gates makes no apologies. "Any operating system without a browser is going to be f——— out of business," he says. "Should we improve our product, or go out of business?" Later, on his trip to Japan, he returns to the subject in a two-page E-mail. "Customers are benefiting here in the same way they benefited from graphical interfaces, multitasking, compressions and dozens of other things," he writes. "If improving a product based on customer input is willful maintenance of trying to stay in business and not have Netscape turn their browser into the most popular operating system, then I think that is what we are supposed to do."

Though the stakes are clear, the law (which was developed in the era of railway barons) is not. After deadlocking, the Federal Trade Commission in 1993 surrendered jurisdiction over Microsoft to the Justice Department. FTC Commissioner Christine Varney, an expert in the field, says it's hard to apply antitrust law in a fluid situation. "My concern is with the law's ability to keep pace with market conditions in fields that change so rapidly," she says. "Once it's clear a practice is anticompetitive, the issue may already be moot."

Longtime competitors raise a more philosophical issue about Gates: his intensely competitive approach has poisoned the collaborative hacker ethos of the early days of personal computing. In his book *Startup,* Jerry Kaplan describes creating a handwriting-based system. Gates was initially friendly, he writes, and Kaplan trusted him with his plans, but he eventually felt betrayed when Gates announced a similar, competing product. Rob Glaser, a former Microsoft executive who now runs the company that makes RealAudio, an Internet sound system, is an admirer who compliments Gates on his vision. But, he adds, Gates is "pretty relentless. He's Darwinian. He doesn't look for win-win situations with others, but for ways to make others lose. Success is defined as flattening the competition, not creating excellence." When he was at Microsoft, for example, Glaser says the "atmosphere was like a Machiavellian poker game where you'd hide things even if it would blindside people you were supposed to be working with."

It comes down to the same traits that his psychologist noted when Gates was in sixth grade. "In Bill's eyes," says Glaser, "he's still a kid with a startup who's afraid he'll go out of business if he lets anyone compete." Esther Dyson, whose newsletter and conferences make her one of the industry's fabled gurus, is another longtime friend and admirer who shares such qualms. "He never really grew up in terms of social responsibility and relationships with other people," she says. "He's brilliant but still childlike. He can be a fun companion, but he can lack human empathy." "If we weren't so ruthless, we'd be making more creative software? We'd rather kill a competitor than grow the market?!?" Gates is pacing around his office, sarcastically repeating the charges against him. "Those are clear lies," he says coldly. "Who grew this market? We did. Who survived companies like IBM, 10 times our size, taking us on?" He ticks off the names of his rivals at Oracle, Sun, Lotus, Netscape in an impersonal way. "They're every bit as competitive as I am."

"We win because we hire the smartest people. We improve our products based on feedback, until they're the best. We have retreats each year where we think about where the world is heading." He won't even cop a plea to the charge that Microsoft tends to react to competitors' ideas—the graphical interface of Apple, the Web browser of Netscape—more than it blazes new trails of its own. "Graphical interfaces were done first at Xerox, not Apple. We bet on them early on, which is why Microsoft Office applications became the best."

Gates is enjoying this. Intellectual challenges are fun. Games are fun. Puzzles are fun. Working with smart people is superfun. Others may see him as ruthless, cold or brutal; but for him the competition is like a sport, a blood sport perhaps, but one played with the same relish as the summer games at Hood Canal. He sprawls on a couch, uncoils and pops open a Fresca. Though rarely attempting the social warmth of his mother (he doesn't actually offer me a Fresca but acquiesces when I ask), Gates has an intensity and enthusiasm that can be engaging, even charming. He takes a piece of paper and draws the matrix of strategies he faced when creating applications to compete with WordPerfect and Lotus. See what an exciting puzzle it was? His language is boyish rather than belligerent. The right stuff is "really neat" and "supercool" and "hardcore," while bad strategies are "crummy" and "really dumb" and "random to the max."

His office is rather modest, sparsely decorated and filled with standard-issue furniture. The biggest piece of art is a huge photo of a Pentium processor chip. There are smaller pictures of Einstein, Leonardo da Vinci and Henry Ford, though he admits that he has little admiration for the latter. The few personal pictures include one of the original dozen Microsoft employees (most with scruffy beards, except him), one of Ann Winblad on a trip to Germany, and one with Melinda and nine friends on a 1995 vacation to Indonesia. There are no pictures of Jennifer displayed, but he pulls a snapshot out of his desk showing him proudly cradling her.

He hopes to be running Microsoft for another 10 years, he says, then promises to focus as intensely on giving his money away. He says he plans to leave his children about $10 million each. "He will spend time, at some point, thinking about the impact his philanthropy can have," Buffett says. "He is too imaginative to just do conventional gifts." Already he's given $34 million to the University of Washington, partly to fund a chair for human genome-project researcher Leroy Hood; $15 million (along with $10 million from Ballmer) for a new computer center at Harvard; and $6 million to Stanford. An additional $200 million is in a foundation run by his father, and he has talked about taking over personally the funding of Microsoft's program to provide computers to inner-city libraries, to which he's donated $3 million in book royalties. "I've been pushing him gently to think more about philanthropy," his father says. "I think his charitable interests will run, as they do now, to schools and libraries."

Asked about his regrets, Gates talks about not getting a Microsoft E-mail application to the market quickly enough. "We were too busy, and at a retreat where I wrote our next priorities on a board, everyone said I had to take one off, so we took off E-mail."

It is hard to get him to delve more personally. But especially since Jennifer's birth, friends say, he has begun to reflect more on his life and what he might end up contributing. He speaks of the promise of computing, not just in business terms but in social ones. "Everyone starts out really capable," he says. "But as you grow and turn curious, either you get positive feedback by finding answers or you don't, and then this incredible potential you have is discouraged. I was lucky. I always had a family and resources to get more and more answers. Digital tools will allow a lot more people to keep going the next step rather than hitting a wall where people stop giving them information or tell them to stop asking questions."

He has also become less enamored with pure intelligence. "I don't think that I.Q. is as fungible as I used to," he says. "To succeed, you also have to know how to make choices and how to think more broadly."

So has family life dulled Gates' intensity?" Well, predictably, he's pumped and focused on Jennifer," says Ballmer. "He showed a picture of her at our last sales conference and joked that there was something other than Netscape keeping him awake at nights. He may be a bit less exhausting and a bit more civil.

But he still pushes as hard, still keeps score." Gates likes repeating Michael Jordan's mantra—"They think I'm through, they think I'm through"—and the one Intel's CEO Andrew Grove used as a book title, "Only the paranoid survive." As Ballmer says, "He still feels he must run scared." Gates puts another spin on it: "I still feel this is superfun."

And what about his feeling that there is nothing unique about the human mind, that intelligence can someday be replicated in binary code? Has watching a daughter learn to smile at a father's face changed that at all? At our last meeting, these questions don't seem to engage him. As I wander out of his office, he offers none of life's standard see-you-again-someday pleasantries, but he agrees that I should feel free to E-mail him. So I pose the questions, along with some more mundane technical ones, in a message a few days later. Answers to the tech issues come promptly. But he ignores the philosophical ones. Finally, weeks later, a note pops up in my mailbox, dispatched from storm-swept Seattle:

Analytically, I would say nature has done a good job making child raising more pleasure than pain, since that is necessary for a species to survive. But the experience goes beyond analytic description. . . . Evolution is many orders of magnitude ahead of mankind today in creating a complex system. I don't think it's irreconcilable to say we will understand the human mind someday and explain it in software-like terms, and also to say it is a creation that shouldn't be compared to software. Religion has come around to the view that even things that can be explained scientifically can have an underlying purpose that goes beyond the science. Even though I am not religious, the amazement and wonder I have about the human mind is closer to religious awe than dispassionate analysis.

QUESTIONS TO CONSIDER

1 Explain how the technological revolution has changed your lives. Make your own list of how it has profoundly transformed our world. Do you agree that the technological revolution has eclipsed the Industrial Revolution in historical significance?

2 Compare Bill Gates to earlier portraits in this volume of Andrew Carnegie and Henry Ford. Do you agree with Isaacson that Gates "has become the Edison and Ford of our age"? Does Gates possess the "cutthroat instinct" that made those previous business leaders a threat to their competitors? On the more positive side, has Gates, like those earlier entrepreneurs, attempted to give something back to society and to those people less fortunate than himself?

3 How would you describe Gates's personality, work habits, and intellectual curiosity? Does he seem more interested in other people or in himself? Is religion an important force in his life? Why did he and fellow baby boomer Bill Clinton fail to develop a close relationship on their golf outing?

4 Do you think that we can better understand Gates by examining his youth and family background? Gates's father maintained that "winning mattered" even in family games after Sunday dinner. What influence did this have on young Gates? As a boy, was Gates more interested in team or individual sports?

5 Why does Microsoft prefer to hire people based on their intelligence rather than their experience? In what ways does the work environment at Microsoft reflect its founder's personality? How would you describe Gates's management style and his relationship with his employees?

6 Although this selection originally appeared in *Time* before the federal government's antitrust action against Microsoft, what evidence does Isaacson provide to suggest that Gates "tried to leverage, unfairly and perhaps illegally, Microsoft's near monopoly in desktop operating systems"? Does Gates encourage cooperation among his employees at Microsoft? Does he encourage an environment there that rewards an open sharing of information?

32 The Lessons of September 11

JOHN LEWIS GADDIS

"Good of an unpredictable sort can come out of evil."
PAULINE MAIER

Americans of the current generation will never forget the September 11, 2001, terrorist attacks on the twin towers of the World Trade Center in New York City and the Pentagon near Washington, D.C. As President Roosevelt said of Pearl Harbor, September 11 is "a date which will live in infamy." For the rest of our lives, we will remember the scenes of unbelievable horror flickering on our television screens—scenes that were played over and over again that day. The TV cameras first showed one of the Trade Center towers with a gaping hole in it—caused, we initially thought, when a passenger jet accidentally crashed into it. But soon another jet airliner appeared at the corner of our TV screens, suddenly veered, and crashed into the second tower in an explosion of flame and smoke. Then, one by one, the great buildings collapsed, sending enormous clouds of dust, ash, and debris boiling through the streets and engulfing people who were running for their lives. What remained of the twin towers, once masterpieces of modern architecture, engineering, and construction, were mountains of smoldering rubble with an untold number of victims trapped inside. When the TV cameras swept the New York City skyline, there was a huge, haunting hole where the twin towers had once stood.

Thanks to television, we also saw the terrible damage caused by another passenger jet when it crashed into the Pentagon. We soon learned that the three jet airliners, with passengers on board, had been hijacked by Muslim terrorists from the Middle East, who turned the planes into guided missiles. A fourth hijacked airliner, heading for Washington (probably to hit the White House or the Capitol), crashed in Pennsylvania. Investigators believe that some heroic passengers wrested control of the aircraft from the terrorists and crashed the plane in order to thwart their murderous objective.

The strikes against the Pentagon and the World Trade Center were the worst hostile acts by foreign terrorists ever carried out on United States soil. Officials estimate that the attacks killed more than 3,000 people—the exact total may never be known—and wounded and maimed a great many more.

The events of September 11 have forever marked our generation, just as Pearl Harbor marked an earlier generation. Those murderous acts unified the country as no events had done in more than a generation. The inspirational leadership of Mayor Rudolph Giuliani of New York City brought us even closer together. So did the courage and sacrifice of the New York City firefighters and police, many of whom were killed when the towers collapsed. The country gave President George W. Bush an extraordinarily high approval rating when he vowed to bring the guilty parties to justice and to battle terrorists wherever they could be found. He called it "the first war of the twenty-first century."

When American intelligence identified Osama bin Laden and his al-Qaeda terrorist network, based in Afghanistan, as the culprits, President Bush acted swiftly. By his orders, American air and ground forces invaded Afghanistan, vanquished the brutal Taliban regime that had harbored the terrorists, obliterated al-Qaeda training camps, killed countless numbers of al-Qaeda and Taliban fighters, and drove the survivors into mountain hideouts. The vast majority of Americans resolutely supported the war and President Bush's handling of it.

In March, 2003, Bush expanded his war on terrorism by sending American forces to conquer Iraq and depose its dictator, Saddam Hussein. They and their British allies swiftly accomplished that mission in a stunning display of military power. Bush contended that he had to overthrow Saddam Hussein by force of arms, because the president believed that the Iraqi dictator had ties with al-Qaeda terrorists and was secretly developing weapons of mass destruction. Bush never produced evidence that Saddam Hussein had any connections with al-Qaeda terrorists. Nor did American troops ever discover any weapons of mass destruction or the facilities for producing them. Two years later, a commission appointed by the President investigated U.S. intelligence briefings, on which Bush had based his decision to make war on Iraq. The commission's lengthy report concluded that the briefings were "dead wrong" in most of their pre-war assessments of Iraq's arsenal. If the report distressed Bush, he showed no signs of it in public. In fact, he announced that he was implementing some of the commission's recommendations, which included expanding the authority of the newly created director of national intelligence, reorganizing the FBI, and establishing "a directorate of human intelligence based at the CIA."

In the meantime, American troops did capture Saddam Hussein, thus ridding both Iraq and the world of a monstrous tyrant. American and British occupation soldiers went on to supervise free elections of public officials in Iraq, in an effort to convert that long-oppressed country into a democracy. But as this volume goes to press, fighting still rages in Iraq, with pro-Hussein insurgents battling the Americans and British in a perplexing guerrilla war.

Meanwhile, in the aftermath of September 11, Americans across the country were frightened and insecure, all the more so when administration officials warned us to expect further terrorist acts on United States soil. "It's still America the beautiful," said Tom Brokaw of NBC, "but now it is also America the vulnerable, and it will take another great generation to bind up the wounds." The attacks of September 11 were so overwhelming, so unspeakably evil, that they still defy comprehension. How do we find meaning in that cataclysmic day? How did it happen? What does it portend for the future? Can history help us understand it?

In the following selection, John Lewis Gaddis, an expert on the history of foreign policy, discusses the lessons of September 11 from a historical perspective. Focusing on the post–Cold War decade, he explains how the failures and shortcomings of American foreign policy created anti-American feelings in much of the world. Washington officials, in particular, were too insensitive to the fact that American power and wealth "were being blamed" for the inequities caused by the globalization of capitalism. He warns us that September 11 was a historic turning point, thrusting us into a new era that is "bound to be more painful than the one we've just left."

Gaddis believes—and the editors of Portrait of America agree—that a knowledge of history can ease our fears and help us endure the difficult days ahead. As Civil War historian James M. McPherson reminds us, the United States has been tested many times in the past and has "emerged from the trauma stronger and better than before." Historian Pauline Maier finds a lesson in the American Revolution that speaks to us across the centuries. "Americans joined arms and became a nation in the wake of an outside attack. Good of an unpredictable sort can come out of evil."

GLOSSARY

BIN LADEN, OSAMA   The son of a Saudi Arabian billionaire and an extremely wealthy man in his own right, bin Laden created an international terrorist network with bases in Afghanistan. He was responsible for the September 11 terrorist attacks on the Untied States. His hatred for America stems, in part, from the presence of United States troops in Saudi Arabia, where his family fortune was acquired and where the Muslim holy cities of Mecca and Medina are located.

BUSH, GEORGE W. The former Texas governor and son of the forty-first president, he narrowly defeated Al Gore in the presidential election of 2000. He showed courage and leadership following the terrorist attacks of September 11 and rallied the American people behind what he called "the first war of the twenty-first century."

GLOBALIZATION The movement toward universally accepted concepts and values that are a product, in part, of mass communication, interdependent economies, and a common cyberspace vocabulary that diminishes the importance of the borders between nations.

HUSSEIN, SADDAM Iraq's dictator who in 1990 invaded neighboring Kuwait. That action resulted in the Persian Gulf War between Iraq and an international coalition led by the United States. Although the coalition drove Iraqi troops out of Kuwait, inflicting terrible losses in men and equipment, it left Saddam Hussein in power.

MARSHALL PLAN Also known as the European Recovery Program, it was the brainchild of George C. Marshall, Truman's second secretary of state (1947–1949) and former army chief of staff. The program distributed $12 billion in American aid that helped rebuild war-ravaged western Europe.

MARX, KARL He and Friedrich Engels wrote the *Communist Manifesto* (1848), which predicted the fall of capitalism and the creation of a workers' state that would control the means of production.

McCARTHYISM A term that cartoonist Herbert Block ("Herblock") coined to describe the demagogic behavior of Senator Joseph R. McCarthy of Wisconsin and the anti-Communist fervor that plagued the United States in the 1950s.

MILOSEVIC, SLOBODAN The brutal leader of Serbia whose terror-driven regime resulted in the murder of thousands of Bosnian Muslims and Croatians. This so-called ethnic cleansing forced NATO to intervene to ease tensions and prevent Milosevic from killing yet more innocent victims. Although eventually deposed and later imprisoned for his crimes, the Serbian president remained an awful reminder of the ethnic and religious hatreds that had long plagued the Balkans. He died of a heart attack in his cell in March 2006.

NORTH ATLANTIC TREATY ORGANIZATION (NATO) Organized in 1949, NATO was a collective security agreement to

protect the West from Soviet aggression. Part of the containment strategy that President Truman devised following World War II, NATO committed the United States to the defense of member nations that faced an "armed attack." The first countries to commit to NATO were Belgium, Canada, Denmark, France, Great Britain, Iceland, Italy, Luxembourg, the Netherlands, Norway, Portugal, and the United States.

RWANDA Horrible famine and disease, a product of a vicious civil war, struck this poverty-ravaged nation in central Africa. In the summer of 1994, the Clinton administration offered humanitarian aid but refused to intervene in Rwanda, where political tension had produced one million refugees. Gaddis concludes that "we responded to the greatest atrocities of the decade by simply averting our eyes."

SMITH, ADAM (1723–1790) An Enlightenment thinker who believed in *laissez-faire* economics that would allow individuals free access to world markets. He felt that tariffs and trade monopolies were destructive and that governments should not hinder private enterprise.

SOMALIA Factional tension and hunger, the result of severe droughts, plagued this small African nation bordering the Indian Ocean. At first, the United States supported the relief efforts of the United Nations and sent troops to Somalia to help capture a recalcitrant warlord. But when, in the summer of 1993, guerrillas killed twelve American soldiers, President Clinton withdrew the American troops. Gaddis believes that "our reluctance to take casualties of our own revealed how little we were prepared to sacrifice for the rights of others."

UNILATERALISM A foreign policy based on national self-interest that often ignores the concerns and insecurities of other nations. Gaddis argues that this was a failure of American diplomacy in the post–Cold War years. "We seemed to have assumed, perhaps because we were the greatest of the great powers, that we no longer needed the cooperation of the others to promote our interests."

UNITED STATES COMMISSION ON NATIONAL SECURITY IN THE 21ST CENTURY Six months before the terrorist attacks on New York City and Washington, this commission and its chairpersons, Gary Hart and Warren Rudman, warned of the need for "homeland" security.

WARSAW PACT Created in May 1955 in response to NATO, this was a Soviet-dominated alliance of the nations of eastern Europe. It collapsed after the end of the Cold War.

We've never had a good name for it, and now it's over. The post–cold war era—let us call it that for want of any better term—began with the collapse of one structure, the Berlin Wall on November 9, 1989, and ended with the collapse of another, the World Trade Center's twin towers on September 11, 2001. No one, apart from the few people who plotted and carried out these events, could have anticipated that they were going to happen. But from the moment they did happen, everyone acknowledged that everything had changed.

It's characteristic of such turning points that they shed more light on the history that preceded them than on what's to come. The fall of the Berlin Wall didn't tell us much about the post–cold war world, but it told us a lot about the cold war. It suddenly became clear that East Germany, the Warsaw Pact, and the Soviet Union itself had long since lost the authority with which the U.S. and its NATO allies had continued to credit them right up to the day the wall came down. The whole history of the cold war looked different as a result. Having witnessed the end, historians could never again see the middle, or even the beginning, as they once had.

Something similar seems likely to happen now to the post–cold war era. For whatever we eventually settle on calling the events of September 11—the Attack on America, Black Tuesday, 9/11—they've already forced a reconsideration, not only of where we are as a nation and where we may be going, but also of where we've been, even of who we are. Our recent past, all at once, has been thrown into sharp relief, even as our future remains obscure. To paraphrase an old prayer, it's obvious now that we have done some things which we ought not to have done, and that we have not done other things which we ought to have done. How much health there is in us

John Lewis Gaddis, "And Now This: Lessons from the Old Era to the New One," from *The Age of Terror* by Strobe Talbott. Copyright © 2001 by Strobe Talbott and Nayan Chanda. Reprinted by permission of Basic Books, a member of Perseus Books, L.L.C.

will depend, to a considerable degree, on how we sort this out.

———

1.

But first things first. No acts of commission or omission by the U.S. can have justified what happened on September 11. Few if any moral standards have deeper roots than the prohibition against taking innocent life in peacetime. Whatever differences may exist in culture, religion, race, class, or any of the other categories by which human beings seek to establish their identities, this rule transcends them.

The September 11 attacks violated it in ways that go well beyond all other terrorist attacks in the past: first by the absence of any stated cause to be served; second by the failure to provide warning; and finally by the obvious intent to time and configure the attack in such a manner as to take as many lives as possible—even to the point, some have suggested, of the airplanes' angle of approach, which seemed calculated to devastate as many floors of the twin towers as they could. Let there be no mistake: this was evil, and no set of grievances real or imagined, however strongly felt or widely held, can excuse it.

At the same time, though, neither our outrage nor the patriotic unity that is arising from it relieves us of the obligation to think critically. Would anyone claim, in the aftermath of September 11, that the U.S. can continue the policies it was following with respect to its national defense or toward the world before September 11? Americans were not *responsible* for what happened at Pearl Harbor; but they would have been *irresponsible* in the extreme if they had not, as a consequence of that attack, dramatically altered their policies. Nobody—given the opportunity to rerun the events leading up to that catastrophe—would have handled things again in just the same way.

It's in that spirit, I think, that we need a reconsideration of how the U.S. has managed its responsibilities in the decade since the cold war ended, not with a view to assigning blame, indulging in recrimination, or wallowing in self-pity, but rather for the purpose—now urgent—of determining where we go from here. Patriotism demands nothing less.

———————

2.

The clearest conclusion to emerge from the events of September 11 is that *the geographical position and the military power of the U.S. are no longer sufficient to ensure its security.*

Americans have known insecurity before in their homeland, but not for a very long time. Except for Pearl Harbor and a few isolated pinpricks like Japanese attempts to start forest fires with incendiary bombs in the Pacific Northwest in 1942, or the Mexican guerrilla leader Pancho Villa's raid on Columbus, New Mexico, in 1916, the U.S. has suffered no foreign attack on its soil since British troops captured Washington and burned the White House and the Capitol in 1814. There's a macabre symmetry in the possibility that the fourth plane hijacked on September 11—which crashed presumably after an uprising among the passengers—probably had one of these buildings as its target.

Few other nations have worried so little for so long about what is coming to be called "homeland security." The late Yale historian C. Vann Woodward even went so far as to define this lack of concern as a central feature of the American character. "Free security," he insisted, had done as much to shape Americans' view of themselves as had the availability of free, or almost free, land.

The 20th century, to be sure, eroded that sense of safety, but this happened as a result of the larger role the U.S. had assigned itself in world affairs, together with ominous shifts in the European balance of power. It did not arise from any sense of domestic insecurity. We entered World War I to ensure that Germany did not wind up dominating Europe, and we were preparing to do the same thing again in World War II when the Japanese attack, followed by Hitler's own declaration of war, removed any choice in the matter from us.

Even so, the continental U.S. remained secure throughout the long and bloody conflict that followed. Neither the Germans nor the Japanese could bomb our cities or occupy our territory, as we eventually would do to them. And despite the incarceration of some 120,000 Japanese Americans during the war, the only significant fifth-column network operating within the U.S. at the time was that of an ally, the Soviet Union—a fact not discovered until after the war had ended. The world might be unsafe, but homeland security could be taken for granted almost as easily during the total wars of the 20th century as it had been throughout most of the 19th century.

The cold war made the American homeland seem less secure in two ways: when spies working on behalf of the Soviet Union were shown to have betrayed the country; and as the prospect arose that Soviet long-range bombers and later intercontinental ballistic missiles might soon be capable of reaching American soil. The spies were mostly rounded up by the time McCarthyism reached its peak in the early 1950s, a fact that helps to account for why that season of paranoia went away as quickly as it did. The nuclear danger never entirely went away, and for a while it was a palpable presence for Americans who saw their public buildings designated as fallout shelters even as they were being encouraged, for a while, to build their own in their own backyards.

Despite moments of genuine fear, however, as during the Berlin and Cuban missile crises, the only images we had of destroyed American cities were those constructed by the makers of apocalypse films and the authors of science fiction novels. Real danger remained remote. We had adversaries, but we also had the means of deterring them.

Even cold war insecurities, therefore, never meant that Americans, while living, working and traveling within their country, had to fear for their lives. Dangers to the American homeland were always vague and distant, however clear and present overseas dangers may have been. The very term "national security," invented during World War II and put to such frequent use during the cold war, always implied that both threats and vulnerabilities lay *outside* the country.

A second jet airliner commandeered by extremist Muslim terrorists prepares to crash into the World Trade Center's twin towers. Gaddis suggests that the "airplanes' angle of approach" assured maximum devastation. "Let there be no mistake," he says, "this was evil, and no set of grievances real or imagined, however strongly felt or widely held, can excuse it." (AP Photo/Anthony Cotsifas)

Our military and intelligence forces were configured accordingly.

That's why the U.S. Commission on National Security in the 21st Century—often known, for its co-chairs Gary Hart and Warren Rudman, as the Hart-Rudman Report—distinguished between "national" and "homeland" security when it warned of our domestic vulnerabilities, with uncanny prescience, in March 2001. In the aftermath of September 11, we have not only adopted the concept of "homeland security"—it has become synonymous with national security. Such is the revolution in our thinking forced upon us by the events of that day. It means that Americans have entered a new stage in their history in which they can no longer take security for granted: it is no longer free—anywhere, or at any time.

What was striking about September 11 was the success with which the terrorists transformed objects we had never before regarded as dangerous into weapons of lethal potency. There was nothing exotic here like bombs or even firearms. They used instead the objects of everyday life: pocket knives, twine, box-cutters and, of course, commercial aircraft. The terrorists also combined what may seem to us to be a primitive belief in the rewards of martyrdom with the most modern methods of planning, coordination, and execution. We confront, therefore, not only a new category of easily available weaponry, but a new combination of skill and will in using it.

The attack's cost-effectiveness was equally striking. No previous act of terrorism came close to this one in lives lost and damage inflicted. The dead were almost twice the number killed in some three decades of violence in Northern Ireland. They are ten times the toll on both sides in the most recent round of the Israeli-Palestinian *intifada*. They exceed, in deaths suffered on a single day, the most violent battles of the American Civil War. The operation required the lives of nineteen terrorists and expenditures of about $500,000. The "payoff," if we can use such a term for such a brutal transaction, was approximately 5,000 dead and perhaps as much as $100 billion in recovery costs. Ratios like these—some 263 victims for every terrorist, and $2,000 in damages for every dollar expended—cannot help but set a standard to which future terrorists will aspire.

The whole point of terrorism is leverage: to accomplish a lot with a little. This operation, in that sense, succeeded brilliantly—even allowing for the fact that one of the four planes failed to reach its target, and that more planes may have been in danger of being hijacked. As a consequence, the images of terrified New Yorkers running through the streets of their city to escape great billowing clouds of ash, dust, and building fragments; or of the government in Washington forced to seek shelter; or of several days of skies devoid of the contrails we have come to expect aircraft to add to the atmosphere over our heads—these memories will remain in our minds just as vividly as the images, from six decades earlier, of American naval vessels aflame, sinking at their own docks within an American naval base on American territory.

Security, therefore, has a new meaning, for which little in our history and even less in our planning has prepared us.

Billowing smoke engulfs the Pentagon on "Black Tuesday," a day that the current generation of Americans will never forget. Gaddis states: "What was striking about September 11 was the success with which the terrorists transformed objects we had never before regarded as dangerous into weapons of lethal potency." (© Reuters NewMedia, Inc. / Corbis)

3.

That leads to a second conclusion, which is *that our foreign policy since the cold war ended has insufficiently served our interests.*

National security requires more than just military deployments or intelligence operations. It depends ultimately upon creating an international environment congenial to the nation's interests. That's the role of foreign policy. Despite many mistakes and diversions along the way, the U.S. managed to build such an environment during the second half of the 20th century. The Soviet Union's collapse stemmed, in no small measure, from its failure to do the same.

As a consequence, the world at the end of the cold war was closer to a consensus in favor of American values—collective security, democracy, capitalism—than it had ever been before. President George H. W. Bush's talk of a "new world order" reflected a convergence of interests among the great powers which, while imperfect, was nonetheless, unprecedented. Differences remained with the European

Union, Russia, China and Japan over such issues as international trade, the handling of regional conflicts, the management of national economies, the definition and hence the protection of human rights; but these were minor compared to issues that had produced two world wars and perpetuated the cold war. Americans, it seemed, had finally found a congenial world.

What's happened since, though? Can anyone claim that the world of 2001—even before September 11—was as friendly to American interests as it had been in 1991? It would be silly to blame the U.S. alone for the disappointments of the past decade. Too many other actors, ranging from Saddam Hussein to Slobodan Milosevic to Osama bin Laden, have helped to bring them about. But the question that haunted Americans after Pearl Harbor is still worth asking: given the opportunity to rerun the sequence, what would we want to change in our foreign policy and what would we leave the same?

The question is not at all hypothetical. The administration of George W. Bush has already undertaken, in the wake of September 11, the most sweeping reassessment of foreign policy priorities since the cold war ended. Its results are not yet clear, but the tilt is far more toward change than continuity. That is an implicit acknowledgment of deficiencies in the American approach to the world during the post–cold war era that are clearer now than they were then.

One of these, it seems, was unilateralism, an occupational hazard of sole surviving superpowers. With so little countervailing power in sight, such states tend to lead without listening, a habit that can cause resistance even among those otherwise disposed to follow. The U.S. managed to avoid this outcome after its victory in World War II because we had, in the Soviet Union, a superpower competitor. Our allies, and even our former adversaries, tolerated a certain amount of arrogance on our part because there was always "something worse" out there; we in turn, fearing their defection or collapse, treated them with greater deference and respect than they might have expected given the power imbalances of the time.

With our victory in the cold war, though, we lost the "something worse." American ideas, institutions, and culture remained as attractive as ever throughout much of the world, but American policies began to come across as overbearing, self-indulgent, and insensitive to the interests of others. Our own domestic politics made things worse: with the White House in the control of one party and the Congress in the hands of another during most of this period, it was difficult to get a consensus on such matters as paying United Nations dues, participating in the International Criminal Court, or ratifying the Comprehensive Test Ban Treaty, the Land Mines Convention, or the Kyoto Protocol on Climate Change. During most of the cold war, knowing what our enemies would make of our failure to do these things, it would have been easy.

A second problem arose, largely as a result of this unilateralism: we neglected the cultivation of great power relationships. We seemed to have assumed, perhaps because we were the greatest of the great powers, that we no longer needed the cooperation of the others to promote our interests. We therefore allowed our relations with the Russians and the Chinese to deteriorate to the point that by the end of that decade we were barely on speaking terms with Moscow and Beijing. We failed to sustain one of the most remarkable achievements of American foreign policy during the cold war—the success of Richard Nixon and Henry Kissinger in creating a situation in which our adversaries feared one another more than they feared us. . . .

This happened chiefly as the result of a third characteristic of our post–cold war foreign policy, which was a preference for justice at the expense of order. We had never entirely neglected the demands of justice during the cold war, but we did tend to pursue these by working with the powerful to get them to improve their treatment of the powerless. We sought to promote human rights from the inside out rather than from the outside in: sometimes we succeeded, sometimes we did not.

With the end of the cold war, however, we changed our approach. We enlarged NATO against the wishes of the Russians, not because the Poles, the Czechs, and the Hungarians added significantly to the alliance's military capabilities, but rather because these states had suffered past injustices and therefore "deserved" membership. We then used the expanded alliance to rescue the Kosovars and bomb the Serbs, despite the fact that in doing so we were violating the sovereignty of an internationally recognized state without explicit United Nations approval. Unsurprisingly, this angered not just the Russians but also the Chinese, both of whom had discontented minorities of their own to worry about. . . .

A fourth aspect of our post–cold war foreign policy followed from the third: it was the inconsistency with which we pursued regional justice. We were, as it turned out, by no means as adamant in seeking justice for the Chechens or the Tibetans as we were for the Kosovars: Moscow and Beijing, despite their nervousness, had little to fear. But by applying universal principles on a less than universal basis, Washington did open itself to the charge of hypocrisy. It was worse elsewhere, as in Somalia, where our reluctance to take casualties of our own revealed how little we were prepared to sacrifice for the rights of others, or in Rwanda, where we responded to the greatest atrocities of the decade by simply averting our eyes.

Meanwhile, in the Middle East, we tolerated the continuing Israeli dispossession and repression of Palestinians even as we were seeking to secure the rights of the Palestinians; and we did nothing to adjust policy in response to the fact that an old adversary, Iran, was moving toward free elections and a parliamentary system even as old allies like Saudi Arabia were shunning such innovations. There was, in short a gap between our principles and our practices: we proclaimed the former without linking them to the latter, and that invited disillusionment. There are several reasons why the rantings of bin Laden resonate to the extent that they do in so many parts of North Africa, the Middle East, and Asia; but surely this is one of them.

A fifth problem was our tendency to regard our economic system as a model to be applied throughout the rest of the world, without regard to differences in local conditions and with little sense of the effects it would have in generating inequality. The problem was particularly evident in Russia, where we too easily assumed a smooth transition to market capitalism. Our efforts to help came nowhere near the scope and seriousness of the programs we'd launched to rebuild the economies of our defeated adversaries after World War II.

Meanwhile, Washington officials were less sensitive than they should have been to the extent to which American wealth and power were being blamed, throughout much of the world, for the inequities the globalization of capitalism was generating. Capitalism would have expanded after the cold war regardless of what the U.S. did. By linking that expansion so explicitly with our foreign policy objectives, however, we associated ourselves with something abroad that we would never have tolerated at home: the workings of an unregulated market devoid of a social safety net. Adam Smith was right in claiming that the pursuit of self-interest ultimately benefits the collective interest; but Karl Marx was right when he pointed out that wealth is not distributed to everyone equally at the same time, and that alienation arises as a result. . . .

Finally, and largely as a consequence, the U.S. emphasized the advantages, while neglecting the dangers, of globalization. There was a great deal of talk after the cold war ended of the extent to which that process had blurred the boundary between the domestic and the international: it was held to be a good thing that capital, commodities, ideas and people could move more freely across boundaries. There was little talk, though, of an alternative possibility: that danger might move just as freely. That's a major lesson of September 11: the very instruments of the new world order—airplanes, liberal policies on immigration and money transfers, multiculturalism itself in the sense that there seemed nothing odd about the hijackers when they were taking their flight training—can be turned horribly against it. It was as if we had convinced ourselves that the new world of global communication had somehow transformed an old aspect of human nature, which is the tendency to harbor grievances and sometimes to act upon them.

What connects these shortcomings is a failure of strategic vision: the ability to see how the parts of one's policy combine to form the whole. This means avoiding the illusion that one can pursue particular policies in particular places without their interacting with one another. It means remembering that actions have consequences: that for every action there will be a reaction, the nature of which won't always be predictable. It means accepting the fact that there's not always a linear relationship between input and output: that vast efforts can produce minimal results in some situations, and that minimal efforts can produce vast consequences in others. . . . Finally, it requires effective national leadership, a quality for which American foreign policy during the post–cold war era is unlikely to be remembered.

So what might we have done differently in the realm of foreign policy? Quite a lot, it's now clear, as we look back on a decade in which it appears that our power exceeded our wisdom.

————

4.

Where do we go from here? Will the events of September 11 bring our policies back into line with our interests? Can we regain the clarity of strategic vision that served us well during the cold war, and that seemed to desert us during its aftermath? Shocks like this do have the advantage of concentrating the mind. Those of us who worried, during the 1990s, about the difficulty of thinking strategically in an age of apparent safety need no longer do so. As was the case with Pearl Harbor, a confusing world has suddenly become less so, even if at horrendous cost.

What's emerging is the prospect, once again, of "something worse" than an American-dominated world—perhaps something much worse. The appalling nature of the attacks on New York and Washington forged a new coalition against terrorism overnight. The great power consensus that withered after 1991 is back in place in expanded form: the U.S., the European Union, Russia, China and Japan

are all on the same side now—at least on the issue of terrorism—and they've been joined by unexpected allies like Pakistan, Uzbekistan, and perhaps even, very discreetly, Iran. Terrorism can hardly flourish without some state support; but September 11 brought home the fact that terrorism challenges the authority of all states. Everybody has airplanes, and everything that lies below them must now be considered a potential target. Just as fear of the Soviet Union built and sustained an American coalition during the cold war—and just as the prospect of nuclear annihilation caused the Soviets themselves ultimately to begin cooperating with it—so the sudden appearance of "something much worse" is a paradoxical but powerful ally in the new war that now confronts us.

Maintaining this coalition, however, will require tolerating diversity within it. That was one of our strengths during the cold war: the U.S. was far more successful than the Soviet Union in leading while listening, so that those we led felt that they had an interest in being led. NATO survived, as a consequence, while the Sino-Soviet alliance and the Warsaw Pact did not. If the global coalition against terrorism is to survive, it will demand even greater flexibility on the part of Americans than our cold war coalition did. We'll have to give up the unilateralism we indulged in during the post–cold war era: the Bush administration, prior to September 11, had seemed particularly to relish this bad habit. We'll have to define our allies more in terms of shared interests, and less in terms of shared values. We'll have to compromise more than we might like in promoting human rights, open markets, and the scrupulous observance of democratic procedures. We'll have to concentrate more than we have in the past on getting whatever help we can in the war against terrorism wherever we can find it. Our concerns with regional justice may suffer as a result: we're not likely to return soon to rescuing Kosovars, or to condemning oppression against Chechens and Tibetans. The compensation, one hopes, will be to secure justice on a broader scale; for terrorism will offer little justice for anyone.

Even as we pursue this path, we'll need to address the grievances that fuel terrorism in the first place.

Once again, there are cold war precedents: with the rehabilitation of Germany and Japan after World War II, together with the Marshall Plan, we fought the conditions that made the Soviet alternative attractive even as we sought to contain the Soviets themselves. . . . Can we apply the same strategy now against the conditions that breed terrorists in so many parts of what we used to call the "third" world? We'd better try, for some of these regions are at least as much at risk now as Europe and Japan were half a century ago.

The era we've just entered—whatever we decide to call it—is bound to be more painful than the one we've just left. The antiterrorist coalition is sure to undergo strains as its priorities shift from recovery to retaliation. Defections will doubtless occur. Further terrorist attacks are unavoidable, and are certain to produce demoralization as well as greater resolve.

But it does seem likely, even at this early stage in the war they have provoked, that the terrorists have got more than they bargained for. "What kind of a people do they think we are?" Winston Churchill asked of the Japanese in the aftermath of Pearl Harbor. It's worth asking the same of our new enemies, because *it can hardly have been their purpose to give the U.S. yet another chance to lead the world into a new era, together with the opportunity to do it, this time, more wisely.*

QUESTIONS TO CONSIDER

1 Why does Gaddis view the events of September 11 as an example of pure evil, which existed at a level "well beyond all other terrorist attacks in the past"? What must the United States now reevaluate, in a manner similar to the reassessment after the Japanese attack on Pearl Harbor?

2 Do you agree with Gaddis that "the geographical position and the military power of the U.S. are no longer sufficient to ensure security"? Why has America, throughout its history, failed to place "homeland security" as a high priority? During the Cold War, why did many Americans feel vulnerable to outside attack and realize that the era of "free security" was over?

3 Why does Gaddis state that the "striking" thing about the events of September 11 was that the terrorists changed "objects we had never before regarded as dangerous into weapons of lethal potency"? Explain his conclusion that the attacks were cost effective and helped America's enemies gain "leverage."

4 The author claims that at the end of the Cold War the United States "had finally found a congenial world" that supported American interests and values. Why does he feel that America's foreign policy in the post–Cold War years "insufficiently served our interests"?

5 Since the end of the Cold War, how has unilateralism resulted in an American foreign policy that tends "to lead without listening"? Why has it failed to cultivate positive relationships with other significant nations like Russia and China? Do you agree with the author that recent U.S. diplomacy promotes "justice at the expense of order" and has inconsistencies between "principles and practices"?

6 How has globalization made the United States more vulnerable to terrorism? Does Gaddis's essay help you understand why many less fortunate people in the world might resent America's wealth and power? How have the events of September 11 helped develop new bonds between the United States and other nations?